WAR IN THE SHADOWS

WAR IN
THE SHADOWS

THE GUERRILLA IN HISTORY

Volume I I

ROBERT B. ASPREY

AN AUTHORS GUILD BACKINPRINT.COM EDITION

AN AUTHORS GUILD BACKINPRINT.COM EDITION

Published by iUniverse, Inc.

For information address:
iUniverse, Inc.
5220 S. 16th St., Suite 200
Lincoln, NE 68512
www.iuniverse.com

Originally published by William Morrow & Company, Inc.

ISBN: 0-595-22594-2

Printed in the United States of America

PART FOUR

THEN UNTIL NOW: A SURVEY

ernment • The jihad (holy war) declared by mujaheddin guerrillas • Collapse of the Afghan army • The Soviet army versus the guerrillas • Soviet military deficiencies • Mujaheddin disunity • Pakistan's role • U.S. military aid to the mujaheddin • Military stalemate • The Mohammed Najibullah regime • Mikhail Gorbachev pulls out • The war continues: Gulbuddin Hakmatyar versus Ahmed Shah Massoud • The drug factor • United Nations attempts to end the fighting fail • The war continues

CHAPTER 57

Castro in Mexico • Che Guevara joins • Return to Cuba • Early disaster • The fugitives • Sanctuary in Sierra Maestra • Castro's plan • Urban support • Early guerrilla operations • Castro's problems • The Matthews interview • A myth begins • Guerrilla tactics • Batista's countertactics • American army influence • Dissension in Washington • Ambassador Smith • Pact of the Sierra • Urban guerrillas • War in the countryside • The balance sheet • The American position • Eisenhower's arms embargo • The climax approaches • Operation Summer fails • Castro's counterattack • The revolution spreads • Batista exits • Castro takes over • Che Guevara on guerrilla warfare • His heterodoxy • His exodus • Che's Bolivian expedition • Capture and execution • Che's failure analyzed

IN LATE SPRING OF 1955, Fidel Castro traveled to the United States, where he raised several thousand dollars for "the cause." In Mexico City, he rounded up other Cuban exiles, mostly middle-class dissidents belonging to the Movement, and put them on a ranch to train for invasion—the task of one Colonel Alberto Bayo, a former Cuban air force officer, a veteran of the Spanish civil war, and supposedly an expert in guerrilla fighting.[1]

Enter Ernesto Guevara Lynch.

Che Guevara was twenty-six years old when he met Castro in Mexico. Son of a left-wing Argentinian architect, he had extended a medical career to revolutionary politics. He had participated in several unsuccessful attempts to depose Juan Perón, and the previous year had allegedly served in a minor capacity in Arbenz's Guatemalan Communist government. After Arbenz's overthrow, he went to Mexico and was working either in a heart institute or as an itinerant photographer (the record is cloudy) when he met Castro. Politically, he was far left, though

not necessarily a Communist. He was well read in Marx and Lenin—he carried their books with him—and he was anti-United States, mainly because of the CIA's role in Guatemala.[2] He enthusiastically joined the Movement and, despite chronic asthma, devoted himself to serious guerrilla training, serving also as the army's doctor.[3]

Castro himself paid little attention to operational matters. Instead, he continued to seek support both inside and outside Cuba. The internal situation was scarcely conducive to his plans. Batista seemed stronger than ever. After rigged elections returned him to the presidency, he received a fulsome Vice-President Nixon and, later, Allen Dulles, head of CIA. In early 1956, he offered an olive branch to opponents and began the short-lived *Diálogo Cívico*. Cuba's economy was expanding and, to the casual observer, Batista's government appeared stable.[4]

Batista's refusal to negotiate in depth with opposition groups and to restore civil rights had created a good deal of dissidence, however, not only outside government but inside and particularly in the army. Serious incidents including assassination of Batista's intelligence chief plagued the government during 1955 and 1956. Splinter opposition groups formed and dissolved; students continued to protest through the FEU's newly formed militant group, the DR (Directorio Revolucionario), which agreed to support Castro, although most of these groups did not recognize Castro and the Movement as the key to Batista's overthrow. Castro did gain other new allies from the remnant MNR, notably Frank País, a Baptist and former teacher in Santiago, whom Castro named as head of all "action groups" in Cuba, and Armando Hart and Faustino Pérez in Havana. Cuban exiles in the United States and Mexico also supported him.

Castro was plagued by Batista's secret police, who arranged raids by Mexican police on his various headquarters and even arrested him. Such were the vicissitudes of Cuban politics that Castro now gained an important backer: Prío Socarrás, Cuba's former President, who was spending millions in trying to overthrow Batista, donated at least fifty thousand dollars to Castro. Castro used fifteen thousand dollars to buy a battered yacht, *Granma;* he also procured arms and supply, and in late 1956, *Granma* sailed for Cuba with Castro and eighty-two guerrillas aboard. Castro planned to land with the help of local guerrillas. The new army would then attack Manzanillo garrison to capture arms and equipment. Simultaneously, urban terrorists would attack various targets, and finally a general strike would bring down the government. In case of a general uprising, Castro's force would arm the peasants and march on Havana; in case of trouble, it would escape to the mountain vastness of the Sierra Maestra to organize and train a volunteer army.[5]

This was an extremely optimistic plan. Frank País, Castro's agent in Santiago, had warned him against it. In the event, no local guerrillas met *Granma*. Badly overloaded, she landed late and off course, disgorging passengers in a swamp where much food and supply were lost. Even before she landed, País' people, some three hundred young rebels, had attacked various targets in Santiago, a fiasco, as it turned out. Most other "action groups" remained inactive.

No general uprising—no local uprising. A Cuban frigate spotted *Granma;* troops and planes rushed to the coast. With help of a turncoat guide, soldiers cornered the guerrillas in a cane field and killed or captured about seventy. Twelve or fifteen survivors, including Castro, his brother Raúl, and Che Guevara, who was wounded, escaped to the Sierra Maestra. For several weeks, they lived precariously, unable to trust most peasants, almost constantly hounded by army patrols.

This was what Che later categorized as "favorable ground" for guerrillas, and though patrols often came close, they never captured the errants. The Sierra Maestra was too big, the terrain too difficult, for troops to plug all exits. Moreover, the peasants, including large numbers of impoverished *precaristas,* or squatters, proved receptive to revolutionary propaganda, notably the old song Land to the Landless. In time, Castro established a "safe" base and set to the task of revolution.[6]

The original plan to overthrow Batista's government having failed, Castro adopted a two-front strategy: warfare in cities and warfare in the country, the one (the *Llano*) to support the other (the *Sierra*)—or vice versa. Urban warfare—strikes, riots, and terrorism—fell to Civic Resistance (*Resistencia Cívica*) movements in Havana and Santiago, which forced the government to keep numerous army units in cities and thus ease pressure on guerrillas in the Sierra Maestra; urban units also sent money, arms, supply, and recruits to the mountain sanctuary. Rural guerrillas began to enlarge the mountain base by enlisting peasant cooperation while training a regular army. Simultaneously, Castro's guerrilla units began to strike small army outposts such as La Plata, which yielded arms and ammunition. This and other attacks goaded the army into ever more repressive measures that ensured revolutionary growth in both cities and countryside.

For a long period the urban effort sustained the rebellion. The "peasant revolution" later claimed by Castro and publicized by Che Guevara, Régis Debray, and C. Wright Mills did not exist—neither at this time nor later. Unlike Mao Tse-tung and Ho Chi Minh, Castro had not prepared the peasantry; he and his lieutenants were intellectuals, and neither class easily identified with the other. Rather than turning peasants of Oriente province into a grand army, Castro had all he could do to prevent peasants from turning him in. Life in the mountains also proved hard: morale plunged. Castro concerned himself more with security and sustenance than with fighting.

At this point, February 1957, the outside world knew little either of Fidel Castro or the rebellion. Taking the government's word, United Press and the *New York Times* had reported Castro's death in early December. Batista, who, in private, referred to the guerrillas as "a bunch of bandits," seemed to control the situation, and the Eisenhower administration continued to bless him. An American military advisory group daily strengthened his army; Batista and his officers received American decorations, and American officers received Cuban decorations.[7] The Cuban economy was booming, with large increases in American investments. Batista's propaganda machine continued to insist that Castro was dead; his security forces added to the illusion by promptly and ruthlessly suppressing local outbreaks. On Christmas Day 1956, a provincial commander rounded up, tortured, and executed twenty-two men and boys, a stupid act exploited by rebels as "Batista's Christmas Present."[8]

To dispel the notion of security and to broadcast his intentions to the world (following Grivas' example in Cyprus), Castro arranged a rendezvous with a senior *New York Times* editor, Herbert Matthews, a fifty-seven-year-old peripatetic reporter nudging the Richard Harding Davis tradition. In mid-February 1957, Castro agents shepherded Matthews to Castro's camp in the mountains. Castro immediately impressed him: " . . . a powerful six-footer, olive-skinned, full-faced, with a shapely beard. He was dressed in an olive grey fatigue uniform and carried a rifle with a telescopic sight of which he was very proud."[9] They spent the night talking, or, rather, whispering, since, according to Matthews' dramatic account, Batista's soldiers were hovering nearby. Castro evidently whispered persuasively: Matthews, who was with him less than a day, became as pro-Castro as Ambassador Gardner was pro-Batista. The first of three articles opened:

> Fidel Castro, the rebel leader of Cuba's youth, is alive and fighting hard and successfully in the rugged, almost impenetrable fastnesses of the Sierra Maestra.

Matthews found Castro's personality " . . . overwhelming. It was easy to see that his men adored him. . . . Here was an educated, dedicated fanatic, a man of ideals, of courage and of remarkable qualities of leadership . . . one got a feeling that he is now invincible." As for his aims:

> . . . His is a political mind rather than a military one. He has strong ideas of liberty, democracy, social justice, the need to restore the Constitution, to hold elections. . . . The program is vague and couched in generalities, but it amounts to a new deal for Cuba, radical, democratic and therefore anti-Communist.

701

Castro whispered to the reporter:

> ... We have been fighting for seventy-nine days now and are stronger than ever. ... The soldiers are fighting badly; their morale is low and ours could not be higher. We are killing many, but when we take prisoners they are never shot. We question them, talk kindly to them, take their arms and equipment, and then set them free. ... Batista has 3,000 men in the field against us. I will not tell you how many we have, for obvious reasons. He works in columns of 200; we in groups of ten to forty, and we are winning. It is a battle against time and time is on our side.[10]

The articles caused a furor in the United States. Batista had recently lifted censorship, and they were also published in Cuba where officials immediately denied that a meeting had taken place. The *New York Times* replied by publishing a photo of Castro and Matthews in the mountains. Cuban dissidents reacted enthusiastically to the story, with many townspeople joining Civic Resistance units. Like the poet Byron, Castro and the Movement awoke famous. A CBS television documentary filmed in the mountains a few weeks later added to Castro's now considerable fame in North America.

Matthews had bought a gold brick. No one, probably including Castro, knew his political loyalties at this time. A complex man, Castro, " ... as much demagogue as idealist, as much adventurer as revolutionary, as much anarchist as Communist or anything else"—superficially a bright man, but an undisciplined man whose brain was not to cope with the challenge of democratic government, whose quixotic personality was to take refuge in the role of twentieth-century "Leader," with the disaster it entailed.[11] But all this lay ahead. At the time of the Matthews visitation, Castro's background was known. Despite relatively moderate social, economic, and political reforms called for in the "History Will Absolve Me" speech, he obviously was an angry young man who stroked and sometimes embraced far-left philosophies. Matthews found Raúl Castro "slight and pleasant" but said nothing of his known Communist background, nor did he mention Che Guevara, much less *his* background.

Matthews also falsely reported Castro's strength. What seemed an endless flow of guerrillas in and out of the Castro camp was the same group, herded by brother Raúl. This was the force that " ... had been fighting for seventy-nine days"—fighting mainly to stay alive. By Castro's later admission, his "army" at this time consisted of eighteen men![12]

Thus the foundation of a myth: in part, the result of sensational, as opposed to in-depth, reporting. How to explain this monumental aberration on the part of a senior *New York Times* editor? Matthews helped us when he later wrote: " . . . I knew I had a sensational scoop. I exulted at the fact that at the age of fifty-seven I could still show a younger generation of newspapermen how to get a difficult and dangerous story, and how to write it. And I was moved, deeply moved, by that young man."[13]

Pride first, emotion second. But on what other grounds did Matthews justify his positive assertions? Where was the discipline of objectivity? Matthews later tried to justify his reporting, but it remains cheap and tawdry stuff—a costly episode that should come to the minds of those persons who write words for publication and who are tempted to abnegate the tremendous responsibility involved.

Despite Matthews' publicity, Castro's situation remained precarious. An influx of fifty recruits allowed him to organize his force into platoons, which often lived and fought independently. These units worked hard in attempting to win over local peasants, but their support probably depended as much on repressive army counterguerrilla measures and on landlords seizing land temporarily vacated by precaristas (at army orders) as on Castro's blandishments. This does not detract from the work and accomplishments of the various columns, and Che Guevara's account of life in the mountains is well worth reading as a primer on guerrilla warfare.[14]

Castro and Che claim to have developed guerrilla techniques independent of either Mao's or Giap's teachings.[15] Whatever the truth, they bore a marked resemblance to these teachings. They concentrated on agitation and propaganda techniques to win over peasants and gain their support, both active and passive—what Guevara called " . . . dressing the guerrillas in palm leaves."[16] Small bands raided army outposts and ambushed army columns and convoys to gain arms and supply and prisoners (treated well and released) and to provoke the government to extreme countermeasures. In May, the guerrillas were strong enough to carry out a successful frontal attack in daylight against a defended village.

The main accomplishment was survival during a critical period— what Guevara called the nomadic phase. Whether we like it or not, Castro was (and is) a charismatic figure with tremendous appeal to a large number of his countrymen. By keeping the standard of revolt flying in the Sierra Maestra, he succeeded in polarizing opposition elements that daily became more daring in the cities. Urban guerrilla tactics proved a two-edged weapon, particularly when they were uncoordinated and lacked single political purpose, and various urban movements suffered some serious defeats. Time favored the guerrillas only because Batista failed to cope intelligently with the situation. Political mistakes aside (though here lay the key to his ultimate defeat), his counterguerrilla tactics proved inept. Conventional efforts to "seal" the guerrillas in the mountains and to bomb and starve them into submission were expensive flops. Summary evacuation of precaristas played into landlord hands and increased already wide dissatisfaction to bring more security and recruits to Castro. His strength in 1957 amounted to only about two hundred guerrillas operating in small units that defied the keenest bombardier's eye. The guerrillas daily were growing tougher and, for some time, had existed, when necessary, on one meal a day. As with other guerrilla units throughout history, Castro's people were becoming increasingly self-sufficient. Small workshops appeared, a dispensary, armory, a shoe factory; the guerrillas printed and circulated a mimeographed newspaper and, in time, built a cigar factory! And all in remote mountain valleys approachable only through most difficult and hostile terrain.[17]

By early 1957, press and television coverage was making Cuba a domestic political issue in America with Castro rapidly emerging as Hero against Villain Batista. That spring, Eisenhower removed Ambassador Gardner (no easy task) in favor of a generous Republican backer, Earl Smith, a fifty-four-year-old investment broker with Ivy League background—his first wife was Consuelo Vanderbilt—who lacked diplomatic experience. Eisenhower's choice was unfortunate. The situation demanded a master, not a student, a person trained in professional diplomacy with sufficient local knowledge to unravel the complex political snarl. The Eisenhower administration was veering toward what it called a "neutral" attitude. Smith was instructed to " . . . alter the prevailing notion in Cuba that the American Ambassador was intervening on behalf of the government of Cuba to perpetuate the Batista dictatorship."[18] Considering decades of involvement, American neutrality was as ludicrous as the attempted "neutral" role of the British in Palestine after World War II—a fact that a competent ambassador would have stressed to the Secretary of State. It perhaps would have done no good. The Administration, the State Department, and the military were split into pro- and anti-Batista factions, a split that carried to the Havana embassy, where the CIA was operating virtually independently of the ambassador. The situation called for a united stand on the part of his embassy—and perhaps no one could have achieved this, considering the military-political schisms of the day and the bewildered man in the White House.

Eisenhower apparently did not realize the rotten structure of Batista's government. Batista's crusade against "communism," his expanding economy and so-called stable rule were daily attracting diverse American investments, which only added to the strength of the pro-Batista lobby in Washington. And yet American officials, diplomats, CIA agents, and newspapermen were reporting the sordid and increasingly obvious facts.

Positive action in mid-1957 might not have salvaged anything in the end, but it was the only hope: To let matters continue on a disaster course, to pursue a policy of diplomatic "neutrality" not only solved nothing but caused considerable harm. For "neutrality," as defined by the Administration, meant arms and shipments to Batista and harassment of anti-Batista forces in the United States; it meant continued presence of the American military mission in Havana—and all this, in Cuban minds, spelled support of the regime. This produced two results. So long as Batista felt that he could count on continued American support, he refused to change his ways. Yet his regime was growing so distasteful that theretofore moderate and *attentiste* Cubans were veering toward the opposition. A scholar of the period later concluded:

> ... It would appear that American policy in this period was so inept and ineffectual that it was pro-Batista to Castro and pro-Castro to Batista. On the whole, however, Batista was favored as long as he was capable of benefiting from favors, and this period constitutes a sorry and sometimes shameful interlude in the history of recent Cuban-United States relations.[19]

Throughout summer of 1957, the threat to Batista's government steadily grew in scope. In July, two opposition leaders from Havana, Raúl Chibás, of the Ortodoxos, and Felipe Pazos, a respected economist, visited Castro to work out an alliance. The Pact of the Sierra called for a united revolutionary front to oust Batista in favor of free elections and democratic government. Significantly, it asked Washington to stop sending arms to Batista and otherwise not to intervene in Cuban affairs.

Meanwhile, terror in the towns continued to do Castro's work for him. Toward the end of July, his chief organizer, Frank País, fell to police bullets in Santiago. The funeral brought a massive and impressive demonstration by Santiago mothers. Ambassador Smith witnessed this sad group, which Batista's police broke up with a violence that caused the new ambassador's public protest (and, in turn, elicited Batista's protest against Smith's statement). A strike followed, which police and troops savagely broke within a week.

By autumn of 1957, civil war existed in Cuba. In September, dissident naval elements working with the 26th of July Movement (and probably the CIA) attempted a mutiny, an abortive effort called off at the last minute. Not getting the word, Cienfuegos rebels rose, captured the base, and seized most of the town. Troops, supported by armor and aircraft, arrived in the afternoon and soon eliminated all opposition, killing perhaps three hundred rebels. The revolt made headlines in the

United States. A small anti-Batista bloc in Congress objected to American arms being used to suppress internal disorders and there was criticism of Batista's strong-arm methods in the press. Some State Department officials began talking about prohibiting further arms shipments to Cuba.[20] Influential voices spoke just as loudly in defense of such shipments, and there the matter rested—for the moment.

Castro's guerrillas meanwhile made several small but successful attacks on outposts, and at least one ambush of a relief column. Castro now controlled about two thousand square miles of Oriente province and was strong enough to send two columns from the mountains: one, seventy men, of whom only twenty-eight were armed, under Juan Almeida, to work slowly toward Santiago; the other, sixty-five partially armed men under brother Raúl, to work north toward the Central Highway.[21] Local columns, one commanded by Che Guevara, continued to expand the Oriente base, striking at army outposts in fringe areas. All was not roses for Castro, however. His people remained desperately short of arms, and supply was also difficult. In early 1958, the American reporter Dickey Chapelle visited Castro: " . . . at one point I lived on raw sugar cane for two days, and at another time I ate only one meal a day for five days in a row."[22] Contrary to sensational reporting by American correspondents, Castro's total force numbered closer to three hundred, than to the several thousand alleged. His army lacked discipline, while a good many peasants refused his blandishments and had to be coerced and (foreshadowing the future) sometimes executed.[23] In December, he ordered widespread burning of the sugar crop which caused considerable resentment and was later canceled. Representatives of various opposition groups meeting in Florida presented him with the Miami Pact, which called for a joint resistance effort under a Council of Liberation, a notion he angrily rejected while criticizing Prío Socarrás' followers for storing arms in Havana, where they most likely would be captured, when they were needed in the countryside.

Batista, on the other hand, counted some positive gains. Despite bombings and murders and the fighting in Oriente, the Cuban economy continued to prosper and more capital to flow in, mostly from the United States.[24] The U.S.A. was also providing weapons including armored vehicles. Security forces in cities kept terrorists splintered and frequently on the run.

Neither CIA nor State Department officials favored Castro so much as they condemned Batista. While he burbled on about spring elections, police and troops continued to operate with such undisguised violence that theretofore-neutral agencies began to swing over to the revolutionary cause. The Communists, whom Batista had been blaming all along, only started to veer toward Castro's support in February 1958. Significantly, prominent church leaders and judges also began protesting. In mid-March, a Havana magistrate ordered indictment of two of Batista's hatchet men (and barely escaped with his life). Batista suspended constitutional guarantees, reimposed censorship, and postponed scheduled elections. The university long had been closed; secondary schools now closed. Urged by resistance leaders in the city, Castro ordered a general strike for early April, to be followed by a massive civil-disobedience campaign throughout the country.

A blow to Batista far worse than these was about to fall. The American public had become increasingly upset by Batista's brutality and by liberal press reports that portrayed Castro as a liberator who "promised genuine representative government."[25] Cuba had become a domestic political issue. Eisenhower could no longer watch, he had to act. Citing the charter of the Organization of American States, he placed an embargo on further arms shipments to Batista.

The arms themselves were not so important as the moral effect of the deed. Batista at once ordered arms from Europe and England. He could not replace the tacit support of the Eisenhower administration, even though, ambiguously enough, the Administration bowed to Pentagon pressures and left the military advisory mission in Havana. Ambassador Smith remained close to Batista, and the U. S. Army tactlessly decorated one of Batista's pet colonels with the Legion of Merit (for prior services on the Inter-American Defense Board). The arms embargo nonetheless proved a welcome shot in the arm to the rebels, who hastened plans for a general strike. They may have moved too rapidly. Some evidence suggests that Castro himself did not really favor the tactic, perhaps because of its organizational difficulties, perhaps because success would have allowed a junta to take over. Whatever the case, the strike, or what Hugh Thomas more accurately calls an urban uprising, failed, and caused Castro to resume guerrilla tactics in both cities and countryside.* Batista answered in two ways, the first being increased counterterror, with emphasis on students who were " . . . blamed as the main troublemakers. . . . It became safer for young men to take to the hills than to walk in the streets."[26]

Next came Operation Summer, the biggest military operation in Cuban history, launched toward end of May and designed to eliminate Castro. Thirteen combat teams of about three hundred fifty men each—some forty-five hundred troops—supported by tanks, artillery, naval gunfire, and aircraft, and supplemented by Rural Guard units, pushed in from two directions toward Castro's headquarters.

The attacks progressed satisfactorily for a few weeks, then petered out. Batista's two senior commanders loathed each other. Like Rennen-

---

* Castro would have been wise to have read Chorley on the efficacy of the general strike in the history of revolutionary warfare.

707

kampf and Samsonov, who brought the Russian armies to disaster at Tannenberg in 1914, they refused to co-operate either with each other or with the General Staff. Batista's orders tied up about a quarter of the troops in guarding coffee and sugar plantations in Oriente. Army morale, in general, was poor; most units were untrained for guerrilla warfare. Upon leaving the lowlands, they succumbed to fatigue and disease; the rainy season slowed them even more.[27] They pushed on, however, and, by mid-June, had boxed Castro into a four-square-mile area; in his later words: " . . . Our territory was reduced and reduced until we could not reduce any further."[28] But now columns lacked sufficient strength to deliver a *coup de grâce,* nor were reinforcements available to help them.

Nor had the push fragmented the guerrillas. Learning of Batista's plans in ample time, Castro pulled in his outposts and his roving units. As soldiers advanced, he retreated. Knowing literally every move made by the army, he kept one step ahead. When the columns reached the end of their tether, he attacked. One army column, nearly a thousand men, lost two thirds of its strength in killed and wounded, not to mention loss of arms, radios, and code books.[29] Batista's army was soon on the run. The retreat yielded rifles, machine guns, mortars and bazookas, even a 14-ton tank.[30] The entire action cost the guerrillas perhaps twenty-seven killed and fifty wounded.

Batista's army was still extricating itself from the Sierra Maestra when Raúl Castro's guerrillas struck in the north to protest American delivery of rockets to the army by kidnaping a number of American and Canadian mining employees, along with twenty-seven American sailors and marines from Guantánamo and several officials of United Fruit Company. This bold act caused ranking officials in Washington to argue for armed intervention against the guerrillas, but the storm blew over when Raúl released them and they reported that they had been well treated.[31]

Batista's failure in the countryside, graphically described to the Cuban people by Radio Rebelde broadcasting from the Sierra, brought near panic in top government circles. Batista attempted to counter Castro's growing popularity with incessant propaganda and large rewards, such as a hundred thousand dollars offered for the capture of the bearded guerrilla leader. In cities, police rounded up thousands of "suspects" in a desperate attempt to quell growing revolution fed by rebel broadcasts. In July, in Caracas, agents of the Movement brought together representatives of other underground groups (Communists excluded) to form a Junta of Unity (Frente Cívico Revolucionario Democrático), which designated Castro commander in chief of revolutionary forces· and issued a revolutionary manifesto. Although Batista prevented publication in Cuba, it was published in the United States and elsewhere in the hemisphere and was broadcast in Cuba both from stations in Caracas and from Radio Rebelde.[32] About this same time, the Communists, who had been edging closer to Castro and the Movement since early in the year, saw the light and sent a representative to the Sierra, much to the delight, no doubt, of Raúl Castro and Che Guevara.

Failure of Operation Summer sounded the knell to Batista's hope of restoring control in southern Oriente. A large part of the area now lay under Castro's direct or indirect command, to the extent that local mills paid him a tribute of fifteen cents per 250-pound bag of sugar shipped to Havana—an income, according to Batista, of millions of dollars used to bribe more soldiers and buy more weapons. In August, Castro established central headquarters in the hills above La Plata. A few weeks later, his units started toward the coastal city of Santiago. Simultaneously, Guevara and another lieutenant, Cienfuegos, led columns west, toward Las Villas province, where Guevara was to establish a new base and take command of Directorio guerrilla groups fighting in the Escambray area. Both Guevara and Cienfuegos have written graphically of the hardships of this forty-day march. Although the enemy shot up one of Guevara's units, the guerrillas received considerable help from local Communists; they may also have bribed Batista's local commander in Camagüey—the suggested figure is one hundred thousand dollars—to let them transit the province. By end of October, Guevara and Cienfuegos had absorbed the Directorio and Communist units and were controlling a large portion of Las Villas, even going so far as to distribute privately owned land to local peasants. Guevara now began working across the island to sever the government's east-west communications.

Castro's columns meanwhile had snaked toward Santiago and other towns and were cutting communications and ambushing increasingly demoralized army units. Castro increasingly resembled an army theater commander more than a provincial guerrilla leader. Political envoys, couriers, and foreign correspondents arrived and left the La Plata headquarters in a steady stream. The guerrillas were on the offensive and would remain so until Batista's fall.

Batista fell with surprising swiftness. A rigged election of a new President in November, a Batista candidate, Rivero Agüero, fooled no one. Although Rivero attracted limited American support, mainly from the pro-Batista lobby, the government's situation was deteriorating beyond salvation. Panic in Havana washed over Washington. Eisenhower's later words unintentionally emphasized the poverty of his Cuba policy:

> . . . During the rush of these last events in the final days of 1958, the Central Intelligence Agency suggested for the first time that a

Castro victory might not be in the best interests of the United States. (Earlier reports which I had received of Castro's possible Communism were suspect because they originated with people who favored Batista.)

"Communists and other extreme radicals appear to have penetrated the Castro movement," Allen Dulles said. "If Castro takes over, they will probably participate in the government." When I heard this estimate, I was provoked that such a conclusion had not been given earlier.

One of my advisers recommended that the United States should now back Batista as the lesser of two evils. I rejected that course. If Castro turned out to be as bad as our intelligence now suggested, our only hope, if any, lay with some kind of nondictatorial "third force," neither Castroite nor Batistiano.[33]

Eisenhower was about five years too late. Guevara now cut the island in half and continued to receive surrender of principal city garrisons. At year's end, Batista gathered wife and children and, with a personal entourage " . . . of bodyguards, retainers, and erstwhile military and political accomplices" who filled five airplanes, flew into an exile that would end in Florida—no great hardship, in view of a personal fortune estimated as high as $300 million.[34]

Batista's exodus was Castro's victory. In early January 1959, Che Guevara and his ragged band entered Havana and took control of government. Castro triumphantly followed, the Liberator claiming the country for the Movement.

The political revolution was over, the social revolution about to begin—with results disastrous to Cuba and her long-suffering people.

From the standpoint of guerrilla warfare, Che Guevara's expedition to Bolivia constitutes an important postscript to the Cuban revolution. Daniel James, who translated and edited Che's captured diaries, offers an excellent account of this ill-fated expedition in his book *The Complete Bolivian Diaries of Ché Guevara*, on which the following brief account is largely based.[35]

Almost immediately upon assuming power, Castro began to alter facts of the multifaceted revolutionary experience. A combination of arrogance of ignorance and political opportunism caused him and Che to invent a theme that, by means of a peasant uprising, the rebels had established a peculiar "Latin American way" to revolution. Che Guevara developed the theme:

. . . We consider that the Cuban Revolution made three fundamental contributions to the laws of the revolutionary movement in

710

the current situation in America [i.e., Central and South America]. They are: Firstly, people's forces can win a war against the army. Secondly, we need not always wait for all the revolutionary conditions to be present; the insurrection itself can create them. Thirdly, in the underdeveloped parts of America the battleground for armed struggle should in the main be the countryside.[36]

Che foresaw a continental struggle brought on by a series of local insurrections—the famous *foco insurreccional*.[37] Here was a sort of revolutionary *tache d'huile* concept that, in time, Che supposed would result in a large revolutionary base from which to carry on the armed struggle:

> ... As Fidel said, the Andes will be the Sierra Maestra of America, and all the immense territories that make up this continent will become the scene of a life-and-death struggle against the power of imperialism.[38]

This grandiose dream might have died, except for a peculiar combination of factors. One was Castro's and Che's belief, probably genuine, in historical determinism:

> ... We cannot tell when this struggle will acquire a continental character nor how long it will last; but we can predict its advent and its triumph, because it is the inevitable result of historical, economic and political conditions and its direction cannot be changed.[39]

Allied to this factor was Castro's determination to retain his own revolutionary personality, particularly as regards Soviet influence. Castro and Che's revolutionary thesis was a synthesis owing much more to Mao Tse-tung and Ho Chi Minh than to the Soviets. This was all right so long as Castro did not have to depend on the U.S.S.R. for survival. When that unhappy state of affairs arose, the unorthodox revolutionary line could scarcely be tolerated, and, indeed, from 1961 onward, Guevara found himself in nasty fights with doctrinaire Communists at home and abroad.

Add to this Che's own performance as president of the Cuban National Bank and as Minister of Industry. Dr. Guevara's treatment of the Cuban economy very nearly killed the patient. His ineptness both in economics and in politics brought him into increasing conflict with Castro, whom he was beginning to criticize, albeit guardedly, and who saw him as a rival in any event.

In late 1964, Che evidently fell from grace, leaving Havana and becoming a sort of revolutionary ambassador without portfolio, in some

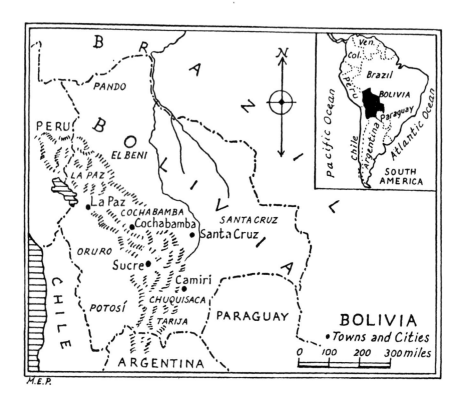

ways a romantic figure—a Walt Whitman with machine gun. In New York, he delivered a fiery address to the United Nations attacking both the United States and the Soviet Union as imperialist powers; he went on to Africa, made more bellicose speeches, and returned to Havana in March 1965, apparently impressed with the revolutionary possibilities offered by Congo troubles. He now went underground, resigning all official positions and renouncing Cuban citizenship, his goal to carry revolution abroad.[40]

Backed by Castro, he took 125 Cuban guerrillas to join the Kinshasa rebellion in the Congo. This effort totally failed, and he returned to Havana in autumn of 1965. He next decided to carry revolution to South America by establishing an insurrectional *foco* in Bolivia—a plan approved by Castro, who allowed him to recruit and train some twenty Cuban guerrillas and also supported him financially. At first glance, Bolivia seemed just the country in which to launch an agrarian revolution. The population was predominantly peasant. Terrain favored guerrilla warfare. The Barrientos government was authoritarian and seemed to Che and Castro to resemble Batista's former government. The army was small and ill-trained. A local Communist Party existed to carry revolution to the cities.

Disguised as a traveling salesman, Che arrived in Bolivia in November 1966. The young French Communist Régis Debray had arrived ear-

712

lier " . . . to make a geopolitical study of the selected zone."[41] Che now organized a headquarters for his small group, which included twenty-nine Bolivians. After a short training program, he started his force, about fifty, on a training march designed to learn the terrain, to perfect guerrilla tactics, and to recruit local peasants. In late March, the guerrillas successfully ambushed an army patrol, a success repeated in April.

Also in April, an army patrol elsewhere captured Régis Debray and two followers, and the Barrientos government agreed to accept a sixteen-man team of American Special Forces advisers to train a regiment of Rangers in counterinsurgency tactics. By May, considerable steam had gone out of Che's operations. Che was recording frequent quarrels in the ranks; lack of food and general illness were slowing his movements; he had recruited no peasants. Although he remained optimistic and, in July, briefly "captured" a town, he was forced to split his group and, in general, to keep moving. By now, Bolivian army intelligence had closed in on his earlier headquarters and had identified him and most of his lieutenants. By August, he admitted he was in " . . . a difficult situation." Matters steadily worsened. In early October, Ranger units surrounded his small group. He was wounded, captured, and presumably summarily executed.

What went wrong?

Castro's and Che's estimate of the situation was nearly as faulty as that made by Lyndon Johnson, Eugene Staley, Maxwell Taylor, and Walt Rostow in Vietnam in 1961 (see following chapter). The terrain in southeastern Bolivia favored guerrilla warfare only so long as one *knew* the terrain. Neither Che nor his Cubans nor his Bolivians knew the terrain, which meant that they had to depend largely on the peasants.

Che miscalculated badly here. The peasants, in this case Indians, who constituted more than two thirds of Bolivia's 4.25 million people, were not to be stirred. As Daniel James noted,

> . . . The National Revolution had radically transformed the life of the Bolivian Indian . . . and that was probably its greatest single accomplishment. It had done so, first, through an agrarian reform law enacted in 1953, which made landholders of the virtually landless Indian peasantry and gave them pride of ownership, even if it was but a little plot they were given. Second, the whole body of revolutionary legislation had the effect of raising the Indian out of age-old serfdom and enabling him to exert his rights as a citizen.

Guevara's chief selling point of revolution—Land to the Landless—automatically fell flat when pitched to Indians with land. But, more than that, in Che's area of operations, his *foco insurreccional* in southeastern Bolivia, the Indians were a particular sort, parochial and suspicious of any outsiders. Che and his guerrillas had studied the dominant Indian language, Quechua, but, in the Southeast, the Indians spoke Guaraní: " . . . Not one of the guerrillas, including the Bolivians, could speak it. . . . "[42] Lacking a valid sales pitch and easy communication, Che failed not only to win over peasants but to gain even limited co-operation. His monthly analysis for April included the ominous statement: " . . . The peasant base has not yet been developed although it appears that through planned terror we can neutralize some of them; support will come later. Not one enlistment has been obtained."[43] The May analysis included this statement: " . . . Complete lack of peasant recruitment, although they are losing their fear of us and we are beginning to win their admiration. It is a slow and patient task. . . . "[44] In June, he noted: " . . . The lack of peasant recruits continues. It is a vicious circle: to get this enlistment we need to settle in a populated area, and for this we need men."[45] And the last analysis, in September: " . . . the peasants do not give us any help and are turning into informers."[46]

Peasants had been informing all along. Though no great shakes, the Barrientos government and the Bolivian army impressed the peasants far more than did Che's guerrillas. This was partly because of land reforms, partly an "ingrained fear and respect" of the army, and partly because it was a peasant army and its recruits were aware that the government had been trying to help peasants. American army advisers had been on hand since 1958, their influence evident in a Civic Action Program which, by late 1963, had the army spending 20 per cent of its time in civil works, mostly in the countryside. Che's early successes caused peasant organizations throughout Bolivia to denounce "the invaders" and to organize armed peasant detachments to fight them, the prelude to a later formal "alliance of the peasantry with the Armed Forces."[47] For this reason, the army gained intelligence it needed to run down guerrillas; guerrillas lacked intelligence needed to survive, prosper, and grow.

Che fared no better with local revolutionary groups. Two such could have helped: the Communist Party, or PCB, headed by Mario Monje, with primarily an intellectual-student following; and the miners, helped by one Guevara (no relation). Castro and Che alienated Monje with their initial decision to use Bolivia as a revolutionary comfort station, a decision taken without consulting him.

Debray added to conflict by dealing with miners instead of with Monje—a futile gesture that resulted in only a few, undesirable recruits for Che. Che's own insistence on leading a rural revolution with the military struggle predominant over the political struggle completed Monje's alienation. Monje " . . . saw the revolution in more orthodox

Leninist terms, as emerging from a mass uprising in the cities"[48] as soon as a national crisis occurred. Monje, moreover, felt that he should lead the effort. When Che refused to consider this, the two fell out—to Guevara's great cost.

Even had Monje remained co-operative, he could have offered only limited help. He could have supplied Bolivian recruits, but whether they would have known terrain and Indians any better than Che is problematical. He also could have kept open a line of communication to Che, but whether Fidel Castro would have filled that line with revolutionary needs—arms, supply, and money—is also problematical: Daniel James suggests that Castro was not sorry to be rid of his old lieutenant.

That his old lieutenant was failing seems to have been the case. From his arrival in Bolivia, he had begun violating his own basic tenets of guerrilla warfare. By June, he was a sick man gradually losing control of himself and his group. It is possible that he wanted to die a martyr. He had seen his economic theories refuted. He might have believed that Castro was compromising Marxism-Leninism by accepting an imperialistic Soviet presence. He had failed in the Congo, and almost daily, despite various euphoric diary entries, he was seeing his theories fail in the Bolivian wilderness. Whether asthma and general debilitation dulled his senses or whether he underestimated the army, he refused to cut out for the border in time to avoid capture. On the basis of diary entries, not to mention his previous behavior and personality in general, we can conclude that Che's ego overcame his common sense. We don't know where his body lies but if ever a plaque is erected it should bear only two words, as fatal to a guerilla as to those who fight guerrillas: VANITAS VANITATUM.

CHAPTER FIFTY-SEVEN

1. Taber, 50 ff., for details of this training.
2. Goldenberg, 154. The author, himself a former Communist, described Che as a Marxist closely linked to international communism. See also, James, *Che Guevara* . . .
3. Guevara, *Reminiscences* . . . , 14, 38 ff.
4. Thomas, *Cuba* . . . , 874.
5. Guevara, *Reminiscences* . . . , 38–41.
6. Ibid., 131 ff., 196 ff.
7. Draper, *Castro's Revolution* . . . , 162.
8. Taber, 84. Rebels later assassinated the responsible officer.
9. H.L. Matthews, *The Cuban Story*, 36. See also, Pflaum, 16. The author found Castro shorter than six feet, pudgy, and with sloping chin.
10. H.L. Matthews, *The Cuban Story*, 27–39.
11. Draper, *Castro's Revolution* . . . , 56.
12. Ibid., 190. See also, Guevara, *Reminiscences* . . . This is scarcely an original *ruse de guerre*. While Castro at this time could have commanded a meaningful force, that was not proof that he *did* command one—and it was a reporter's responsibility to either discover the strength or report it with qualification.

13. H.L. Matthews, *The Cuban Story*. See also, Draper, *Castro's Revolution*... 191–2. On March 11, 1966, Draper wrote Matthews:

> ...I strongly doubt that your articles would have had such an electrifying effect if you had not personally vouched for Castro's large and winning force. You now claim that you "guessed at the time that he had about forty men." Then why did you report at the time, without any hint of skepticism, his boast that he had "groups of ten to forty"? And you gave a different version of this matter in your book.

14. Guevara, *Che Guevara on Guerrilla Warfare*.
15. Debray, 20–1: Castro relied politically on Marx, Martí, Lenin; militarily on Engels and Hemingway's *For Whom the Bell Tolls*,

> ...not so much as sources as ... coincidences; Fidel found in them only what he was looking for. Mao Tse-tung's *Problems of Strategy in Guerrilla War Against Japan* [sic] came into Fidel's and Che's hands after the 1958 summer offensive: to their surprise they found in this book what they had been practising under pressure of necessity.

16. Guevara, *Reminiscences*..., 197.
17. Ibid., 205.
18. Thomas, *Cuba*..., 958. See also, Smith.
19. Draper, *Castro's Revolution*..., 162–3.
20. Taber, 204.
21. Ibid., 210.
22. Chapelle.
23. Guevara, *Reminiscences*, see, for example 246–7.
24. H.L. Matthews, *The Cuban Story*, 66, 236–7. See also, ibid., 246: "... in 1958, United States interests controlled 80 per cent of Cuban utilities, 90 per cent of the mines, 90 per cent of the cattle ranches, all of the oil refining and distribution (with the Royal Dutch Shell) and 40 per cent of the sugar industry"; Draper, *Castroism*...; Mills; Thomas, *Cuba*..., 967.
25. Draper, *Castro's Revolution*..., 16.
26. Ibid., 14.
27. Mallin.
28. Thomas, *Cuba*..., 997. See also, H.L. Matthews, *Castro*...
29. Thomas, *Cuba*..., 997.
30. Ibid., 998. See also, Taber.
31. H.L. Matthews, Castro..., 106. See also, Taber; Mallin. From the guerrilla standpoint, the kidnapings made sense. Raúl's idea was to force the United States to negotiate and thus grant the rebels a sort of diplomatic recognition important for propaganda purposes; the divisive kidnapings also demonstrated widespread guerrilla control of the area.
32. Special Operations Research Office, *Casebook on Insurgency and Revolutionary Warfare*, 186:

> ...The agreement called for cooperation in the common cause, continued cooperation after victory, the arming of the people, and the cooperation of labor and business in a general strike to be called to aid the military front when needed. The manifesto called on the soldiers to desert, and on everybody else to support the revolution. Above all, it stressed the theme of unity.

33. Eisenhower, *Waging Peace*..., 521. See also, H.L. Matthews, *The Cuban Story*, 172: The Deputy Director of CIA, General C.P. Cabell, testified to the Senate Internal Security Committee on November 5, 1959, that his organi-

zation believed that Castro was not a member of the Communist Party, and did not consider himself to be a Communist.

34. Thomas, *Cuba* . . . , 1027. See also, H.L. Matthews, *The Cuban Story.*
35. James, *The Complete Bolivian Diaries* . . . See also, Guevara, *Bolivian Diary.*
36. Lavan, *Che Guevara Speaks* . . . , 75, for his interview with two Chinese Communist journalists in April 1959.
37. James, *The Complete Bolivian Diaries* . . .
38. Lavan, *Che Guevara Speaks* . . . , 86.
39. Ibid.
40. Ibid., 98, 102. See also ibid., 139–41 for his "Farewell Letter to Fidel": ". . . Other nations of this world call for my modest efforts."
41. James, *The Complete Bolivian Diaries* . . . , 11, 32.
42. Ibid., 59–61. See also, Fagg.
43. James, *The Complete Bolivian Diaries* . . . , 151.
44. Ibid., 164.
45. Ibid., 176.
46. Ibid., 219.
47. Ibid., 22, 60.
48. Ibid., 62–4.

CHAPTER 58

John Kennedy inherits a war • General Lansdale's estimate of the situation • Kennedy's strategic appraisal • His early errors • Lyndon Johnson's report • Hawks versus doves • Military versus political strategy • The Staley Plan • The Taylor mission • The military solution • Kennedy's reservations • Roger Hilsman dissents • De Gaulle's warning • Kennedy acts • His relations with Diem • The situation in South Vietnam

SINCE 1951, John Kennedy had interested himself in the Vietnam scene, on several occasions pressing his views on fellow legislators and the nation.[1] For nearly ten years, protests of dissident officials had claimed his ear. He had listened to such Saigon veterans as Robert Blum and Edward Gullion, and he knew and approved of some of Colonel Edward Lansdale's views.

In June 1956, the young senator told a meeting of American Friends of Vietnam: "... What we must offer [the Vietnamese people] is a revolution—a political, economic, and social revolution far superior to anything the Communists can offer—far more peaceful, far more democratic, and far more locally controlled."[2]

Kennedy's error, and that of hundreds of influential and well-intentioned Americans, was the assumption that President Ngo Dinh Diem both wished and was able to effect such a revolution—an assumption unfortunately voided by Diem's behavior, which increasingly caused some of his most enthusiastic American supporters to have second thoughts on his performance. Although the Eisenhower administration was preparing to send more advisers and more aid, Ambassador Durbrow "... had been required to bear so many messages of disapproval from the United States that he had not been welcome at the presidential palace in Saigon for several months."[3]

Although Vietnam played no prominent role in 1960 U.S. presidential elections, Kennedy entered office displeased with the situation in

Indochina. He was scarcely reassured when, in early February 1961, presidential assistant Walt Rostow handed him a memorandum prepared by the Pentagon's leading expert on guerrilla warfare, Brigadier General Edward Lansdale, who, in Robert Shaplen's words,

> . . . felt that the Vietnamese military structure and military methods of operation (which the Americans, in their pale advisory role, were countenancing) were all wrong. He felt that if the bitter conflict stood any chance of being won, we would have to be firm in insisting on a complete reorganization of the government's fighting machine; we would have to make it a force capable of dealing with Communist subversion in a meaningful and imaginative way, much as Magsaysay had done in the Philippines in 1951–52.[4]

Kennedy read the paper through and turned to Rostow: "This is the worst yet," he said. "You know, Ike never briefed me about Vietnam."[5]

Kennedy early concluded that guerrilla warfare—what he termed "internal" or subterranean" war—was the real challenge of the sixties and ordered Secretary of Defense Robert McNamara to begin weaning the United States from dependence on the Eisenhower-Dullesian massive-retaliation strategy of nuclear warfare. The Lansdale report so impressed Kennedy that he decided to send its author back to Vietnam as American ambassador. The threat of Lansdale's disruptive presence to sacrosanct bureaucratic and military empires caused a storm of protest from Washington and Saigon officialdom.[6] Unfortunately, the young President succumbed to these forces (which he would never quite tame), and dispatched Frederick E. Nolting as his new ambassador. A soft-spoken Virginian, Nolting was a fifty-year-old former philosophy professor turned diplomat, a man without experience in Southeast Asia,

> . . . a big, soft-spoken man who was so comfortable to be with that almost everyone used his nickname, Fritz. He was ideal for the job of restoring good relations with Diem and attempting to influence him toward concessions that would bring his regime wider support from within Vietnam and make it politically easier for the United States to give him the aid he requested.[7]

Instead of getting off to a good start, then, Kennedy kept the pot of South Vietnam bubbling as it had been for the previous five years. A change of faces and additional American aid meant no fundamental improvement of a worsening situation. Instead, it meant privately compounding past and present errors while publicly defending them as a viable program. A number of reasons exist for Kennedy's disappointing performance in this troubled area, and we shall discuss them in due course. But first we must present in brief the turbulent events of these crucial years of the insurgency.

In spring of 1961, Kennedy and his advisers were still deeply concerned about the American role in Vietnam and particularly in Laos, where the Joint Chiefs of Staff (JCS) had recommended committing American ground troops. General James Gavin, whom Kennedy had appointed ambassador to France, hotly opposed the idea, and bluntly told Kennedy:

> ... that Laos was a landlocked area in which it would be very difficult to bring U.S. power to bear in any meaningful way, even if it should be in the U.S. interest to do so. I felt Laos would turn into a bottomless pit into which we would pour soldier after soldier. I recounted for the President the history of the debate inside the Pentagon after Dien Bien Phu and said I felt this new situation was similar. There was little to be gained and a great deal to be risked by U.S. military action.[8]

While a special task force of ranking officials studied the problem, Kennedy sent Vice-President Lyndon Johnson on a general tour of Southeast Asia. In Saigon, the lanky Texan talked to Diem and his officials, promised increased aid, and stated the Administration's confidence in the Diem government. Ngo Dinh Diem, he told reporters, was the Winston Churchill of Southeast Asia. Far worse, he told Kennedy that

> ... the basic decision in Southeast Asia is here. We must decide whether to help these countries to the best of our ability or throw in the towel in the area and pull back our defenses to San Francisco and a "Fortress America" concept.

Johnson "did not consider Southeast Asia lost, 'and it is by no means inevitable that it must be lost.' " Diem was

> ... a complex figure beset by many problems. "He has admirable qualities, but he is remote from the people, is surrounded by persons less admirable than he. The country can be saved—if we move quickly and wisely."[9]

Johnson's mission produced varied, generally unfortunate results. Perhaps the most harmful was to reinforce the concept of South Vietnam as a "strategic necessity" to the United States, along with the notion of Diem's indispensability—not only in his and his intimates' minds

720

but in those of the Administration and the American public. Johnson made plain his attitude, on the plane flying from Saigon, when a reporter started discussing Diem and his faults. " . . . Don't tell me about Diem," Johnson answered. "He's all we've got out there."[10]

Kennedy simultaneously fell victim to another pernicious influence, his Secretary of State, Dean Rusk, a small man in a big job:

> . . . While the President and a number of his advisers saw the insurgency primarily as a civil war . . . Rusk tended to ignore the highly complex causes and history of the insurgency and developed the theme of "aggression from the North," which was to become increasingly prominent as the American-sponsored efforts of the Saigon regime proved ineffective against the rebellion. As early as 1961, Rusk was speaking of "the determined and ruthless campaign of propaganda, infiltration, and subversion by the Communist regime in north Viet-Nam to destroy the Republic of Viet-Nam."[11]

Rusk's indignation was shared by Secretary of Defense Robert McNamara and, to a lesser degree, by Kennedy's national security adviser, McGeorge Bundy, an "establishment intellectual" who, along with Rusk and McNamara, favored a military strategy. Bundy's deputy, Walt Rostow, was particularly hawkish and epitomized the dubious talent with which Kennedy surrounded himself. Forty-five years old, he was a Yale man, a Rhodes scholar, an economist and historian long associated with government; in World War II, he had served with the OSS in Burma. Rostow shared Rusk's belief in "aggression from the North" (or perhaps Rusk shared Rostow's belief). Rostow made his thinking known publicly at West Point, in spring of 1961, where he argued that emerging nations must be protected against external Communist aggression to the point that it might be necessary to " . . . seek out and engage the ultimate source of aggression."[12] Although Hanoi at this time was helping insurgents in the South, the effort nowhere near approached that claimed by Rusk and Rostow, and they were as much at fault for preaching this as others were for denying its existence.

Still other presidential advisers, most of them close to Kennedy, though admitting the North's unsavory role in the South, wanted to counter it, along with the actual insurgency, with a political strategy that would have sharply subordinated military operations. This group, which would be termed doves, included Robert Kennedy, Averell Harriman, George Ball, Roger Hilsman, and Michael Forrestal.

The hawks—Johnson, Rusk, McNamara, Rostow, and the JCS—formed a formidable pressure group. Although Kennedy, in general, favored a political strategy, he could not ride roughshod over those who favored a military strategy. He was also increasingly incensed, as were many Americans, with Viet Cong terrorist tactics, and he realized that implementation of a political policy would involve military aspects, which posed the problem of preparing the nation to follow him. Heretofore restrained in public utterances on the subject, he now began emphasizing the theme of Communist revolutionary warfare and external aggression, telling a joint session of Congress in late May:

> ... their aggression is more often concealed than open. They have fired no missiles; and their troops are seldom seen. They send arms, agitators, aid, technicians and propaganda to every troubled area. But where fighting is required, it is usually done by others, by guerrillas striking at night, by assassins striking alone, assassins who have taken the lives of 4,000 civil officers in the last 12 months in Vietnam, by subversives and saboteurs and insurrectionists, who in some cases control whole areas inside of independent nations.[13]

Kennedy next dispatched Professor Eugene Staley, who spent summer of 1961 preparing a report on Diem's needs. Although not made public, Staley's recommendations included " . . . a number of changes in the administration of aid, as well as certain reforms of a political nature."[14] He also allegedly recommended increasing Vietnamese army strength to 170,000, doubling the Civil Guard to a total 120,000, equipping the Self-Defense Corps with modern small arms and radios, and constructing a network of fortified, or strategic, hamlets.[15] Kennedy was mulling over the Staley Plan when Diem sent an anguished plea for help. Kennedy now dispatched a larger mission, headed by sixty-year-old General Maxwell Taylor, a former army chief of staff whom he had consulted in the Bay of Pigs fiasco, assisted by Walt Rostow. Kennedy wanted to know in particular if the Diem government could be "saved." Taylor (and Rostow) " . . . was dismayed by a number of things he thought were wrong with the Diem regime and he recommended a tougher approach." He recommended among many other things

> ... that we stand firm on our demand that Diem and Nhu decentralize their administration, both in its civilian and its military aspects, and that we insist on a revamping of the muddled system of collecting and interpreting intelligence about the Vietcong. Taylor also felt strongly that certain political reforms should be instituted and that bona fide nationalist leaders who were in jail should be freed.[16]

On the positive side:

... their collective answer to Kennedy's question was that South Vietnam had enough vitality to justify a major United States effort ... they recommended increased American intervention—in effect, a shift from arm's length advice to limited partnership. While only the Vietnamese could finally beat the Viet Cong, Americans at all levels, Taylor and Rostow argued, could show them how the job was to be done.[17]

Taylor's recommendations meant openly refuting the manpower ceiling laid down by the Geneva Agreements. The American role would be enlarged, " ... essentially through the penetration of the South Vietnamese army and government by American 'advisers,' attached to Vietnamese military units or government offices and designed to improve the level of local performance";[18] these included American helicopter and air-reconnaissance units for logistics-support purposes. The report also called for committing American ground troops (which the JCS had recommended a few months earlier): an eight-to-ten-thousand-man task force would be provided as "engineers" to help in flood-control work; such a force, in addition to raising Vietnamese morale and demonstrating United States determination to Hanoi, Peking, and Moscow, would be capable of conducting " ... combat operations for self-defense and perimeter security and, if the Vietnamese Army were hard pressed, of providing an emergency reserve." In case this force provoked invasion from the North, additional troops would be required. Moreover—and here was Catch-22—" ... Taylor and Rostow *hoped* that *this* program would suffice to win the civil war—and were sure it would *if only* the infiltration from the north could be stopped. But if it continued, then they could see no end to the war. ... "[19] Finally, " ... the whole program was only an important first step in the direction of the longer-run goal, eventually to contain and eliminate the threat to the independence of South Vietnam ... for final victory the U.S. might have to strike the source of the aggression (though this decision could be deferred)."[20]

Here was a qualitative change in addition to a quantitative change of means to realize the grand ambition: *stop communism*. Taylor and Rostow's rationale was as fascinating as it was dangerous. Instead of appreciating the political nature of an insurgency, he was attempting to change the rules. As Roger Hilsman later noted,

> ... The mission of these American troops—revealing the continued focus in General Taylor's mind on the possibility of a conventional, Korea-type attack—would be to hold the ring against invasion from the north by regular North Vietnamese divisions and to man the northern borders against infiltrators, while the South Vietnamese dealt with the guerrillas in the rear.[21]

Far from being the far-sighted strategist that Kennedy needed, Taylor might as well have donned an air force uniform and stood in the public pulpit to preach the virtues of massive retaliation. Far from approaching the problem with imagination and flexibility (and caution), he was thinking primarily in conventional-force terms.

Apparently, Taylor and his fellows were either ignorant of or oblivious to the estimate of the situation that General Matthew Ridgway had presented in 1954 (see Chapter 48) and that emphasized incompatibility between the American military machine and the tactical environment of Vietnam. In 1961, the highest American military councils unfortunately lacked any semblance of Ridgway's intelligent restraint. Only that spring, General Lyman Lemnitzer, chairman of the JCS, had returned from an inspection trip to Vietnam and, according to newspaper reports,

> . . . felt that the new administration was 'oversold' on the importance of guerrilla warfare and that too much emphasis on counter-guerrilla measures would impair the ability of the South Vietnamese Army to meet a conventional assault like the attack on South Korea by the ten or more regular North Vietnamese divisions.

In early November, speaking at Fordham University, General Earle G. Wheeler, army chief of staff, told his audience

> . . . that what the United States was committed to support in Vietnam was "military action. . . . Despite the fact that the conflict is conducted as guerrilla warfare," Wheeler went on to say, "it is nonetheless a military action. . . . It is fashionable in some quarters to say that the problems in Southeast Asia are primarily political and economic rather than military. I do not agree. The essence of the problem in Vietnam is military."[22]

Taylor now was proposing a course of action consonant with Lemnitzer and Wheeler's antiquated reasoning—a course of action that, if it did provoke the enemy to conventional counteraction, would lead to an escalation projected by the JCS in a report on Laos: If landing American troops in Thailand, South Vietnam, and government-held portions of the Laotian panhandle did not produce a cease-fire, the JCS

> . . . recommended an air attack on Pathet Lao positions and tactical nuclear weapons on the ground. If North Vietnamese or Chinese then moved in, their homelands would be bombed. If massive Red troops were then mobilized, nuclear bombings would be threatened and, if necessary, carried out. If the Soviets then inter-

vened, we should "be prepared to accept the possibility of general war." But the Soviet Union, they assured the President, "can hardly wish to see an uncontrollable situation develop."[23]

Taylor's plan contained no less a number of "x" factors. Rostow was an even more outspoken advocate of escalation, arguing " . . . for a contingency policy of retaliation against the north, graduated to match the intensity of Hanoi's support of the Viet Cong. . . . "[24] Secretary of Defense Robert McNamara also reported to the President a conclusion shared by his deputy secretary Roswell Gilpatric, and by the JCS,

> . . . that the chances were against, probably sharply against, preventing the fall of South Vietnam to Communism by any measures short of the introduction of U.S. forces on a substantial scale . . . though of great help to Diem, even the initial U.S. task force of about 8,000 men, would not convince the other side that we meant business, unless we accompanied the introduction of the initial force with a clear commitment to the full objective of preventing the fall of South Vietnam to Communism and warned Hanoi through some channel that continued support of the VC would lead to punitive retaliation against North Vietnam. . . . If the proposed commitment and force deployment were undertaken, the President was warned of the possibility that Hanoi and Peiping might intervene openly, in which case as many as, but (given logistic difficulties of the other side) not more than six U.S. divisions, or about 205,000 men would be required.[25]

The Taylor-Rostow mission evoked several responses. Not long after the mission's return, Kennedy met with his close friend and adviser Arthur Schlesinger, Jr.:

> " . . . They want a force of American troops," he told me early in November. "They say it's necessary in order to restore confidence and maintain morale. But it will be just like Berlin. The troops will march in; the bands will play; the crowds will cheer; and in four days everyone will have forgotten. Then we will be told we have to send in more troops. It's like taking a drink. The effect wears off, and you have to take another." The war in Vietnam, he added, could be won only so long as it was *their* war. If it were ever converted into a white man's war, we would lose as the French had lost a decade earlier.[26]

Although pressured by the JCS and by some principal advisers to commit a task force of American troops, Kennedy refused. The Bay of Pigs disaster had made him suspicious of experts, especially when other experts disagreed.[27] One important dissenter was Roger Hilsman. A West Pointer ('43) from Texas, forty-one-year-old Hilsman had served with OSS in Burma; after the war, he had earned a Ph.D. from Yale, left the army, and taught international affairs until entering the State Department, in 1961, as director of its intelligence section. Hilsman differed sharply with the Pentagon and with Rusk and Rostow as to Vietnam. He saw the challenge as political—as a war of ideas that demanded essentially a political strategy designed to gain popular support:

> ...that government existed for the benefit of the people, that a government could really *care,* was as revolutionary in most of Asia as anything the Communists had to offer....

He concluded that a viable strategy " ... would require an emphasis on political, economic, and social action into which very carefully calibrated military measures were interwoven."[28] Militarily, guerrillas must be fought with guerrilla, rather than conventional, tactics. This opinion, shared by other experts, military and civil, struck a responsive note with the President, who a few months earlier had been warned by Charles de Gaulle that

> ... to intervene in this region [Indochina] will be to catch yourself in the cogs of a machine. ... the more you become involved there fighting Communism, the more Communists will appear as champions of national independence. ... We, the French, have experience of that. You, the Americans, wanted to take our place in Indo-China. Now you want to take over where we left off and restart the war which we ended. I predict that you will sink bit by bit into a bottomless military and political swamp however much you pay in men and money.[29]

Kennedy moved cautiously. He probably hoped that the psychological effect of committing more "advisers" and logistics-support troops such as helicopter units would warn Hanoi that he meant business, would revive South Vietnamese morale, would cause Diem to reform his government, and would satisfy administration hawks. He also ordered his military chiefs " ... to be prepared for the introduction of combat troops, should they prove to be necessary."[30] In addition, he authorized continued CIA support of agents infiltrated into North Vietnam and Laos to work up covert resistance against the Communists, a program started in the Eisenhower administration.[31]

What he did not do—and this is one of his great failures—was to pursue his doubts. What he did not do was to call for a re-examination of what was passing for political policy and military strategy. He badly needed a devil's advocate with intelligence and courage sufficient to question underlying assumptions held by the majority of his advisers. He turned down recommendations to commit troops in Laos and Vietnam partly because the JCS and the CIA had so terribly misjudged the Cuban situation. What made him think that prevailing notions of policy and strategy in Southeast Asia were any more valid, particularly in view of General Ridgway's earlier dissent? That the domino theory could hold up under intelligent analysis? That the Pentagon would be content to remain in an advisory role? That Diem was indispensable? That Nolting and Harkins could manage Diem? That he himself could foist the Diem regime on the world as free, democratic government? That, had the American people been properly informed, they would not have trusted him and backed him in a "risk" strategy necessary to straighten out the Diem regime? Instead, he remained a prisoner to this regime, to his own bellicose advisers, and to his own unsure self.

The Taylor report had brought explosive response from the Diem government in Saigon and from the Vietnam lobby in the United States, and this alone should have caused doubts to arise in the minds of the military missionaries in the White House and Pentagon. Stung by Taylor's criticisms and prompted by brother Nhu, the Vietnamese President huffed and puffed about his country's sovereignty. In Shaplen's words, " . . . what followed over a period of several weeks was a game of bluff, which the Vietnamese won hands down."[32] Instead of pressing the issue to final conclusions, the Administration yielded and pretended to find solace in Diem's empty promises. This was a vital error. Diem had consistently refused to allow either a political opposition or a coalition government in order to broaden his support. Diem was incapable of understanding representative government, and, by 1962, this fact was obvious. Despite such sops as a National Economic Council and provincial councils, Diem and his ruling oligarchy had refused to relinquish any real powers. Millions of American dollars continued to fall into their hands—$300 million in army credits alone in 1961—and, either in cash or kind, precious little of these funds reached the countryside, where the war was being fought. U.S. protests aroused only further threats from Diem and his advisers. At Ambassador Nolting's urging, the Administration agreed to a "soft" approach in hope that Diem would change his ways.[33]

Instead of political reforms, Diem pushed through his rubber-stamp assembly such restrictive legislation as the Public Meetings Law, " . . . a law that forbade all kinds of meetings unless they were authorized by the government," and the Bill for the Protection of Morality, a piece of legislative nonsense sponsored by Mme. Nhu and one comparable to Chiang Kai-shek's New Life Movement. Total censorship prevailed and Nhu's secret police prowled everywhere to pounce on dissidence:

... by 1962 there were some thirty thousand prisoners in about fifty jails throughout the country, about two-thirds of whom were classified as political prisoners. Many were captured Vietcong insurgents, but there were also a lot of "suspects" who had languished in jails for months or even years. Among the prisoners were some three hundred non-Communist liberals arrested solely for having expressed anti-Diem views or for being suspected of having spoken out in favor of the abortive 1960 coup.[34]

The regime's suspicions extended to the army, which continued to stir restlessly despite Diem's efforts to control it:

... Promotion on the basis of personal loyalty rather than ability, the use of informers, the banishment of men of integrity and initiative, and the domination of all strategy had not made the Army more loyal; these methods had merely brought about a tenuous control, and badly compromised and diluted a military force which was in a fight to the death with a tough enemy.[35]

A confused and demoralized army not only could not fight a successful counterinsurgency, but its ranks became increasingly vulnerable to the enemy's proselyting effort, the *binh van* program, which one expert believed was " ... the most deadly weapon" in the Viet Cong arsenal.[36] In emphasizing the Communist and northern-aggression themes that so appealed to American officials and politicians and in steadfastly refusing to recognize his real enemy, the NLF and the emphasis it placed on the "armed struggle," particularly the political struggle, Diem remained bent on polishing the veneer of government at a time when termites were gnawing away its essential supports.

CHAPTER FIFTY-EIGHT

1. Kennedy, *The Strategy of Peace*, 57.
2. Buttinger, II, 936.
3. Hilsman, 419–20.
4. Shaplen, *The Lost Revolution*, 148.
5. Schlesinger, *A Thousand Days*, 320. See also, Sidey, for a slightly different version; Clifford who, as Kennedy's "transition planner," arranged a briefing on Southeast Asia in January 1961. Clifford later wrote:

   My notes disclose the following comments by the President [Eisenhower] ... [who] said, with considerable emotion, that Laos was the key to the entire area of Southeast Asia. He said that if we permitted Laos to fall, then we would have to write off all the area. He stated we must not permit a Communist takeover.

6. Mecklin, 85. See also, Hilsman, 421–2, 439. The State Department recommended sending Lansdale out on three subsequent occasions without success; in 1965, Lodge finally insisted on his presence.
7. Hilsman, 420.

8. Gavin, *Crisis Now*, 51.
9. Schlesinger, *A Thousand Days*, 542–3. See also, Johnson, *The Vantage Point* . . .
10. Halberstam, *The Making of a Quagmire*, 69.
11. Kahin and Lewis, 127.
12. Rostow, "Guerrilla Warfare . . . "
13. Kennedy, *Public Papers of* . . . , I, 397.
14. Shaplen, *The Lost Revolution*, 153.
15. Fall, *The Two Viet-Nams* . . . , 332. See also, Lacouture.
16. Shaplen, *The Lost Revolution*, 153–4.
17. Schlesinger, *A Thousand Days*, 546. See also, Ellsberg, who points out that the reports called for the short-run goal of "frustrating" the Communists; i.e. " . . . halting or reversing a current downward trend or spiral of deterioration," and the long-run goal of "defeating" them; i.e. the " . . . ultimate goal of eliminating the Communist threat."
18. Schlesinger, *The Bitter Heritage* . . . , 22.
19. Schlesinger, *A Thousand Days*, 546. My italics. See also, Hilsman.
20. Ellsberg:

> . . . Taylor underlined the urgency by making explicit his recognition of an impressive list of disadvantages of the proposed move, including weakness of the U.S. strategic reserve; increased engagement of U.S. prestige; difficulty of resisting pressure to reinforce the first contingent if it were not enough (with no limit to the possible commitment, unless we attacked the source in Hanoi, if we sought ultimately to clean up the insurgents); and the risk of an escalation into a major war in Asia. It was in the face of all these possible drawbacks that he made his recommendation to introduce a Task Force without delay: made it on the grounds that a U.S. program to save South Vietnam simply would not succeed without it.

See also, Hilsman.
21. Hilsman, 423.
22. Ibid., 415–16, 426.
23. Sorenson, 644–5.
24. Schlesinger, *A Thousand Days*, 546–7. See also, Halberstam, *The Making of a Quagmire*.
25. Ellsberg.
26. Schlesinger, *A Thousand Days*, 547. See also, Sorensen, 654:

> . . . He had watched the French, with a courageous well-equipped army numbering hundreds of thousands, suffer a humiliating defeat and more than ninety thousand casualties. Now the choice was his. If the United States took over the conduct of the war on the ground, he asked, would that not make it easier for the Communists to say we were the neo-colonialist successors of the French? Would we be better able to win support of the villagers and farmers so essential to guerrilla warfare—than Vietnamese troops of the same color and culture? No one knew whether the South Vietnamese officers would be encouraged or resentful, or whether massive troop landings would provoke a massive Communist invasion—an invasion inevitably leading either to nuclear war, Western retreat or an endless and exhausting battle on the worst battleground he could choose.

27. Sorensen, 644, 652.
28. Hilsman, 433 ff., 425, 435.
29. *The Sunday Telegraph* (London), November 11, 1970. See also, De Gaulle, *Memoirs of Hope*.
30. Sorensen, 654. See also, Hilsman.

31. *The Times* (London), June 23, 1971.
32. Shaplen, *The Lost Revolution,* 154.
33. Lacouture, 63.
34. Shaplen, *The Lost Revolution,* 156–7.
35. Halberstam, *The Making of a Quagmire,* 59.
36. Pike, 253.

CHAPTER 59

NLF organization • The People's Revolutionary Party (PRP) • Hanoi's influence in the South • NLF aims • "The struggle movement" • Agit-prop techniques • Diem's failings • Increased American aid • American military influence • Viet Cong setbacks • American optimism • Tactical chimeras • The Viet Cong recovers • Disaster at Ap Bac • ARVN failures • The strategic-hamlet program • Diem's increasing intransigence • The American commitment increases • Buddhist revolts • Shifting NLF strategy • Washington changes direction • Diem's death

WHAT OF THE ENEMY written off so comfortingly by General Myers and Ambassador Durbrow in 1959? As we have seen, in December 1960 the National Liberation Front (NLF) appeared in the South, published a "Ten-Point Manifesto" that called for a democratic, coalition government, and embarked on an "action program" to achieve this end. A year later, it gained a leader in the person of Nguyen Huu Tho, a fifty-two-year-old Saigon lawyer and Marxist who had escaped after five years of imprisonment for political activities.

The interworkings of NLF leadership in these years are not particularly well documented in the West (despite the capture in 1966 of some six thousand NLF documents). NLF leaders remained underground. They did not reside at a permanent headquarters, they met infrequently, and those of their records later captured are sketchy. By the time Tho joined his comrades, Communists both in the South and in Hanoi apparently were worried about ultimate control of the liberation movement. In January 1962, militant Communist elements of the NLF established a revolutionary front, the People's Revolutionary Party (PRP), which now became the radical branch of the movement, the "vanguard" of the revolution. The PRP, most experts believed, was

" . . . the Southern branch of the Lao Dong [Communist] party which rules Hanoi," its main function being "to insure political control of the military arm of the NLF and to guide the movement's political struggle."[1] This did not mean, as asserted by South Vietnamese and American officials at the time, that Hanoi either absorbed the movement or thenceforth directly controlled it. Professor Donald Zagoria, among other experts, concluded that " . . . the NLF includes very significant political forces that are not Communist and still harbor long-held apprehensions about both Communist domination and domination by Northerners."[2] In other words, the NLF remained a specific political entity and, despite the extent of Hanoi's control, it might have been wiser to recognize it as such if only to influence its non-Communist and even some of its Communist members.

Two months later, in March 1962, the NLF held its first congress, which elected Nguyen Huu Tho president and Nguyen Van Hieu, a mathematics professor believed by many to have been the real driving force of NLF, secretary-general of the Central Committee. The congress also announced a new objective: independence of South Vietnam, an objective extended in July to making " . . . south Viet-Nam, Laos, and Cambodia a neutral zone with all three states enjoying sovereign rights." Simultaneously, the NLF continued appealing to all " . . . parties, sects, and groups representing all political tendencies, social strata, religions, and nationalities of South Vietnam."[3] The Geneva Agreements of 1962, which resulted in a neutralized Laos (in theory), strengthened the NLF (and Hanoi) in demands for a neutral, coalition government in the South.

No matter the ultimate NLF and PRP intention, which Communist leadership cunningly concealed during formative years; at a time when Diem was adamantly refusing representative government, his enemy was stressing its desire for such, a brilliant tactic in the propaganda war. Continued U.S. association with and support of the Diem regime also offered a superb propaganda target for Communists to exploit. In 1962, NLF leaders introduced the term *special war*—" . . . described as a form of neocolonialism in which a colonial power, no longer able to use expeditionary forces to assert its control, worked through a clique of compradors whom it 'advised,' with the rank-and-file military force being supplied by the colonialized nation."[4]

The NLF, or anyway its Communist leadership, sought to gain either direct control of the South Vietnam Government through a general uprising, or to gain indirect control by establishing a coalition government and working on from there. Essential to the process was "the struggle movement," a two-pronged program well described by Douglas Pike:

... Within the generic term "struggle," there were two types of struggle movements; The political struggle (*dau tranh chinh tri*) and the armed, or military struggle (*dau tranh vu trang*). To the NLF, as to the Viet Minh and Chinese Communists before it, victory would be achieved through the proper balance of political and military activities or, in Communist terms, by the proper combination of the political struggle and the armed struggle.

The political struggle, which, in accordance with Mao's teachings, gained primary ascendancy, called for a three-pronged program: consolidation of areas already controlled by Viet Cong; the "liberated areas" or base sanctuaries so essential to further revolutionary activity (the *dan van,* or "action among the people"); organization of the countryside under GVN control, the agit-prop task discussed earlier (the *dich van,* or "action among the enemy"); proselyting of ARVN and the GVN civil service (the *binh van,* or "action among the troops"). The military struggle, which at first remained subordinate to the political struggle, consisted " ... not simply [of] guerrilla military attacks but kidnappings, assassinations, executions, sabotage"—what Pike succinctly calls the "violence program." Military organization strongly resembled that of the Viet Minh earlier discussed (see Chapter 39). Operations remained the responsibility of the "People's Self-Defense Armed Forces Committee." As with other national committees, this extended downward through provincial and district organizations. The Liberation Army consisted of two parts: Main Force regiments, or what might be called regulars; the Guerrilla Popular Army or paramilitary forces—peasants by day, guerrillas by night—organized in small units that varied in function from village militia duty (generally covert) to active combat often in conjunction with Main Force or regional units. The Guerrilla Popular Army formed the reservoir of men that supplied the regular units. It also maintained three-man "special activity cells," which

... would strike anywhere at any time. From the roster of these cells were drawn the assassination teams, the volunteer grenade hurlers, the death or suicide squads. Most of the spectacular acts of sabotage, assassinations of province chiefs, or daring military escapades were the work of a special activity cell, sometimes working with demolition experts or other military specialists supplied by the provincial-level central committee.

Although the importance of the political and military struggles would vary, each complemented the grand design.

... Vo Nguyen Giap wrote that if an uprising was an art, the chief characteristic of its leadership was the ability to change the struggle form in accordance with changed events. At the beginning, he said, the political struggle dominated and the armed struggle was secondary. Gradually the two assumed equal roles. Then the armed struggle dominated. In the end came the return to the political struggle. Struggle was *the word*. Its goal, toward which the cadres pledged themselves, toward which each Vietnamese was expected daily to contribute a little, was the General Uprising, the nationwide, simultaneous grand struggle movement.[5]

By 1962, the NLF controlled large areas of South Vietnam, including two rich areas in the Mekong Delta. While they busily converted these into "liberated areas," Viet Cong units continued to ambush ARVN columns and attack ARVN and police outposts. Terrorists struck at government officials, particularly village officials and school teachers. Hideous tactics these, but not often promiscuous and less hideous in final result than quantitative military tactics: mass artillery bombardment or aerial bombings. Above all, tactics with a purpose, tactics that formed part of a relentless propaganda war designed to consolidate and expand a peasant base that Communist leaders realized was essential to future operations.

The song had not changed, and now, after more than twenty years of singing, the voices were good. The communism that Kennedy was endeavoring to stop did not enter the picture. Human misery did. John Mecklin later described the Communist target, a typical Vietnamese hamlet of fewer than a thousand people:

> ... a cluster of straw and bamboo huts with earthen floors and straw sleeping mats. The land between the huts was a quagmire of ankle-deep black mud in the rainy season, choking dust in the dry season. The peasant's wife or children often walked as much as three or four miles and then waited in line an hour or two for the daily drinking water. In the dry season the distance was often further because the regular well became saline. There was seldom electricity, frequently no road of any sort to the outside world, and no communication except by foot.
>
> [The peasant] was beset by insects, by rats that could literally make a hamlet uninhabitable and become fierce enough to attack humans (in one province alone, some five million rats were killed in a two-month, U.S.-sponsored drive in 1962), by floods and by droughts. He was seared by the sun and whipped by the rain, and his bare feet became calloused, unfeeling boards. The beauty of his women was destroyed by their mid-twenties, and by the midthirties they were hags, wracked by years of merciless burden, and often by disease.

And forever there were the flies, chiltering the stinking fish at the village market, swarming the open sores in the skin of his infant son, harassing his sleep. To survive his mind became numb, reconciled forever to submission and pain without end.[6]

Then strangers appeared in the night. They brought no gifts, no money, no food. Sometimes they asked for food, paying if they could. They sat by the fire, they talked, they listened, and because they had once been of these hamlets themselves, they soon did not seem strange. They brought sympathy, understanding, and compassion. They brought what no one had ever brought before: genuine interest in the peasant's welfare. They brought a solution to pernicious poverty, the National Liberation Front which would seize the country from foreign hands to give them a land of peace and freedom—and sufficient land for the crops to feed often hungry mouths. They preached more. They carried a materialistic bible with thousands of appealing verses. These agit-prop agents did not hurry to convert the listener. At first they settled for passive acceptance. Their continued interest and honeyed words of promise often produced the desired effect, and that was to arouse hope and, with it, new-found dignity. The peasant now had something to fight for.[7] Now he would lend his children to the Viet Cong, the younger as messengers, the older as fighters. Now he would donate to the cause, now he would pay taxes, now he would supply food and sanctuary and guides who would help guerrillas transit twenty-five miles of tortuous terrain in five hours of night marches. The agent recruited the female as well. He organized the guerrilla version of a Fem-Lib movement. He stressed the ghastly lot of women during the French colonial and the Diem regimes. The PRP pledged itself to " . . . total liberation of women in every respect . . . for economic equality, political equality, cultural equality, social equality . . . and equality in the family."[8]

Having aroused the peasant, the Viet Cong kept him aroused: "struggle meetings," "denunciation meetings," "ceremonial meetings," "people's conventions"; dozens of front organizations, each tailored to a specific target; newspapers, leaflets, theatrical troupes, cultural teams, radio, motion pictures—an altogether-well-organized, massive propaganda effort almost constantly misunderstood and underrated by South Vietnamese and American officials. The American-Diem military effort helped to sustain the propaganda effort. Each bomb dropped, each machine-gun bullet fired, each gallon of defoliant, was worth a thousand persuasive words.

Probably not one Viet Cong agent in a thousand could read English, yet each knew the truth long-before written by Lawrence of Arabia: " . . . A province would be won when we had taught the civilians in it to die for our ideal of freedom. The presence of the enemy was secondary. Final victory seemed certain, if the war lasted long enough for us to work it out."[9]

The prevailing political atmosphere in Saigon could hardly have engendered a national will so necessary to combating Communist influence in the countryside. Diem's continued failure to allow urgently needed economic, agrarian, and social reforms and to decentralize political control meant an apathetic peasantry who remained peculiarly prone to propaganda and blandishments offered by NLF and PRP cadres.[10]

So long as peasants remained apathetic or hostile, the military effort against the Viet Cong could not succeed—no matter how expansive it became. Unfortunately, this unpalatable truth, emphasized repeatedly since 1945 and preached by vigorous, intelligent, and experienced voices, did not wash against the American military priesthood who were well on their way to the fateful formula for disaster that combined arrogance of ignorance with arrogance of power.

Kennedy's decision to go along at least in part with the Staley and Taylor-Rostow recommendations tipped an expansion that by early 1962 reached impressive proportions. The Vietnamese task force already existed. The Pentagon soon opened an Office on Counter-Insurgency and Special Activities, headed by Major General V. H. Krulak, a marine officer who enjoyed direct access to the Joint Chiefs of Staff and also to McNamara. The State Department set up a "counter-insurgency course" to train civil officials; the armed forces began similar specialized training. In Saigon, Ambassador Nolting headed the Country Team of civil and military officials, and he also headed the Country Task Force, which, in theory, functioned " . . . as an extension of the Vietnam Task Force in Washington." In reality, General Paul Harkins, who arrived in March 1962 as head of MACV (formerly MAAG), almost at once became the dominant figure, which meant, among other things, that the military effort continued to receive priority over the civil effort. By early 1962, the United States was funding a hefty increase in South Vietnam's armed forces and it was also financing what it hoped would prove to be a widespread "strategic hamlet" program. American army and marine helicopters began ferrying Vietnamese troops to and from "combat areas." By spring, some six thousand Americans were serving in Vietnam; a significant portion of field advisers and helicopter crews were being shot at; some military advisers were beginning to shoot back, as were armed helicopter crews. Special Forces teams working with the CIA were active in the central highlands and in the North, trying to woo heterogeneous Montagnards to fight on the government's side.

In the South, in the Mekong Delta area, the infusion of weapons and material sparked a great series of "offensives," of "search-and-destroy" operations, of regimental and division sweeps supported by T-28 and B-26 aircraft strafing and bombing (too often on speculation) and burning out "enemy" complexes with napalm. Communiqués sounded like those issued by the French in the late 1940s. According to one source, enemy battle deaths were running between four and five hundred a month, with another thousand men being wounded or taken prisoner. Mobility offered by helicopters allowed ARVN forces to catch numerous units off guard and posed a tactical challenge not immediately met by the Viet Cong. Captured NLF and PRP documents showed Communist consternation, as did increased terrorist tactics including kidnapings and assassinations. In some areas, the Viet Cong forcibly recruited guerrilla replacements and kept them in line by threatening reprisals against their families; they kept families in line by threatening to punish the sons. Wilfred Burchett, the peripatetic Australian Communist reporter in Hanoi at the time, later wrote that the Viet Cong were on the point of yielding the Mekong Delta and withdrawing to the mountains.[11]

All this was heady stuff that impressed a good many American officials. Secretary of Defense Robert McNamara returned from Vietnam, in May 1962, and stated: " . . . Every quantitative measurement we have shows we're winning this war." General Maxwell Taylor returned from a second trip to Saigon impressed by "a great national movement" that would destroy the Viet Cong. In January 1963—the American presence in Vietnam had increased to nearly ten thousand—President Kennedy, in his State of the Union message, said: " . . . The spearhead of aggression has been blunted in South Vietnam."[12]

These and other glossy statements were unduly optimistic. Tactical gains amounted to little more than a gossamer sheen woven by temporary technological superiority. Despite intensification of fighting, the problem remained essentially a guerrilla suppression problem and for this the Vietnamese army and a large proportion of American advisers proved singularly ill-prepared, not only showing themselves unable either to adjust tactically or to exploit tactical gains by a forceful and effective civil-affairs program. Not understanding basic tenets of guerrilla warfare, Vietnamese and American senior officers converted fatalities into "victories." This was a great mistake: Dead bodies do not mean destroyed infrastructure. Dead bodies, particularly those of innocent peasants, mean a strengthening, not a weakening, of the insurgent cause. The NLF and PRP were down, but scarcely out. At the time retreat was being discussed, an NLF delegation headed by Nguyen Van Hieu, secretary-general of the NLF Central Committee, was touring Eastern Europe to introduce the NLF to the world. At the same time, southern cadres who had been living in the North took to what was to become famous as the Ho Chi Minh Trail to infiltrate back to the South. About thirty-seven hundred had arrived in 1961, according to Douglas Pike, who suggested that in 1962 another fifty-eight hundred arrived.[13] More would come the next year.

As 1962 turned to autumn, the Viet Cong began to display a new and disturbing aggressiveness. If they were not yet actively picking fights with ARVN troops, they were not avoiding them either. And they were continuing to strike Civil Guard and Self-Defense Corps outposts, both to supply themselves with new American arms and to prove their power to the peasants. Such was their success that to American advisers the outposts became known as Viet Cong PXs.[14]

Nor was ARVN showing well. As the Viet Cong recovered and began to shoot back, Diem's army seemed reluctant to fight. The battle of Ap Bac, in January 1963, exposed the awkward truth.[15] A task force of more than three South Vietnamese battalions, lifted in part by helicopters and armored personnel carriers, failed to destroy a Viet Cong battalion though having had it surrounded and greatly outgunned. ARVN's failure underlined the futility of trying to fight a guerrilla war with a conventional army that lacked both will and know-how. The U. S. Army's training program had denied it necessary flexibility. Armored personnel carriers and artillery had sharply decreased cross-country mobility. Confined to roads, ARVN units, just like French units formerly, remained vulnerable to ambush. Units lifted by helicopter could not long sustain themselves in the field without logistic support they had been taught to expect. ARVN staff work remained haphazard, particularly in vital intelligence sections. Operations remained uncoordinated. Diem refused to establish a supreme commander and general staff, instead running what virtually amounted to a war-lord arrangement. This meant spotty operations with slow response to hit-and-run guerrilla tactics. Intelligence, the vital ingredient in counterguerrilla warfare, was missing to a disastrous degree, the inevitable result of governmental failure to identify with peasants. Lacking intelligence on which to base small, selective, surprise raids, army units resorted to "sweeps," which often damaged and destroyed crops and hamlets but generally failed to kill or capture significant numbers of enemy. Troop looting and torture of villagers to obtain information nullified any psychological gain from show of force. If ARVN did clear an area of enemy, failure to occupy, consolidate, and protect villagers soon brought back the Viet Cong. U. S. Army advisers, with few exceptions and almost none at senior levels, could not be persuaded to adopt a proper counterinsurgency strategy: viable search-and-hold operations with concomitant political and military pressure on Diem to force his government to initiate a genuine strategic-hamlet program.

Over-all failure only sapped ARVN of remaining will and made its ranks more prone to enemy propaganda—the *binh van* (proselyting) program. Although the Viet Cong sought to induce desertions whenever possible, they also relied on internal disintegration, on the process the French called *pourrissement*. This was generally a private deal between the NLF and the low-level village official in which the latter escaped death in return for neutralizing government programs:

This could be done by a slowdown, by snarling the program in red tape, or by outright falsification of reports to higher headquarters. For instance, a strategic-hamlet chief could go through the motions of creating a village security apparatus that only appeared to have succeeded in separating the guerrillas from the villagers. Vietnamese Information Service posters and leaflets arriving from Saigon could be distributed only superficially, in areas where district officials would be likely to notice them, and the rest destroyed. A military patrol leader could lead his patrol noisily down a well-travelled path and after an hour return to the hamlet, never having made a serious effort to determine whether guerrillas were in the area but with his superiors being none the wiser. The effect was to place a premium on mediocrity in low-level administration at a time when excellence was vital . . . many ARVN military operations were ruined by Vietnamese military or civil servants gratuitously passing on information to NLF agents or persons they presumed to be in contact with the NLF, simply in an effort to ingratiate themselves with the NLF—as a sort of life insurance policy.[16]

The CIA and Special Forces found lucrative operational possibilities in the central highlands, where more than a hundred thousand Montagnards had fled their villages, the result of NLF failure to capture their loyalty.[17] American teams began recruiting and training Montagnard units to return to the hills to fight the Viet Cong.[18] Initial successes here also proved illusory: The Montagnards, while willing in some instances to fight as mercenaries in American pay, refused to transfer loyalty to the Diem government; to the South Vietnamese, they were known as *moi*, or savages, treated similarly, and responded predictably. So long as Americans remained, the effort prospered; with their departure, it failed.

By end of 1962, the highly touted "strategic hamlet" program, which aimed to fortify eleven thousand, or two thirds, of the country's hamlets by 1963, had also bogged down. In theory, this was an excellent idea. Its genesis traces not to Eugene Staley but to the head of the British Advisory Mission to Viet-Nam, Robert Thompson, who arrived in Saigon in autumn of 1961.[19] A veteran of Orde Wingate's follies in Burma in World War II and of the later Malayan Emergency, Thompson had been instrumental in relocating Chinese villages in order to cut insurgents from local sources of intelligence, supply, and recruits, as well as protecting villagers from insurgent infiltration and attacks. (See Chapter 46.) The idea was not original. As Gallieni and Lyautey realized, protection is an essential part of pacification. Area clearance had been used subsequently in emergencies, for example by General Weyler in Cuba, by the American army in the Philippines, by Kitchener in the Boer War, more recently by the French in Indochina and Algeria, and by the British in Malaya and Kenya. The present concept called for the army to clear and hold an area while the government helped villagers fortify hamlets into defensive complexes defended with militia, civil guards, and police, with regular troops on call. The Diem government refused Thompson's original suggestion because brother Nhu did not like it. When Staley favored it, which spelled American financing, Nhu swung around and made it his own project—something quite different from what Thompson or Roger Hilsman had in mind.

Though valid enough, the concept, at best, was no panacea, which Thompson would have been the first to point out. Like most pacification measures, it called for a patient, methodical, and selective approach best illustrated by Lyautey's phrase *tache d'huile*. It had several drawbacks. The Mekong Delta, for example, was rich enough to feed guerrillas, fortified hamlets or no. The concept demanded efficient administration, and particularly effective internal and external security arrangements. When it worked, it worked well, and might have proved the key to solving the pacification problem but for two major defects. The first was a failure to integrate the strategic-hamlet program into a single, over-all strategy evolved by Hilsman and others and discussed above. Thompson and Hilsman wanted the program to start in the heavily populated Mekong Delta and work slowly out from there. Instead, under Nhu's aegis, strategic hamlets sprang up like rice shoots. The government could not possibly provide enough civic action and security teams necessary to revamp hamlets and to organize and train peasant militia, nor did police exist in sufficient quantity to ferret out Viet Cong agents and sympathizers from within defended complexes. Once again, massive American aid, dollar and material, filtered through venal fingers to lose intended impact. In most areas, the program mired in ooze of bureaucratic corruption and ineptitude.

This was bad enough in its own right. But, as it was happening, the enemy was admitting the threat and, once again, was adjusting tactics. NLF leadership judged the threat of such proportions that it began subordinating the political struggle to the armed struggle and made the strategic-hamlet program a priority tactical target—at a time when ARVN and local militias were particularly vulnerable. Many of the hastily constructed complexes lacked adequate fortifications and remained physically vulnerable to Viet Cong propaganda, infiltration, and attacks. Rudimentary communications and regular army inefficiency slowed reaction time and thus lowered promised protection. Battery-operated transmitter-receiver radios to provide village-to-garrison communications proved of slight value since " . . . calls for help were so rarely answered [by ARVN], or answered so slowly as to be useless."[20]

A second major defect centered on Nhu's ulterior motives. As with the previously unsuccessful *agrovilles* and "fighting hamlets," Nhu saw fortified hamlets as a convenient form of population control, with neighbor reporting on neighbor.[21] In places, they became little more than concentration camps full of unwilling guests. These were peasants who until the government-enforced move had been listening to a siren song, his deception the greater because his ears had never before heard music. Then, suddenly, he was scooped up, placed in a strategic hamlet—and found the same miserable life of old, the same arrogant and corrupt officials, the same squeeze, the same sicknesses. A song became a nightmare and a program went to pot.

Here was the real failing, not alone of the strategic-hamlet program but of the entire counterinsurgency effort. The Diem government and its foreign advisers may not have known it, but they were fighting essentially an idea, and fortifications, in the long run, are invalid against ideas. As Hilsman had discerned, the only valid weapon against an idea is a better idea—and Ngo Dinh Diem's abortive doctrine of Personalism, which the Eisenhower and Kennedy administrations kept trying to insist was democracy, did not fill the bill. The Diem government may have given peasants barbed wire and advisers and even a civil-guard unit, but failure to provide vigorous counterideas—to give the peasant something to fight for—left hamlets and villages as vulnerable as ever to vigorous NLF and PRP propaganda.

Far from protecting the peasant, the strategic-hamlet program frequently alienated him. Despite strenuous efforts of some American field advisers and a good many Vietnamese officers and officials, this unhealthy situation continued into 1963. Whether the situation could have been retrieved then is debatable; if Diem could have brought himself to initiate legitimate reforms, it is possible that he still could have claimed the upper hand.

This was not to be. Kennedy's kid-glove treatment of the Diem hierarchy had backfired. Diem and his circle of intimate advisers grew increasingly difficult to deal with. At times, Diem held himself practically inaccessible; on other occasions, he granted audiences and then subjected ranking callers such as Nolting or Harkins to hours-long monologues. To most observers, he appeared firmly under the thumb of brother Nhu and Mme. Nhu, and, to some observers, the former was as mad as the latter was corrupt and ambitious.

What was the official American reaction? It was as if Diem and his failures did not exist. In March 1963, the Secretary of State, Dean Rusk, stated that the war was "... turning an important corner ... Government forces clearly have the initiative in most areas of the country." In April,

> ... he discerned a "steady movement toward a constitutional system resting upon popular consent," declared that "the 'strategic hamlet' program is producing excellent results," added that "morale in the countryside has begun to rise," assured his listeners that "to the Vietnamese peasant" the Viet Cong "look less and less like winners" and concluded, "The Vietnamese are on their way to success. . . . "[22]

Roger Hilsman later reported an April meeting in Honolulu between Harkins and McNamara:

> ... General Harkins gave us all the facts and figures—the number of strategic hamlets established, number of Viet Cong killed, operations initiated by government forces, and so on. He could not, of course, he said, give any guarantee, but he thought he could say that by Christmas it would be all over. The Secretary of Defense [McNamara] was elated. He reminded me that I had attended one of the very first of these meetings, when it had all looked so black—and that had been only a year and a half ago.[23]

In May, when the NLF was collecting taxes in forty-one of South Vietnam's forty-four provinces, Harkins told Saigon reporters that the war would be won "... within a year." A month later—American troops in Vietnam now numbered over fifteen thousand—Ambassador Nolting told reporters: "... South Viet-Nam is on its way to victory over communist guerrillas."[24] To gain that victory, the administration had progressively raised its commitment from six hundred to fifteen thousand troops; as an adviser had warned Dean Acheson in 1950: "... These things have a way of snowballing."

The brilliance of official statements suddenly dimmed in the flare of Buddhist revolts. The Buddhist problem had been building for a long time. Like the peasant problem, it was essentially political, although it held religious overtones. South Vietnam is overwhelmingly Buddhist, with some eleven million persons carrying the appellation. Like all great religious movements, Buddhism had splintered into many variations, and perhaps four million could be called orthodox Buddhists.[25] The disillusionment of this majority bloc began when Diem installed northern, Catholic refugees in the more important and lucrative administrative posts and otherwise favored the minority (1.5 million) Catholic population. Buddhist grumblings grew increasingly severe in 1961. Instead of righting wrongs and admitting Buddhist leadership into his government, Diem, as usual, relied on repression. Open rebellion broke out in May in Hué when government troops, attempting to disperse a Buddhist crowd, opened fire and killed nine Buddhists. Although the Diem government blamed this on Communist agitators, it gave in to some Buddhist demands. During negotiations a Buddhist fanatic, following an ancient sacrificial custom, burned himself to death in a public ceremony in Saigon, an act photographed by Malcolm Browne and one that helped turn world opinion sharply against the Diem regime.[26] Subsequent immolations kept the issue alive and brought continuing demands from the Kennedy administration for a settlement. Instead, Nhu, prodded by his wife (who heartlessly described the suicides as "barbecues"), persuaded Diem to declare martial law followed by police raids of Buddhist pagodas throughout South Vietnam—his police supplemented by Vietnamese Special Forces, a unit organized with CIA aid and one supposedly dedicated to counterguerrilla warfare.

With these acts, Diem and Nhu signed the death warrant of their government and, as it turned out, themselves. The raids brought thousands of protesting students into Saigon and Hué streets, where their arrest by army troops caused additional thousands of vociferous protests. Meanwhile, the NLF was shifting emphasis to the armed struggle. This was partly at the instigation of its own leaders and of the PRP, partly at Hanoi's instigation. In April 1963 in Hanoi, the secretary-general of the Lao Dong, Le Duan, " . . . made the case for a violent versus a peaceful path to power [in the South]."[27] Hanoi also sent south a particularly skillful leader, Tran Nam Trung (an alias), who became secretary-general of the PRP, which held responsibility for the armed struggle. The NLF continued to step up guerrilla operations—the armed struggle was about to command the political struggle. The situation was far from simple. Dissident groups existed in the NLF and also in Hanoi. Moscow did not want the war escalated, but Peking did. Apparently, moderates in both South and North still controlled the situation—in any event, the NLF and Hanoi now released peace proposals sufficiently concrete to cause General de Gaulle to ask for neutralization of the area.

President Kennedy also dispatched a new ambassador, Henry Cabot Lodge, who was instructed to maintain a " . . . posture of silent disapproval" vis-à-vis the Diem government. Kennedy further suspended $12 million of monthly aid and, as a particular snub to Nhu, Lodge arranged for recall of the CIA chief, John Richardson, who was overtly sympathetic to the regime. The American Government's new firmness began jelling an incipient army revolt that had been brewing for over a year and now joined hands, albeit obliquely, with a more recently formed generals' plot.

Although the Kennedy administration would willingly have continued to support Diem in return for sincere political and economic reforms, Diem's continued intransigence and particularly the anti-American raillery indulged in by Nhu and his vicious wife finally wore Kennedy's patience thin. In a famous speech of early October 1963, he told a television audience that " . . . a change of policy and perhaps personnel" was required in the Saigon government.

Rightly or wrongly, the generals plotting a coup regarded the President's words as a green light, and they seem to have been further encouraged by some American officials, both in Washington and Saigon, who had been made aware of their plans:

> . . . On October 10th, the American go-between informed [General Duang Van] Minh that the United States would not stand in the way of a coup if it took place, and that if it was successful and if a new regime could improve military morale and effectiveness, could obtain popular support, and could deal on a practical basis with the American government, it would receive aid.[28]

Plots and counterplots developed during the next three weeks. The coup began in earnest on the first day of November. Diem activists such as Colonel Tung, who commanded the dreaded Special Forces, lost their lives on the first day; Diem and Nhu refused Ambassador Lodge's offer of sanctuary and flight and, on the following day, were arrested and summarily executed by army officers.

The coup might have solved many problems, particularly had the American administration followed with a firm policy vigorously pursued. Unfortunately, less than three weeks after Diem and Nhu met their deaths, President Kennedy was assassinated.

CHAPTER FIFTY-NINE

1. Zagoria, 112–16. See also, Pike, 136 ff.
2. Zagoria, 116–17.
3. Lacouture, 59–60.
4. Pike, 55.
5. Ibid., 85 ff.
6. Mecklin, 75–6. See also, Pike, 109–10 for a contrasting description. Other personal observations, my own included, not to mention sociological statistics, favor Mecklin's report.
7. Tanham, *War Without Guns,* 13 ff. See also, ibid., 20: Dr. Tanham interviewed a guerrilla prisoner in Thailand. The man said he had become dissatisfied with his government in June 1959. Pressed as to why the date was so specific, he answered: " . . . A man told me I was unhappy with certain things and I suddenly realized he was right."
8. Pike, 174.
9. Lawrence, "Guerrilla Warfare."
10. Tanham, *War Without Guns,* spells out many of these. See also, Pike, 60:

Diem's land-reform program lasted only " . . . 3 years and aided only about 10 per cent of the landless."

11. Burchett.
12. Schlesinger, *The Bitter Heritage* . . . , 24–5.
13. Pike, 324.
14. Mecklin, 97.
15. Hilsman, 447–50. See also, Halberstam, *The Making of a Quagmire*, 147, 150, 157.
16. Pike, 257–8.
17. Ibid., 205.
18. Mecklin, 68: In 1963, Special Forces took over the program and eventually trained 20,000 troops with varying success. See also, Pike.
19. Robert Thompson, *Defeating Communist Insurgency*. See also, Clutterbuck, *The Long Long War;* Mecklin; Tanham, *War Without Guns*.
20. Mecklin, 67. See also, Tanham, *War Without Guns*.
21. Pike, 64 ff. See also, Halberstam, *The Making of a Quagmire;* Warnke.
22. Schlesinger, *The Bitter Heritage*, 25.
23. Hilsman, 466–7.
24. Schlesinger, *The Bitter Heritage*, 25.
25. Shaplen, *The Lost Revolution*, 192.
26. *The Times* (London), January 29, 1971:

> . . . The ancient custom which Thich Quang Duc [the 73-year-old monk who burned himself to death] revived takes its origin in a Mahayana Buddhist text written in India in the first century A.D. Called the Saddharma-pundarika-sutra, it tells the story of Bhaishayjaraja, who ate incense, drank oils, and bathed in essences for 12 years before setting fire to himself as an offering to Buddha.
> This text was translated into Chinese (about 223 A.D.) and the cult first became established in China and Vietnam in the fifth century A.D. In the next 500 years there are records of at least 25 Buddhists (including two nuns and one layman) ceremonially burning themselves. The fanatics commonly dieted before igniting themselves, to make their bodies more combustible. Others made more modest offerings by cutting off and burning fingers or hands.

See also, Lacouture, whose authority is M. Folliozat, a specialist in the tradition of Indian Buddhism:

> . . . One may see in these acts primarily an affirmation of eminent dignity and purification. By burning his arm—which is the most traditional gesture—or his body, the initiate, who is "free" or "awakened," freely disposes of what he has come to know to be simple appearance. No longer attached to things, he heroically demonstrates that he understands real values, a deeper order, and in this fashion condemns the attitude of those who persecute his coreligionists.
> F. adds that such cremations could also be gestures of protest, condemnation, or vengeance; he states, too, that these acts constitute exploits of an extraordinary psychosomatic technique which, it seems, reduces the sufferings caused by the sacrifice. . . .

27. Zagoria, 108.
28. Shaplen, *The Lost Revolution*, 203–4.

CHAPTER 60

Kennedy's failure analyzed • The Administration's ignorance concerning South Vietnam • Ambition versus policy • Vietnam's low priority • Pentagon and CIA influence • False reports • Kennedy's advisers • Guerrilla warfare and American armed forces • Special Forces (the Green Berets) • CIA's role • The tactical problem analyzed • General Griffith's warning • Quantitative versus qualitative warfare • American military advisers • American dependence on technology • Helicopters • ARVN tactics • The war escalates • Nolting and Harkins' dream world • Warnings from the field • Wishful thinking in Saigon • American Government versus the press • The Hilsman-Forrestal report • Kennedy condones the great deception • Pierre Salinger's warning • McNamara's volte-face • Kennedy's private doubts

WHY DID JOHN KENNEDY fail in Vietnam?
The reasons are several and complex. Taken together, they do not compliment the man's historical image, nor do they present a comforting picture of American officialdom, military or civil, and the decision-making process. Taken together, they emphasize the theme of this book—the arrogance of ignorance—and they must be analyzed, if only briefly, for us to understand subsequent events in Vietnam, the continuing and ever expanding rift in American political, diplomatic, and military circles, the resultant widening and in many ways dangerous schism between government and people, and the precarious moral position in which the United States finds itself vis-à-vis the world today.

Although Kennedy had interested himself in Indochina since 1951, his was a politician's interest, in his case a well-meaning, liberal desire to put matters right, but scarcely a profound understanding of basic issues. Kennedy never recovered sufficiently from initial ignorance to give Indochina the priority attention it required. The situation demanded a dynamic, imaginative, courageous, and even incautious policy on Kennedy's part. Instead, he remained wedded to the inherited ambition: *stop communism.* This presupposed that communism is a physical thing like a tank or a division of troops or a bullet, and not an abstract idea so theoretically appealing as to have survived elaborate corruptions placed upon it by a dozen pinchpenny dictators. Stopping communism was an ambition that disallowed occasional short-term "defeat" in the process of winning long-term "victory." Hindering communism while proving the virtues and strengths of democracy is a policy that demands a planned course of conduct based on a realistic recognition of "strategic conveniences" as opposed to "strategic necessities," and one that accepts temporary setbacks in the process of insuring healthy survival with potential growth.

Kennedy's tense political situation—" . . . The margin of voices that proclaimed him President was so thin as to be almost an accident of counting"[1]—dissuaded him from disowning his inheritance. Instead, he bowed to forces of fear, both Republican and Democratic—and, almost to the end, remained prisoner to the Diem regime and to those officials who favored a predominantly military approach to a political problem.

Two other bonds held him in thrall. One was Vietnam's relatively low priority in international affairs. Kennedy no sooner entered the White House than, like Truman and Eisenhower before him, he faced a host of major international and domestic problems. "Each day the crises multiply," was his plaintive cry to his countrymen soon after he took office. "I must inform the Congress that . . . in each of the principal areas of crisis—the tide of events has been running out and time has not been our friend."[2]

Kennedy assumed office during the Laotian blow-up, with Vietnam a secondary problem. Before he could come to grips with Vietnam, he was involved in the Berlin crisis, with resultant political strains at home. Then the moratorium on nuclear testing, the Bay of Pigs fiasco, the missile challenge, the 1962 Congressional elections, the quarrel with Great Britain over Skybolt, the De Gaulle crisis, the civil-rights battle, the confrontation with the Soviet Union over Cuba—one followed the other, a political TV serial, a house of troubles with the Vietnam issue now and again popping in like an unwanted relative. Not until the Buddhist revolts in spring of 1963 did Vietnam become an Administration "crisis area." Until late 1963, only three American news media—Associated Press, United Press International, and the New York *Times*—maintained full-time staff correspondents in Vietnam.[3]

A second bond strengthened the first. Kennedy, essentially, was a positive person. He entered office as a young and healthy man with a sincere belief in himself and his philosophy of government. This was one of the most appealing things about the man: his belief in America and America's greatness. He had not yet defined the meaning of or need for humility. He had not yet defined sufficiently the word "force" to realize that, in addition to virtues, it contains defects; that it is a word of nuance and limit; indeed, that use of force is engendered by fear, a subtle truth that explains, among other things, the remarkable success of judo and karate.

Kennedy's refusal to disown his inheritance of an impractical ambition was in part the result of the tense political situation—its genesis was the fall of Chiang Kai-shek—but it also resulted in part from Kennedy's insistence on playing a crusader role. At a time when polarized communism was defrosting, Kennedy embraced the monolithic theory which threatened the engulfment of the "free" world.[4]

Kennedy was full of himself and his country, and insisted on having that confidence justified. He wanted to believe reports of responsible officials who, when it came to insurgency warfare, were as enthusiastic, confident . . . and ignorant as he himself—and for some time, for too long, he believed them.

Kennedy welcomed dissent no more than most of us. Despite severe and persevering contradictions offered by the historical record and presented by talented, courageous, and knowledgeable civil and military experts, historians, and correspondents—a cumulative body of intelligent opinion derived from historical and contemporary experience—Kennedy refused what President Eisenhower had refused before him: to force a political settlement to what was in essence a political, not a military, problem.[5]

By allowing the military mastiff to overshadow the political cat, Kennedy erred egregiously, thus insuring the frequently pernicious and often unchallenged pre-eminence of the Pentagon in determining national security policy. It was partly his own fault in that he had appointed a man of limited stature as Secretary of State. A more effective stance would have been difficult to achieve in any case, but, as Roger Hilsman has pointed out, Dean Rusk " . . . regarded Vietnam as essentially a military problem even though a number of his colleagues in the State Department disagreed."[6] To worsen matters, Kennedy appointed Walt Whitman Rostow, an unmitigated hawk, as his national security adviser, which turned out to be a disaster of the first order.

Neither did McNamara or Taylor serve the President well. Not understanding the complexities of insurgency warfare himself, he could not know that they had escaped the conventional mind of Taylor and the computer mind of McNamara, both of whom often accepted false reports from the field, quantitative reports presenting a dangerously inaccurate picture. Perpetrators of these reports probably intended no deception at first. Alike untrained in insurgency warfare, military and civil advisers and observers, with some splendid exceptions, misread field developments to report extravagant tactical gains that so excited Washington officialdom in 1962. This is understandable if scarcely commendable. Top officials, military and civil, were putting careers on the line. Vanity was at work and so was ambition, but over these rode an appalling ignorance that produced an unhealthy, indeed fatal, arrogance that would admit of no error. When the bloom wore off, these people refused to accept that the tactical flower had died, and when mourners turned up for the funeral, they were brusquely advised there was no funeral.

Although several factors combine to explain this unfortunate fact, it was due primarily to American military ascendancy in Vietnam affairs since 1954 and concomitant insistence on seeking a military solution to an essentially political problem. Once the military began to rule the American presence, arrogance of ignorance asserted itself to begin eliminating rational thought. And when rational thought disappears, error multiplies finally to explode into catastrophe—which is what happened to the U.S. effort in Vietnam.

To understand this is to understand something of the American military profile at the time. Most of our military leaders did not grasp the concept of limited war. Thanks to Korea (and to MacArthur's inept strategy), the generals privately agreed that a limited ground war in Asia must be avoided in the future, that the requirement demanded an all-or-nothing strategy. They failed to agree on which arm was to accomplish the inane concept of "massive retaliation" strategy, with the result that the armed forces became more divisive than ever, with each grabbing for a disproportionate piece of the budgetary pie (a morbid condition that continues today).

Kennedy did not take kindly to either the military strategy or the military plant that he inherited. He did not wish to rely entirely on massive retaliation, which he feared would bring a nuclear war, and he did not trust so-called "tactical" nuclear weapons.[7] Prompted by Maxwell Taylor, who had argued against air force predominancy in a controversial book, *The Uncertain Trumpet*,[8] Kennedy returned to a conventional-force strategy, in short: " . . . a limited Communist conventional action . . . could best be deterred by a capacity to respond effectively in kind."[9] At this stage of the cold war, however, the Communists were no longer interested in waging costly conventional actions such as that in Korea. Kennedy now realized that the U.S. military was " . . . wholly unprepared to fight—or even to train others to fight—a war against local guerrillas."[10] To repair this tactical ignorance, he directed the Department of Defense to a priority effort.

Enter Special Forces—the Green Berets—who belonged to the army, a small unit operating under such a cloak of secrecy that, in the mid-

1950s, it very nearly secreted itself out of existence.[11]

Special Forces was and is a valid operational concept. Without going into detail, it attempted to amalgamate the best features of SOE/OSS World War II guerrilla operations to come up with teams based on the Jedburgh and OG prototypes (see Chapter 25). These teams varied in size, but each consisted of specialists trained to infiltrate into a target area and there contact and organize indigenous guerrilla forces either known, or believed by intelligence, to exist. In the mid-fifties, the U.S.S.R. and its satellites formed the major targets, but another Special Forces unit, based on Okinawa, was undoubtedly casting covetous eyes on China's hinterland. Despite some favorable publicity, Special Forces remained small and relatively unimportant until 1961.[12]

Special Forces skyrocketed to fame when President Kennedy recognized its elite status, authorized its unofficial emblem, the green beret, and increased its numbers and scope of responsibility. In effect, Kennedy made Special Forces what it was never intended to be and what it had not trained for, a counterinsurgency force.

The United States possessed still another agency which, perhaps unconstitutionally, had concerned itself with guerrilla warfare. This was the CIA, concurrently operating in Laos, clandestinely arming, supporting, and transporting pro-Western Laotian units to meet Pathet Lao guerrilla incursions supported by North Vietnam. In spring of 1961, by presidential authority, the CIA began infiltrating South Vietnamese forces into southeastern Laos " . . . to locate and attack Communist bases and lines of infiltration." The agency also began infiltrating agents into North Vietnam, where they were to form " . . . networks of resistance, covert bases and teams for light harassment inside North Vietnam." Judging from results and from later events, these operations were not very successful, though better than other efforts.

Nor was the CIA successful in the political field. The conflict between intelligence collection and analysis and executive operations had already emerged in the agency. The CIA in Laos and Vietnam was in the policy-making business to an alarming degree, its recommendations based on reports written by its chief, John Richardson, who insisted to one reporter that Diem's villainous brother, Nhu, " . . . was a great nationalist."[13]

At the beginning of the Kennedy administration, then, the country possessed precious little guerrilla expertise. The armed forces were operating in a state of flux, each more concerned with trying to maintain a state of readiness necessary to carry out conventional missions than in probing unconventional depths of insurgency warfare. A military correspondent in 1961 was asked to cover NATO Operation Wintershield, in Bavaria, not MAAG activities in Vietnam, and was ticked off by the air force for writing critically of its concentration on strategic bombers at the expense of tactical air support.[14] Insurgency and guerrilla warfare were not subjects of general military discussion. The *Marine Corps Gazette* scooped its competitors by devoting its January 1962 issue to guerrilla warfare: President Kennedy was so moved that he wrote the editor a personal letter of congratulation and directed the Pentagon to pay special attention to what he would soon tell the graduating class at West Point:

> . . . This is another type of war, new in its intensity, ancient in its origins—war by guerrillas, subversives, insurgents, assassins; war by ambush instead of by combat; by infiltration, instead of aggression, seeking victory by eroding and exhausting the enemy instead of engaging him. . . . It requires in those situations where we must counter it . . . a whole new kind of strategy, a wholly different kind of force, and therefore a new and wholly different kind of military training."[15]

But, in spring of 1962, when the first American helicopter units were flying in South Vietnam, Kennedy nevertheless entertained the Shah-in-Shah of Iran by taking him to Camp Lejeune, North Carolina, where hordes of marines performed a conventional amphibious landing. And in spring of 1962, a military correspondent could ask the chief of staff of Fleet Marine Force, Atlantic, what the immense command—some forty thousand ground and air troops—was doing about counterinsurgency, and could hear in reply: "What is it?"[16]

Kennedy had yet to learn that a presidential directive cannot work miracles. He failed to respect the soldier's fondness for tradition. It had taken a century to remove the soldier from the horse, once the rifle claimed the battlefield. A piece of paper could not overnight reorient armed forces that had grown up on gasoline, especially when most senior commanders agreed with Army chief of staff General George Decker that " . . . any good soldier can handle guerrillas." Convinced that the challenge was primarily military, commanders of all services, including twenty-two American army generals in Saigon,[17] began trying to convert an unorthodox area of operations into an orthodox theater of war. Not understanding the new rules, they could not tactically adapt. Whatever the President said about guerrilla warfare, these officers, in general, secretly believed that military professionalism would prove more than a match in any battle with "irregulars." Although, in time, some of the younger advisers would realize this error, the bulk remained convinced that professionalism—by which they meant adherence to Western military doctrines—would *win the war*. They had never heard of Major Callwell's writings on small wars, so they would never have pondered his sage advice to regard the native as the professional, the newcomer as the amateur (see Chapter 12). They had never studied Gallieni's and Lyautey's pacification campaigns (see Chapter 13). They had never heard of General Gwynn and so did not realize that, in countering an insurgency, the military was fulfilling a police role and had to apply *minimum*, not maximum, force; nor would they have known of his warning that a lull in guerrilla action is usually a danger sign, not a "victory" (see Chapter 23).

Some of their own people tried to educate them—with no success. As early as 1950, a regular marine officer, an Annapolis graduate, wrote a series of articles on guerrilla warfare in the *Marine Corps Gazette*. This was Colonel Samuel B. Griffith, who had served in Nicaragua, had personally observed Mao Tse-tung's tactics in China and was the first to translate his writings into English, and had served with great distinction as a Raider commander in World War II. Griffith stressed that " . . . modern arms and techniques have greatly increased the capabilities of partisans":

> . . . Ten thousand partisans organized into a number of columns can easily tie up 10, 20, or 30 times their own number of regular troops. Radio makes possible concerted partisan effort in widely separated areas. It also insures close strategic and tactical coordination between conventional and partisan forces and provides a means for the uninterrupted flow of information.

The partisan can be defeated, the author went on, but not by conventional military operations:

> . . . Anti-partisan operations embrace political, economic, and psychological measures, as well as those of a military nature. Indeed, the latter are of the least significance. The basis of partisan operations is in the people, or at least in a proportion of them. It becomes the first task then to win away important segments of this support, a task which requires correct policies in the three fields named. These policies will also make it possible to recruit one's own partisans, who should constitute the major part of the anti-partisan forces. Partisans must be beaten at their own game. This means that mobile columns must be the primary military agency. These columns should be equipped with the lightest weapons consonant with delivery of maximum fire effect . . . [they] cannot be dependent upon supply trains; supply, replacement, and evacuation must be carried out by aircraft so that the columns need not be tied to a base. Equipment must be transportable by light aircraft and helicopters in order that an entire column may be moved from place to place within its operating area with the greatest possible rapidity. Two or three anti-partisan "flying columns" of several

hundred men each would thus, even if operating in an area of one hundred miles square, never be out of mutually supporting distance. . . . Too much centralization of control over operations of anti-partisan columns must be avoided. . . . Operational rigidity can result only in disaster.[18]

Lacking suitable background, the American command did not realize that Western-style warfare is quantitative and that insurgency warfare is qualitative. To fight the latter successfully is frequently to reverse normal standards of measurement, just as trick mirrors in an amusement park make a fat person thin and a thin person fat. From the beginning, the American command erred by trying to use maximum, not minimum, force, and by designating the guerrilla the primary target rather than the population that supported him. Dead guerrillas became "victories"—enough "victories" would "win" the war. They did not understand that an insurgency is not "won"—except that it fades into relative quiescence. Unlike the Western battlefield, a rising body count in an insurgency is a danger sign. So is the necessity for "surprise" encounters, no matter how successfully fought. Progress is not made in an insurgency situation until local peasants are protected sufficiently and have sufficient reason to support government forces and supply necessary information on which to base operations. The oft-expressed American desire to persuade the Viet Cong "to stand and fight," a desire inherited from the French, was another pathetic fallacy. These were professional guerrillas who would not stand and fight—except on their own terms.

The Americans also failed to understand that qualitative warfare calls for careful target selection—that "saturation" of a battle area contains a number of built-in booby traps in an insurgency situation. The more units involved, the more-attenuated the lines of communication, thus the more targets available to the enemy. Rusk, Rostow, and the JCS could bleat their combined heart out about arms and supply from the North—the grim fact remained that the Viet Cong was deriving the bulk of its arms and supply from ARVN, exactly as Mao Tse-tung had done from the armies of Chiang Kai-shek. Worse than this, saturation of a battle area invariably damaged the peasants' crops and villages, frequently killing innocent people, thereby alienating the very persons the government needed to "win."

Our military commanders could not understand this. When General Harkins " . . . was asked about the political consequences when villages were hit with napalm, he replied that it 'really puts the fear of God into the Viet Cong.' 'And that,' he said, 'is what counts.' "[19]

* * *

A large part of the American failure in South Vietnam derived from ignorance of respective forces. A long time ago, Sun Tzu advised military commanders: " . . . Know the enemy and know yourself; in a hundred battles you will never be in peril. When you are ignorant of the enemy but know yourself, your chances of winning or losing are equal. If ignorant both of your enemy and of yourself, you are certain in every battle to be in peril."[20]

Prompted by Diem and Nhu, who, like Chiang Kai-shek, regarded guerrillas as "Communist bandits," American commanders in Saigon in large part oversimplified the enemy and particularly his goals. They would not accept that he was waging revolutionary warfare as defined by Mao and modified by Ho Chi Minh and Vo Nguyen Giap. Our senior officers refused to differentiate between the "political struggle" and the "armed struggle" or realize the importance of the former and its determinant influence on the course of war. They accepted militarily "quiet" areas as "won" areas, where, often, the reverse was true and they were politically "active" areas calling for the greatest concentration of government counteractivity. Such was their arrogance, such their ignorance, that they refused to respect adverse reports filed by subordinates from the field—reports that frequently contradicted information being fed to Washington.

Conversely, they found it difficult, if not impossible, to understand the temperament and mentality of the ARVN troops they were advising. They did not understand the evolutionary requirement of making a military silk purse out of a native sow's ear. They would not admit that expensive American-trained ARVN was avoiding contact with the VC, not seeking it—that the Civil Guard and Self-Defense Corps, which were running on slim budgets, were taking the bulk of casualties in defending static positions against VC night assaults. They failed to realize that the edifice had to be scrapped and rebuilt, with will a cornerstone, if a viable army was to result. As corollary to this failure, they did not understand that defectors gained by the government's Open Arms (Chieu Hoi) program did not necessarily mean loyal government supporters—that, in a larger sense, diminishing NLF strength did not mean added Diem strength.

With a few splendid exceptions, American advisers did not understand very much. They came with confidence instead of caution; they taught before they learned. From Nolting on down, too many of them resembled Alden Pyle—Graham Greene's Quiet American, " . . . who was impregnably armored by his good intentions and his ignorance."[21] The insurgencies of our time, not to mention those of history, might never have happened. The lessons they furnished weren't so much lost— they were never learned. To accomplish the military goal in Vietnam, to "win the war," to achieve "victory," the American military command sought to repair doctrinal deficiencies with machines. It relied on technology as opposed to motivation, on helicopters and jeeps and trucks and armored personnel carriers, aircraft and ships as opposed to men. It did precisely what the American military command in China had done nearly twenty years earlier. It attempted to remedy political, social, and economic deficiencies with metal.

The advisers were not at first discouraged because the new technology brought illusory success. The South Vietnamese Government estimated that the Viet Cong began the year with about sixteen thousand hard-core guerrillas. They estimated that in 1962 they had killed about twenty thousand "guerrillas" (I use quotation marks because we shall never know how many innocents were included in the figure). Yet VC strength, they estimated, had increased to twenty thousand! " . . . At the same time," Roger Hilsman later wrote, "captured documents, interrogation of prisoners, and other intelligence indicated that *at the most* only three to four thousand infiltrators had come down the Ho Chi Minh trail."[22] The other replacements came from hamlets and villages, and if some arrived under duress, a great many others came freely.

Despite ARVN "victories," the Viet Cong retained control of major areas. In summer of 1962, this writer flew several missions with U. S. Marine Corps helicopter squadrons operating out of Soc Trang, south of Saigon, the mission being to haul ARVN units to this or that threatened area. Fuel for these machines came from Saigon by tank truck, the Saigon trucker paying the Viet Cong a "toll" in order to pass to Soc Trang. This meant that at any moment the Viet Cong could prevent marine helicopters from flying. This rarely if ever happened—should it not have occurred to MACV that the effort could scarcely have been hurting the Viet Cong if the choppers were allowed to keep flying?

The fallacy of the new approach was already becoming evident. Initial Viet Cong fright soon turned to bewilderment; analysis followed to produce countertactics. Night operations increased, since helicopters at first did not fly at night. Assassinations and kidnapings greatly increased, the reasons being to enforce discipline, demonstrate determination, and gain recruits. By spring of 1962, the Viet Cong were beginning to fight back, and, by autumn, were not only pursuing active guerrilla tactics but were standing against ARVN units.[23] Once again, Viet Cong countertactics were immensely aided by intelligence derived from peasant networks that, while on the defensive, were scarcely defunct. Marines at Soc Trang and American field units elsewhere were living, to use Bernard Fall's term, in a fishbowl, their every movement, their take-off and landing, their resupply, noted and reported by Viet Cong agents.

The new technology did nothing to repair the existing gap between Vietnamese army units and peasants; indeed, helicopter delivery widened the intelligence gap by flying troops *over* villages and thus eliminating personal contact with the peasants—perhaps a good thing in the case of rapacious army units. The new vehicles also proved expensive. Helicopters and armored personnel carriers require large workshop and storage complexes, installations that in Vietnam demanded ground troops to provide security and nonetheless remained vulnerable to guerrilla attack, as did their lines of communication to major supply centers. Troops so assigned inevitably assumed a static role, to the guerrilla's benefit. Armor plate and motors did not erase poorly conceived plans. American and Vietnamese planners were trying to strike the enemy all over the place. All too often, these were random strikes, because the commands lacked proper intelligence on which to base specific and profitable operations. Where good intelligence existed, Viet Cong intelligence frequently countered it. Helicopters and APCs are noisy, and a black-pajama-clad Viet Cong did not take long to ditch his weapon and either commence work in the field or hide along the reeded bank of a nearby canal. By summer of 1962, frustrated American airmen had begun developing new tactics, for example "eagle flights," whereby helicopters landed a unit in a suspect area. If contact resulted, other, lingering helicopters immediately brought in reinforcements. The poverty of this tactic is too obvious for comment.

When the Viet Cong recovered from surprise and started to shoot, helicopter crews shot back.[24] At first, this was primitive; a crew member firing from the cargo doorway. Then Vietnamese planes, T-28s, sometimes piloted by American advisers, began strafing missions prior to helicopter landings. In late 1962,

> ... the armed helicopters arrived, with four mounted machine guns and sixteen rocket pods; they were to escort the unarmed helicopters into battle and were not to fire until fired on. ... By mid-1963 the armed helicopters were often serving as fighter planes, carrying out strafing missions.[25]

The net result was an increase in quantitative tactics—or escalation of the tactical effort.

CIA and Special Forces operations in the central highlands produced two results. One was a diminution of effort on part of the Vietnamese when left to their own resources. Once American teams moved on, Montagnard projects wilted and died to create tribal disillusionment and thus fertile ground for Viet Cong propaganda. The other was an extension of the war by building military outposts such as that at Pleiku, outposts that had to be defended, supplied—and finally evacuated.

At the same time, the civil effort burst into fresh bloom. This concentrated on the expensive strategic-hamlet program, which, as we have seen, was rapidly becoming dangerous in that false reports were endeavoring to prove it a success. Not only were the hamlets host to the sea of troubles already discussed, but they in no way answered the root problem of land reform. The reader will perhaps remember that highly restrictive land-distribution laws had made about 20 per cent of total ricelands available for peasant purchase. By the end of 1962, only about 25–30 per cent of the available land had been transferred to peasant hands. The former big landowners, rich Vietnamese, French *colons*, and the Catholic Church remained principal owners, with members of Diem's family and government claiming huge chunks of sequestered lands. Despite Diem's promises to American officials, nothing had changed. John Mecklin later wrote of " . . . at least one area where we found tax collectors attached to military units. The idea was that this was a convenient way to collect back taxes for absentee landlords in hamlets where government authority had totally collapsed, often several years later."[26]

The fallacy of the American approach did not escape certain observers. A small press corps almost unanimously contradicted optimistic statements of various American officials. Official statements emanating from Saigon and Washington, they wrote, scarcely reflected true feelings of American advisers in the field. The war admittedly had picked up speed, but, to what ultimate purpose, was not clear. Certainly by the turn of the year, it was obvious that the South Vietnamese army was not doing its share, the result of manacled command and poor morale, and it was obvious that the strategic-hamlet program had bogged down. Some disillusioned American field advisers had learned the difference between right and wrong, and were increasingly passing their observations to perceptive journalists. Roger Hilsman later noted that " . . . every faction was so passionately convinced of the rightness of its cause that leaking to the press became a patriotic act."[27] As befits a democratic system, a number of these journalists avoided the subjective thinking that crowned the Saigon mission and attempted to report the situation objectively.[28] Their accounts of what was happening conflicted at almost every point with what Saigon *wanted* to be happening. The official reaction was attempted news management and suppression in the totalitarian tradition—thus, a State Department directive of February 1962 that virtually ordered reportage favorable to the regime while denying " . . . newsmen access to whole segments of U.S. operations."[29] American reporters reacted predictably, and a feud of massive proportions developed. Contradiction crowned contradiction until a veritable communications breakdown developed—with awesome results in the United States.

Some evidence exists that President Kennedy was already worried about the Pandora's box of power he had opened. Faced with a pessimistic report from Hilsman's office in December 1962, he sent Hilsman and Michael Forrestal (son of the former Secretary of Defense) on still another "fact-finding" mission. The two emissaries found Harkins and Nolting " . . . strongly and quite genuinely optimistic," despite the battle at Ap Bac (which Harkins insisted was a "victory"). As for the strategic-hamlet program, the British expert Robert Thompson, though admitting certain shortcomings, was now " . . . the most optimistic" of all. Their report to the President began: " . . . The war in South Vietnam is clearly going better than it was a year ago." After a review of facts, the report continued:

> . . . Our overall judgment, in sum, is that we are probably winning, but certainly more slowly than we had hoped. At the rate it is now going, the war will probably last longer than we would like, cost more in terms of both lives and money than we had anticipated, and prolong the period in which a sudden and dramatic event could upset the gains already made.

The report went on to object to a lack of an over-all plan, to an inadequate police system, and to a predominance of "search-and-destroy" and "elaborate, set-piece" tactics; it also questioned the " . . . increasing use of air power." A top-secret "eyes only" annex, after listing other serious failures, went on in damning words:

> . . . The real trouble, however, is that the rather large U.S. effort in South Vietnam is managed by a multitude of independent U.S. agencies and people with little or no overall direction. No one man is in charge. What coordination there is results mainly from the sort of treaty arrangements that we arrived at in the country team meetings. . . . The result is that the U.S. effort is fragmented and duplicative. . . . What is needed ideally is to give authority to a single strong executive, a man perhaps with a military background but who understands that this war is essentially a struggle to build a nation out of the chaos of revolution. . . . [30]

How much credence the President attached to this report is not known, but Hilsman's promotion to Assistant Secretary of State for Far Eastern Affairs seemed to lend it at least presidential grace. In spring of 1963, Lieutenant Colonel John Vann, a senior field adviser, returned to Washington to report his dissent with ARVN performance, a bit of healthy heterodoxy that probably reached White House ears. In April, John Mecklin personally reported to the President the unsavory relationship between officialdom and press in Saigon. William Truehart, Nolting's deputy, was beginning to express grave doubts about the Diem regime. In September, Rufus Phillips, who headed the $20-million

Rural Affairs program in Vietnam, told President Kennedy that, despite Phillips' own earlier optimism, the program was failing. When Henry Cabot Lodge arrived in Saigon as the new ambassador, William Flippen, deputy chief of AID, who had been in South Vietnam for six years, "... delivered a bitter attack on our previous policy. Flippen added that the American military had been consistently wrong in its reports and interpretations ever since he arrived in Vietnam, and stated flatly that the war was being lost."[31]

Such dissidents formed a minority. Nolting, Richardson, and Harkins refused to admit that the American effort had turned sour. By spring of 1963, these people resembled company directors surrounded by charts and statistical reports showing favorable production and sales at a time when, unknown to them, the factory was shutting down. Their obdurate attitude found reflection in visiting officials, some of whom should have known better. At one point, Major General V. H. Krulak, an incisive little man jocularly known to his Marine Corps associates as "the Brute," arrived in Saigon as McNamara's counterinsurgency expert. At a time when the strategic-hamlet program was bursting at the seams, Krulak, although aware of Vann's strong feelings on this and other matters, reported favorably to McNamara. Later, when Rufus Phillips flew to Washington to acquaint Kennedy with disaster, he "... was immediately and bitterly challenged by Krulak, who doubted his veracity and his competence ... "[32]—a curious stand, considering Krulak's lack of background in guerrilla warfare.

The conflict between Saigon and the field—between wishes and facts—had already produced a chilling corollary: extreme intolerance, on the part of both the Saigon regime and the American mission, of journalists who questioned the validity of allied performance. In March 1962, Mme. Nhu had begun persuading President Diem to expel three troublemakers, the veteran news correspondents Homer Bigart of the *New York Times*, François Sully of *Newsweek*, and James Robinson of NBC, each of whom was increasingly harassed by the Saigon government, as were other correspondents who, in Joseph Buttinger's words, were "... accused of being part of an international Communist-inspired conspiracy to slander the regime."

... The U.S. mission was anything but forceful in defending these correspondents against abuse and ill-treatment, and almost apologetic in explaining that these men were merely trying to live up to the American concept of a free press. Ambassador Frederick E. Nolting, Jr., and General Paul Harkins in particular were incensed by the American newsmen's attacks on the regime.... They, as well as their superiors in Washington, spoke repeatedly of the "slanted" or even "irresponsible" press reporting out of Saigon, convinced not only that the correspondents who criticized the regime did harm to U.S.-South Vietnamese relations, but also that they were wrong.[33]

Nolting and Harkins took it upon themselves to deny the democratic right of free speech, and it is to John Kennedy's shame that, while publicly calling for journalistic freedom,[34] he tried to muzzle the outspoken Halberstam by suggesting to his publisher, Arthur Hays Sulzberger, " . . . that he might give Halberstam a vacation to remove him from Vietnam."[35] Sulzberger refused, and Halberstam, along with Malcolm Browne, went on to win a Pulitzer prize. Another dissident, Charles Mohr of *Time,* who reported pessimistically on the deteriorating situation, found his copy suppressed by senior editors, and resigned in disgust.[36] Reporters who wrote favorable accounts, among them Marguerite Higgins, Joseph Alsop, and Richard Tregaskis, received comforting little pats for their part in what was rapidly becoming the great deception. The Administration was running scared.

The double standard of reporting continued into 1963. As each new allied effort flared and wilted, MACV continued to insist that the war was being won; the press, in general, continued to insist that it was being lost. If conditions were somewhat dicey in the Mekong Delta, briefing officers said, it was because " . . . the guerrillas had been pushed south by successful operations in northern areas."[37] If conditions were somewhat dicey in the delta, reporters wrote, it was because the strategic-hamlet program was failing—the inevitable result of a despot-ridden regime whose venality and corruption penetrated the entire command system of ARVN. (The reader should take note that almost every disclosure made by American reporters earlier and at this time was confirmed, and then some, by discoveries made after Diem's death!)

The eye-opening Buddhist revolts favored the reporters, however. Throughout summer of 1963, some of the truths they had been writing began emerging in official reports. National Security Council meetings grew more tense and acrimonious as the civil-versus-military battle mounted in Administration circles. In September, the President sent out still another civil-military fact-finding team, consisting of Krulak, the Pentagon's expert on insurgency warfare, and J. S. Mendenhall, a veteran diplomat with extensive service in Vietnam. In due time, they returned to Washington and a meeting of the National Security Council. Krulak reported enthusiastically on the situation, Mendenhall unfavorably. So diametrically opposed were the reports that President Kennedy dryly commented, " . . . Were you gentlemen in the same country?"[38] The President was probably not impressed, either, with General Harkins, who stated in October: " . . . I can safely say the end of the war is in sight."[39]

The end of the war, though not as Harkins meant it, might have been in sight had President Kennedy lived. In September 1963, one of his most trusted advisers, Robert McNamara, theretofore an optimist, returned from Saigon to report a *volte-face* that brought Kennedy up short. On previous inspection tours, McNamara had been sold a bill of goods by Harkins and Nolting that bore but slight resemblance to facts. Henry Cabot Lodge had replaced Nolting and was dissatisfied with what he found, apparently, pressing his views with considerable vigor on McNamara. McNamara back in Washington " . . . reportedly told Kennedy that the military had been wrong, that the war was not going well and that the official version of military events was inaccurate."[40] McNamara and Taylor nonetheless continued to insist on a military approach, reporting

> . . . their judgment that the major part of the United States military task can be completed by the end of 1965. . . . They reported that by the end of this year [1963] the U.S. program for training Vietnamese should have progressed to the point that one thousand U.S. military personnel assigned to South Vietnam can be withdrawn.[41]

Despite this optimism, misplaced as usual, the situation continued to deteriorate with such rapidity that, shortly after McNamara's return, Kennedy decided to dump Diem or at least not stand in the way of those who wished him dumped.

A former presidential aide, Kenneth O'Donnell, disclosed in 1970 that Kennedy, for some time, had been entertaining private personal doubts as to the American role in Vietnam. In late 1962, Senator Mike Mansfield had urged that the President stop escalating the American effort and withdraw all American forces from what was a civil war.

> . . . A continued steady increase of American military advisers in South Vietnam, the senator argued, would lead to sending still more forces to beef up those that were there, and soon the Americans would be dominating the combat in a civil war that was not our war . . .

When Mansfield continued to press the argument, Kennedy called him to the White House in spring of 1963, a private meeting witnessed by O'Donnell:

> . . . The President told Mansfield that he had been having serious second thoughts about Mansfield's argument and that he now agreed with the senator's thinking on the need for a complete military withdrawal from Vietnam.

"But I can't do it until 1965—after I'm re-elected," Kennedy told Mansfield.

President Kennedy felt, and Mansfield agreed with him, that if he announced a total withdrawal of American military personnel from Vietnam before the 1964 election, there would be a wild conservative outcry against returning him to the Presidency for a second term.

After Mansfield left the office, the President told me that he had made up his mind that after his re-election he would take the risk of unpopularity and make a complete withdrawal of American forces from Vietnam. "In 1965, I'll be damned everywhere as a Communist appeaser. But I don't care. If I tried to pull out completely now, we would have another Joe McCarthy red scare on our hands, but I can do it after I'm re-elected. So we had better make damned sure that I *am* re-elected."[42]

What the President allegedly thought is not what the President told the public. Neither doubts nor maturity embossed his statement given at a news conference in September 1963: " . . . we have a very simple policy in that area. In some ways I think the Vietnamese people and ourselves agree: we want the war to be won, the Communists to be contained, and the Americans to go home. That is our policy. . . . "[43]

As we said earlier, that was no policy, that was an ambition. What would have happened had the President lived and been re-elected is futile to speculate. We know that, until his death, he continued publicly to support the American commitment to Vietnam. His successor, Lyndon Johnson, chose to expand it.

CHAPTER SIXTY

1. White, *The Making of the President 1960*, 349.
2. Kennedy, *Public Papers of . . .* , I, 22–3.
3. Mecklin, 122. Robert Shaplen also covered the area for *The New Yorker* magazine.
4. Zagoria, 26:

   > . . . During the decade in which the triangular relationship [among Moscow, Peking, and Hanoi] replaced the bipolar, the United States was slow to appreciate its own role in the process. Top American officials recognized the existence of the Sino-Soviet dispute only belatedly, then were extremely cautious about acknowledging it, and were always at a loss to know whether or how to exacerbate it.

5. Ellsberg: " . . . In early 1952, writing to the President to argue against sending combat units to Vietnam or otherwise deepening our involvement, J. K. Galbraith spoke of his fears that the bright hopes of the New Frontier would be sunk in the rice paddies of Southeast Asia." See also, Hilsman, 423: Chester Bowles argued for extending the area of neutrality beyond Laos to include Vietnam, Burma, Thailand, and Malaya; although Kennedy took no action, he seemed to favor a neutral Southeast Asia as a long-term goal.

6. Hilsman, 421.
7. Sorensen, 625–6:

> ... some of these "small" weapons carried a punch five times more powerful than the bomb that destroyed Hiroshima. Those ready for use in Europe alone had a combined explosive strength more than ten thousand times as great as those used to end the Second World War. If that was tactical, what was strategic?

8. Maxwell Taylor, *The Uncertain Trumpet*.
9. Sorensen, 626.
10. Ibid., 651.
11. The near disaster caused a change of public-relations heart, and in 1956 this writer was given an open-arms welcome as a military correspondent by the Special Forces unit headquartered in Bad Tölz, Bavaria.
12. In 1956, after a period in field and garrison at Bad Tölz, I wrote a favorable article for *Army* magazine. Alas! the secrecy cloak had not lifted to mini-size: My relatively short article was returned with fifty-five security violations noted, one of which was a recommendation to give Special Forces units on-the-job training in Vietnam. My article was not published. In 1961, as special correspondent for *Army* magazine, I revisited the scene of my earlier crime, was again welcomed and again impressed. Whether I was less perceptive or whether army security precautions had relaxed, my article was finally cleared and published, and it even elicited a congratulatory letter from the chief of the army's Information Section upon its inclusion in a volume on special warfare. See also, Sorensen, 632: Special Forces consisted of " ... only eighteen hundred men ... preparing for a wholly different kind of action in a general war in Eastern Europe. Their equipment was outmoded and insufficient, unchanged since the Second World War."
13. Halberstam, *The Making of a Quagmire*, 223.
14. I was the correspondent. Scene: U. S. Air Force Public Information Office, Pentagon. Serious Major Sunderman tapping copy of offensive article in *Army* magazine: " ... I must inform you, Mr. Asprey, that you have ruined General LeMay's afternoon."
15. Hilsman, 411.
16. Again, I was the correspondent. This brings to mind Admiral Ernest King's lament in early 1942: "I don't know what the hell this 'logistics' is that [General] Marshall is always talking about, but I want some of it." Griffith, *The Battle for Guadalcanal*, 30.
17. Hilsman, 455.
18. Griffith, "Guerrilla."
19. Hilsman, 442. See also, Shaplen, private letter to the author: Harkins' attitude at times approached the incredible. In 1962, the highly respected and experienced *New Yorker* correspondent Robert Shaplen brought a CBS television documentary to Saigon. Called *The End of an Empire*, it was a photographic record of the Viet Minh fighting at Dien Bien Phu—"by far the most graphic picture of its kind ever filmed." Harkins refused to let it be shown to either American advisers or South Vietnamese officers because it would "frighten" them to see how well the Viet Minh had fought!
20. Griffith, *Sun Tzu . . .* , 84.
21. Graham Greene, 214.
22. Hilsman, 450–1. See also, Pike; Halberstam, *The Making of a Quagmire*; Bushell.
23. Author's personal observation. See also, Mecklin; Halberstam, *The Making of a Quagmire*.
24. Mecklin, 66: By the end of 1962 American combat deaths numbered 21; in 1963, 97 were killed.
25. Halberstam, *The Making of a Quagmire*, 81. See also, Harvey.

26. Mecklin, 86.
27. Hilsman, 499.
28. More subjective reporting, e.g., by Halberstam and Browne, came later—induced in part, it should be added, by the hopeless corruption and inefficiency of the Diem regime, in part by obtuse and obdurate behavior of American civil and military officials.
29. Mecklin, 115. See also, Salinger, 323.
30. Hilsman, 453, 462, 464–6.
31. Halberstam, 249.
32. Ibid., 254. See also, Hilsman.
33. Buttinger, II, 989. See also, Mecklin.
34. Kennedy, *Public Papers of . . .* , I, 304.
35. Salinger, 325. See also, Halberstam, 268.
36. Halberstam, 269 ff.
37. Ibid., 172.
38. Schlesinger, *A Thousand Days,* 993.
39. Schlesinger, *The Bitter Heritage,* 25.
40. Halberstam, 258. See also, Hilsman, 509: McNamara " . . . came back doubting the statistics he loved so well—or at least recognizing that unquantifiable political factors might be more important than he had been willing to believe before"; Kahin and Lewis.
41. Hilsman, 509.
42. O'Donnell.
43. Hilsman, 506.

CHAPTER 61

Enter President Lyndon Johnson • Duong Van Minh's provisional government • Political anarchy in the South • Revolutionary pressures • Nguyen Khanh takes over • McNamara's report (I) • Operation Plan 34A • Intelligence experts dissent • JCS hawks • Nguyen Khanh's reforms • McNamara's report (II) • Renewed VC offensives • The situation deteriorates • The Lodge plan: "carrot and stick" • Johnson backs the hawks • CIA rebuttal • Seaborn's mission to Hanoi • Hanoi hawks • Taylor relieves Lodge: the military situation • The new Saigon team • The Tonkin Gulf incident • William Bundy's Congressional resolution

NOTHING in President Johnson's background presaged a healthy change of policy in Vietnam. So far as that dismal situation went, he assumed office with one foot in a trap, albeit a trap he had helped set. Like John Kennedy, Johnson embraced a number of simplistic tenets. Unlike Kennedy, he was unable to question and perhaps outgrow them. He was wedded to the grand ambition: *stop communism*. He accepted the "aggression from the North" theory, and if the monolithic-Communist-conspiracy theme had developed a major crack, Peking conveniently replaced Moscow as master villain. The new President regarded South Vietnam as a military rather than a political problem; drawing on Prometheus and Robert Frost, he " . . . held with those who favored fire" for its solution.

Johnson faced a presidential election within a year, and that, rather than personal doubts, at first checked his use of overt force. As Kennedy had done in 1961, Johnson ordered a program greatly enlarged from the earlier civilian effort, but he also embraced force to compel the North to stop the war.

* * *

President Diem's demise had opened the way for a reform government that, properly pressured by the American Government, could possibly have retrieved the situation in South Vietnam. Instead, a provisional government showed itself weak and divided. Headed by a cardboard premier, it consisted of twelve generals who chopped off as many pro-Diem heads as possible—and then sat still, content to collect eggs from the American golden goose while their country went down the drain. In a situation that demanded firm and vigorous domestic policy carried out by trustworthy, trained, and confident officials, Duong Van Minh and his fellow generals proved themselves incapable of rule, indeed even of trusting one another.

Here was a power vacuum that a determined effort on the part of American advisers might have filled. But lack of viable American policy dictated inaction at a crucial time. As Robert Shaplen put it:

> . . . we dealt repeatedly in tired shibboleths, in continued bland expressions of optimism; and in consequence our policy, if indeed we had one, was obscured in a welter of words that unfortunately soon became involved in a Presidential political campaign. The admission must be made that we had no more of a post-coup plan than the Vietnamese had.[1]

With government fragmented by Diem's death and daily challenged by the Viet Cong, the situation soon grew calamitous. In the cities, political parties proliferated—sixty-two of them within a month and a half of the coup! The factious bodies in no way influenced the junta government into framing and passing reform legislation. A Council of Notables, which was supposed to draft a new constitution (but never did), included " . . . no representatives of the peasantry or of the labor movement."[2]

Although the junta removed some important pro-Diem officials, a number of them survived in office, as did thousands of lesser bureaucrats imbued with mandarin philosophy. Part of the reason was necessity: Trained officials remained in short supply. But part was political: Each junta member held ties to the old regime, his power resting, in part, on cliques and cabals within the framework of Diem's government, including the army. Power had merely shifted from one house of rule to another, with no seeming intention to improve the peasant's lot, no seeming recognition that here was a political revolution being overwhelmed by demands for a social revolution.

In autumn of 1963, the politically organized NLF-PRP was on hand to exploit the very real desire in the South for social revolution in cities and countryside. Within a month after the junta had assumed power, Viet Cong guerrillas opened carefully planned offensives throughout

South Vietnam. By December, guerrillas had ARVN on the run; once again, a cloud of jeopardy covered the land.

The failure of Minh's junta government promoted increasing intrigue that resulted in a bloodless military coup in late January 1964—General Nguyen Khanh now replaced Duong Van Minh.

Shortly after taking office, President Johnson conferred with Ambassador Lodge and with CIA Chief John McCone. Johnson later described Lodge as "optimistic" (as opposed to McCone):

> . . . I told Lodge that I had not been happy with what I had read about our Mission's operations in Vietnam earlier in the year. There had been too much internal dissension. I wanted him to develop a strong team; I wanted them to work together; and I wanted the Ambassador to be the sole boss. I assured him of full support in Washington. . . . [3]

We still don't know the exact relationship of that period. We do know that a stronger man than Lodge was needed to halt the internecine warfare being fought between not only American civil and military missions, but between sections within each. We also know that McCone's pessimism was justified. In December 1963, President Johnson sent Secretary of Defense Robert McNamara to Saigon for a two-day visit. McNamara reported that " . . . the situation is very disturbing. Current trends, unless reversed in the next 2–3 months, will lead to neutralization at best and more likely to a Communist-controlled state"; the new Saigon government was " . . . the greatest source of concern. It is indecisive and drifting." The "second major weakness," McNamara reported, was the Country Team, or *ad hoc* civil-military U.S. committee that was supposed to co-ordinate the American effort:

> . . . It lacks leadership, has been poorly informed, and is not working to a common plan. . . . [Ambassador] Lodge has virtually no official contact with Harkins. Lodge sends in reports with major military implications without showing them to Harkins, and does not show Harkins important incoming traffic. My impression is that Lodge simply does not know how to conduct a co-ordinated administration.

McNamara told the President that the situation has " . . . been deteriorating in the countryside since July to a far greater extent than we realize because of our undue dependence on distorted Vietnamese reporting." Infiltration of men and equipment from the North also played a part: " . . . The best guess is that 1000–1500 Viet Cong cadres entered

South Vietnam from Laos in the first nine months of 1963." In order to co-ordinate the American effort, McNamara wanted major operational changes, better U.S. staff personnel to improve reporting, improved pacification measures, and covert action—sabotage and psychological warfare operations—against North Vietnam.[4]

Johnson was sufficiently impressed to order significant changes in reporting methods from the field including direct " . . . detailed weekly reports from Ambassador Lodge which pulled no punches in describing problems as well as progress."[5] He also authorized additional American personnel, both civil and military, for the Saigon missions, as well as covert operations in the North. The latter effort, known as Operation Plan 34A, called for a variety of actions ranging from U-2 flights to commando-type raids designed " . . . to result in substantial destruction, economic loss and harassment"—what the Pentagon called "destructive undertakings." Two other covert operations complemented Plan 34A. One was an air effort directed by the CIA in Laos, where a force of twenty-five to forty T-28 fighter-bombers interdicted Pathet Lao operations. The other consisted of U. S. Navy destroyer operations in the Gulf of Tonkin. Code-named DeSoto patrols, they were mainly designed as a show of force, but " . . . the destroyers collected the kind of intelligence on North Vietnamese warning radars and coastal defenses that would be useful to 34A raiding parties."[6]

Along with other Administration officials, McNamara was apparently convinced from radio intercepts " . . . that Hanoi controlled and directed the Vietcong." McNamara recommended Plan 34A to the President in the hope that " . . . progressively escalating pressure from the clandestine attacks might eventually force Hanoi to order the Vietcong guerrillas to halt their insurrections." The plan went into effect in February 1964. Two important bodies remained unimpressed with the covert effort. The first was the intelligence community in general, which held that raids would not affect NLF operations in the South. Taylor and the JCS argued that "a much higher level of activity" was necessary, meaning raids into Laos, aerial bombing of the North, and committing American troops in sufficient numbers to meet the combat challenge in the South, including any specific response from the North such as invasion in the Korean style.[7] In large part, this parroted JCS thinking on Laos in 1961 and also bore direct resemblance to the Taylor-Rostow plan of late 1961. Walt Rostow, once again in the State Department, continued to press his "aggression from the North" thesis, urging punitive action against Hanoi. Ho Chi Minh, he informed Dean Rusk, " . . . has an industrial complex to protect: he is no longer a guerrilla fighter with nothing to lose."[8]

As with earlier plans, the new JCS plan glossed over the danger of escalating local insurgency into thermonuclear war, but whatever the danger, " . . . The Joint Chiefs of Staff consider that the strategic importance of Vietnam and of Southeast Asia warrants preparations" for the recommended escalation.[9]

In Saigon, meanwhile, General Nguyen Khanh was trying to rule through a mélange of vice-premiers, a Cabinet, and an enlarged Military Revolutionary Council. His top officials consisted mainly of Dai Viet nationalists, his government, in general, excluding other important nationalist groups and parties.

In March 1964, presumably prodded by American advisers, Khanh announced a Program of Action that included ambitious and bold political, social, economic, and military reforms. In place of Nhu's defunct strategic-hamlet program, Khanh substituted a concept called New Rural Life Hamlets. Theoretically a reversion to Lyautey's *tache d'huile* concept of pacification, Khanh's plan called for clearing, consolidating, and defending specific rural areas. Unlike former programs, however, the new effort bowed to NLF success in mobilizing from the inside. Integral to it were Advance People's Action Groups:

> . . . Directed by Vietnamese after being organized and trained by the United States Central Intelligence Agency, they were, specifically, guerrilla outfits of six men each who, dressed in black pajamas, like those worn by the Vietcong, surreptitiously entered a Vietcong-controlled hamlet, usually at night, engaged in direct armed counterinsurgency action against the Communists; and followed this up, once the Vietcong were dispersed, by staying on the scene and helping the people harvest their rice and repair whatever damage had been done.[10]

By going after what one counterinsurgency expert, Richard Clutterbuck, aptly terms "the man with the knife," the groups were attacking the fundamental fear that allowed Communist agitation/propaganda agents to organize the infrastructure essential to guerrilla operations. Once covert groups had removed Viet Cong agents, political and social action would consolidate the gain, new areas would be cleared and held . . . and so on until South Vietnam lived free of Viet Cong. To aid the process, Khanh wanted the Civil Guard brought up to strength, some eighty thousand, and joined to the regular army; the Self-Defense Corps would also be brought up to its authorized strength, seventy-two thousand. Specific land reforms would win over peasant groups, while "national mobilization" would eliminate inequities in conscription laws.[11]

To some American observers, Khanh appeared determined to lead South Vietnam out of chaos created by Diem and subsequent junta governments. Secretary of Defense McNamara

... found many reasons for encouragement in the performance of the Khanh government to date [March 1964]. Although its top layer is thin, it is highly responsive to U.S. advice, and with a good grasp of the basic elements of rooting out the Viet Cong.

McNamara advised Johnson to instruct appropriate government agencies:

... To make it clear that we are prepared to furnish assistance and support to South Vietnam for as long as it takes to bring the insurgency under control. ... To make it clear that we fully support the Khanh government and are opposed to further coups. ... [12]

The United States, already contributing directly $500 million a year to South Vietnam, now added another $50 million a year.

Alas, the new strong man could not lift the weight of government. Not only did he fail to fuse dissident political and religious elements into a governing whole, but he also fell victim to a self-made legacy of quarreling, jealous, and ambitious generals, not to mention veteran nationalist politicians. In protecting his flanks of power, he slowed and ultimately doomed forward movement. In contrast, the NLF-PRP became increasingly aggressive, passing in 1964, so Hanoi claimed

... to the tactic of conducting an uninterrupted offensive against the enemy. ... Efforts to kill Americans have developed with great vigor and on a large scale in all regions, and particularly in Saigon proper. [13]

Black-clad agit-prop teams proclaimed Khanh another American lackey in the Diem tradition, and made capital propaganda out of his attempts to cut losses by abandoning weak and isolated strategic hamlets as Viet Cong attacks continued. ARVN remained the VC's major supply depot, contributing an average one thousand weapons per month. [14]

The South Vietnamese army seemed no more able to halt the rot than previously. McNamara and Taylor reported upon their return from Saigon in March 1964 that " ... the situation has unquestionably been growing worse." About 40 per cent of the countryside was " ... under Viet Cong control or predominant influence." Civil and military morale was low, ARVN and para-military desertion rates high, draft-dodging extensive. The report recommended contingency plans capable of putting " ... new and significant pressures upon North Vietnam" by limited ARVN incursions into Laos and Cambodia and "retaliatory bombing strikes" of the North by South Vietnamese and American planes. [15]

President Johnson accepted the bulk of McNamara's recommendations, agreeing with him that it was too early to take overt military action against the North,[16] particularly since " . . . we expect a showdown," as he cabled Lodge, "between the Chinese and Soviet Communist parties soon and action against the North will be more practicable after than before a showdown."[17]

Johnson's other immediate concern was increasing indigenous sentiment in Saigon for a neutralist settlement in form of a coalition government with the NLF, a solution that he and his advisers deemed tantamount to Communist victory, in view of Khanh's fragile government. Lodge was to knock " . . . the idea of neutralization wherever it rears its ugly head."[18]

Various courses of action were discussed at a high-level strategy meeting of American officials in late April in Saigon. In general, two schools of thought were at work: a go-slow and a go-fast. The major check on go-fast escalation, aside from American and international public opinion, was lack of adequate information " . . . concerning the nature and magnitude" of infiltration from the North. Its appeal, however, to the bulk of the President's top advisers, was only too obvious. The JCS had already approved a plan submitted by Commander-in-Chief, Pacific (CINCPAC) Admiral Harry Felt:

> . . . It tabulated how many planes and what bomb tonnages would be required for each phase of the strikes, listed the targets in North Vietnam with damage to be achieved, and programed the necessary positioning of air forces for the raids. A follow-up operation plan . . . calculated the possible reactions of China and North Vietnam and the American ground forces that might be necessary to meet them.[19]

William Bundy, who headed Intelligence Security Affairs—a sort of private State Department in the Department of Defense—was also preparing a sixteen-point "scenario" for escalation. Bundy and Rusk had questioned a tacit assumption that the insurgency's continuing success hinged on aid from the North. Rusk sent a former *New York Times* correspondent, William Jorden, to Saigon to assemble available data. What became known as the Jorden Report apparently convinced Rusk and Bundy that sufficient infiltration existed to justify attacks against the North—sufficient, at least, to justify such attacks to the American public. In late May, Bundy drafted a resolution for Congress that would free the President's military hand.[20]

In May, Pathet Lao offensives in Laos heated up that situation and caused the Administration to commit American navy and air force planes to low-level reconnaissance flights. Although this crisis blew over, continuing deterioration in South Vietnam did nothing to dampen hawk enthusiasm. At another high-level meeting in June, Ambassador Lodge, theretofore moderate, began arguing for bombing the North, believing that " . . . most support for the VC [Viet Cong in South Vietnam] would fade as soon as some 'counterterrorism measures' were begun against the D.R.V. [North Vietnam]." In discussing the necessity for a Congressional resolution to free the President's hand prior to escalating military action, McNamara noted that it might be necessary " . . . to deploy as many as seven [U.S.] divisions," while Rusk

> . . . noted that some of the military requirements might involve the calling up of reserves, always a touchy Congressional issue. He also stated that public opinion on our Southeast Asia policy was badly divided in the United States at the moment and that, therefore, the President needed an affirmation of support.

According to William Bundy's memorandum:

> . . . General Taylor noted that there was a danger of reasoning ourselves into inaction. From a military point of view, he said the U.S. could function in Southeast Asia about as well as anywhere in the world except Cuba.

Although the assembled notables advised President Johnson to delay overt action in order to gain time " . . . to refine our plans and estimates,"

> . . . Mr. [William] Bundy emphasized the need for an "urgent" public relations campaign at home to "get at the basic doubts of the value of Southeast Asia and the importance of our stake there."[21]

At a subsequent JCS meeting, enemy reaction to escalation was discussed. Admiral Felt asked for the option to use nuclear weapons, " . . . as had been assumed under various plans":

> . . . Secretary McNamara then went on to say that the possibility of major ground action also led to a serious question of having to use nuclear weapons at some point. Admiral Felt responded emphatically that there was no possible way to hold off the Communists on the ground without the use of tactical nuclear weapons.[22]

During this crucial period, President Johnson continued to follow a wait-and-see policy, but one that held aggressive overtones. He permitted

American aircraft to engage in combat operations in Laos; he evidently authorized official leaks to emphasize the Administration's determination " . . . to support its allies and uphold its treaty commitments in Southeast Asia"; he authorized military preparations for troop movements to the area. But doubt apparently entered his mind, at least to the extent that he formally asked the CIA: " . . . Would the rest of Southeast Asia necessarily fall if Laos and South Viet-Nam came under North Vietnamese control?" Neil Sheehan, who studied these particular highly classified documents, later wrote that the CIA replied on June 9:

> . . . With the possible exception of Cambodia, it is likely that no nation in the area would quickly succumb to Communism as a result of the fall of Laos and South Vietnam. Furthermore, a continuation of the spread of Communism in the area would not be inexorable, and any spread which did occur would take time— time in which the total situation might change in any number of ways unfavorable to the Communist cause.
> . . . The C.I.A. analysis conceded that the loss of South Vietnam and Laos "would be profoundly damaging to the U.S. position in the Far East" and would raise the prestige of China "as a leader of world Communism" at the expense of a more moderate Soviet Union. But the analysis argued that so long as the United States could retain its island bases, such as those in Okinawa, Guam, the Philippines and Japan, it could wield enough military power in Asia to deter China and North Vietnam from overt military aggression against Southeast Asia in general.[23]

The CIA analysis said, in effect, that South Vietnam was a strategic convenience, *not* a strategic necessity. If ever a green light flashed for a President and his advisers to accept facts, re-examine objectives, reform priorities, and realign effort—to change from a collision course to a crafty and intelligent course designed to attain national aims at a reasonable cost—it was in June 1964. We don't know Johnson's reaction to this reply. Judging by subsequent events, he was unimpressed; at least, he appears not to have questioned sharply those spurious and dangerous postulates pleaded by those around him. Instead he sent a Canadian official, Blair Seaborn, on a secret mission to Hanoi to warn Premier Pham Van Dong that, if he he did not stop supporting the Viet Cong, the action would escalate.[24] The premier's alleged humble acceptance of the warning was at decided odds with his and others' hawkish belief that it was only a matter of time until the Saigon government collapsed.

Hoping to forestall more overt action, at least until after the presidential election, Johnson continued to approve massive doses of American aid to the South. In June, he recalled Ambassador Lodge, who had never quite made "the team" and now wanted to campaign for the Republican presidential nomination. He replaced Lodge with a powerful "team": General Maxwell Taylor as ambassador and U. Alexis Johnson, a hawkish career diplomat, as deputy ambassador—appointments that confirmed priority of the military over the political role. General William Westmoreland already had replaced General Harkins; Admiral Ulysses S. Grant Sharp would soon replace Admiral Harry Felt as CINCPAC. A corps of American military and civil specialists descended on Saigon to help Khanh revive his moribund Program of Action.

The influx of American advisers did not serve Khanh well. At Taylor's insistence, South Vietnamese officials directly controlled materials provided by American aid, which resulted in two major disasters: First, relatively little reached the essential target, the peasants, whose cooperation was vital to neutralizing VC operations; and second, in siphoning off and selling American arms, equipment, and material to make personal fortunes, GVN officials and ARVN officers (frequently the same) furnished the enemy with more equipment than was arriving from Hanoi. The Americans found themselves enmeshed in corruption and intrigue that made most thrillers read like nursery stories. Lacking linguistic ability, not to mention an understanding of insurgency warfare, they floundered while attempting to repair inadequate performance by quantitative methods: American agencies quickly proliferated into numerous bureaucratic empires staffed by highly paid civil servants who, like war lords of old, too often fought each other instead of the common enemy. To add to Taylor's problems, as the internal situation worsened during summer of 1964—at this time the NLF-PRP correctly claimed to control much of South Vietnam—Khanh sought to save his neck by carrying the war into North Vietnam, a "March North" propaganda campaign squelched only with difficulty by Taylor.

Covert operations involving " . . . trained sabotage teams, electronic intelligence-gathering equipment, C-123 transports for the airdrops and fast PT boats for the coastal raids" mounted in scope and intensity. At the end of July, one of MACV's South Vietnamese naval commando teams raided two North Vietnamese islands. Two days later, enemy patrol boats searching the area attacked a DeSoto patrol destroyer, USS *Maddox*. Her guns and American carrier planes knocked out three of the boats, and *Maddox* sailed South. The next day, President Johnson ordered *Maddox* and another destroyer back north along with air cover.[25] On August 1 and 2, T-28 planes bombed North Vietnamese villages on the Laotian border; and on the night of August 3, MACV launched two more covert attacks by South Vietnamese-manned PT boats. On the following night, North Vietnamese patrol boats allegedly attacked the two American patrol destroyers.[26] Washington reacted promptly. Planes from two U.S. aircraft carriers struck DRV naval installations along a hundred miles of coast. President Johnson ordered previously alerted aircraft squadrons to South Vietnam, as called for in JCS strike plans; he also alerted army and marine ground forces for deployment against North Vietnamese or Chinese reaction to the raids. In announcing these momentous events that night on television, the President assured his audience, " . . . we still seek no wider war."

This might have been so, but Johnson nonetheless wanted authority to wage wider war if necessary. Bundy's resolution was now dusted off, altered slightly, and introduced into Congress.[27] In secret and hastily held Congressional hearings, Robert McNamara threw up a verbal dust screen to inquisitive senators. To Senator Wayne Morse, who had learned of the August 3 raids and suggested that McNamara was aware of them and that the American navy had been involved, he replied:

> . . . First, our Navy played absolutely no part in, was not associated with, was not aware of, any South Vietnamese actions, if there were any. . . .
> I did not have knowledge at the time of the attack on the island. There is no connection between this patrol and any action by South Vietnam.[28]

Partly on the basis of this and presumably other false, distorted, and incomplete testimony from top American officials, an alarmed and emotional Congress passed the Southeast Asia Resolution (commonly known as the Tonkin Gulf Resolution), which authorized the President " . . . to take all necessary steps, including the use of armed force, to assist any member or protocol state of the Southeast Asia Collective Defense Treaty requesting assistance in defense of its freedom." Although some critics, including two senators, dissented on the grounds that DRV attacks were shrouded in mystery and that the resolution partially abrogated Congressional responsibility for placing the nation in war, the bulk of American people seemed to accept it with equanimity and trust—even with pride.

CHAPTER SIXTY-ONE

1. Shaplen, *The Lost Revolution*, 214.
2. Ibid., 224–5. See also, Pike; Carver; Lansdale, "Viet Nam: Do We Understand Revolution?"
3. Johnson, *The Vantage Point* . . . , 44.
4. Sheehan, Smith, Kenworthy, and Butterfield, 271–4. See also, Johnson, *The Vantage Point* . . .
5. Johnson, *The Vantage Point* . . . , 64.
6. Sheehan et al., 240.
7. Ibid., 274–7.

8. Ibid., 241.
9. Ibid., 277.
10. Shaplen, *The Road from War,* 38.
11. Shaplen, *The Lost Revolution,* 238–9.
12. Sheehan, et al., 277–83.
13. Lacouture, 177–8.
14. Ibid., 185:

> ... Between January 1 and October 1, 1964, the Viet Cong took nine thousand arms from government troops, that is an average of eight hundred per month between January and July, and close to fifteen hundred per month between July and October.

15. Sheehan et al., 278–83.
16. Johnson, *The Vantage Point . . .*, 66–7. See also, ibid., 119: Chief of CIA John McCone, according to Johnson, also wished to escalate the action, believing that McNamara's measures were " . . . too little, too late."
17. Sheehan et al., 285–6. See also, Johnson, *The Vantage Point . . .*, 66–7, whose stated reason later became the necessity to avoid massive Communist intervention.
18. Sheehan et al., 285–6.
19. Ibid., 247.
20. Ibid., 286.
21. Ibid., 250–2.
22. *The Sunday Times* (London), June 27, 1971.
23. Sheehan et al., 254.
24. Ibid., 256.
25. Ibid., 259. See also, Johnson, *The Vantage Point . . .*; *Public Papers of . . . (1963–64).*
26. Sheehan et al., 305. A number of qualified observers, including a senior marine intelligence officer, have informed me that it is doubtful if the North Vietnamese attacks ever occurred. Confidential information in the author's files. See also, Corson, 63: The chief sonarman of the *Maddox* reportedly stated " . . . that the North Vietnamese PT boats used harassing movements, but they did not fire shells or torpedoes;" *International Herald Tribune,* July 12, 1993:" . . . Admiral Stockdale [a U.S. Navy pilot] witnessed what happened that day [August 4, 1964, in the Tonkin Gulf] and reported to his superiors that there was *no* attack on a U.S. vessel and no sign of enemy boats." [My italics]
27. Sheehan et al., 264. See also, Johnson, *The Vantage Point . . .*; *Public Papers of . . . (1963–64);* William P. Bundy.
28. Sheehan et al., 265–6.

CHAPTER 62

General Taylor reports from Saigon • William Bundy's program of escalation • Admiral Sharp's recommendations • Taylor's operational plans • Pentagon voices • Johnson: "... we still seek no wider war" • September meeting in the White House • Enemy estimate of the situation • Douglas Pike's analysis • Edward Lansdale's analysis • The Bien Hoa attack • John McNaughton's adjusted aims • "Fast full squeeze" and "hot-blood actions" • Rostow on power • George Ball's doubts • Taylor's pessimism • The intelligence panel dissents • Khanh's dictatorship • Dissent in Saigon • Tran Van Minh takes over

ADMINISTRATION HAWKS had won the day. Shortly after American planes had bombed North Vietnam, United Nations Secretary-General U Thant proposed a meeting between Ho Chi Minh and U.S. envoys. Ho Chi Minh accepted, Lyndon Johnson did not.[1] Ambassador Taylor, when secretly queried in Saigon as to the advisability of an international conference, replied:

> ... Rush to conference table would serve to confirm to Chicoms [Chinese Communists] that U.S. retaliation for destroyer attacks was transient phenomenon and that firm Chicom response in form of commitment to defend NVN [North Vietnam] has given U.S. "paper tiger" second thoughts. ...[2]

Taylor would shortly report to McNamara and the JCS that the Khanh government, "... beset by inexperienced ministers who are jealous and suspicious of each other ... has a 50/50 chance of lasting out the year." Since there was "no one in sight to replace Khanh," we must "do everything possible to bolster the Khanh government." The American Government must "... be prepared to implement contingency plans against North Vietnam with optimum readiness by January 1, 1965."[3]

At the same time, William Bundy, now working in the State Department, where he had replaced Roger Hilsman as Assistant Secretary of State for Far Eastern Affairs, was drawing up an action memorandum calling for

> ... a combination of military pressures and some form of communication under which Hanoi (and Peiping) eventually accept the idea of getting out. Negotiation without continued pressure, indeed without continued military action, will not achieve our objectives in the foreseeable future.

Bundy and John McNaughton in the Pentagon agreed with Taylor that the United States must not consent to an international conference on Vietnam, at least until North Vietnam was "hurting" from retaliatory pressures.[4] Bundy's program called for "military silence" for the rest of August, then for "limited pressures," both covert and overt, until the new year, then "more serious pressures" such as interdicting " ... infiltration routes and facilities" leading up to bombing oil depots, bridges, and railroads and mining Haiphong harbor.[5] Admiral Sharp in Honolulu sharply rejected this gradual program:

> ... Further demonstration of restraint alone could easily be interpreted as period of second thoughts about Pierce Arrow [U.S. bombing attacks] and events leading thereto as well as sign of weakness and lack of resolve. ... A conference to include Vietnam, before we have overcome the insurgency, would lose U.S. our allies in Southeast Asia and represent a defeat for the United States.

Sharp next got to the nub of his and the Saigon mission's desires:

> ... [W]e must recognize that immediate action is required to protect our present heavy investment in RVN [South Vietnam] ... a successful attack against Bien Hoa, Tan Son Nhut, Da Nang ... would be a serious psychological defeat for U.S. MACV reports that [sic] inability of GVN to provide requisite degree of security and therefore we must rely on U.S. troops. ... consideration should [also] be given to creating a U.S. base in RVN [to] provide one more indication of our intent to remain in S.E. Asia until our objectives are achieved. ... Such a base should be accessible by air and sea, possessed of well developed facilities and installations, and located in an area from which U.S. operations could be launched effectively. Da Nang meets these criteria. ... [6]

Sharp's recommendations introduced a sinister note into the proceedings. The general Administration view at this time, at least as outlined in a joint State and Defense departments publication, did not call for committing American combat troops:

> ... The military problem facing the armed forces of South Viet Nam at this time is not primarily one of manpower. Basically it is a problem of acquiring training, equipment, skills, and organization suited to combating the type of aggression that menaces their country. . . . U.S. combat units would face several obvious disadvantages in a guerrilla war situation of this type in which knowledge of terrain, language, and local customs is especially important. In addition, their introduction would provide ammunition for Communist propaganda which falsely proclaims that the United States is conducting a "white man's war" against Asians.[7]

Although Taylor ostensibly remained cool to massive U.S. troop deployment, he nonetheless developed two operational plans which ultimately would bring this about. The first was a go-slow plan—U-2 overflights of North Vietnam, resumption of 34A coastal raids and destroyer patrols, and air and ground strikes against infiltration routes in Laos—which the United States would implement in return for Khanh's promise " . . . to stabilize his government and make some progress in cleaning up his operational backyard." This, Plan A, called for a specific "precautionary military readiness": " . . . Hawk [anti-aircraft] units to Da Nang and Saigon, landing a Marine force at Da Nang for defense of the airfield and beefing up MACV's support base." Course B, a go-fast plan, would ask

> ... virtually nothing from the Khanh Government, primarily because it is assumed that little can be expected from it. It avoids the consequence of the sudden collapse of the Khanh Government and gets underway with minimum delay the punitive actions against Hanoi. Thus, it lessens the chance of an interruption of the program by an international demand for negotiation by presenting a fait accompli to international critics.

Taylor added,

> ... it increases the likelihood of U.S. involvement in ground action since Khanh will have almost no available ground forces which can be released from pacification employment to mobile resistance of DRV attacks.

Taylor recommended adopting Course A, " . . . while maintaining readiness to shift to Course of Action B." The JCS preferred Taylor's Course B: " . . . an accelerated program of action with respect to the

DRV is essential to prevent a complete collapse of the U.S. position in Southeast Asia."[8]

All this contrasted starkly with President Johnson's " . . . we still seek no wider war" theme, which he was laboring against his Republican opponent, Senator Barry Goldwater, who was calling for all-out air strikes against North Vietnam. In late August, Johnson told a crowd at an outdoor barbecue in Texas:

> . . . I have had advice to load our planes with bombs and to drop them on certain areas that I think would enlarge the war and escalate the war, and result in our committing a good many American boys to fighting a war that I think ought to be fought by the boys of Asia to help protect their own land.[9]

While Johnson was soothing Texas constituents, one of his top officials, John McNaughton in the Pentagon, was writing still another operational memorandum designed " . . . to reverse the present downward trend. Failing that, the alternative objective is to emerge from the situation with as good an image as possible in U.S., allied and enemy eyes." McNaughton's proposals included a significant enlargement of " . . . the U.S. military role in the pacification program . . . e.g., large numbers of U.S. special forces, divisions of regular combat troops, U.S. air, etc., to 'interlard' with or to take over functions of geographical areas from the South Vietnamese armed forces" as well as for actions against North Vietnam that would cause the enemy to react in such a way as to give the American Government initiative to escalate the action at will. At best, McNaughton suggested, this program would cause Hanoi to call off its support, thus allowing pacification of the South. It might result in either "explicit settlement" or "tacit settlement": " . . . If worst comes and South Vietnam disintegrates or their behavior becomes abominable, to 'disown' South Vietnam, hopefully leaving the image of 'a patient who died despite the extraordinary efforts of a good doctor.' "[10]

Administration officials thrashed out various points of view at the White House in early September, finally agreeing that air attacks against North Vietnam would have to be employed, but on a go-slow, "low-risk" basis, since Khanh's government was too weak to withstand probable enemy reaction to rapid escalation by American forces. Undoubtedly with the rapidly approaching election in mind, Johnson agreed to this course, but approved various covert actions along with a significant increase in expenditures inside South Vietnam.[11]

Hanoi did not react passively to the continuing American counteroffensive. In mid-September, North Vietnamese patrol boats attacked DeSoto patrol destroyers, an action that President Johnson let slide. Administration nerves again jangled in October, when Communist China exploded a nuclear pile. Also in October, Saigon observers reported an increase in infiltration, including a GVN claim that ARVN had captured four North Vietnamese soldiers in South Vietnam. American intelligence analysts did not seem overly worried about action from the North. A Special National Intelligence Estimate (SNIE) of early October read in part:

> ... While they [Hanoi and Peking] will seek to exploit and encourage the deteriorating situation in Saigon, they probably will avoid actions that would in their view unduly increase the chances of a major U.S. response against North Vietnam (DRV) or Communist China. If despite Communist efforts, the U.S. attacks continued, Hanoi's leaders would have to ask themselves whether it was not better to suspend their support of Viet Cong military action rather than suffer the destruction of their major military facilities and the industrial sector of their economy. ... [12]

This estimate fell considerably wide of the mark, as did American insistence that the fulcrum of insurgency lay in Hanoi. The NLF-PRP had by no means decided on a specific course of action during these momentous months. Ever since major American intervention in 1962— the beginning of what the NLF called Special War—the enemy had been debating how to win the war. As Douglas Pike has pointed out, this was a major doctrinal problem that occupied enemy minds during 1963 and 1964.

Three options existed:

> ... the military ending, or third stage; the social ending, or General Uprising; and the political-infiltration and takeover ending, or the negotiated settlement. All three were doctrinally acceptable ...

In 1964 the NLF was defending the "dominant doctrine of the General Uprising" while

> ... the regular cadres from the North held for increased militarization of the effort, a calculated military challenge to the ARVN, and greater emphasis on military assaults, including assaults on exclusively American military installations in Vietnam. For a time, as the debate raged, the armed struggle took on a schizoid character: NLF activities for a few weeks would be predominantly military, then switch to political approaches, and then back to military actions. ... In the end the Northerners won the NLF debate, and military activities increased in scope, tempo, and nature. [13]

Though allowing that the fulcrum of insurgency lay in the South, the Johnson administration continued to believe that its *raison d'être* came from the North. They could not understand the true situation as explained, for example, by Edward Lansdale. After discussing favored Administration options, he wrote: " . . . The anomaly in these reactions is that each falls short of understanding that the Communists have let loose a revolutionary idea in Viet Nam and that it will not die by being ignored, bombed or smothered by us. Ideas do not die in such ways." He then called for essentially a political approach, which would

> . . . oppose the Communist idea with a better idea and to do so on the battleground itself, in a way that would permit the people, who are the main feature of that battleground, to make their own choice. A political base would be established. The first step would be to state political goals, founded on principles cherished by free men, which the Vietnamese share; the second would be an aggressive commitment of organizations and resources to start the Vietnamese moving realistically toward those political goals. In essence, this is revolutionary warfare, the spirit of the British Magna Carta, the French "Liberté, Egalité, Fraternité" and our own Declaration of Independence.

South Vietnam had to have a "cause," and the American effort primarily had to go

> . . . on helping the Vietnamese leadership create the conditions which will encourage the discovery and most rapid possible development of a patriotic cause so genuine that the Vietnamese willingly will pledge to it "their lives, their fortunes, their sacred honor.

After suggesting a number of ways in which this could be done, Lansdale warned that the most urgent function is " . . . to *protect* and *help* the people":

> . . . When the military opens fire at long range, whether by infantry weapons, artillery or air strike, on a reported Viet Cong concentration in a hamlet or village full of civilians, the Vietnamese officers who give those orders and the American advisers who let them "get away with it" are helping defeat the cause of freedom. The civilian hatred of the military resulting from such actions is a powerful motive for joining the Viet Cong.[14]

On November 1, the Viet Cong launched a surprise mortar attack against Bien Hoa, the American airbase outside of Saigon, killing four airmen and destroying a number of B-57 aircraft. Although Lyndon Johnson was elected President two days later by a large majority, he did not use the Bien Hoa attack as an excuse to escalate the war—despite urgings by the JCS for extensive reprisal action. The Pentagon Papers reveal beyond question that ranking officials of the Department of Defense, the JCS, the State Department, and the American mission in Saigon intended to escalate the war;[15] it was a matter of when and how, as it had been for some months. From the standpoint of the American public, the record is one of dissembling, if not outright fraud. Thus, a draft paper dated November 5, prepared on Johnson's instruction by an interagency working group under William Bundy,[16] reads in part:

> ... Congress must be consulted before any major action, perhaps only by notification if we do a reprisal against another Bien Hoa, but preferably by careful talks with key leaders ... Query if it should be combined with other topics (budget?) to lessen the heat.
>
> We probably do not need additional Congressional authority [to that granted in the Tonkin Gulf Resolution], even if we decide on very strong action. A session of this rump Congress might well be the scene of a messy Republican effort.
>
> We are on the verge of intelligence agreement that infiltration has in fact mounted, and Saigon is urging that we surface this by the end of the week or early next week. Query how loud we want to make this sound. Actually Grose in the Times had the new estimate on Monday; so the splash and sense of hot new news may be less. We should decide this today if possible. .... In general, we all feel the problem of proving North Vietnamese participation is less than in the past, but we should have the Jorden Report updated for use as necessary. .... [17]

Apparently as a result of this thinking, the State Department sent another representative, Chester Cooper, to Saigon to report on infiltration, meanwhile stressing the fact of mounting efforts from Hanoi by means of "leaks."[18]

McNamara's assistant secretary, John McNaughton, was also drafting a paper that adjusted Administration aims in South Vietnam. The task now became, according to McNaughton and presumably McNamara:

> ... (a) To protect U.S. reputation as a countersubversion guarantor.
>
> (b) To avoid domino effect especially in Southeast Asia.
>
> (c) To keep South Vietnamese territory from Red hands.
>
> (d) To emerge from crisis without unacceptable taint from methods.

Although admitting that the real problem of South Vietnam lay in the South, McNaughton noted that " . . . action against North Vietnam is to some extent a substitute for strengthening the government in South Vietnam. . . . " McNaughton offered a three-option plan. Option A called for continuing the present course of action: In essence, go-slow, low-risk operations against the North with reprisals when necessary. Option B called for " . . . fast full squeeze . . . with pressure actions to be continued at a fairly rapid pace and without interruption until we achieve our central present objectives." Option C called for

> . . . progressive squeeze-and-talk. Present policies plus an orches-
> tration of communications with Hanoi and a crescendo of addi-
> tional military moves against infiltration targets . . . [and] other
> targets in North Vietnam . . . designed to give the U.S. the option
> at any point to proceed or not. . . .

In his opinion, reaction from the North was not a vital worry:

> . . . The DRV and China will probably not invade South Vietnam,
> Laos or Burma, nor is it likely that they will conduct air strikes on
> these countries. The USSR will almost certainly confine herself to
> political actions. If the DRV or China strike or invade South Vi-
> etnam, U.S. forces will be sufficient to handle the problem.

McNaughton showed considerable concern for the effects of escalation on South Vietnam:

> . . . Military action against the DRV could be counterproductive
> in South Vietnam because (1) the VC could step up its activities,
> (2) the South Vietnamese could panic, (3) they could resent our
> striking their "brothers," and (4) they could tire of waiting for
> results.

However, McNaughton continued,

> . . . Should South Vietnam disintegrate completely beneath us, we
> should try to hold it together long enough to permit us to try to
> evacuate our forces and to convince the world to accept the unique-
> ness (and congenital impossibility) of the South Vietnamese case.[19]

Apparently, neither Department of Defense nor State Department senior officials seriously considered holding the line with Option A. William Bundy and McNaughton were said to favor Option C. The JCS, however, preferred Option B—" . . . fast full squeeze," with what the Pentagon called "hot-blood actions"—" . . . with something like Option C as a fall-back alternative."[20]

Still another voice sounded a cry for escalation. In mid-November, Walt Rostow wrote McNamara his feeling that the American Government must clearly "signal" Hanoi its intentions, including escalation if desired. Rostow was " . . . convinced that we should not go forward into the next stage without a U.S. ground force commitment of some kind." A few days later, he expanded his thinking in a memorandum to Secretary of State Rusk. Convinced that Hanoi wished to avoid destruction of its industrial plant (as postulated in the October SNIE), Rostow wrote:

> . . . Our most basic problem is, therefore, how to persuade them that a continuation of their present policy will risk major destruction in North Viet Nam; that a preemptive move on the ground as a prelude to negotiation will be met by U.S. strength on the ground; and that Communist China will not be a sanctuary if it assists North Viet Nam in counterescalation.

Calling for retaliation against the North " . . . for continued violation of the 1954–1962 [Geneva] Accords" and " . . . the introduction of some ground forces in South Viet Nam and, possibly, in the Laos corridor," Rostow wanted to go further:

> . . . Perhaps most important of all, the introduction into the Pacific Theater of massive forces to deal with any escalatory response, including forces evidently aimed at China as well as North Viet Nam, should the Chinese Communists enter the game. I am increasingly confident that we can do this in ways which would be understood—and not dangerously misinterpreted—in Hanoi and Peiping.

But deployment of forces and " . . . even bombing operations in the north" would not form a "decisive signal." The situation called for " . . . that kind of Presidential commitment and staying power" familiar to the Berlin and Cuba crises. In Rostow's mind, the danger existed that Hanoi would either " . . . pretend to call off the war in South Viet Nam, without actually doing so," or would " . . . revive it again when the pressure is off." American troops in South Vietnam, as well as an American naval blockade, were essential to prevent this and to force Hanoi to stop supporting the NLF and the PRP. In summing up, Rostow wrote:

> . . . Considering these observations as a whole, I suspect what I am really saying is that our assets, as I see them, are sufficient to

see this thing through if we enter the exercise with adequate determination to succeed. I know well the anxieties and complications on our side of the line. But there may be a tendency to underestimate both the anxieties and complications on the other side and also to underestimate that limited but real margin of influence on the outcome which flows from the simple fact that at this stage of history we are the greatest power in the world—if we behave like it.

"The greatest power in the world," according to Rostow, could bring limited Utopia to " . . . the Asian community," provided that it acted swiftly and surely. Among other deeds, he called for:

> . . . immediate direct communication to Hanoi to give them a chance to back down before faced with our actions, including a clear statement of the limits of our objectives but our absolute commitment to them.

Should this fail, as was likely, physical actions were in order.[21]

In late November, a select committee of the National Security Council (NSC) met to discuss the working group's draft proposals. Present at this meeting of ranking Administration officials was Under Secretary of State George Ball, who challenged basic Administration postulates, a brave act, considering the prevailing temper of his associates. According to William Bundy's memorandum of this meeting,

> . . . Mr. Ball "indicated doubt" that bombing the North in any fashion would improve the situation in South Vietnam and "argued against" a judgment that a Vietcong victory in South Vietnam would have a falling-domino effect on the rest of Asia.[22]

As Neil Sheehan later wrote,

> . . . While the working-group sessions had been in progress, the [Pentagon] study discloses, Mr. Ball had been writing a quite different policy paper "suggesting a U.S. diplomatic strategy in the event of an imminent GVN collapse."
>
> In it, he advocated working through the U.K. . . . who would in turn seek cooperation from the U.S.S.R., in arranging an international conference . . . which would work out a compromise political settlement for South Vietnam. . . .

Although Ball alone stood for this particular approach, other dissent emerged during the meeting. Secretary of State Rusk said

. . . that while he favored bombing North Vietnam, he did not accept an analysis by Mr. McNaughton and William Bundy that if the bombing failed to save South Vietnam "we would obtain international credit for trying."

"In his view," the [Pentagon] analyst writes, "the harder we tried and then failed, the worse our situation would be."

McGeorge Bundy [the President's special assistant for national security affairs] demurred to some extent, the account goes on, but Mr. Ball "expressed strong agreement with the last Rusk point."

General Wheeler [who had replaced Maxwell Taylor as chairman of the JCS], reflecting the viewpoint of the Joint Chiefs, argued that the hard, fast bombing campaign of Option B actually entailed "less risk of a major conflict before achieving success," in words of the study, than the gradually rising air strikes of Option C.[23]

The meeting ended with no decision as to which option would be recommended to the President. On the following day, Ambassador Taylor joined the select group of officials to report on the Vietnam situation. His words could not have been more gloomy. A new civilian government in Saigon was proving no more effective than the former military government, either in the capital or in the provinces. The Viet Cong everywhere had advanced and were threatening to cut the country in half. Despite heavy casualties produced by an increasingly stronger professionally competent ARVN (!), the Viet Cong not only were making good their losses but were adopting new and improved tactics:

> The ability of the Viet-Cong continuously to rebuild their units and to make good their losses is one of the mysteries of this guerrilla war. . . . [We find] no plausible explanation of the continued strength of the Viet-Cong if our data on Viet-Cong losses are even approximately correct. Not only do the Viet-Cong units have the recuperative powers of the phoenix, but they have an amazing ability to maintain morale. Only in rare cases have we found evidences of bad morale among Viet-Cong prisoners or recorded in captured Viet-Cong documents.

One reason for continued Viet Cong growth, Taylor continued, was increasing infiltration from the North. Although the real problem lay in the South, where effective government had to be established in order to run an effective counterinsurgency, pressure also had to be brought on the North by a combination of methods already discussed. Not only could escalating American military operations cause Hanoi to back off from the war, but they could also be used to gain the South Vietnamese Government's promise to promise more effective government. Taylor added ominously, however, " . . . In any case, we should be prepared for emergency military action against the North if only to shore up a collapsing situation." For the moment, he favored carrying on with Option A; once Saigon leaders promised to reform, he favored the first actions in Option C.[24]

One more voice remained to be heard from, however. Bundy's working group included an "intelligence panel" composed of representatives from CIA, the State Department's Bureau of Intelligence and Research, and the Pentagon's Defense Intelligence Agency. This panel faulted the prevailing desire for air strikes against the North. It did not believe the chances were great of " . . . breaking the will of Hanoi"; it suggested that such strikes would cause a much wider war; and it did not attach much weight to Walt Rostow's thesis, embraced by a good many top military officers, that Hanoi would back down in order to preserve its industrial base:

> . . . We have many indications that the Hanoi leadership is acutely and nervously aware of the extent to which North Vietnam's transportation system and industrial plant is vulnerable to attack. On the other hand, North Vietnam's economy is overwhelmingly agricultural and, to a large extent, decentralized in a myriad of more or less economically self-sufficient villages. Interdiction of imports and extensive destruction of transportation facilities and industrial plants would cripple D.R.V. industry. These actions would also seriously restrict D.R.V. military capabilities, and would degrade, though to a lesser extent, Hanoi's capabilities to support guerrilla warfare in South Vietnam and Laos. We do not believe that such actions would have a crucial effect on the daily lives of the overwhelming majority of the North Vietnam population. We do not believe that attacks on industrial targets would so greatly exacerbate current economic difficulties as to create unmanageable control problems. It is reasonable to infer that the D.R.V. leaders have a psychological investment in the work of reconstruction they have accomplished over the last decade. Nevertheless, they would probably be willing to suffer some damage to the country in the course of a test of wills with the U.S. over the course of events in South Vietnam.[25]

No one seems to have respected the intelligence panel's doubts, which (correctly) refuted official thinking, particularly Rostow's optimistic thesis. Ignoring professional opinion, the principals agreed on a course of action more or less as outlined by Taylor. For the moment, the go-slow school prevailed, and William Bundy's intention " . . . to publicize the evidence of increased DRV infiltration" at the earliest feasible date was shelved. The plan presented to the President in early December, in essence, called for a two-pronged course of action: Phase I—go-slow, low-risk until the South Vietnamese Government swung around to making a real war effort; then Phase II—increasing air strikes against the North while concentrating on the pacification program in the South. The President seems to have accepted the plan, at least sufficiently to brief Prime Minister Wilson on its operational aspects and send various emissaries off to inform other allies of its salient points.[26]

The Tonkin Gulf action served South Vietnam's Nguyen Khanh well. In mid-August, he submitted a constitutional charter " . . . that gave him virtually complete powers"; the Military Revolutionary Council approved it and elected him President of South Vietnam.[27] The new charter immediately brought protests from such important elements as students and Buddhists. Instead of trying to placate them, Khanh chose imperial aloofness. Dissenters responded with mass demonstrations against the government. Catholic groups spilled out to fight them. Viet Cong infiltrators effectively fanned rampant hatreds. Riots in Saigon spread to Hué and Da Nang. Khanh refused to accept dissident demands, summoned the Military Revolutionary Council, and resigned as president! He was reinstalled as prime minister in a caretaker government headed by himself and Generals Minh and Khiem—a deceptively simple solution for a most complex problem.[28]

The new government brought a shaky end to demonstrations by promising a better constitution than the one framed by Khanh. The new constitution would be written by a new High National Council; as soon as possible, government would return to civilian hands.

The dust had not settled when a group of disgruntled generals attempted another coup. This failed, in part because some younger and powerful officers remained loyal to Khanh, notably the head of the Vietnamese air force, Air Commodore Nguyen Cao Ky, a former pilot in the French air force, and an ambitious young man whose slick mustache, purple scarf, and Captain Midnight flight suit would soon become prominent on the Vietnamese scene.

Civil government succeeded no better than military government. The new premier, a sixty-year-old former schoolteacher and mayor of Saigon, Tran Van Huong, quickly fell prey to now-familiar dissident elements. Although he received American backing, his hands were tied, in part by General Khanh, who retained real power in the form of ARVN. Beset by various demonstrations in cities and by military reverses in the countryside, the new government soon foundered. The High National Council splintered into opposing cliques, and, in December, the young generals "purged" it in favor of an Armed Forces Council. This was not to Ambassador Taylor's liking. On Christmas Eve, he assembled a group of errant officers, including General Nguyen Van

Thieu and Air Commodore Nguyen Cao Ky. "... Do all of you understand English?" the ambassador asked. When the officers indicated that they did, the ambassador-general lowered the boom:

> ... I told you all clearly at General Westmoreland's dinner we Americans were tired of coups. Apparently I wasted my words.... I made it clear that all the military plans which I know you would like to carry out are dependent on governmental stability. Now you have made a real mess. We cannot carry you forever if you do things like this.[29]

Taylor could not understand the mess, let alone straighten it out. He now backed Huong, who backed down. General Khanh next launched a virulent anti-Taylor, anti-American campaign, at a time when the American Government was attempting to preserve South Vietnam's identity by spending $1.5 million per day. Although Taylor advised Huong to defy the purge, the premier instead reached a shaky compromise with the young generals. Khanh allied himself briefly with the Buddhist cause, the Buddhists opened their own anti-American campaign, the young generals ousted the Huong government—and Khanh again was in power.

But not for long. His new government, headed by Premier Phan Huy Quat, proved no more stable than its predecessors. Plots and counterplots swirled through the capital.[30] On February 19, 1965, an attempted military coup succumbed to counterforces. But Taylor notwithstanding, the young generals had had enough of Khanh. They now deposed him as army commander in chief in favor of General Tran (Little Minh) Van Minh.

CHAPTER SIXTY-TWO

1. Zagoria, 44–5.
2. Sheehan et al., 346.
3. Ibid., 291–4.
4. Ibid., 295.
5. Ibid., 294–8.
6. Ibid., 298–300.
7. Department of State Publication 7724.
8. Sheehan et al., 349–55.
9. Ibid., 311.
10. Ibid., 355–7.
11. Johnson, *The Vantage Point* ... , 120–1. See also, Sheehan et al., 357–60.
12. Sheehan et al., 419–20.
13. Pike, 105–8. Pike does not emphasize that these were NLF or Viet Cong attacks. Although he asserts that militarizing the effort in late 1964 "... included ordering thousands of NorthVietnamese regular army soldiers to the South," he cites no evidence for this statement. Administration officials subsequently claimed that regular North Vietnamese army (PAVN) units ap-

peared in the South in late 1964, but these contradictory and confusing claims tend to validate contrary assertions that regular PAVN units did not appear in appreciable numbers until after mid-1965 and then mainly in the central highlands and the North.

14. Lansdale, "Viet Nam: Do We Understand Revolution?"
15. Sheehan et al., 322. See also, Johnson, *The Vantage Point* . . . , 121.
16. Sheehan et al., 363–4.
17. Ibid.
18. Ibid., 338. See also, Cooper.
19. Sheehan et al., 365–8.
20. Ibid., 368–70.
21. Ibid., 418–23.
22. Ibid., 325–6.
23. Ibid.
24. Ibid., 370–3.
25. Ibid., 331–2.
26. Johnson, *The Vantage Point* . . . , 128.
27. Shaplen, *The Lost Revolution*, 270–1.
28. Ibid., 275–7. See also, Carver. This article by a CIA official examines political compatibilities in the South where, the author stresses, a social revolution was occurring, as distinct from a northern-imposed insurgency.
29. Sheehan et al., 379–81.
30. Shaplen, *The Lost Revolution*, 283 ff., for a splendid account of this political maelstrom.

CHAPTER 63

Fresh Viet Cong offensives • William Bundy's dilemma • McGeorge Bundy's memorandum • The attack at Pleiku • McGeorge Bundy's report • The White Paper • American marines land • Early results • Westmoreland demands more troops (I) • Johnson's Baltimore speech • Hanoi's investment in the South • ARVN offensives • More American aid • The enemy retreats • More American troops • Taylor dissents • Rostow's optimism • Renewed guerrilla offensives • The Thieu-Ky dictatorship • Westmoreland demands more troops (II) • Senator Fulbright's analysis • George Ball's secret warning • Clifford and Mansfield's pessimism • Ball's solution • Johnson's intransigence • The deception continues

THE INTERNECINE WAR in Saigon scarcely benefited the real war. Each crisis and each coup expended untold amounts of energy that could better have been used in the countryside. Even optimum government would have made the outcome "a near-run thing." Inept government resulted in continuing VC gains of such importance as to decide Hanoi and the NLF-PRP to launch the third, or all-out offensive, phase of the insurgency.

Fresh VC offensives caused something akin to panic among American officials in Saigon and Washington. By end of December 1964, the Saigon trinity—Taylor, Alexis Johnson, and Westmoreland—apparently despaired of rigging a stable South Vietnamese government and notified Washington that the air campaign should start " . . . under any conceivable alliance short of complete abandonment of South Vietnam."[1] In early January, Johnson received a report from Taylor that concluded, " . . . we are presently on a losing track and must risk a change. . . . To take no positive action now is to accept defeat in the fairly near future."[2]

This attitude gained currency among Administration officials in January. Both William Bundy and McNaughton openly favored air strikes and the possibility of committing "limited" numbers of American ground troops to South Vietnam. Secret preparations for more overt action continued during the month, as pessimistic reports continued to roll in. In late January, McGeorge Bundy sent a memorandum to the President stating that he and McNamara were " . . . pretty well convinced that our current policy can lead only to disastrous defeat." President Johnson later wrote:

> . . . Bundy and McNamara saw two alternatives: either to "use our military power in the Far East and to force a change of Communist policy" or to "deploy all our resources along a track of negotiation, aimed at salvaging what little can be preserved with no major addition to our present military risks." They said that they were inclined to favor the first alternative—use of more military power—but they believed that both courses should be studied carefully and that alternative programs should be developed and argued out in my presence. . . . The January 27 memo concluded by pointing out that Dean Rusk did not agree with the McNamara-Bundy assessment. . . . "What he [Rusk] does say," the memo stated, "is that the consequences of both escalation and withdrawal are so bad that we simply must find a way of making our present policy work. This would be good if it was [sic] possible. Bob [McNamara] and I do not think it is."

President Johnson responded by asking " . . . Rusk to instruct his experts once again to consider all possible ways for finding a peaceful solution." In addition, he sent McGeorge Bundy and a team of experts to Saigon to make still another report.[3]

In early February, Viet Cong guerrillas attacked two American camps in the central highlands, Pleiku and Camp Holloway, killing nine and wounding a hundred and forty American troops. While helicopter-borne troops pursued and killed a substantial number of guerrillas, American naval aircraft and South Vietnamese bombers carried out an attack on North Vietnamese barracks and staging areas at Dong Hoi, some forty miles north of the 17th parallel. The President also ordered American dependents withdrawn from South Vietnam. A few days later, Viet Cong guerrillas struck again, attacking both American and South Vietnamese installations on the central coast. U.S. naval jet fighter-bombers and bombers responded by striking North Vietnamese "installations." Political confusion in Saigon largely negated morale benefits derived from this new and tough line. While South Vietnamese politicians continued to behave as if no national crisis threatened, Viet Cong attacks continued in the central highlands. Johnson earlier had authorized Westmoreland to commit combat aircraft in support of ARVN. Now, to prevent the enemy from slicing off the northern provinces, Westmoreland released U. S. Air Force F-100 fighter-bombers and B-57 light jet bombers to bomb and strafe alleged VC concentrations in support of South Vietnamese troops.

McGeorge Bundy and his team of experts were in Saigon when the VC attacked Pleiku. On his way back to Washington, he wrote a memorandum for the President that began,

> ... The situation in Vietnam is deteriorating, and without new U.S. action defeat appears inevitable—probably not in a matter of weeks or perhaps even months, but within the next year or so. There is still time to turn around, but not much...

... Arguing that a negotiated withdrawal of American forces would mean " ... surrender on the installment plan," Bundy instead proposed a policy of " ... graduated and continuing reprisal" against North Vietnam. He also pointed to specific courses of action in the South, " ... such as helping to strengthen the Vietnamese political structure and improving pacification," and concluded:

> ... There is one grave weakness in our posture in Vietnam which is within our own power to fix—and that is widespread belief that we do not have the will and force and patience and determination to take the necessary action and stay the course.
>
> This is the overriding reason for our present recommendation of a policy of sustained reprisal. Once such a policy is put in force, we shall be able to speak in Vietnam on many topics and in many ways, with growing force and effectiveness.
>
> One final word. At its very best the struggle in Vietnam will be long. It seems to us important that this fundamental fact be made clear and our understanding of it be made clear to our own people and to the people of Vietnam. Too often in the past we have conveyed the impression that we expect an early solution when those who live with this war know that no early solution is possible. It is our own belief that the people of the United States have the necessary will to accept and to execute a policy that rests upon the reality that there is no short cut to success in South Vietnam.[4]

An annex, apparently written by John McNaughton, recommended sustained reprisal against North Vietnam:

> ... We cannot assert that a policy of sustained reprisal will succeed in changing the course of the contest in Vietnam. ... What we can say is that even if it fails, the policy will be worth it. At a

minimum it will damp down the charge that we did not do all that we could have done, and this charge will be important in many countries, including our own. Beyond that, a reprisal policy . . . will set a higher price for the future upon all adventures of guerrilla warfare, and it should therefore somewhat increase our ability to deter such adventures. We must recognize, however, that that ability will be gravely weakened if there is failure for any reason in Vietnam.[5]

Other Administration hawks, particularly Rostow and members of the JCS, did not adopt such a pessimistic attitude. This school held that strategic bombing of the North would "win" the war. What it could not ignore was that strategic bombing of the North could well lead to a nuclear war. Primarily for this reason, President Johnson adopted the lesser course of action, " . . . a policy of sustained reprisal" against North Vietnam.[6]

The Administration's justification for escalation rested fundamentally on the aggression-from-the-North theme. The State Department now added a diplomatic exclamation point to military plans by publishing a fourteen-thousand-word treatise called "Aggression from the North—The Record of North Viet-Nam's Campaign to Conquer South Vietnam." This White Paper, which William Bundy had called for in his "escalation scenario" of May, made it clear that the Johnson administration held North Vietnam fully responsible for fomenting, directing, and supporting the VC insurgency in the South.

In early March 1965, U.S. and South Vietnamese planes struck a North Vietnamese ammunition depot and naval base. A few days later, an American marine expeditionary force of two reinforced battalions— some thirty-five hundred troops—landed at Da Nang to defend the airfield against VC reprisal attacks. At a news conference at his Texas ranch in late March, the President repeated a pledge he had made a year before:

> . . . For ten years, under three Presidents, this Nation has been determined to help a brave people to resist aggression and terror. It is and it will remain the policy of the United States to furnish assistance to support South Viet-Nam for as long as is required to bring Communist aggression and terrorism under control.

A few days later, he repeated this sentiment in a formal presidential statement. The American public may not have known it, but their country had gone to war.[7]

*   *   *

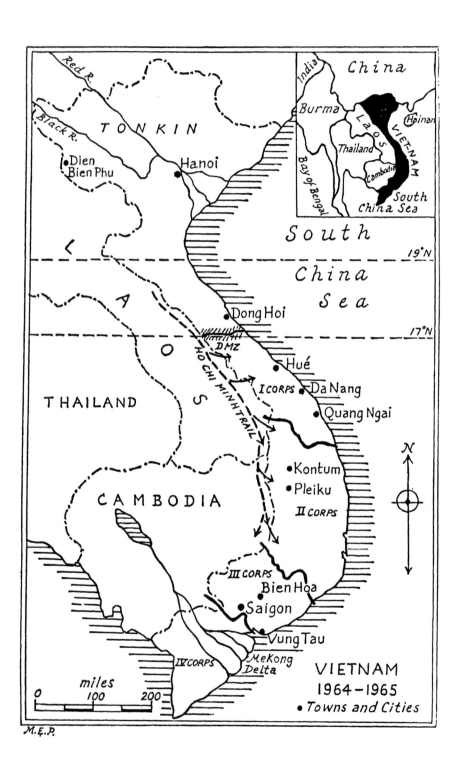

VIETNAM
1964–1965
• Towns and Cities

American air strikes against the North, what became known as Operation Rolling Thunder, coupled with American marines landing in Da Nang, bolstered GVN and ARVN morale, particularly at top echelons, but did little to improve existing deficiencies in either government or armed forces. Nor, as Robert Shaplen pointed out, did it imbue ARVN with the offensive attitude so heavily desired by American military advisers. Improved morale at top levels soon gave way to renewed political turbulence and crises that continued to inhibit beneficial governmental action in the countryside, where the bulk of South Vietnam's peasants—that is to say, the bulk of the South Vietnamese people—did not share Saigon's enthusiasm for a widening war. American actions alarmed many peasants who, contrary to what most people in the United States believed, had yet to be touched by insurgency. In numerous areas of the South, the war still resembled a distant cloud of locusts, and escalation seemed a threatening wind that moved this cloud uncomfortably closer. When it exploded to release phosphorus and napalm bombs, streams of machine-gun bullets, high-explosive artillery shells, and nausea-producing gases, all of which too often failed to distinguish between Viet Cong and innocent folks, it also unleashed a counterstorm of world opinion that included many vociferous voices in the United States.

By spring of 1965, the Johnson administration's escalation policy had failed on two counts: North Vietnam seemed singularly unimpressed either by American air strikes or by grim warnings that they would continue. And, despite an expenditure of millions, the landing of several thousand troops, and the presence of over twenty-five thousand advisers, the American Government seemed as far from accomplishing the necessary task of establishing viable government in South Vietnam as it ever had.

As one result, President Johnson faced a situation familiar in embryo to Presidents Eisenhower and Kennedy. Reduced to simplest terms, it called for the American Government to demand that the Saigon government produce or else stand (or fall) alone. It was not an easy ultimatum but it was the one action, short of arbitrarily terminating aid and withdrawing, that might have fused dissident elements sufficiently to fight a counterinsurgency.

Where Eisenhower and Kennedy failed, so did Johnson. Instead of demanding an about-face from the Saigon government, instead of confining the war to the South and treating it for what it was, a politically motivated civil conflict, the President attempted to convert it to an international ideological conflict that had to be resolved by American arms with or without the tacit co-operation of either the South Vietnamese or American people.

Throughout March, air strikes mounted in intensity. Although President Johnson authorized use of napalm early in the campaign, he confined air strikes to south of the 19th parallel, which infuriated service chiefs as well as Ambassador Taylor in Saigon. Pressures mounted during March for a sustained bombing program north of the 19th parallel. Also in March, the JCS and General Westmoreland began calling for SEATO ground forces (which would have to be predominantly American) both to hold coastal enclaves and to patrol northern and northwestern border areas. Westmoreland wanted about seventy thousand troops by June " . . . and indicated that more troops might be required thereafter if the bombing [of the North] failed to achieve results." The JCS recommended sending in three divisions, two American and one Korean, " . . . for offensive combat operations against the guerrillas." Ambassador Taylor argued against the requests, " . . . because he felt the South Vietnamese might resent the presence of so many foreign troops—upwards of 100,000 men—and also because he believed there was still no military necessity for them."[8] McNamara tended to support the requests, but his deputy, John McNaughton, wanted them integrated into a specific course of action.[9] CIA chief John McCone held still other ideas. In line with Walt Rostow's thesis, McCone believed that " . . . forcing submission of the VC can only be brought about by a decision in Hanoi." A decision in Hanoi, in turn, could only result from a massive air campaign that would impose "unacceptable damage" and threaten the DRV's "vital interests":

> . . . We must hit them harder, more frequently, and inflict greater damage. Instead of avoiding the MIG's, we must go in and take them out. A bridge here and there will not do the job. We must strike their airfields, their petroleum resources, power stations and their military compounds. This, in my opinion, must be done promptly and with minimum restraint. . . . [10]

President Johnson met with his top advisers at the White House in early April. Although VC guerrillas had just blown up the American embassy in Saigon, the President declined to take drastic overt action (other than asking Congress for a million dollars in order to build a new one), but instead set the stage further. Among other decisions, he authorized two more marine battalions and one marine air squadron for the Da Nang enclave, and a further eighteen to twenty thousand support troops for South Vietnam. More important, he authorized marines to change from defensive to offensive operations in the Da Nang area.

In early April, in what became known as his Baltimore speech, the President set forth the Administration's position in Southeast Asia. Like Kennedy before him, he was Prometheus on the podium. He left no doubt as to the villains: " . . . The first reality is that North Viet-Nam has attacked the independent nation of South Viet-Nam. Its object is total conquest." Hanoi, however, was not acting unilaterally: " . . . Over this war—and all Asia—is another reality: the deepening shadow of Communist China. The rulers in Hanoi are urged on by Peiping. . . . The contest in Viet-Nam is part of a wider pattern of aggressive purposes." As for American presence in South Vietnam:

> . . . We are there because we have a promise to keep. Since 1954 every American President has offered support to the people of South Viet-Nam . . . over many years, we have made a national pledge to help South Viet-Nam defend its independence. . . . To dishonor that pledge . . . would be an unforgivable wrong. We are also there to strengthen world order. . . . Let no one think for a moment that retreat from Viet-Nam would bring an end to conflict. The battle would be renewed in one country and then another. The central lesson of our time is that the appetite of aggression is never satisfied. To withdraw from one battlefield means only to prepare for the next. We must say in Southeast Asia—as we did in Europe—in the words of the Bible: "Hitherto shalt thou come, but no further."

What did the United States wish to accomplish?

> . . . Our objective is the independence of South Viet-Nam and its freedom from attack. We want nothing for ourselves—only that the people of South Viet-Nam be allowed to guide their own country in their own way. We will do everything necessary to reach that objective, and we will do only what is absolutely necessary.

Having applied the stick, the President offered the carrot that General de Gaulle had recommended to President Kennedy four years earlier. The United States had been and remained ready " . . . for unconditional discussions" in order to bring an end to the fighting. If fighting stopped, he would ask Congress to fund a billion-dollar investment program in Southeast Asia that would bring a new and better life to the peoples of Southeast Asia, including those of North Vietnam.[11]

If President Johnson expected his words to propel Ho Chi Minh to the conference table, he was quickly disappointed. Although, at one time, the United States might have influenced the Communist leader to conciliatory action, since 1950 the U.S.A. had emerged as archenemy in northern eyes. That did not mean that they stood ready to rush army divisions to the South. Thanks to Pentagon and State Department fulminations, we tend to forget that Hanoi's investment in the southern rebellion was still minimal. Hanoi had contributed by training Southerners who had come North and who returned to work up the insurgency. During 1964, Hanoi began infiltrating *northern* cadres, at the most probably twenty-five hundred. These people joined an extremely viable organization that was Communist-dominated in part by means of the PRP, but one that was largely self-supporting. For years, the NLF had controlled large areas of the South; it collected taxes, sold war bonds, extorted money, captured arms, ammunition, medical supplies, and other material from ARVN—all this to a remarkable degree, described in detail by Douglas Pike who estimated that the 1964 NLF budget was $75 million with Hanoi contributing about 20 per cent, a minimum investment that kept the pot of rebellion not only boiling but daily growing more savory.[12]

In this respect, Johnson and his coterie of hawks were aiming at the wrong target. Not only was the NLF-PRP carrying on the war, but Hanoi would have had its hands full in persuading the southern organization to stop fighting. Put another way: successful negotiations with the NLF-PRP could have stopped the war. At this point, Hanoi was still conforming to standard Communist revolutionary doctrine as defined by Moscow and Peking, whose leaders believed that a rebellion had to come from within although it could be helped from without. Hanoi's help remained contingent on satisfactory progress of the southern insurgency. This is the essence of protracted revolutionary warfare; it is a political axiom derived from a tactical tenet: If an insurgency fails, back off, wait, and try again. This is very important to understand, for it means that the fulcrum of insurgency is interior, not exterior.

By spring of 1965, Hanoi's commitment to the southern insurgency was remarkably slight and for good reason. Years of toil had produced a formidable southern guerrilla force that from some five thousand in 1959 numbered in early 1965 an estimated fifty-five to eighty thousand—"perhaps the toughest, most experienced guerrilla fighters to be found anywhere on earth."[13] In view of this growth, Hanoi would have been foolish to interrupt local dynamics, the more so because the insurgency continued to expand. The 1964 decision to concentrate on a military solution did not mean seriously involving North Vietnam's fourteen regular infantry divisions (though this army might have been tempted into overt invasion had the American military acted wisely). It was to be a southern-based military solution, as it had to be if only some twenty-five hundred Northerners came South in all of 1964.[14]

In 1965, Hanoi infiltrated an estimated eleven thousand Northerners, but this figure must be qualified: Considering NLF-PRP strength, it was neither impressive nor was it necessarily accurate. Dean Rusk told the Senate Foreign Relations Committee in April 1965 that the 325th North Vietnamese division had moved across the border " . . . as a division" between November 1964 and January 1965[15]—a presence repeatedly referred to by Lyndon Johnson in his memoirs as justification for subsequent attacks against the North.[16] But Rusk and Johnson apparently were not using William Bundy's intelligence sources. Bundy later stated,

" . . . we know that one North Vietnamese regiment entered South Vietnam by December 1964, and we know that several other regiments entered in the spring of 1965. . . . Hanoi, as we suspected then and later proved, had taken major steps to raise the level of the war before the bombing began."[17]

Enter Westmoreland, who told an interviewer that " . . . in 1965 he [the enemy] began to move regular North Vietnamese Army units into Vietnam through Laos."[18]—but Rusk said that the enemy began to do this in 1964! Now enter McNamara, who, in the same month that Rusk testified before the Senate committee, revealed that

. . . it was not until the end of March [1965]—four weeks after the systematic bombing of North Vietnam was initiated and three weeks after the Marines had landed—that intelligence confirmed the presence of North Vietnamese troops in South Vietnam. Moreover, McNamara indicated, the unit was only one battalion of 400 to 500 men from the North Vietnamese Army's 325th Division. Tacitly it was noted that the 325th Division was still in North Vietnam.[19]

By August 1965, according to General Wheeler, chairman of the Joint Chiefs of Staff, approximately fourteen hundred North Vietnamese troops were serving in the South (as opposed to seventy-five thousand American troops); by year's end, North Vietnamese troops numbered fourteen thousand, U.S. troops two hundred thousand![20]

American reinforcements which followed the President's reassuring speech once again seemed to breathe new life into the Saigon government and ARVN. After blunting the Viet Cong's winter offensives, ARVN had moved against the enemy in the Mekong Delta area, the central coastal areas, and the North; government troops had killed impressive numbers of guerrillas and had opened major roads in several areas.

In April, another three thousand American marines reached the Da Nang area to build the commitment to some eight thousand men supported by artillery, armor, aircraft, and naval gunfire. Marine patrols were now fanning out from Da Nang, the first steps in contesting Viet

Cong control of that area. McNamara and the JCS subsequently persuaded President Johnson to enlarge the ground role by committing an American airborne brigade to the Bien Hoa-Vung Tau areas, outside of Saigon, " . . . to secure vital U.S. installations."[21] Despite these reinforcements, the situation in South Vietnam remained fragile in the extreme. As usual when ARVN forces made substantial gains, they failed to exploit them by consolidating operational areas. Instead, they withdrew to defensive positions.

If the Viet Cong had failed to divide South Vietnam, it did not mean that they were defeated. In the best guerrilla tradition they withdrew to the hills to fortify villages, lick wounds, and reorganize units with replacements and supply obtained locally and from the North. Fresh American efforts again had caused them to think twice about the war. An ominous portent of their thinking emerged in a CIA report of late April, which identified a regiment of the North Vietnamese army [PAVN] in the province of Kontum.[22]

Most American principals now agreed that bombing the North was not going to bring "victory" (but nevertheless most wanted it intensified). At a high-level meeting in Honolulu, John McNaughton noted general agreement that the decision would be gained in the South: " . . . The current lull in Vietcong activity was merely the quiet before a storm. The victory strategy was to 'break the will of the D.R.V./VC by denying them victory.' "[23] Members of the JCS, Westmoreland, and other hawks continued to argue for aggressive tactics to bring the war home to the enemy. They accordingly asked for more troops from the United States and other countries. Ambassador Taylor, according to the Pentagon study, " . . . protested the 'hasty and ill-conceived' proposals for the deployment of more forces with which he was being flooded" and called for " . . . a clarification of our purposes and objectives."[24] The Honolulu conference ended in a clear victory for the Pentagon, which recommended a 100 per cent increase in American troop strength, raising the total from about forty thousand to over eighty thousand; in addition, another seventeen battalions, eleven American and six South Korean, could be deployed at a later stage.[25]

The President was still hopeful that extraneous action would force the North to call off the war. In May, he proposed a bombing halt of the North to coincide with Buddha's birthday. A paragraph in a message sent to Ambassador Taylor offers an interesting insight into presidential thinking at this stage:

> . . . You should understand that my purpose in this plan is to begin to clear a path either toward restoration of peace or toward increased military action, depending upon the reaction of the Communists. We have amply demonstrated our determination and our

commitment in the last two months, and I now wish to gain some flexibility.[26]

Three days later, the President suspended air strikes, a four-day halt that brought no response from Moscow, Hanoi, or Peiping (formerly Peking). Although he resumed Operation Rolling Thunder, he refused to authorize strikes in the vicinity of Hanoi. His obdurate attitude infuriated the JCS, just as his cryptic statement that " . . . a military victory is impossible" alarmed one of the more bellicose of his civil advisers, Walt Rostow. Rostow informed Rusk in late May that there was no reason the U.S.A. could not win a clear victory in South Vietnam. In Rostow's mind, Hanoi, which in February had hoped to obtain victory through political collapse and subsequent coalition government in Saigon, was now

> . . . staring at quite clear-cut defeat, with the rising U.S. strength and GVN morale in the South and rising costs in the North. That readjustment in prospects is painful; and they won't in my view, accept its consequences unless they are convinced time has ceased to be their friend, despite the full use of their assets on the ground in South Viet-Nam, in political warfare around the world, and in diplomacy.[27]

While Rostow was writing this remarkable prognosis, the situation in South Vietnam was deteriorating at an alarming pace. In late May, VC guerrillas ambushed an ARVN battalion to open an action that " . . . completely decimated" two ARVN battalions. In June, two VC regiments attacked an ARVN outpost and then ambushed reinforcements. Around Da Nang, U. S. Marine Corps patrols were encountering increasing numbers of enemy, and in April and May suffered about two hundred casualties. Johnson's decision to widen the bombing effort in the North by way of reprisal brought still another ominous reaction, when Britain's Prime Minister Harold Wilson "dissociated" his country from it.[28]

In Saigon, the political situation remained as confused and torn as ever. Renewed fighting between Buddhist and Catholic factions led to the generals' ousting Premier Quat in early June. In place of civil government appeared a National Leadership Committee headed by forty-two-year-old General Nguyen Van Thieu. The ten-man committee included most of the familiar military faces, among them thirty-five-year-old Nguyen Cao Ky, the airman who now became premier. Although Ky imposed a number of dictatorial measures including summary trial and execution of terrorists, black marketeers, speculators, and corrupt officials, government remained weak and ineffective.[29]

With a Viet Cong offensive obviously developing, General Westmoreland reported to the JCS, via CINCPAC, on June 7:

> ... In pressing their campaign, the Viet-Cong are capable of mounting regimental-size operations in all four ARVN corps areas, and at least battalion-sized attack in virtually all provinces. . . .
> ARVN forces on the other hand are already experiencing difficulty in coping with this increased VC capability. Desertion rates are inordinately high. Battle losses have been higher than expected; in fact, four ARVN battalions have been rendered ineffective by VC action in the I and II Corps zones.

Force ratios on which earlier estimates had been made were thus upset, Westmoreland continued. His solution was to become a MACV theme song:

> ... I see no course of action open to us except to reinforce our efforts in SVN with additional U.S. or third country forces as rapidly as is practical during the critical weeks ahead.

Westmoreland now requested a whopping increase in outside troop strength, to a total of forty-four battalions. Admiral Sharp (CINCPAC) endorsed the request with approval and noted: " ... We will lose by staying in enclaves defending coastal areas." The JCS were not antagonistic to the request but wanted to know " ... where Westmoreland intended to put this force in Vietnam." Westmoreland's reply, according to a Pentagon analyst,

> ... was extremely important, for in it [he] spelled out the concept of keeping U.S. forces away from the people. The search and destroy strategy for U.S. and third country forces which continues to this day [1967–68] and the primary focus of RVNAF (ARVN) on pacification both stem from that concept. In addition, Westmoreland made a big pitch in this cable for a free hand to maneuver the troops around inside the country.[30]

Westmoreland's request aroused considerable controversy inside the government. At the same time, however, Johnson's decision to allow American troops to indulge in combat operations had slowly leaked to the public, segments of which were already uneasy by a supplementary appropriation of $700 million authorized by Congress in early May " ... for military needs in Viet-Nam." Mounting intensity of fighting due to the Viet Cong's monsoonal offensive now caused some critical questioning of Administration policy. In mid-June, Senator J. W. Fulbright addressed his fellow senators:

... It is clear to all reasonable Americans that a complete military victory in Viet-Nam, though theoretically attainable, can in fact be attained only at a cost far exceeding the requirements of our interest and our honor. It is equally clear that the unconditional withdrawal of American support from South Viet-Nam would have disastrous consequences. ... Our policy therefore has been—and should remain—one of determination to end the war at the earliest possible time by a negotiated settlement involving major concessions by both sides.

In view of the then-current Viet Cong offensive and advantages derived by them from the monsoonal season, Fulbright warned of American setbacks:

... As the ground war expands and as American involvement and American casualties increase, there will be mounting pressure for expansion of the war.

Indeed, such pressures already existed, and the President must continue to ignore them in favor of "restraint and patience":

... we must persuade the Communists that Saigon cannot be crushed and that the United States will not be driven from South Viet-Nam by force; second, we must continue to offer the Communists a reasonable and attractive alternative to military victory.[31]

Fulbright's tolerance was shared neither by the JCS nor by Westmoreland, whose hand was steadily being reinforced by the deteriorating political and military situation in South Vietnam. In May, President Johnson had authorized Westmoreland " ... to use his forces in combat support if it became necessary to assist a Vietnamese unit in serious trouble." In June, the President authorized him to use his forces "independently" of South Vietnamese forces. At the end of June, Westmoreland committed an airborne brigade to a search-and-destroy operation in conjunction with an ARVN battalion and an Australian battalion northwest of Saigon. Meanwhile, General Wheeler, chairman of the JCS, asked Westmoreland " ... if the 44 battalions were enough to convince the enemy forces that they could not win." According to the Pentagon study, Westmoreland replied

... that there was no evidence the VC/DRV would alter their plans regardless of what the U.S. did in the next six months.
The 44-battalion force should, however, establish a favorable balance of power by the end of the year. If the U.S. was to seize

the initiative from the enemy, then further forces would be required into 1966 and beyond.[32]

A few days later, the JCS approved a planned deployment of nearly two hundred thousand American troops in South Vietnam. In mid-July, influenced by a new report from McNamara, President Johnson authorized this build-up and also gave Westmoreland authority to commit American troops to combat at his discretion.[33]

Although these measures remained secret, at least for the moment, they caused considerable consternation within the Administration. On July 1, Under Secretary of State George Ball submitted a lengthy memorandum to President Johnson:

> . . . The South Vietnamese are losing the war to the Viet Cong. No one can assure you that we can beat the Viet Cong or even force them to the conference table on our terms, no matter how many hundred thousand *white, foreign* (U.S.) troops we deploy.
>
> No one has demonstrated that a white ground force of whatever size can win a guerrilla war—which is at the same time a civil war between Asians—in jungle terrain in the midst of a population that refuses cooperation to the white forces (and the South Vietnamese) and thus provides a great intelligence advantage to the other side.

The President, Ball stated, had one question to decide:

> . . . Should we limit our liabilities in South Vietnam and try to find a way out with minimal long-term costs?
>
> The alternative—no matter what we may wish it to be—is almost certainly a protracted war involving an open-ended commitment of U.S. forces, mounting U.S. casualties, no assurance of a satisfactory solution, and a serious danger of escalation at the end of the road.

The President, Ball believed, had to decide on the answer now:

> . . . So long as our forces are restricted to advising and assisting the South Vietnamese, the struggle will remain a civil war between Asian peoples. Once we deploy substantial numbers of troops in combat it will become a war between the U.S. and a large part of the population of South Vietnam, organized and directed from North Vietnam and backed by the resources of both Moscow and Peiping. . . . Once we suffer large casualties, we will have started a well-nigh irreversible process. Our involvement will be so great that we cannot—without national humiliation—stop short of achieving our complete objectives. *Of the two possibilities I think*

humiliation would be more likely than the achievement of our objectives—even after we have paid terrible costs.

Ball did not recommend a unilateral withdrawal from South Vietnam. Instead, he proposed a total troop commitment of seventy-two thousand men to support restricted combat operations; he also agreed to the present bombing program. Simultaneously, he called for a diplomatic offensive by unilateral approach to Hanoi, the general idea being that Johnson could pressure the Saigon government and Ho to bring the NLF to the conference table to hammer out " . . . a multi-national agreement guaranteed by the U.S., the Soviet Union and possibly other parties, and providing for an international mechanism to supervise its execution."[34]

Ball next examined short-term costs of a compromise solution. Astute diplomacy could hold these to a minimum. The United States had good allies in Southeast Asia and would continue to support them. If South Vietnam fell to Communist control, Burma, Cambodia, and Indonesia would probably enter the Eastern orbit—but they were scarcely in the Western orbit at this time. Other nations could be expected to hold, with proper backing from the U.S.A. As for Thailand: " . . . Providing we are willing to make the effort, Thailand can be a foundation of rock and not a bed of sand in which to base our political/military commitment to Southeast Asia." As for U.S. world-wide credibility: With the possible exception of West Germany,

> . . . [our NATO allies] will be inclined to regard a compromise solution in South Vietnam more as new evidence of American maturity and judgment than of American loss of face. . . . On balance, I believe we would more seriously undermine the effectiveness of our world leadership by continuing the war and deepening our involvement than by pursuing a carefully plotted course toward a compromise solution. In spite of the number of powers that have— in response to our pleading—given verbal support from feeling of loyalty and dependence, we cannot ignore the fact that the war is vastly unpopular and that our role in it is perceptively eroding the respect and confidence with which other nations regard us. We have not persuaded either our friends or allies that our further involvement is essential to the defense of freedom in the cold war. . . .[35]

Neither Johnson nor the majority of his advisers was to be swayed by this memorandum, which, although a bail-out course that need never have been necessary had proper measures originally been taken, was at the time a bold, imaginative, and courageous policy that had been needed since 1954. Ball further dissented from Administration thinking

807

during a late-July session with Johnson. At Camp Aspen a few days later, Johnson also found his close adviser Clark Clifford " . . . in a reflective and pessimistic mood":

" . . . I don't believe we can win in South Vietnam," he said. "If we send in 100,000 more men, the North Vietnamese will meet us. If North Vietnam runs out of men, the Chinese will send in volunteers. Russia and China don't intend for us to win the war."

He urged that in the coming months we quietly probe possibilities with other countries for some way to get out honorably. "I can't see anything but catastrophe for my country," he said.

Senator Mike Mansfield, who had dissented from Johnson's February decision to begin bombing North Vietnam, also expressed " . . . serious doubt and opposition" to the present course.[36]

Refined and properly applied, this dissentient thinking, echoed variously by influential citizens throughout the country, might have led to a solution that would have given Lyndon Johnson that place in American history he so obtrusively desired. Instead, he rejected compromise in favor of a "win" strategy. At a press conference in late July he said:

. . . The lesson of history dictated that the U.S. commit its strength to resist aggression in South Vietnam. . . . I have asked the commanding general, General Westmoreland, what more he needs to meet this mounting aggression. He has told me. We will meet his needs.

Having declared a collision course with disaster, the President still thought it was necessary to deceive the American public. A reporter asked,

. . . Mr. President, does the fact that you are sending additional forces to Vietnam imply any change in the existing policy of relying mainly on the South Vietnamese to carry out offensive operations and using American forces to guard American installations and to act as an emergency back-up?

At a time when an American airborne brigade had already sharply engaged the Viet Cong in a search-and-destroy mission, at a time when marines were seeking out Viet Cong and were planning a major search-and-clear operation, at a time when McNamara, Westmoreland, and the JCS were flexing military muscles to "come to grips" with the enemy[37]—at this time, the President of the United States replied:

. . . It does not imply any change in policy whatever. It does not imply change of objective.[38]

808

CHAPTER SIXTY-THREE

1. Sheehan et al., 337.
2. Johnson, *The Vantage Point* . . . , 122.
3. Ibid., 122–3.
4. Ibid., 126–7. See also, Sheehan et al., 423.
5. Sheehan et al., 423–7.
6. Johnson, *The Vantage Point* . . . , 128–9. See also, Sharp.
7. Johnson, *Public Papers of* . . . , 1965, Book I, 300.
8. Sheehan et al., 399.
9. Ibid., 438.
10. Ibid., 440–1.
11. Johnson, *Public Papers of* . . . , 1965, Book I, 394–7. See also, ibid., Johnson's statement to the press, "Tragedy, Disappointment, and Progress" in Vietnam, April 17, 1965.
12. Pike, 304. See also, O'Neill.
13. Pike, 238–9. See also, ibid., 232–52, for excellent detail on Viet Cong organization and tactics.
14. Ibid.
15. Corson, 63–4.
16. Johnson, *The Vantage Point* . . . , see, for example, 121–2, 232.
17. William P. Bundy.
18. *U.S. News and World Report*, November 28, 1966.
19. Corson, 64–5.
20. Ibid., 65.
21. Sheehan et al., 402–3.
22. Ibid., 409: Statements of Administration officials aside, this would appear to be the first major PAVN unit in the South.
23. Ibid., 407. See also, Johnson, *The Vantage Point* . . .
24. Sheehan et al., 406–7, 443–6.
25. Ibid., 408.
26. Ibid., 446–7.
27. Ibid., 448. See also, Gilpatric, whose recital of American strengths and weaknesses was tempered only by the possibility that the American people would not want to fight a prolonged war.
28. Sheehan, 448–9.
29. Shaplen, *The Lost Revolution*, 345–6.
30. Sheehan, 409–10, 413. See also, Johnson, *The Vantage Point* . . .
31. Raskin and Fall, 205–10, for full text of Senator Fulbright's speech.
32. Sheehan et al., 413–14.
33. Johnson, *The Vantage Point* . . . , 153. See also, ibid., 145–6. McNamara, according to Johnson, reported a seriously deteriorating situation that could be met with one of three courses of action: cut losses and withdraw under the best conditions that could be arranged; continue at present level; expand promptly and substantially. McNamara recommended the third course.

 . . . With the force that he and the others were proposing, McNamara was convinced that the South Vietnamese and allied armies could reverse the downward trend and move to the offensive. He said that the military commanders planned to locate, engage, and destroy the North Vietnamese and Viet Cong main-force units. At the same time, they believed we should press our anti-infiltration campaign by hitting enemy supply lines by air and on the sea. We would also carry the air war more intensively into Viet Cong base areas in the South.... [Ibid., *Public Papers of...*, 1965, Book I, "The President's News Conference of July 13, 1965"]

34. Sheehan et al, 449–54.
35. Ibid.
36. Johnson, *The Vantage Point...*, 148.
37. Sheehan et al., 457–8.
38. Johnson, *Public Papers of...*, 1965, Book II, 795–801.

CHAPTER 64

The fighting escalates • Viet Cong setbacks • American and ARVN gains • The air war • Westmoreland's strategy • Search-and-destroy tactics • The American build-up • Westmoreland's four wars • The "other war" • American arms and equipment • Army operations in the central highlands • Westmoreland's "spoiling" tactics • Operation Crazy Horse • Marine operations in I Corps area • Walt's pacification program • PAVN crosses the DMZ: Operation Hastings, Operation Prairie • Operations in III Corps area • The air war escalates • The naval war • The "other war": the Honolulu Conference • Ky's Revolutionary Development program • Elections in the South • The Manila Conference • General allied optimism

AMERICAN INFUSION OF STRENGTH again steadied the fibrillating heart of South Vietnam's government and army. If the Viet Cong nowhere accomplished its major objective of permanently dividing the country in vicious fighting during summer and autumn of 1965, its battalions and regiments, increasingly reinforced by PAVN units from the North, cut road and rail communications, attacked ARVN outposts almost at will, ambushed ARVN forces sent to relieve beleaguered garrisons, and continued a campaign of sabotage and terror against South Vietnamese and American installations and personnel. But ARVN units, in some cases supported by American forces, also generally fought hard, and new American units showed every willingness to fight,[1] even if hamstrung by MACV's overly cautious and utterly impracticable *Rules of Engagement,* " . . . specifically the one that precluded a U.S. soldier firing his weapon if not fired upon."[2] " . . . In guerrilla-controlled areas," a marine lieutenant later wrote, one could not fire "at unarmed Vietnamese *unless they were running.*"[3] Thus hindered, American marines based at Da Nang mounted Operation Starlight in August, a sweeping operation designed to evict Viet Cong from Chu Lai Peninsula. In a several-day action, marines recorded fifty killed and one hundred and fifty wounded, but claimed over five hundred Viet Cong deaths. Meanwhile, the American army's 1st Cavalry (Airmobile) Division set up shop at An Khe, in the central highlands—a base from which units would attempt to screen the neighboring Cambodian border while clearing enemy from the immediate area. When North Vietnamese units, an estimated two regiments, attacked a Special Forces camp at Plei Me, near the Cambodian border, the American garrison held out and then mounted a counterattack, which led to bloody fighting in the Chu Phong and Ia Drang area. The Americans recorded two hundred and forty killed and four hundred and seventy wounded, but claimed over fifteen hundred enemy deaths.[4]

Simultaneously, air strikes against the North rose impressively. During the summer, the purpose of Operation Rolling Thunder had changed from breaking Hanoi's will to " . . . cutting the flow of men and supplies from the North to the South."[5] In addition to striking barracks, ammunition depots, and staging points, pilots at their own discretion attacked vehicles, locomotives, and barges. Sorties increased from nine hundred a week in July to fifteen hundred a week in December; by end of 1965, fifty-five thousand sorties had been flown and thirty-three thousand tons of bombs dropped.

As troops continued to arrive in South Vietnam, General Westmoreland and his chief of operations Brigadier General William DePuy increasingly implemented an attrition strategy—a dependence on superior American military manpower, firepower, and mobility to wear down and finally force the enemy from the war. This was the World War I syndrome, a meaningless and costly concept challenged by a host of thinking military professionals for the last five decades. Lieutenant General Dave Palmer, for example, taught his students when he was an instructor at West Point: " . . . attrition is not a strategy, but the absence of any strategy, and . . . the commander who resorts to it admits his failure to conceive an alternate strategy."[6] Precedents for Westmoreland's choice already had appeared during the Eisenhower and Kennedy administrations, which had adopted increasingly quantitative approaches for fighting this insurgency but had managed to retain limited objectives. The Johnson administration enlarged the concept to embrace an all-out "win" strategy. America's armed forces implemented this strategy by relying on quantitative, or search-and-destroy, tactics: find the enemy—fix him—kill him. By the end of 1965, Westmoreland's strategy and tactics had yielded results deemed favorable by military leaders. Westmoreland had received about one hundred and fifty thousand of a promised two hundred thousand troops. New units were arriving daily, as were tons of equipment and supply. Energetic com-

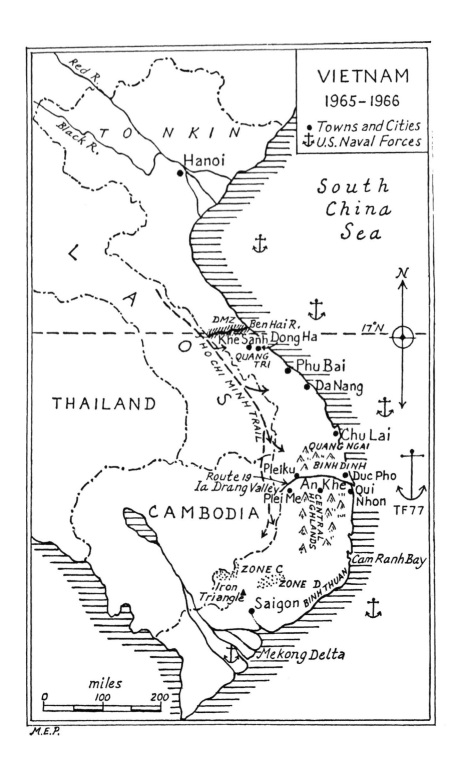

VIETNAM
1965–1966
• Towns and Cities
⚓ U.S. Naval Forces

Red R.

Black R.

T O N K I N

Hanoi

South
China
Sea

DMZ Ben Hai R.
Khe Sanh Dong Ha
QUANG
TRI
Phu Bai
Da Nang

17°N

N

THAILAND

HO CHI MINH TRAIL

Chu Lai
QUANG NGAI
BINH DINH
Pleiku
Route 19
Ia Drang Valley
Plei Me
An Khe
Duc Pho
Qui
Nhon

CENTRAL HIGHLANDS

TF77

CAMBODIA

ZONE C
Iron
Triangle
ZONE D
BINH THUAN
Saigon

Cam Ranh Bay

Mekong Delta

miles
0   100   200

M.E.P.

manders were slowly sorting out initial supply snags while simultaneously pushing the enemy on several fronts. American commands were working around the clock. American planes were striking enemy units in North and South. American patrols were seeking contacts and fighting when possible. A pervasive air of aggression was pushing aside the stale air of defeatism. That winter in South Vietnam even the most cynical observer had to admit that the Americans were obviously determined to impose their will on the enemy.

The man chosen to command the American military effort in Vietnam, General William Childs Westmoreland, seemed ideally fitted for the task. A South Carolinian and West Pointer (1936), he had served as an artillery commander in World War II in Africa and Europe, and had commanded an airborne regiment in Korea. Promoted to brigadier general at thirty-eight years, he had served subsequently as secretary of the general staff, commanding general of the 101st Airborne Division, and superintendent of West Point, adding a star for each new billet. Now fifty-one years old, he stood nearly six feet tall, a rugged, fit man of one hundred and eighty pounds, a devout Episcopalian who frowned on swearing, smoking, and hard drinking, and who was said to keep a Bible on his desk and to read it.[7]

General Westmoreland soon found himself fighting four distinct, though intimately related, shooting wars: the "original" guerrilla, or counterinsurgency, war that challenged the NLF-VC organized in regular and paramilitary units throughout the country; the quasi-conventional ground war in the central highlands and south of the Demilitarized Zone (DMZ) that was fought against VC and regular units of the North Vietnamese army (PAVN); the naval war; and the air war. Each of these efforts bred certain political, economic, and psychological problems, which, taken together, influenced what some called "the other war," the contest to win people's "hearts and minds"—what a few persons accurately called "the only war."[8]

To fight the shooting wars, General Westmoreland disposed of a force so impressive as to bring to mind the prophet Jeremiah's description of the ancient army that would irrupt into Judah: " . . . his chariots shall be as a whirlwind: his horses are swifter than eagles. . . . Their quiver is as an open sepulchre. . . . " From the standpoint of technology, the world had never seen a more sophisticated armed host than that committed by the Americans in South Vietnam. Literally no expense had been spared in equipping and training these infantry and airborne and marine divisions and air units and naval armadas before committing them to combat.

In addition to standard arms and equipment, troops received rapid-firing Armalite rifles, at first the controversial M-16, later the improved M-14 which fired a lighter, 7.62-mm. round. Each squad carried flame throwers, light machine guns, and grenade launchers; in addition to fragmentation and smoke grenades, troops were equipped with a variety of nauseous gases and rocket launchers. Platoons and companies carried such organic support weapons as 60- and 81-mm. mortars and 90- and 106-mm. recoilless rifles. Supporting artillery units carried 4.2-inch mortars and 105-mm., 155-mm., and eight-inch howitzers. More effective artillery shells appeared, for example the 105-mm. "Beehive," which, upon detonation, released eight thousand steel "fléchettes"—tiny darts to tear through whatever body got in the way. Small-unit communications were vastly improved, as were tropical clothing, boots, ancillary equipment, field rations. Combat troops also received such sophisticated identity aids as electronic sensory devices, or "man sniffers," infrared night-sighting equipment, short-range ground radars. A galaxy of specialist units—medical, engineer, communications—supported ground operations; where necessary, commanders could count on heavy artillery, armor, and, along the coast and inland waterways, naval-gunfire support.[9]

Commanders also relied on armored personnel carriers and on large numbers of helicopters for improved mobility. The U. S. Marine Corps, a pioneer in helicopter "vertical assault" tactics, brought its own "chopper" squadrons as integral components of its air wings. The U. S. Army, which employed helicopter companies organic to the ground division, went so far as to build two divisions around this machine. Each "airmobile" division consisted of approximately sixteen thousand troops equipped with 434 aircraft, mostly helicopters, and sixteen hundred land vehicles (compared to a normal army division's one hundred organic aircraft and over three thousand vehicles).

A vast flotilla escorted troop-carrying helicopters into action. Conventional aircraft often "prepared" the "target": F-100, F-104, F-105, F-4C, and F-5 planes, to name a few, not only bombed and machine-gunned but also carried a varied and highly destructive kit that included conventional high-explosive bombs, delayed-action bombs, white-phosphorus bombs, napalm, and rockets. Some of these were tailored for the tactical situation, for example "daisy-cutters"—bombs fitted with a delayed fuse so as to detonate in water and destroy by concussion any Viet Cong hiding there—and CBUs, or Cluster Bomb Units, which contained thousands of small metal balls released on impact and scattered lethally by compressed air. Huey gunships—helicopters armed with 7.62-mm. machine guns, rockets, and grenades—usually accompanied troop-carrying helicopters (also armed with machine guns) to furnish immediate fire support in case of enemy fire during approach and landing or in later retrieval operations. Ground commanders also were supported by specially fitted aircraft, old and slow-flying Douglas DC-3s and C-47s, for night defense. These relics, known as Puff the Magic Dragon and Smokey the Bear, circled for hours, dropping magnesium flares and pouring in thousands of rounds from three electrically operated rapid-fire machine guns, each capable of firing six thousand rounds per minute.

Helicopters also played an immensely important support role. Small, fast machines that land most anywhere whipped commanders around extended battle areas to give a tactical cohesion unfamiliar since Napoleonic warfare—or so it was claimed. Larger machines landed reinforcements and supply to hard-pressed units, and evacuated the wounded. Medical evacuation (MedEvac) techniques became so polished that the American army claimed a "save" ratio of eighty-two out of a hundred men wounded (as opposed to seventy-one out of a hundred in World War II); the Marine Corps pointed out that no wounded man was "... more than 30 minutes ... from a fully staffed and equipped hospital."[10]

The quasi-conventional ground war at first centered north of Saigon, specifically in the central highlands of II Corps area and the northern coastal provinces of I Corps area. Having foiled the enemy's 1965 plan to cut South Vietnam in half, Westmoreland turned to the twofold task of preventing the enemy from resuming the offensive, then eventually isolating and destroying him in detail while energetically pacifying areas reclaimed from enemy control. To accomplish the first task, Westmoreland depended primarily on a wide variety of search-and-destroy missions, or what he called "spoiling" tactics, that is, blocking and enveloping actions designed to keep the enemy off-balance and thus "spoil" his plans.

Operations in the central highlands were carried out by the 1st Cavalry (Airborne) Division, based at Camp Radcliffe, a huge complex protected by a ten-mile-long barrier beneath Hong Kong mountain. This division "fed" a variety of permanent and temporary fortified bases in the surrounding area. These, in turn, supported numerous operations ranging from small patrols to task-force "sweeps" but including special missions by other units, for example Civilian Irregular Defense Groups (CIDG) composed of Special Forces teams and friendly Montagnard tribesmen.

In winter and spring of 1966, the division was carrying out a threefold mission: countering enemy operations in the central highlands; interdicting border areas where six or seven PAVN regiments were believed to be hovering across the line, in Cambodia; protecting communications from Pleiku along Highway 19 to the sea.

Division operations almost always utilized helicopters. The American army believed that extreme mobility offered by these machines was the key to fighting successful counterinsurgency warfare. Early in the division's operations, William DePuy, now a major general commanding the division, told Frank Harvey: " . . . the VC needs ten days to transfer three battalions. We manage five battalions in a day."[11]

Standard operating procedure in the highlands called for extensive patrolling designed to find the enemy, then fix him and destroy him. Based on information derived from such as aerial observation, Special Forces units, and friendly local peasants, preliminary action generally fell to a special Reconnaissance Squadron so organized as to first locate and then, circumstances permitting, engage the enemy.

Exploitation assumed a number of forms. One was an ambush patrol, usually carried out by special teams infiltrated into the target area by helicopters using appropriate deceptive techniques. Another was the combat patrol, which sought out and engaged the enemy. If action developed favorably, division could escalate it to a major operation, thanks to mobility offered by helicopters and to fire support supplied by base artillery, helicopters, and tactical (and even strategic) aircraft. If a fire fight developed adversely, the local commander could usually evacuate his patrol, including wounded and dead, by helicopter under cover of supporting fire.

These actions were generally very confused, and co-ordinating them into a meaningful whole taxed the ability of competent senior commanders. The flamboyant American military correspondent, S. L. A. Marshall, described one such operation, known first as Crazy Horse, later as the battle of Vinh Thanh Valley, in detail. The action began when a CIDG patrol surprised an enemy patrol and killed five PAVN soldiers, including a lieutenant. Captured documents indicated that PAVN had moved 120-mm. mortars into the area and was probably going to attack the CIDG base camp in battalion strength (as had been rumored by local villagers). The division commander, Major General Jack Norton, turned the problem over to First Brigade, which was tactically responsible for the area. Although strapped for troops, its commander, Colonel John Hennessey, committed a company-strength patrol into an area "fed" by Landing Zone (LZ) Savoy and, beyond that, by LZ Hereford. When the patrol encountered substantial resistance—it was ambushed and mauled—another company joined the action. Suspecting a lucrative target, Norton enlarged the operation to brigade strength.

According to Marshall, who monitored the action, its purpose was twofold: " . . . to purge the mountain country beyond LZ Hereford of Communist forces and to make it so costly to them that they would be loath ever again to attempt using it as a sanctuary."

Subsequent patrols did not encounter many enemy units, at least not on favorable terms. Although captured enemy documents soon confirmed that the Americans were fighting elements of five battalions from two PAVN regiments, as well as local Viet Cong units, none of the patrols captured prisoners or attracted defectors, who could have offered precise enemy locations, strength, and intentions. As one result, operations continued on a hit-and-miss basis. Patrols sometimes "found" the enemy, too often by virtue of stumbling into ambushes, but their troop back-up rarely succeeded in "fixing" and "destroying" him. Although the "kill" ratio at times was favorable, it was never decisive. At home in the terrain, the enemy seemed to have little difficulty in breaking off an action at will and in evading pursuit. Within two weeks, the operation bogged down.

This was only one of dozens of such operations. Task forces ranging from reinforced companies and battalions to brigades and even divisions tramped through the highlands and border country to the west in almost constant pursuit of the elusive enemy. So successful did MACV deem search-and-destroy tactics that over sixty operations a month were mounted in South Vietnam in the first six months of 1966, an effort that, according to MACV, yielded a "kill" figure of over sixteen thousand PAVN/VC troops.[12]

An equally impressive effort simultaneously was occurring in the more heavily populated I Corps areas on the coast. Here the build-up of III Marine Amphibious Force had been rapid and efficient. Commanded by Major General (soon to be Lieutenant General) Lewis Walt, the force soon numbered nearly sixty thousand troops, including air units.

We have already discussed the marines' early and, in some ways, successful clearing of Chu Lai Peninsula. Before that area could be pacified—that is, the Viet Cong infrastructure rooted out and replaced by government authority—Walt had been forced to expand his command area: In just over a year, it would grow from eight square miles to eighteen hundred-plus square miles, mostly under Viet Cong control. His mission also had altered: In addition to defending airfields at Da Nang, Chu Lai, and Phu Bai, he was supposed to destroy PAVN and main-force Viet Cong units in the area and root out VC infrastructure, as part of an extensive pacification program.[13]

Tactical operations at first remained at small-unit level and consisted primarily in patrol and ambush work essential to command security. By summer of 1966, marine units had carried out thousands of patrols, while helicopters and marine fixed-wing aircraft had flown thousands of sorties, an activity that resulted in several thousand confirmed enemy dead[14]—though how many were enemy and how many were peasants is a moot question.

For some time, marines relied on search-and-destroy tactics favored by the American army. Two reasons explained the choice. One was command ignorance. General Walt later explained that, when he assumed command in Vietnam, he did not understand the nature of the war.[15] Senior marine commanders echoed Walt's confusion (with some exceptions) and attempted to fight the war with conventional methods. The second fact was I Corps area, which had been under VC control for a long time. I Corps area comprised five provinces (about ten thousand square miles) and over 3 million people, 90 per cent of whom lived in the narrow coastal strip. Although the South Vietnamese Government exercised some control in the cities, the countryside, in general, belonged to the Viet Cong. Marine units sent to outlying areas such as Duc Pho, in Quang Ngai province, lived in a sea of hostility provoked both by regional resentments of Saigon government and by fear of the Viet Cong. A marine who had served in Duc Pho later told Jonathan Schell

> ... that for the first month they had been unable to travel five hundred yards beyond their camp without running into heavy enemy fire. After receiving reinforcements, they had moved out farther but had still been unable to penetrate many areas.[16]

An important result of this tactical impasse was lack of intelligence on which to base operations—a complaint common to all allied commands in Vietnam, and one generally met by random destruction of "suspected" VC hideouts. Schell, who was appalled at the amount of destruction in Quang Ngai province, explained its etiology:

> ... The villages had been destroyed in many ways and in a great variety of circumstances—at first by our Marines and later by our Army. In accordance with the local policy of the 3rd Marine Amphibious Force, a village could be bombed immediately and without the issuing of any warning to the villagers if American or other friendly troops or aircraft had received fire from within it. This fire might consist of a few sniper shots or of a heavy attack by the enemy. Whatever the provocation from the village, the volume of firepower brought to bear in response was so great that in almost every case the village was completely destroyed. A village could also be destroyed if intelligence reports indicated that the villagers had been supporting the Vietcong by offering them food and labor, but in such a case the official 3rd Marine Amphibious Force rules of engagement required that our Psychological Warfare Office send a plane to warn the villagers, either by dropping leaflets or by making an airborne announcement ... There was no official ruling on when troops on the ground were permitted to burn a village, but, generally speaking, this occurred most often after fire had been received from the village, or when the province chief had given a

specific order in advance for its destruction. In some cases, the villagers had been removed from an area in a big-scale operation and then the area had been systematically destroyed. . . . [17]

Such tactics did not endear the allied cause to local populations. So long as peasants remained hostile or apathetic, marines were not going to obtain information on enemy locations and movements, which they needed in order to fight successfully. In a relatively short time, they set about obtaining this information by introducing civic programs designed to win over local people. These varied considerably in effectiveness. Some of them proved outstanding. One enterprising commander instituted the Golden Fleece program, wherein marines guaranteed four villages a secure rice harvest in return for information on local Viet Cong. Other programs seemed to prosper, but progress remained slow, owing both to interruptions caused by enemy attacks and to widespread xenophobia and peasant apathy, perhaps the inevitable result of this particular civil war. A second method was more efficacious. Beginning with villages south of Da Nang, marines provided medical services and began assisting in various construction projects. This necessitated working with I Corps commander Lieutenant General Nguyen Chanh Thi, a suspicious Buddhist nationalist who shortly would be involved in a minor civil war with the Saigon government. Walt nonetheless persuaded Thi to co-operate in establishing a joint area-pacification council of civil and military members, under whose aegis the pacification program slowly spread to a nine-village area. Not content with creeping progress, Walt borrowed a page from the old Nicaraguan campaign and persuaded Thi to go along in establishing a Combined Action Group—an integrated company of marines and Popular Forces (local militia) designed to provide village security. First tried at Phu Bai, the experiment worked almost at once. Robert Shaplen, who visited the village in early 1966, observed marines and militia working together and even learning each other's language:

> . . . As a result of these joint patrols, the Vietcong network in four villages around Phu Bai has been measurably damaged, though the Communists still slip in eight or ten armed agents at a time to collect food and taxes from the population and nothing as advanced as a Census/Grievance and Aspiration unit can yet function safely. Road traffic in this area has picked up noticeably, and hamlet markets now attract buyers and sellers from as far off as two kilometers, which may not sound like much but is a lot compared with what the safe-travel radius was six months ago.[18]

Such was the impact of Combined Action Groups that Walt extended the program as rapidly as possible, his goal being seventy-five groups by year's end.

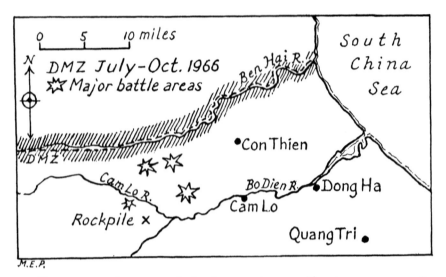

Two events interrupted the burgeoning pacification program. In March 1966, Buddhist riots in Hué, which involved Thi and brought an eyeball-to-eyeball confrontation between ARVN and Walt's marines, seriously set matters back. By the time this crisis ended, intelligence was reporting indications of a planned North Vietnamese attack through the DMZ. This was the so-called "neutral strip," established by the Geneva Accords, at the 17th parallel. It ran almost sixty miles inland to the Laotian border and extended three miles on either side of the parallel. Although Hanoi had used it for infiltration purposes (as undoubtedly had the South for covert purposes), the bulk of their troops and supply were reaching the South either by means of the Ho Chi Minh Trail through Laos and Cambodia, or by the sea route.

U.S./ARVN counteroperations in the central highlands and to the south were probably beginning to make the long land route less attractive, as were air and naval interdiction operations. A political factor also entered. The Viet Cong had controlled large parts of I Corps area for years; the Buddhist riots in Hué—in effect a civil war—must have further enhanced the area in the eyes of the North. All these factors have been discussed in still another brilliant *New Yorker* article by Robert Shaplen, whose book *The Road from War* is essential to an understanding of these crucial years.

In spring of 1966, at least four PAVN divisions were known to be immediately north of the DMZ. Intelligence reports increasingly confirmed that PAVN units were crossing the line and busily " . . . preparing the battlefield" for subsequent operations. Communist movement began in late May, when vanguard units of Division 324B crossed the DMZ into the rugged terrain of northern Quang Tri province. This was a "regular" army division, some ten to twelve thousand troops well armed and equipped, though perhaps not so well fed. Soldiers carried

821

Chinese copies of Soviet weapons, the AK-47 assault rifle with fifty to a hundred rounds of 7.62-mm. ammunition, RPD light machine guns, SKS carbines, RPG-2 rocket launchers, and grenades. Shaplen later wrote:

> ... Each man's supplies further consisted of two khaki, green, or purple uniforms, a canteen, a canvas bag, a raincoat, a pair of rubber sandals, a pair of boots, a hammock, a blanket, a mosquito net, some halazone water-purification tablets, some quinine tablets, some vitamin pills, a small can of chicken or shrimp, a kilogram and a half of salt, and seven kilograms of rice. According to information obtained later from prisoners and from captured documents, food, especially rice, was in very short supply, and several of the battalions had to be pressed into service as transport units, going back and forth a number of times to bring more rice down from North Vietnam before crossing the Ben Hai River for good.[19]

General Westmoreland in Saigon had been keeping a close eye on the situation, as had General Walt in Da Nang, and had worked out contingency plans that involved both Marine Corps and ARVN units. In July, a small marine reconnaissance team reported enemy presence in strength, reports confirmed by ARVN units who had taken some prisoners in the same area. Operation Hastings now began. It called for "spoiling" operations by a marine force of seven battalions plus artillery units—Task Force Delta, some eight thousand troops, commanded by Brigadier General Lowell English. While Delta operated well to the northwest, an ARVN force of five infantry and airborne battalions—about three thousand men—moved into the eastern and southcentral zones.

English hoped to surprise the enemy by landing two battalions by helicopter at either end of a valley about a mile south of the DMZ and northeast of a prominent terrain feature known as the Rockpile. The enemy reacted instantly, furiously, and effectively. He first prevented a juncture of the two battalions; by the time they joined fighting was so intense that English broke it off in favor of a new attack from the south, a withdrawal that provoked more severe fighting. English meanwhile committed other battalions to block the southern portion of the area. For several days, marines fought a series of hot actions ranging from squad to battalion strength while a small reconnaissance team occupied the Rockpile to call in air, artillery, and naval gunfire on nearby PAVN columns. ARVN units to the south and east also, on occasion, engaged enemy units, and claimed several hundred enemy lives.

Operation Hastings ended in early August with a general backing off of PAVN regiments. Pointing to enemy losses—nearly nine thousand confirmed killed and several thousand wounded—Marine Corps spokesmen claimed a "victory" of major proportions. In some respects, however, it was a Pyrrhic victory: The marines lost over two hundred killed and several hundred wounded. If PAVN division 324B had been knocked out, it was temporary, and three other divisions remained in the immediate area. Finally, as General Walt later noted, the enemy accomplished two major objectives: " . . . they had slowed the pacification of the I Corps area by forcing me to commit men into the largely barren north, and they had made many headlines in the United States about escalation and American casualties."[20]

Operation Hastings gave way to Operation Prairie. Increasingly bloody contacts soon confirmed that Division 324B, despite its pummeling, was still active in the DMZ, where it was fortifying the area in the vicinity of the Rockpile. In frustrating this plan, the marines fought another series of bloody actions, in some cases using tanks. The description of the fighting at the time in various papers and magazines reminded more than one marine veteran of both World War II and Korean actions, particularly the assault and capture of Hills 400 and 484, which dominated the enemy's main line of resistance in the DMZ and forced him once again to withdraw to the North. Operation Prairie terminated in early October. The marines claimed over twelve hundred "counted" dead, with another sixteen hundred "probable," at a cost of about two hundred marine lives. The area would remain a hot spot; further action would center on Khe Sanh, not many miles to the south.[21]

While army and marine units fought in the central highlands and coastal areas, Westmoreland continued to build up forces and to undertake operations in III Corps area, which included Saigon, and in IV Corps area, the Mekong Delta, which was almost completely a guerrilla challenge.

The enemy was strong in both these corps areas. In III Corps area, Zones C and D and the Iron Triangle had been Viet Minh centers of resistance and were extremely well fortified and organized. Early in 1966, a combined ARVN-U.S. force had swept part of Zone D in Binh Duong province to capture over six thousand enemy documents and large amounts of supply and munitions. Probing efforts continued during the year and consisted both of search-and-destroy and more permanent, clear-and-hold operations such as those undertaken by an Australian task force southeast of Saigon and very well described in a book by an Australian soldier and scholar, Robert O'Neill, *Vietnam Task*.

Throughout 1966, allied troops, including Australians, a few New Zealanders, and the vanguard of a Korean division, continued to arrive in South Vietnam. Once sufficient numbers were on hand, the American command directed a series of giant "sweeps" through sanctuary zones. Toward the end of 1966 and in early 1967, such operations as Attleboro, Cedar Falls, and Junction City uncovered and destroyed miles of tunnel defenses, underground hospitals, and supply depots.

Simultaneously, other troops were fighting other wars.

The air war consisted of two parts. One was the out-country war already familiar to us—the strategic bombing of North Vietnam and tactical interdiction of supply routes leading to and running through Laos and Cambodia. Rolling Thunder utilized both B-52 bombers (carrying 500- and 750-pound bombs) flying from Thailand and Guam, and a host of air force, navy, and marine planes flying from immediate land and carrier bases. In spring of 1966, President Johnson yielded to pleas of military advisers and authorized strikes against oil-storage depots, including those around Hanoi and Haiphong. In December, Johnson authorized strikes against the theretofore prohibited inner ring of Hanoi. In 1966, pilots flew 138,000 missions to drop 128,000 tons of bombs on targets in the North. In February 1967, B-52 flights would increase from sixty to eight hundred monthly (including missions over South Vietnam).[22]

Air force, navy, and marine planes, including giant B-52 bombers, also carried on an in-country aerial war consisting of conventional strategic bombing of alleged VC base areas and defensive complexes, tactical interdiction of supply routes along borders and inside South Vietnam, and tactical and logistic support of ground units. During 1966, air force pilots alone " . . . flew more than 70,000 attack sorties in South Vietnam." During the first three days of Operation Attleboro, air force planes delivered three hundred thousand pounds of rations, ammunition, and other supplies to the ground forces.

The air war also involved a host of special missions including around-the-clock rescue of downed airmen. High-flying planes bombarded Vietnam with millions of Chieu Hoi (Open Arms) amnesty leaflets, which exhorted the enemy to surrender (and prosper thereby)—according to the air force, these leaflets brought in over nineteen thousand "ralliers" by end of 1966.[23] RB-57s, RB-66s, " . . . supersonic RF-101 Voodoos and double-sonic RF-4C Phantoms" patrolled the skies on thousands of reconnaissance missions, each utilizing highly sophisticated techniques to photograph targets that ranged from the immediate ground battle scene to enemy lines of communication and suspected enemy concentration areas. During 1966, air force technicians processed four million feet of film a month, while aerial reconnaissance furnished " . . . 85 per cent of all immediate intelligence data in Southeast Asia."[24] Still another aerial effort involved chemical defoliation, the theory being to deprive the enemy of natural cover as well as of food in his base areas. This mission fell to the Ranch Hand Squadron, whose motto, according to correspondent Frank Harvey was: "Only You Can Prevent Forests." The squadron's motivation was noteworthy for its brevity: " . . . Dresser showed me around the squadron rooms. It was a spartan place. The familiar sign, FUCK COMMUNISM, which was painted horizontally in stripes of red, white and blue, was tacked to one wall." Ranch Hand pilots performed the hazardous duty of spraying chemical defoliants from a hundred fifty feet at a slow speed over generally enemy-infested areas. An eleven thousand-pound pay load, which cost five thousand dollars, took four minutes to spread and killed everything green over three hundred acres.[25]

The American navy was also fighting two wars: an out-country effort, which attempted to intercept coastal junks bringing arms and supply from North to South, and the in-country effort, which involved coastal and inland-waterway patrols to intercept supplies intended for the Viet Cong. The out-country naval war included a support role for American marines and ARVN units in I Corps area, a role later expanded southward to include operations in the Mekong Delta.

Both efforts quickly escalated to majestic proportions. The out-country interdiction task fell to Task Force 77, an armada of five aircraft carriers, four hundred aircraft, about twenty-five support ships, and over thirty thousand men operating from "Yankee Station," in Tonkin Gulf. A pamphlet issued by Seventh Fleet described the mission in precise enough terms. Besides aerial bombardment (planes were soon flying thousands and even tens of thousands of missions), TF 77's surface arm—" . . . the guided missile cruisers, frigates and destroyers— are prowling the Vietnamese coast, foiling attempts to infiltrate by sea and pumping tons of ordnance into shore battery positions and coastal supply routes."[26] Interdiction of coastal operations north of the DMZ became the task of destroyers charged with Operation Sea Dragon, which, in its first six months, destroyed or damaged more than one thousand barges and junks that were allegedly carrying supplies South. Still another armada, of radar picket escorts and smaller craft, both navy and coast guard, carried out Operation Market Time, below the DMZ, in an effort to disrupt infiltration of supplies along the thousand miles of coastline. Naval-gunfire support hinged on another armada, of heavy and light cruisers, guided-missile destroyers and frigates, destroyers, destroyer escorts, and radar-picket escorts. This combined might could send eight-inch 55-caliber shells, each weighing over 250 pounds, some fifteen miles, or six-inch, five-inch, or three-inch shells to a lesser range.[27] This effort would soon be garnished with a battleship, USS New Jersey, removed from mothballs and reconditioned at a cost of $40 million.

The in-country, or riverine, warfare also quickly grew. Fought mainly in the Mekong Delta, it introduced a host of specially adapted craft ranging from PGM patrol gunboats to PBR river patrol boats and " . . . unsinkable styrofoam and fiber-glass swimmer support boats, Swift Boats, patrol air cushion vehicles (capable of traveling over 65 knots, combat loaded, over land or water), and an impressive list of modified amphibious craft, including monitors and armored troop carriers, sampans and junks." These operated either on their own or in conjunction with American and ARVN troop units. Sea-air-land, or SEAL, teams extended the offensive aspect of river patrol operations inland, and the Navy-Army Mobile Riverine Force, an amphibious strike force of two army battalions, eventually began to penetrate fortified Viet Cong areas.[28]

There remained the final war, the "other war," the war for people's "hearts and minds," the real war. This had also gained impetus in mid-1965 when, reappointed as American ambassador, Henry Cabot Lodge brought with him as principal assistant a counterinsurgency expert, veteran of the earlier Philippine and French Indochina campaigns, Edward Lansdale. Lansdale had always advocated grass-roots pacification as the key to revolutionary warfare. As opposed to centralized direction of the program from Saigon down to hamlet level, Lansdale wanted to begin at hamlet level and work outward and upward—a decentralized, horizontal concept practiced with such telling effect by the National Liberation Front.

Like previous regimes, the Thieu-Ky government opposed such an approach, since it would force Saigon to yield partial control not only of provinces and of pacification cadres but of immensely valuable supplies daily arriving from the United States and daily adding to personal fortunes of South Vietnamese officials. In addition to Vietnamese bureaucracy, Lansdale also found himself at odds with a vast number of American agencies, a proliferation of bureaucracy, civil and military, so ably described by Robert Shaplen.[29]

The end result was a sluggish pacification program. Thanks mainly to Lansdale, the Johnson administration was not allowed to forget this vital failure, and pressure continued on the Thieu-Ky government to take necessary action.

In February 1966, President Johnson met with South Vietnamese leaders in Honolulu, where Ky impressed the President by his determination to build " . . . a really democratic government, one which is put into office by the people themselves and which has the confidence of the people." The pacification program, Ky promised, would go ahead full steam. Unaware that Ky's speech had been written by his American advisers,[30] the grateful President responded by promising full support, albeit with an expectation of rapid results. By the next meeting between the South Vietnamese and Americans, he wanted " . . . coonskins nailed to the wall."[31]

Thieu and Ky already had established a Ministry of Revolutionary Development, headed by Major General Nguyen Duc Thang, whose principal assistant was Major Nguyen Be. Thang and Be had recognized for some time the inadequacy of the principal pacification instrument, the forty-man People's Action Team, which was neither large enough nor sufficiently motivated to eliminate hamlet deficiencies. A new fifty-nine-man Revolutionary Development Group, trained at Be's special center, was to carry out a new program which emulated existing Communist doctrines. Its over-all objective was two-fold: to pacify the hamlet and to help build a better life for its people. Once a hamlet was militarily secure, government forces would concentrate on rooting out VC infrastructure while simultaneously helping the people to build a viable "community of responsibility."

The new program faced a number of difficulties, which we shall discuss later. Buddhist riots in spring of 1966 added to manifold problems, and the RD program failed to make significant headway during the summer. An effective pacification program depended, as always, on an effective government, and here some progress seemingly did appear. At American urging, in September 1966, the junta held elections for a constituent assembly that would write a new constitution. Although polls opened in only 55 per cent of the country, American officials applauded a turnout of " . . . 81 per cent of over 5 million registered voters, in spite of Vietcong intimidation and terrorism."[32] In general, American observers commented favorably on electoral procedures. If the mechanism appeared clumsy and in places questionable, no one could deny that the elections introduced the "democratic idea" to the South Vietnamese.

And few denied that definite progress was being recorded in general. The enthusiasm of both governments was plain at a conference in Manila in October 1966, which produced " . . . specific plans for the postwar and long-term civil development of Viet Nam." A Joint Development Group, " . . . an organization composed of a private American company . . . and a group of Vietnamese professionals," was charged with " . . . the task of postwar planning, of creating a design and a strategy for the transition from a wartime to a peacetime footing, and of making an objective assessment of the prospects of South Viet Nam's economy in the years ahead."[33]

As the year ended, a new optimism seemed to have emerged in South Vietnam, and with some justification. ARVN forces totaled 285,000, with another 284,000 Regional and Popular troops, plus about 130,000 police and some thirty thousand Revolutionary Development cadres. The infusion of American strength was daily freeing

ARVN units for pacification duties. Although the Viet Cong continued to control over half of the countryside, American counteraction, without doubt, had blunted their offensive plans. American troops numbering 350,000 were in South Vietnam, and more were on the way—though not as many as Westmoreland and the JCS would have liked. The ground, naval, and air wars continued to escalate. More than ever, the U.S.A. seemed determined to win the war.

CHAPTER SIXTY-FOUR

1. Leftwich.
2. Hackworth, 466.
3. Caputo, 74.
4. Hackworth, 484.
5. Sheehan et al., 468.
6. Rice, 103.
7. Ibid.
8. See Mulligan for a description of enemy forces in detail. See also, Shaplen, *The Lost Revolution;* Pike; Marshall; O'Neill; *U.S. News and World Report,* November 28, 1966, for General Westmoreland's description of the war as he saw it.
9. West. See also, Mulligan; Duncan.
10. U.S. Air Force. See also, Harvey; Asprey, "Tactics."
11. Harvey, 117. See also, Hackworth, 562, for a professional appraisal of DePuy's strategy and tactics.
12. O'Ballance, "Strategy in Viet Nam." See also, Duncanson, "The Vitality of the Viet Cong."
13. Walt, *Strange War, Strange Strategy.* See also, Stolfi, for a detailed description of this transition period.
14. U.S. Marine Corps, "III Marine Amphibious Force . . . " See also, West.
15. New York *Times,* November 18, 1970. See also, Walt.
16. Schell, 16.
17. Ibid., 14–15, who points out that printed warnings often failed in purpose because villagers were illiterate. We have pointed out that a similar situation existed in the Rif rebellion (Chapter 22).
18. Shaplen, *The Road from War,* 44–5. See also, Mulligan; Corson; Stanford; Evans; Stolfi.
19. Shaplen, *The Road from War,* 97.
20. Walt, *Strange War, Strange Strategy,* 141.
21. Shaplen, *The Road from War,* 118.
22. Sheehan et al., 480. See also, U.S. Air Force; Fall, "Viet Nam in the Balance": According to Fall, who quoted McNamara, the 1966 "bombing plan" called for expending 638,000 tons of "aerial munitions"—thirty-eight thousand tons *more* than dropped in the Pacific theater in *all* of World War II.
23. Harvey, 69. See also, U.S. Air Force.
24. U.S. Air Force.
25. Harvey, 69.
26. U.S. Seventh Fleet, "Task Force 77."
27. U.S. Seventh Fleet, "Cruisers and Destroyers in Vietnam." See also, U.S. Navy.
28. U.S. Navy.
29. Shaplen, *The Road from War,* 27–30. See also, Corson.
30. Karnow, 431.

31. Johnson, *The Vantage Point* . . . , 243–4.
32. Thompson, *No Exit from Vietnam*, 102. See also, Shaplen, *The Road from War*, 83, who questions the 81 per cent figure as optimistic; Tran Van Dinh, who offers interesting background on electoral problems.
33. Lilienthal.

CHAPTER 65

Blurs on the operational canvas • Failure of Operation Rolling Thunder (I) • Increasing cost of aerial warfare • Shortcomings of attrition strategy and search-and-destroy tactics • The refugee problem • Manpower facts • The numbers game • Russian and Chinese aid to the North • The ground war • Increasing American costs (I) • The logistics picture • The Jurassic dinosaur

A NUMBER OF BLURS marred the operational canvas in Vietnam. One was the failure of Operation Rolling Thunder—bombing North Vietnam—to accomplish its objectives (already being variously changed by Administration officials). The theory advocated by the JCS and such presidential advisers as Walt Rostow was to hurt the North sufficiently to cause Hanoi to call off the war in the South. Top-level intelligence reports at end of 1965 confirmed that bombing had indeed " . . . reduced industrial performance," but: " . . . the primary rural nature of the area permits continued functioning of the subsistence economy." Moreover, reports agreed, Hanoi seemed as determined as ever to support the war in the South. Although a greatly expanded bombing effort in 1966 reportedly destroyed 70 per cent of North Vietnam's original oil storage capacity,[1] it soon became clear that the enemy could get by on fuel dispensed in drums. According to a CIA estimate, the total bombing effort " . . . accomplished little more than in 1965."[2] In 1966, American planes encountered " . . . the most sophisticated and concentrated air defense network ever faced in any war."[3] Although American fliers shot down thirty-six MIGs and otherwise carried out bombing and interdiction missions, the effort cost another 147 American aircraft—a total of 318 crews and machines lost. Direct operational costs rose from $460 million in 1965 to $1.2 billion in 1966.[4]

Rolling Thunder also continued to reap heavy criticism within and without the Administration. Reports of heavy civilian casualties raised an uproar in the world press, the more so since Harrison Salisbury of the *New York Times* was reporting directly from Hanoi at the time. Although the Johnson administration denied the accusation, top-secret CIA estimates put the casualty figure in North Vietnam at thirty-six thousand for 1965 and 1966; of this figure, about 80 per cent were civilians.[5] The new effort may also have caused Hanoi to back off from talks that some hoped would lead to negotiation. According to John Hightower, AP diplomatic correspondent in Washington, the Soviet Union and European satellites brought considerable pressure on North Vietnam at the Bulgarian Party Congress in November 1966 to open the way for a peace conference. Negotiations by Polish intermediaries were allegedly proceeding favorably when the bombing of Hanoi's outskirts caused Hanoi to break off proceedings. President Johnson later made light of this effort in his memoirs; Mr. Hightower, however, suggested that Johnson realized the bombing was a major blunder and that this was the major reason for the later, four-month halt in bombing Hanoi as well as for a secret peace initiative (admitted, in part, by Johnson).[6]

A second blur centered on the ground war and Westmoreland's choice of attrition strategy and search-and-destroy tactics. The problem faced by allied forces was essentially pacification that demanded a qualitative and selective approach. The tactical task was to clear an area of Viet Cong so that civil teams could move in to build a viable and secure community. The military tactic thus required was clear-and-hold. The first task was to free an area from main-force guerrilla control. This called for fragmenting, dispersing, and destroying main-force units.

But that was only the beginning. Having cleared an area, military units had to "hold" it—that is, they had to provide area security while helping police forces to root out the all-important Viet Cong infrastructure, while, simultaneously, other specialized government forces undertook area rehabilitation and established viable government. Military strength was insufficient to clear and hold *all* enemy-infested, or even challenged, areas simultaneously. This meant that priority areas of operation had to be established, along with "economy of force" areas, which received only limited military pressure. Some challenged areas would perforce have had to be ignored until later in the pacification process. The real target was the peasant, not the guerrilla, and the only way the peasant's support could be gained was by establishing secure and viable local-area government—a slow and difficult task amply demonstrated throughout history.

American strategy and tactics did not respect this essential requirement. Large "sweeps" through an area, though uncovering supply dumps and killing a few enemy, essentially answered nothing. Neither did search-and-destroy tactics respect the essential military task. On rare occasions, enemy concentrations, such as those in certain areas of the

DMZ, could be countered by conventional-warfare methods. As a rule, such methods inflicted grievous damage on people whose co-operation was necessary if the over-all mission was to be accomplished. Instead of clearing and holding small areas as first essential steps in winning peasant support, marine and army units pushed out in all directions in huge, awkward attempts to "kill" the enemy. The results were several, and each contained the seeds of important failure.

The first was to widen the war. Up to spring of 1965, fighting in South Vietnam had remained selective, on the whole. Douglas Pike, an official and careful observer and analyst, later wrote:

> Thousands of Vietnamese villagers lived through the entire 1960–1965 period without being involved in, and hardly ever being inconvenienced by, either the NLF's armed struggle or the GVN's military operations. Although subjected to great NLF organizational and political attention, the average rural Vietnamese was seldom if ever a direct victim of its violence program.... The result was that he did not perceive the situation in Vietnam as a "war" in the same way that Americans regard the Vietnam "war." Thus the frequently stated observation that the Vietnamese peasant "has known nothing but war for twenty years," although technically accurate, is also misleading ... [7]

Escalation inevitably changed this low-key situation. By July 1965, over four hundred thousand refugees had fled South Vietnam's countryside. The bulk of these unfortunates either ended in ghastly shantytowns around larger cities or in hastily constructed and very primitive camps. Their potential importance was tremendous. Roger Hilsman testified before the Senate in late 1965:

> ... The refugees are, in my judgment, a key [to an effective counterguerrilla program]. ... What I am suggesting is that the refugee program should not be just to feed, house, and care for these people, but to train them for the job of making their villages guerrilla proof when they return—to train them as village defenders, as school teachers, medical technicians, agricultural advisers and so on. If an imaginative, positive effort is made, in sum, the refugees can become the vanguard of a peaceful revolution in the Vietnamese countryside sponsored by the free world—which is the only way that the bloody, Communist revolution can be circumvented.

Wesley Fishel, who was originally involved in Ngo Dinh Diem's government as head of the Michigan State University team (see Chapter 50), warned the same Senate committee:

> ... If this refugee problem is badly handled, these people ... could further intensify the political instability of South Vietnam and create even greater problems for the Government than it now faces.
>
> If this situation is treated with some intelligence, then these 600,000 refugees of the moment could become a major asset to the Vietnamese Government. ... If these people are handled well the Saigon government is going to secure the manifest loyalty which it needs. ...

The refugees were not being well handled. AID officials had estimated a hundred thousand refugees in 1965 and was unprepared to cope with a larger number. GVN's 1965 budget called for 370 million piasters for refugees; as of July just less than 25 million piasters had been spent. The committee concluded that the refugee program

> ... reflected the absence of an overall strategic concept and program which fully integrates the political, economic, and social aspects of the Vietnamese conflict with the needed military effort.[8]

The second result of promiscuous search-and-destroy tactics was frequent damage to either person or property or both of peasants who remained and whose strength was necessary to effectively counter the insurgency. The third result was frequently to tire the troops with "Yorkish" operations that produced no real benefits:

> The noble Duke of York,
> He had ten thousand men,
> He marched them up to the top of the hill,
> and he marched them down again.

The fourth result was to flood the country with foreign troops. The fifth result was to increase the troop commitment and eventually relieve ARVN of combat duties, which, in turn, called for a larger American military investment that merely compounded incipient failures.

By end of 1966, then, it was becoming clear that American troops had undertaken a task for which they were neither organized nor trained, a task that they did not understand—indeed, a task that could only have been accomplished by the South Vietnamese themselves. It is a great pity that the innate ineptness of Westmoreland's strategy and tactics was not more obvious. Unfortunately, the "indicators," or criteria selected by the military, to judge progress in Vietnam seemed reasonable to many Americans, who at first trusted their government and armed forces. But, as any number of experts had earlier pointed out and as Bernard Fall once again emphasized in 1966, MACV and the

JCS continued to judge progress by such military measurements as troop increases, expended ammunition, enemy dead, structures destroyed, rice confiscated, and weapons captured—conventional criteria meaningless in a counterinsurgency.[9] " . . . Our mission was not to win terrain or seize positions," Lieutenant Philip Caputo later wrote,

> but simply to kill. . . . Victory was a high body-count, defeat a low kill-ratio, war a matter of arithmetic. The pressure on unit commanders to produce enemy corpses was routine, and they in turn committed it to their troops. This led to such practices as counting civilians as Viet Cong. 'If it's dead and Vietnamese, it's VC,' was a rule of thumb in the bush.[10]

The military's chief criterion was "kill" figures; as James Reston wrote, " . . . death became the official measure of success." Commanders had to succeed in order to satisfy their superiors which, as David Hackworth noted, soon made "everyone a bounty hunter and a liar," with concomitant injury to the traditional and healthy concept of military honor.[11]

Pointing to an alleged forty to fifty thousand enemy dead a year and many more wounded and deserters, MACV, the JCS, and Administration hawks argued that enemy morale would have to crumble. There was nothing new about the argument. It was the old World War I syndrome. In Vietnam a half century later, the enemy did not seem to have much difficulty in keeping units up to strength or in bringing in fresh units from the North. Despite an estimated sixty thousand battle deaths, local VC recruitment continued at thirty-five hundred a month. By mid-1966, VC-PAVN forces in the South had increased within a year from 110,000 to 270,000, the bulk of which came from the South.[12] Four PAVN divisions were deployed north of the DMZ, nine more divisions farther north, and the Chinese army north of there. Soviet aid, already half a billion dollars in 1965, substantially increased in 1966 and included " . . . ground-to-air missiles, 'complex antiaircraft guns with radar guidance systems, and antiaircraft automatic guns of 'large caliber,' " along with some fighter aircraft. Later in the year, the Soviet Union agreed to contribute another $800 million worth of aid. Hanoi was successfully playing off Moscow against Peking, which was also supplying arms and equipment and very probably stood ready to supply "volunteers" if necessary.[13]

A more subtle difficulty also existed. This was the fallacy inherent in the numbers game. Owing in large part to Robert McNamara's influence in the Pentagon, American military analysts had become slaves to statistical studies. Testifying before the Senate Foreign Relations Committee in February 1966, Maxwell Taylor stated:

. . . Since history has shown that the government forces successfully opposing a guerrilla insurgency in the past have required a
much greater preponderance of strength, ten to one or twelve to
one for example, it was quite clear the Vietnamese could not raise
forces fast enough to keep pace with the growing threat of the Viet
Cong in time. It was this sobering conclusion that led to the decision to introduce American ground forces with their unique mobility and massive fire power to compensate for the deficiency in
Vietnamese strength. With such forces available, it was felt that
the ratios of required strength cited above would lose much of their
validity.[14]

Taylor was misquoting history. As Major General Richard Clutterbuck,
the British counterinsurgency expert, pointed out in 1966, the 12:1 or
10:1 soldier versus guerrilla ratio is virtually meaningless, since the
guerrilla's strength derives from the people, and his numbers must include not only those persons sympathetic to his aims but those too
frightened or too apathetic to contest those aims. Successful Roman
commanders in Spain had realized this before the birth of Christ. In
1775, General Gage had warned that American rebels would not be
easily subdued (see Chapter 5):

> . . . Since other colonies would undoubtedly come to the aid of the
> north, " . . . he urged that the Ministry estimate the number of men
> and the sums of money needed, and then double their figures."

When another realist, William Tecumseh Sherman, was asked how
many men he would need to pacify the Cumberland area during the
Civil War, he replied: "Two hundred thousand" (see Chapter 9).

American bombing and interdiction of supply routes in the North
and Laos and in South Vietnam were only partially successful in interrupting the flow of supply south. Planes could bomb and strafe roads
and railroads and warehouses and vehicles, but thousands of peasants
repaired roads and bridges, and trucks continued to travel at night, as
did hundreds of thousands of bicyclists carrying " . . . 100-pound loads
for long distances," children easily carrying " . . . their own weight."[15]

The Viet Cong also received supply from sampans sailing from the
North, from peasants sympathetic to the rebel cause, from corrupt
South Vietnamese officials, and, not least, from attacks on government
outposts, hamlets and villages. Such was the extent of local support and
participation that Dennis Duncanson termed Vietnam a *symbiotic insurgency:* " . . . one, that is, in which, for the great bulk of its resources,
the revolutionary movement draws its requirements from the supplies
of its adversaries"[16]

Thus it was all the more necessary to use Lyautey's qualitative tactics, a slow, methodical approach in order to win peasant alliance rather than Westmoreland's search-and-destroy tactics defined by one senior American commander in Vietnam as " . . . Grab 'em by the balls and the hearts and minds will follow."[17] Too often this was warfare at its most violent and stupid, and those who ordered it and condoned its excesses were placing themselves in a dangerous legal and moral position.[18] The inane order issued to Marine Corps units not to fire on unarmed Vietnamese *unless they were running* " . . . left us bewildered and uneasy," Lieutenant Caputo later wrote. " . . . What if we shot a Vietnamese who turned out to have a legitimate reason for running? Would that be a justifiable act of war or grounds for court-martial?"[19]

The choice of search-and-destroy tactics was perhaps inevitable, considering the tactical "shape" of American units—and this introduces still another blur. Despite emphasis placed on counterinsurgency warfare since 1961, U.S. divisions, regiments, and battalions were neither organized nor properly trained to wage irregular warfare. Colonel David Hackworth later wrote of the dangerously inadequate individual and small-unit training at Fort Benning where, instead of running around in meaningless regimental and division exercises, the soldier should have learned " . . . the stuff that keeps you alive."[20] Westmoreland's quantitative approach was necessarily expensive in manpower and resources. In 1965, the U.S. officer death rate in Vietnam rose above the 5 per cent rate of World War II and Korea. By spring of 1966, U.S. casualties totaled four thousand killed and twenty-one thousand wounded, cumulative totals that would rise sharply by year's end. Also upsetting, of 240,000 U.S. troops in South Vietnam, " . . . only 50,000 at most were actual combat troops"—and those suffered the bulk of casualties.[21] Westmoreland perforce developed an insatiable appetite for troops, only a relatively small percentage of whom could undertake combat/pacification tasks. Added to this was a personnel policy that limited a tour of duty to one year: thus, those who fought the enemy did so for only twelve months before returning to the United States—in the case of draftees, for discharge.[22] But, such was the American military's administrative requirement, that roughly three months were spent coming, three months going. And such was the peculiar nature of the war that a man needed the other six months to learn how to fight it. If he survived enemy mines and booby traps and ambushes and pungi stakes and jungle rot and malaria—if he lived and remained intact in body and mind—he was just becoming valuable when he went home.

An enormous logistics requirement adversely affected the situation in several ways. In the opening months, indeed well into 1966, combat troops were forced to subsist mainly on C-rations, a poor diet at best but a criminal diet in a tropical jungle-mountain environment. Army fatigues and Marine dungarees were too hot for jungle warfare (for which the troops were untrained in virtually every respect, particularly in countering mines and booby traps, which accounted for a large proportion of casualties); boots and field shoes soon fell to pieces and were only slowly replaced with light canvas jungle boots. Units lacked such necessaries as preservative oil and cleaning patches for weapons that needed cleaning several times a day. Search-and-destroy tactics in a hostile environment utilized an expenditure of ammunition that is difficult to comprehend. The official explanation for abrogation of what older soldiers know as "fire discipline" is to the effect that, lacking sufficient numbers to fight the war, American forces had to compensate by increased mobility and firepower. Lieutenant Caputo described a marine action, Operation Blast Out, in August 1965: " . . . Three thousand Marines and ARVN soldiers, supported by tanks, artillery, planes, and the six-inch guns of a U.S. Navy cruiser, managed to kill two dozen Viet Cong in three days. . . . "[23] In describing one marine patrol action in mid-1966, Captain Francis J. West wrote:

> . . . Less than two minutes after reception of the message, the guns were firing. So swift was the reaction that the message alerting the patrol of an impending fire mission reached the patrol via the relay station after the shells had fallen. The battery fired 1,188 pounds of high explosives to discourage the trackers. It did.
> Twenty minutes later, from task force headquarters came the order to blanket the entire target area. At higher headquarters, the thinking was that, if the North Vietnamese had organized a pursuit, they must have returned to their base camp and been in the process of digging out. The battery fired another area saturation mission, dropping 10,692 pounds of high explosives in the stream bed, base camp, and hill complex.[24]

This was theater policy and far too often it amounted to promiscuous firing that accomplished very little, often damaged a great deal—and was very expensive.

Quasi-conventional operations were equally expensive. To field what amounted to nearly a marine division during Operation Hastings required a supply effort that suggested a World War II amphibious landing. To give the 1st Cavalry (Airmobile) Division helicopter mobility meant supplying five hundred tons of material a day.[25] Such was the appetite of conventionally organized American units that a division required a logistics "tail" of over forty thousand troops.

Another factor inexorably exacerbated the supply problem. With exception of a few elite units, American armed forces had grown used to comfort, and even elite units expected amenities provided by no other armed forces in the world or in history. This disturbing trend began after World War II and stemmed in part from a national pride of an affluent society buttressed by swollen defense budgets. By the time of Korea, it had grown sufficiently for one commander, General Mark Clark, to complain. Shortly after assuming command in Korea, he later wrote,

> . . . I felt strongly that we would have to pull in our belts, cut off some fat. We have always wanted the best of everything for our men. . . . In Korea that search for the best went so far as to make ice cream an item of regular distribution to front-line units. . . . But the amenities in the American Army will have to be the first casualty in any big war with communism.[26]

By the end of 1966, the amenities in South Vietnam had increased, particularly in the rear echelons, and they added heavily to the logistics requirement.

The logistics burden otherwise adversely influenced the tactical situation. As General Matthew Ridgway's 1954 report had emphasized, the theater of war was not compatible with the support requirement of conventional forces. Base development, as Ridgway forecast, proved an enormous task. Westmoreland himself later wrote that, lacking " . . . a fully developed logistic base" to support combat units rushed into South Vietnam, he had to use " . . . backed-up ships as floating warehouses."[27] What he did not point out was the large number of combat troops initially tied up in base-construction tasks during this crucial period. But conventional organization also meant undue reliance on mechanical transport and on supporting weapons that tended to "tie" small units to centralized operations and also consumed "combat troops" in administrative and support duties. Each new installation produced a new security requirement, both to protect the installation and to provide security for convoys carrying material to combat units, and this, in turn, demanded more troops. As base camps grew in size, so did guerrilla attacks against them—which meant providing even more troops for static security duty, less for field operations. At one base camp, one third of an airborne brigade was tied up in guard duty, at a time when some infantry companies were fighting at 50 per cent of combat strength.[28]

A second result was more indirect but equally invidious. To supply the insatiable hunger of a few combat divisions, base supply areas developed and rapidly expanded. Each held thousands of troops who could not but influence local economies—too often, adversely. A heavy expenditure of piasters contributed to an already ugly inflation. A black market invariably sprang up, one not alone fed by millions of dollars' worth of PX and commissary supplies but often by combat equipment and arms—significant quantities of each ultimately ending in Viet Cong hands. Bored garrison soldiers also constituted a problem: bars, dance halls, whorehouses, each multiplied to exacerbate already difficult community relations, particularly between American and ARVN soldiers. Large numbers of Vietnamese employees—around a hundred thousand, many in servile occupations—inside American bases not only upset local economies but insured that Americans continued to live inside a fish bowl.

All these factors combined to produce a highly unsatisfactory military profile. By the end of 1966, Westmoreland's military plant, which should have been lean and fit, resembled the Jurassic dinosaur, which became weaker as it grew larger.

CHAPTER SIXTY-FIVE

1. Sheehan et al., 480.
2. Ibid., 523. See also, ibid., 462, 469, 494, 502–9, 518, 522.
3. U.S. Air Force.
4. Sheehan et al., 523.
5. Ibid., 513–15, 523.
6. Zagoria, 60. See also, Johnson, *The Vantage Point* . . . ; Brandon, who discusses this in detail.
7. Pike, 372–3.
8. U.S. Senate, *Refugee Problems in South Vietnam.*
9. Fall, "Viet Nam in the Balance."
10. Caputo, xviii. See also, Hackworth, 667–8.
11. Hackworth, 572.
12. Fall, "Viet Nam in the Balance."
13. Parry. See also, Zagoria.
14. Fulbright, *The Vietnam Hearings.*
15. Rogers.
16. Duncanson, "The Vitality of the Viet Cong."
17. Corson, 68.
18. Telford Taylor for an interesting study of this difficult and controversial subject.
19. Caputo, 74.
20. Hackworth, 454–5.
21. Fall, "Viet Nam in the Balance."
22. Barclay.
23. Caputo, 203.
24. West.
25. Weller.
26. Mark W. Clark, 190.
27. *U.S. News and World Report*, November 28, 1966.
28. Hackworth, 556.

CHAPTER 66

More blurs on the canvas • American tactical problems • Operation Gibraltar • Ia Drang—the enemy learns • Operation Attleboro • Marshall and Hackworth's mission • Operation of Paul Revere IV • Operation Crazy Horse • Colonels Henry Emerson and John Hayes define the tactical challenge • U. S. Marine Corps operations • Captain Miller's observations • The intelligence failure • Mines and booby traps • VC intelligence network • Captain Jim Cooper's discovery • The pacification failure • Continued South Vietnamese governmental abuses • ARVN's failure • Dissent in the U.S.A. • The Vietnam hearings • The thoughts of James Gavin and George Kennan • The secret thoughts of Robert McNamara • Escalation pressures • The hawks win again

FOUR OTHER BLURS had appeared on the allied operational canvas by end of 1966. One was the difficulty of American combat units in adapting to the tactical challenge; one the proclivity of MACV in announcing fictitious "victories" to the world; one the continued inept performance of South Vietnam's government and army; and one the influence of these on American opinion, both official and public.

American combat units faced severe tactical problems in South Vietnam, most of which resulted from trying to impose Western tactical doctrines on an insurgency environment. Contemporary accounts of fighting in 1965 and 1966 leave little to be desired regarding individual and unit bravery. Young officers, non-commissioned officers, soldiers, marines, sailors, and airmen generally fought hard and sometimes gave more than they got. But were they fighting wisely?

Operation Gibraltar, the seizure of An Khe from the Viet Cong by units of the 101st Airborne Division, was broadcast by Westmoreland as a "great victory." More accurately, one officer participant termed it "a blundering success"; another stated that "the VC saved [our] day by walking away."[1] One helicopter assault landed " . . . dead in the middle of the 95th [Viet Cong] Battalion's training base and was shot to ribbons." "Friendly" American fire killed thirteen and wounded twelve of our own troops.[2]

The highly touted "victory" at Ia Drang had more holes than a Swiss cheese. In addition to heavy casualties from "friendly" fire, " . . . inadequate [air] lift and piecemeal commitment," one battalion landed " . . . virtually at the enemy's front door," and thus was "incredibly outnumbered."[3] Wounded officers from this battalion later spoke of " . . . annihilation, almost to the man of . . . units as big as company size." These unpalatable facts of what Westmoreland called "an unprecedented victory" were not announced to the American Congress or to the public.[4] The enemy's heavy losses at Ia Drang were cited by MACV as proof of the validity of an attrition strategy. In truth, as noted by a prescient American army-officer-turned-civil-adviser, the legendary John Paul Vann, whose short life is so well told by Neil Sheehan's *A Bright and Shining Lie*, they were suffered by the enemy in order " . . . to figure out how to beat the Americans' incredible firepower and amazing mobility." Although badly hurt, they learned " . . . to hug the 'belt' of their enemy," as David Hackworth later wrote,

> . . . to come in as close as they could in order to neutralize the killing power of our artillery and air support. At Ia Drang, the North Vietnamese *learned how to fight us* . . . even if the battle was an unprecedented victory for the Americans in our war of attrition, it was an equally unprecedented victory for our enemy in their protracted guerrilla war.[5]

Neither did such giant search-and-destroy sweeps through sanctuary zones like Operation Attleboro live up to MACV's claims of success. David Hackworth, who earlier had made his mark as a battalion commander and at this time was escorting the well-known military journalist S. L. A. Marshall on an official fact-finding tour, later revealed that their in-depth study of Attleboro confirmed that " . . . the same lethal mistakes" on the battlefield were "being made again and again . . . ":

> the operation (which claimed 155 U.S. lives and another 741 wounded in action) was just another case of dancing to the tune, a tune written years before during the Indochina war. The tactics the NVA and Main Force VC employed were right out of [Bernard Fall's] *Street Without Joy*. . . .

Detailed interrogation of officers, NCOs and men who carried out this operation

> ... revealed that the VC initiated or controlled almost every action. (During Attleboro, they sucked U.S. units into well-prepared killing zones ... and then ate the Americans up at eyeball-to-eyeball range. All our men could do was try their damnedest to extricate their dead and wounded and themselves, and get some distance so they could hammer the enemy with our unbeatable firepower.) And yet, when I asked the company and battalion commanders who'd participated in Attleboro whether they'd read Bernard Fall's basic primer on the war, few could answer in the affirmative.[6]

Marshall and Hackworth's detailed examination of Operation Paul Revere IV along the Cambodian border, a "classic encounter," as a briefing team told Robert McNamara and Generals Wheeler and Westmoreland,

> ... revealed that there was almost *no correlation* between the official Army report ... and what actually happened on the ground. ... If Paul Revere IV were viewed as it had to be, from the perspective of the war of insurgency that it was, then we did *not* win and we were *not* brilliant. In fact, we were stupid, lethally so. ... The enemy sucked the American units into well dug-in killing zones along the Cambodian border, killing more than 140 and wounding more than 560 of our men on terrain that favored them completely (once they'd accomplished their mission, they could scoot right across the border to regroup).

Hackworth for the first time

> ... realized that probably no one at the very top had any idea that the reports were wrong. ... These reports ... made it all the way back to Washington unchallenged. And there they became the basis of critical decisions made on the war.[7]

Subsequent operations showed little tactical adaptation or invention. We looked briefly at Operation Crazy Horse and its negative results in Chapter 64. Did anyone at corps or division or brigade level consider the possibility of accomplishing the mission by beating the enemy at his own game? The CIDG had made a good start by bushwhacking an enemy patrol—a prosperous tactic that should have impressed senior commanders. Marshall does not suggest alternate plans. No mention is made of carrying on as usual while setting a trap for the enemy lurking up in the mountains.

Estimate of enemy intentions is relatively simple: He is going to attack the CIDG camp—a small and minor installation—or he is going to shell Camp Radcliff with mortars, or he is going to do nothing until more reinforcements reach him by means of routes shown on the captured map. To accomplish either of the first two objectives, he would have to bring forward his units and thus subject them to ambush. What would have been the result had not one ambush team of the type described by Marshall (which is larger than necessary) but a score or forty or eighty such teams spotted the few routes of approach? What would have happened had similar teams staked out ingress routes?

Put another way, why hurry to ferret out the enemy on other than your own terms? The war was not going to end the next day. Senior commanders knew enough of the area to know their ignorance concerning enemy strength and locations. Intelligence had furnished some reasonable indications of enemy presence in strength. By this time, senior commanders knew that the enemy rarely acted impulsively—that he prepared the battlefield, in this case his mountain base. Lacking patience to prepare a reception for the enemy, did no one want to find out more before committing a company? What was the matter with using the CIDG force, which operated extremely well in the mountains? Lacking this force, where were the small guerrilla teams that were needed to work the area? Why an orthodox approach, when, from beginning to end, the units would be operating in the blind? Marshall's only explanation is unsettling in the extreme:

> . . . So it became agreed, as it was later done, an inspiration of which nothing better can be said than that it seemed to look good at the time. At the top level of the cavalry division there was still no firm belief that the hills so close to home base were loaded with big game.[8]

Almost nothing of the subsequent operation suggests even normal tactical savvy. PAVN repeatedly used both ambushes and envelopment with telling effect. American units twice walked *through* areas holding sizable numbers of enemy, hidden, weapons zeroed in, patiently waiting for a propitious moment to strike. The American soldiers paid for their carelessness.[9]

A few commanders learned, most did not. Lieutenant Colonel Henry Emerson, commanding a battalion in the 101st Airborne Division, soon learned the rewards to be gained from small-unit tactics, for example by infiltrating a company into the bush during darkness and from there having seven-man patrols fanned out to comb the land.

> . . . At the end of each day, these small teams became ambush patrols spread out all over the battle area. Besides regularly draw-

ing blood, continuity allowed us to interdict the enemy's ingress-egress routes—in essence, to take the battlefield away from our foe.... Slowly the men began to understand a little more about their enemy and to respond in kind. Slowly they began to develop patience, that VC strong point.[10]

Another paratrooper battalion commander formed

... an all-volunteer, Raider-like unit ... [which] gave the battalion a long range reconnaissance and ambush element that would operate independently, as well as the flexibility of a handy fourth maneuver element.[11]

Colonel John Hayes tossed the book out the window in commanding Delta Force which, in Hackworth's opinion,

... pound for pound and weighed against its cost, was the most effective fighting force in Vietnam [in late 1966].... Delta Force was infinitely successful with its tactics, doctrine, and a basic philosophy at odds with the Army's regular units."[12]

Marines up north also found the tactical going extremely difficult, be it in fighting guerrilla warfare south of the DMZ or in fighting larger, quasi-guerrilla operations in and around the DMZ. Part of the problem was normal: that of adapting to a new tactical environment made the more difficult by insufficient training for counterinsurgency warfare and by inadequate logistic support. " ... The Marines in I Corps lived hard," Lieutenant Philip Caputo, who landed at Da Nang early in the war, later wrote. " ... Dirt, filth and mosquitoes filled our hooches at night. Our one cooked meal seemed always to be rice and beans. C-rations constituted the other two meals."[13] Caputo graphically described his first search-and-destroy mission, his platoon being part of a two-company force:

... Lemmon's men moved out first. A machine-gunner sprayed the jungle on the far side of the field. This was called "reconnaissance by fire," a fancy term for what amounted to shooting at bushes to see if they shot back.... It took us all morning to cover the three miles between the [helicopter] landing zone and the village. Four hours to walk three miles, and the company had not once run into significant enemy resistance. It was the land that resisted us, the land, the jungle, and the sun.[14]

An experienced veteran of these early days, Captain John Miller, later offered a remarkably candid analysis of small-unit actions and problems encountered by the newcomers. Miller found the climate to be hostile:

> . . . The constant heavy rains of the wet monsoon can swell rifle stocks to the point where the trigger cannot be depressed completely and where disassembly and assembly are out of the question. Rust and corrosion of metal surfaces are, of course, accompanying side effects.

Marines had to learn how to keep as dry as possible and avoid omnipresent evils such as immersion foot (from wet socks) and flu/pneumonia (from generally wet surroundings). Terrain, too, posed immense problems:

> . . . The unit leader must constantly fight the recurring problem of canalization. Both the thickly wooded highlands and the open paddy areas tend to force his unit—be it squad or company—into a column, vulnerable to directional mines, ambushes, and similar evils. His choices are limited. If he departs from a jungle trail, he must cut his own—and pay the price in terms of slow movement plus wear and tear on his trailbreakers. If he leaves the paddy dikes, he can count on the same slow pace in moving through the muck and (sometimes) high water and high grass. In deciding, he must constantly weigh the requirements of his mission against his vulnerability, adopting whatever dispersion and security measures he can effect.[15]

Miller also commented feelingly about "the load" as did another marine officer, Captain Francis J. West, who described a patrol with the 9th Marines:

> . . . The Marines wore helmets and flak jackets. Each rifleman carried 150 rounds of ammunition and 2 or more hand grenades. The men of the two machine gun crews were draped with belts of linked cartridges totalling 1,200 rounds. The two 3.5-inch rocket launcher teams carried five high explosive and five white phosphorus rockets. Four grenadiers carried 28 40mm shells apiece for their stubby M79s. Sergeant Cunningham had given six LAAWs [a 66-mm. one-shot disposable rocket launcher for use against tanks] to some riflemen to provide additional area target capability. . . .
>
> The platoon moved out at 1100. There was no breeze and no shade. The temperature was 102 degrees. Within five minutes, every Marine was soaked in sweat. . . . [16]

Although the patrol acquitted itself well, the weight problem continued to bother unit commanders.

One of the most difficult problems faced was enemy use of booby traps and mines. Whether planted passively or electrically detonated by guerrillas, they extracted a heavy toll, not alone from the initial explosion but often in subsequent pursuit actions that involved enemy-prepared terrain and ambush. Discussing small-unit operations in spring of 1966, Captain West pointed out that of ten marines killed and fifty-eight wounded in one company in five weeks, " . . . two men were hit by small arms fire, one by a grenade. Mines inflicted all the other casualties."[17] As one senior intelligence officer pointed out to this writer, the peasant *invariably* knew the location of booby traps and mines but for one or more reasons, usually fear of the VC, would not warn the intended victims, thereby further eliciting American fury.

These and other substantial problems usually stemmed, at least in part, from a supreme problem: lack of intelligence. Marine patrols, more often than not, were operating in the dark, trying to guess enemy locations while keeping oriented with unsatisfactory, 1:50,000 maps. Captain John G. Miller noted that:

> . . . target acquisition is one of the rifleman's biggest problems. The presence of civilians on the battlefield requires each Marine to exercise the finest degree of judgment in applying any number of local rules of engagement. This situation sometimes puts Marines in the unhappy position of having to "lead with their chins" in order to make contact with the enemy.[18]

Leading with their chins was exactly what the enemy wanted marines to do. The enemy reacted in one of several ways. Sometimes they slipped away, usually leading the marine unit a merry chase before so doing. Sometimes they fought and, though suffering themselves, usually inflicted relatively high casualties on the marine units involved; but, more important than that from the enemy standpoint, he usually arranged the firefight so that peasants tasted marine wrath.

What allied forces in Vietnam refused to recognize, at least for some time, was what Callwell had pointed out nearly a hundred years earlier: In a guerrilla situation, the guerrilla is the professional, the newcomer the amateur. A veteran marine intelligence officer later wrote of a VC intelligence officer, " . . . a wizened little man wearing black pajamas and tire-tread sandals":

> . . . Ai No U does not have aerial observers; no infra-red, no SLAR, no TV; no digital data "real time" readout computerized equipment. But he is successful. This confounds Americans. The

result is a communist psychological operation by accident; more effective than if by design. How does he do it?

Ai No U relies upon two things: (1) the People's Military Intelligence Concept, and (2) the American Military penchant for the SOP [standard operating procedure], a commander's tactical signature.

American tactical predictability frequently contributed to enemy successes. Fragmentary reports (frequently from VC sympathizers) too often tipped the American commander's hand and allowed a VC unit to disperse. The ensuing operation, while accomplishing no concrete result, often further antagonized the peasants, strengthening VC control over them.[19]

The key remained the peasant. Despite the aggression-from-the-North theme, constantly hammered home by senior American officials and officers, the real enemy was indigenous to the area; as Viet Minh, he had fought the French; as Viet Cong, he was fighting ARVN and the Americans. He had lived in this area for a long time; he had devoted his every effort to his task. He held a detailed knowledge of most operational areas, knowledge gleaned from personal reconnaissance, often over the years and sometimes even decades, and from information supplied either by guerrillas or local peasants. He also profited from an adaptive ability noted by one experienced marine officer: " . . . His techniques and tactics are not exotic innovations; his strength lies only in the ability to apply fundamentals and to adjust his tactics to those of his opponent."[20]

This was precisely the challenge faced by marines. They were fighting to clear an area infested by gophers: For too long, their answer was to rip up terrain in an attempt, vain of course, to kill the gophers rather than to make that terrain sufficiently unpleasant for the gophers to go away. Some commanders twigged the essential problem and tried to do something about it. In mid-1966, one company commander, Captain Jim Cooper, saw the futility of operating from an isolated combat outpost on top of a hill. Cooper moved his people into a hamlet of about three hundred fifty peasants, one of several in a village complex of some six thousand population, set up proper security, increased patrols and ambushes, and slowly integrated a theretofore isolated Popular Forces unit into hamlet life: " . . . The hamlet chief moved from the ARVN fort back into his own home. . . . Cooperation followed friendship. The hamlet chief showed the Marines the favorite ambush and hiding places of the Viet Cong." Cooper was on to the real secret of fighting an insurgency. But, despite his impressive success, he learned by a cunning maneuver that VC sympathizers and informers continued to live *in the hamlet,* while VC units shifted operations elsewhere. Converting the village to the government's side would have taken a major effort and much patience and time.

> ... Less than a month after their arrival, the Marines did leave to go on an operation. They left the marks of their influence behind in the village and especially in the hamlet. The Vietnamese had reopened two schools and a pagoda. They were washing. Their medical ills had been treated. A Vietnamese public health nurse and two school teachers had come to the village. The hamlet and village chiefs had returned. The Popular Forces were acting more like disciplined troops.
>
> What would happen in the future, Cooper was not about to guess. . . .[21]

What happened to that particular village, we are not told. What frequently happened both in I Corps area and elsewhere was a return of the VC the moment allied troops departed.[22] Once again, the situation cried for clear-and-hold tactics followed by a viable pacification or rehabilitation campaign. General Walt and his marines finally came to understand this, at least in part, and were on the right track with Combined Action Groups. In time, marines might have overcome the language obstacle and even innate corruption of most Saigon and I Corps area officials, who did not want viable government in the villages and sabotaged the American effort at almost every turn.[23] But marines lacked time and, so long as Giap sucked marine units into quasi-conventional warfare, they lacked men. The marine pacification effort was never more than a drop in the bucket. In 1966, the Viet Cong controlled about three quarters of I Corps area, either outright or through parallel hierarchies. By mid-1966, of 169 villages within the marine area, only thirty-seven were regarded as 80 per cent or more pacified; less than half of the area's nine hundred thousand people lived therein.[24]

Prime Minister Ky's highly touted Revolutionary Development program, so fervently embraced by President Johnson, suffered from two perhaps irreconcilable difficulties. The first was a definition of terms. The democracy that the Johnson administration wanted in South Vietnam was an ambition, not a feasible goal; the assumption that this was a form of government also wanted by Thieu and Ky and the special interests they represented was false. As the *enfant terrible* of the Marine Corps, Lieutenant Colonel William R. Corson, put it:

> ... we call it democracy—they call it obedience. [The] Honolulu [Conference of February 1966] left unanswered the questions

848

"What is pacification?" and "What are we really trying to do?" The generalized and idealized statements about a "better world," "hearts and minds," and such are not, and were not then, operational. You can't sell a product if you can't define it.[25]

The situation in South Vietnam did not fit the picture being reported by Lodge and Westmoreland, whose claims of significant pacification progress were frequently broadcast to the nation by its President, despite his being informed to the contrary by Robert McNamara (among others). While Johnson promised Thieu and Ky the moon and a piece of cheese at the Manila conference in October 1966, *all* governmental abuses so far discussed continued in force. No matter who was elected to the constituent assembly or what type of constitution would result, neither Thieu nor Ky nor the ruling junta of generals intended to liberalize government, much less institute a representative government that would appeal to either peasants or dissident sects or Buddhist or minorities or classes or professions—that would appeal to those complex elements constituting the political invention of South Vietnam. The generals stood as far removed from peasant aspirations as their American counterparts. A preponderance of northern Catholics occupied major posts both in Saigon and the countryside. The peasants were as badly off as formerly, and in some cases worse. Land reform was a dead issue: Landlords continued to accompany troops to claim back taxes from peasants, and to invoke heavy, usually illegal rents.[26] Friction continued, not only with increasingly militant Buddhists, but with other dissident southern groups such as remnant Cao Dai and Hoa Hao. GVN failure to live up to promises made to the Montagnards also cost heavily: More than two thirds of the two hundred fifty-man Montagnard garrison at Plei Me had defected the day prior to the Viet Cong attack, and some Montagnards had subsequently gone over to the enemy.[27]

Government failure meant that old abuses continued. The administration's chief hatchet man, General Nguyen Ngoc Loan, used the most violent methods to eliminate political opponents. Jails remained jammed with political prisoners; favored sons remained exempt from military duty; bribery and corruption claimed almost every transaction. At virtually each level of government, officials extracted "squeeze." Peasants bringing vegetables and fish to market paid squeeze to the police for protection; people buying and selling commodities paid squeeze for necessary licenses; students wanting scholarships to the U.S.A. paid for them; sick people wanting treatment on American hospital ships paid for it; peasants and refugees wanting food and clothes supplied by American funds paid for them.

This would have been bad enough under normal circumstances, but, considering South Vietnamese needs, it proved catastrophic. A dangerous political climate suppressed intelligent opposition and discouraged worthy Vietnamese who had fled abroad from returning at a crucial time. As one example, of the country's eight hundred doctors, five hundred served the army, a hundred fifty served private patients, and a hundred fifty treated fifteen million people;[28] yet, over seven hundred Vietnamese doctors were in Paris and refused to return![29]

Continuing VC gains in the countryside and the infusion of American troops exacerbated the situation. Rampant inflation developed, as did an enormous black market—an economically confused situation ably exploited by VC resident agents and infiltrators in two ways: by buying or stealing military needs from American stockpiles (while MACV and the JCS continued to worry about enemy supply lines from the North), and by agitation and propaganda among the hundreds of thousands of refugees generated from search-and-destroy tactics.

Governmental failure inevitably influenced ARVN, which contained nearly as many organizational and operational flaws as previously. The advisory system, in which so much hope had been placed, had already backfired—just as it had in the case of Chiang Kai-shek's Kuomintang army. A good many American army advisers were ill-equipped for the task and proved ineffective and, in some cases, dishonest and dangerous. The turbulent military situation, language deficiencies, and a one-year tour of duty combined to thwart the hard work of a good many capable and courageous Americans. Try as they would, they could not overturn a ruling mandarin philosophy and get ARVN units into the boondocks and keep them there. ARVN increased in 1965 from 493,000 to 640,000, but it counted ninety-three thousand desertions for the year.

Continued government and ARVN failures explained the second difficulty of the Revolutionary Development program, which was operational. Few GVN officials and ARVN officers shared Major Be's expressed idealism (see Chapter 64). Although ARVN units became increasingly available to provide hamlet security (as American soldiers and marines took over virtually the entire combat role), they proved, in general, as unsatisfactory in pacification as in combat. One American adviser, Dwight Owen—a highly motivated and sincere young man who left a postgraduate course to serve in Vietnam, where he would shortly die—wrote of this period:

> ... At present the ARVN has little or no responsibility or responsiveness to the people of Vietnam. They fight but do not build. ... Garrisons in towns and villages are notoriously inactive in CA [civic action] work. Often this is because they lack initiative and spirit. ... Good pay, promotions, decent quarters, good rations, leave, and many other benefits most armies enjoy are lacking in

many respects in the Vietnamese army. This undercuts morale and thus troop effectiveness. . . . [30]

ARVN soldiers from corps commanders to privates received squeeze to the extent that peasants saw little difference between friends and enemies. Ky's Revolutionary Development program soon brought to mind Ngo Dinh Nhu's earlier efforts to control the peasant population rather than win it to the government's side (see Chapter 59). William Corson, who was intimately involved in the pacification effort in I Corps area, later wrote:

> . . . The 30,000 members of the Armed Combat Youth (ACY) are a bargain-basement mob of thugs who counterterrorize the Vietnamese people while promoting "democracy" GVN style. The ACY units—or as they are being renamed, the Revolutionary Development Peoples' Groups (RDPG)—are organized to promote Nguyen Cao Ky's "strength through joy" approach to individual liberty. Through this borrowed Hitlerian concept Ky is attempting to build up an absolute form of political control that makes Nazi Germany look like Thomas More's "Utopia." . . . The fear generated by the presence of the ACY in a hamlet is exceeded only by presence of one of the "elite" ARVN units such as the Rangers, Airborne, or Vietnamese Marines.[31]

Nor did the American-directed reorganization result in streamlined operations that were needed. Province advisers at all levels found themselves enmeshed in bureaucratic and military corruption that sometimes defied imagination. Some of these advisers were conscientious, hard-working, and brave persons. Others were not. Most did not speak the language and had to rely on interpreters. Most knew little of customs of the people they were trying to help, and their aid estimates frequently lacked practicality or proper priority. Most were also endowed with the desire to do the job themselves. In the same letter quoted above, Dwight Owen wrote:

> . . . Our pacification effort is not making significant headway. The first major problem is a lack of realistic appraisal by U.S. officials of what is needed. Plans have been grandiose and have not considered the realities of the situation—too much and too fast. We have not allowed pacification cadre adequate time in hamlets by assigning them a quota of so many hamlets a year, which allows them about 2–3 months per hamlet. The plans have lacked follow-through. After the cadre leave, the job is considered finished, when, in reality, it is only beginning. . . .

Agency infighting frequently ruled an American camp, and agencies often collided with the military, both ARVN and American. A British adviser on counterinsurgency, Robert Thompson, later told a seminar audience, " . . . when I added up the intelligence organizations which were operating in Saigon in 1966 against the Vietcong, there were seventeen, both American and South Vietnamese, and none of them were talking to each other!"[32]

What possibly could have been a viable pacification program became just another in a long series of flaccid, money-wasting efforts—a development incessantly harped on by NLF-PRP-Hanoi propaganda which exhorted South Vietnamese peasants to fight against U.S. imperialists and their Saigon lackeys.[33] If Hanoi ever displayed nervousness, it was over the allied pacification effort. In a major speech delivered in January 1967, Vo Nguyen Giap returned to the subject with the reluctant persistence of Raskolnikov returning to his evil deeds in Dostoyevsky's *Crime and Punishment*. And well he might: Pacification was the key to combat in the South, a fact repeatedly proved by history, ancient and modern, a fact never understood by American military planners who refused to fight a complex war of nuance and subtlety in preference to a good old black-and-white shooting match, a fact never understood by Johnson or his hawkish advisers who refused to formulate objectives consonant to fact in preference to wild ambition that demanded an undefinable and thus unrealizable nothing called "victory."

By early 1966, a good many doubts had risen in public and private minds within the United States as to the wisdom of American actions in Vietnam. Taken together, they began to suggest that the Johnson administration had bought a gold brick made the more fraudulent by size and weight. In February 1965, the *New York Times* had published a petition, "An Open Letter to President Johnson," signed by over four hundred New England academics, including sixty-six from the Massachusetts Institute of Technology and sixty-two from Harvard. In this " . . . careful, cautious and even generous letter," the signatories pointed to the deteriorating position in Vietnam and called for a negotiated peace: " . . . If we are not to widen the war beyond all conscience, as reasonable men we must negotiate while there is still time."[34] A letter to Dean Rusk, signed by nearly seven hundred academics, appeared in the *Times* in May—a strong rebuttal to a speech in April by Rusk, who had attacked academic critics of the war. A distinguished scholar, Professor Hans Morgenthau, a political scientist and government consultant, next questioned the Johnson administration's policy in Vietnam in a televised debate with McGeorge Bundy in June 1965 in which Bundy came out second best. Morgenthau followed this effort with a lengthy article, "Vietnam: Shadow and Substance," in the *New York Review of Books* in September 1965. After defining the nature of foreign policy and national prestige, Morgenthau explained " . . . the realities of power and the American misunderstanding of those realities." The prestige of France, he went on, was never lower than during its wars in Indochina and Algeria; only after it liquidated those enterprises did its prestige rise " . . . to heights it had not attained since the beginning of the Second World War." Moving to the moral plane, Morgenthau wrote that victory in a guerrilla war can be achieved only by genocide. " . . . We have tortured and killed prisoners; we have embarked on a scorched-earth policy." Morgenthau warned that this indiscriminate killing would get worse as our armed forces became brutalized, that this was our dirtiest war, and there was no end and no justice in sight. The reader worried about national prestige, he concluded, should reflect on " . . . the kind of country America will become when it emerges from so senseless, hopeless, brutal and brutalizing a war."[35] In late October 1965, over 650 professors removed the velvet glove in another letter to President Johnson, published in the *Times,* which forcefully told the President to " . . . stop the bloodshed in Vietnam."[36] In February 1966, the *New York Review of Books* published an article, "Call to the American Conscience," which was sponsored by a score of notable authors who invited readers to " . . . a read-in for peace in Vietnam" to be held at Manhattan's Town Hall. In this same month, the *Times* published an "Open Letter on Vietnam" in which nearly thirteen hundred academics voiced their protest and warning: " . . . U.S. bombs, napalm, and chemical warfare are making a desert of the country. The only peace that can be achieved in this way is the peace of the grave. We recoil in horror."[37] Such was the continuing flow of petitions and articles that a contemporary historian, David Schalk, has recently concluded that in 1966 Lyndon Johnson had become to the dissenting academics and other members of the antiwar movement, " . . . a subject of antipathy, mockery, savage satire and devastating caricature."[38]

Nor were the academics and other conscience-stricken Americans standing alone. In February 1966, *Harper's Magazine* published a letter-article from a retired soldier with a fine World War II combat record and a lengthy postwar record of distinguished public and private service. This was General James Gavin, who now challenged the logic of escalation. What became unfairly known as a demand for "enclave strategy" was an intelligent attempt to reassess a complex situation, and fit limited resources to realistic goals.

Gavin's article was published shortly before the Senate Foreign Relations Committee, whose chairman was William Fulbright, opened what became the famous Vietnam hearings. These televised sessions left little doubt that the situation was not as black-and-white as the Johnson administration proclaimed. The Administration's position was presented by Dean Rusk and Maxwell Taylor, each of whom reaffirmed the domino theory and aggression-from-the-North-under-Peking-aegis thesis (and each of whom was pretty well worked over in question periods).

As devil's advocates, the Senate called on General Gavin and Ambassador George Kennan. Gavin warned the Foreign Relations Committee and the listening American public of dangers inherent in further expanding the war, particularly since no tactical need existed. As he had already written in *Harper's Magazine:*

> ... Today we have sufficient forces in South Vietnam to hold several enclaves on the coast, where sea and air power can be made fully effective. By enclaves I suggest Camranh Bay, Danang, and similar areas where American bases are being established. However, we are stretching these resources beyond reason in our endeavours to secure the entire country of South Vietnam from the Viet Cong penetration. This situation, of course, is caused by the growing Viet Cong strength.

To expand the American presence and the war would create new problems, for example Chinese intervention or a new war in Korea. Instead, the United States should pursue a strategy compatible to the area's importance and to the tactical challenge: " ... if we should maintain enclaves on the coast, desist in our bombing attacks in North Vietnam, and seek to find a solution through the United Nations or a conference in Geneva, we could very likely do with the forces now available. ... "

Frederick the Great, in speaking of his foray from Silesia against the Austrians, noted that " ... this plan was simple, proportionate to the possibility of execution, and adapted to circumstances; there was therefore every reason to hope it would succeed." The same could be said of the Gavin plan, but such was the power of the hawks that it became perverted into a strategy of defeat and would not soon have the chance to prove itself. Such was the Administration's outcry against the "enclave theory," that few persons paid attention to what possibly was Gavin's most important point. As Mao Tse-tung had suggested some years before, Gavin believed that warfare had radically changed:

> ... Since the advent of the Space Age, there has been a revolution in the nature of war and global conflict. The confrontation in Vietnam is the first test of our understanding of such change, or our lack of it. The measures that we now take in Southeast Asia must stem from sagacity and thoughtfulness, and an awareness of the nature of strategy in this rapidly shrinking world.[39]

Ambassador Kennan already had challenged the wisdom of American commitment to South Vietnam.[40] Once again, he contradicted Administration hawks who proclaimed that South Vietnam was of vital strategic interest to the United States:

> . . . if we were not already involved as we are today in Vietnam, I would know of no reason why we should wish to become so involved, and I could think of several reasons why we should wish not to. Vietnam is not a region of major military, industrial importance. It is difficult to believe that any decisive developments of the world situation would be determined in normal circumstances by what happens on that territory.

After expatiating on this statement, which must have shaken thoughtful senators, Kennan suggested that, since we had become militarily involved, we could not hastily abandon our posture. But that was no reason to enlarge the posture. The political situation in the South permitted no easy solution; American military might could not overcome such factors as enemy space and manpower, and an attempt to subdue the North by invasion would probably draw China into the fray. As it was, the war was severely damaging American relations with the U.S.S.R. and Japan. Kennan wanted the American presence liquidated as soon as possible:

> . . . In matters such as this, it is not, in my experience, what you do that is mainly decisive. It is how you do it, and I would submit that there is more respect to be won in the opinion of this world by a resolute and courageous liquidation of unsound positions than by the most stubborn pursuit of extravagant or unpromising objectives.

As for the "obligation" maintained by Johnson and his advisers, Kennan, sounding like a diplomatic Socrates, continued:

> . . . I would like to know what that commitment really consists of, and how and when it was incurred.
> What seems to be involved here is an obligation on our part not only to defend the frontiers of a certain political entity against outside attack, but to assure the internal security of its government in circumstances where that government is unable to assure that security by its own means.
> Now, any such obligation is one that goes obviously considerably further in its implications than the normal obligations of a military alliance. If we did not incur such an obligation in any formal way, then I think we should not be inventing it for ourselves and assuring ourselves that we are bound by it today. But if we

did incur it, then I do fail to understand how it was possible to enter into any such commitment otherwise than through the constitutional processes which were meant to come into play when even commitments of lesser import than this were undertaken.

Although Kennan felt the deepest personal sympathy for the South Vietnamese and repugnance toward the Viet Cong, he nonetheless maintained that

> ... our country should not be asked, and should not ask of itself, to shoulder the main burden of determining the political realities in any other country, and particularly not in one remote from our shores, from our culture, and from the experience of our people. This is not only not our business, but I don't think we can do it successfully.[41]

Three months later, another hard-charging soldier spoke up. This was David Shoup, a retired four-star Marine Corps general, winner of the Medal of Honor at Tarawa, former commandant of the Marine Corps, member of the Joint Chiefs of Staff, and unofficial military adviser to President Kennedy. Speaking in Los Angeles in May 1966, Shoup denied South Vietnam's strategic importance:

> ... The Administration, he said, has never realistically assessed whether the United States' own self-interest is at stake in Southeast Asia. The Administration has never presented a timetable proving that there would be "irreparable effects upon this nation at the end of five, ten, fifteen, fifty years" if South Vietnam were overrun by the Communist Vietcong guerrillas.

Pointing to drastic changes in the world Communist order, Shoup declared that Administration reasons for American intervention in South Vietnam " . . . are too shallow and narrow for students, as well as other citizens. Especially so, when you realize that what is happening, no matter how carefully and slowly the military escalation has progressed, may be projecting us toward world catastrophe." In case any one missed the point, General Shoup stated: " . . . I don't think the whole of Southeast Asia, as related to the present and future safety and freedom of the people of this country, is worth the life or limb of a single American."[42]

So it was that in 1966, influenced by Morgenthau, Gavin, Kennan, Shoup, and myriad other voices, large numbers of America's educators were becoming opponents of Johnson's war. Although Lyndon Johnson publicly treated these and other dissentient voices with insouciance tinged with contempt, members of his own inner circle continued to express certain doubts that could not altogether be ignored. These were occasioned mainly by the increasing expense of the war as fought by Westmoreland and the JCS.

No sooner had Johnson authorized committing nearly two hundred thousand troops by the end of 1965 than Westmoreland, in July of that year, informed McNamara that these would suffice only to stop the enemy offensive by the end of the year. In order to resume the offensive in priority areas and to continue the pacification program, Westmoreland requested another 112,000 troops for the first half of 1966; he also warned McNamara that he would need even more troops to defeat the enemy by the end of 1967. A few months later he asked for another 154,000 bodies.

After considerable soul-searching, McNamara agreed: If a bombing pause failed to produce a satisfactory reaction from Hanoi, he recommended a troop increase to seventy-four battalions, or about 400,000 men, by the end of 1966, but warned that at least two hundred thousand additional troops would perhaps be needed in 1967! McNamara concluded his memorandum to the President in somber but ambivalent words that bring to mind the western-front syndrome of World War I:

> ... We should be aware that deployments of the kind I have recommended will not guarantee success. U.S. killed-in-action can be expected to reach 1000 a month, and the odds are even that we will be faced in early 1967 with a "no-decision" at an even higher level. My over-all evaluation, nevertheless, is that the best chance of achieving our stated objective lies in a [bombing] pause followed, if it fails, by the deployments mentioned above.[43]

McNamara's recommendation for a bombing halt touched off an intra-Administration quarrel that would continue to the end of Johnson's administration. Johnson later wrote that he viewed McNamara's proposal to halt the bombing with a "deep skepticism" shared by Mc-George Bundy, Dean Rusk, and Ambassador Lodge, not to mention military chiefs and advisers. Pertinent factors slowly brought some of these persons around. In private discussions, McNamara went so far, according to the President, as to question " ... assurance of military success in Vietnam," stating that " ... we had to find a diplomatic solution":

> ... I asked him whether he meant that there was no guarantee of success no matter what we did militarily. "That's right," he answered. "We have been too optimistic. One chance in three, or two in three, is my estimate."[44]

McNamara also pointed out that if the pause failed to move Hanoi to the conference table, " . . . it would at least [demonstrate] our genuine desire for a peaceful settlement and thereby temper the criticism we were getting at home and abroad."[45] International diplomatic activity, particularly from the U.S.S.R. and Hungary, also seemed to promise negotiations if the bombing halted. In the end, according to the President, McGeorge Bundy and Rusk joined McNamara and George Ball in urging the halt. Against JCS advice, the President stopped the bombings in late December. When Hanoi showed no inclination to come to the conference table—critics of the Administration pointed to Johnson's intractable conference position as one reason—the President ordered bombing resumed at the end of January.

The hawks were now definitely in the ascendancy. In February 1966, the *New York Times Magazine* published an article, "The Case for Escalation," by veteran military analyst Hanson Baldwin. Arguing that the domino theory was valid, Baldwin seemed willing to accept war with China if that was necessary to defeat North Vietnam; meanwhile, he called for declaration of a national emergency and a greatly expanded war.[46]

The next round started with the Buddhist revolts in March 1966, which precipitated a new crisis and forced the Thieu-Ky government to use ARVN units to recapture the cities of Hué and Da Nang. Again the Washington administration split on the issue. Pessimists argued that Ky could never form an effective government, which meant that he could not maintain a viable pacification program; optimists pointed out that he commanded enough loyalty, at least in the army, to settle the issue and that, as a bonus, the government and Buddhists agreed to elections for a constituent assembly to draw up a new constitution. Although the crisis occasioned another fierce argument within the Administration (with Under Secretary of State Ball once again calling for disengagement), President Johnson sided with those who favored pursuing the current program, escalating as necessary. With the appointment of Walt Rostow as presidential assistant (replacing McGeorge Bundy as presidential adviser on national security in deed if not in word), the hawks won a major round, and the American commitment continued to increase.

The doubts that had already formed in Secretary of Defense Robert McNamara's mind now began to develop dramatically. In August of 1966, the Secretary received an unpleasant, if not entirely unexpected, surprise: a report from forty-seven of the nation's top scientists whom he had secretly mobilized to study the effects of Operation Rolling Thunder and to consider alternate means of stopping enemy infiltration from the North. Their report stated that not only had the twin objectives of Rolling Thunder—to reduce infiltration and to force Hanoi to call off the insurgency—failed (a conclusion previously reached by CIA reports), but that an expanded bombing program would probably fail to accomplish either objective. Instead, the group recommended building a sophisticated barrier across the southern border of the DMZ and curling on the Laotian panhandle—all together some forty to sixty miles—this to comprise new and secret mines and sensors that would locate infiltrators, who would then be destroyed by patrolling troops and supporting arms. The system would cost perhaps a billion dollars to build and about $800 million a year to operate.[47]

McNamara was still digesting the morbid contents of the scientists' findings when he received another unpleasant surprise: a new request from General Westmoreland to provide a total 570,000 troops in South Vietnam by end of 1967. A few weeks later, the JCS, which approved Westmoreland's newest request (favorably endorsed by Admiral Sharp), " . . . urged what the Pentagon study calls 'full-blown' mobilization of 688,500 Army, Navy, Air Force and Marine reservists to help provide more troops for Vietnam and also to build up the armed forces around the world."[48]—a move pressed on the American public by Hanson Baldwin in the October *Reader's Digest*.[49]

The Westmoreland-Sharp-JCS-Baldwin thinking was not to McNamara's liking. In October, he again flew to Saigon (where an attempt was made on his life). Upon his return to Washington, he reported in detail to President Johnson that, although

> . . . We have done somewhat better militarily than I anticipated . . . my concern continues . . . in other respects. This is because I see no reasonable way to bring the war to an end soon. Enemy morale has not broken—he apparently has adjusted to our stopping his drive for military victory and has adopted a strategy of keeping us busy and waiting us out (a strategy of attriting our national will). He knows that we have not been, and he believes we probably will not be, able to translate our military successes into the "end products"—broken enemy morale and political achievements by the GVN.

The September elections in South Vietnam were healthy enough, he opined, but the South Vietnamese Government had not come to terms with the real problem:

> . . . Pacification is a bad disappointment . . . [and] has if anything gone backward. As compared with two, or four, years ago, enemy full-time regional forces and part-time guerrilla forces are larger; attacks, terrorism and sabotage have increased in scope and intensity; more railroads are closed and highways cut; the rice crop expected to come to market is smaller; we control little, if any,

more of the population; the VC political infrastructure thrives in most of the country, continuing to give the enemy his enormous intelligence advantage; full security exists nowhere (not even behind the U.S. Marines' lines and in Saigon); in the countryside, the enemy almost completely controls the night.[50]

In McNamara's opinion, the United States had to " . . . continue to press the enemy militarily" and also to make "demonstrable" progress in pacification, but

> . . . we must add a new ingredient forced on us by the facts. Specifically, we must improve our position by getting ourselves into a military posture that we credibly would maintain indefinitely—a posture that makes trying to "wait us out" less attractive.

McNamara called for " . . . a five-pronged course of action": contrary to Westmoreland's, Sharp's and JCS desires, he wished to limit troop increases to seventy thousand which, in the current round, would give a total of 470,000—enough, he believed, to neutralize enemy operations and get on with pacification; to save troops, and thus avoid mobilizing reserves, and to find an effective substitute for expensive and relatively useless bombing of the North, he recommended building an electronic barrier across the DMZ as suggested by the earlier-mentioned scientists' report; he called for stabilizing Operation Rolling Thunder: eighty-four thousand attack sorties had failed to attain stated objectives. We were then flying twelve thousand attack sorties per month (at an operational cost of $250 million per month), which was sufficient to " . . . continue the pressure and would remain available as a bargaining counter to get talks started (or to trade off in talks)." Moreover,

> . . . At the proper time . . . I believe we should consider terminating bombing in all of North Vietnam, or at least in the Northeast zones, for an indefinite period in connection with covert moves toward peace. Pursue a vigorous pacification program—if necessary, reorganize. Press for negotiations.

He did not believe that either military action or negotiations offered more than a "mere possibility" of ending the war. As opposed to Westmoreland and the JCS, McNamara believed that

> . . . The solution lies in girding, openly, for a longer war and in taking actions immediately which will in 12 to 18 months give clear evidence that the continuing costs and risks to the American people are acceptably limited, that the formula for success has been found, and that the end of the war is merely a matter of time. All

of my recommendations will contribute to this strategy, but the one most difficult to implement is perhaps the most important one—enlivening the pacification program. The odds are less than even for this task, if only because we have failed consistently since 1961 to make a dent in the problem. But, because the 1967 trend of pacification will, I believe, be the main talisman of ultimate U.S. success or failure in Vietnam, extraordinary imagination and effort should go into changing the stripes of that problem.

President Thieu and Prime Minister Ky are thinking along similar lines. . . . They expressed agreement with us that the key to success is pacification and that so far pacification has failed. They agree that we need clarification of GVN and U.S. roles and that the bulk of the ARVN should be shifted to pacification. Ky will, between January and July 1967, shift all ARVN infantry divisions to that role. . . . Thieu and Ky see this as part of a two-year (1967–68) schedule, in which offensive operations against enemy main force units are continued, carried on primarily by the U.S. and other Free-World forces. At the end of the two-year period, they believe the enemy may be willing to negotiate or to retreat from his current course of action.

Neither Westmoreland nor the JCS agreed with McNamara's conclusions. The JCS vigorously dissented from stabilizing the air campaign against the North, calling instead for a radical expansion of the effort along with an increase in targets and additional naval action.[51] Other hawks agreed, and President Johnson was inclined to agree with the hawks.

McNamara did persuade Johnson to limit troop increases, but only for a short time. In November, McNamara, obviously with presidential assent, informed the JCS that Westmoreland could have 469,000 troops at his disposal by mid-1968.[52]

CHAPTER SIXTY-SIX

1. Hackworth, 468–9, 474.
2. Ibid.
3. Ibid., 486.
4. Ibid., 487.
5. Ibid., 488–9.
6. Ibid., 559–60.
7. Ibid., 569–70.
8. Marshall, 42. See also, Hackworth, 545 ff., 568–71, 582–6, for a professional appraisal of this veteran military correspondent.
9. Marshall, 43 ff.
10. Hackworth, 513.
11. Ibid., 485.
12. Ibid., 572.
13. Caputo, 65.
14. Ibid., 86–7.

15. Miller.
16. West.
17. Ibid. See also, O'Neill.
18. Miller.
19. Grier.
20. Rogers. See also, Mack, "Ambuscade."
21. West.
22. O'Neill, 137–58, who writes feelingly on the subject.
23. Clement. See also, Corson.
24. U.S. Marine Corps, "III MAF . . . "
25. Corson, 59.
26. Fall, "Viet Nam in the Balance."
27. Corson, 91.
28. U.S. Senate, *Refugee Problems in South Vietnam.*
29. Corson, 273.
30. Dwight Owen, private letter in the author's files.
31. Corson, 91.
32. Royal United Service Institution Seminar.
33. Vo Nguyen Giap, "The Strategic Role . . . " See also, Snepp, 11–12: CIA personnel alone numbered 600. See also, ibid., *Big Victory, Great Task.*
34. Schalk, 118–19.
35. Ibid., 53–4.
36. Ibid., 120.
37. Ibid., 121.
38. Ibid.
39. Gavin, "A Soldier's Doubts." See also, Fulbright, *The Vietnam Hearings.*
40. Raskin and Fall. See, for example, Kennan's testimony before the House Committee on Foreign Affairs, May 1965, 15–31.
41. Fulbright, *The Vietnam Hearings.*
42. Deakin.
43. Sheehan et al., 487–9.
44. Johnson, *The Vantage Point . . . ,* 234–6.
45. Ibid., 234.
46. Baldwin, "The Case for Escalation."
47. Sheehan et al., 483–5, 502–9.
48. Ibid., 48.
49. Baldwin, "To End the War in Vietnam, Mobilize!"
50. Sheehan et al., 542–51. See also, Giap, "The Strategic Role . . . "
51. Sheehan et al., 552–3.
52. Ibid., 520–1.

CHAPTER 67

The war continues • President Johnson's optimism • The February bombing halt • Operation Cedar Falls • Fighting in the highlands • The marine war • New tactical techniques • Khe Sanh defended • Air and naval wars • Ambassador Bunker and pacification • South Vietnam's political progress • Allied profits for the year • "... Light at the end of a tunnel"

IN HIS STATE OF THE UNION MESSAGE in early January 1967, President Johnson once again justified American presence in Vietnam in the strongest possible terms. Once again he spoke of specific "commitments" and the evil that would follow should the United States fail to uphold them. He promised no easy way out of what he called this "limited war":

> ... I wish I could report to you that the conflict is almost over. This I cannot do. We face more cost, more loss, and more agony. For the end is not yet. I cannot promise you that it will come this year—or come next year. Our adversary still believes, I think, tonight, that he can go on fighting longer than we can, and longer than we and our allies will be prepared to stand up and resist.

The answer to that was to continue Westmoreland's attrition strategy:

> ... Our men in that area—there are nearly 500,000 now—have borne well "the burden and the heat of the day." Their efforts have deprived the Communist enemy of the victory that he sought and that he expected a year ago. We have steadily frustrated his main forces. General Westmoreland reports that the enemy can no longer succeed on the battlefield.
> So I must say to you that our pressure must be sustained—and will be sustained—until he realizes that the war he started is costing him more than he can ever gain.[1]

His speech made it clear that he was committed to a hawk strategy and did not want to change.

The President continued to place great faith in the bombing of the North. He approved none of McNamara's "stabilizing" suggestions made the previous autumn and, indeed, drastically raised the number of authorized B-52 missions, to take effect in late February. Although international pressures caused him to halt bombing the North for a few days in February, he ignored the British prime minister's plea to hold off until the Soviet premier could discuss negotiations with Hanoi. How much this was due to his own belief and how much to the work of hawks is anyone's guess. The President made his attitude clear in two documents, however. In a secret letter of early February to Ho Chi Minh, his moral indignation at Hanoi's transgression is apparent—it is all he can do to swallow it and offer to stop bombing the North if Hanoi would stop infiltration into the South. Ho replied, in effect, that the U.S.A. had no right to bomb the North in the first place and that discussions between the two countries could occur only when bombing and other unjustified acts of war ceased.[2]

Not only was bombing the North morally and legally justified in the President's mind, but, contrary to reports from the nation's top intelligence analysts, he insisted that the bombings were producing very real effects. Although Johnson emphasized in his memoirs that he did not expect bombing of the North to win the war, the record strongly suggests that he regarded air power as his chief punitive weapon and could not understand why Hanoi did not submit in order to call off the punishment. In any event, the air war, both North and South, escalated to frantic proportions in 1967.

The President did not exercise such active control over the ground war in the South as he did over bombing of the North. He nonetheless vigorously supported Westmoreland. By year's end, South Vietnam's armed forces climbed to over seven hundred thousand (at least on paper); American troop strength approached half a million with 525,000 authorized; Korea supplied forty-five thousand troops; Australia, six thousand; Thailand, twenty-five hundred, with the promise to furnish a division; New Zealand, a few hundred. Direct operational costs for the year zoomed to over $25 billion. By October 1967,

> . . . 40 percent of our combat-ready divisions, half of our tactical air-power, and at least a third of our naval strength . . . were waging full-throated war on the Southeast Asian peninsula.[3]

One analyst aptly called it more of the same.

In January, Operation Cedar Falls—an allied force spearheaded by the American army's 1st Division—began to sweep through a B-52-bomb-plastered Iron Triangle, northwest of Saigon. In this traditional Viet Cong defense complex, troops discovered an "underground city" and seized half a million enemy documents and enough rice to feed " . . . an estimated 13,000 soldiers for one year."[4] More sweeps followed to push the enemy from the Iron Triangle and from Zones C and D and keep him on the defensive while bringing alleged stability to surrounding provinces. An active and tactically profitable year in vital III Corps area: by December, U.S.-ARVN-allied forces claimed 22,500 enemy dead; more important, Viet Cong main-force units had retreated north to Cambodian border areas. Summarizing the war at year's end, *Newsweek* magazine quoted Lieutenant General Frederick Weyand, commanding U.S. forces in III Corps area: " . . . The three enemy divisions that used to ring Saigon are now 80 and 90 miles away from the capital, where their targets are outside the key areas. . . . The enemy can't suck me out of the populated areas now by attacking an outpost. We now have the strength to respond to such attacks and still maintain control of the population."[5]

Farther south, in IV Corps area, U.S.-ARVN forces also reported significant gains and claimed to be destroying one thousand Viet Cong guerrillas per month. Where once enemy units had proved elusive, contacts now were frequent: " . . . The units we fight now will break and run," says one general. "Two years ago you couldn't pry them out."[6] Particularly productive in this corps area were riverine warfare operations conducted by U. S. Navy personnel often in conjunction with American and Vietnamese ground units.

Similarly, large-scale "spoiling" operations in II Corps area, both along the coast and in the central highlands, were said to be keeping the enemy temporarily off balance. These sophisticated operations differed only in quantity and location from ones earlier discussed. American army operations continued in the two coastal provinces throughout summer and autumn. The correspondent Jonathan Schell found operations virtually unchanged from previous months. American army units continued to sweep hostile areas and to call in air and artillery strikes on suspect villages. Each operation strongly resembled the others; each depended on the quantitative approach that had now become the hallmark of American tactics.[7]

In October, enemy forces again became active in the northwest. To prevent them from seizing the provincial capital of Kontum, Westmoreland broke off coastal operations to fight a number of fierce actions in the vicinity of Dak To. Then, in mid-November, in III Corps area, in the south, two enemy regiments attacked an allied outpost at Loc Ninh, a town only nine miles from the Cambodian border, a fierce action that claimed 926 confirmed North Vietnamese dead, with another two or three thousand wounded. Another attack, against Dak To, was beaten back with five hundred Communist dead claimed; week-long fighting cost 177 American dead and 761 wounded, and 279 ARVN dead.[8] In early December, the enemy again attacked the base camp at Dak To, a vicious five-day battle that again resulted in heavy Communist casualties: 1,599 confirmed dead at a cost of 150 U.S. paratrooper lives and 250 wounded. Another attack, a week later, at Bo Duc was also beaten off.

In the North, in I Corps area, Walt's marines had been kept busy fighting three wars: one against main-force Viet Cong and PAVN units in and around the DMZ, one against VC units south of the DMZ, and finally, the "other war," that which involved protecting hamlets and villages while trying to win peasants to the government's side.

Marines fought the first war from a series of strong points designed to prevent infiltration south by PAVN units crossing the DMZ or entering from Laos. The effort involved screening enemy movements and harassing or disrupting them by ground action and/or artillery, air, and naval fire when possible. Although major fire fights continued to exact heavy enemy casualties, the enemy seemed no less strong, and as the year wore on, he began employing " . . . sophisticated Russian howitzers, artillery, mortars and rockets"—the result of increasing Soviet aid.[9] Action flared variously in the area, in general the marines reacting rather than acting. One marine strong point was at Khe Sanh, a scrubby, isolated combat base with airstrip, originally the home of a CIDG—some two hundred Vietnamese irregulars and Special Forces advisers.[10] A few miles from the Laotian border, the base was held by a reinforced company. As with other combat bases, Khe Sanh filled a dual role: Patrols constantly issued forth to observe and sometimes interdict enemy movement, and to respond, along with base supporting weapons, to calls from neighboring Combined Action units.

In April 1967, a marine patrol from Khe Sanh had set up an observation post on Hill 861, part of a nearby triangular terrain feature. Unknown to marines, elements of two PAVN regiments had been moving to these hills, presumably in preparation for an attack on Khe Sanh itself. When enemy attacked the marine patrol on Hill 861, a fire fight of major proportions developed, to culminate in a marine counteroffensive: violent assault and capture of Hills 861, 881 North, and 881 South, actions that reminded older marines of World War II operations. The twelve-day battle ended in a marine "victory" in that the PAVN regiments retired, having lost, according to marine figures, nine hundred lives with two or three that number wounded. Marine casualties numbered 138 dead and 397 wounded.[11]

An even more frustrating war continued against VC units south of the DMZ. Although marines fought this war with grim determination, they possessed neither tactics nor strength essential to clear and hold areas that, long since, had been dominated by VC cadres. Every time a quasi-conventional action developed in the DMZ area, the effort to the south suffered. In early spring of 1967, VC units were sufficiently strong to open a general offensive, shelling Hué and Da Nang and even over-running Quang Tri, while other units struck at pacification teams throughout the provinces.

VC gains led to important reorganization of the area. Marine units, now some seventy-five thousand strong, concentrated in the three northern provinces. South of them, a new army unit moved in, the Americal Division, whose four brigades were reinforced with a fifth, airmobile brigade. ARVN troops were increased to some thirty thousand, and units began fighting in conjunction with American troops. In June, Lieutenant General Robert Cushman, U. S. Marine Corps, replaced General Walt in command of III MAF, whose operational area had grown to over two thousand square miles in I Corps area (which comprised five provinces and some three million people and was commanded by Lieutenant General Huong Xuan Lam). In addition to troops listed above, the area held a Korean brigade, CIDG units, eighteen thousand American sailors, and seven thousand American airmen, not to mention countless civil and military advisers.

That summer and autumn, fast and furious actions continued to be fought throughout the long coastal area and in the north. In summer, marine and ARVN units began Operation Beau Charger, designed to root out VC forces in and south of the DMZ prior to making it a "free fire zone"—a complicated and costly task that, among other things, meant relocating some thirteen thousand civilians, to add to refugee hordes already crowding Da Nang and Hué.[12] In autumn, as engineers began surveying terrain as the first step in constructing McNamara's "fence" across the southern boundary of the DMZ, marine units fought frequent savage actions in defending strong points such as Cam Lo and Con Thien—"spoiling" operations that bore heavy price tags: In September alone, marine casualties totaled over twenty-two hundred.[13]

The scope of fighting, not only in I Corps area but throughout South Vietnam, is difficult to comprehend. By August 1967, marine units had mounted over three hundred thousand patrols—over 1,200 a day since early 1967—set 114,000 ambushes, and fought over two hundred battalion-size or larger actions. Marine fixed-wing aircraft had flown 128,000 missions; marine helicopters registered a total of 859,000 flights. At year's end, the claimed kill figure for I Corps area would reach thirty-eight thousand.[14]

Pacification also showed impressive gains. Of 219 villages (with a population exceeding 1.2 million) in the marine area, forty-three (with a population of five hundred thousand) were declared 80 per cent or more pacified by late autumn. ARVN units had been working in the area for over a year, and Combined Action Platoons now numbered seventy and were to expand to 114. Navy doctors attached to marine units had treated over two million Vietnamese, dentists over a hundred thousand. Marines had distributed over four million pounds of food, had helped build or rebuild a hundred schools and a hundred other buildings such as churches and dispensaries; they had dug over a hundred wells, built forty-nine bridges, and serviced four hundred miles of roads.[15] Pacification techniques were improving, as witness this account of an operation called County Fair:

> ... A Marine unit in cooperation with Vietnamese units surrounds a hamlet or village usually before dawn and cordons it off to prevent anyone from leaving. After the people are assembled, Vietnamese officials with Marine support begin a series of actions to gain their confidence. A census is taken. A field dispensary is set up and medical attention given to those who need it. Sometimes a dentist accompanies the party. Meals are cooked and served. Lectures and movies are presented. A Marine band may play for an hour or so. Much of this activity takes place under canvas which probably accounts for the name County Fair. A careful house-to-house search is aimed at VC guerrillas and VC political personnel who may be part of the local cadre. .... The County Fair technique has had excellent results and is now a routine type operation, although each one varies in its specifics.[16]

The marines also improved techniques in an attempt to repair intelligence deficiencies. A long-overdue step involved recruiting scouts from enemy defectors, the Kit Carson Scout Program, variations of which had proved so successful in Malaya and Kenya (see Chapters 46 and 52), indeed in the Philippines at the turn of the century (see Chapter 11). Marine intelligence officers recruited these people from Viet Cong and North Vietnamese who had surrendered under the Chieu Hoi program. After training, they were normally assigned in pairs to an infantry battalion deployed in search-and-destroy missions. The former enemy soldiers proved invaluable in detecting ambush sites and booby traps, and also in acting as interpreters. When possible, they were employed in areas where they were familiar with the terrain, people, and their former units. Marines initially procured fifty per division, later a hundred; the program was so successful that the army adopted it.

A complementary solution involved developing a unit's own scouts in the form of small, long-range patrols that came to be known as Sting Ray operations, similar to those practiced by a few enlightened army

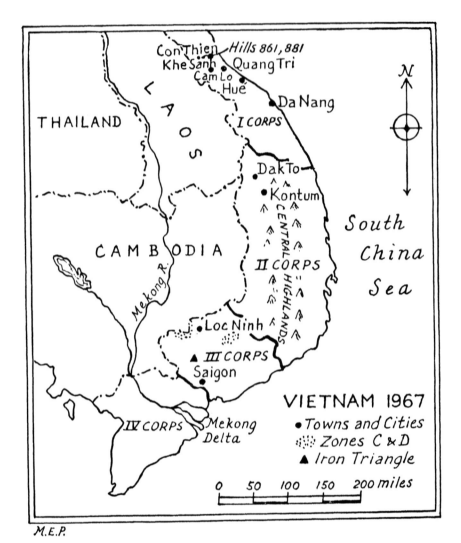

Con Thien
Khe Sanh
Cam Lo
Hills 861, 881
Quang Tri
Hue
Da Nang
I CORPS
THAILAND
L A O S
Dak To
Kontum
CENTRAL HIGHLANDS
II CORPS
CAMBODIA
Mekong R.
South
China
Sea
Loc Ninh
III CORPS
Saigon
IV CORPS
Mekong
Delta
VIETNAM 1967
• Towns and Cities
Zones C & D
▲ Iron Triangle
0   50   100   150   200 miles

M.E.P.

units in the central highlands and the Mekong Delta. Such a patrol consisted of a few highly trained men equipped to find the enemy, then call in friendly air, artillery, or naval gunfire by radio. A patrol infiltrated either on foot or by helicopter operated normally for five days, gathering intelligence and employing disruptive tactics by establishing appropriate ambushes. If a fire fight developed unfavorably, a patrol sought to extricate itself either by guerrilla tactics of fading into the terrain, or by helicopter call-in; one enterprising marine lieutenant, when greatly outnumbered, ordered his men to don gas masks, then saturated the area with tear gas, which held off the enemy until helicopters arrived.

This same officer, who led patrols over a period of several months, obtained a final kill ratio of 226 confirmed VC dead to the loss of a few wounded marines, a figure he believed would have been five times greater had an assault company, controlling its own helicopter transport, been instantly available to exploit numerous chances for severely punishing observed enemy units.[17] Still another tactic involved two-man sniper teams that were especially trained to stake out a position and wait for opportunity. The 1st Marine Division claimed that, in eight months, its ninety snipers recorded over four hundred fifty confirmed kills against four marine dead. Called "13-cent killers," because of the price of a rifle cartridge, the tactic was carried out by some five hundred army and marine snipers during the year.[18]

Despite improved tactics and techniques, as autumn gave way to early winter, army and marine commanders continued to dance to the enemy's tune. As earlier noted, coastal pacification operations now yielded to meeting new enemy threats around Kontum. In the north, the Khe Sanh area had remained relatively quiet through summer and autumn, but, in October, enemy activity again increased. In November, General Cushman opened Operation Scotland and, by mid-December, had bolstered the small garrison with two reinforced battalions. At year's end, patrols were confirming heavy enemy build-up in western Quang Tri province in general and around Khe Sanh in particular.

Air and naval wars, both in- and out-country, also escalated, with thousands of sorties flown to drop thousands of tons of bombs and napalm and expend thousands of rockets and millions of rounds of ammunition. Naval-marine amphibious groups conducted twenty-three battalion-force landings along the South Vietnamese coast in 1967, which allegedly " . . . kept the enemy off balance, disrupted his logistical support, and denied him profitable coastal areas."[19] From June 1966 to July 1967, the Coastal Surveillance Force " . . . boarded or inspected over 500,000 watercraft" in an attempt to interrupt VC supply lines.[20] In-country naval operations in the Mekong Delta also expanded to involve water-borne search-and-destroy operations in conjunction with American army and ARVN units. Provisional reconnaissance units also appeared in the delta country; these were small groups of former VC guerrillas who had changed sides and were employed mostly as night raiders sent to attack VC camps and strongholds. Where camps could not be attacked, American planes attempted to uncover them and deprive them of food: During 1967, Ranch Hand planes " . . . dumped more than four million gallons of herbicide and defoliation chemicals on South Vietnam . . . four times the annual herbicide productive capacity of *all* American chemical companies."[21]

Simultaneously, the "other war" grew in size and complexity. In spring of 1967, the new American ambassador to South Vietnam, Ellsworth Bunker, once again reorganized the pacification program, at least from the American standpoint. Called now Civil Operations and Revolutionary Development Support (CORDS), it was headed by a deputy ambassador, former presidential aide Robert Komer, who administered it under MACV's jurisdiction with large amounts of funds going directly to the South Vietnamese government. The general idea was to coordinate military aspects, particularly security, which had always been a weak point, with civil aspects. During 1967, the Revolutionary Development program grew to some fifty-five thousand cadres, including nearly five hundred Revolutionary Development Teams. Their work was measured by Komer's people, using an elaborate computerized system called Hamlet Evaluation System (HES). Data furnished by U.S. advisers, who monthly reported on eighteen criteria, went into computers, which then graded villages anywhere from totally secure ("A") to VC-controlled ("V"). By year's end, Komer claimed that two thirds of the population lived under government control—" . . . only one South Vietnamese in six now lives under VC control."[22]

Administration voices also emphasized substantial political progress in South Vietnam. At Guam, in March, Thieu and Ky had unveiled their new constitution, a document heralded by President Johnson as slightly more important than the Magna Carta, particularly since he secretly exacted a pledge from the two Vietnamese not to break up the fragile South Vietnamese Government by reason of personal vendettas. Spring elections followed in about eight hundred villages and four thousand hamlets. An autumn presidential election placed Thieu in power, with Ky as vice-president; voters also elected a sixty-man senate and a 137-man house of representatives.

The Administration's line was clear: By continuing to pursue a winning strategy, the President was going to give the American people a well-deserved victory in South Vietnam. In various speeches around the United States, Lieutenant General Walt assured audiences that we were "winning" (at least in I Corps) and that it would be folly to stop now: " . . . wise or unwise, we have committed ourselves in Vietnam; weakness, vacillation, irresolution here at home are being paid for on the battlefields of Vietnam with the lives and blood of our fighting men."[23] MACV spokesmen in Saigon continued to report positive gains during the summer. In October, General Westmoreland told newsmen that " . . . the enemy is in the worst posture he has been in since the war started." Prior to leaving for Washington, in November, Westmoreland told newsmen that he was " . . . more encouraged than at any time since I arrived here."[24] Ambassador Bunker and Robert Komer, Bunker's pacification chief, reflected Westmoreland's optimism; indeed, according to *Time,* " . . . all three brimmed with confidence." At a White House meeting, Bunker told the President, " . . . It's going to be all right, Mr. President. Just let's keep on, keep on."[25] At President Johnson's request, Westmoreland addressed a joint session of Congress, which learned " . . . that the war was being won militarily. He outlined 'indicators' of progress and stated that a limited withdrawal of American combat forces might be undertaken beginning late in 1968."[26] As the year closed, President Johnson said, " . . . General Abrams tells me that the ARVN is as good as the Korean Army was in 1954."[27] At the turn of the year, Secretary of State Rusk spoke optimistically of " . . . a clear . . . turn of events on the ground."

Although the President wrote in his memoirs that the tactical situation was very crucial at this time, and that he had warned of "kamikaze tactics" to come, the record does not show that he disapproved of Westmoreland's strategy or was in any mind to heed warning voices. Shortly before the new year, he stated that the Communists " . . . can't point to one single victory" in Vietnam. His State of the Union address in January 1968 implied satisfactory progress, with more to come. General Westmoreland's annual report, delivered on January 27, included the following paragraph:

> . . . Interdiction of the enemy's logistics train in Laos and NVN [North Vietnam] by our indispensable air efforts has imposed significant difficulties on him. In many areas the enemy has been driven away from the population centers; in others he has been compelled to disperse and evade contact, thus nullifying much of his potential. The year ended with the enemy increasingly resorting to desperation tactics in attempting to achieve military/psychological victory; and he has experienced only failure in these attempts.[28]

CHAPTER SIXTY-SEVEN

1. Johnson, *Public Papers of . . .* , 1967, Book I, 12.
2. The letters are published in *Survival,* June 1967.
3. Hoopes, 57.
4. Johnson, *The Vantage Point . . .* , 258.
5. *Newsweek,* January 1, 1968.
6. Ibid.
7. Schell, 35 ff.
8. *Reuters,* Saigon, November 16, 1967. See also, Shaplen, *The Road from War,* for details of these actions.
9. Shaplen, "Viet-Nam: Crisis of Indecision."
10. Walt, "Khe Sanh—The Battle That Had to Be Won."
11. U.S. Marine Corps, "The Battle for Hills 861 and 881." See also, Corson, 72, who cites 155 dead and 425 wounded.
12. Corson, 69.
13. *Time,* October 6, 1967.
14. *Newsweek,* January 1, 1968.

15. U.S. Marine Corps, "III MAF Force . . . " See also, Wagner.
16. McCutcheon. See also, Walt, *Strange War, Strange Strategy.*
17. Private information in the author's files. See also, Asprey, "Guerrilla War-fare"; ibid., "Tactics"; West.
18. *Time,* October 27, 1967.
19. Department of the Navy.
20. U.S. Navy.
21. Corson, 76.
22. *Newsweek,* January 1, 1968. See also, Snepp, 12.
23. Walt, "Our Purpose in Vietnam." See also, ibid., "Are We Winning the War in Vietnam?"
24. *Time,* November 17, 1967.
25. Ibid., November 24, 1967.
26. Kissinger, "The Viet Nam Negotiations." See also, Johnson, *The Vantage Point . . . ,* 376: Westmoreland told the President that his "central purpose" over the next two years was to transfer additional responsibility to the South Vietnamese. Westmoreland, the President wrote, " . . . was convinced that within that time—that is, by the end of 1969—we could safely begin with-drawing American forces."
27. Corson, 103.
28. Sheehan et al., 593.

CHAPTER 68

More blurs on the canvas • Allied losses • Failure of Operation Rolling Thunder (II) • The numbers game • Westmoreland wants more troops (III) • John McNaughton: " . . . A feeling is widely and strongly held that 'the Establishment' is out of its mind." • McNamara's new policy paper • The President's middle course • Increasing American costs (II) • MACV headquarters: "Disneyland East" • Senior commanders' life-style • The fallacy of attrition warfare • The other war • Have we killed all the enemy? • Failure of the Revolutionary Development program • Komer's "indicators" • South Vietnam's government corruption • Failure of land reform • Electoral restrictions and irregularities • Increasing opposition to the war at home and abroad • Press and TV coverage The experts dissent • The Clifford mission • Johnson's San Antonio offer • Thwackum and Square

As WESTMORELAND'S OPERATIONAL CANVAS expanded in 1967, the blurs that had appeared in 1966 grew more prominent. Physical losses and financial cost sharply increased. During 1967, nine thousand Americans were killed in Vietnam and over sixty thousand were wounded, to make cumulative totals of about sixteen thousand dead and one hundred thousand wounded since 1961.[1] Other allies lost fifteen hundred killed. South Vietnamese deaths were reported at sixty thousand, of which ten thousand were ARVN deaths. Steadily improving anti-aircraft defenses in the North exacted increasing toll of aircraft. In December, an official American spokesman put cumulative U.S. losses at 1,822 planes and 1,416 helicopters.[2]

The air offensive was proving no more effective than in 1966, despite official claims to the contrary. Testifying before a Senate subcommittee in August 1967, Robert McNamara pointed out that North Vietnam had the capacity to import fourteen thousand tons of supply per day, but was importing only fifty-eight hundred tons. North Vietnam and Viet Cong forces in the South, he told senators, required under one hundred tons of supply per day from the North.[3] American air power was not preventing this small amount from reaching the enemy, nor would it do so. Townsend Hoopes later wrote that, by October 1967, " . . . the cold, unhypothetical fact remained that the flow of men and supplies from North Vietnam to South Vietnam had definitely increased in absolute terms."[4]

Almost incessant bombing, far from breaking Hanoi's will, was cementing its intransigence and was drawing increasing criticism, from critics within and without the United States. As in previous years, it continued to frustrate well-intentioned efforts by intermediaries to bring both sides to a conference table. Prime Minister Wilson of Great Britain was particularly offended by Johnson's attitude in February during behind-the-scenes negotiations. Wilson ascribed the hard-line attitude to "mentally confused" hawks and later wrote, undoubtedly with Rostow in mind, " . . . The more I saw of certain White House advisers, the more I thought Rasputin was a much maligned man."[5]

Despite official claims that enemy units could not win a major tactical victory in the South and could not maintain main-force units close to cities, the Viet Cong seemed more active than ever, while PAVN forces continued to call the play in the highlands and in the North. MACV's claims of some eighty thousand enemy dead and three or four times that number wounded in 1967 seemed irrelevant in that the enemy apparently had ample human resources and ammunition, not to mention open supply lines from both China and the U.S.S.R. and to the South. VC terrorists murdered 3,820 people, double the count for 1966; nearly six thousand Southerners were kidnaped as part of a determined effort to display continuing strength in and control of specific areas. If enemy morale suffered, as captured soldiers attested and as MACV claimed while pointing to twenty-five thousand deserters, it did not show in determined fighting, whether in defense or attack. Confusion as usual obfuscated MACV figures. This headquarters had stated in 1966 that 280,000 enemy were fighting in South Vietnam; in 1967, the figure had risen to 378,000, a dramatic increase scarcely in keeping with official claims of enemy casualties and one weakly explained in Saigon as owing to a new method of calculating enemy strength.

The new figures brought further dissension among President Johnson's close circle of advisers and officials. To regain the "tactical initiative," Westmoreland requested more troops: a "minimum essential force" of about one hundred thousand; an "optimum force" of about two hundred thousand, which would have meant a total of some 670,000 Americans in South Vietnam. The JCS passed this request on, with favorable endorsement, to McNamara. The JCS in turn proposed

> . . . the mobilization of the reserves, a major new troop commitment in the South, an extension of the war into the VC/NVA sanctuaries (Laos, Cambodia and possibly North Vietnam), the mining of North Vietnamese ports and a solid commitment in manpower and resources to a military victory. The recommendation not unsurprisingly touched off a searching reappraisal of the course of U.S. strategy in the war.[6]

In late April, Westmoreland returned to the United States to argue his case before the President. According to notes made by John McNaughton, Lyndon Johnson was not pleased at future prospects:

> . . . When asked about the influence of increased infiltration upon his operations the general [Westmoreland] replied that as he saw it "this war is action and counteraction. Anytime we take an action we expect a reaction." The President replied: "When we add divisions can't the enemy add divisions? If so, where does it all end?"

Westmoreland explained that, with the minimum increase he requested, the war could continue for three years; with the maximum increase, for two years. General Earle G. Wheeler, the hawkish chairman of the Joint Chiefs of Staff warned that American troops would possibly have to invade Cambodia, Laos, and North Vietnam; he also pointed out that the air effort had nearly run out of targets and would have to be extended to port areas.[7]

Almost no ranking civilian official agreed with the proposed new and aggressive strategy. Townsend Hoopes, who had been promoted to Under Secretary of the Air Force, argued that, despite American bombing, Hanoi, " . . . in absolute terms," was sending more, not fewer, men and materials to the South. He himself had concluded " . . . that the Administration's Vietnam policy had become a quietly spreading disaster from which vital U.S. interests could be retrieved only if the policy were reversed or drastically altered."[8] William Bundy argued strongly against extending ground operations to North Vietnam, " . . . asserting that the odds were 75 to 25 that it would provoke Chinese Communist intervention."[9] He also warned that an attack on northern ports could bring Soviet counteraction, a position supported by CIA reports. A call-up of reserves, in Bundy's opinion, was to be avoided for domestic political reasons. Walt Rostow, theretofore as hawkish as the generals, did not agree with mining North Vietnamese harbors or bombing ports; in his opinion, this would make Hanoi more dependent on China and would increase United States tensions with the Soviet Union and China.[10] Instead, he wanted to concentrate the air effort " . . . on the 'bottom of the funnel,' the lines of communication and infiltration routes in southern North Vietnam and through Laos. . . . "[11] Dr. Alain Enthoven, Assistant Secretary of Defense for Systems Analysis, held that the requested troop increases would not produce proportionate enemy casualties:

> . . . On the most optimistic basis, 200,000 more Americans would raise [the enemy's] weekly losses to about 3,700, or about 400 a week more than they could stand. In theory we'd wipe them out in 10 years.[12]

John McNaughton, slated to become Secretary of the Navy, was equally firm. Hoopes described him at this time as

> . . . physically exhausted and deeply disenchanted with the Administration's Vietnam policy . . . [he was] appalled by the catastrophic loss of proportion that had overtaken the U.S. military effort in Vietnam. "We seem to be proceeding," he said to me in barbed tones, after returning from a particular White House session, "on the assumption that the way to eradicate Viet Cong is to destroy all the village structures, defoliate all the jungles, and then cover the entire surface of South Vietnam with asphalt."[13]

McNaughton wanted the air war shifted to lines of communication south of the 20th parallel, a definite cutback, designed primarily to save American pilots and planes; any significant troop increase was merely " . . . more of the same" and would resolve nothing. In early May, McNaughton advised McNamara (belatedly)

> . . . that the "philosophy" of the war should be fought out now so everyone will not be proceeding on their own major premises, and getting us in deeper and deeper; at the very least, the President should give General Westmoreland his limit (as President Truman did to General MacArthur). That is, if General Westmoreland is to get 550,000 men, he should be told, "That will be all, and we mean it."

McNaughton, who was to die shortly in an air crash, continued:

> . . . A feeling is widely and strongly held that "the Establishment" is out of its mind. The feeling is that we are trying to impose some U.S. image on distant peoples we cannot understand (any more than we can the younger generation here at home), and we are carrying the thing to absurd lengths.

Related to this feeling is the increased polarization that is taking place in the United States with seeds of the worst split in our people in more than a century.[14]

On the basis of these and other arguments, Robert McNamara submitted a major policy paper to President Johnson which recommended a scaling down of the air effort and very limited troop increases.[15] Even more important, he recommended that the ambitions enunciated by President Kennedy and carried on by President Johnson in National Security Action Memorandum 288 be changed to reasonable political goals. He attempted first to quiet unreasonable fears by abolishing the domino theory he himself had once embraced. He went on in words made the more intelligent, bold, and courageous in that they reflected his own reversal of thought at a time when the President was embracing force more than fact:

> . . . The time has come for us to eliminate the ambiguities from our minimum objectives—our commitments—in Vietnam. Specifically, two principles must be articulated, and policies and actions brought in line with them: (1) Our commitment is only to see that the people of South Vietnam are permitted to determine their own future. (2) This commitment ceases if the country ceases to help itself.
>
> It follows that no matter how much we might *hope* for some things, our *commitment* is *not*:
> —to expel from South Vietnam regroupees [Viet Cong], who are South Vietnamese (though we do not like them),
> —to ensure that a particular person or group remains in power, nor that the power runs to every corner of the land (though we prefer certain types and we hope their writ will run throughout South Vietnam),
> —to guarantee that the self-chosen government is non-Communist (though we believe and strongly hope it will be), and
> —to insist that the independent South Vietnam remain separate from North Vietnam (though in the short-run, we would prefer it that way). (Nor do we have an obligation to pour in effort out of proportion to the effort contributed by the people of South Vietnam or in the face of coups, corruption, apathy or other indications of Saigon failure to co-operate effectively with us.) We *are* committed to stopping or offsetting the effect of North Vietnam's application of force in the South, which denies the people of the South the ability to determine their own future. Even here, however, the line is hard to draw. Propaganda and political advice by Hanoi (or by Washington) is presumably not barred; nor is economic aid or economic advisors. Less clear is the rule to apply to military advisors and war matériel supplied to the contesting factions.

The importance of nailing down and understanding the implications of our limited objectives cannot be overemphasized. It relates intimately to strategy against the North, to troop requirements and missions in the South, to handling of the Saigon government, to settlement terms, and to US domestic and international opinion as to the justification and the success of our efforts on behalf of Vietnam.[16]

McNamara, in effect, was recommending a dramatic shift to viable policy; he was recognizing (after a long hiatus) that South Vietnam was a "strategic convenience" and should be treated as such. If it could be held with a limited effort, fine; but its retention was not worth a world war and was not worth a deepening schism inside the U.S.A. If the South Vietnamese could not come to terms with themselves, the country would be "lost" and could be "lost" without undue damage to American interests in Southeast Asia (which had never "owned" it, to start with). McNamara recognized that he was asking the President to adopt a difficult course of action, which would be sharply criticized and possibly would cause a government crisis in South Vietnam: " . . . Not least will be the alleged impact on the reputation of the United States and of its President. Nevertheless, the difficulties of this strategy are fewer and smaller than the difficulties of any other approach."[17]

President Johnson did not agree with Secretary McNamara, and this document probably marks the beginning of McNamara's decline and fall from presidential grace. Indeed, the Secretary allegedly offered to resign at this time. His own doubts were reflected the following month, when he commissioned what since has become known as the Pentagon report—a highly secret attempt to explain how and why the United States became and remained involved in South Vietnam.

Neither did the President altogether agree with hawks who refuted McNamara's conclusions and recommendations with practiced fervor and ability similar to those of Viet Cong agit-prop agents. Although he refused to alter what he liked to call Administration policy, he did not authorize troop increases requested by Westmoreland, Sharp, and the JCS. Instead, he sent McNamara to Saigon to work out still another compromise with Westmoreland. Early in August, he announced an increase of fifty-five thousand troops, to bring total American commitment to 525,000. He did, however, authorize expanding the air war to include targets in Hanoi and in the China buffer zone.[18]

The war was also costing more and more money. Direct war expenditures totaled $24–27 billion in 1967 and billions more in indirect costs. Part of the expense was due to the technology of war as Americans fought it. Airplanes, helicopters, APCs, self-propelled artillery, tanks, vast naval armadas, all cost a great deal of money to manufacture, maintain and replace if destroyed. Part of the expense stemmed from the vast logistics effort which tied up some 80 per cent of the armed forces in supporting about 20 per cent of combat troops. This shameful situation started in Saigon or rather in the U. S. Army and MACV headquarters (the latter known to the field troops as "Disneyland East"), each of which was "incredibly plush," the home of hordes of rear-echelon commandos (known to the field troops as "rear-echelon motherfuckers"), all wearing pressed jungle fatigues and new canvas boots, all drawing the same combat pay as the guys getting wounded and killed.[19] It continued in Field Force or Corps headquarters. David Hackworth described Lieutenant General Julian Ewell's generals' mess as

> ...the most lavish I'd ever seen...he had a very large general staff, all of whom, when I arrived, were in the middle of their cocktail hour, mingling with martinis in perfectly starched jungle fatigues and camouflage scarves, a million miles away from the war of the grunt, which ran along unabated just beyond the berm of Long Binh's base camp.[20]

It was the prodigal life-style familiar to senior allied and German command headquarters on the western front in World War I. It carried to other base camps such as that at Di An where Hackworth

> ...was assigned to share an air-conditioned bungalow (complete with a bar in the corner of the living room and a full-time Viet maid who kept shoes polished, clothes washed and pressed, and beds made with perfectly starched white sheets... [The assistant division commander] emerged from his room each morning wearing pajamas and a dressing gown...[21]

Senior officers and important visitors at the 1st Air Cavalry headquarters, An Khe, lived in Hilton-standard suites:

> ...throughout each evening's three course, five-star quality gourmet meal (presented on fine china embossed with the Cav insignia and served by black waiters in white starched jackets...[with] after-dinner cigars, liqueurs, coffee and conversation...[22]

Finally, a large portion of the logistics burden stemmed from Westmoreland's quantitative strategy whereby commanders defended vast ammunition expenditures on grounds of saving lives. At Dak To in November a *single* B-52 raid dropped one hundred and fifty thousand pounds of bombs,[23] " . . . a million-dollar strike . . . responsible for some [estimated] two hundred enemy casualties."[24] Put another way: The official claim of 1,644 enemy killed depended in part " . . . on 2096 air strikes (about one and a half air strikes per enemy dead), and the expenditure of 151,000 rounds of artillery (92 rounds per enemy dead) . . . "[25] Thus the battle of Dak To in which 344 American soldiers were killed (twenty by "friendly" aerial bombing) and 1,441 wounded,[26] scarcely a satisfactory ratio so long as Ho Chi Minh was willing to lose ten of his men for one of the enemy. Jonathan Schell summed up a search-and-destroy operation up north, not a particularly big one, in which an armored brigade in two weeks destroyed an estimated 65 per cent of the houses of perhaps seventeen thousand natives in the Chu Lai area:

> . . . On August 28th, when Operation Benton came to a close, Task Force Oregon announced that the troops taking part in it had killed, and counted the bodies of, three hundred and ninety-seven of the enemy, and that forty-seven American soldiers had been killed. Into an area of ten by twenty kilometres they had dropped 282 tons of "general-purpose" bombs and 116 tons of napalm; fired 1,005 rockets (not counting rockets fired from helicopters), 132,820 rounds of 20-mm. explosive strafing shells, and 119,350 7.62-mm. rounds of machine-gun fire from Spooky flights; and fired 8,488 artillery rounds. By the end of the operation, the Civil Affairs office had supervised the evacuation of six hundred and forty of the area's seventeen thousand people, to the vicinity of government camps.[27]

During the twelve-day battle for Hills 861 and 881, in the marine area, gunners fired over eighteen thousand artillery rounds,[28] tactical aircraft dropped 1,375 tons of bombs, and B-52 aircraft dropped 1,750 tons of bombs.[29] Small-unit commanders relied on supporting artillery and aircraft fire as probably no commanders in history. The "mad minute" became standard operating procedure in many units. In the Vietnam version of this World War I tactic, at first light the unit fired every available weapon for at least sixty seconds, the theory being to disrupt an attack *in case* the enemy had infiltrated "close in" during the night. If on occasion it scored a major hit, this was rare enough. Had the U.S. forces been fighting the war correctly, the tactic would not have been necessary except on singular occasion. American supporting arms, particularly from warships and B-52 bombers, responded to later Communist attacks of Con Thien with what Westmoreland called the heaviest concentration of firepower " . . . on any single piece of real estate in the history of warfare."[30]

Most accounts of army and marine operations in this period stress use of supporting weapons employed by commanders to rectify tactical disadvantages caused by inadequate intelligence. Spoiling tactics were scarcely the precise operations implied by MACV; for the most part, they were "encounter" battles often initiated and almost always broken off by the enemy when he wished. Valiant as was the American effort to hold defensive outposts or "capture" prominences, it didn't really solve anything. It proved once again that an enemy was hard put to stand against either a determined defense backed by co-ordinated supporting fires (the major tactical lesson of the 1905 Russo–Japanese War and of World War I) or against a determined offense also backed by co-ordinated supporting fires (the major tactical lesson of World War II)—but in South Vietnam damage inflicted on the enemy was scarcely decisive, particularly when that enemy held ample reserves and reasonably secure lines of communication.

These actions continued to demonstrate the fallacy of American attrition strategy. So long as American commanders lacked good intelligence (that could only come from the locals), they would have to fight in the most expensive possible way. Trumpeted to the world as American "victories," encounter battles, in view of cost in human lives and suffering and in material versus tactical results did little more than illustrate the truth of an ancient axiom: " . . . from no victory shall the ass's kick be missing." Or, as Captain Roeder had put it while watching Napoleon's army invade Russia: " . . . Every victory is a loss to us."

It was so unnecessary. History repeatedly had shown its basic fallacy. Why did American commanders, faced with unpalatable facts, keep insisting that this was the way to "win" the war? Why had no attention been paid to the prognoses of such professionals as Matthew Ridgway, Roger Hilsman, and James Gavin? The crime is compounded by the fact that a few commanders, realizing the error of doctrinaire ways, successfully revised their thinking to fashion valid small-unit tactics and, in the case of such as Colonel Henry Emerson, to reach tactical parity with the professional guerrilla. Early in 1967, David Hackworth discovered that General Willard Pearson, commanding an airborne brigade at Phan Rang, had developed what he called " . . . "semiguerrilla" tactics—stealth, deception, and surprise, units infiltrating the battlefield at night and without the use of choppers or accompanying H&I [harassing and interdicting fire]." These economy of force tactics resulted in outambushing the enemy with commensurate rewards: in one instance a fifteen-man ambush team " . . . killed nineteen NVA, took one prisoner and eighteen weapons for no casualties of their own"; in another instance they gained a " . . . very high weapon-to-body count ratio (143 weapons . . . to 149 enemy dead) . . . [plus] seventy-six prisoners."[31]

Claimed enemy casualties were increasingly dubious. Marine commanders would have been hard put to explain the discrepancy between a claim of 28,455 "confirmed enemy dead" and 3,952 weapons captured. American army claims were rendered suspect not alone by various factors discussed in earlier chapters, but by tactical surprises such as that at Bo Duc in early December. The previous month, at Loc Ninh, Major General John Hays' 1st Infantry Division claimed to have inflicted almost 50 per cent casualties on the two regiments of the 9th VC Division, with Hays predicting " . . . that it would be three to six months before the 9th VC Division . . . would be able to fight in force again."[32] One of the "decimated" regiments attacked at Bo Duc less than a month later. Granting that enemy casualties were heavy, the enemy nonetheless initiated the actions that caused the casualties—and for good reason. His attacks in the central highlands caused Westmoreland to divert units from pacification operations in the coastal provinces. His continued presence in and around the DMZ, his attacks at Khe Sanh and Con Thien, his continued probes in the general area— all slowed marine pacification efforts by causing General Cushman to commit battalions and resources needed for pacification duties, and by adding to a refugee flow that, in late 1967, numbered some five hundred thousand in I Corps area alone.

Thus we return to the other war. Despite the barrage of statistics fired by MACV and III MAF at all visitors, pacification was not going well anywhere. The marines in I Corps area erred in several respects. As elsewhere in South Vietnam, search-and-destroy tactics continued to antagonize people who had to be won over. Marines were operating in a vast sea of fear that could easily turn to hatred, and frequent fire fights, no matter how carefully conducted, could not but exacerbate the situation—moving bullets are promiscuous. Marine bands could play, and marines could distribute food and clothing, and doctors could help villagers, but these advantages paled when one, two, or more villagers were killed in a fire fight or by bombs, rockets, naval shells, or napalm. Marines attempted to prevent this in two ways: either to evacuate villages or to help them to protect themselves. In 1967, nearly three hundred thousand of half a million refugees were living in hastily constructed camps, sometimes in appalling conditions. Far from being rehabilitated and trained for the day when they could return to their hamlets, they were fortunate to survive, considering the rapacious officialdom that surrounded them. Since numerous Viet Cong agents accompanied refugee groups, the camps presented a bewildering security problem, as did 176 villages that were under 80 per cent pacified.

In attempting to protect villages, marines erred by trying to do the job themselves: Marines could hold "county fairs" until doomsday, but,

unless carried to fruition, they were not only meaningless but dangerous, in that they brought forward either friendly or potentially friendly
villagers who were subsequently exposed to VC wrath. Nothing was
new about the county-fair technique; Lyautey used almost an identical
procedure, but Lyautey was smart enough to back it with reasonably
honest administration that improved tribal life, at least initially. Moving
in government development teams too often subjected villagers to rents
and various forms of squeeze that soon neutralized attendant advantages. As far as the psychological approach went, the Viet Cong did it
better: Few Vietnamese peasants would prefer to hear a marine band
in preference to Vietnamese acting out dramas and operas in their own
tongue and their own cultural traditions. Although marines made better
progress in pacification than either the American army or ARVN, their
program left considerable to be desired, and, in view of South Vietnamese civil and military corruption, it is doubtful if it would ever have
succeeded. One of the most tragic cameos to come from I Corps area
is this, related by a senior marine intelligence officer:

> . . . one day [in 1966] the commanding general remarked to me,
> "We've been doing well lately. Don't you think we are now really
> eliminating the enemy? Haven't we just about killed them all?"
> Looking out the window, I thought of the hundreds of thousands
> of peasants living on that vast rice plain; of the patient and thor-
> ough way in which a highly-motivated enemy for decades had been
> organizing that society at all levels. I answered only, "No, sir. We
> haven't killed all the enemy."[33]

The pacification effort elsewhere in South Vietnam caused the largest blur to occur on Westmoreland's operational canvas. The reader
may remember that one reason for an extensive American build-up was
to replace ARVN combat units with American units, so that ARVN
could reorganize while undertaking the major task of protecting the
pacification program. This program worried the enemy more than any
other action, because, where it worked, it seriously challenged his presence. Unfortunately, it did not work in many places. Although the Revolutionary Development program had expanded drastically during 1967
under Robert Komer's aegis, the performance of ARVN units assigned
to protect the teams proved disappointing, and VC terrorism increased
substantially in some areas during the year. Increased South Vietnamese
control of funds and materials added to already widespread corruption
to further hinder the program's effectiveness. Despite widespread failures noted and reported by a host of observers, Komer continued to
claim substantial progress based on "indicators" that, like those used
by the American military, were not always pertinent to a counterinsur-

gency situation. A particularly hostile critic of Komer, William Corson, later wrote concerning one of CORDS's projects:

> ... When the General Accounting Office (GAO) reviewed AID/CORDS stewardship of the funds for War Relief and Support [about $70–75 million annually], it was not misled by Komer's reports. Under Komer, progress is indicated by the amount of money pushed into the hands of the GVN. However, the GAO noted that in the October 1967 report only one out of ten "scheduled" houses had been rebuilt, one out of eight "New Life" hamlets constructed, one out of nine public-health sanitation facilities erected, and more than half of the refugees had received *no* assistance. Senator Edward Kennedy, in commenting on the GAO report, said that the findings "show that the refugee program and the medical program in South Vietnam are a scandal." ... [34]

Komer also claimed substantial progress in regaining control of hamlets, his indicator here being the Hamlet Evaluation Estimate program. But William Lederer noted that " ... the evaluation of the conditions in approximately 13,000 hamlets is made by U. S. Army officers who are advisers to Vietnamese district chiefs. They send in Hamlet Evaluations monthly. I estimate that 99 percent of the U. S. Army advisers have neither language facility nor the knowledge of Vietnamese culture to know what is happening in their own district." Lederer continued:

> ... I have seen samples of the Hamlet Evaluation Estimates sent to headquarters by U. S. Army advisers. These estimates are fraudulent, or, to be charitable, they are distorted with errors. Under the present system they can be no other way. It is not only that the U. S. advisers and their interpreters are intellectually and culturally unable to make accurate estimates, but the taint of dishonesty has swept through the entire United States government reporting system in Vietnam. This pollution sinks down from the top. In Washington, Walt Rostow (who advises President Johnson) suggests—sometimes even insists—that his colleagues de-emphasize unfavorable facts. Occasionally when his assistants refuse to alter facts Rostow goes into tantrums. Once he threw a water pitcher at a colonel who showed that Rostow's figures were biased. Unwillingness to face unwelcome facts has spread throughout the government, and it has of course reached Saigon and down to the Army advisers in remote South Vietnamese districts.[35]

A RAND analyst, Konrad Kellen, included the pacification program as one of eleven American fallacies,

... aside from the fact that Pacification is impossible because our Pacification aims and methods are unacceptable to the people in the Vietnamese countryside, there is another aspect to this which makes Pacification a doubly impossible aim: the choice of Americans entrusted with it. ... One need only to have met a member of AID and Army representatives to know that all these men, despite their great goodwill, and ample knowledge of local detail, can never do anything but confuse and antagonize any foreign population, and disorganize, if not destroy, its social fabric. And there are no other men to do the job, which cannot be done in the first place.[36]

The people who should have taken on the pacification task, the South Vietnamese, could not accomplish it owing to government inefficiency, pervasive corruption, and lack of individual will or even desire. Horrified U. S. senators learned that only half of an estimated four million refugees received the fourteen ounces of rice and five cents a day that the South Vietnamese Government was supposed to be providing—at U.S. expense. The same report alleged that numerous refugees never received a $42 resettlement allowance and a six-month rice supply.[37] One American official, John Vann, senior adviser in IV Corps area, " ... managed to have 75 GVN officials removed for corruption, only to find all of them reinstated within six months in equal or better jobs."[38] William Lederer was informed by one knowledgeable Vietnamese that the black market in South Vietnam involved about $10 *billion* a year, all American goods and moneys, an incredible situation that " ... could not exist without American collusion." He described a visit to a black-market warehouse in Saigon:

> ... The place looked like a U. S. Army Ordnance Depot. Everything seemed to be painted brown and to smell of either oil or fresh paint. Ordnance equipment was arranged in orderly lines, and neatly printed price tags hung from everything. Automatic rifles were $250. A 105 mm mortar ... was priced at $400. ... There were about a thousand American rifles of different kinds standing neatly in racks. M16s cost $80. On one side of the loft were uniforms of all services. ...

So much American military transport had been stolen, that " ... the American military has been renting its own stolen jeeps from black-market operators at $250 a month. The same double indignity and multiple cost applies to U.S. government trucks." Lederer pointed out that, in three years, South Vietnam's gold reserves increased from $130 to $450 million (all at American expense) and that, according to Swiss and Chinese informants, approximately $18 *billion* " ... has been sent to foreign banks by private Vietnamese individuals since 1956. Not so long ago, Madame Nhu, through a silent partner, purchased outright the second largest bank in Paris, for cash."[39]

The same blatant corruption pervaded the pacification program. Land reform remained a bad joke. As two congressmen, John Moss and Ogden Reid, informed Secretary of State Dean Rusk in December 1967, " . . . Land distribution in South Vietnam has been at a virtual standstill since 1962." Their letter continued:

> . . . Of 2.47 million acres acquired by the Government of Vietnam only 667,000 acres have been distributed to 128,000 families since 1954, including 51,800 acres to 12,000 families in 1967.
>
> Of 566,000 acres of choice rice land acquired by the government in 1958 from French owners, 240,000 have been rented to small farmers, but no actual distribution was made until October 1966, eight years after the land was expropriated. . . . [40]

Landlords frequently violated rent-control laws. Although limited by law to paying 25 per cent of the principal crop as maximum rent, " . . . four out of five peasants pay a land rent equal to more than fifty per cent of the crop because there is no valid attempt to enforce the provisions of the land-rent law."[41]

Aid programs similarly suffered: Almost without exception, South Vietnamese officials and ARVN officers sold food and material to hamlets and villages, a shocking corruption freely admitted by American personnel in the field and in Saigon.[42] The political progress applauded by MACV and embassy spokesmen was in many ways meaningless. Townsend Hoopes later wrote that American efforts to produce a South Vietnamese constitution and elections had resulted only in continuing military rule.[43]

Thus despite escalation, despite increasing costs in lives and money, despite official optimism, the U.S.A. and South Vietnam were no closer to "winning" the war than ever and, in some respects, were even farther from this ambition. President Johnson's expressed determination to persevere unto "victory" was also in jeopardy. *Ramparts,* an outspoken, militant anti-Vietnam periodical, reached a U.S. circulation of three hundred thousand in 1967.[44] Increasingly influential and strident voices were questioning not only the conduct but the very *raison d'être* of the war. In February 1967, Noam Chomsky's explosive essay, "The Responsibility of Intellectuals," appeared in the *New York Review of Books* and thereafter was widely circulated—one of the " . . . key documents in the intellectual resistance to the Vietnam War,"[45] in that it called for the nation's intellectuals, who passively opposed American participation in the war, to become *engagé*—in David Schalk's term— and even *embrigadé* or counterlegal if necessary " . . . to speak the truth and to expose lies."[46] In this watershed essay, Chomsky blasted such "establishment intellectuals" as Arthur Schlesinger, Jr., Walt W. Rostow, McGeorge Bundy, and Henry Kissinger

> ... for their abandonment of the critical role that should fall to them because of their privileged status. These academics who had entered politics displayed a kind of "hypocritical moralism" that hid American imperialism with pieties and masked and apologized for aggression, especially American aggression in Vietnam.[47]

Other influential voices added to the fire of protest, a debate characterized in British Prime Minister Harold Wilson's words by " ... great passion, great feeling, and great emotion." In early 1967, Walter Lippmann challenged the desire of such Congressional hawks as Mendel Rivers " ... to flatten Hanoi if necessary and let world opinion go fly a kite." If the United States adopted genocide as a national policy, Lippmann wrote, it would find itself dangerously isolated. It would not only earn the suspicion and hatred of neutrals but even of allies: " ... We would come to be regarded as the most dangerous nation in the world, and the great powers of the world would align themselves accordingly to contain us." The President, Lippmann went on, found himself confronted

> ... with the agonizing fact that limited war has not worked because *limited war can be effective only for limited objectives.* The reason why the President is confronted with the demand for unlimited war is that he has escalated his objectives in Vietnam to an unlimited degree.[48]

In April anywhere from a quarter of a million to a million antiwar demonstrators in New York marched from Central Park to the United Nations Plaza—the "spring demonstration" that horrified the White House and Congress. In June, a petition called "Individuals Against the Crime of Silence," holding that the war was immoral and illegal, stated that " ... the conscience of America is not dead."[49] More and more American citizens believed that Lyndon Johnson had lost control of the situation—that the praying mantis of earlier portraits had become a preying menace to common sense. Businessmen were speaking up and so were some congressmen. Capable journalists were continuing to report adversely, their copy often reflecting dissident views of American civil and military officials, particularly at lower levels, with official policy. TV coverage of battle areas increasingly brought home the agony of war in all forms. What some American officials called distorted camera coverage in reality emphasized the stupidity of search-and-destroy tactics and, at the same time, questioned optimistic claims of military spokesmen. Embarrassed Administration officials continued to blame press and television correspondents for twisting news, an accusation frequently implied by President Johnson and one that scarcely modified the growing antagonism between press and government. Although a few correspondents did allow personal emotion to overcome objective reporting, a great many did not, and the Administration erred grievously in attempting to cast doubt on the veracity of many courageous and intelligent observers whose analyses often contained constructive criticism.

In October, still another anti-war petition signed by such well-known dissenters as the Jesuit priest Philip Berrigan, Noam Chomsky, Herbert Marcuse, Edgar Snow, and Dr. Benjamin Spock appeared in the *New Republic* and the *New York Review of Books,* the petitioners asserting that the war was unconstitutional and illegal and that American troops were indulging in "crimes against humanity."[50] The famous march on the Pentagon followed to further embarrass the Administration.

Interested and experienced observers such as Generals Gavin, Ridgway, and Shoup added to the criticism, as did portions of the business world—thenceforth, the BEM (Business Executives Move for Peace in Vietnam), whose military board included one of the United States' few genuine guerrilla-warfare experts, Brigadier General Sam Griffith, would become increasingly influential and, through its publication, *Washington Watch,* hostile to Administration policy. Other new voices were heard: In mid-November, General Lauris Norstad, former NATO chief and subsequently a top business executive, told a Los Angeles audience that Washington should seriously consider such moves as an unconditional halt of bombing and unilateral cease-fire in South Vietnam if these would move Hanoi to the conference table.[51]

Writing in the *New York Times,* John Kenneth Galbraith pointed to a shifting tide of feeling within the United States and within Congress:

> ... I next assume that public opinion in the United States has turned very strongly against the war—and especially against those who hope to bring it to a military solution. The public opinion polls show it. So do the altered stands of political and other leaders ...

The Administration's credibility, Galbraith continued, was rapidly approaching ground zero:

> ... The consequence of this ghastly sequence of promise and disappointment is that now nearly everything that is said in defense

889

of the war is suspect. This, in turn, nullifies the natural advantage of the Administration in access to press and television. There isn't much advantage in being able to get your side before the people if they no longer believe what you say or do not listen.

Since " . . . it is now a war that we cannot win, should not wish to win, and which our people do not support," it was essential for the Administration to change objectives and reverse present policy.[52]

Senator Eugene McCarthy was equally critical: In his best-selling book *The Limits of Power,* the senator from Minnesota called for a fundamental change in general foreign policy and as swift an exodus as possible from Vietnam.[53] At year's end, Senator Fulbright told constituents that national pride, not national security, is the reason that Americans are fighting in Vietnam. Experts added persuasive testimony: Douglas Pike, in his quasi-official work *The Viet Cong,* identified the real enemy; George Tanham, in his quasi-official work *War Without Guns,* pointed to errors in American aid programs. Foreign experts also contributed: Richard Clutterbuck's *The Long Long War* and Robert Thompson's *Defeating Communist Insurgency* threw considerable, if not always pertinent, light on the Vietnamese challenge as seen by two veterans of the Malayan emergency. The British strategist Alastair Buchan, in the January 1968 issue of *Encounter,* warned that Vietnam was the greatest tragedy that had befallen the U.S.A. since the Civil War. By diminishing American influence, it was giving superb diplomatic advantage to its adversaries while destroying the confidence of its own people in their vision of law and order and international justice. In December, a group of scholars and former Administration officials and officers that included General Ridgway and Roger Hilsman produced a short analysis, the "Bermuda Statement," which urged the Administration to de-escalate the war and start giving it back to the South Vietnamese Government. All this and more caused American citizens to begin questioning the fact of war, and this particularly applied to campuses, to students and teachers, and if emotion sometimes colored the questioning process, it was usually genuine emotion expressed by youngsters who eventually would probably wind up in Vietnam fighting a war for which, more and more, they saw less and less reason.

Johnson and the majority of his advisers either ignored what they regarded as minority voices or, when these spoke too powerfully to be ignored, brushed them aside with considerable petulance that too often questioned the dissenter's loyalty to his country.

Dissent was not to disappear. In late summer, Johnson had sent one of his closest advisers, Clark Clifford, and Maxwell Taylor on a tour of Southeast Asia, an informal attempt to persuade concerned countries to increase troop support of the war. The dominoes that had played such a major role in shaping the American commitment seemed unusually inert. Thailand, South Korea, Australia, and New Zealand showed no interest in increasing minimal contributions (which, in the case of Korea and Thailand, were subsidized by the United States); the Philippines government asked President Johnson to avoid sending the team to Manila, for political reasons! The experience deeply impressed Clifford: " . . . It was strikingly apparent to me that the other troop-contributing countries no longer shared our degree of concern about the war in South Viet Nam." In his later words:

> . . . I returned home puzzled, troubled, concerned. Was it possible that our assessment of the danger to the stability of Southeast Asia and the Western Pacific was exaggerated? Was it possible that those nations which were neighbors of Viet Nam had a clearer perception of the tides of world events in 1967 than we? Was it possible that we were continuing to be guided by judgments that might once have had validity but were now obsolete? In short, although I still counted myself a staunch supporter of our policies, there were nagging, not-to-be-suppressed doubts in my mind.

What portion of these doubts brushed against President Johnson is problematical, but, in late September, at San Antonio, he did offer to halt bombing in the North if Hanoi wished to negotiate (an offer already made privately to Hanoi by Henry Kissinger, acting as presidential agent). Although Clifford and other advisers found this a step in the right direction, their optimism was brief:

> . . . As I listened to the official discussion in Washington, my feelings turned from disappointment to dismay. I found it was being quietly asserted that, in return for a bombing cessation in the North, the North Vietnamese must stop sending men and matériel into South Viet Nam. On the surface, this might have seemed a fair exchange. To me, it was an unfortunate interpretation that— intentionally or not—rendered the San Antonio formula virtually meaningless. The North Vietnamese had more than 100,000 men in the South. It was totally unrealistic to expect them to abandon their men by not replacing casualties, and by failing to provide them with clothing, food, munitions and other supplies. We could never expect them to accept an offer to negotiate on those conditions.[54]

Thus, bombing continued and so did the ground war. In late September, General Westmoreland asked Washington to speed the arrival of promised troops. Worried by reports of a general enemy build-up, Johnson agreed. Once again, McNamara tried to prevent further escalation and in early November sent the President another general analysis of the war. Rejecting increased military actions because of the risks they entailed in widening the war, he wanted Johnson to halt bombing in the North by end of the year, to stabilize operations in the South with no increase in American troop strength, and to reshape the southern effort in order to give the South Vietnamese a larger share of responsibility in fighting the war.

This precipitated a new Administration row. Johnson later wrote that, after careful consideration of the views of various advisers, he decided against the proposal in view of an increasing enemy build-up. The record contradicts the carefully drawn self-portrait of studied calm presented in his memoirs. If his public utterances are to be believed, he ended the year as firmly convinced of a pending American victory as at year's beginning. In discussing the President's performance at one point, the British Prime Minister evoked the image of the czar's court. That was wrong: In 1967, Johnson did not sound so much like Czar Nicholas as he did George III, who, during the American Revolution, forever demanded "total submission" of American colonists.

But even George III could not match Johnson's ideological motivation. The President spoke and wrote at this time and later as if he were St. George bent on destroying the dragon of communism. Whether writing to Senator Jackson to explain resumption of bombing the North, or addressing the Tennessee legislature and announcing "a new team" for South Vietnam, or in introducing David Lilienthal and Robert Komer to discuss their optimistic appraisal of the situation in South Vietnam, or in lengthy news conferences where star performers such as Robert McNamara or William Westmoreland or Ellsworth Bunker confirmed his expressed optimism, or at Guam or Canberra or Cam Ranh Bay—whenever and wherever possible, in discussing the war, the President sounded like Thwackum and Square discussing Tom Jones' frequent aberrations. And if he identified Ho's intransigence without understanding it, he nonetheless made it clear to any who would listen that the transgressor would be punished—no matter the time, no matter the effort, no matter the cost.

CHAPTER SIXTY-EIGHT

1. Institute for Strategic Studies, "The United States," *Strategic Survey, 1967.*
2. Reuters, December 15, 1967. See also, Hoopes: From February 1965 to December 1967, the United States lost, from all causes, in Vietnam some 3,000 aircraft (including helicopters), at a cost of $2.9 billion.
3. Hoopes, 87.
4. Ibid., 81.
5. Wilson.
6. Sheehan et al., 528. See also, Johnson, *The Vantage Point . . .* , 259; Hoopes.
7. Sheehan et al., 567–8. See also, Johnson, *The Vantage Point . . .* : According to Johnson, Westmoreland

> ... pointed out that heavy infiltration and continuing recruitment in the South were making up for battle casualties, but he was hopeful that the 'crossover' point—when losses exceeded the ability to replace those losses—might be reached reasonably soon.

8. Hoopes, 92.
9. Sheehan et al., 530–1.
10. Ibid., 533.
11. Ibid., 573–7.
12. Ibid., 531.
13. Hoopes, 51.
14. Sheehan et al., 534–5.
15. Ibid., 577–85. See also, Johnson, *The Vantage Point* . . .
16. Sheehan et al., 583–4.
17. Ibid., 585.
18. Johnson, *The Vantage Point* . . . , 369:

> ... I rejected the suggestion that we use air power to close the port of Haiphong and knock out part of the dike system in the Red River delta. I felt that there was too grave a risk of Communist Chinese or even Soviet involvement if those measures were carried out, and I wished to avoid the heavy civilian casualties that would accompany destruction of the dikes.

19. Hackworth, 552.
20. Ibid., 708.
21. Ibid., 556–7.
22. Ibid., 555.
23. *Time*, November 17, 1967. See also, Sheehan et al., 525.
24. Hackworth, 542.
25. Ibid., 610. See also, Atkinson, 240–53.
26. Ibid.
27. Schell, 178–9.
28. U.S. Marine Corps, "The Battle for Hills 861 and 881."
29. Shaplen, *The Road from War*, 138.
30. *Time*, October 6, 1967. Perhaps the general forgot about Hiroshima and Nagasaki?
31. Hackworth, 566.
32. *Time*, December 8, 1967.
33. Private information in the author's files.
34. Corson, 216 ff., who offers numerous illustrations of gross incompetence, maladministration, and corruption—all bad enough in their own right as damaging American aid programs—but damage *always* compounded by a high percentage of missing items and supplies ending up in the enemy camp.
35. Lederer, *Our Own Worst Enemy*, 160–2.
36. Kellen.
37. *Time*, October 20, 1967.
38. Kellen.
39. Lederer, *Our Own Worst Enemy*, 97–8, 132, 164–5.
40. Corson, 127.
41. Ibid., 129.
42. Lederer, *Our Own Worst Enemy*, 137 ff.
43. Hoopes, 72–3.
44. Schalk, 9.
45. Ibid., 57.
46. Ibid., 142–3.
47. Ibid., 143.
48. *Newsweek*, January 16, 1967.

49. Schalk, 122.
50. Ibid., 123.
51. *Time,* November 17, 1967.
52. Galbraith, 25–32.
53. McCarthy, 187 ff.
54. Clifford.

CHAPTER 69

The Pueblo fiasco • The Tet offensive • Enemy aims and accomplishments • Defeat or victory? • The Johnson-Westmoreland stand • General Wheeler's report • MACV objectives • Westmoreland demands more troops (IV) • Hawks versus doves • Dean Acheson: " . . . With all due respect, Mr. President, the Joint Chiefs of Staff don't know what they're talking about." • The Clifford Group • Action in the North • The other war • Dissension within America • Johnson's compromise • Westmoreland is relieved • Johnson steps down • Paris peace talks • Saigon's intransigence • The second Tet offensive • Operation Phoenix: pros and cons • Westmoreland's swan song • Creighton Abrams takes command • The 1968 price tag

THE CONFIDENT if not ebullient pose maintained by the Johnson administration was transmitted to Congress and the American people by the President in his annual State of the Union message in mid-January 1968. In this major speech, the President listed what he regarded as major gains in South Vietnam. Although he noted that " . . . the enemy continues to pour men and material across frontiers and into battle, despite his continuous heavy losses," he left little doubt that the situation was under control: " . . . Our patience and our perseverance will match our power. Aggression will never prevail."[1]

The President later wrote, in his memoirs: " . . . Looking back on early 1968, I am convinced I made a mistake by not saying more about Vietnam in my State of the Union report. . . . I did not go into details concerning the build-up of enemy forces or warn of the early major combat I believed was in the offing. . . . "[2]

This would have been well-advised. The first of a series of military disasters had already struck by the time General Westmoreland's comforting report reached the White House in early 1968 (see Chapter 67).

In late January, patrol boats of the North Korean navy attacked and captured an American ship, the USS *Pueblo*. Although the *Pueblo* carried highly sensitive and top-secret electronic gear, with which she was intercepting North Korean communications, she was sailing in international waters, her mission common to both American and Soviet ships. As her captain, Lloyd Bucher, later made clear in his book, neither officers nor crew were fully trained in destruction procedures, and her armament was virtually non-existent; Bucher's messages to higher authorities elicited no response—no planes, nothing.[3]

The Western world was still stunned with this act of piracy and seeming American impotence to contest it, when tragedy reverted sharply to Vietnam. Despite official optimism, MACV and the marines had been worried about a continuing enemy build-up in the South. Since the turn of the year, the enemy had repeatedly struck positions in III and I Corps areas, attacks beaten off only with fighting described by Westmoreland as " . . . the most intense of the entire war."[4] In the first two weeks of 1968, VC units had shelled forty-nine district and provisional capitals, attacking eight of them and twice occupying two within thirty miles of Saigon—activity suspiciously at odds with General Weyand's comfortable claims of superiority made less than a month before (see Chapter 67). During those two weeks, MACV claimed to have killed five thousand enemy, and Westmoreland announced that " . . . the Communists seem to have run temporarily out of steam."[5]

Westmoreland nonetheless was carefully watching Khe Sanh, where the enemy was daily building up attacking forces. The presumed importance of Khe Sanh can be gathered from later official statements. General Walt regarded the place " . . . as the crucial anchor of our defenses along the demilitarized zone."[6] General Wheeler would shortly stress its strategic and tactical importance as the Western anchor of the American defensive line. " . . . To lose it," Wheeler said, "would allow a deep Communist penetration into South Vietnam."[7] General Cushman, probably with Dien Bien Phu in mind, allegedly was not happy about tying up several marine combat battalions in a static defense of a position vulnerable to long-range enemy artillery fire, tactically dominated by heights, some of them enemy-held, and at the fog-shrouded end of a twenty-seven-mile supply line that guerrilla interdiction made dependent solely on air delivery. In any event, Westmoreland expected a major attack against the garrison either before or after the Tet holiday, and, at his instigation, Cushman continued to build up the garrison while other units moved north to bolster defenses in the DMZ area. By month's end, the Khe Sanh garrison comprised four marine infantry battalions, one marine artillery battalion, one ARVN ranger battalion, U. S. Air Force and Seabee detachments. Armament included 105-mm. howitzers, 90-mm.-gun tanks, and 106-mm. recoilless rifles. During the final twelve days of January, the garrison fired thirteen thousand artillery and mortar rounds and was supported by nearly four thousand tactical air missions and 288 B-52 bomber missions.[8] Meanwhile, Westmoreland was said to have moved over half of his combat battalions north.

This was not, however, the tragedy referred to, though it would play a significant part. At the end of January, with allied eyes anxiously watching Khe Sanh, the enemy opened what soon became famous to the world as the Tet offensive—so named because it began during the Tet, or lunar new year, holidays, when a truce had been established and large numbers of South Vietnamese soldiers were on leave. For some days prior to January 31, Viet Cong and North Vietnamese commando squads had infiltrated areas around allied bases and in principal cities and towns, where they were hidden by VC sympathizers. Simultaneously, battalion-size units had worked into the surrounding countryside. Numbering between fifty and sixty thousand, the attack force consisted predominantly of Viet Cong units reinforced by about six thousand PAVN soldiers. Early in the morning of January 31, the commandos attacked key targets in cities and towns while their fellows attacked from without. In addition to Saigon and Hué, the enemy struck thirty principal towns and seventy district towns. The targets included human beings: Special squads sought out and executed military and police officers, civil officials, and their families. In Saigon, a VC commando unit (whose ranks included Vietnamese working for the U.S. government) penetrated American embassy grounds while other units captured the radio station and attacked Joint General Staff Headquarters (where Westmoreland was), near the airport, and naval headquarters near the Saigon River. Extensive damage included some 125 planes and helicopters fully or partially destroyed.

In most places, heavy fighting lasted a week or two. As perhaps foreseen by the enemy, ARVN and American counterattacks caused tremendous damage; in Hué, where the enemy held out almost to the end of February, allied counterattacks destroyed perhaps half the city and inevitably added to civilian casualties. About four thousand American and South Vietnamese troops lost their lives, and some twelve thousand were wounded. Thousands of civilians were killed or wounded and thousands more made homeless. Continuing rocket and mortar attacks from surrounding countryside added to general carnage. But the enemy did not escape unscathed; according to government figures, thirty-six thousand Communists were killed by February 18, a figure that probably included large numbers of non-Communists.[9]

The psychological effect could not have been greater. Many readers will remember the force of surprise and shock that hammered America—the futility that one felt upon seeing blood-spattered bodies, friendly and enemy, in the American embassy compound, or the famous black-and-white photograph of General Loan about to shoot a manacled VC officer through the head, or the statement made by an unwitting American army major to the Australian correspondent Peter Arnett as the two looked over the smoking ruins of Ben Tre: " . . . The city had to be destroyed in order to save it." The sum formed an overdraft on the meager balance of credibility maintained by the Johnson administration, " . . . seriously damaging," as an Institute of Strategic Studies bulletin later noted, "the reputation of those analysts who had concluded that the ability of the enemy to organize military action on a national or regional scale had been eliminated during 1967."[10] The Tet attacks brought home to the American people that, despite official optimism, the war was likely to continue *ad nauseam.* As surely foreseen by Hanoi, they added a particularly volatile fuel to the already blazing row within top echelons of the Johnson administration. Perhaps the main accomplishment of the Tet offensive, from the enemy standpoint, was to finally polarize existent but theretofore divergent opposition to Administration policy in Vietnam.

Johnson, the JCS, Sharp, Westmoreland, and other hawks at once adopted a simplistic stand on the attacks. At a news conference in early February, the President told correspondents:

> . . . We have known for several months, now, that the Communists planned a massive winter-spring offensive. We have detailed information on Ho Chi Minh's order governing that offensive. Part of it is called a general uprising.
>
> We know the object was to overthrow the constitutional government in Saigon and to create a situation in which we and the Vietnamese would be willing to accept the Communist-dominated coalition government.
>
> Another part of that offensive was planned as a massive attack across the frontiers of South Vietnam by North Vietnamese units. We have already seen the general uprising.

After emphasizing maximum enemy and minimum American casualties, the President announced that " . . . the biggest fact is that the stated purposes of the general uprising have failed." However, he warned,

> . . . we may at this very moment be on the eve of a major enemy offensive in the area of Khe Sanh and generally around the Demilitarized Zone.

The enemy's second objective, Johnson explained, was to attain a psychological victory, and he was trying to prevent that from being achieved. In this lengthy conference, he implied that nothing of the situation was surprising and that matters were firmly under control; as for further deployment of U.S. troops: " . . . There is not anything in any of the developments that would justify the press in leaving the impression that any great new overall moves are going to be made that would involve substantial movements in that direction."[11]

The salve of this business-as-usual approach comforted almost no one, and the President probably would have been wiser to share some of his apprehensions with the American people. If his later writings are to be believed, these must have been considerable:

> . . . This is not to imply that Tet was not a shock, in one degree or another, to all of us. We knew that a show of strength was coming; it was more massive than we had anticipated. We knew that the Communists were aiming at a number of population centers; we did not expect them to attack as many as they did. We knew that the North Vietnamese and the Viet Cong were trying to achieve better co-ordination of their country-wide moves; we did not believe they would be able to carry out the level of co-ordination they demonstrated. We expected a large force to attack; it was larger than we had estimated. Finally, it was difficult to believe that the Communists would so profane their own people's sacred holiday.[12]

In Saigon, Westmoreland went Johnson one better. The American commander's ebullience reminds one of Lord Cornwallis insisting that the battle of Guilford Courthouse (see Chapter 6) was a "victory"—a victory, perhaps, responded the *Annual Register*'s scribe, but a victory " . . . productive of all the consequences of defeat." In reviewing dispatches of the time, one would suppose that the American general had himself planned the Tet offensive. On February 2, he told newsmen that there was evidence to suggest that the enemy " . . . is about to run out of steam."[13] Westmoreland interpreted the attacks as designed to drive American troops from Khe Sanh, which was the enemy's real objective: The Communist attacks, he told newsmen, were prelude to a "go-for-broke" attack on Khe Sanh and the two northern provinces.[14] This plan would fail, as had the rest of the enemy plan—by February 6, Westmoreland believed that enemy losses, which he put at 21,330 dead, " . . . may measurably shorten the war."[15] Westmoreland, in short, viewed the attacks as a desperate move of a dying enemy: He went so far as to tell a disbelieving André Beaufre " . . . that he compared this decision [of Giap's] with that of Hitler on the eve of the Ardennes offensive in the autumn of 1944, that is to say a decision of despair by an enemy at his wit's end."[16]

* * *

The plot now thickens, the record suggesting something like the following. Early in the Tet offensive the President asked Westmoreland how he could help him—a reasonable and sympathetic request. On February 3, Wheeler allegedly cabled Westmoreland: " . . . The President asks me if there is any reinforcement or help that we can give you." On February 8, having received no reply [!] from Westmoreland, Wheeler cabled:

> . . . Query: Do you need reinforcement? Our capabilities are limited. We can provide 82d Airborne Division and about one-half a Marine Corps division, both loaded with Vietnam veterans. However, if you consider reinforcements imperative, you should not be bound by earlier agreements [i.e., a troop limit of 525,000]. United States Government is not prepared to accept defeat in Vietnam. In summary, if you need more troops, ask for them.

Westmoreland immediately requested the units named by Wheeler and also asked " . . . that the President authorize an amphibious assault by the marines into North Vietnam as a diversionary move." A day later, he outlined his need for additional troops to contain the enemy's "major campaign" in the north and " . . . to go on the offensive as soon as his attack is spent," to otherwise carry out previous campaign plans, to bolster a weakened ARVN, and " . . . to take advantage of the enemy's weakened posture by taking the offensive against him."[17] According to the President, Westmoreland

> . . . saw the situation as one of heightened risk but of great opportunity as well.
> "I do not see how the enemy can long sustain the heavy losses which his new strategy is enabling us to inflict on him," he reported. "Therefore, adequate reinforcements should permit me not only to contain his I Corps offensive but also to capitalize on his losses by seizing the initiative in other areas." He believed that exploiting the opportunity "could materially shorten the war."[18]

When Westmoreland requested early delivery of troops, the JCS pointed out that such a deployment would compromise the strategic reserve and should be deferred—a tactic allegedly designed to cause Johnson to call up the reserves, a major step in full-scale mobilization, which had so long been desired by the JCS. According to Johnson, debate centered on sending Westmoreland six maneuver battalions, or about ten thousand men, and all agreed to do this while holding off on the subject of a reserve call-up. The JCS also requested presidential authority to bomb closer to the centers of Hanoi and Haiphong—a request opposed by McNamara and by Paul Warnke, who had replaced John McNaughton, and one finally turned down by the President.

Johnson now sent Wheeler to Saigon, from where he reported that " . . . the current situation in Vietnam is still developing and fraught with opportunities as well as dangers." The enemy offensive had hurt ARVN more psychologically than physically. Nonetheless, two to three months were needed to recover equipment losses; three to six months to regain pre-Tet strength. The worst damage occurred to the Rural Development Program; in many areas, the VC now openly controlled the countryside. In order to put things right, Westmoreland wanted a " . . . 3 division-15 tactical fighter squadron force"—a whopping levy of over two hundred thousand more troops to be deployed by end of 1968.[19] Responsible commanders, Wheeler reported, regarded 1968 as "the pivotal year" and warned that, without the troop increase, " . . . we might have to give up territory, probably the two northern-most provinces of South Vietnam. . . . " The troop increase requested by Westmoreland and the JCS placed the President in an extremely awkward position. Hawk that he was, he was also politician, and he was naturally upset at the national furor generated by the Tet offensive. In his later words,

> . . . I did not expect the enemy effort to have the impact on American thinking that it achieved. I was not surprised that elements of the press, the academic community, and the Congress reacted as they did. I was surprised and disappointed that the enemy's efforts produced such a dismal effect on various people inside government and others outside whom I had always regarded as staunch and unflappable. Hanoi must have been delighted; it was exactly the reaction they sought.[20]

It was also a reaction justified in large part by specific facts. Hanson Baldwin, parroting the official line, may have concluded in an article in the March *Reader's Digest* that " . . . the enemy can no longer find security in his South Vietnamese sanctuaries,"[21] but the enemy seemed to be doing pretty well without security. Astute advisers also questioned Westmoreland and the JCS's interpretation of the attacks as a desperation move on the part of the NLF-PRP-VC and Hanoi. Costly though the attacks proved to the enemy, the NLF still disposed of over sixty thousand hard-core guerrillas, augmented by twice that many active supporters and by some sixty thousand more PAVN troops, with impressive reserves untouched in North Vietnam (not to mention China, which, as James Reston once noted, was down to her last 700 million men). Advisers such as Clark Clifford questioned the magic number of 205,000, where perhaps a half million to a million men would be required. Advisers such as Philip Habib pointed to divided opinions in the Saigon mission as to the wisdom of sending *any* large reinforcement as opposed to insisting on the South Vietnamese doing the job.[22] Subordinate but influential voices added to the general protest. Townsend Hoopes later wrote:

> ... In the Pentagon, the Tet offensive performed the curious service of fully revealing the doubters and dissenters to each other, as in a lightning flash. Nitze suddenly spoke out on "the unsoundness of continuing to reinforce weakness," and wrote a paper that argued that our policy in Vietnam had to be placed in the context of other U.S. commitments in the world. Warnke thought Tet showed that our military strategy was "foolish to the point of insanity." Alain Enthoven ... confided that, "I fell off the boat when the troop level reached 170,000" ... and other influential civilians expressed their strong belief that the Administration's Vietnam policy was at a dead end.
>
> One thing was clear to us all: The Tet offensive was the eloquent counterpoint to the effusive optimism of November. It showed conclusively that the U.S. did not in fact control the situation. ... [23]

Johnson was so insulated by Rostow from dissident opinions that it is doubtful if these attitudes reached him. Nonetheless, he remained keenly aware of the national mood, and he was also brought abruptly to heel by a senior adviser, Dean Acheson. Acheson had no love for Johnson and did not eagerly accept his summons to the White House in late February. Townsend Hoopes later described the meeting:

> ... When the President asked him his opinion of the current situation in Vietnam, Acheson replied he wasn't sure he had a useful view because he was finding it impossible, on the basis of occasional official briefings given him, to discover what was really happening. He had lost faith in the objectivity of the briefers: "With all due respect, Mr. President, the Joint Chiefs of Staff don't know what they're talking about." The President said that was a shocking statement. Acheson replied that, if such it was, then perhaps the President ought to be shocked.[24]

The sum of these factors persuaded the President to two important moves. He asked Acheson to make an independent study, drawing on expert testimony at subordinate levels of government; and he ordered his new Secretary of Defense, Clark Clifford, to convene his most responsible officials to study the Westmoreland-JCS request, indeed to appraise fully the situation in Vietnam.

Sixty-two years old, Clark Clifford had recently replaced the disillusioned McNamara. A well-known Washington attorney, a close friend of the President and loyal supporter of Johnson's Vietnam policy, he had served for years as a confidential adviser. The previous summer, as we have related, he had undertaken a presidential mission to persuade Asian countries to increase troop support in Vietnam, an unsuccessful effort that caused him to entertain certain doubts concerning the war.

What became known as the Clifford Group included Secretary of State Dean Rusk, Secretary of the Treasury Henry Fowler, Under Secretary of State Nicholas Katzenbach, Deputy Secretary of Defense Paul Nitze, General Wheeler, CIA director Richard Helms, presidential assistants Walt Rostow and Maxwell Taylor, and numerous other ranking officials. Subsequent meetings predictably accentuated the current rift between hawks and doves. General Maxwell Taylor presented the prevailing JCS view in a memorandum both to the group and directly to President Johnson:

> ... We should consider changing the objective which we have been pursuing consistently since 1954 [!] only for the most cogent reasons. There is clearly nothing to recommend trying to do more than we are now doing at such great cost. To undertake to do less is to accept needlessly a serious defeat for which we would pay dearly in terms of our worldwide position of leadership, of the political stability of Southeast Asia and of the credibility of our pledges to friends and allies.[25]

Doves did not agree. Prompted by CIA reports, most civilian members of the group apparently argued that any substantial increase of American forces could be easily offset by North Vietnamese troops. Dr. Alain Enthoven typified the realistic pessimism of the doves:

> ... While we have raised the price to NVN [North Vietnam] of aggression and support of the VC [Viet Cong], it shows no lack of capability or will to match each new U.S. escalation. Our strategy of "attrition" has not worked. Adding 206,000 more U.S. men to a force of 525,000, gaining only 27 additional maneuver battalions and 270 tactical fighters at an added cost to the U.S. of $10-billion per year raises the question of who is making it costly for whom. ... We know that despite a massive influx of 500,000 U.S. troops, 1.2 million tons of bombs a year, 400,000 attack sorties per year, 200,000 enemy K.I.A. [killed in action] in three years, 20,000 U.S. K.I.A., etc., our control of the countryside and the defense of the urban areas is now essentially at pre-August 1965 levels. We have achieved stalemate at a high commitment. A new strategy must be sought.[26]

Enthoven and other experts argued that Westmoreland should call off search-and-destroy attrition strategy in favor of protecting population centers while the South Vietnamese Government and armed forces developed effective capability—which was more or less what General James Gavin had recommended in 1965.

Nothing better illustrates the abject poverty of Administration thinking than Clifford's later account of these high-level meetings:

> ... In the colloquial style of those meetings, here are some of the principal issues raised and some of the answers as I understood them:
>
> "Will 200,000 more men do the job?" I found no assurance that they would.
>
> "If not, how many more might be needed—and when?" There was no way of knowing.
>
> "What would be involved in committing 200,000 more men to Viet Nam?" A reserve call-up of approximately 280,000, an increased draft call and an extension of tours of duty of most men then in service.
>
> "Can the enemy respond with a build-up of his own?" He could and he probably would.
>
> "What are the estimated costs of the latest requests?" First calculations were on the order of $2 billion for the remaining four months of that fiscal year, and an increase of $10 to $12 billion for the year beginning July 1, 1968.
>
> "What will be the impact on the economy?" So great that we would face the possibility of credit restrictions, a tax increase and even wage and price controls. The balance of payments would be worsened by at least half a billion dollars a year.
>
> "Can bombing stop the war?" Never by itself. It was inflicting heavy personnel and matériel losses, but bombing by itself would not stop the war.
>
> "Will stepping up the bombing decrease American casualties?" Very little, if at all. Our casualties were due to the intensity of the ground fighting in the South. We had already dropped a heavier tonnage of bombs than in all the theaters of World War II. During 1967, an estimated 90,000 North Vietnamese had infiltrated into South Viet Nam. In the opening weeks of 1968, infiltrators were coming in at three to four times the rate of a year earlier, despite the ferocity and intensity of our campaign of aerial interdiction.
>
> "How long must we keep on sending our men and carrying the main burden of combat?" The South Vietnamese were doing better, but they were not ready yet to replace our troops and we did not know when they would be.

When Clifford asked for a military plan, he was told that no plan for victory existed " . . . in the historic American sense" due to presidential limitations that prohibited invading North Vietnam, pursuing into Laos and Cambodia, and mining Haiphong Harbor. Clifford now asked:

. . . "Given these circumstances, how can we win?" We would, I was told, continue to evidence our superiority over the enemy; we would continue to attack in the belief that he would reach the stage where he would find it inadvisable to go on with the war. He could not afford the attrition we were inflicting on him. And we were improving our posture all the time.

I then asked, "What is the best estimate as to how long this course of action will take? Six months? One year? Two years?" There was no agreement on an answer. Not only was there no agreement, I could find no one willing to express any confidence in his guesses. . . .

A disturbed man now asked a disturbed question:

. . . "Does anyone see any diminution in the will of the enemy after four years of our having been there, after enormous casualties and after massive destruction from our bombing?"

The answer was that there appeared to be no diminution in the will of the enemy. . . .

The total experience was salutary if dismal. It had reinforced Clifford's earlier doubts:

. . . I was convinced that the military course we were pursuing was not only endless, but hopeless. A further substantial increase in American forces could only increase the devastation and the Americanization of the war, and thus leave us even further from our goal of a peace that would permit the people of South Viet Nam to fashion their own political and economic institutions. Henceforth, I was also convinced, our primary goal should be to level off our involvement, and to work toward gradual disengagement.[27]

The Clifford report attempted to resolve the contretemps by compromise. Although Clifford later wrote that he favored a reversal of strategy, the hawks proved sufficiently strong to prevent this recommendation. The final document did not question present strategy except by indirection, in that it recommended limiting troop reinforcement to a maximum twenty-two thousand. It did not recommend a new peace initiative or a proposed cutback in the bombing of the North.[28]

Clifford's group paid considerable attention to the air question. The JCS submitted three general plans for consideration: an increase in bombing, including expansion of targets around Hanoi and Haiphong to include railroad equipment in the Chinese buffer zone and the dike system that supported the North's agriculture, and mining Haiphong Harbor; a shift in bombing away from the Hanoi-Haiphong area in favor of striking roads and supply trails in the southern part of North

Vietnam, including the Laotian Panhandle; an interdiction campaign in the South " . . . designed to substitute tactical airpower for a large portion of the search-and-destroy operations currently conducted by ground forces, thus permitting the ground troops to concentrate on a perimeter defense of the heavily populated areas." Wheeler, Taylor, and Rostow wanted the first course of action; other principals held for the second and third.

Since the report left matters largely as they were, it pleased no one. One of the President's objections to the document centered on its negative approach to negotiations. The CIA had reported to the Clifford group that if the United States were to call off bombing of the North, " . . . Hanoi would probably respond to an offer to negotiate, although the intelligence agency warned that the North Vietnamese would not modify their terms for a final settlement or stop fighting in the South."[29] In discussing the possibility of renewed negotiations, Secretary of State Dean Rusk suggested a bombing halt in the North during the rainy season except in battle zone areas. His suggestion continued the argument already being waged within Administration circles, one that would intensify during the rest of March.

The Clifford report kicked off what proved to be an exciting, exasperating, and crucial month in American affairs. The military situation was by no means as favorable in Vietnam as Westmoreland was reporting. Although enemy attacks had been beaten back, enemy units surrounding towns and cities continued to strike and interdict road communications while rebuilding bases in the countryside. At Khe Sanh the marine-ARVN garrison continued to withstand severe buffeting while the greatest aerial bombing effort in history pounded the besiegers. The situation worried Westmoreland to the extent that he considered using "a few small tactical nuclear weapons" or possibly chemical agents.[30]

Westmoreland's preoccupation with Khe Sanh did not lessen the real and devastating importance of the other war. In contrast to claims advanced by MACV and Washington, Robert Shaplen offered an eyewitness account of the scene:

> . . . Since the Tet attack, the Communists have maintained their countrywide harassment of cities, airfields, and various Allied installations, primarily with rocket and mortar fire. They have made occasional fresh ground assaults against about a dozen cities, mostly in the Delta, and particularly on March 3rd and 4th, when it seemed that a second wave of the offensive might be beginning. They have recruited as many as thirty thousand new troops, ranging in age from fifteen to forty. Most of the recruiting has been

done in the Delta, where the Communists moved in to fill the vacuum in the countryside following the withdrawal of American and government troops to positions of defense around the cities and the towns. Hanoi has continued to infiltrate troops both to reinforce the North Vietnamese forces now totalling a hundred and twelve thousand men in South Vietnam (five more North Vietnamese divisions are said to be alerted to move south) and to build up the main-force Vietcong units that suffered the heaviest losses during Tet. . . .

The attacks had not only badly hurt ARVN and halted the pacification program, but had further splintered the Saigon government, widening the dangerous rift between Thieu and Ky. Once the emergency had passed, a sense of shock set in. Shaplen noted

> . . . a continuing erosion of morale and a growing sense of foreboding. Vietnamese I have known for many years are as frank as they are sad these days in their prognoses; they sound more and more like men who know they are suffering from an incurable malady.[31]

Pessimism so prevalent in Saigon found ample voice throughout the United States. At the end of February 1968, George Kennan told a Newark audience that we " . . . have pushed stubbornly and heedlessly ahead, like men in a dream, seemingly insensitive to outside opinion, seemingly unable to arrive at any realistic assessment of the effects of [our] acts."[32] Large numbers of influential Americans, including leading business executives, agreed. Throughout the country, campus demonstrations, draft-card burnings, and civic protestations were becoming the order of the day. Norman Mailer's incendiary *Armies of the Night* further heated already hot tempers. Congress was becoming increasingly rebellious. The Senate Foreign Relations Committee opened televised hearings on the Foreign Aid Bill and called Dean Rusk before it. Almost at once, the hearings became a debate on Vietnam. For almost two days, a beleaguered Rusk fielded generally hostile questions with what many persons believed were less than candid answers—altogether a performance that further fueled nationwide fires of dissent.

The pressure was telling on the President. The veteran British correspondent Henry Brandon later wrote:

> . . . Anyone who had the opportunity of seeing President Johnson around March 11, 1968, in person and in private, was taken aback by the near-exhaustion that had overcome him. He was a man in torment as I had never seen one before. His face was ashen, his eyes sunken, his skin flabby, and yet, underneath, his expression was taut.[33]

The President was to find little relief ahead. Almost no one agreed with anyone else. Ambassador Bunker, although a hawk who agreed with the necessity of supplying Westmoreland with more troops, wanted a limit of seven battalions, since he felt that more men would dissuade the South Vietnamese from putting their own army right. Rusk and Clifford pointed to a practical difficulty: The United States could not supply an additional half million men with weapons and at the same time furnish modern arms to an expanding ARVN. Civilian dissension was also increasing: Paul Nitze, Clifford's deputy, allegedly asked to be excused from appearing before the Senate committee to defend Administration policy in Vietnam. Then came Eugene McCarthy's near victory in the New Hampshire primary elections—McCarthy was a dove and outspoken critic of Johnson's Vietnam policy. A few days later the President received another unpleasant surprise in the form of Dean Acheson, who had been conferring with numerous officials on the Vietnam question. At a private luncheon,

> ... Acheson told the President he was being led down a garden path by the JCS, that what Westmoreland was attempting in Vietnam was simply not possible—without the application of totally unlimited resources "and maybe five years." He told the President that his recent speeches were quite unrealistic and believed by no one, either at home or abroad. He added the judgment that the country was no longer supporting the war. . . . [34]

The following day, the President's real political nemesis, Robert Kennedy, announced his candidacy for the Democratic nomination.

It was all too much for tired old Johnson. After a final show of truculence, he accepted facts and acted accordingly. In late March, he announced Westmoreland's imminent relief. He also convened a senior advisory group of prominent civil and military officials, past and present, including Dean Acheson, George Ball, Arthur Dean, Henry Cabot Lodge, McGeorge Bundy, and Matthew Ridgway. Meeting for two days in late March, this group, known as the Wise Men, heard a special briefing delivered by an interdepartmental executive team that included the army's Major General William DePuy, the State Department's Philip Habib, and CIA's George Carver. Although opinions differed in detail, only three of fourteen members agreed with Administration policy; seven, including former hawk McGeorge Bundy, argued for a basic change; four expressed grave doubts. Johnson's reaction to this new dissension, particularly on the part of McGeorge Bundy, brings to mind Mrs. Western's furious words to her brother, the squire: " . . . Thou art one of those wise men whose nonsensical principles have undone the nation; by weakening the hands of our Government at home, and by discouraging our friends, and encouraging our enemies abroad." Johnson was allegedly so upset that he insisted on hearing the same briefing, which he later said contained information that he had been receiving all along.[35]

Johnson now decided to send only a token troop reinforcement to South Vietnam, although he did ask Congress for an additional $4 billion defense appropriation. He also announced that the American Government would concentrate on building up ARVN (a task begun thirteen years earlier!) so that it could relieve American forces of major combat tasks. Finally and more important, he summarily halted bombing of North Vietnam beyond the 20th parallel. At the same time, he asked Hanoi to begin talks that would lead to peace, and he attempted to underline his sincerity by withdrawing from coming presidential elections.

In this dramatic speech, President Johnson offered to meet the enemy "anywhere." When Hanoi responded favorably, American officials rejected one place after another, to settle finally on Paris, where peace talks opened officially on May 13. Meanwhile renewed fighting in Vietnam flared in the background like an ancient omen of evil, and while American and North Vietnamese delegations argued about protocol— who would sit where—many thousands of human beings bled and died. Once again, ARVN and allied forces pushed from beleaguered cities and towns to try to reclaim the countryside from the VC or at least open communications between cities. Once again, MACV announced "successful" offensives with such improbable code names as "Complete Victory"; once again, MACV stressed enormous enemy losses: fifteen thousand dead at Khe Sanh alone; seventy-one thousand dead since Tet began. And once again, in early May, the enemy launched another, a second Tet offensive, that undeniably hurt the South, psychologically, by again demonstrating a strength he wasn't supposed to have, physically, by causing more casualties and destruction. The total carnage was ghastly: The two offensives resulted " . . . in 13,000 civilians killed, 27,000 wounded, 170,000 homes destroyed or damaged; and created 1,000,000 refugees with property damage estimated at $173,500,000."[36] American and allied casualties shot upward and would continue to rise.

Westmoreland, about to leave for the United States, claimed that the offensives had hurt the enemy worse than he admitted. He pointed to some impressive facts: Nowhere had the enemy succeeded in realizing military objectives. Having failed to take Khe Sanh, in early April he had lifted the siege and stolen away—at a cost of an estimated ten to fifteen thousand dead (an action we shall discuss later). Elsewhere he was neutralized by American "spoiling" tactics, which were effectively keeping him off balance. Although damage done by the Tet offensives was great, the Saigon government and country had survived. Meanwhile, pacification operations slowly revived, as did Operation Phoenix, a long-overdue effort to identify, infiltrate, and destroy Communist political networks in the south.[37]

The Phoenix program, which has been condemned as an "instrument of civilian terror," is still a subject of considerable controversy among historians. It was basically a CIA concept, in theory an excellent one in that it was designed to eliminate the Viet Cong infrastructure (including "the man with the knife") that infested villages to hold back or even prevent the pacification process. This was the job of CIA-supported Provisional Reconnaissance Units (PRUs),[38] altogether about 4,500 South Vietnamese "advised" by several hundred Americans who infiltrated target villages to smoke out the VC infrastructure, be it "the man with the knife," be it the men, women, and youths who secretly supplied the VC with food and information. In 1968, over thirteen thousand persons were handed over to the authorities, thousands more were interrogated and released. Frequent assassinations of suspected VC were carried out, although the defenders of the program insist that these were "killings" resulting from shootouts with security forces. During the next few years

> . . . the program assertedly accounted for about seventeen thousand members of the Viet Cong infrastructure who had been amnestied, twenty thousand who had been killed, and twenty-eight thousand who had been captured and, in the majority of cases, sentenced to imprisonment.[39]

Critics of the program point to its promiscuous, corrupt, and cruel character, not to mention its general ineffectiveness.

> . . . Despite all the intelligence effort devoted to the program, only about two percent of those claimed as having been eliminated from the infrastructure had been specifically targeted: The names and whereabouts of the vast majority of its personnel were not known. Indeed, nine out of ten of those killed, many of them in the course of military operations, were killed anonymously, and only later identified—or misidentified—as members of the infrastructure.[40]

Such was the corruption in the South Vietnamese security forces that one critic claimed that "70 percent of the Vietcong suspects captured bought back their freedom."[41] As had happened in earlier fighting, such was the pressure to kill that any civilian victim of a shootout was automatically listed as a VC. Village officials

> . . . also rounded up innocent peasants in order to inflate police blotters, then spared those who could pay them off, and they fre-

quently tortured villagers on no more evidence than the accusation of jealous neighbors.[42]

Undoubtedly to his surprise, the writer of those words, Stanley Karnow, years later heard top officials confirm the damage done to the Communists by Phoenix. "We never feared a division of troops," a veteran VC leader told him, "but the infiltration of a couple of guys in our ranks created tremendous difficulties for us." A senior officer complained of "the loss of thousands of our cadres"; another called it "extremely destructive"; still another said that it "wiped out many of our bases" in South Vietnam, forcing army and Viet Cong troops to take sanctuary in Cambodia.[43]

This perhaps is true but it is also true that in many areas VC operations continued. Had the program been a part of a genuine pacification program from the beginning, there might well have been a more satisfactory result. By the time it got going, the VC had won a large and dedicated following that it was impossible to eradicate:

> . . . at the village level the infrastructure was highly decentralized and could operate autonomously, regardless of what happened to cadres of the vertically organized command structure.[44]

General Creighton Abrams, Westmoreland's deputy who for over a year had been trying to reshape ARVN also reported considerable progress. Asked by the President to compare the South Vietnamese effort with the earlier Korean effort, Abrams replied, "I would say the Vietnamese are doing as well, if not better, than the Koreans."[45] In April, General Westmoreland personally reported to the President that "militarily, we have never been in a better relative position in South Vietnam."[46]

Westmoreland continued to display the optimism so admired by the President. Shortly before his return to the United States to take up the post of army chief of staff—surely the most extraordinary appointment since King James I knighted a piece of beef—he launched into a vigorous defense of his generalship. Dismissing enclave strategy as "defeatist," and "oil-spot" strategy as impractical in view of a limited number of troops [!], Westmoreland told reporters:

> Our strategy in Viet Nam is most definitely not a search-and-destroy strategy, and it is unfortunate that it has been so characterized by some. Search and destroy is merely an abbreviated version of a time-honored infantry mission: "Find, fix, fight and destroy the enemy." It is not a strategy or a tactic; it is a mission. . . .

The general repeated what he had told the President: "The allies are in the strongest relative military position in Viet Nam today that we have yet achieved."[47]

At this point, a good many Americans refused to take Westmoreland or his pronouncements seriously. Not only Westmoreland but Pentagon "spokesmen" had become a supreme embarrassment to the Democratic Party and its leading candidate Hubert Humphrey. Unable to dissociate himself from Vietnam policy, Humphrey attempted to chart a cunning course that elevated Vietnam tactical issues to world strategic issues, where he could say more without almost automatically being contradicted by unpalatable fact. The leading Republican contender, Richard Nixon, on the other hand, blasted American policy in Vietnam and spoke mysteriously of a "new plan" to end the American involvement and regain American "superiority" in strategic matters.

While political debate claimed the American scene in summer and autumn of 1968, fighting continued sporadically in Vietnam, with Saigon frequently under rocket bombardment and VC/PAVN troops showing little hesitation in attacking where and when they wished. Although the enemy was hurting and infiltration from the North had slowed, it nonetheless continued at an estimated ten thousand men per month, a figure that allegedly, on occasion, approached thirty thousand.[48] In the country, some hope appeared in a fundamental tactical change reportedly made by Westmoreland's successor, fifty-three-year-old Creighton Abrams, a West Pointer (1936) and World War II tank commander. As later reported in *Time:*

> ... Abrams has found that forays by sub-battalion-size units—companies, platoons, even squads—can be mounted more quickly, more often and in more places [than battalion and brigade actions]. Such surprise sweeps also achieve better results. Thus the general's sting-ray tactics, designed to interdict the movement of North Vietnamese units and supplies, involve the same number of men but hundreds and sometimes thousands more of what Abrams prefers to call "initiatives" rather than "offensives." As Abrams explained it ... " ... all our operations have been designed to get into the enemy's system. Once you start working in the system that he requires to prepare his offensive operations, you can cause him to postpone his operations or to reduce their intensity or length."[49]

This was a diluted version of Sting Ray tactics, which the Marine Corps and a few army units had been using for over two years in an overdue effort to respect Roger Hilsman's dictum of fighting guerrillas with guerrillas—a qualitative approach calling for small, highly trained patrols experienced in guerrilla tactics, as opposed to a quantitative approach, yet one that still tied units to artillery protection. Unfortunately, what Abrams ordered and what army and marine unit commanders did were frequently two different things. So wedded were some commanders to search-and-destroy tactics that they sabotaged the new directives in favor of the old.[50] Elsewhere, the tactical environment defeated them. In early July, Abrams abandoned the Khe Sanh position (a sensible move that nonetheless further bewildered an already bewildered American public, who, thanks to Westmoreland and Walt, regarded it as of Verdun-like importance). But other fire bases remained, and so did the problem of keeping open communications.

Nor did Hanoi appear in any hurry to sit down at the Paris conference table and hammer out the longed-for peace. In retaliation for Hanoi's refusal to admit the Saigon government to the talks, as well as to stop fighting in the South, Johnson authorized resumption of limited bombing in the North:

> . . . I said [to Abrams] that we had reached the crucial stage of both military and diplomatic operations. We would never achieve the kind of peace we wanted unless the enemy was kept on the run, unless he realized he could never win on the field of battle. I instructed Abrams to use his resources and manpower in a maximum effort to achieve that goal and to inspire the South Vietnamese army to do the same.[51]

Matters were still at a standstill when the two presidents met in Honolulu in mid-July. Prior to the meeting, Secretary of Defense Clifford flew in from Saigon. The Secretary was

> . . . oppressed by the pervasive Americanization of the war: we were still giving the military instructions, still doing most of the fighting, still providing all the matériel, still paying most of the bills. Worst of all, I concluded that the South Vietnamese leaders seemed content to have it that way.[52]

Johnson described President Thieu as " . . . more confident than I had ever seen him." Thieu spoke of the splendid job of reorganizing ARVN and privately told Johnson that the United States would be able to start withdrawing forces in mid-1969, perhaps sooner.[53]

Johnson's honeymoon with Thieu was short-lived. In October, the North Vietnamese delegation in Paris quietly signaled that they would admit Saigon to the talks in return for a bombing halt. Johnson and his advisers, including the JCS, went along with this. Thieu refused to send a delegation, and was persuaded to do so only with considerable difficulty and delay—an attitude that reinforced Clifford's belief that " . . . the goal of the Saigon government and the goal of the United States were no longer one and the same, if indeed they ever had been. . . . "[54] Johnson later wrote, " . . . It was one of those rare occasions, in my years of dealing with them, that I felt Thieu, Ky, and their advisers had let me down. More important, I felt that their action put in peril everything both governments had worked so long and sacrificed so much to achieve. . . . "[55] The President scarcely veiled his annoyance in a major speech at the end of October, when he announced a total bombing halt of the North and implied that South Vietnam would henceforth take over a larger share of the fighting.[56]

As American voters went to the polls to elect Richard Nixon the thirty-seventh President of the nation, American and North Vietnamese officials in Paris continued to argue over the shape of the conference table, a momentous issue still unsettled by year's end.

Whatever the results in Paris, the United States would not rejoice. At the end of 1968, a tally offered by a responsible organization read as follows:

> From 1961 to 1967, 16,022 American troops had been killed in action in Vietnam. 14,592 more were killed during 1968. When deaths from accident and disease were added, 35,724 Americans had lost their lives in Vietnam since 1961. Communist casualties were far greater still: the United States claimed over 191,000 of the enemy killed during 1968 alone. In all, the war had caused more than half a million deaths in South Vietnam within eight years. Even the high Communist casualties had cost the United States dearly. Allied forces used conventional munitions in Vietnam during 1968 at a rate of nearly $14 million a day. The value of equipment destroyed was hardly less remarkable. Since 1961, combat action had claimed 919 American aircraft and 10 helicopters over North Vietnam, together with 327 aircraft and 972 helicopters over South Vietnam, 1,247 aircraft and 1,293 helicopters had been destroyed on the ground or in accidents. The cost of this attrition of aircraft alone was at least $4,800 million [$4.8 billion]. Figures for the complete cost of the war to the United States were incalculable, but $27,000 million [$27 billion] was a reasonable estimate for 1968.[57]

These figures, which are conservative, represented only part of the price paid. The direct result of escalation and attrition strategy, they did not include the cost of a nation torn, with no visible means of immediately repairing the damage, and at a peculiar historical time of particular stress from within and without. The human and material costs, however, emphasized the poverty of a strategy founded on ignorance and executed in arrogance, a strategy whose failure drove a

President from the White House—a defeated man, " . . . unwept, un-honored and unsung."

CHAPTER SIXTY-NINE

1. Johnson, *Public Papers of* . . . , 1968, Book I, 25.
2. Johnson, *The Vantage Point* . . . , 380. Johnson here characteristically attempted to shift blame to the press corps: " . . . I relied instead on the 'background' briefings that my advisers and I, as well as the State and Defense departments, had provided members of the press corps for many weeks. In those briefings we had stressed that heavy action could be expected soon." See also, Westmoreland, 321: " . . . In retrospect, I believe that I and officials in Washington should have tried to do more to alert the American public to the coming of a major offensive. . . . "
3. Bucher. See also, Gallery. Although the North Koreans released the crew eleven months later, they kept the ship and her secrets.
4. *Time*, January 19, 1968.
5. Ibid., January 26, 1968.
6. Walt, "The Nature of the War in Vietnam."
7. UPI, Washington, February 5, 1968.
8. U.S. Marine Corps, "Khe Sanh Wrap-Up."
9. Shaplen, *The Road from War*, 192, 212–13. See also, Karnow, 523–66, for a comprehensive account of this action.
10. Institute for Strategic Studies, "The United States," *Strategic Survey*, 1968.
11. Johnson, *Public Papers of* . . . , 1968, Book I, 155–8.
12. Johnson, *The Vantage Point* . . . , 384. See also, Schandler, 74–91, for a concise analysis of the action and its public effect.
13. AP, UPI, Saigon, February 2, 1968.
14. UPI, Saigon, February 2, 1968.
15. UPI, Saigon, February 6, 1968. See also, Westmoreland, 332, who claims 37,000 enemy killed.
16. Beaufre.
17. Kalb and Abel, 209–10. See also, Sheehan et al., 594–5.
18. Johnson, *The Vantage Point* . . . , 386.
19. Sheehan et al., 615–21. See also, Hoopes; Shaplen, *The Road from War*, 192–3: "American officials estimate that the whole [pacification] program, which was just beginning to make some small headway, has lost three or four months, and maybe more."
20. Johnson, *The Vantage Point* . . . , 384.
21. Baldwin, "The Foes Is Hurting."
22. Johnson, *The Vantage Point* . . . , 389.
23. Hoopes, 145–6.
24. Ibid., 204–5. See also, Brandon.
25. Sheehan et al., 600. See also, Johnson, *The Vantage Point* . . . ; Hoopes.
26. Sheehan et al., 600–1.
27. Clifford.
28. Sheehan et al., 601–3. See also, Hoopes, 176.
29. Sheehan et al., 599.
30. Westmoreland, 338. See also, Schandler, 90.
31. Shaplen, *The Road from War*, 210–11, 208.
32. Kellen.
33. Brandon. See also, Heren.
34. Hoopes, 205.
35. Ibid. See also, Ridgway, "Indochina: Disengaging"; Brandon, 133:

To Acheson's surprise, his views were shared by more among those present than he had expected. The one who mattered most, because he too had been a strong supporter of the war, was McGeorge Bundy. He summed up for those supporting Acheson's views and admitted, in self-flagellating mood, that "for the first time in my life I find myself agreeing on this issue with George Ball."

36. Personal letter from General Walt to the author.
37. Institute for Strategic Studies, "The United States," *Strategic Survey,* 1968. See also, Colby, 168–9, 231–4, 267–86.
38. Colby, 234.
39. Rice, 108. See also, Blaufarb, 246–8; Colby, 234, 266–76; Lewy.
40. Rice, 108. See also, Lewy.
41. Hackworth, 736.
42. Karnow, 602.
43. Ibid.
44. Rice, 108
45. Johnson, *The Vantage Point* . . . , 417.
46. Johnson, *Public Papers of* . . . , 1968, Book I, 499.
47. *Time,* May 10, 1968.
48. Ibid., June 21, 1968.
49. Ibid., June 6, 1969.
50. Jenkins.
51. Johnson, *The Vantage Point* . . . , 523.
52. Clifford. See also, Johnson, *The Vantage Point* . . . , 511, who did not find Clifford so pessimistic.
53. Johnson, *The Vantage Point* . . . , 512.
54. Clifford. See also, Kissinger, "The Viet Nam Negotiations," which questions the advisability of American insistence on Saigon's participation in the first place.
55. Johnson, *The Vantage Point* . . . , 524.
56. Johnson, *Public Papers of* . . . , 1968, Book I, 1099 ff.
57. Institute for Strategic Studies, "The United States," *Strategic Survey,* 1968.

CHAPTER 70

*The summing up (1): the Bible and the Sword • Not "reason good
enough" • Communists and dominoes • Inside South Vietnam •
Economics • Government versus press: America—the communications
failure*

LYNDON JOHNSON FAILED in Vietnam for many of the same
reasons that John Kennedy failed (see Chapter 60). The key
to failure lay in substituting ambition for policy. *Stop communism* appealed to Johnson, a man of " . . . little background and much uncertainty in foreign affairs" (in the words of one subordinate),[1] even more
than it had appealed to Kennedy. A Texas Baptist, Johnson had been
raised in shadows of GOOD and EVIL. He was a great believer in the
Bible and the Sword, and while he quoted one, he wielded the other.
When neither faith nor force served him well, he was lost.

Johnson's downfall began before he was elected President. Like
other worthy but myopic Americans, he accepted the "strong man"
thesis that resulted in the American government's prostrating itself before the pudgy form of Ngo Dinh Diem. As a southern Democrat, Johnson wore scars from the Republican excoriation that followed the loss
of Nationalist China to Mao's Communists. In spring of 1954, following the Geneva Conference, he said, " . . . American foreign policy has
never in all its history suffered such a stunning reversal. . . . We stand
in clear danger of being left naked and alone in a hostile world."[2] He
did not believe that his party could survive another such loss, and when
Diem—whom he had called the Winston Churchill of Southeast Asia—
failed him, he turned to force.

The President early displayed his line of thought in a National Security Action Memorandum which he approved shortly after assuming
office and which read in part:

> . . . It remains the central objective of the United States in South
> Vietnam to assist the people and Government of that country to

win their contest against the externally directed and supported communist conspiracy. The test of all U.S. decisions and actions in this area should be the effectiveness of their contribution to this purpose.[3]

Johnson greatly expanded this relatively mild statement in his famous Baltimore speech of April 1965 (see Chapter 63), where he repeated misplaced ambition emphasized by misdirected appeal, neither to change during the next three years. His eloquence not only failed to propel Ho Chi Minh to the conference table, but it prompted a rather negative reaction both in the United States and throughout the world. This should have warned Johnson and his advisers. In his peroration, he had asked the American people: " . . . Have we, each of us, all done all we can do? Have we done enough?" The true leader leads by example. Had Johnson asked himself this question, he would have had to reply no. In his crusading zeal, the President was forgetting wise Demades' admonition to the assembly " . . . to have a care lest in guarding heaven they should lose earth." Like an emperor of old, he was crying, "Justice must be done, even if the world should perish."[4] The President should have respected the dissident opinions of those who attempted to warn him of Demades' words. Critics with such credentials as George Kennan, Matthew Ridgway, James Gavin, and David Shoup should not have been lightly dismissed. Sufficiently disturbing currents were at work at the beginning of Johnson's administration to call for the most penetrating examination of policy. The President might have asked himself, as for example Edward Lansdale, an expert on Vietnam, later asked *himself*, " . . . What is it exactly, that we seek in Viet Nam? . . . We have to answer the question *fully*. . . . Without a sound answer, the seemingly endless war in Viet Nam becomes just that—seemingly endless. Alternatively, it may be headed for an end that could be dishonorable, with profound consequences."[5] He could have listened to intelligent and courageous officers such as General Matthew Ridgway, who in 1967 warned:

> . . . A war without goals would be most dangerous of all, and nearly as dangerous would be a war with only some vaguely stated aim, such as "victory" or "freedom from aggression" or "the right of the people to choose their own government." Generalities like these make admirable slogans, but authorities today must be hardheaded and specific in naming exactly what goal we are trying to reach and exactly what price we are willing to pay for reaching it. Otherwise, we may find that, in spite of ourselves, the whole conduct of the war will be left in the hands of men who see only victory as the proper objective and who have never had to define

that word in terms plain enough to be understood by all the world's people.

Ridgway continued in words strengthened by simplicity:

> ... A limited war is not merely a small war that has not yet grown to full size. It is a war in which the objectives are specifically limited in the light of our national interest and our current capabilities. A war that is "open-ended"—that has no clearly delineated geographical, political and military goals beyond "victory"—is a war that may escalate itself indefinitely, as wars will, with one success requiring still another to insure the first one. . . . [6]

Had Johnson pursued this question of specific goals, had he demanded that civil and military advisers answer it fully, had he taken counsel not so much of fears as of unpalatable facts, he would not have weakened his position, as he did, by basing it on arguable premises. To pursue the strategy foisted by his military and civil advisers, demanded "exquisite reason," but, unlike Sir Andrew, the President lacked even "reason good enough." At a time when he and his advisers should have been questioning, they were accepting. Townsend Hoopes, who became Deputy Assistant Secretary of Defense for International Security Affairs in January 1965, discerned no " . . . central guiding philosophy" in American foreign policy, only hit-and-miss efforts motivated by the belief of Johnson and his principal advisers in a monolithic Communist threat, despite both Russia's traditional disinterest in Southeast Asia and her current quarrel with China (indisputably the most significant international development since Tito's defection and Chiang Kai-shek's fall). Dean Rusk, McGeorge Bundy, Robert McNamara, Walt Rostow, Maxwell Taylor, William Westmoreland, members of the JCS—each spoke frequently and feelingly of "Communist aggression," while never fully defining the term or fitting the facts to the precise situation in Vietnam. Hoopes later wrote that " . . . to the President's men in early 1965, there seemed no logical stopping point between isolationism and globalism." Perhaps even more dangerous, he found these men supremely confident of militarily stopping the North Vietnamese and, with that, all "wars of national liberation."[7]

The President and his advisers grossly erred in trying to make a complex problem so simple. Unduly influenced by American economic and military power, frightened by the bogeyman of international communism, they accepted shibboleths bequeathed by Eisenhower and Kennedy and polished them with perfervid rhetoric made the more specious by crusade-like appeal. With one or two exceptions, they were yesterday's men living in tomorrow's world—like great-power exponents of another century, they tried to stop the clock of history and succeeded only in producing cacophonous chimes. Listen to Lyndon Johnson writing on the September 1964 White House meeting:

> ... As one gloomy opinion followed another, I suddenly asked whether anyone at the table doubted that Vietnam was "worth all this effort." Ambassador Taylor answered quickly that "we could not afford to let Hanoi win in the interests of our overall position in Asia and in the world." General Wheeler strongly supported the Ambassador's view. It was the unanimous view of the Chiefs of Staff, he said, that if we lost South Vietnam we would lose Southeast Asia—not all at once, and not overnight, but eventually. One country after another on the periphery would give way and look to Communist China as the rising power of the area, he said. John McCone agreed. So did Secretary Rusk, with considerable emphasis.[8]

Johnson failed to add that a great many experts, including top CIA analysts, did not agree with these views.

During the next two years, opposing voices, many of them expressing experience and study of decades, made it clear that the issues at stake were anything but black-and-white. With one or two exceptions, presidential advisers refused to listen. Maxwell Taylor and William Bundy continued to stress but in slight disguise the monolithic-Communist thesis that produced the domino theory: If one falls, all fall. Johnson and most of his advisers persisted in this belief despite demonstrable facts: that a good many insurgencies of two decades stood remote from communism; that insurgency in South Vietnam could not have lasted a month without peasant support; that by threatening Hanoi's existence, American arms had nearly brought rapprochement between China and Soviet Russia, they had brought an internal political development inside China whose full effects might well threaten America's best interests, and they had brought the Soviet presence into an area in which, historically, Russia had displayed little interest.[9] The President and his advisers could have heard these facts from a score of highly qualified and eminently patriotic observers at home and abroad. C. P. Fitzgerald, for example, a distinguished scholar who lived in China for twenty-five years, demolished the domino theory (as others had done earlier): His article in *The Nation,* June 28, 1965, "The Fallacy of the Dominoes," should have been required Administration reading. Fitzgerald pointed out that since if one falls, all fall, then it follows that if one stands, all stand. But this was patently false at a time when Indonesia was in more danger of being taken over by Communists—their own—than Vietnam. He denied the validity of regional protective pacts, for clearly stated historical reasons; in short, he said here was an immensely complicated political situation with deep historical roots:

> ...All these ancient claims and quarrels are more important, more real and more urgent to the peoples of South-East Asia than the conflict of communism backed by China and anti-communism backed by the United States. That contest is seen essentially as the quarrel of two great outsiders, to be used for promoting national ambitions or thwarting those of traditional foes, but in itself extraneous to the countries themselves. The Asians may well be wrong to take such an attitude, but the West is also much deluded when it thinks of these states as being without personalities of their own, willing to enlist on one side or the other in a global conflict, obedient to the behests of Washington or Peking.

The real appeal in these countries, evidence suggests, is nationalism, and this is one reason why the presence of Western armed forces, which provide an anti-nationalist target, is so dangerous. The challenge calls for a much more subtle approach and for extremely limited objectives: "... it must be remembered that this area is the region adjacent to China, in which its influence through the centuries has always been present, sometimes powerful and active, at other times dormant, but by the mere facts of geography, never extinct."[10]

Not a word do we find of such heretical notions either in official statements of the day or in the Pentagon papers. Were similar opinions reported by American diplomats throughout the area? Were such opinions debated in high councils? Perhaps someday we shall know the answers. Some argument must have existed, though Johnson's memoirs are lacking substance in this respect. In the January 1967 issue of *Foreign Affairs*, we find McGeorge Bundy carefully disclaiming the theretofore sacrosanct domino theory, but, by then, Bundy had left the government;[11] we also find indirect confirmation in later disillusionment expressed by Clark Clifford and Townsend Hoopes. In 1965, however, and for the next two years, any government official daring to question the cornerstone of Administration policy would have been tagged a "nervous Nellie" and relegated to limbo.

The President's top civil and military officials equally could insist on Hanoi's dominant role in the war as proclaimed in the 1965 White Paper.[12] But this did not wash with a good many American and foreign observers and experts, who were aware of the early minimum role played by Hanoi, particularly in troop and supply categories. If a "constant stream" of trained men and supplies was flowing from North to South, a veritable flood of such had already flowed from West to East.[13] Similarly, Communist China's participation in the conflict had been minimal, despite menacing growls from Peking. The partnership between Ho and Mao implied by the President did not exist. Writing in 1967, Donald Zagoria pointed out that

> ... any careful study of Chinese foreign policy during the past fifteen years would have to conclude that although China is a revolutionary power opposing the present status quo, it does not aim to bring about change by its own military force.
>
> ... [It is] one of the key messages in Lin Piao's article [September 3, 1965] and one of the basic principles of "liberation wars"—that Communist revolutionaries throughout the world must make their revolutions on their own. Far from giving any notice of any intention to intervene aggressively in Vietnam or in other "people's wars," Lin Piao was rationalizing Peking's unwillingness to intervene directly and massively in such wars. He was reiterating what is essentially a "do-it-yourself" model of revolution for foreign Communists.[14]

In 1965, Ho was walking a tightrope between Chinese and Soviet camps, and President Johnson's attempts to stress the Chinese threat while not mentioning the theretofore prominent villain, the Soviet Union, did not impress intelligent auditors.

The President's "national pledge" was equally specious: " ... We are there because we have a promise to keep." What promise? When? President Eisenhower said that the United States would supply limited aid to South Vietnam, providing Diem carried out essential reforms. Here was a reasonable proposition. Nothing was new about it. It was the beginning of a temporary alliance with presumed attendant advantages to each party. Such alliances crowd the pages of history, and such have been commented on through the ages as, for example, by Spinoza, who, as Leopold Ranke noted,

> ... starts from the principle that states permanently subsist in a state of nature with respect to one another, and does not hesitate to assert that a treaty has force only so long as the causes of it— fear of injury or hope of gain—exist; that no ruler is to be reproached with faithlessness for breaking an alliance he had formerly concluded, as soon as any of the causes which determined him to it should have ceased, since that condition is equal for both parties.

This is little more than common sense. Yet, in less than a decade, Eisenhower's casual alliance became promoted, mostly by American military voices, into a "promise" and now into "a national pledge to help South Viet-Nam defend its independence." Listen to Maxwell Taylor, writing in 1967:

... If we are convinced, as I am, that the stake is important, that we are honor-bound to obtain for the people in South Vietnam the right to freedom, then every dollar and every man we have committed in my opinion is justified.[15]

By right to freedom, Taylor undoubtedly included rule by Diem and Nhu and Thieu and Ky and whatever other national war lords would appear in the future—neither Taylor nor any of the other ancient citizens who surrounded the President, with the possible exception of Clifford, realized that Administration ambitions for South Vietnam bore almost no resemblance to the relatively simple goal of the Saigon government, which was to maintain and enlarge its own power structure while yielding minimum freedoms to its peoples. And if the U.S.A. was honor bound to intervene in South Vietnam, then why not in Rhodesia, South Africa, Greece, most of the South American and all the Iron Curtain countries, indeed in any country whose government did not conform to American system or desire?

Attempting to put the record in proper perspective, in 1967 Senator Eugene McCarthy wrote:

> ... It is said that we fight to ensure the credibility of our commitments, to show the world that we honor our treaty obligations. This is the rationale of our politico-military prestige. Yet we have already demonstrated our reliability in Korea and in the protection of Taiwan as well as in Europe.
>
> It is said that we must carry on the war in Vietnam in order to preserve and defend our national honor. Our national honor is not at stake, and should not so readily be offered. In every other great war of the century, we have had the support of what is generally accepted as the decent opinion of mankind. We do not have that today. We cannot, of course, depend only on this opinion to prove our honor; it may not be sound. But always in the past we have not only had this support, but we have used it as a kind of justification for our action.[16]

As for the unforgivable wrong of abandoning " ... this small and brave nation to its enemies, and to the terror that must follow," the President again was indulging in fiction. The homogeneous national picture that he implied did not exist. Viet Cong cadres had controlled large areas of South Vietnam since 1954; in 1965, the enemy controlled probably 90 per cent of the countryside. In 1965, as in 1955, Saigon rule was remote in some areas, ruthless in other areas. A large percentage of peasants did not care who ruled so long as they could till crops and get a fair shake in the market place. The peasants' main concern was not democracy but survival with dignity, and the splendid rhetoric that burbled from Washington and Saigon officialdom was virtually meaningless to bent bodies laboring in rice paddies and on rubber plantations. No one had shown peasants that democracy was worth fighting for, because no one had shown them democracy. As Johnson spoke, the gulf between the Saigon government, the sects, and the peasants was as wide as ever, growing wider.[17]

People who would have been eliminated by a Communist takeover constituted, for the most part, a rapacious ruling minority whose greed and intransigence were keeping the nation, such as it was, in its turbulent, impotent condition. And here was Johnson, like Kennedy and Eisenhower before him, compounding the damage by unfounded fears and loose rhetoric. Once again, Johnson was saying that the West could not survive without this geographical neutrino, this whirling nothing of a country. So many Americans had insisted that a dubious political entity called South Vietnam was an indispensable ally in the war against communism, that South Vietnamese Catholics, Buddhists, mandarins, generals, landowners, merchants, intellectuals, and students began to believe it—so indispensable, that, on occasion, South Vietnamese government leaders such as Khanh could indulge the most virulent language and defiant behavior to the country that was keeping them alive. About this time, a Vietnamese political observer told Robert Shaplen: " . . . In a way, after all the pent-up years under the French and under Diem, we are like children letting off steam. Maybe there will have to be yet another half-dozen coups before we settle down—even though we know we can't afford them."[18] He was wrong. South Vietnam could afford them—as long as the United States insisted on bestowing unqualified support on a rump government whose totalitarian characteristics contradicted a heritage held sacred by thoughtful American citizens. In spring of 1965, a firm threat to abandon South Vietnam was perhaps the only action that could have produced the social-political cohesion necessary to make a nation. The Vietnamese politicians may not have admitted it, but they were in a classic "backs-to-the-wall" position. President Johnson's "solution," his Baltimore speech, removed the wall.

No one could fault the President's assertion of great stakes in play in the international power game. But if retreat from Vietnam would not bring an end to conflict, neither would "victory" in Vietnam. The President was trying to produce a black-and-white center-ring act from a multicolored sideshow. Neither Moscow nor Peking particularly wanted the war to escalate: Moscow did not want to upset its détente with Washington; Peking did not want a strong American military presence on the Asian mainland. However, once the United States made a major commitment in South Vietnam, Moscow and Peking rolled with the punch and moved to exploit the situation. No matter how big, powerful, and rich the U.S.A., no nation could be everywhere at once. While

President Johnson was talking to the world, Chinese money and Chinese technicians were on their way to Tanzania to begin construction of a sixteen-hundred-mile railroad into the interior of Africa; Soviet money and Soviet technicians were working in Cairo's defense ministry; satellite money and satellite technicians were scouring underdeveloped parts of the world for investment and prestige purposes. While American priority effort went to a strategically unimportant country, the Soviet Union and China reinforced their presence in Africa and the Middle East—indeed anywhere that dangerous insurgencies were brewing—to the detriment of the West and with the knowledge that the U.S.A. could not launch a maximum countereffort.

The President's stated objective of "independence" for South Vietnam also rang hollow. Whether the United States or South Vietnam liked it or not, the tragic rump would remain economically and militarily dependent on the United States, just as had Cuba and the Philippines for so many decades, just as Taiwan and Korea were doing.

In trying to justify the American action, the President resembled a boy whistling his way past a cemetery on a dark night. The most cursory reader of American newspapers, magazines, and books knew that the President's stated resolution was not shared by an increasingly influential portion of the nation, including legislators who were beginning to hold second thoughts about the Tonkin Gulf Resolution. Leaving aside domestic and major international problems that were crying for enormous expenditures of expertise and money, nothing in the American character suggested the qualities of patience that Lyndon Johnson claimed in pursuing his ambitions. His statements presupposed a national interest and stamina that did not exist—and for several reasons. The first was a failure in communications that we have already discussed with regard to the Kennedy era. Speaking in 1954 as a senator, Johnson had said: " . . . We will insist upon clear explanations of the policies in which we are asked to cooperate. We will insist that we and the American people be treated as adults, that we have the facts without sugar coating."[19] When, during the Kennedy administration, the press attempted to give the facts, a good many senior American officials bridled and a minor war developed. Kennedy's press representative, Pierre Salinger, warned of the coming storm in 1963, and Vice-President Johnson must have been aware of the dangerous situation. As President he foolishly exacerbated it, and relations between press and officialdom continued to deteriorate. In an article in *Foreign Affairs* in July 1966, veteran correspondent James Reston again warned of a communications breakdown. Far from heeding him, Johnson increasingly scorned the press (which he criticized throughout his memoirs).

As one result, a good many senior officials in Saigon and Washington continued to dissemble; some reporters continued to distort. So complex was the Vietnamese scene that even highly talented correspondents had their hands full in communicating its complex turbulence to the American public. With a few splendid exceptions, not many, publishers unfortunately did not present the war in depth. A British expert on counterinsurgency, Major General Richard Clutterbuck, after visiting South Vietnam, accused three journalist friends

> ... of reporting only what occurred above 12,000 feet. If you put cloud over the world at 12,000 feet, the only things that stick up are rugged and spectacular, and that is what gets reported. They agreed that that was what they did, and said that if they reported anything below 12,000 feet, it would not get into their papers anyway; no one would read it if it did, and they would lose their jobs. We had to leave it at that, and so the real blame falls on the public.[20]

While newspaper publishers, TV-station owners, and public admittedly were culpable, the statement is not altogether true. Reporting in depth (by far the most accurate and intelligent coverage came from Robert Shaplen of *The New Yorker*) was well received by impressive segments of the public, who became aware that the situation scarcely resembled the black-and-white situation described in presidential platitudes.

But for every informed American citizen and even vaguely informed American citizen, dozens existed who had only the foggiest notion of what was going on in Vietnam. Even had it wished to, the Administration could not have alleviated national ignorance by a well-conceived and well-executed educational program because it had already decided that the issues were black and white, and that it was a question of imposing American military will on Hanoi—and damn any American citizen who didn't agree.

The communications problem, which resulted in continuing national ignorance (thus frustration and resentment), gave rise to an even more serious condition. Johnson had embarked on a crusade that the American public did not understand but at first supported, though by no means eagerly, because it trusted its national leaders and its military and civilian officials and because it shared, at least in part, their arrogance of ignorance. But not very long after the Tonkin Gulf Resolution, a tradition began quietly to assert itself. As Bill Moyers, Johnson's press man, later pointed out, the American democratic concept embraces not only a tradition of dissent, but also of consent:

> ... Our system assumes a sense of participation by the people in the making of critical national decisions. When that sense of involvement is absent, when the public feels excluded from the judg-

ments that are made in its name, a policy is doomed from inception, no matter how theoretically valid it may be.

Translating this to Vietnam, Moyers continued:

> ... War is clearly one of those questions on which a government—a democratic government—dare not act without evidence of genuine support. In this case, that support was not deliberately withheld—it simply was not sought. And it was not sought because few if any officials anticipated the war would ever reach the proportions that would require a declaration.[21]

Rather than leveling with the American people, Johnson and his advisers continued in the hope that they could clean up matters—that they could "win"—before the American public realized quite what had happened. That this hope was doomed by a false military strategy did not at first occur except to a very few advisers, and these Johnson ignored and later banished. When truth began leaking out, when casualties and expenses rose out of all proportion to gained results, impressive portions of the American public rebelled.

Parts of the United States were already rebelling at the time of Johnson's Baltimore speech in the spring of 1965. Although Communist leaders in South and North Vietnam were provincial and often naïve, they sensed currents at work in the United States that suggested France of an earlier day. These leaders had experienced protracted warfare, many had been fighting since 1943 and even earlier (some since 1932), and from 1946 onward, they had witnessed the pressures of protracted guerrilla warfare at work on Western countries. In their minds, protracted warfare had gained one victory. It could now gain another. An American president could proclaim that his nation would not be defeated or would not grow tired—but Communists had only to read American newspapers and magazines to realize that this was proclamation without solid national support. Throughout his memoirs, the President repeatedly stressed Hanoi's unwillingness to negotiate a peace in these crucial years. Never once, apparently, did it occur to him to ask himself why; never once does he suggest that, being human, he was fallible and his basic precepts could have been fallacious.

CHAPTER SEVENTY

1. Hoopes, 2.
2. *New York Times*, May 7, 1954, quoted in Eden, *Towards Peace in Indo-China*, 7.
3. Johnson, *The Vantage Point* . . . , 45.
4. *Fiat justitia, pereat mundus.*
5. Lansdale, "Viet Nam—Still the Search for Goals." This article demon-

927

strates only a few contradictions that occur when ambition is substituted for policy.

6. Ridgway, *The Korean War*, 232, 245.
7. Hoopes, 1, 16.
8. Johnson, *The Vantage Point* . . . , 120.
9. Zagoria, *Vietnam Triangle* . . . , 27 ff.
10. Quoted in *Survival*, September 1965. See also, C.P. Fitzgerald; Zagoria, "Who Fears the Domino Theory?"; Harries, "Should the U.S. Withdraw from Asia?" for a dissenting opinion; Reischauer, an acknowledged expert on the Far East and Asia, whose telling arguments as to the minimal importance of a Communist "victory" in Vietnam were validated by that very "victory"; Soedjatmoko; Harris; Salisbury, "Image and Reality in Indochina," which discusses distorted viewpoints of both sides.
11. McGeorge Bundy.
12. See, for example, Taylor, *Responsibility and Response*, 26: " . . . as early as 1961 when I headed a mission to Vietnam . . . the mission called attention to the fact that the real source of the guerrilla strength in South Vietnam was not in South Vietnam but in North Vietnam. It was perfectly clear that the direction, the supplies, the reinforcements, and the leadership came from the North. . . . "
13. Morrock, "Revolution and Intervention in Vietnam," in Horowitz, *Containment and Revolution*, 244–5. Hans Morgenthau commented: " . . . Let it be said right away that the (State Department) white paper is a dismal failure. The discrepancy between its assertions and the factual evidence adduced to support them borders on the grotesque." See also, U.S. Department of Defense, "Working Paper on the North Vietnamese Role in the War in South Vietnam," which asserts, rather than proves, Hanoi's dominant role from the beginning; Tanham and Duncanson:

> . . . In reality, the Marxist-Leninists of the East not only take pride in winning power with a minimum contribution from their own side, but have found from experience that this is a more reliable road to victory. Besides concealing the directing hand, it leaves the door open to repudiation of unsuccessful insurgencies. . . .

Lacouture, 182, cites Pentagon advice " . . . that the deliveries from the North were . . . on the order of fifteen to twenty per cent [of Viet Cong needs]."
14. Zagoria, *Vietnam Triangle* . . . , 79. See also, H.L. Duncan.
15. Maxwell Taylor, *Responsibility and Response*, 37.
16. McCarthy, 190–1.
17. Duncanson, *Government and Revolution in Vietnam*.
18. Shaplen, *The Road from War*, 7.
19. Deakin.
20. Royal United Service Institution Seminar: Brigadier Kenneth Hunt of the Institute for Strategic Studies also complained of a press deficiency:

> . . . The most dispiriting thing is to go to a Press conference in Saigon. It is not merely because the quality of the briefing is kindergarten, that it comes out in a dead-pan American style. The quality of the questions asked by reporters is also often poor and amateurish. That is reflected in what comes back and is printed.

21. Moyers.

CHAPTER 71

The summing up (II): use of air power • The Douhet theory • Strategic bombing in World War II • The paradox of nuclear stalemate • Lessons of the Korean War • American expectations in North Vietnam • Historical factors • Harrison Salisbury reports from the North • Bombs and international diplomacy

THE PRESIDENT'S DECISION to carry the war to the North undoubtedly came as an unpleasant surprise to Hanoi. But this decision could not change the axis of war, which remained in the South. Moreover, the intention to alter enemy will by use of aerial bombardment introduced several factors that seem to have escaped official cognizance.

The use of air power produces both moral and material results, and the tally means one thing to the user, another to the receiver. On advice of his military chiefs, Johnson was embracing a modified Douhet theory of aerial bombing when he agreed to send American planes over North Vietnam. This theory emerged in 1921, when Giulio Douhet, an Italian air officer, wrote a small book, *The Command of the Air.*

Douhet correctly foresaw the importance of the new arm:

> . . . By virtue of this new weapon . . . the battlefield will be limited only by the boundaries of the nations at war, and all of their citizens will become combatants since all of them will be exposed to the aerial offensives of the enemy. There will be no distinction any longer between soldiers and civilians . . . All of this must inevitably effect a profound change in the form of future wars. . . .

Air power, Douhet prophesied, would prove omnipotent as it already had in World War I despite " . . . anti-aircraft guns, and reconnaissance and pursuit planes." Douhet made no claim to selectivity or subtlety:

... The complete destruction of the objective has moral and material effects, the repercussions of which may be tremendous. To give us some idea of the extent of these repercussions, we need only envisage what would go on among the civilian population of congested cities once the enemy announced that he would bomb such centers relentlessly, making no distinction between military and non-military objectives.

In Douhet's mind, as in Foch's before him, the moral was as important as the physical:

... We should always keep in mind that aerial offensives can be directed not only against objectives of least physical resistance, but against those of least moral resistance as well. For instance, an infantry regiment in a shattered trench may still be capable of some resistance even after losing two-thirds of its effectives; but when the working personnel of a factory sees one of its machine shops destroyed, even with a minimum loss of life, it quickly breaks up and the plant ceases to function.[1]

Professional airmen in the West such as Billy Mitchell in the United States and Hugh Trenchard in England, who were attempting to build air forces and were obstructed at every turn by army and navy traditionalists, embraced Douhet's theory as another argument in favor of the new arm. In the late twenties, Mitchell sacrificed his career by demonstrating that bombs could sink a battleship; as we have seen, the British claimed strategic-tactical successes in Iraq and in northwestern frontier provinces in India, as did U. S. Marines in Nicaragua (see Chapter 23). Goering's Luftwaffe experimented with the theory during the Spanish civil war, at one point eliminating the town of Guernica; at another, testing results of carpet bombing.

Variations appeared early in World War II. Older readers will remember horrendous pictures of Stuka dive bombers preparing cities such as Rotterdam for paratroop invasion and later attacking refugee columns in France in order to cause panic and impede military movement. The Battle of Britain raised the psychological level of the theory, but the Luftwaffe failed to bring England to its knees. When skillful and determined RAF opposition produced heavy German losses in aircraft and pilots, which could not easily be replaced, Hitler terminated the campaign.

The theory did not die with this failure. RAF and American strategic air bombings attempted to destroy Hitler's industrial plant and thereby force Germany from the war. RAF saturation bombings culminating in the destruction of Dresden attempted to break the German people's will; American fire bombings of Tokyo and the final destruction of Hiroshima and Nagasaki by atomic bombs did play a major role in breaking Japanese will to continue war.

Thus the Douhet theory: At its nicest, strategic bombing; at its ugliest, genocide. And this is why the theory is fallacious: first, the more bombs dropped, the lower the morale—but not necessarily a significant lessening of will to resist. This is a challenge situation familiar to psychology. Challenge, discipline, and incentive all play major roles; resistance is never easily analyzed. These factors help to explain why medieval fortresses held out against overwhelming odds, why, in World War I, neither side would yield on the western front, why men in battle, for example American marines on Guadalcanal in those black days of late 1942, tolerated weeks of bombing and shelling by Japanese aircraft and ships without losing their will to fight. Civilians of London, Berlin, Tokyo, and numerous other cities reacted similarly. Aerial bombings subverted civil will to resist only by killing the holders of that will. Conventional strategic bombing did not kill enough holders of that will fast enough; atomic bombing did.

The advent of the atomic bomb seemed to fructify Douhet's theory, but only as long as one side held a monopoly. Even then, moral aspects outweighed the practical: Premeditated genocide is not an acceptable clause in the Western code of civilization, as the Germans discovered. And not only the Germans. At the height of allied bombing in World War II, the American air force general Carl ("Tooey") Spaatz caviled at the RAF's saturation bombing program. The American people's reaction to the atomic bombings of Hiroshima and Nagasaki was also disturbed, and if those of us who were training for the invasion of Japan proper were pleased with the war's sudden termination, this did not erase a feeling of guilt, however nebulous, in the national conscience. As General Matthew Ridgway wrote in 1956, when discussing the use of strategic air power: " . . . to my mind, such mass destruction is repugnant to the ideals of a Christian nation. It is incompatible with the basic aim of the free world in war, which is to win a just and enduring peace".[2]

Once the Soviet Union broke atomic monopoly, the atomic bomb's omnipotence evaporated in an air of retribution. The paradox of nuclear stalemate—of destructive impotence—resulted. Both moral and practical aspects prevented American use of atomic bombs in Korea and in North Vietnam. At the height of the bombing of North Vietnam, in October 1967, Robert McNamara laid the issue on the line in a top-secret memorandum to President Johnson:

> . . . It is clear that, to bomb the North sufficiently to make a radical impact upon Hanoi's political, economic and social structure, would require an effort which we could make but which would

931

not be stomached either by our own people or by world opinion; and it would involve a serious risk of drawing us into open war with China.[3]

Material results of strategic bombing are something else again. Strategic-bombing proponents have frequently overstated their case, which is usual with minority arguments. World War II offered excellent examples of bombing's strength and weaknesses. Any interested reader can find myriad statistics in the postwar *Strategic Bombing Survey,* whose directors included George Ball, John Galbraith, and Paul Nitze. The survey cited impressive accomplishments of allied air forces, giving fliers their due and then some; but it also established that workers did not flee an area when first bombs fell, as Douhet and later strategic-bombing proponents had it. Bombing, although interrupting production, rarely halted it, at least until the very end, when allied ground forces already had invaded Germany. Permanent damage was not nearly so great as current estimates had suggested, and in some areas production even increased, while in others reserve stocks and emergency measures provided short-term compensation for havoc wrought. Bombing raids in July and August 1943 on Hamburg killed some sixty to a hundred thousand people and destroyed 55–60 per cent of the city, including three hundred thousand homes. Yet

> . . . Hamburg as an economic unit was not destroyed. It never fully recovered from the bombing but in five months it had regained 80 per cent of its former productivity, despite the fact that great areas of the city lay, and still lie, in dust and rubble. As in the case of industrial plants where it was found much easier to destroy the buildings than the machines within, so also it is much easier to destroy the physical structures of a city than to wipe out its economic life.

Saturation bombings, what the RAF called "area raids," also provided startling "kill" figures. The Strategic Bombing Survey estimated that bombs eliminated 3.6 million homes, or approximately 20 per cent of Germany's total dwelling space; bombs killed about three hundred thousand people and injured some 780,000. Although " . . . bombing appreciably affected the German will to resist," bombs did not crumble that will:

> . . . War production is the critical measuring rod of the effects of lowered morale in the German war effort. Allied bombing widely and seriously depressed German civilian morale, but depressed and discouraged workers were not necessarily unproductive workers.

932

As has been seen, armaments production continued to mount till mid-1944.

Strategic bombing also received a setback from a cost-analysis standpoint. It proved very expensive in both lives and cost of bombers and bombs. The establishment required to operate a peak twenty-eight thousand combat planes numbered 1.335 million men. Nearly eighty thousand American and eighty thousand British airmen were lost in action, while eighteen thousand American and twenty-two thousand British planes were lost or damaged beyond repair. Up to VE-day, the American air effort in Europe alone cost over $43 billion! A final factor emerged after the war: Industrial complexes that had been damaged and destroyed, not to mention surrounding urban areas, had to be rebuilt, with the victors, primarily the U.S.A., picking up the tab.[4]

Strategic-tactical bombing and interdiction also proved chimerical. Lavish claims advanced by proponents of air power were often matched by lavish failures. Few, if any, interested persons disputed tactical advantages derived from command of the air. We have glanced at these in the 1920s and 1930s. But, as Gwynn pointed out in 1934, air power was not a tactical panacea and could not apply in all places at all times. In World War II, tactical air power proved a tremendous boon to allied armies, not only in clearing skies of enemy aircraft but in close air support, a fine art developed particularly by U. S. Marines. But such accomplishments did not obliterate shortcomings: Tactical air power did not "win" ground battles, any more than strategic air power "won" the war. Writing years later, General Matthew Ridgway recalled that limitations of air power " . . . were never better illustrated than in World War II, when the Germans were able to maintain some twenty-six divisions south of the Alps in Italy, using a few mountain passes to keep them supplied for two years, regardless of uncontested Allied air supremacy."[5]

The Korean War added to lessons already learned (but either ignored or forgotten by proponents of aerial warfare). Air Force, Navy and Marine aircraft controlled the skies, destroying every industrial target in North Korea, flying thousands of tactical missions, interdicting enemy communications and supporting allied ground troops—but air power did not prevent ammunition, food, and replacements from reaching the enemy's front-line units. "For the Air Force," General James Gavin wrote,

> . . . Korea had been a disillusioning and frustrating experience. Air Force leaders had assumed that air superiority, air surveillance and air attacks would smash the North Korean drive and demolish the North Korean military establishment. They had trumpeted this

point of view both to the public and to the President. When the bombing failed to halt the North Korean war effort they developed the myth of the Yalu sanctuary. If only they could bomb Red Chinese Manchuria, which lay beyond the Yalu River, they said, everything would turn out all right. Thus the Air Force was able to avoid, at least in public, confronting the evidence that in Korea both strategically and tactically air power had failed. Unfortunately from their frustration sprang a readiness to answer any challenge to American power with threats of total nuclear war.[6]

In those momentous months of 1964 and 1965, Johnson and his advisers displayed massive historical ignorance of air power. Johnson himself had fallen victim to a powerful civil-military lobby that preached virtues of air power without mentioning its severe limitations. Ignorant of the true nature of the war in Vietnam, frustrated at lack of progress in "winning" it, and frightened by recent and substantial reverses, Johnson proved particularly prone to panaceas.

Judging from later events, he probably also believed that he could control the action, that he needn't place all military eggs in one basket. In his mind, he could turn air power on and off like a water tap, and if this did not succeed, he could follow with ground and sea power, a rationale enthusiastically preached by the JCS and some top civil advisers. This fallacious reasoning is of interest, first because as bombing began and failed it changed; second because the Nixon administration would bring it back to life. Maxwell Taylor early wrote:

> . . . by February, 1965, it had become perfectly apparent that we must strike at this external base [North Vietnam] and do so for three reasons . . . to let the people of South Vietnam feel that for the first time, after eleven years of bitter warfare, they were striking back against the source of all their troubles [!] . . . to utilize our superiority in the air to strike military targets which, if destroyed, would have the effect of restraining or making more difficult the infiltration of men and supplies from North Vietnam into South Vietnam . . . to remind the leadership in Hanoi, the men who were directing this war in the South, that little by little through the progressive, restrained application of force by bombing, they would pay an ever-increasing price for a continuation of their aggression in the South. In other words, we were following the basic military principle applicable to all wars—that the objective of military action is the will of the enemy—in the conviction that, by the use of our air power, we could operate on that will and eventually create in the minds of the leadership of Hanoi a picture of the inevitability of defeat and the realization of the prohibitive cost of continued aggression. . . . [7]

Some hawks went even further. Admiral Sharp would inform a *Reader's Digest* audience in 1969 that the secret to "winning" the war in Vietnam was relatively simple: " . . . All that we had to do to win was to use our existing air power—properly."[8] Sharp, as well as members of the JCS and other hawks, argued from the beginning for the Pentagon's Option B: " . . . fast full squeeze" with "hot-blood actions" (see Chapters 62 and 63). He and his "colleagues in the field" wanted " . . . to bring the economy of North Vietnam to a halt," naturally by bombing. Parroting Rostow's earlier thesis, Sharp argued that " . . . the primary purpose of the air campaign against North Vietnam should have been to disrupt the enemy's economy and thus destroy his ability to wage war." Sharp wanted " . . . a sustained, maximum-effort attack on all of the enemy's war-supporting industries, transportation facilities, military complexes, petroleum-storage depots . . . "; he wanted Haiphong Harbor mined and the port closed. Although he understood that " . . . the Joint Chiefs of Staff supported my position 100 percent," most of his requests were denied by Secretary of Defense McNamara, who " . . . arbitrarily and consistently discarded the advice of his military advisers."

About all the reader can say is thank God he did, for Sharp goes on:

> . . . It may well be that our civilian leadership believed that to use our military tools properly, to eliminate the enemy's ability to make war would have been to risk a nuclear confrontation with the Soviet Union. Personally, I believe the risk was minimal; in any case, a nation which is not willing to take calculated risks to achieve its objectives should never go to war in the first place. Further, I believe that once a political decision is made to commit American troops to battle, we are morally obliged to use our military power in such a way as to end the fighting as quickly as possible.[9]

If Taylor and other advisers did not go as far as Rostow, Sharp, and the JCS, they nonetheless erred, not only in estimating strategic effects of air power but also in estimating tactical effects of air power in guerrilla warfare. It is a great pity that these influential experts had never studied such recent insurgencies as those in Indonesia, the Philippines, Malaya, Cyprus, and French Indochina, where interdiction air raids played about as effective a role in the ground action as Drake's naval raids on the Spanish Main played in England's war against Spain. In the same work quoted above, Taylor pointed to

> . . . the inability of the enemy to maintain and keep in action an indefinite number of men supported only by a clandestine logistic system. Their logistic problem increases if we continue to conduct

air attacks against their lines of supply. It grows if, by the use of our mobile offensive capability, our heli-borne forces keep attacking the main forces of the Vietcong, requiring them to defend themselves, to consume ammunition and supplies, and to suffer heavy casualties. Under such pressures, they probably cannot maintain much larger forces than they have now.[10]

Taylor was seeing the enemy in Taylor's terms, failing to realize that PAVN had not attained Western military sophistication and that its logistic demands were not to be compared with American demands. Tactical bombing against conventional armies brings meager rewards—against quasi-guerrilla armies, it brings virtually no rewards. American intelligence estimated that the *entire* Viet Cong needed twelve tons of outside supply per day[11] (versus five hundred tons daily needed to support operations by the 1st Cavalry [Airmobile] Division alone!) to carry on. How are you going to interdict effectively such a meager supply requirement?

President Johnson's decision in 1965, then, ignored two primary lessons concerning air power. The first was that chances were virtually nil of bending Hanoi's will to the extent of bringing a cringing North Vietnamese government to the conference table. Unless, it should be added, atomic bombs were employed—but this was unacceptable from both moral and practical viewpoints, and the President knew this.

The second was that aerial interdiction could impede but not stop passage of men and supplies from North to South. Neither could it noticeably halt production in North Vietnam, because the industrial complex essential to furnishing targets to bombers did not exist. To halt cottage production meant eliminating cottages, a lengthy, repugnant, and expensive task, as we learned in the strategic-bombing effort against Japan in World War II. To stop arms and equipment from entering North Vietnam meant risking war by interdicting Chinese and Soviet supply lines, and since the Administration wished to avoid war with either nation, this meant that supply lines would remain open.

These lessons proved valid. Almost everything that history either had suggested or confirmed about aerial bombing was demonstrated in North Vietnam and along the Ho Chi Minh Trail by end of 1967. The first outstanding fact was expense in American lives and machines. Although North Vietnam possessed neither an air force nor early-warning systems, the Soviets and Chinese vied in supplying anti-aircraft guns and missiles. Soviet SAM missile sites soon appeared around priority objectives. As early as 1966, American pilots were reporting that North Vietnam bridges were protected by " . . . an awesome curtain of exploding steel,"[12] words similar to those used by American pilots flying over Dien Bien Phu in 1954. Hundreds of aircraft were shot down;

those pilots and crews not killed were to languish in ghastly North Vietnamese prison camps.

The second fact was operational cost compared to results obtained. It is difficult even for a student of warfare to comprehend the vastness of the American air effort. By end of 1967, American airplanes—air force, navy, and marine—had dropped more bombs on Vietnam than the allied total expended on Germany in World War II. We must add to this hundreds of thousands of rockets and machine-gun bullets and tons of napalm. Initial operational costs shot upward and continued to rise, not a matter of millions of dollars, but of billions, which did not include more billions of indirect cost.

The third fact was international opprobrium wrought by bombings. In Ramsey Clark's words,

> ... Few people in Asia, Africa or Latin America can identify sympathetically with well-fed representatives of a rich society journeying ten thousand miles to pilot multimillion dollar B-52s and drop death and destruction on underfed Indochinese in miserable villages or along jungle trails.[13]

In early 1966, George Kennan warned the Senate Foreign Relations Committee that strategic bombing would jeopardize American relationships with Japan and other nations:

> ... Our motives are widely misinterpreted, and the spectacle ... of Americans inflicting grievous injury on the lives of a poor and helpless people, and particularly a people of different race and color, no matter how warranted by military necessity or by the excesses of the adversary our operations may seem to us to be or may genuinely be, produces reactions among millions of people throughout the world profoundly detrimental to the image we would like them to hold of this country.[14]

International voices soon confirmed the validity of this warning. In Charles de Gaulle's words, " ... We find it totally detestable that a small country should be bombed by a very big one." Arthur Schlesinger concluded that bombings have brought

> ... the rise of a new form of anti-Americanism, emotional rather than ideological, leading toward a serious estrangement between Europe and America. ... When we began to bomb the oil deposits, James Reston wrote, "There is now not a single major nation in the world that supports Mr. Johnson's latest adventure in Hanoi and Haiphong. ... "[15]

Other difficulties were unique to Vietnam. Townsend Hoopes, who was Assistant Secretary of the Air Force in 1967, later listed " . . . four adverse and intractable factors" when it came to bombing effectiveness in the North: the relatively small supply needs of the North, both for its own purposes and to pursue war in the South; the North's ability to keep going under heavy bombardment; poor weather from late September to early May (" . . . visual bombing attacks were possible on the average of only five days per month, and were frequently precluded for from two to three weeks at a time"); this meant not only diminution of attacks, but inaccurate bombing (" . . . in bad weather the bombs fell, on the average, between 1,500 and 1,800 feet from the target center"). Due to the military policy of "massive retaliation" during the Eisenhower era, " . . . bombing accuracies had improved hardly at all in the period between Korea and Vietnam."[16]

What was the net accomplishment?

Very little, except once again to disprove the Douhet theory and confirm Sir Robert Thompson's later suggestion that " . . . the bombing of the North was probably the greatest of the strategic errors of the war."[17] In fairness to Douhet, and as any number of American air force officers and other hawks have repeatedly stated, the American effort was selective (in theory, anyway) and not a saturation-bombing program. At President Johnson's insistence, planes bombed and strafed "military" targets only. Major targets at first consisted of forward supply depots and installations and of "choke points," for example key bridges or railroad yards or warehouses and oil depots. As these were neutralized or destroyed, air intelligence officers furnished secondary targets, usually smaller depots and railheads. Planes flying "armed reconnaissance" also fired on targets of opportunity, such as convoys and trains, repair parties, occasional troop units; if nothing else, planes dropped bomb loads on roads and rail lines.

As bombs and bullets killed more bridges and culverts and roads, then exploded on factories and refineries, then crept around and into Hanoi and killed and wounded thousands of civilians, and as General Curtis LeMay spoke of bombing the North Vietnamese back to the stone age—the moral and material fallacies were becoming more apparent. Harrison Salisbury, veteran correspondent of the *New York Times*, visited Hanoi in December 1966 and January 1967. He found the city in a state of defense, with thousands of individual concrete shelters " . . . spaced three or four feet apart along every boulevard and street in the city, round dark cavities with concrete lids." Rather than shocked and frightened, the people struck him as determined:

... I seldom talked with any North Vietnamese without some reference coming into the conversation of the people's preparedness to fight ten, fifteen, even twenty years in order to achieve victory. ... I began to realize that this was a national psychology. It might have been inspired by the regime, but it certainly was entirely natural. And, I believed, it suited the North Vietnamese temperament. ...

The regime had little trouble in exploiting this feeling into strength. Mr. Salisbury was shown what could hardly have been a staged scene: the wreck of the Vandien truck park, on the outskirts of Hanoi,

> ... listed as one of the major targets of our December 13 [1966] attack. It was not a formidable target when I viewed it from Route Nationale No. 1—just a half-dozen loading sheds, blasted by American bombs. But in attacking these the bombers had wrecked what was called the Polish Friendship School, probably half a mile distant on the other side of the highway. ... I could accept the bombing of the school as an accident. But I was not surprised to find that the North Vietnamese thought it was deliberate. ...

The "major" target, incidentally, contained twelve or fourteen broken-down buses and trucks. As Salisbury rhetorically asked: " ... For this kind of target was it worth jeopardizing $2 million dollar planes and the precious lives of American pilots?"[18]

The North Vietnamese Government constantly exploited, from the propaganda standpoint, other bombing mistakes, such as destruction of Namdinh village in an attempt to neutralize its rail yards. Even without mistakes, the government would have had little difficulty in exploiting the people's hatred. Fixed installations were few in North Vietnam; they had been built by personal sacrifice, and the people could hardly refrain from hating that which destroyed them. The government went so far as to arm factory workers and some citizens in Hanoi with ordinary rifles, which they fired at attacking planes. A Communist diplomat in Hanoi told Salisbury: " ... I think something like this happened in England ... in the days when the German Air Force attacked the British. As a Communist I have been interested to see the ideological propaganda gradually being replaced by national patriotic appeal. Maybe you remember something like this in the Soviet Union during the critical days of the German attack."[19]

Not only did Hanoi's will survive bombing, but substantial material gains failed to result. As expert and experienced voices soon pointed out, interdiction was not materially influencing the flow of men and supply to the South. A bomb can hit a train or a truck only with difficulty; it can rarely hit a coolie pushing a loaded bicycle along a narrow jungle trail. A bomb can interdict a bridge, which a mass labor force can either repair, replace, or bypass in a night. A bomb can interdict roads and slow traffic. But, as the French learned, mass labor can repair roads quickly; supply will get through and so will small guerrilla forces marching at night or under jungle cover to evade eyes flying overhead.

If air strategists such as Taylor, LeMay, Sharp, and Wheeler had studied Harrison Salisbury's report, they might have had second thoughts. Salisbury personally saw what past experience and present photographic reconnaissance already had demonstrated: that bombs had closed neither roads nor railroads to traffic:

> . . . We had certainly destroyed sections of the railroad time and again. I could see bridges that had been blasted beyond repair. I bumped over stretches of highway that had been relaid several times. Yet traffic was moving. It was moving in very large quantities. And this, I quickly learned, was not just because a Christmas truce was on. . . . Never, so far as I could learn, had it been seriously impeded. Difficulties, yes. Barriers, no.[20]

Even by the time of Mr. Salisbury's visit, the maximum effect of American bombing had been achieved, and it was little enough. It had not stopped Chinese and Soviet supplies from entering Vietnam, and it had slowed, but in no instance stopped, those supplies from going south. Escalation of the air war and a change of emphasis from North to South and then back again resulted in few substantial accomplishments, with almost no effect on the war in the South. The greatest accomplishment of the air war in the North lay in the reconnaissance field. On occasion, infrared radar cameras spotted troop build-ups such as that north of the Demilitarized Zone in the spring of 1967, and resulted in profitable bombing operations—isolated instances that did not alter the program's destructive failure.

Like a medicine that failed to cure a disease, bombing of the North resulted in unpleasant side effects. Selective bombing did not prevent civil casualties, which Hanoi from the beginning exploited internationally. North Vietnam had no air force and at first only primitive air defenses to counter American planes, and to some, the United States appeared as an aggressive bully, a posture exploited by Communist propaganda everywhere. Another side effect concerned Hanoi's relations with Moscow and Peking. In late 1964 and early 1965, the U.S.S.R. cautiously favored another Geneva conference, a notion rejected by Peking, which was posing as friendly protector to Hanoi. In February 1965, Soviet Russia's Premier Kosygin made an important bid to replace Chinese influence in the North Vietnamese capital. He led a strong delegation to Hanoi, where he found some support for settlement by negotiation—despite American air attacks, which Washington hastily explained were taken in "retaliation" for an NLF attack against Pleiku. The situation was later analyzed by a particularly astute observer, Professor Donald Zagoria:

> . . . It thus appears that as of early 1965, Moscow was anxious to bring about negotiations, Peking was trying to forestall them, and the Hanoi leadership was somewhere in the middle—ready to listen to American proposals, but internally divided on whether to continue applying military pressure on the south or to negotiate.

The March bombings, followed by a massive commitment of American troops, placed Hanoi moderates in an impossible position and thus altered the diplomacy of the U.S.S.R. As Zagoria wrote, " . . . Hanoi's position began to harden and the Russians became increasingly sensitive to Chinese criticism that they were anxious to make a deal with the United States to end the war on terms disadvantageous to Hanoi." The Soviet Union, in other words, had to react to the new set of rules imposed by the American government, and so did China. Where, formerly, aid to Hanoi was spasmodic and never particularly generous, now it became a token in the Sino-Soviet conflict—to Hanoi's profit. And along with that, Moscow ditched any hope for a negotiated settlement, or, as Zagoria wrote, " . . . the Russians moved to the diplomatic sidelines, letting initiatives pass to North Vietnam and the NLF.[21]

But that was only one facet of this complicated situation. By spring of 1965, the rift between Peking and Moscow had grown very wide. Officials in both capitals displayed a loquacious virulence that has few parallels in historical non-shooting situations. American diplomacy had played almost no part in developing this rift. So far as the West was concerned, it came as a bonus from the historical process; it was the greatest boon to the West since Tito's defection, in 1947, and was far more momentous, and it should have been carefully nurtured and exploited by American diplomacy. As we have seen, the Kennedy administration seemed surprisingly unaware of the developing rift. The Johnson administration seemed almost bewildered by it. Far from appreciating its importance, Johnson continued with the one policy that could have led to rapprochement between the two titans. Khrushchev's departure from the Soviet Government, coupled with the March bombings, touched off a political quarrel in Peking, where influential members of the army argued for a common front with the U.S.S.R. to resist American aggression. The quarrel exploded into civil war, which Mao Tse-tung won only with the greatest difficulty.

All this was bad enough, but whatever the attitude of the Soviet Union and China, Hanoi could not have remained complacent in response. Whether Ho Chi Minh and his advisers wanted the North to participate more actively in the South is not known. We do know that, at the time (and later), the Hanoi power group contained hawks and doves, just as did the NLF in the South. This was only natural: The war in the South had created definite stresses in the North, and there were those who wished to terminate it and those who wished to escalate it and those who wished to pursue a middle course. By reducing and even eliminating these intraparty stresses, American bombings gave Hanoi hawks virtually a free hand to escalate the action further.

CHAPTER SEVENTY-ONE

1. Douhet, 14, 22, 24.
2. Ridgway, *Soldier* . . . , 275.
3. Sheehan et al., 542–51.
4. U.S. Government, *The United States Strategic Bombing Survey* . . .
5. Ridgway, *The Korean War,* 244.
6. Gavin, *Crisis Now,* 43.
7. Maxwell Taylor, *Responsibility and Response,* 26–8.
8. Sharp.
9. Ibid. See also, Johnson, *The Vantage Point* . . .
10. Maxwell Taylor, *Responsibility and Response,* 36.
11. Browne. See also, McNamara's analysis in Sheehan et al., 550–1, 577–85; Hoopes; Weller.
12. Harvey, 141.
13. Ramsey Clark.
14. Fulbright, *The Vietnam Hearings.*
15. Schlesinger, *The Bitter Heritage* . . . , 56.
16. Hoopes, 77–8.
17. Royal United Service Institution Seminar.
18. Salisbury, *Behind the Lines—Hanoi,* 43, 144, 68. See also, Schoenbrunn, "Journey to North Vietnam"; ibid., *Vietnam.*
19. Salisbury, *Behind the Lines—Hanoi,* 147.
20. Ibid., 87–8.
21. Zagoria, *Vietnam Triangle* . . . , 45–9.

CHAPTER 72

*The summing up (III): the war on the ground • Westmoreland's strategy
• Westmoreland, Walt, and the enemy • The helicopter • Khe Sanh
• The tactical challenge • American frustration and atrocities •
Failure of the school solution • The Australian success story • Colonel
David Hackworth's extraordinary achievement • The pacification fiasco
• American tactics: mobility without purpose and purpose without
mobility*

THE STRATEGY CHOSEN to fight the war in South Vietnam
was another major reason for President Johnson's failure. It
was not altogether his fault: President Kennedy had yielded to military
control in Vietnam, and Johnson also supposed he could trust the
knowledge and judgment of such responsible military advisers as the
Joint Chiefs of Staff, theater commanders, and special advisers such as
Maxwell Taylor.

This was a mistake.

A long time ago, Clausewitz noted that " . . . the most important
single judgment a political or military leader can make is to forecast
correctly the nature of war upon which the nation is to embark. On
this everything else depends." Johnson's military advisers failed to forecast correctly the nature of this war; Johnson held neither knowledge
nor experience to question their judgment, and he lacked inclination to
consult those who could have helped him. Once he had erred, first by
bombing the North, second by committing a large number of conventional American troop units, he compounded error by permitting further
escalation. It would have taken a much more intelligent and courageous
man to withstand surrounding pressures and do otherwise. He did otherwise only when a greater pressure—American public opinion—forced
him to it.

* * *

The United States armed forces were relatively well organized for either nuclear or non-nuclear war when they were committed in strength to Vietnam, in spring of 1965. They were neither well organized, properly equipped, nor adequately trained to cope with insurgency warfare.

We have already discussed Westmoreland's attrition strategy—a dependence on superior U.S. military manpower, firepower, and mobility to wear down and finally force the enemy from the war. This was a quantitative, as opposed to a qualitative, or selective, strategy: an open-ended strategy in a challenge that called for task-force strategy. If so many men and machines could not "win," its proponents argued, more men and machines could "win." Considering size and weight of the American military machine, commanders probably felt much as Roman commanders had felt when setting out to subdue recalcitrant Iberian tribes, or as Napoleon's generals felt two thousand years later when leading armies into Spain. Our own command confidence was as misplaced. It is a great pity that our officers and officials had not analyzed these and other irregular campaigns, that they had not heeded warnings such as that delivered by Jomini in 1838:

> ... All the gold of Mexico could not have procured reliable information for the French [in Spain]; what was given was but a lure to make them fall more readily into snares.
>
> No army, however disciplined, can contend successfully against such a system applied to a great nation, unless it be strong enough to hold all the essential points of the country, cover its communications, and at the same time furnish an active force sufficient to beat the enemy wherever he may present himself. If this enemy has a regular army of respectable size to be a nucleus around which to rally the people, what force will be sufficient to be superior everywhere, and to assure the safety of the long lines of communication against numerous bodies?
>
> The Peninsular War should be carefully studied, to learn all the obstacles which a general and his brave troops may encounter in the occupation or conquest of a country whose people are all in arms....[1]

American command ignorance was not justified in Vietnam. The Viet Cong repeatedly had demonstrated that they could fight and fight well.

Hanoi's failure to panic when American bombs started dropping in the North was surely significant, as was Vo Nguyen Giap's statement, in June 1965, that the Viet Cong would fight "... only to the point that the enemy could be brought to the conference table and there defeated"—which was the position of the Viet Minh vis-à-vis France in 1954. The Viet Cong offensive in summer of 1965 added weight to

Giap's words, as did the first appearance in strength of North Vietnamese (PAVN) regiments. When the American build-up blunted the enemy effort—essentially a VC effort—still another cautionary voice sounded from the enemy camp. This was Mao's top general, Lin Piao, who, in September 1965, wrote a lengthy and somewhat ambiguous article on liberation wars. If some persons interpreted his words as warning to Hanoi not to expect active Chinese involvement in Vietnam, he nonetheless made it clear that Hanoi held the option of changing strategy and fighting a protracted war.

Such was the initial success of American arms in the South that this thought seemingly did not intrude itself into American strategic thinking. The military bias of American strategy effectively shielded the political bias of enemy strategy. Westmoreland and other military leaders, and civilians as well, could not but see the war in conventional terms despite its guerrilla trappings. They consistently underestimated the enemy's military potential. Westmoreland believed that the enemy was unimaginative and inflexible. In November 1966, he was asked: "What are the chances of the Viet Cong main-force units reverting to strictly guerrilla warfare?" He made this incredible reply:

> . . . Of course, if the enemy did this, he would be going contrary to his doctrine. He has rigidly followed Mao Tse-tung's three-phase doctrine for Communist insurgency warfare. Under this doctrine, phase one provides the political structure, phase two the guerrilla force, and phase three large, conventional-type formations that can fight open warfare. If he moved back to phase two, it would be admitting defeat. And I think this would be hard on the morale of the leadership and the troops.[2]

Westmoreland's words suggest that he had never studied either Mao Tse-tung's writings (see Chapter 21) or Giap's campaigns against the French (see Chapters 37–41 and 47–48). His confusion was matched only by the first marine commander in Vietnam, Lieutenant General Lewis Walt, who, according to the *New York Times,* told newsmen in Washington, in November 1970,

> . . . that when we went to Vietnam in the summer of 1965, he did not understand that this was primarily a guerrilla war. Like many officers who were over-optimistic in the early years of the war, he thought in terms of World War II and the Korean War, when the enemy was easy to identify.
>
> To illustrate what he termed his naiveté, he said he had once interviewed a man in a Vietnamese village who claimed to be the village chief and who gave him an optimistic report. Later he felt a tug at his pocket and found that a village woman had slipped a

note into his pocket warning him that he had been talking to the regional chief of the Vietcong.[3]

Walt further expressed his confusion in his book *Strange War, Strange Strategy,* and explained it in these extraordinary words:

> . . . Before our involvement in Vietnam we knew practically nothing of its people. As late as 1958 there was no history of them printed in the English language. There are only two or three today, none widely read.[4]

If the reader will turn to my bibliography, which does not include extensive intelligence studies of Indochina available to the author in the early 1950s (and surely to General Walt), he will note that the general errs. As for Walt's stigmatization in his book of Giap as an inept commander, this is a matter of criteria. One thinks of Foch walking in his garden at critical times in World War I and asking himself, "De quoi s'agit-il?"—What is the problem? It appears that Giap held a rather more fundamental grasp of the problem than either Walt, Westmoreland, the JCS, or those amateur strategists in the White House.

Having committed the military crime of underrating the opponent, our military leaders fell victim to tactical panaceas occasioned by technology. Early ground actions caused a good many commanders, not all, to believe that they had found the key to fighting insurgency warfare. The key was the helicopter, which furnished mobility essential to locating the enemy and bringing superior firepower to bear on him. So impressed was Secretary of Defense Robert McNamara with early operations of the 1st Cavalry (Airmobile) Division, that he said the helicopter marked " . . . the beginning of a new era in land warfare."

But dissident voices also spoke. As early as February 1966, Sir Robert Thompson, a veteran counterinsurgency campaigner, complained of American misuse of helicopters in general, pointing out that they should primarily support clear-and-hold operations rather than chase " . . . Viet Cong guerrilla units around the jungle." Thompson astutely observed that extensive availability of helicopters " . . . has exaggerated two great weaknesses of the American character in counterinsurgency—impatience and aggressiveness."[5]

Other shortcomings in American tactics soon appeared. Increased mobility proved expensive. The army's airmobile concept, while sacrificing armor, armored personnel carriers, and firepower heavier than the 105-mm. howitzer, nevertheless demanded hefty logistic support— " . . . as much as 500 tons per day if the entire division is in combat"— and could be met by air transport delivery only at virtually prohibitive cost.[6] Thus land communications, in this case from the coast to An Khe, had to be kept open—a supporting operation that neither broke up guerrilla units nor brought relief to peasants, yet furnished targets to guerrillas. The security requirement of the base camp, a huge area essential to house and feed the helicopters, also proved onerous, as did security requirements of outlying bases, permanent or temporary. If a hundred thousand troops were needed to maintain twenty thousand combat troops, then fifteen thousand combat troops were needed to produce five thousand troops actively pursuing the enemy.

Neither did the initial impact of the helicopter last long. Guerrillas heard and recognized helicopters, which meant that the user often forfeited tactical surprise. Although commanders developed decoy techniques and low-level approaches, the deception nonetheless alerted the enemy that something was up. More often than not, he slipped away before the machines landed, or he fired on machines and then slipped away, or he engaged landing parties and then slipped away. Sometimes American soldiers and marines killed, wounded, or captured him, but he also shot down a great many helicopters, ambushed a great number of ground units, and killed a great many soldiers and marines.

The increase in command communications offered by the helicopter also proved a mixed blessing. Properly exploited, it helped bring a new cohesion to the battlefield. But, as one disgruntled colonel told me, " . . . In a tactical environment where the company and battalion commanders should rule, the command helicopter often brought the brigade or division commander to the small unit tactical scene before either the company or battalion commander could arrive—the net result was to dissipate further the lower level commander's already tenuous operational control."

At the same time, American units wasted time, effort, and money in blindly pursuing the enemy. Noise limitation combined with excellent enemy intelligence caused a veteran if disillusioned marine combat officer to claim that " . . . less than two percent of all U.S. offensive operations produce any contact whatsoever with the Viet-Cong."[7]

Neither did blocking operations prosper. Units along Cambodian and Laotian borders expended great effort in blocking Viet Cong lines of communication only to find, as commanders had discovered throughout history, that they expended the bulk of their strength in static defense duties while the enemy made end runs around them. The United States could not furnish enough troops to seal off borders, and strength in one area meant weakness in another. If defense concentrated on a particular zone, the Viet Cong, unburdened by maintenance of large barrack areas and supply depots, ceased operations in favor of striking elsewhere.

Blocking actions in the north, in I Corps area, proved no more decisive. Lacking intelligence, marines blundered into costly fire fights in and south of the DMZ, where they defended strong points such as Khe Sanh only at considerable effort and cost. General Walt subsequently called the siege of Khe Sanh the most important battle in the war.[8] As he explained to a *Reader's Digest* audience, but for the "holding" action at Khe Sanh, two North Vietnamese divisions would have been able to attack Hué during the Tet offensive.

Walt's claim seems meaningless to this writer. At the time of the Khe Sanh build-up, no one in the American or South Vietnamese camp, with the possible exception of some newspaper correspondents, dreamed of a massive Tet offensive against cities and towns. This offensive did not depend on PAVN troops, whether in the Khe Sanh area or elsewhere: The enemy used only a few thousand of an available sixty thousand PAVN troops *already* in South Vietnam. What neither Walt nor Westmoreland nor their planners nor other hawks seemed to appreciate was Giap's momentum tactics: If a battle prospered, pursue it no matter the cost; if a battle did not prosper, take your losses and get out. (Giap had learned this the hard way while fighting the French.) Had the Tet offensive succeeded (assuming that Giap was calling the signals), had the South Vietnamese people risen, Giap had no less than four divisions immediately north of the DMZ that he could, and probably would have committed, along with a substantial troop reserve in South Vietnam. During the fighting at Khe Sanh, marines discovered a secret road *south* of Khe Sanh, which the enemy was using to infiltrate men from Laos.

Khe Sanh was one more American effort in a chimerical series to create a battle of Dien Bien Phu, one that American firepower would "win." Khe Sanh was neither "blocking" nor "holding." It was a tactical excrescence and was recognized as such three months after the American "victory"; in July, marines evacuated the place, which, according to a marine division commander, Major General Ray Davis, was " . . . a yoke around my neck." Despite heavy enemy casualties, Giap continued to hold the initiative in and around the DMZ and tie down thousands of marines and ARVN troops needed for counterinsurgency operations.[9]

Westmoreland's "spoiling" and "blocking" tactics may have unbalanced the enemy on occasion, but they did not gain the Americans the initiative. Even worse, as quantitative tactics, they contained the seeds of their own destruction. They called for combat troops that Westmoreland did not have and could not have so long as the American military machine yielded one combat soldier per ten soldiers. They produced maximum friendly casualties for results obtained. They proved incredibly expensive in supporting arms, and in the end they proved unacceptable to the American people, whose support was necessary if the war was to continue to escalate.

Why did Westmoreland use "spoiling" tactics, and why did the JCS condone them? The first reason was ignorance both of irregular and counterinsurgency warfare. Prior to departing for Vietnam to serve as Harkins' deputy, Westmoreland called on General Douglas MacArthur for paternal advice:

> ... Do not overlook the possibility, he [MacArthur] concluded, that in order to defeat the guerrilla, you may have to resort to a scorched earth policy. He also urged me to make sure I always had plenty of artillery, for the Oriental, he said, "greatly fears artillery."[10]

So armed, Westmoreland implemented an attrition strategy and search-and-destroy tactics that defied historical precedent. One has to search no farther than Marshal Lyautey's *tache d'huile* concept, which employed clear-and-hold tactics. Whether moving against an active or a potential enemy, the commander's strength limited his ambition. He had to move slowly, forcing himself to build a "show-piece" community of such dimensions as to attract loyalty and support of people on the spot and the attention of peoples yet to be pacified. Successful application of the concept called for a slow and methodical approach—the will to resist encroachment into "asleep" areas until means became available to clear and hold them. Then came adequate protection of the inhabitants, the issuing of identification cards, the digging out of the VC, "the man with the knife," be it by normal police methods or, those failing, by more radical Phoenix-like measures. It was slow-slow-slow, but when an area was pacified in the true meaning of the word, when the peasant enjoyed fair land distribution, fair rents, fair crop prices, adequate protection—then and only then did the word pass to make other areas receptive, a slow, often painful but ultimately rewarding process. The reader may ask, what of the enemy forces? The answer is that our all-too-few successful pacification gains nearly drove them crazy. It was the one thing that truly frightened them and in every case they reacted violently. Had the pacification process developed in a qualitative, orderly, and intelligent manner, the enemy probably would have attacked in force and been flattened by unquestionably superior firepower.

Westmoreland's refusal to accept this basic precept was shared by most of his military contemporaries—the inevitable result of "molding" American officers to staff and command norms as if they were some kind of human dough. It was an attempt to solve an unconventional tactical situation with conventional weapons and tactics, an attempt to make ordinary war out of extraordinary war. The Joint Chiefs of Staff,

Westmoreland, and various planning staffs did not and possibly could not understand that this was a war to be fought for the people rather than against a physical enemy. No matter that information was available to prove this a thousand times over—one had only to read Douglas Pike's *Viet Cong*—our people would not accept it. Little was new about the situation, either politically or tactically. Throughout history, aggressors and defenders have been faced with extraordinary political and military challenges. Those who responded wisely, those who adapted to meet the task at hand are the great captains; the others rest in Valhalla, or, hopefully, in Limbo, where they bore only their fellows with tales of battles almost but not quite won.

Having gotten priorities wrong, Westmoreland and his fellows in the Pentagon failed to realize that a quantitative effort in the highlands and the North was counterproductive. Conventional firepower possessed little validity or effectiveness in an insurgency situation. Conventional weapons "killed" without question—but they killed quantitatively. "Free fire zones" were but an admission of tactical poverty. The tactical problem was one of identifying and neutralizing enemy and reversing the political orientation of a peasantry motivated by terror, if not conviction, to anti-Western attitudes. When weapons killed the innocent, they contributed positively to the insurgent cause. And when weapons were used in such abundance as they were used in Vietnam in 1965–68, they killed many innocents.

The problem of enemy identification constantly plagued American commanders. Lacking an enemy actually firing a weapon or attempting to hide same, the American soldier was forced to identify on the basis of observation (a patrol, for example, sighting an enemy unit) and interrogation. His best intelligence source remained the peasant, but, in addition to usual hazards of obtaining military intelligence from civilians and of obtaining exact information from Orientals, the linguistic block asserted itself in nearly all cases, as did fear, distrust, and general xenophobia.

The collection process is difficult enough under the most favorable circumstances. In South Vietnam, the American soldier's distrust of the native complicated it. His superiors could speak loud and long about "hearts and minds," and President Johnson could continue to praise those "true democrats," Thieu and Ky, but the words didn't mean very much. Excepting a few isolated instances, Americans did not readily identify with South Vietnamese, toward whom they generally displayed contempt, sometimes genial, sometimes not—at worst reflected in such tactical savagery as that occurring at My Lai.

The young soldier, like his superiors totally untrained in the psychology of insurgency warfare, could not be blamed for this attitude. It was more an exuberance of confidence than of innate arrogance, more a blind belief in the American way of life. The monthly pay of an American private exceeded that of senior South Vietnamese officials and army officers. The young American raised in a technological society could not be expected, without a great deal of training which he did not receive, to respect Vietnamese peasants, the more so since he could not communicate with them. Despite the claims of many American servicemen to a Christian ethos, the bulk of them regarded peasants as gooks or slope-heads; they were human beings, yes, they should be fed and protected where possible, yes—but they were an inferior race.

This probably did not surprise the peasant, who had suffered decades of humiliation from the French and from ruling Vietnamese mandarins and army. It added, however, to a fundamental xenophobia that further widened the gulf to damage greatly the intelligence-collection process with the concomitant result of repeated tactical failures and ever-mounting casualties.

In time, and not a very long time, the young soldier began to feel that anyone not in American uniform was against him. As jungle environment told, as fevers appeared, as sores opened and festered, as men fell victim to mines and booby traps, as units walked into ambush, tired and nervous men grew more tired and more nervous and, if fired upon, sometimes did not hesitate to invoke the available total wrath of the American equivalent of Zeus. Commanders who were enjoined to kill as many enemy as possible at cost of the fewest American lives, too often failed to delimit the target before committing the vast armory at their disposal. When such fury failed to evoke expected results, tempers flared further and sometimes innocent people suffered as a result. Early denunciations of ARVN cruelty to villagers horrified many Americans. Yet, as the war continued, American forces sometimes indulged in the fatal error of promiscuous brutality. One disillusioned marine combat officer, Lieutenant Colonel Corson, charged that " . . . search-and-destroy tactics against VC-controlled areas have degenerated into savagery. The terrorism of the enemy has been equally matched by our own."[11] Corson's indignant cry was dismissed by hawks as that of a malcontent. Unfortunately, his words soon gained currency when My Lai became a part both of the American vocabulary and American shame.[12]

The shame of My Lai was not singular. American marines were not long in the field when they began to answer VC atrocities in kind. "We paid the enemy back, sometimes with interest . . . ," Philip Caputo wrote of those early days. "Some line companies did not even bother taking prisoners; they simply killed every VC they saw, and a number of Vietnamese who were only suspects."[13] As David Hackworth later put it, " . . . It really was a wonder there were not more My Lais."[14]

The reader may well ask: Was there a way around this difficulty, a solution? The answer is yes, and it is not an answer of hindsight since in part it was demonstrated with favorable results.

The first solution would have been to choose civil and military commanders who understood insurgency warfare and were mentally and morally equipped to report realities, not dreams, to Washington. This would have dictated two complete turn-arounds in American policy. It would have demanded a supreme commander, a single director of civil and military operations—a temporary dictator, if you will, but a qualified one that would have been jammed down Ngo Dinh Diem's unwilling patrician throat. It would also have demanded a clear-and-hold pacification strategy, a qualitative approach demanding more time and far less physical and financial investment as onus was slowly but methodically transferred to local, indigenous authority.

On the tactical level, a primary solution would have been to utilize native talent. Robert Shaplen has pointed out to the writer that, whereas Americans find the Vietnamese language difficult to learn, the Vietnamese learn English fairly well and quickly, if properly taught.[15] A viable teaching program did not develop, and as one result, most ARVN soldiers did not speak English, which made it even more difficult to integrate them into American units. Moreover, thanks to early American army influence, most ARVN soldiers were not counterguerrilla-oriented and did not often respect the peasant or identify with him.

One answer was the Kit Carson scout program, which, in general, worked very well. The surprising fact, in view of the historical precedent of such programs, is that it took so long to initiate and remained so limited.

The army and marines were also on the right track with long-range reconnaissance patrols, probably the most successful tactic employed by either service in Vietnam. It remained to go a step further and cut the umbilical cord to artillery and air support—in other words, to fight guerrillas with guerrillas, as Roger Hilsman, among others, had recommended years earlier, and as a few outstanding field-grade and company-grade army and marine officers were doing. To have fought guerrillas with guerrillas would have dictated an entirely different tactical approach. American military doctrine does not accept decentralized tactical control. Reluctance of senior commanders, from Pentagon to battalion level, to turn this war over to small-unit commanders was a major tactical deficiency that neither time nor experience repaired. The Australians did not so err. Having analyzed the tactical problem in their area of operations, they " . . . concentrated solely on jungle warfare at a ten-thousand-acre tropical rain forest training ground." Eschewing battalion- and company-size tactics, they " . . . used squads to make a contact, and brought in reinforcing elements to do the killing; they planned in the belief that a platoon on the battlefield could do anything 'including get out' . . . the Australians understood the war better than our guys ever would."[16]

Young American soldiers, both officers and non-coms, often resented the doctrinaire approach, especially in such a variegated combat environment. Young, active, bright, confident, and often imaginative, they respected without fearing the enemy. My friend Lieutenant X, cited in a previous chapter, like dozens of others, proved time and again that he and his men were as capable of sneaking through and fighting in the boondocks as the Viet Cong. Had such men been encouraged to perfect appropriate tactics, the war could have been fought with minimum expenditure to gain maximum results. So impressed was Lieutenant Colonel Hackworth with the Australian doctrine that, when commanding a battalion, he sent three platoon leaders to train with them, even though he had been refused official permission to do so—"selective insubordination," he called it, in this case to save lives.[17]

Hackworth later commanded a battalion, composed mostly of recent draftees, in the Mekong Delta where he faced a main-force VC regiment. Employing a great deal of effort and ingenuity, he managed to convert the battalion into a genuine counterinsurgency force, with each of four rifle companies intensely trained in one operational specialty, be it day and night, long- and short-range ambush; be it day and night small-unit patrols; be it sniper teams operating from helicopters or equipped with starlight scopes, flying at night in choppers to fire tracers on VC groups so that following gunships could work them over; be it inserting two-man sniper teams by night into "enemy" country to wait-wait-wait, then WHAM! By means of an intelligent admixture of " . . . surprise, deception, mobility, imagination, and familiarity with the terrain," he attained the vital shock action and flexibility necessary to " . . . out-guerrilla the guerrilla." The result? An early success that resulted in 143 dead VC at a cost of eight lightly wounded American soldiers. Then 120 hard-core VC dead versus four lightly wounded American soldiers. In a few months, over 2,500 VC dead in return for twenty-five American lives. Here was counterinsurgency warfare as it should have been fought from the beginning. Here is what history, what Hilsman and Gavin and Griffith had recommended. Higher echelons duly honored Hackworth's achievement, as well they should since it belonged in the *Guinness Book of Records* and since he had been wounded four times in achieving it. He was awarded more medals. " . . . And yet no one tried to copy us. . . . Even General Abrams said that all his battalions should fight like 4/39, but no effort was made to make sure they did. . . . So in the end, yet again, there were no lessons learned, and the same mistakes were allowed to be made, day after day after day."[18]

Higher echelons of the American military had no intention of departing from traditional command and staff doctrines. The inevitable result was reliance on what the military calls "the school solution." Secondary operations such as Sting Ray patrols were tolerated but not particularly encouraged. The writer attempted to discuss the success of small, long-range patrols with a senior marine officer only to be told, " . . . Oh, we have dozens such patrols—one's the same as the other." Had other patrols scored the tactical success of the ones the writer was attempting to discuss, half of General Walt's tactical problems would have been solved. But as Frederick the Great sagely pointed out, " . . . The jackass who experienced twenty of [Prince] Eugene's campaigns was none the better tactician for it."

Small-unit tactics, no matter how well conducted, would have been wasted without the other essential: a strong political base from which they could be launched and which could be expanded as they succeeded—in effect, Lyautey's *tache d'huile* concept. Nothing better illustrated the disparity in thought in top military and civil echelons than this requirement. Despite MACV's authority, it did not command a unified effort. The Saigon government and ARVN remained outside its administrative and operational control, as did such allied units as the Koreans. This meant a variety of pacification efforts, each with its own administrative complex. But MACV also faced internal problems. U. S. Army commanders did not see the pacification task in the same light as Foreign Service officers in CORDS. The U. S. Air Force, U. S. Navy and U. S. Marine Corps, which reported directly to CINCPAC, generally did not agree with the army concept. So far apart were the U. S. Army and U. S. Marine Corps on the pacification issue, that the situation became reminiscent of nineteenth-century warfare, when commanders, separated and out of touch, waged the type of campaign each deemed best.

MACV held for occupation of "liberated" areas by ARVN units working in conjunction with the Saigon government's Revolutionary Development program—an inadequate solution (as discussed earlier) in that ARVN units furnished neither adequate military security nor economic sustenance to peasants, with whom they did not seem able to identify. The marines approached the problem differently, and made some substantial progress. William Lederer pointed out that, during 1967, the number of villages under NLF-PLP control increased " . . . except in one small area where the United States Marine Corps combined action platoons (CAP) are operating." In his opinion, it was " . . . the only successful American project of any kind whatsoever in Vietnam."[19] A British counterinsurgency expert, Richard Clutterbuck, reported that the marine effort represented one of " . . . two grains of encouragement" in Vietnam in 1968. Clutterbuck was impressed because the CAP tackled the basic village problem of VC intimidation—in his effective phrase, " . . . the man with the knife":

> . . . The normal popular force [militia] in Vietnam now does not live in the village at night, but outside. In the village at night the man with a knife can get in. If 15 Marines and 35 Popular Forces live inside the village at night, you get somewhere, and you can also patrol the village street at night.

At the time of Clutterbuck's visit, eighty CAPs had been formed, and in 80 per cent of the concerned villages " . . . the hamlet chief can sleep, whereas he can only do so in 20 per cent of the villages in the rest of Vietnam." Although CAPs suffered high casualties, " . . . they are only 50 per cent of the casualties of the normal infantry or marine battalions being flown around by helicopter on large scale operations."[20] Clutterbuck did not add that casualties would radically lower as village complexes were consolidated, policed, and redeveloped.

What went wrong with CAP?

A number of things. By mid-1968, the program included nearly two thousand Americans and twenty-seven hundred Vietnamese militia working in a hundred different hamlets. These figures are not impressive: I Corps area comprised five provinces, with a total 2.7 million population. The prototype program could only expand if additional combat personnel were made available. These would have had to come from one of two sources: from operational units, which would have meant adopting a defensive posture, in other words severely limiting or even ending search-and-destroy or "spoiling" tactics; or from fresh units sent from the United States.

But Westmoreland (later Abrams), MACV, and the JCS held no intention of abandoning large-scale actions. Another British observer, Brigadier K. Hunt of The Institute for Strategic Studies, was also favorably impressed with the CAP program, but " . . . when I went down to MACV and referred to this, they said that I had been fixed by the Marines, been brain-washed! They did not agree and said that in any case it would be too expensive."[21] MACV refused to accept early successes and went out of its way to sabotage the program by forcing Walt to commit increasing numbers of combat units to the DMZ fighting. To emphasize displeasure, Westmoreland created a new command in the north under an army general, which exacerbated already tense command relations between the two services.[22]

But even MACV's intransigent attitude was not the major stumbling block to a viable pacification program. Walt and Westmoreland could have committed a hundred thousand American troops to the effort and still drawn a blank—so long as the South Vietnamese Government failed to govern properly.

By end of 1968, then, American tactics continued to provide mobility without purpose and purpose without mobility. They continued to expend American lives and dollars for minimum combat results while destroying the vital ingredient of counterinsurgency warfare: peasant co-operation. In trying to win the shooting war, American military strategy was contributing to the loss of the real war. How to reverse the situation or at least to salvage some semblance of national self-respect from it was perhaps the chief problem inherited by Richard Milhous Nixon.

CHAPTER SEVENTY-TWO

1. Jomini, 32.
2. *U.S. News and World Report, November 28, 1956.*
3. *New York Times,* Washington, November 18, 1970.
4. Walt, *Strange War, Strange Strategy, 92.*
5. Robert Thompson, "Feet on the Ground."
6. Weller.
7. Corson, 147.
8. Walt, "Khe Sanh—The Battle That Had to Be Won."
9. UPI, Saigon, July 5, 1968. See also, Hackworth, 610–11. Neither did Mc-Namara's fence solve anything. Fences, walls—barriers of all kinds—had been tried from the dawn of history, and most had been found wanting in even favorable terrain. The difficult terrain of the DMZ, ground hotly contested and often controlled by VC and PAVN units, ground interdicted by long-range artillery, made such a project initially impractical. Neither was sensor technology so advanced as scientists claimed. Finally, the enemy had never infiltrated through the DMZ to the extent reported, but rather through Laos by the Ho Chi Minh trail, which it continued to use. See O'Ballance, "The Ho Chi Minh Trail." In the event, McNamara's folly was quietly dropped—after an expenditure of several million dollars.
10. Westmoreland, 40.
11. Corson, 68.
12. Hersh, "My Lai 4."
13. Caputo, 178.
14. Hackworth, 694.
15. Private letter to the author.
16. Hackworth, 494–5.
17. Ibid., 498.
18. Ibid., 700–4.
19. Lederer, *Our Own Worst Enemy,* 158, 186.
20. Royal United Service Institution Seminar. See also, Mulligan.
21. Royal United Service Institution Seminar.
22. Saipan all over again! See Vandegrift and Asprey, 259–64.

CHAPTER 73

Richard Nixon's promise • His position on Vietnam • Enter Henry Kissinger • His plan for disengagement • General Creighton Abrams' tactics • Cambodian sanctuaries • Le petit prince Norodom Sihanouk and Cambodian neutrality • The Bowles mission • President Nixon's decision to bomb enemy sanctuaries in Cambodia • Operation Menu

AS THE KOREAN WAR had influenced 1952 presidential elections, the Vietnam War produced heated debate throughout 1967 up to the November elections of 1968.[1] Richard Nixon not only secretly criticized President Johnson's Vietnam policy, but implied that he had a secret plan to win the war. As he told prospective voters in New Hampshire early in the year:

> . . . I pledge to you the new leadership will end the war and win the peace in the Pacific. . . . I do not suggest withdrawal from Vietnam. I am saying to you that it is possible if we mobilize our economic and political and diplomatic leadership it can be ended. The failure in Vietnam is not the failure of our fighting men in Vietnam but the failure of our leadership in Washington, D.C., to back them up.[2]

In his inaugural address, he spoke of moving from " . . . an era of confrontation to an era of negotiation." In March 1969, he would tell his cabinet that " . . . I expect the war to be over in a year."[3] (So Nixon, and Kissinger along with him, joined the ranks that from the beginning had underestimated Hanoi's resilience and determination.) If Nixon supporters imagined that he was going to pull an Eisenhower—visit Vietnam and bring about a cease-fire (a dramatic effort with disappointing results in the case of Korea)—they were soon disappointed. Nixon was a man of covert compromise, and in his mind Vietnam called for a particularly careful political approach which in essence was to be

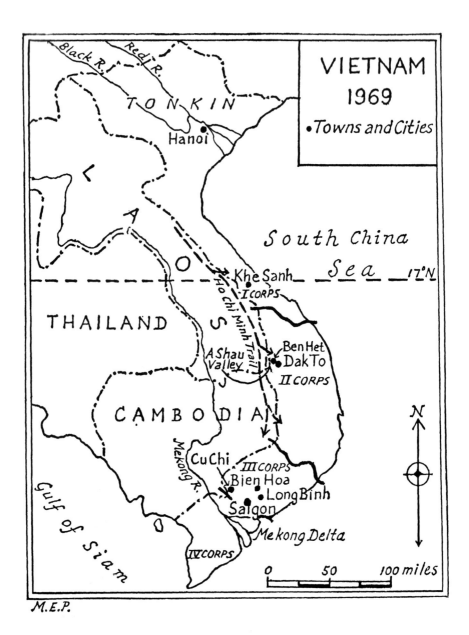

VIETNAM
1969
• Towns and Cities

M.E.P.

based on gunboat diplomacy, in this case massive aerial bombing, and, when this failed, enlarged ground action.

Nixon entered office a prisoner of three major forces: his own fears of communism, which he had repeatedly emphasized by provocative and even bellicose statements and actions in refuting the idea of negotiation as a proper basis for ending the Vietnam War; a hawkish military strategy (he had " ... favored the use of American bombers to rescue the French at Dien Bien Phu and asserted that 'tactical atomic explosives are now conventional and will be used against the target of any aggressive forces' ");[4] the South Vietnamese Government, which he had helped to build. From 1962 onward, he consistently pushed for escalation of the war in Vietnam in order to prevent Chinese hordes from overrunning all of Asia. In 1966, he told an American Legion audience:

> . . . In the event that Vietnam is either lost at the conference table or on the battlefield, it will mean that the Pacific will become a Red Sea, that Communist China will become the dominant power in that area of the world, and that World War Three will be inevitable.[5]

Although he began to backtrack in 1968, he could not summarily cut the bonds of these forces, and he never did. At some point after his election, he told one of his keepers, H. R. Haldeman, that his strategy rested on military threat:

> . . . I call it the Madman Theory, Bob. I want the North Vietnamese to believe I've reached the point where I might do *anything* to stop the war. We'll just slip the word to them that "for God's sake, you know Nixon is obsessed about Communism. We can't restrain him when he's angry—and he has his hand on the nuclear button"—and Ho Chi Minh himself will be in Paris in two days begging for peace.[6]

Shortly after taking office, Nixon relieved negotiator William Averell Harriman in favor of Henry Cabot Lodge, whom he instructed to avoid private negotiations at the Paris talks. At the same time, he permitted General Creighton Abrams, Westmoreland's successor in South Vietnam, to continue attrition strategy by keeping pressure on the enemy. So far, this was "more of the same," but the new President also made an appointment that surprised a good many persons: he named Henry Kissinger to the influential post of presidential adviser on national security affairs.

Kissinger's appointment would have raised eyebrows under normal circumstances. Forty-five years old, he had come to America in 1938, a German-Jewish refugee who studied at Harvard and subsequently became a professor of government there. Within the Establishment he was well known as a theoretician and writer on national strategy and limited war—indeed, about the only Republican with such a background. One of his early outpourings called for replacing John Foster Dulles' insane doctrine of "massive [nuclear] retaliation" with "limited nuclear war," an equally insane doctrine preached by, among other military futurists, Herman Kahn, and later watered down by Kissinger to the more sensible limited conventional war.[7] Kissinger had advised three administrations on international affairs; he had for some time been involved in behind-the-scenes diplomacy concerning Vietnam during which he had made several fact-finding trips to that country,[8] and he had served a " . . . short, unhappy stint in McGeorge Bundy's National Security Council" before returning to Harvard and to Governor Nelson Rockefeller's political fiefdom.[9]

Kissinger considered himself brilliant, witty, and charming, and some agreed with that assessment. Others considered him overly pedantic, short-tempered, arrogant, and rude, an intellectual opportunist who wanted power and more power. He also considered himself a man of honor—to my knowledge he never defined the term—who was intent on saving America and the world from the evils of communism. Some of his judgments did show a certain prescient brilliance, for example in 1968 he declared that Richard Nixon was "unfit to be President"—"the most dangerous" of the candidates.[10] Events quickly altered those harsh judgments. According to Nixon, Kissinger shortly before the 1968 presidential election was using his contacts with the Democrats " . . . to uncover foreign policy information that he passed on to help Nixon's campaign."[11]

From the hawk standpoint, Kissinger initially appeared to be a disappointing selection. He was not a military man nor did he necessarily embrace force as a proper solution to political problems. He was willing to listen to those who favored a military solution, but he did not suffer fools gladly, and he had an annoying habit of producing facts and figures that weighed heavily against those cited by various hawks. The latter's fears were greatly increased when the January 1969 issue of *Foreign Affairs* carried his work, "The Viet Nam Negotiations," as its lead article. After briefly reviewing the situation in South Vietnam, Kissinger discounted American attrition strategy, which " . . . failed to reduce the guerrillas and was in difficulty even with respect to the North Vietnamese main forces." A predominant military influence " . . . caused our military operations to have little relationship to our declared political objectives. Progress in establishing a political base was excruciatingly slow; our diplomacy and our strategy were conducted in isolation from each other." This explained, among other things, the failure of the pacification program. The Tet offensive, which militarily Kissinger judged an American "victory," was " . . . a political defeat in the countryside for Saigon and the United States." This action

> . . . marked the watershed of the American effort. . . . Denied the very large additional forces requested, the military command in Viet Nam felt obliged to begin a gradual change from its peripheral strategy to one concentrating on the protection of the populated area. This made inevitable an eventual commitment to a political

solution and marked the beginning of the quest for a negotiated settlement.

Kissinger went on to review earlier, behind-the-scenes negotiations, and emphasized the difficulties that had to be overcome before meaningful talks could occur. A variety of factors were at work in each of the interested countries, and these combined in a dozen ways to affect internal and external relationships, thereby limiting each country's freedom of maneuver. At best, Kissinger believed, the United States could expect " . . . prolonged negotiations progressing through a series of apparent stalemates."[12]

The newly elected President was not familiar with this article, so the story goes, when he tapped its author for the new and responsible job of national security adviser. His choice implied tacit acceptance of Kissinger's somewhat vague and convoluted thinking. Kissinger's appointment, however, spelled no immediate or drastic action, at least in connection with the Vietnam War. Kissinger's main effort in the early days seemed to concentrate on reorganizing, with the help of able assistant Morton Halperin, the National Security Council in such a way as to effectively seal off the Departments of State and Defense from the President's office.[13] This was done by setting up a number of powerful committees, each chaired by Kissinger, who in a short time held more titles than ever dreamed of by Poo-Bah. (Halperin would soon be accused of trying to thwart the monster he had helped to create. After having had his telephone tapped and suffering other indignities, he resigned as did other top assistants including Roger Morris, who later described the National Security Council as " . . . a seizure of power unprecedented in modern American foreign policy.")[14]

So armed, Kissinger turned to the major problem of carrying out Nixon's "plan," which apparently existed only in embryo. As for Kissinger's article, several of its points had been raised over a year earlier by a proven authority on Indochina, Robert Shaplen, also writing in *Foreign Affairs*.[15] Instead of a specific program, Kissinger offered general guidelines. The disparate factors he had discussed that existed in Hanoi, Saigon, and Washington exerted themselves on the new Administration just as they did on Saigon and Hanoi governments. Top American officials, civil and military, were still divided into hawks and doves. Three months after Nixon assumed office, *Newsweek* reported that a canvass of the Pentagon, the State Department, the American embassy in Saigon, and the American team in Paris made it clear

> . . . that none of these governmental "satrapies" could agree on the facts of the Vietnam conflict, much less on what conclusions to draw from those facts. As a result, at the first full-dress National

Security Council meeting devoted to Vietnam, the participants were asked to consider no fewer than nine possible courses of action to end the war—four military and five political.[16]

Shortly after Abrams relieved Westmoreland, American tactics had begun to alter. Although Abrams was a World War II tank commander wedded to conventional Western military thinking, he apparently entertained some doubts about Westmoreland's attrition strategy with emphasis on large-unit search-and-destroy operations. As stated earlier, he converted in part to Sting Ray tactics—smaller patrols instead of battalion and brigade actions essential to successful prosecution of this type of war.

Three factors lessened the beneficial effects derived from this tactical modification. The first was that Abrams did not seem to understand the nature of this war any more than had Westmoreland. He insisted on gaining a military solution by keeping "maximum pressure," so-called "pile-on" tactics, against an enemy willing to fight back. In time, perhaps, Abrams' tactical adaptation might have produced sufficiently important results to bring a change from the quantitative to the qualitative, with emphasis on political aspects of the war. But now the second factor emerged: Abrams' changes, minor enough, encountered doctrinal hostility from *within the U. S. Army* whose senior commanders were lukewarm to *any* tactical changes, the more so because they still did not and perhaps never would comprehend the nature of this war, much less its tactical challenges. Related to this was a third factor: each arm attempting to outdo the other in staking its claim as the arm most suitable for fighting counterinsurgency warfare and, in the process, frequently operating in such a way as to reduce or totally neutralize beneficial effects of civil pacification programs.

Lack of progress had of course to be justified. In addition to a claimed insufficiency of troops; a temporary lid on the bombing of the North; American civilian, press, and television hostility, the favorite scapegoat was enemy sanctuary in Cambodia with alleged vast amounts of arms and equipment from China reaching the Communists through the port of Sihanoukville. Never mind that it had been obvious from the beginning that the guerrillas would rely on this sanctuary just as had the Viet Minh in the war against the French. As American clear-and-destroy operations multiplied, Viet Cong and PAVN units, when caught short or when tired or when needing resupply, merely slipped across the border into the mountains and forests of northeast neutral Cambodia, which in time housed a complex that supported an estimated forty thousand troops.[17] It was natural enough for MACV and ARVN to want to invade the sanctuaries and thereby, as it was believed, eliminate the potential threat of a massive attack on Saigon only twenty-five to thirty miles from the border.

The difficulty was that Cambodia, a French protectorate-cum-colony since 1864, had gained independence with its neutrality guaranteed by the 1954 Geneva Agreements. For some years its ruler, Prince Norodom Sihanouk—a flamboyant, irascible, anti-American playboy—was willing to ignore the restricted VC and PAVN intrusions, just as his forefathers had accepted the existence of bandits in the mountainous southwest, the pirates that infested the rivers, and the Khmer Loeu hill tribes in the northeast mountains.[18] Such was Sihanouk's erratic but dictatorial rule that his political base in Phnom Penh was far from firm. Although he was a virtual god to the feudal peasantry (a very important fact consistently overlooked by American planners), he had to rule through a variety of fiefdoms controlled by various powerful war lords. He had no army to speak of, he feared the traditional Vietnamese enemy, and he wanted desperately to keep Cambodia out of the war. A major complication had been solved after the Geneva Agreements when several thousand Cambodian Communists went into voluntary exile in North Vietnam (where they were trained in insurgency warfare). The few Communists who remained—Sihanouk named them *les Khmers Rouges*—poised no immediate challenge to an essentially conservative peasantry, nor did a nationalist guerrilla group, the *Khmer Serai,* cause great concern. Sihanouk's main purpose was not to rock his very vulnerable ship of state, as reflected in his refusal to join John Foster Dulles' cardboard alliance called SEATO, thus raising American ire another degree (see Chapter 49).[19] Not-so-subtle American attempts to change this policy resulted in increasing estrangement marked by Sihanouk's concomitant move toward Russia and China, a move paralleled by the CIA's support of Sihanouk's rival, Son Ngoc Thanh, and by a disruption campaign as stupid as it was vicious designed to woo the urban elite and the officer corps from supporting Sihanouk, an effort so threatening that an enraged Sihanouk broke diplomatic relations with the United States in 1965 and subsequently permitted the VC and later PAVN units to take sanctuary in the east and to allow China to ship arms to the port of Sihanoukville from where they eventually reached Viet Cong and PAVN units.

Details of the sanctuary area were vague. Covert American and South Vietnamese intelligence-collection operations inside Cambodia—Programs Salem House and Daniel Boone—carried out by CIA and Special Forces' recruited Civilian Irregular Defense Groups (CIDG) had met with only limited success: " . . . in 1,835 missions over four years they captured twenty-four prisoners."[20] MACV nonetheless reported and aerial reconnaissance partially confirmed the alleged existence of fifteen enemy bases in the border area. To his credit, President Johnson refused to subvert international law by condoning overt retaliation. He did not share the State Department's aversion to Sihanouk—"Everything I hear about the Prince suggests that we ought to get on well with him," he told his staff in 1966[21]—and he did not believe that America could violate Cambodia's sovereignty with impunity.

That a severe threat both to South Vietnam and potentially to Cambodia existed was beyond doubt. Taken with Sihanouk's fear of massive retaliation against the sanctuaries by the Americans, it caused him to seek rapprochement with the Johnson government. In late 1967 he told a journalist, Stanley Karnow, that

> . . . he would grant the U.S. the right of "hot pursuit" against the North Vietnamese and Vietcong in Cambodia—so long as no Cambodians were harmed. . . . Plainly trying to prevent Cambodia from becoming a battlefield, Sihanouk said: "We are a country caught between the hammer and the anvil, a country that would very much like to remain the last haven of peace in Southeast Asia."[22]

An official mission headed by Chester Bowles, U.S. ambassador to India, soon arrived in Phnom Penh. Exactly what was or was not agreed to is not clear. William Shawcross writes that the State Department subsequently edited and excised official records (which has happened before and after). Nixon later wrote that Sihanouk requested American retaliation " . . . either with 'hot pursuit' on the ground or by bombing the sanctuaries."[23] The somewhat cloudy record does not substantiate Nixon's statement, and neither Bowles nor mission members agreed with it:

> . . . The State Department notes that by the end of the visit the Bowles party believed that "there seemed little doubt that on the Cambodian side fears of 'hot pursuit' [by American and South Vietnamese forces] had been allayed." The Americans, for their part, stressed that a catastrophic widening of the war had been averted and that the Bowles mission had succeeded in overcoming many of the problems which had embittered United States-Cambodian relations.[24]

Shawcross later wrote that Sihanouk told Bowles that " . . . he was ready to restore relations with Washington if only the Americans would recognize the inviolability of Cambodia's existing borders."[25] There is a serious contradiction in the record here, but President Johnson's refusal to violate the border other than with small covert raids suggests that this was no black-and-white affair, at least in the international tribunal. Sihanouk is a very quixotic little man, and indeed may have said different things to different people. In the end it did not matter what he said since Nixon and Kissinger summarily judged that " ... the concerned territory ... was no longer Cambodian in any practical sense."[26]

President Nixon was perfectly willing to resume relations with Cambodia on a quid pro quo basis that he and Kissinger hoped would wean Sihanouk from neutrality. The sanctuary problem seemed to offer a good beginning. How could the United States best "quarantine" Cambodia was an early question Nixon put to the JCS. The reply came from Saigon where MACV had steadily invoked the Cambodian sanctuary as the reason for the continuing failure of American and ARVN strategy and tactics, and in so doing had created a mythical picture of an enemy Pentagon in the middle of the Cambodian jungle. In early February, General Creighton Abrams informed the JCS that " ... recent information gives us hard intelligence on COSVN Hq [North Vietnam's Central Office for South Vietnam] facilities in Base Area 353."[27] Abrams predicted

> ... a large-scale enemy offensive around Saigon in the near future. An attack on COSVN, he argued, "will have an immediate effect on the offensive and will also have its effect on future military offensives which COSVN may desire to undertake."[28]

Abrams recommended " ... a short-duration, concentrated B-52 attack of up to sixty sorties. ... There is little likelihood of involving Cambodian nationals if the target boxes are placed carefully."[29] This fitted nicely with Nixon's question, and when the North Vietnamese launched a new offensive in February, which Nixon interpreted as a test of his determination and which in three weeks cost over a thousand American lives and far more South Vietnamese lives, he approved Abrams' recommended bombing program—providing it was carried out in total secrecy. Operation Menu began with Breakfast on March 18. Each B-52, flying from Guam, carried thirty tons of bombs which were dropped on a " ... box ... about a half mile wide by two miles long": " ... forty-eight of such boxes were stamped upon neutral Cambodia by the express order of the President."[30] Breakfast was succeeded by Lunch, Snack, Dinner, and Dessert—in fourteen months, 3,630 B-52 raids were carried out against a neutral country.[31]

Nixon and Kissinger's aerial offensive was unique in several respects. Elaborate precautions were taken to maintain secrecy. Congressional authority was not sought. According to Nixon and Kissinger, only a few of the people's representatives were informed. They included Senators Richard Russell and John Stennis of the Senate Armed Services

Committee: " . . . both men," Nixon wrote, "thought that the bombing was the right decision, and both said they would back me up in the event that it became public."[32] Neither the Secretary nor the Chief of Staff of the Air Force was told. Defense Secretary Melvin Laird and Secretary of State William Rogers were informed and they argued against it; Laird at least wanted it to be made public but Kissinger and Nixon refused to consider this. A week after the Breakfast bombing began, the *New York Times* reported that Abrams had requested air strikes against the Cambodian sanctuaries. The White House issued a "qualified denial."[33] Ironically, when the *Times* and other papers broke the story in April and May no one, including members of pertinent Congressional committees, paid attention except Nixon and Kissinger, who in their fury at the leak had a number of assistants, officials, and journalists wiretapped by the FBI.[34] Other than that blip, secrecy and deniability were achieved by a system of dual reporting so involved that " . . . the bombing was not merely concealed; the official, *secret* records showed that it never happened."[35] Indeed it was not until 1973 that the scam was exposed by a conscience-stricken radar officer who blew the whistle to his senator. In a subsequent series of Senate hearings, the principals either disclaimed knowledge or responsibility or both, or swore that Sihanouk had sanctioned the raids. General Brent Scowcroft, one of Kissinger's principal aides, stated that " . . . the falsification was done on direct White House orders."[36] The investigation possibly would have gone deeper except that America was tired of the war and for some time Watergate had replaced it as the country's chief interest.

What did the bombings achieve? They certainly killed some of the enemy and eliminated some rude enemy installations. Although General Abrams and Ambassador Ellsworth Bunker, according to Melvin Laird, were convinced that " . . . Menu has been one of the most telling operations of the war,"[37] there is considerable evidence that the multimillion-dollar operation did not live up to tactical expectations—bombings rarely do especially if you are bombing forest and jungle. Roger Morris, also a principal Kissinger aide, later wrote that " . . . according to the best CIA and Pentagon intelligence fourteen months [and over 100,000 tons of bombs] later . . . [it had] no appreciable effect on enemy capabilities in enemy areas."[38] A special stand-by infantry team was told prior to the first bombing that " . . . if there was anybody still alive out there they would be so stunned that all [we would] have to do [was] walk over and lead him by the arm to the helicopter." The team duly moved in immediately after the strikes and was slaughtered by enemy fire. A second team refused to go in—its members, when threatened with arrest, were legally advised that " . . . you can't be arrested for refusing to violate the neutrality of Cambodia."[39]

Enemy units dispersed by Operation Menu merely moved farther west to set up new camps. Bringing the war closer to the Cambodian people complicated Sihanouk's position even more—and perhaps that was the Administration's intention. There remains the question of civilian casualties inflicted by the bombings. Nixon and Kissinger later insisted that the target areas were free of Cambodian civilians.[40] That does not appear to be accurate:

> ... Classified documents published later were to disclose that Abrams and other top officers, knowing the targeted areas to be populated by civilians, had secretly conceded that "some Cambodian casualties would be sustained in the operation."[41]

According to William Shawcross:

> ... The Joint Chiefs themselves informed the administration as early as April 1969 that many of the sanctuary areas were populated by Cambodians who might be endangered by bombing raids.[42]

Base Area 353, for example, was believed to have had " ... a total population of approximately 1,640 Cambodians, of whom the Joint Chiefs reckoned 1,000 to be peasants."[43] One should keep in mind that the peasants had neither warning nor air raid shelters. There is no doubt that many of them, as harbinger of the future, were killed and wounded—no one knows how many.

CHAPTER SEVENTY-THREE

1. U.S. Congress, "The Candidates' Views." See also, White, *The Making of the President 1968*.
2. U.S. Congress, "The Candidates' Views."
3. Nixon, *Memoirs*, 390.
4. Shawcross, 76.
5. Reichley, 106.
6. Haldeman, 83.
7. Shawcross, 75. See also, Morris, 53.
8. Kissinger, *The White House Years*, 232–5.
9. Shawcross, 75. See also, Reichley, 114.
10. Shawcross, 79. See also, Karnow, 584–5; Fallaci, 37: In 1972, Oriana Fallaci, an exceedingly perceptive Italian journalist, asked Kissinger:

> O.F.: Power is always alluring. Dr. Kissinger, to what degree does power fascinate you? ...
> H.K.: ... You see, when you have power in your hands and have held it for a long period of time, you end up thinking of it as something that's due you ... what interests me is what you can do with power. Believe me, you can do wonderful things.

11. Shawcross, 79.
12. Kissinger, *The White House Years,* 234 ff.
13. Mollenhoff, 156 ff. See also, Morris, 47 ff., 78–83.
14. Karnow, 587. See also, Haldeman, 100–3, for the etiology and subsequent developments of the FBI wiretaps " . . . inspired by Henry's rage and ordered by Nixon"; Morris, 154–63, on wiretaps.
15. Shaplen, "Viet-Nam: Crisis of Indecision."
16. *Newsweek,* April 7, 1969.
17. Nixon, *Memoirs,* 381.
18. Shawcross, 37. See also, Sihanouk.
19. Sihanouk, 75 ff. See also, Colby, 149–50, who mistakenly dates the rupture from 1959.
20. Shawcross, 65. See also, Kiernan, 385.
21. Shawcross, 66.
22. Karnow, 590.
23. Nixon, *Memoirs,* 382.
24. Shawcross, 70–1.
25. Ibid., 71, 94.
26. Kissinger, *The White House Years,* 240, 246.
27. Shawcross, 19.
28. Ibid., 20. See also, Nixon, *Memoirs,* 380.
29. Shawcross, 20. See also, Kissinger, *The White House Years,* 242–3.
30. Shawcross, 23.
31. Ibid., 27. See also, Nixon, *Memoirs,* 383–5.
32. Nixon, *Memoirs,* 382. See also, Kissinger, *The White House Years,* 253; Karnow, 592 ff.
33. Shawcross, 33.
34. Nixon, *Memoirs,* 389–90. See also, Kissinger, *The White House Years,* 252–3; United States Senate, *Role of Dr. Henry A. Kissinger in the Wiretapping of Certain Government Officials and Newsmen;* Note 14 above.
35. Shawcross, 31.
36. Ibid., 95. See also, ibid., 287–91, for a detailed discussion of Nixon and Kissinger's responsibility for the bombing campaign, despite their subsequent attempts to deny it.
37. Kissinger, *The White House Years,* 249.
38. Morris, 156.
39. Shawcross, 25.
40. Kissinger, *The White House Years,* 240 fn. General Abrams, according to Kissinger, assured Nixon in February " . . . that *the target* was at least a kilometer distant from any known Cambodian hamlets . . . " (my italics). The trouble is, there was no *target,* there were *targets,* each of which was a "box" a half mile wide by two miles long; See also, ibid., 250, 252, 254.
41. Karnow, 591.
42. Shawcross, 28.
43. Ibid.

CHAPTER 74

*The war escalates • Lieutenant Colonel Herbert's charges • Operation
Dewey Canyon • Operation Hamburger Hill • ARVN's failure at Ben
Het • President Nixon reverses course • Dissent on the home front
• The hawks and the Hellespont • Soedjatmoko speaks out •
Stalemate in Paris • Kissinger's secret talks with Hanoi • Saigon
obstructionism • The President's new plan • First troop withdrawals
• The Midway meeting • The Clifford Plan (I)*

OPERATION *MENU* had not long been under way when it became obvious that the overt American military operations
under Abrams' command differed not in kind but only in degree. All
the wars previously discussed—air, naval, and ground—continued to
escalate. As search-and-destroy operations blossomed anew throughout
South Vietnam, so did the attendant evils earlier discussed. A heavily
decorated army officer, Lieutenant Colonel Anthony Herbert, later testified that in mid-February 1969 he witnessed a battle with the Viet
Cong near Cuu Loi:

> . . . after the fire fight, I walked up on these [civilian] detainees—
> there were about 15 of them—and they were in the custody of an
> ARVN unit and an American lieutenant.
>
> There were four dead already, and when I walked up, they had
> a knife at the throat of a woman. Her baby—there were several
> kids in the bunch—her baby was screaming and grabbing at her
> leg, and her other child . . . was being suffocated by an ARVN who
> was pushing its face into the sand with his foot.
>
> I ordered them to stop, but with me just standing there look-
> ing, they proceeded to slit the woman's throat. I asked the lieuten-
> ant what the hell was going on and then I ordered him to get his
> tail out of the area and take his ARVN with him. They left and I
> sent one of my sergeants with the detainees to the L.Z. [landing

zone]. I told him to get them out and back so they could be processed.

Well, it wasn't long after he left that I heard firing in the direction he'd taken them. He came running back, yelling, mad as hell.
He told me the American lieutenant and the ARVNs had jumped
him, overpowered him and killed all the detainees. I followed him
back and found the bodies. All of them. The children, too.

Herbert subsequently witnessed torture of prisoners by American military intelligence personnel. His insistent reports of these criminal activities won him only opprobrium of his seniors, Lieutenant Colonel J.
Ross Franklin and Major General John Barnes, and he was shortly relieved of his command and sent to military limbo.[1]

Other evils appeared. Despite intense security, Viet Cong guerrillas
continued to penetrate American base areas such as that at Cu Chi
where special raiding teams, covered by rocket and small-arms fire, destroyed nine and severely damaged three Chinook helicopters in a brief
night action, an estimated $16-million loss described by MACV as
"light material damage."[2] In warding off a Tet attack on the big American base at Long Binh, American aircraft were forced to level the village of Bien Hoa, a frantic action that resulted in heavy enemy casualties
and was, once again, claimed by MACV as a "victory." Contrarily, a
captured enemy document noted that the spring offensive

... was a significant tactical and a great strategic victory ... we
killed more Americans than we did in the 1968 spring offensive.
[It] upset Nixon's plan, because U.S. forces were heavily hit....
The antiwar movement in the U.S. flared up again strongly demanding the withdrawal of U.S. troops.[3]

Matters did not greatly improve in I Corps Area where American
marines seem to have learned few lessons. In February, the 3rd Marine
Division in conjunction with ARVN units had kicked off Operation
Dewey Canyon, an immense sweep of tortuous terrain running west to
the Laotian border. Although few enemy contacts resulted, marine
spokesmen called the operation one of " ... the most successful of the
war" and insisted on the importance of captured weapons and matériel
(some 450 tons) to justify 121 dead marines, several hundred wounded,
and units exhausted. Marines followed this with sweeping operations
around Khe Sanh while air and naval units continued to pound enemy
positions in and around the DMZ, a gigantic effort that included USS
New Jersey firing one-ton shells on suspected bunker positions.

In late May, paratroopers of the 101st Airborne Division, while
carrying out a months-long sweep of A Shau Valley south of the marine
area of operations, "surprised" an enemy force dug in on Ap Bia Hill.

The mission of the paratroopers, in the words of a company commander participant, Captain Bob Harkins, was " . . . to find and destroy NVA [North Vietnamese Army] units and supply bases . . . to insure that a recurrence of the previous [1968] 'Tet' did not happen."[4] The 101st at this time was so dispersed that it was impossible to mass what forces were available. In view of this and of the enemy's estimated strength, the local commander might have decided to isolate the hill complex and eliminate or at least badly hurt the dug-in enemy by a mixture of air strikes and artillery fire. Instead, presumably never having studied Napoleon's treatise on mountain warfare, much less the expensive lessons learned by the U. S. Army in northern Italy in World War II, he chose to make that most difficult maneuver, an uphill attack—an effort approved by the division commander, and one that would soon resemble lead soldiers storming a red-hot stove. For several days, well-disciplined and very brave paratroopers fought up what became famous as Hamburger Hill. It was "captured" at a cost of eighty-four dead and 480 wounded against an estimated six hundred enemy dead. It was evacuated a few days later. When North Vietnamese troops again occupied it, the division commanding general announced " . . . that if ordered to take the hill again, 'I am prepared to commit everything that it takes, up to the entire division, to do the job.' "[5]

While paratroopers were bleeding and dying on Hamburger Hill, Giap as usual was preparing another unpleasant surprise for allied forces. This time he chose the old battle areas around Dak To and Ben Het, the latter defended primarily by ARVN units. In May, South Vietnamese patrols had attempted to upset Giap's plans, but the newly reorganized army that American advisers were boasting about did not hold together. By early June, the South Vietnamese were dug in at Ben Het. By mid-June, PAVN units had cut the strong point from the American garrison at Dak To, besieged it for a month, and disappeared, having taken an estimated three thousand casualties mainly from massive doses of napalm and bombs dropped by American aircraft. Despite the fact that an ARVN relief force thinned by 20 to 30 per cent desertion, reached the besieged garrison several days *after* the enemy had departed, MACV touted the relief as a "great victory," certain proof that Vietnamization was working. Colonel David Hackworth, who investigated the action, concluded that " . . . whatever the hype, the truth was that ARVN had failed dismally in its first real test."[6]

The Administration had already suggested that matters were not going to improve radically overnight. In early March, the President defended his policy, blaming it on the enemy:

> . . . we had no other choice but to try to blunt the offensive. Had General Abrams not responded in this way, we would have suf-

fered far more casualties than we have suffered, and we have suffered more than, of course, any of us would have liked to have seen.[7]

In view of the current offensive, the President said, " . . . there is no prospect for a reduction of American forces in the foreseeable future." In mid-March, Secretary of Defense Melvin Laird warned that the United States could not reduce troop commitment until North Vietnam withdrew its troops; according to military commanders in South Vietnam, another two years would be required to bring the situation "in hand."[8]

The Administration's "more of the same" attitude unleashed increasingly vocal and hostile voices in the United States. In late March, a protesting congressman placed the names of 31,379 American dead in the *Congressional Record*. In early April, Henry Niles, chairman of the increasingly influential BEM (Business Executives Move for Peace in Vietnam), complained that " . . . over 2,000 Americans have been killed since President Nixon took office. . . . The honeymoon is over. We want peace."[9] A *New York Times* dispatch from Saigon of May 22 stated that U.S. commanders in Vietnam

> . . . are still under orders to pursue the enemy relentlessly, using every tactic and weapon at their command, to deny the North Vietnamese and Vietcong troops any strategic advantage as a result of the halt in bombing. The United States commanders in the field have followed the order to the letter, and have dramatically stepped-up the number of offensive operations initiated by the allies.[10]

Edward Kennedy reminded fellow senators that Nixon had not ordered or intended to order any reduction of military activity in Vietnam; he continued:

> . . . President Nixon has told us, without question, that we seek no military victory, that we seek only peace. How then can we justify sending our boys against a hill a dozen times or more, until soldiers themselves question the madness of the action? The assault on "Hamburger Hill" is only symptomatic of a mentality and a policy that requires immediate attention.[11]

A month earlier in the April issue of *The Atlantic,* a former marine commandant, General David Shoup, warned the public of a new and dangerous American militarism, "a poisonous weed" that would have to be exterminated.[12]

Shoup's article caused a major furor in Administration circles as did continued press criticism of military actions in Vietnam. Assistant Commandant of the Marine Corps General Lewis Walt charged that " . . . news coverage of the war, assessment of the caliber of the South Vietnamese army and allegations of corruption in the Saigon government" were "inadequate or misleading." Chief of Naval Operations Admiral Moorer " . . . complained of the reporting on American military morale and the 'so-called existence of an evil military-industrial complex.' " The *Washington Post* noted: " . . . Criticism of press and television has joined ABM [anti-ballistic missile] boosterism as a predictable ingredient in top Defense Department speeches."[13]

Military hawks were fighting a losing battle. In taking on the national press, they were going to prove as effective as Xerxes when he tried to punish the Hellespont for destroying his bridge.* Like the Hellespont, the nation's press was too big, powerful, and insensitive, particularly when intelligent and politically influential observers around the world were pointing out fallacies that had underlain American policy in Vietnam. One of the most intelligent voices belonged to the Indonesian ambassador in Washington, Soedjatmoko, who told a Honolulu audience on the same day that President Nixon addressed the nation,

> . . . the future of the South-east Asian region will not be determined solely by the outcome of that war. . . . Firstly, the population of Vietnam, or even of the whole of erstwhile Indo-China together, constitutes less than one-third of the total population of South-east Asia. On the other hand, Indonesia's population alone accounts for almost half of that total. In keeping the Vietnam war in its proper proportions, it is important to realize that if Indonesia had become a Communist country, any military gains in the Vietnam war would have been nullified.

The domino theory, still popular in American administration circles, was fallacious because it did not respect regional facts:

> . . . It is, therefore, not the political color of a regime that counts in the end, but its capacity for nation-building and development. More important than the question whether a country will turn towards Communism—however important that may be to the

---

* Herodotus, 369: " . . . [Xerxes] straightway gave orders that the Hellespont should receive three hundred lashes, and that a pair of fetters should be cast into it. Nay, I have even heard it said, that he bade the branders take their irons and therewith brand the Hellespont."

country concerned—is the question whether in doing so it will become a satellite of outside forces or not. For underlying my whole argument is the conviction that in the present world situation no outside power can for long force any South-east Asian country to do its bidding. The South-east Asian nations do not constitute lifeless entities that automatically fall one way or the other, depending on which way their neighbor falls. History does not operate that way. What matters is the will, the political will, the determination of a nation to preserve its own identity. Out of our own national experience, we in Indonesia more than ever believe that this is the crucial element in the equation. Without such a will and determination, the infusion of external power will fail to make much difference. The domino theory, therefore, is to us rather a gross over-simplification of the nature of the historical processes that go on in the area. It obscures and distorts rather than illuminates our understanding and offers no guide-lines for realistic policy.

So long as China pursued its present policy, the ambassador continued, the primary threat to South-east Asian nations "is one of internal subversion and insurgency." But:

> . . . It is not primarily a nation's military capability that will determine its capacity to overcome these threats to internal security, but rather the cohesion of its political system, the viability and the effectiveness of its government in dealing with the problems of poverty, social inequalities and injustices, in bringing about economic development and in continually expanding its base for popular participation. Here again it is not only factors of economic growth, but beyond that the elements of will and determination that are decisive, as well as the people's loyalty to the government and faith in its purposes.[14]

At some point in this spring of 1969, President Nixon decided to temper overt hawkish desire for military victory with an attempt to win a negotiated settlement (but meanwhile continuing to impress the enemy with his determination by such as Operation Menu and continued furious bombing of Laos. His decision did not make the deed. Although some observers drew comfort from the limited action of the 1969 Tet offensive, the action nonetheless showed an unhealthy enemy strength, as did expensive encounter actions in the DMZ and particularly along the Cambodian border which continued to take a high toll of American lives. Enemy intransigence also showed in Paris, and was complemented by President Thieu's lukewarm attitude in Saigon until virtually an impasse had been reached. Mounting criticism at home alarmed Administration officials while Nixon's continued silence infuriated critics.

Finally in a speech in early April, the President hinted that secret talks were taking place with Hanoi:

> . . . we think we are on the right track but we are not going to raise false hopes. We are not going to tell you what is going on in private talks. What we are going to do is our job and then, a few months from now, I think you will look back and say what we did was right.[15]

Meanwhile, he told his audience, he wanted time. As for Administration intentions, Secretary of State William Rogers informed a Senate committee two days later, " . . . We're prepared, if the other side is prepared, to have a [troop] withdrawal over a very short period of time."

The other three sides—the Saigon government, the Communists in the South, and the Hanoi government—did not seem in a hurry to begin productive talks. About the last action desired by the Thieu regime was an American withdrawal. As it had attempted to sabotage every major American effort toward de-escalating the war in the previous three years, so now it obfuscated major issues with dreary dilatory procedures that tried American officials nearly as much as the NLF and Hanoi's mouthings of all or nothing. Writing from Paris in early May, Stewart Alsop concluded that the Communists "presently have no intention whatever" of agreeing to mutual withdrawal: " . . . to believe that the Communists have any interest in a reasonable settlement it is necessary, like the Red Queen, to 'believe six impossible things before breakfast.' "[16]

Nixon was in a position where he had to believe *more* than six impossible things before breakfast, and he chose to make the best of a difficult situation. Administration spokesmen pointed to indications of a possible breakthrough: The enemy was sitting at a table in Paris along with Saigon government representatives. That government had tabled a six-point peace proposal; Hanoi had countered with a four-point plan. In May, the NLF proposed a ten-point plan. If all this seemed relatively meaningless, particularly to the combat soldier in Vietnam, the Nixon administration accepted it as necessary window-dressing to Kissinger's secret talks, disappointing as they had been.

Just how far the Administration had moved from the previous public bellicose attitude became apparent in mid-May when the President appeared on television to make a major policy speech " . . . on our most difficult and urgent problem."[17] Nixon had temporarily concluded that the get-tough approach was a failure. Nor did Hanoi buy Kissinger's secret approach: " . . . They insisted that political and military issues were inseparable, that American troops must be withdrawn unilaterally, and that Thieu must be deposed as a precondition to serious talks." An effort to involve Russia in the negotiations had proved useless.[18] The political stalemate, coupled with increasing domestic opposition, now decided the Administration that some American forces must be withdrawn and that the war must become Vietnamized, that is " . . . that we could train, equip, and inspire the South Vietnamese to fill the gaps left by departing American forces . . . it was largely on the basis of Laird's enthusiastic advocacy that we undertook the policy of Vietnamization."[19]

Bits and pieces of the new strategy appeared in the President's speech. He defended the American presence in Vietnam as necessary to accomplish the American objective, which he now defined as " . . . the opportunity for the South Vietnamese people to determine their own political future without outside interference." This and other bromides (" . . . we seek no bases . . . we insist on no military ties") were to be expected. But he also " . . . ruled out attempting to impose a purely military solution on the battlefield," committed the Administration (and, by implication, the Thieu-Ky government) to negotiation, formal or informal, and offered a one-year plan for mutual troop withdrawals under international supervision. Once a final cease-fire was negotiated, national elections could be held.[20]

Although *Time* magazine greeted the plan as a sort of political Sermon on the Mount, its importance did not lie in the relatively vague proposals to the enemy, or even in Nixon's expressed willingness to negotiate theretofore *verboten* points such as the Saigon-NLF relationship and an interim provisional government. Its importance lay in Nixon's determination to proceed with negotiations, a not-so-hidden message that the Administration had no intention of maintaining the status quo; thenceforth the South Vietnamese would begin to share the combat burden and would search for a satisfactory internal political solution. Prior to the speech, Administration officials leaked the existence of a plan for unilateral withdrawal of American troops.

Thieu's government reacted quickly and sharply. Thieu at once rejected any talk of coalition government and in so doing emphasized his respect for democratic procedures by banning distribution of American magazines that covered the speech. But the Administration refused to budge. At Midway Island where Thieu and Ky met with Nixon in early June, they learned not only that Washington intended to push for elections in South Vietnam, but that it intended to emphasize its desire for negotiated settlement by slowly withdrawing American combat support. The Administration, Nixon announced, was unilaterally withdrawing twenty-five thousand troops to evidence pacific intentions: " . . . We have opened wide the door to peace," Nixon announced back in Washington in words sounding as if Billy Graham had written them, "and now we invite the leaders of North Vietnam to walk with us."[21]

The message was intended for both North and South Vietnam. Although Thieu at Midway had promised the usual reforms (including still another land-distribution program) and spoken optimistically of ARVN's increasing ability to take over the military load, the Nixon administration emphasized its intentions when Secretary of Defense Laird suggested that further withdrawals would be considered come August.

The President's action did not silence important critics at home. Writing in the July 1969 issue of *Foreign Affairs,* Clark Clifford, former secretary of defense in the Johnson administration, called for a complete reappraisal of American policy in Vietnam. Pointing to profound, and from the Western standpoint favorable, political changes in Southeast Asia and in Asia generally, Clifford argued that South Vietnam could stand increasingly on its own feet and should be left with minimum American logistic and air support. Clifford wanted a hundred thousand American soldiers withdrawn by end of 1969, the remainder by end of 1970.[22] Stung by this and other attacks, Nixon suggested further imminent troop withdrawals. Although White House aides nervously suggested that the President had not committed himself, Nixon privately spoke of a desire to virtually end American military participation by the last day of 1970.

CHAPTER SEVENTY-FOUR

1. Wooten.
2. *The Times* (London), February 26, 1969.
3. Shawcross, 609.
4. Private letter to the author, September 26, 1991.
5. *Time,* June 27, 1969. Hamburger Hill almost instantly became the most hotly criticized operation of the Vietnam War, and it played a vital role in bringing what one experienced combat commander later described as "such large scale madness" to an end. It remains a controversial issue. Twenty years after the slaughter, the on-the-spot (in a helicopter) brigade commander, Colonel Joe Conmy, described the battle as a "success" which " ... probably saved thousands of American and Vietnamese lives." Conmy blamed the subsequent criticism of "politicians and members of the press" for the public outcry. (*International Herald Tribune,* June 3–4, 1989, citing Conmy's letter to the *Washington Post.*) I asked Colonel David Hackworth to comment on Conmy's revisionist remarks and received the following reply:

   > ... Hamburger Hill was a classic example of how not to fight in Vietnam. Conmy's remarks reinforce my long-held conclusion that few American senior officers who commanded there understood the nature of that war. ... The seizing of a jungle mountain-top like Ap Bia [Hamburger Hill] was total madness. Such a misuse of our combat forces would be like charging into entrenched German machine guns with mounted cavalry. ... Had I been the theater commander I would at once have arrested and court-martialed [Melvin] Zais [commanding 101st Airborne] and Conmy on grounds of criminal negligence." [Private letter to the author, September 7, 1991.]

Conmy's assertion that the hill *per se* was a tactical necessity is refuted by the company commander (now Colonel Robert Harkins) quoted in my text: " . . . The Hill was worthless. What made it important was the fact that there were 'bad guys' *on the* Hill. Once again our mission was to find and destroy NVA units. We had done exactly that. It was never our intent to hold the Hill." (Private letter to the author, September 26, 1991.) This returns us to the question, Why try to take the hill against such adverse tactical odds, particularly when units could have been drawn back to let air and artillery fire neutralize it? The reader will probably not be surprised to learn that General Westmoreland later condoned the attacks as " . . . a feature of American tactics throughout the war. Aggressive tactics may produce sharp initial losses, but they save lives in the long run, for in a protracted battle, as in a protracted war, casualties inevitably accumulate." (Westmoreland, 152.) But this would seem to contradict his earlier statement: " . . . To have left the North Vietnamese undisturbed on the mountain [sic] would have been to jeopardize our control of the valley and accept a renewed threat to the coastal cities." (Ibid., 151.) Surely the threat was renewed when the enemy again occupied the hill?

6. Hackworth, 712–13.
7. *Nixon, Public Papers of the President 1969,* Vol. 1, 211.
8. *The Times* (London), Washington, March 19, 1969.
9. Ibid., April 9, 1969.
10. *Washington Watch,* May 26, 1969.
11. Ibid.
12. Shoup and Donovan.
13. *Washington Watch,* June 23, 1969.
14. Soedjatmoko.
15. *Newsweek,* April 7, 1969.
16. Ibid., May 5, 1969.
17. Nixon, *Public Papers of the President 1969,* Vol. 1, 369 ff.
18. Ibid., 390–1.
19. Ibid., 392.
20. Ibid., 369 ff.
21. Ibid., 443, 451. See also, Nixon, *Memoirs,* 393.
22. Clifford.

CHAPTER 75

The Hanoi scene • Emergence of the PRG • Combat action drops • General Wheeler's stand • The doves reply • Dissent increases • Nixon's decision • Kissinger's secret talks in Paris • The Nixon Doctrine • Administration problems • CIA and Special Forces • Averell Harriman out, Henry Cabot Lodge in • CIA operations in Laos • Ho Chi Minh's death • Nixon strikes again • Further troop withdrawals • Progress in South Vietnam • The President and the silent majority • The Thompson report • Blurs on the canvas

WE DO NOT KNOW the exact effect of President Nixon's June 1969 overtures in Hanoi or in enemy ranks in the South. They could not have been unwelcome, however. Considerable friction existed in party ranks both in Hanoi and in the South prior to the 1968 Tet offensive. While hawks such as Truong Chinh, Vo Nguyen Giap, and probably Le Duan continued to demand total victory in the South, more moderate voices including those of Ho Chi Minh and Premier Pham Van Dong could point to devastating losses, morale problems occasioned by heavy casualties and supply shortages, severe economic difficulties in part brought on by floods, and suggest that some form of negotiated settlement was in order, particularly if it would result in an American exodus which would leave the North free to undermine the Thieu-Ky government and eventually take over the South.

Dissident factions apparently compromised in June when the National Liberation Front (NLF) announced creation of a new "Provisional Revolutionary Government of the Republic of South Vietnam," the PRG, which was quickly recognized as a legitimate government by the Soviet Union and twelve other nations. The announcement created a brief flurry of interest, which subsided when the North Vietnamese delegation in Paris failed to follow with specific proposals. That something was astir, however, became apparent in early July when the enemy suddenly broke off a major attack against an ARVN post, Ben Het. Action elsewhere faded and American killed-in-action figures dropped to the lowest in 1969, one hundred fifty a week. Three North Vietnamese regiments reportedly withdrew north across the DMZ while intelligence also reported a significant drop in infiltration via the Ho Chi Minh trail. Although spasmodic guerrilla attacks continued, the action further slowed until in late July American fatalities numbered under a hundred a week.

The over-all trend set off an explosive if secret debate in Washington. Pentagon and State Department hawks argued that enemy disengagement was meaningless. General Wheeler, chairman of the JCS, announced in Saigon at the end of a brief inspection tour that the recent lull did not appear to be politically significant; he disputed reports that PAVN regiments had withdrawn north and seemed to imply that American military de-escalation was not justified.[1] Wheeler praised the continued development of ARVN—the U. S. Army had been "developing" ARVN since 1954, the current project costing over $6 *billion*—and said that allied forces " . . . are well prepared for any new military initiatives the enemy may attempt." He also said in words undoubtedly intended for presidential ears " . . . that the [South] Vietnamese could not take over the full war effort by the end of 1970."[2] In a secret briefing of the Senate Armed Services Committee at month's end, he allegedly said that " . . . the Nixon plan to de-Americanize the war had been dropped. He inferred a more aggressive strategy was needed to win the war."[3]

Doves retorted that the lull was politically significant just as it had been after President Johnson halted the bombing. The military had erred then, the argument ran, by keeping up military pressure after Hanoi had withdrawn three PAVN divisions north of the DMZ. This time, doves insisted, Hanoi must be given a chance to show true intentions, particularly since it apparently had forsaken military conquest and reverted to political struggle as suggested by the creation of the new Provisional Revolutionary Government (PRG) in the South.[4]

Nixon had already decided to wind down the shooting war. Hanoi's reactions aside, he was in serious political trouble. Early in July, the figure of American dead in South Vietnam had gone over the thirty-seven-thousand mark. Official figures admitted loss of 5,666 aircraft including nearly 2,900 helicopters—a total financial loss of above $3 billion.[5] These and other unpalatable facts and figures were being spewed to the nation not only by the daily press but by a powerful underground press that in 1969 amounted to almost five hundred newspapers with a circulation approaching five million.[6] The American people, not only students and other "troublemakers," were slowly realizing that an era of militarism was bankrupting the United States both spiritually and financially. More than two thirds of federal expenditure since World War II—over $1 *trillion*—had gone to armaments and armed forces. Vietnam expenditures for fiscal year 1968–69 would come to $30 billion.[7] The 1970 defense budget topped $80 billion. Military leaders were clamoring for new weapons systems, new bombers, strategic missiles, tanks, aircraft. While poverty claimed large areas of the United States, while the population was outgrowing schools and social services, while American cities were coming apart at the seams, the Vietnam war would take $28 billion in *direct* costs in the new fiscal year. As David Calleo of the Washington Center of Foreign Policy Research put it:

> ...It is not isolationism that is reviving in the United States but humanism. Prodded by the prolonged agony of Vietnam many Americans now perceive grotesque distortions in their Government's values. The United States, they believe, is sacrificing the quality of its national life to the demands of a military empire.[8]

Widespread dissent continued to show itself, not only in draft-card burning and student demonstrations, but in the intellectual fabric of America and increasingly in Congress. In that summer of 1969, Nixon in many ways was facing an incipient rebellion, and it is a great argument for the worth of democracy that, though he favored force, public opinion was pushing him toward disengagement.

Nixon in mid-July wrote to Ho Chi Minh to offer negotiation or military escalation, the choice to be made by the first of November at the latest. This led to a secret meeting between Kissinger and Xuan Thuy in Paris, the first of a three-year series. In late July, Nixon sent orders to Abrams not only to cut down offensive missions but to begin withdrawing American units from combat positions as rapidly as ARVN units could replace them. Nixon now undertook a tour of Asia to spread a new gospel that became known as the Nixon Doctrine: America would thenceforth offer economic and limited military aid to those nations willing to supply the manpower necessary to defend themselves.[9] Although the United States would honor its commitments in Southeast Asia, the President explained to leaders in Djakarta, Saigon, and Bangkok, it would thenceforth emphasize economic rather than military action. The time had come, Nixon proclaimed, to end a war and build a peace.

If Nixon hoped to quiet American critics by such oratory, he was quickly disappointed. A series of shocks now befell the Administration and particularly the armed forces. In late July, a Congressional subcommittee, in a report on the *Pueblo* disaster (see Chapter 69), rapped the military soundly on the knuckles:

... The inquiry reveals the existence of a vast and complex military structure capable of acquiring almost infinite amounts of information but with a demonstrated inability ... to relay this information in a timely and comprehensible fashion to those charged with the responsibility for making decisions.[10]

Further adverse publicity spilled over the U. S. Navy a month later when it announced that the USS *New Jersey,* the battleship that had been refitted for service in Vietnam waters at a cost of $40 million, was being mothballed after eighteen months' service. In early August, a scandal broke in Saigon with the arrest of one Huynh Van Trong and some fifty associates. Trong was special assistant and confidant on political affairs to President Thieu. He was charged with running an espionage ring for North Vietnam. The American public was still digesting this upsetting development when MACV announced the arrest of eight Special Forces soldiers including the Green Beret commander in South Vietnam, Colonel Robert Rheault, for murdering a Vietnamese civilian. The victim, who allegedly worked for both CIA and Special Forces, was said to have been "doubled" by the Communists. When that was discovered, CIA ordered him "terminated with extreme prejudice"—a death sentence allegedly carried out by Special Forces.

The case caused tremendous speculation, mostly critical, concerning American policy. NBC, for example, reported that Special Forces had committed over three hundred political assassinations in South Vietnam including those of senior Vietnamese officials. It also caused problems in the Phoenix program, the joint American-South Vietnamese effort that had been trying to root out VC infrastructure in liberated areas. The covert part of this program involved assassination of enemy agents. Nearly five hundred American "advisers" now wondered if they were to be tried for murder. CIA's refusal to produce witnesses for the prosecution of Rheault and his fellows caused the army to drop the case.[11] Instead of airing policy CIA claimed executive privilege and Nixon allowed the altogether dubious claim. This did not repair damage done to the prestige of Special Forces nor did it quiet critics who objected to CIA's terminating people with or without "extreme prejudice." To a good many intelligent Americans the terminology belonged to SMERSH and James Bond, not to a democracy that claimed to embrace the principle of trial by jury.

More was to come. An article by two American scientists in the August issue of *Scientific Research* condemned the defoliation program in South Vietnam and directly challenged U. S. Army claims that herbicides caused only minimal damage. Pointing to established decreases in rice and rubber production caused in part by killing plants and trees, the scientist-authors claimed that herbicides were causing long-term ecological damage, as was B-52 bombing. They pointed out that in 1968 American bombs had created 2.6 million craters " . . . with currently incalculable consequences for the countryside."[12]

Still more criticism broke over the Administration when President Thieu replaced his civilian prime minister, the rather gentle Tran Van Huong, with General Tran Thien Khiem, who was generally considered a hawk. Administration critics bluntly accused Saigon of pursuing a militaristic policy at a time when the United States was trying to negotiate a peace. In late September, Averell Harriman, whom Nixon had relieved as envoy at the Paris peace talks in favor of Henry Cabot Lodge, stated that the United States must ignore Saigon and forge an agreement with North Vietnam and with the National Liberation Front in the South. The Nixon administration was acting " . . . as though it is some sort of a satellite of the Saigon government . . . the personal interests of President Thieu and Vice President Cao Ky should not be allowed to become the premises of American policy."[13] Also in late September, Senator Mike Mansfield returned from a tour of Asia to state that " . . . the American involvement in Laos had grown to such an extent that it could lead to another Vietnam war." Citing Nixon's new Asian doctrine, he added that " . . . present tendencies in Laos were running directly counter to what should be expected."[14] Mansfield's remarks brought correspondents to the Laotian scene like bees to honey. In late October, the *New York Times* reported details of the private war being run by CIA in Laos. Once again critics had a field day and not a few Americans agreed with Senator Stuart Symington, a one-time hawk who now expressed worry about extensive American commitments in light of a worsening domestic situation: " . . . We spend $44 for every child's education up to college age, but in Vietnam we spend $21,600 in ammunition alone to kill one enemy soldier."[15]

President Nixon did not accept this and additional criticism passively, and his temper was improved by a few streaks of light in otherwise somber skies. Some were transitory. Ho Chi Minh's death in early September brought hopeful prophecies from some Hanoi-watchers of a power struggle that would probably end in a peace party gaining dominance. It did nothing of the sort. Pham Van Dong, who headed the new government, publicly admitted to severe problems but showed himself equally unwilling to respect Nixon's "ultimatum."[16]

Nixon sent two specific signals to the new government. One was a three-day halt of B-52 raids in South Vietnam. When this evoked no response, the raids were resumed. In mid-September, he announced that he was withdrawing at least another thirty-five thousand American troops before the end of 1969, an occasion used to place the onus again on North Vietnam with an appeal to begin "meaningful negotiations." Nixon also canceled draft calls for November and December and dismissed General Lewis B. Hershey, octogenarian head of the draft board and subject of extreme criticism, particularly from students objecting to the draft's bias.

The President also continued his partial-withdrawal policy in South Vietnam, and here he scored a major gain. By late September, most American combat units had been withdrawn from the Mekong Delta area. To the surprise of all but genuine counterinsurgency experts, pacification now proceeded much more rapidly than it had when the military was tearing up the countryside with search-and-destroy missions. Village elections were being held throughout the delta. Assassinations by VC terrorists continued, but the Phoenix program at last seemed to be taking hold. Although military hawks argued that such progress was the result of attrition strategy, other observers insisted that the key lay in withdrawing American combat units. Nixon accepted the arguments of the latter group and MACV turned toward a strategy not dissimilar to that recommended by General James Gavin in 1965—an enclave strategy derided by hawks at the time. If nothing else, however, casualties dropped significantly despite warnings of military experts that they would rise.

Nixon was walking a political tightrope during this autumn and early winter of 1969. Faced with increasing dissent including a nationwide moratorium kicked off by 250,000 anti-war demonstrators in Washington, his major pitch continued to be a plea for time. In late September, he pointed to some hopeful facts, for example that North Vietnamese infiltration into the South was down two thirds from the previous year; American casualties had decreased by a third; combat remained at a minimum level. If the American people formed a popular front behind his peace proposals, the President predicted, the Vietnam war would end the next year.[17]

In early November, the President made another major policy speech, in which he dramatically appealed to "the great silent majority of Americans" to let him continue fighting and negotiating as he thought best. He would not accept defeat, he told his audience; he would not withdraw all of America's military forces from South Vietnam until Vietnamization was a fact.[18] The silent majority, without really having much to go on except innate hope and presidential rhetoric, vocally responded overwhelmingly in favor of its President as did some members of Congress. Another majority continued to stage increasingly large anti-war rallies and university sit-ins while newspapers and television continued to criticize the Administration.

Nixon's confidence grew, however, as good news kept arriving from the war-torn country. The Saigon government announced that in October over five thousand Viet Cong rallied to the government's side to make a total of nearly forty thousand defectors for the year. Lieutenant

General Julian Ewell, commanding III Corps area north of Saigon, told reporters that " . . . the Vietcong were rapidly becoming non-existent, the North Vietnamese were being forced to write off certain units to be withdrawn." The general claimed that 97 per cent of the rural population in his area was " . . . under nominal government control"; 82 per cent of the remaining sixty-one thousand enemy, he continued, were North Vietnamese. The British correspondent Fred Emery, who reported the above, wrote in a dispatch the following day that VC defectors had climbed to twenty-six thousand this year, that Regional and Popular Forces recruitment had doubled, and that a million peasants had joined the People's Self-Defense Forces. High percentages of Mekong Delta villages and hamlets had elected their own officials:

> . . . None of these figures, it is true, supports the contention that people have been swung behind the government. . . . Yet there is little doubt that many people are living freer from direct harassment than they can perhaps remember.[19]

A month later, *Time* correspondent Mark Clark reported from Saigon that although " . . . statements of optimism are far more muted than in the halcyon days that preceded *Tet* in 1968, there is an unmistakable air of confidence." The Thieu regime, Clark reported, " . . . is a going concern. While Thieu is not a popular hero, he heads a government that is stable."[20] A similar report was made to the President in late December by a British counterinsurgency expert, Sir Robert Thompson, whom Nixon sent to Vietnam to "reassess" the situation. Nixon later wrote that in October Thompson was " . . . clearly not in favor of escalation.. . . His estimate was that, continuing the current U.S. policy and assuming South Vietnamese confidence that we would not pull out, victory could be won within two years." Something of Thompson's naïve geopolitical astuteness may be adduced from his reply to Nixon's question " . . . whether he thought it was important for us to see it through." Thompson replied, " . . . Absolutely. In my opinion the future of Western civilization is at stake in the way you handle yourselves in Vietnam."[21]

The corpus of Thompson's subsequent report based on a five-week tour remained secret, but in articles, interviews, and private conversations, he displayed enthusiasm made the more impressive by contrast to the critical and pessimistic tone of his book *No Exit from Vietnam* published in March 1969. Interviewed in London, Thompson optimistically discussed pacification progress and the increasingly stable performance of the South Vietnamese Government and concluded:

> . . . The war in South Vietnam can therefore be won, in the sense that a just peace can be obtained, whether negotiated or not, and

that the South Vietnamese people will be in a position to determine their own future without any interference or compulsion from the North. This after all is the limit of the American aim, and has been very clearly laid down by the President, particularly at the Paris peace talks.[22]

In a major speech in mid-December, Nixon announced that he was withdrawing another fifty thousand American troops, mostly combat units, before April 1970.[23] Two months later, President Thieu emphasized his claim of controlling 93 per cent of the South Vietnamese countryside by staging a 475-mile bicycle race whose seventy-three contestants pedaled the course without VC opposition.

As with optimistic pictures previously drawn by Saigon and Washington administrations, a few blurs marred this canvas. The first was the Administration's negotiating position. Nixon's injured tones in discussing Hanoi's intransigence bore little semblance of reality. Whatever his hopes, he had few reasons to expect Hanoi to negotiate an unfavorable peace after fighting a war that had destroyed much of North Vietnam and, by the American administration's own figures, taken the lives of 450,000 enemy soldiers, not to mention those of thousands of civilians, within the previous six years. The President could resume bombing of the North but, short of people, little remained to bomb. According to one National Security Council official, Kissinger set up a special group to " . . . examine new military options, including . . . possible one-time use of a nuclear device"—the "savage blow" that Kissinger believed would knock North Vietnam out of the war. Fortunately, Melvin Laird learned of the goings-on and told Nixon that bombing people out of existence—Giulio Douhet's strategic-genocide theory—would not be permitted either by American or world civil opinion.[24]

What Nixon and his advisers and a good many American citizens failed to realize was that Hanoi could not be further hurt. It had suffered—but it had survived. Peking continued to vie with Moscow to supply essential needs and, in Moscow's case, to guarantee general postwar rehabilitation. American bombing had long since given the North Vietnamese people a genuine stake in the war. They would continue to exist on a subsistence level—a disciplined people is as essential to protracted war as flexibility in strategy and tactics. Whatever methods had been chosen to fight the war so far, Hanoi never forgot the requirements of protracted war. As Colonel Bouquet had instructed in 1766 and Charles Callwell had repeated in 1899, the "savages" were the professionals in their own environment.

Other factors entered. Hanoi was on the brink of winning a tremendous psychological victory by chasing American forces from the scene. Decades before, Lyautey had protested regarding the Spanish withdrawal in Morocco: " . . . My God! An army retreats when it must but it does not announce the fact to the enemy in advance." Nixon was forced to make this very announcement which increased the influence of Hanoi hawks; negotiations or no, they saw themselves on the verge of obtaining a major objective. Why hurry to negotiate when continuing criticism of the war both in the United States and throughout the world would force Nixon's hand further and further? In mid-November, the scandal of the My Lai killings had broken and though the full effect of the shock on the American people had not yet been wrought, cacophonous voices were already shrilling the shameful facts. Senator Fulbright, a long-time critic of the war, publicly criticized growing presidential power to involve the United States in such areas as South Vietnam where " . . . the United States has no vital security interest."[25] Fulbright kept up his attack in December, stating that Nixon's Vietnamization policy meant " . . . a continuing war of stalemate and attrition." Other legislators reacted adversely to reports of a secret war in Laos, and in mid-December the Senate voted to bar American combat troops from Laos and Thailand.[26] Dissension, in short, now ruled Washington councils as it ruled the nation—all to Hanoi's benefit.

What about the optimistic situation in the South Vietnamese countryside? Here again the Administration exhibited considerable naïveté by treating a lull in guerrilla activity as if it were a major victory—precisely what Sir Charles Gwynn had warned against thirty-five years earlier (see Chapter 23). American commanders would have been wise to have respected the Spartan admonition to Philip of Macedon: "If you imagine that your victory has made you greater than you were, measure your shadow." If parts of South Vietnam were being cleared of enemy, large numbers of enemy remained. In early November, the respected Washington correspondent of *The Times* (London), Louis Heren, reported that of PAVN's 430,000 troops about 130,000 were in the South or in border sanctuaries. He placed VC strength at sixty thousand trained guerrillas, ninety thousand in political cadres, and perhaps fifty thousand in local irregular forces.[27] Fred Emery reported from Saigon in mid-November that the enemy was launching sporadic attacks and that terrorist incidents have "barely gone down at all."

> . . . It is precisely because, whatever the military lull, they can inflict retribution on this scale, discriminately and indiscriminately, that pacification is shown to be rarely the same thing as security. And the difference is vital.[28]

In a later dispatch that quoted General Ewell's optimistic reports concerning eleven provinces north of Saigon, Emery also noted that the

American general envisaged "a war around here somewhere for the next 50 to 150 years."[29] President Nixon in his mid-December speech also noted "one disturbing new development," which was a substantial increase in infiltration—some eight thousand men a month from the North.[30]

Sir Robert Thompson's expressed optimism also glossed over some disturbing facts. Thompson had been enthusiastic before—in 1963 for example—and had been wrong. Whatever the total content of his report to the President, he had to admit to grave deficiencies in the scene that he had surveyed as paid consultant to the Nixon administration. Thompson had always deemed a constable force necessary for defeating an insurgency and maintaining the peace. At a London seminar in early 1969, he had pointed to the South Vietnamese failure to build a viable rural police force, and this had not been repaired. Another deficiency to which he privately admitted was a lopsided economic position by which a country of 17.5 million people with an estimated GNP of $2.5 billion (in large part U.S. subsidized) was supporting an armed force over one million strong (including 472,500 regular troops).[31] This condition could scarcely improve under what Thompson called "a long-haul, low-cost strategy" (with South Vietnam increasingly assuming the military burden) that would be necessary for at least three to five years " . . . before Hanoi is compelled to give up her purpose and to negotiate a real settlement."[32]

Thompson shared *Time* magazine's enthusiasm concerning the Saigon government and publicly spoke admiringly of Thieu, whom he considered a real politician. Thieu might have been a real politician—whatever that meant—but he already had proved himself a strong man in the worst totalitarian tradition: as someone disparagingly remarked, "The brown Sahib has replaced the white Sahib." Thieu's officials censored newspapers as frequently as his secret police arrested political dissidents. Magazines disavowing any of his acts such as *Time* and *Newsweek,* were suppressed; he filled jails with political prisoners (Communists, yes, but also non-Communists); his secret police arrested and held opponents without charge. Some of his legislation was as oppressive as that dreamed up by the Diem-Nhu regime. General Duong Van Minh, leader of the revolt against Diem, returned from a four-year exile in Thailand and almost immediately denounced the minority basis of Thieu's government stating, according to Fred Emery, that " . . . the Government has cut itself off from the people, and he adds that this cannot be."[33]

So long as this government remained authoritarian, so long as Thieu's political base rested on army and secret police and force, so long as a gulf existed between mandarin bureaucracy and peasants, the

Viet Cong would continue to operate. In the enemy's mind, American presence or no, the Saigon government would eventually fall. So the problem for Hanoi and the PRG was what it had always been: helping the process along with flexible tactics of revolutionary warfare.

Incredibly, neither Nixon nor his advisers yet seemed to understand that they were grappling with a political problem. Kissinger already had sounded the key word: *honor*. The Administration was embracing Comines' dictum, "He who has success has honor," while overlooking Talleyrand's remark, "Honor in our age of corruption has been invented in order to make vanity do the work of virtue." Nixon failed to see that victory could come only from within a country whose government was attuned to the demands of its peoples. Failing to see this, he made the fatal error of yielding to bellicose civil and military advisers who forever believed that the threat was external and who, if they had had their way, would have enlarged the action to nuclear-warfare proportions.

CHAPTER SEVENTY-FIVE

1. *The Times* (London), July 20, 1969.
2. Ibid.
3. *Washington Watch,* August 7, 1969.
4. Shaplen, *The Road from War,* 293 ff.
5. *The Times* (London), July 25, 1969.
6. Schalk, 9.
7. Kissinger, *The White House Years,* 235.
8. *The Times* (London), July 29, 1969.
9. Nixon, *Memoirs,* 395.
10. *The Times* (London), July 28, 1969.
11. Mollenhoff, 73.
12. *The Sunday Telegraph* (London), August 10, 1969.
13. *The Times* (London), September 18, 1969.
14. Ibid., September 21, 1969. See also, Grant.
15. *The Sunday Times* (London), November 2, 1969.
16. Nixon, *Memoirs,* 401–2.
17. Nixon, *Public Papers of the President 1969,* Vol. 1, 752. See also, *The Sunday Times* (London), November 5, 1969.
18. Nixon, *Public Papers of the President 1969,* Vol. 1, 901–9. See also, Hackworth, 667.
19. *The Times* (London), November 24, 25, 1969.
20. *Time,* December 26, 1969. See also, Blaufarb, 267.
21. Nixon, *Memoirs,* 404–5.
22. Robert Thompson, "On the Way to Victory."
23. Nixon, *Public Papers of the President 1969,* Vol. 1, 1025–28.
24. Reichley, 118.
25. *The Times* (London), November 13, 1969.
26. Ibid., December 15, 1969.
27. Ibid., November 3, 1969.
28. Ibid., November 11, 1969.

29. Ibid., November 24, 1969.
30. Nixon, *Public Papers of the President 1969*, Vol. 1, 1027.
31. Royal United Services Institution Seminar, 1969.
32. *Time,* December 26, 1969.
33. *The Times* (London), November 14, 1969.

CHAPTER 76

Confused U.S. objectives • Congressional opposition mounts •
Involvement in Laos • President Thieu's stand • President Nixon's
dilemma • The Cambodian invasion • Disappointing results •
Dissent on the home front • Clark Clifford's new plan (II)

CONGRESSIONAL DISAPPROVAL of the President's course in Vietnam continued into 1970. In mid-February, the President submitted a foreign-policy report to Congress that contained no specific statement of international objectives—" . . . a disappointment to those who looked for an ordered definition, as opposed to a declamation, of American interests."[1] A staff study in the same month published by the Senate Foreign Relations Committee concluded that " . . . the assumptions on which American policy [in Vietnam] are based are ambiguous, confusing, and contradictory." Nixon's policy depended on three factors, the study suggested: progressive Vietnamization, the stability of the Saigon government, and lack of enemy interference, each "uncertain" of success: " . . . Dilemmas thus seem to lie ahead in Vietnam, as they have throughout our involvement in this war that appears to be not only far from won but far from over."[2] Individual senators in public hearings bluntly made clear their hostility. Charles Goodell spoke of "illusions" entertained by the Administration and concluded, " . . . We have not Vietnamized the war: we have cosmetized it." Senator Fulbright cogently asked, " . . . In what exact ways have we advanced toward peace? The war, as we know, is still going on. Replacements are still being sent to Vietnam; we are still suffering about 750 casualties a week; and the war is still costing the American people about $70 millions a day." Senators Harold Hughes and Thomas Eagleton proposed a resolution calling on the Saigon government for immediate reforms; in lieu thereof, " . . . the President of the United States should declare officially that our commitment to the present Government of South Vietnam is ended."[3]

Adding to legislative dissatisfaction was the increasingly serious situation in Laos. The 1962 Geneva Agreements confirmed the neutrality of an independent Laos governed by Souvanna Phouma's coalition government. The Soviet Union terminated its supply flights to North Vietnamese army [PAVN] units and to Pathet Lao guerrillas; CIA halted its supply flights to Meo tribesmen guerrillas, and Special Forces withdrew its training teams. When Hanoi did not remove its PAVN units, an estimated seven thousand troops working with the Pathet Lao, CIA and Special Forces recommenced their operations, organizing, training, and supplying Meo tribesmen, who thenceforth fought a formidable guerrilla war against the Pathet Lao-North Vietnamese army.[4] In 1969, the Nixon administration upped the ante by authorizing an all-out bombing campaign that included napalm and phosphorus bombs and centered on and north of the contested Plain of Jars. Such was its intensity that in 1970 few villages remained, their inhabitants having been forced underground. " . . . We never saw the sun," one refugee reported; another stated, " . . . There wasn't a night that we went to sleep that we thought we'd live to see the morning."[5] In January 1970, Hanoi further fueled the situation by suddenly reinforcing its already substantial forces north of the Plain of Jars where Pathet Lao guerrillas were being held in uneasy check, not so much by the Royal Laotian Army, which despite years of American training and the expenditure of millions of dollars, remained " . . . hardly fit to face the enemy,"[6] as by some thirty-six thousand CIA-sponsored Meo guerrillas.[7] The expected enemy offensive opened in mid-February and soon cleared the high ground leading to the plain. After considerable dithering, the White House authorized a small B-52 strike that became known and tripped off Congressional and public accusations of further escalation. Nixon's refusal to deny or confirm alleged American involvement drew strong criticism from Senator George McGovern, who, like most of his brethren, knew of neither the secret Operation Menu bombings of Cambodia nor the simultaneous bombing campaign in Laos. Requesting that the Senate debate the subject *in camera*, McGovern condemned the notion of a secret war:

> . . . It is absolutely incredible that a great nation such as ours could be waging a major military operation in a foreign country without the knowledge of either citizens or its Congress. But that is the fact.[8]

Although Nixon assured Congress that no American ground forces would be sent to Laos, he did not explain the presence of those already there—estimated from one to five thousand—nor did he offer details of the aerial bombing. Secretary of State Rogers scarcely mollified worried congressmen by stating that " . . . the possibility of using American ground forces in Laos could not be ruled out, although there were no plans to do so at present."⁹

Meanwhile the Communist offensive gathered steam and in late March had reached the Long Thieng area, the last stop before the capital of Vientiane. But now the Laotian army, stiffened by "volunteers" from Thailand and by the Meo guerrillas, opened what turned out to be a successful counteroffensive. By end of March, the situation had stabilized and would remain so for the rest of the year.

The incipient American exodus suffered another setback when President Thieu reverted to the hackneyed tack of the domino theory: if the United States withdrew from the Asian mainland, the Chinese would take over Laos, Cambodia, Malaysia, and Indonesia. South Vietnam, Thieu stated, was the key to the entire area: " . . . We have to contain the rush of the Communists right here—not in the U.S., not at Midway or Hawaii or in mid-ocean, but right here on the Asian mainland." Thieu insisted that " . . . there was no fixed timetable for the withdrawal of American troops. The South Vietnamese forces must be given sufficient and adequate means to fight the Communists." Thieu had every reason for maintaining a state of emergency. It was his principal justification for running one of the most repressive and corrupt governments in the world. The American military, both MACV and the JCS, agreed in part with Thieu. Louis Heren wrote that " . . . the [American] Army is resisting further cuts [in South Vietnam]. General William Westmoreland, the Chief of Staff, is reported to be pressing for a six-month delay ostensibly because the rate of 'Vietnamization' is too fast for safety and comfort."¹⁰

In spring of 1970, Nixon was caught between two powerful forces: public opinion at home, military opinion at home and abroad. If for no other than domestic political reasons, he had to continue winding down the war in Vietnam. At the same time, MACV and the Pentagon were pointing to forty thousand Communist troops active in Cambodia and to renewed enemy activity in South Vietnam, and were violently arguing against further troop withdrawals. In trying to satisfy everybody, Nixon satisfied no one. He further erred by reintroducing the bogey of atomic warfare, which alarmed and enraged other countries, friendly, neutral, and enemy. In late April, the President told the nation that he had based his troop-withdrawal program on three criteria. Two had been met. Training and equipping South Vietnamese forces had "substantially exceeded our expectations"; and there had been "extensive progress" in pacification (including a new land-reform bill that, in theory, would provide over three million acres for distribution.¹¹ No progress, however, had been made on the negotiating front. Nonetheless he was planning to withdraw another 150,000 American troops by spring of 1971, more if progress was made in negotiations:

. . . I again remind the leaders of North Vietnam that, while we are taking these risks for peace, they jeopardize the security of our remaining forces in Vietnam by increased military action in Vietnam, in Cambodia, or in Laos. . . . If I conclude that increased enemy action jeopardizes our remaining forces . . . I shall not hesitate to take strong and effective measures.[12]

" . . . It is not too much to say," James Reston noted, "that he will use any weapon at his command, repeat *any* weapon, to avoid the destruction of his remaining soldiers."[13]

Extensive B-52 bombings had not greatly damaged enemy sanctuary areas, but they had driven the enemy considerably deeper into Cambodia, where they had begun clashing with village authorities and Cambodian army troops.[14] Taken with CIA support of Prince Norodom Sihanouk's rival, Son Ngoc Thanh, whose nationalist-guerrilla group, the Khmer Serai, was located in South Vietnam, and of an American-sponsored disruption effort that was moving the urban elite and the officer corps in Phnom Penh away from Sihanouk, the bombings had helped to destabilize Sihanouk's rule at a particularly critical time. In August 1969, Sihanouk had formed a new rightist government with General Lon Nol as prime minister. Lon Nol, an alleged anti-Communist, was as corrupt as another of Sihanouk's rivals, his cousin Prince Sisowith Sirik Matak, indeed as Sihanouk himself. Lon Nol as defense minister had run a lucrative business with the Communist enemy by taking large bribes to permit the passage north of Chinese arms sent to Sihanoukville. But the increasing penetration of the enemy westward had caused Lon Nol to challenge the Communist presence and to persuade Sihanouk to protest to Hanoi. Sihanouk himself seemed to be tilting toward the West by forming a regional balance of power that he hoped would preserve Cambodian independence, but at the same time he was preserving his ties to Moscow and Peking in the hope that they could moderate if not eliminate the North Vietnamese and Viet Cong presence in Cambodia.[15]

Sihanouk made his big mistake in January 1970 by taking himself off to a fat farm on the French Riviera. He was not long departed when Lon Nol and Prince Sirik Matak decided to oust him, a move heartily favored by Son Ngoc Thanh across the border in South Vietnam. We shall probably never know the extent of American involvement in the coup. Nixon and Kissinger claim innocence, but their historical recall is not always to be taken seriously, and there is also damaging evidence later provided by Roger Morris, one of Kissinger's senior analysts: " . . . It was clear in the White House that the CIA station in Phnom

Penh knew the plotters well, probably knew their plans, and did nothing to alert Sihanouk. They informed Washington well in advance of the coup. . . . "[16] Lon Nol had been a strong-man favorite of the Administration for some time, and recently had added to his luster by closing the port of Sihanoukville to Communist arms shipments and by demanding that Hanoi withdraw its troops from the country.[17] A CIA analyst in Saigon later wrote that in early 1970 the CIA was encouraging both Son Ngoc Thanh and Lon Nol to replace Sihanouk. MACV and the CIA believed that if Lon Nol replaced the prince, " . . . he would welcome the United States with open arms and we would accomplish everything"[18]—such as being invited to invade Cambodia and start a second war in Southeast Asia.

Sihanouk did not gracefully accept defeat. Three days after the coup, he conferred with China's foreign minister Chou En-lai and Hanoi's premier Pham Van Dong in Peiping, where he was persuaded to accept leadership of the Khmer Rouge guerrillas, Cambodia's native Communists. After establishing a provisional government-in-exile, he appealed to his countrymen " . . . to engage in guerrilla warfare in the jungles against our enemies," an appeal immediately embraced by the North Vietnamese, who thenceforth would join the Khmer Rouge in waging war against Lon Nol's Cambodian army.[19] A large force of Cambodian Communists who had fled their country in 1954 and who had been trained in guerrilla warfare by the North Vietnamese now marched down the Ho Chi Minh trail into Cambodia, where they would attempt to take command of the guerrilla movement.

If Lon Nol and his officials scoffed at Sihanouk's words, peasants in the countryside listened to them. Riots broke out in towns and villages which the army put down, often brutally. An alarmed Lon Nol, to divert attention, now turned the army loose on the nearly half-million Vietnamese who had remained in Cambodia after the Geneva Accords, insisting that they were all Viet Cong who must be eliminated—and many of them were. Within weeks, the warp and woof of Cambodian society were unraveling in Lon Nol's dangerously ineffective hands.[20]

Whether American-inspired or not, the coup seemed a heaven-sent opportunity to Nixon, Kissinger, the JCS, the bellicose Admiral John S. McCain, Jr., in Honolulu, and Abrams and his MACV planners, and the Thieu government in Saigon. With Nixon's overt approval, Administration hawks at once demanded substantial support for the new ruler. Secretary of Defense Melvin Laird, while in Saigon in February, authorized MACV to give logistical support to South Vietnamese units which were crossing the border into Cambodia to attack enemy supply dumps. In April, responding to North Vietnamese gains in Cambodia and to Lon Nol's request for arms, the President secretly authorized MACV to send him several planeloads of captured Soviet-made AK-47 rifles (the first step in a futile two-year expenditure of $1.7 billion) to arm the burgeoning Cambodian army's seventy thousand volunteers—an order that, leaked to the *New York Times* William Beecher, caused another Congressional confrontation.

That was only the beginning. The JCS and MACV had long been wanting to strike enemy sanctuaries across the border. Planners now dusted off previous contingency plans that soon covered Washington desks. Nixon and Kissinger were fascinated by the prospect of a blue-plate special: COSVN captured, sanctuaries cleansed and closed; the security of U.S. forces assured; Vietnamization to continue its allegedly remarkable progress. Enthusiastic planning continued into April while ARVN troops probed the border areas and more American-supplied arms arrived in Phnom Penh for the army that was being built over-night. Son Ngoc Thanh and his Khmer Serai guerrillas were moved to Cambodia along with other U.S.-trained Khmer units.

There were some problems. In one White House briefing, William Safire pointed out that the proposed invasion did not square with the Nixon Doctrine of keeping American soldiers out of Asian battles. Kissinger explosively told him, " . . . We wrote the goddamn doctrine, we can change it."[21] Other important voices disagreed with Nixon, Kissinger, and the hawks. One of the most frightening, indeed tragic, aspects of the Vietnamese, Cambodian, and Laotian wars was the abject refusal of its American parents to even listen to, much less respect, dissentient opinions of well-qualified professionals. Six days after Prince Sihanouk had been deposed, the veteran diplomat and chargé d'affaires in the American embassy in Phnom Penh, Lloyd Rives, warned about the dangers of escalation. Marshall Green, a senior diplomat who represented the State Department in the Washington Special Action Group, a high-powered committee chaired by Henry Kissinger, agreed with Rives and recommended to Kissinger and Rogers that

> . . . the United States should try to work through the French and the Algerians to find a diplomatic solution to Cambodia's new problems. . . . Green believed that the only hope for Cambodia lay in continuing Sihanouk's policies if not actually helping to restore Sihanouk himself. Green pointed out the paradox that "without massive U.S. support the Government of Cambodia cannot rebuild its position . . . but U.S. support could restrict its neutrality, which is its greatest resource." He argued, moreover, that Congress would see aid to Lon Nol as widening the war and might therefore impose further restrictions on aid to Vietnam. Helping Cambodia could hinder Vietnamization. This is exactly what happened.[22]

By being essentially correct and having the courage to say so, Green earned Administration ire and great harm to his career.

Secretary of State Rogers and Secretary of Defense Laird strongly opposed any move into Cambodia until the international political dust raised by the coup had settled.[23] Each subsequently remained strongly against deploying American troops inside Cambodia. The Nixon-Kissinger answer to this dissent was to eliminate them from the planning process by means of Kissinger's office dealing directly with the JCS and by Nixon and Kissinger using a secret back-channel to deal directly with Abrams and Bunker in Saigon, at the same time pressuring Rogers and Laird to condone the operation. Rogers never did come around. Laird caved in but only because he believed that an ARVN invasion *without* American troops would not push Communist troops farther westward to lessen the threat to Saigon while Vietnamization continued. As for the great Communist central control headquarters, COSVN, Laird accurately told Nixon that " . . . COSVN in that sense did not exist and had never existed."[24]

Nixon decided to employ American troops only at the last minute. Appropriate Congressional committees were not informed, although Administration favorite Senator John Stennis, who had been made privy to Operation Menu, was easily won over when briefed by Kissinger, a touching scene as described by the briefer lacking only darkies, mint juleps, banjoes, and magnolia blossoms.[25] Lon Nol was not informed—he learned of the invasion only after it had begun. Kissinger cut most of his staff out of the planning. When the invasion was announced, three important aides resigned in disgust.[26]

Operation Toan Thang (aka Operation Rock Crusher) kicked off on April 29.[27] American artillery prepositioned in South Vietnam, opened preparatory fire while South Vietnamese fighter-bomber aircraft softened the target area. Three ARVN armored columns—some twelve thousand men with perhaps fifty American advisers—then invaded a border area known as Parrot's Beak. American helicopters including gunships supported the operation as did various logistic and medical-evacuation teams.

Shortly after Vietnamese columns began clanking into Parrot's Beak, a combined task force commenced Operation Prometheus north of the Beak. After preparatory air and artillery fire, some five thousand American troops pushed into an area called Fish Hook, which contained two of Operation Menu's target areas and, according to Abrams, was where COSVN was still functioning—despite the twenty-nine thousand tons of bombs dropped there over the past year.[28] This two-pronged

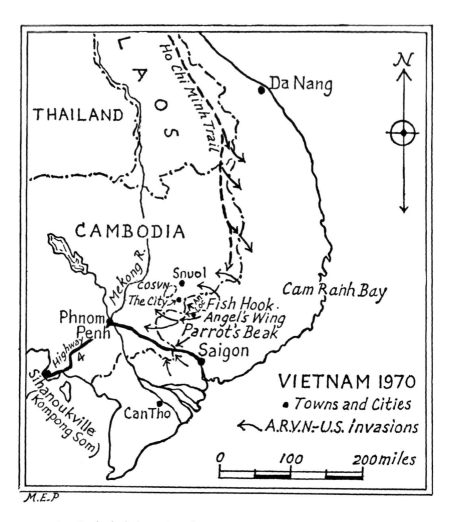

MAP

M.E.P

operation included three South Vietnamese paratroop battalions landed by American helicopters and was designed to close a trap around the enemy. Military spokesmen described the total operation as a "quick-strike" pincers movement converging on COSVN.

The offensive came as a surprise to nearly everyone (except the enemy). President Nixon appeared on television to justify his deeds by pointing out that " . . . the United States had 'scrupulously respected' Cambodia's neutrality for the last five years and had not moved against the sanctuaries," a patent lie " . . . repeated by Kissinger in his background briefings to the press."[29] Nixon went on to explain, somewhat ingeniously, that the invasion was not an invasion. The Cambodian operation was intended to eliminate " . . . the headquarters for the entire communist military operation in South Vietnam. This key control center has been occupied by the North Vietnamese and Viet Cong for years in blatant violation of Cambodia's neutrality." The present limited action, the President explained, was indispensable for the continuing success of the withdrawal program, for ending the war, and for keeping U.S. casualties to absolute minimum.[30] But there was something more, the President insisted, and that was the threat from " . . . the forces of totalitarianism and anarchy . . . [to the] free nations and free institutions throughout the world . . . [if] the world's most powerful nation, the United States of America, acts like a pitiful, helpless giant. . . . "[31]

This was vintage Nixon, but the wine was sour. Senator Edmund Muskie of Maine responded that " . . . this speech confirms a judgment that I've been reluctant to make: the President has decided to seek a military method of ending the war rather than a negotiated settlement." Senator Walter Mondale of Minnesota held that " . . . this is not only a tragic escalation, which will broaden the war and increase American casualties, but is outright admission of the failure of Vietnamization." Other critical voices joined the dissentient chorus, but they were not to down the high-flying President, who at the Pentagon the next day caused several nervous breakdowns by blithely ordering plans made to "take out" *all* the sanctuaries.[32]

Military operations meanwhile proceeded smoothly enough. Major General Ely Roberts, commanding 1st Cavalry (Airmobile) Division, told correspondents, " . . . We think we have them in the bag. In a day or two we shall reach inside the bag and see what we have. We can't be sure."[33] On the fifth day of operations, MACV claimed a total 1,094 enemy killed and 242 captured at a cost of eight American dead and thirty-two wounded. Allied troops also reported capturing large caches of rice and weapons.[34] So far, so good. But not very good. As in the fairy tale, Roberts' bag had grown increasingly lighter—with grim results: he reached inside to find almost no enemy. Had he done so, had enormous "kills" and captures been confirmed, had COSVN headquarters been overrun, had prominent VC and North Vietnamese officers surrendered and been hauled in tumbrels through Saigon streets—had any of this happened, Nixon might have got away with the invasion of Cambodia.

But nothing like this did happen. How could it? How could responsible military officers and civilian officials ever have dreamed of anything like this happening? Had they not by now discovered the basic elements of guerrilla warfare? Did they really believe the nonsense spoon-fed to (in some cases unsuspecting and gullible) correspondents? Did they really believe that " . . . the operational area [to quote one correspondent] which includes the Viet Cong's base areas 352 and 353, 'contains the headquarters of the Central Office for South Vietnam [COSVN], the headquarters of the South Vietnam Liberation Army . . .' . . . a command complex said to be the nerve center for the enemy war effort in the southern half of South Vietnam?" Did they really believe that there in the Cambodian jungles they were going to find the North Vietnamese version of the Pentagon and Fort Meyers? Did they believe that Viet Cong and North Vietnamese forces were going to stand quietly by to await a pitched battle in circumstances overwhelmingly favorable to enemy firepower? Did they believe that in an ARVN and a Saigon government known to be penetrated with Communist agents this operation would surprise the enemy?

Despite MACV's eulogistic communiqués, correspondents soon began to express doubts that made them unpopular with the American command. James Merba of the *New York Times,* for example, pointed out that, as opposed to Administration claims of an immense Communist build-up in South Vietnam, enemy activity according to American intelligence officers had been quite normal. Michael Hornsby of *The Times* (London) reported that observers were questioning the discrepancy between large numbers of enemy killed and captured versus the small number of weapons found on the battlefield—were dead civilians being mistaken for dead enemy? Five days after the beginning of the operation, military leaders were backtracking. Reports to Washington from the Fish Hook area were "not encouraging"; in Washington Ian McDonald of *The Times* (London) wrote that " . . . military commanders now hint that the enemy might have had advance word of the operation."[35]

By this time, President Nixon was undoubtedly sorry that he had ever heard of either the American army or Cambodia. A significant portion of Congress and the nation, on the other hand, was sorry that it had ever heard of Nixon. Nixon later claimed that his subsequent briefing of bipartisan Congressional leadership drew unanimous applause.[36] If so, the euphoria did not last long. Not having taken either the nation's legislators or its citizens into his confidence, the President reaped Congressional and popular wrath. Senator William Fulbright called the operation " . . . a major expansion of the war . . . If you accept the premises on which our justification and objectives have been based, this is consistent with our war policy. It is not consistent with any plan for ending the war."[37] Senator Mike Mansfield complained that " . . . we are sinking deeper into the morass. The feeling of gloom in the Senate is so thick that you could cut it with a knife."[38] Neither was morale exactly high in the White House, where Nixon ordered more wiretaps placed on officials and journalists. State Department officials who had not been advised of the invasion joined the chorus of disapproval, pointing out that Lon Nol's bellicose stand, taken without an adequate army at his disposal, had brought many of his troubles on himself, just as had Nixon who had "isolated himself from his State Department and depended almost entirely on military advice and White House staff work." The invasion of Cambodia caused several officials to resign while three hundred others in the State Department signed memoranda of protest.[39] Senators from both parties quickly moved " . . . to introduce legislation barring the use of funds to support American troops in Cambodia for any reason."[40]

Lon Nol also proved embarrassing. President Nixon reportedly had not taken the head of state into his confidence, but Lon Nol rolled easily with the punches and at once used the rationale of the Nixon Doctrine by requesting " . . . arms for 250,000 men, for helicopters, and equipment for a national army of some four hundred battalions."[41] Forever tied to the South Vietnam syndrome—arms and more arms for an army incapable of using them properly—White House and Pentagon would enable Lon Nol's army to number a theoretical 220,000 within a year.

Nixon also faced growing public hostility. By spring of 1970, the government's overdraft on credibility was considerable, and though large numbers of Americans still listened to their President and in general wanted to believe what he told them, a mean cynicism was pervading the country, particularly when it came to Pentagon and MACV communiqués. Some hostility was not so vague. A number of Harvard professors, Kissinger's former colleagues, called on him in Washington, " . . . a group of people," as their leader explained to Kissinger, "who have completely lost confidence in the ability of the White House to conduct our foreign policy, and we have come to tell you so. We are no longer at your disposal as personal advisers. . . . " After pointing out that

> . . . the invasion could be used by anyone else in the world as a precedent for invading another country in order, for example, to clear out terrorists . . . [Professor Thomas] Schelling told him: "As we see it, there are two possibilities. Either, one, the President didn't understand when he went into Cambodia that he was invading another country; or, two, he did understand. We just don't know which one is scarier.[42]

The National Student Association called for Nixon's impeachment. Violent demonstrations that included the theretofore "moderate middle" of both students and faculties erupted on nearly eight hundred campuses. Student protests in Ohio and Mississippi so alarmed authorities that police and national guardsmen shot twenty-seven and killed four students at Kent State and Jackson State universities—we shall not tolerate dissent.

We will not tolerate dissent—but dissent swirled around the Administration like smoke from an angry jinni's lamp and it did not fail to

1001

engulf an uncomfortable President who had ingeniously de-escalated war by invasion and who now was in trouble, his White House heavily guarded during a demonstration of seventy-five to one hundred thousand irate citizens, his capital invaded by thousands of angry students, his Congress lobbied by lawyers, educators, doctors, corporate executives. Such was Congressional hostility—increased by the Kent State killings—that Nixon promised Congressional leaders of both parties that all American forces would be pulled out of Cambodia within six weeks and that troop withdrawals from South Vietnam would proceed as planned. Meanwhile, Nixon not only wanted but had to have a "victory."

Victory was nowhere in sight. The invasion was not going at all the way the generals had promised. COSVN was not to be found. In searching for it, MACV had launched new incursions into Cambodia; one report estimated that fifty thousand troops were now involved. As invasion became non-invasion, so now non-victory became victory. Military communiqués described in glowing terms the capture of such enemy complexes as "the city" (a group of huts twenty miles west of the Fish Hook area). Two weeks after the operation had begun, MACV claimed 3,740 dead and 1,041 captured along with over three thousand tons of ammunition with but relatively minor American and South Vietnamese casualties.[43]

These figures disguised neither over-all failure of allied action in the South nor an unpleasant political complication. Nixon, like Napoleon after the conquest of Vitebsk, might have asked, "Do you think I have come all this way just to conquer these huts?" Despite continuing exultant press releases, Communist prisoners seemed in short supply. After some three weeks of operations, the Pentagon explained that COSVN " . . . had moved back into Cambodia beyond the 21-mile limit set up for U.S. ground operations."[44] That however, did not mean the end of the operation. Vice-President Ky had stated that ARVN troops would remain in Cambodia after the American withdrawal scheduled for the end of June. How long would they remain? For " . . . several months at the least . . . until the Cambodians were strong enough to defend themselves against North Vietnamese and Viet Cong."[45] Ky's statement further depressed Administration officials—as well it might considering Indochinese historical enmities.

Adding to Nixon's woes was a *Life* magazine article by Clark Clifford, President Johnson's disaffected secretary of defense, a onetime hawk who had become a powerful critic of the war. Clifford accused Nixon of contradicting stated policy with positive action—of widening the war to American and world detriment. After denying validity of the domino theory and pointing to the lack of contributing allies in Southeast Asia, he accused the President of holding a "curious obsession" about Asia in general and Indochina in particular. To consider South Vietnam a strategic necessity—an area where the future of the world would be decided—made no sense: " . . . The war in Vietnam is a local war arising out of the particular political conditions existing in southeast Asia. I consider it a delusion to suggest that it is part of a worldwide program of common aggression." As to the war's nature:

> . . . our problem in Vietnam is due not only to our inability to attain the military goals, despite our great effort, but to the fact that the struggle is basically a political one. The enemy continues to symbolize the forces of nationalism. The regime which we support is a narrowly based military dictatorship.

The Cambodian venture, Clifford went on, was meaningless militarily. The enemy would stay beyond our reach no matter how long troops remained in the area. Once troops were withdrawn, the enemy would return to old haunts. Despite this inevitable result, " . . . a determined effort will be made to portray the entire adventure as a success, even though no major engagements will have taken place and the number of enemy casualties will be woefully small." More than ever a political settlement was needed to end the war. Clifford offered a three-point program that called for total disengagement from combat by end of 1970 and total withdrawal by end of 1971.[46]

CHAPTER SEVENTY-SIX

1. International Institute for Strategic Studies, *Strategic Survey 1970*, "The Super-Powers."
2. Louis Heren, *The Times* (London), Washington, D.C., February 2, 1970.
3. Ian McDonald, *The Times* (London), Washington, D.C., February 3, 1970.
4. Colby, 191–5.
5. Isaacs, 162.
6. Ibid., 163.
7. Colby, 198. See also, Isaacs, 164–9.
8. Louis Heren, *The Times* (London), Washington, D.C., March 3, 1970. See also, Paul, for an analysis of the reason for (and fallacy of) American official silence; Kissinger, *The White House Years*, 450–7.
9. Louis Heren, *The Times* (London), Washington, D.C., March 17, 1970.
10. *The Times* (London), Washington, D.C., March 9, 1970.
11. *Time*, April 6, 1970.
12. *The Times* (London), April 22, 1970.
13. James Reston, *The Times* (London), New York, April 21, 1970.
14. Shawcross, 163.
15. Kissinger, *The White House Years*, 460.
16. Morris, 173.
17. Shawcross, 115 ff. See also, Snepp, 19–20. Although CIA had constantly insisted that the bulk of Communist supplies arrived via the Ho Chi Minh trail, captured Communist records later divulged that " . . . nearly 80 percent of the materiel" came from North Vietnam through the port of Sihanoukville.

18. Shawcross, 115. See also, Kiernan, 300–2.
19. Shawcross, 126. See also, Kiernan, 297–300.
20. Shawcross, 131–2. See also, Kiernan, 303.
21. Karnow, 609.
22. Shawcross, 129.
23. Nixon, *Memoirs,* 447.
24. Morris, 175.
25. Kissinger, *The White House Years,* 496.
26. Nixon, *Memoirs,* 451. See also, Morris, 174.
27. More precisely, Complete Victory 42 and 43, following forty-one earlier Complete Victory operations begun after the 1968 Tet offensive.
28. Shawcross, 140.
29. Ibid., 146.
30. Reuters, Washington, D.C., May 1, 1970.
31. Nixon, *Memoirs,* 452.
32. Ibid., 453–4. See also, Westmoreland, 388.
33. *The Times* (London), May 1, 1970.
34. Sihanouk, 174–5. The South Vietnamese Communist NLF had refused to arm the Khmer Rouge until after Sihanouk's departure and only when it was obvious that the frontier areas would be invaded and the caches of arms captured. Weapons were then freely supplied to the Khmer Rouge and to the "guerrilla Sihanoukists."
35. Ian McDonald, *The Times* (London), Washington, D.C., May 3, 1970.
36. Nixon, *Memoirs,* 451.
37. Ian McDonald, *The Times* (London), Washington, D.C., May 1, 1970.
38. *Time,* May 11, 1970.
39. John Franklin Campbell.
40. Ian McDonald, *The Times* (London), Washington, D.C., April 30, 1970.
41. Shawcross, 130–2. See also, Fred Emery, *The Times* (London), Phnom Penh, April 30, 1970.
42. Shawcross, 156. See also, Kissinger, *The White House Years,* 514, for an injured account of this meeting.
43. *The Sunday Telegraph* (London), May 10, 1970.
44. *The Times* (London), Washington, D.C., May 21, 1970.
45. Michael Hornsby, *The Times* (London), Saigon, May 12, 1970.
46. Clifford.

CHAPTER 77

The Cambodian invasion backfires • ARVN in Cambodia • Congress rebels • The Administration's reply • Nixon's dominoes • PAVN's new threat • The Cambodian sinkhole • Administration reverses • Paris: peace plan versus peace plan • The leaked CIA report • Pacification in South Vietnam: fact versus fiction? • Enemy offensive moves

ALTHOUGH THE American public was not to know, the invasion of Cambodia had upset negotiations outside of and Vietnamization within South Vietnam. A special CIA estimate " . . . showed that United States interests in Indochina had been seriously compromised" by the invasion. A top-level Pentagon report stated that " . . . these operations have not substantially reduced NVA [North Vietnamese Army] capabilities in Cambodia. . . . Captured supplies can be reconstituted in about seventy-five days with opening of additional supply routes through Laos and in Cambodia." A secret State Department analysis " . . . concluded that the invasion had caused 'a traumatic reaction in the world at large' and a blow to American prestige."[1] In short, influenced by his coteries of hawks, by the JCS and MACV, Nixon had made the fundamental error of awakening what Lyautey would have considered, relatively speaking, an "asleep" area.

The Nixon administration remained seemingly oblivious to such classified reports or to other outspoken criticism. At the end of May, the President told the nation that " . . . the Cambodian intervention was the most successful operation of a long and difficult war."[2] His statement found few believers. Twist and wiggle in his wormlike style, Nixon could not evade the fact that he had enlarged the war without accomplishing the stated mission of eliminating the enemy's operational headquarters in Cambodia. MACV spokesmen could jabber on about captured weapons and rice stocks but could not deny that since 1932 the Vietnamese had proved they could go without either and still fight. Hanoi-watchers could discern crisis in the North and point to a burgeoning manpower shortage but could not deny that Moscow and Peking were continuing to supply the enemy and that fresh troops continued to enter South Vietnam. American diplomats in Moscow warned Washington in June that the drain on North Vietnam in Cambodia and Laos was again turning Hanoi toward China; to counter that, Moscow agreed to furnish more weapons and matériel to North Vietnam, thus continuing the vicious circle of great-power escalation of the war.

So it was that enemy strength in the South remained basically unaltered: about a hundred thousand North Vietnamese either in the border areas or in South Vietnam and perhaps a hundred thousand "regular" Viet Cong supported by sixty thousand provincial guerrillas and a civilian network of supporters and sympathizers. The real challenge remained in South Vietnam, where the highly touted ARVN was scarcely showing professional brilliance in the Cambodian operations and was otherwise beset with the cancer of command corruption that was gradually killing the body politic. Colonel David Hackworth, an experienced ARVN adviser, told one journalist that " . . . Vietnamization is a word which must be a product of Madison Avenue. It's a public-relations dream. I haven't seen an improvement in ARVN. . . . Perhaps from a cosmetic viewpoint they look a little better in that they wear their helmets and keep their equipment on."[3] Hackworth's blunt words were reinforced by the normal ARVN desertion rate of eight thousand a month rising to twelve thousand a month.[4] One American adviser watched his ARVN battalion, 525 strong, melt to two hundred combat effectives within thirty days, not from enemy action but from desertion.[5] " . . . Raping, looting and burning" were the orders of the day in claimed retaliation for Lon Nol's recent bloodbath of resident Vietnamese in Cambodia.[6] Hackworth, who accompanied ARVN paratroopers in the invasion, was appalled by the

> . . . wholesale destruction of Cambodian towns and villages . . . and the looting was almost unimaginable. As the days passed, whenever I looked into the sky, I saw furniture, motorcycles, and luxury automobiles (Mercedes, Peugeots, Citroëns) flying along, suspended from Vietnamese Air Force (VNAF) choppers bound for some senior ARVN or VNAF officer's home, garage, or other stash point.

For many ARVN soldiers it was their first combat experience and it didn't wash well. " . . . In all, Cambodia was mines and booby traps, snipers and small hit-and-run attacks on our units, which pretty well eroded whatever fighting spirit our ARVN charges had had." Most

ARVN units moved like glue. One supporting American rocket battalion plastered enemy forces reported by ARVN units " . . . with more than ten thousand rounds"—more than a million dollars' worth of ammunition to kill seven enemy.[7]

As always, inept military strategy had created more problems than it solved. Having supported Lon Nol's regime without being requested to do so, Nixon could not leave the country open to enemy vengeance. The Administration now veered to supporting a continued ARVN presence in Cambodia and even requested Congress to extend the deadline for American troop withdrawal. Congress was having none of it. Not only did a Senate vote defeat the amendment but a week later the Cooper-Church amendment was passed, which demanded that Nixon recall at once all American troops in Cambodia, and which prohibited the Administration from using funds to support U.S. operations in that country—" . . . the first restrictive vote ever cast on a President in war time," Nixon later fumed, ignoring the fact that the country was not officially at war.[8]

The Administration and MACV now ignored the nation's law. American planes were already overflying "limits" stated by Nixon and were attacking Communist supply routes in western Cambodia. As with Operation Menu, the bombing reports were falsified and there was almost no "bomb damage assessment"[9]—God alone knows how many more Cambodian civilians were blown up. MACV quietly assured the Saigon government of continued support of its troops in Cambodia. When the last American troops headed for South Vietnam in late June, " . . . leaving behind a lingering form of tear gas, blown bridges and damaged roads in an effort to slow communist reoccupation of the area," thirty thousand ARVN troops remained behind. The Administration publicly continued to insist that it had gained an impressive victory while privately admitting that the enemy controlled one third of Cambodia, moved freely in another third, and was expected to reoccupy its old border sanctuaries within a few months.[10]

President Nixon completed the last act of a play within a play by appointing a new ambassador to the Paris peace talks, seventy-three-year-old David Bruce, and by again making a public appeal to Hanoi: " . . . We are prepared, by negotiation, to bring out all of our forces and have no forces at all in South Vietnam if the enemy . . . will withdraw theirs." The American government attached only two conditions, the President continued. The South Vietnamese must remain free to determine their own future, and the United States would not impose a coalition government. What if the people chose a Communist government? Nixon would accept their judgment since he was sure that this would not happen—no Communist government had ever been freely elected.* However, he would not hand over South Vietnam to the Communists. The domino theory, the President insisted, was still valid:

> ... Now I know there are those that say, "Well, the domino theory is obsolete." They haven't talked to the dominoes. They should talk to the Thais, Malaysians, to Singapore, to Indonesia, to the Philippines, to the Japanese, and the rest.
>
> And if the United States leaves Vietnam in a way that we are humiliated or defeated, not simply speaking in what are called jingoistic terms but in very practical terms, this will be immensely discouraging to the 300 million people from Japan clear round to Thailand and in free Asia.
>
> And even more important, it will be ominously encouraging to the leaders of Communist China and the Soviet Union who are supporting the North Vietnamese. It will encourage them in their expansionist policies in other areas.[11]

So the presidential voice sounded on that final day of June 1970. It might have been Eisenhower in 1956, Kennedy in 1962, Johnson in 1966. The record was the same. After ten years, nearly forty thousand American lives and over $100 billion the United States was returning to square one.

More of the same followed. In early July, the American chief of the Vietnamization program in the Mekong Delta, John Paul Vann, personally reported to President Nixon that the enemy effort had been reduced to " ... dispersed and dispirited units of five North Vietnamese regiments." Citing the NLF's latest directive, Vann's report spoke of waning enemy confidence. This in part was brought on by the fallout of the Tet offensive—VC losses that led to increased taxes and enforced recruitment in VC-occupied areas, and by a South Vietnamese land reform program under which nearly one million hectares of land would be redistributed to peasant tenant farmers.[12] The NLF now admitted the possibility of a cease-fire, in which case " ... only continuing guerrilla warfare can achieve our purpose in the ensuing complicated situation. ... Strike now at only a few objectives over a wide area. Where necessary and so directed, local cells will go into retirement and await opportunity and orders."[13]

Several developments tempered Vann's expressed optimism. One was increasing enemy activity inside South Vietnam. MACV already had reported that in the last two weeks of May, 221 Americans had been killed in South Vietnam compared to 138 in Cambodia.[14] Two

---

*The President evidently forgot the Chilean elections.

weeks after Vann had submitted his report, an American military spokesman warned of a pending Communist offensive in the central highlands. Five thousand ARVN troops and some fifteen hundred American marines pushed west from Da Nang in a search-and-destroy mission designed to disrupt the enemy build-up. While that was occurring, enemy units attacked an American airborne division base camp eleven miles from the Laotian border, killing at least thirty-two Americans, wounding 148 and forcing evacuation of the area.[15] The action continued to build until in mid-August MACV launched one of the heaviest air interdiction efforts of the war: nearly a hundred B-52 bombers struck North Vietnamese supply and staging areas on both sides of the Laotian border.[16] In early September, enemy reinforcements were coming down the Ho Chi Minh trail while local cadres were reoccupying old border bases in Cambodia.

Cambodia itself was proving a sinkhole. The $7.9 million in arms hastily authorized in May did not go very far; the Nixon administration slated $25 million for military aid in fiscal year 1970–71 but that figure quickly shot to $75 million. In early September, twenty-one South Vietnamese battalions supported by 25 per cent of South Vietnamese air strikes (all paid for by the United States government) were operating in Cambodia,[17] while in Washington the Senior Review Group, chaired by Kissinger, in effect ended Cambodia's "neutrality": the subsequent JCS plan would soon result in a greatly enlarged U.S. advisory team in Phnom Penh, its task to convert the Cambodian army into a conventional force some 220,000 strong plus a paramilitary force of 143,000[18]—precisely what had happened in South Vietnam in the formative early sixties. Throughout summer of 1970, Lloyd Rives in the American embassy in Phnom Penh had warned of Lon Nol's " . . . 'over-grandiose dreams,' and in one cable begged for help to bring Nol 'out of the clouds of his planning.' "[19] In August, the CIA station chief in Phnom Penh reported " . . . the inability of the [Nol] government to communicate at all with the people . . . [and] he believed 'the initial enthusiasm generated by the overthrow of Norodom Sihanouk has dissipated to a large extent.' "[20] Owing to the fighting in the countryside, refugees in Phnom Penh had increased from six hundred thousand to two–three million; rubber production was at a standstill; rice production was diminishing. " . . . By the end of 1970 the government . . . [would be] spending five times its revenue and earning nothing abroad."[21] Corruption controlled the government. The austerity program was a joke—millions of dollars' worth of luxury goods were flowing into Phnom Penh. Corrupt army commanders were receiving pay for soldiers who existed only on paper. The sale of weapons and ammunition to the enemy was commonplace. Some commanders sold rations provided for the troops; hungry soldiers stole from villagers, who soon leaned toward the enemy. These deficiencies would not be repaired in the fighting ahead. They would only increase until ended by defeat.[22] It was the China-Vietnam syndrome apparently unfamiliar to Nixon and his cohorts.

As had been the case in China and Vietnam, the U. S. government was in large part footing the bill. Despite not-so-subtle hints from American officials, SEATO and other Asian nations proved reluctant to help erect a new Cambodian bulwark against communism. These were the "dominoes" referred to by President Nixon, the ones who stood in fear and trembling of the Communist threat: Domino Australia sent a little civil aid, dominoes New Zealand and Korea sent some medicines, domino Thailand refused Lon Nol's request to send troops. In late July, domino Cambodia " . . . rejected the idea of Cambodian membership in SEATO. Reiterating his government's policy of neutrality, Lon Nol said Cambodia had no intention of taking arms against her enemies if they withdrew from Cambodian territory."[23]

The Nixon administration was faring no better on either the Saigon or the home front. Fighting in Cambodia had returned Vietnam to national and international front pages and little escaped notice. In early July, the story broke of appalling conditions in South Vietnamese prisons—the inhuman "tiger cages." This led to a rash of survey stories mostly critical of Thieu's dictatorship. In America, a Congressional committee investigating the My Lai massacre concluded that:

> . . . all details of the killing were covered up at the divisional level. There was, the investigation states in a report released tonight, "a concerted effort among military and State Department officers to suppress all evidence of the allegation and its investigation."
>
> It said that senior officers in both the Americal Division and the State Department were guilty of casting "a blanket of silence" over the massacres.[24]

Then came the Scranton report on the extent of unrest in American colleges and universities: " . . . The divisions splitting American society [were] 'as deep as any since the Civil War . . . nothing is more important than an end to the war' in Vietnam."[25]

In Paris, meanwhile, the Communist delegation put forward a new, eight-point peace plan, which David Bruce dismissed as new wine in old bottles. Kissinger's secret negotiations in Paris had come to naught: in late September he broke off still another fruitless meeting and refused to reschedule a new one. In early October, with midterm elections less than a month away, President Nixon offered what he fondly described as a "peace offensive." Addressing the nation on television, the President announced that his new initiative had been made possible by the remarkable success of the Vietnamization policy of the past eighteen months, and that it had won the concurrence of the South Vietnam, Laos, and Cambodia governments. As for his plan, vintner Nixon was offering old wine in old bottles. Like the magician who promised to produce an elephant and came up with a mouse, his proposals were a diluted version of Henry Kissinger's 1969 plan that itself remarkably resembled a plan presented by Robert Shaplen in 1967. Nixon now called for a cease-fire in place to be "effectively supervised" by international observers (a qualification realistically dismissed by Shaplen), a new international conference, negotiated troop withdrawals, and immediate release of all prisoners of war.

The Communist delegation in Paris shortly and sharply rejected a cease-fire in place, as Shaplen had warned they would if inhibited by international supervision. Thieu in Saigon made it known that he violently disagreed with Nixon: he did not want a cease-fire; he would not accept neutrality; he wanted the Communists to leave his country and American troops to remain; and he would not release forty thousand Communist prisoners. To some observers in the United States the proposal seemed so politically inspired as to deserve contempt. As James Reston put it,

> ... All governments operate on two levels—the moral and the political—but seldom in recent history has any administration matched the Nixon Administration's spectacular combination of priggish moralizing and political expediency. One day it sounds like Billy Graham and the next it acts like Machiavelli.[26]

Considering election results, Nixon failed to derive much political profit from his diplomatic ploy. Too many factors were operating against him. The momentous issue of Vietnam had been steadily tearing Americans from normal loyalty to the executive. We saw the beginning of this process in the early sixties when pro and anti sides steadily leaked classified information to suit their purposes (see Chapter 60). A certain amount of official leakage has always been a part of American government—a case can be made for it as integral to the system of checks and balances. But major leakages of what are called "state secrets" were now developing. In May, the CIA had circulated a top-secret report on South Vietnam that contained devastating information of Communist infiltration of the South Vietnamese government. Concerned U.S. officials took it upon themselves to inform the *New York Times* of this document. In mid-October, the *Times* carried the story written by veteran reporter Neil Sheehan. According to the CIA report, shortly after the 1968 Tet offensive the Communists

... decided to shift their long-range strategy from intense military activity to political erosion. They stepped up their infiltration of secret agents into various branches of the South Vietnamese government.

Most of the agents were natives of the southern part of divided Vietnam, and they were infiltrated into the armed forces, the police force and the South Vietnamese intelligence organizations whose task it was to eradicate the Vietcong and their North Vietnamese allies.

The Communists, the report continued, had infiltrated over thirty thousand agents into the South Vietnamese Government " . . . in an apparatus that has been virtually impossible to destroy." Some twenty thousand of the agents operated in ARVN. According to the report,

> . . . the enemy network could not exist without the tacit complicity whether from fear, sympathy or apathy, of the majority of South Vietnamese soldiers and policemen and [the report] says that such feelings provide evidence that the Saigon government could not command the deep loyalty of the men on whom it depends to defend itself.

With virtually unlimited intelligence at its disposal, the enemy would have little trouble in surviving military pressures to emerge (and presumably take over control) once the United States had withdrawn its troops.[27]

White House officials downplayed the importance of the report. It was "overly pessimistic," they claimed, and plainly contrary to present progress. President Thieu insisted that 98 per cent of South Vietnam's population was under government control, and if this figure contradicted an official U.S. estimate of 75 per cent, no one could deny that progress was being made in pacification. American troops were daily withdrawing from actual combat; U.S. deaths were down to about forty a week. Over-all troop withdrawal was proceeding on schedule. Forty thousand more troops were to leave by year's end. By spring of 1971, all combat troops would be gone, leaving some 270,000 "support" troops in the area. President Thieu, Administration spokesmen emphasized, was actively widening his political base in preparation for presidential elections scheduled for autumn of 1971. Thieu's seat would be challenged by General Duong Van Minh, who reportedly would campaign on a "peace" ticket—if that wasn't democracy, what was?

A pretty picture, but more blurs. Ninety-eight per cent of the population under government control? Seventy-five per cent? This was fine except some qualified observers suggested that " . . . the indices upon which such assessments are based . . . [are] largely meaningless."[28] Until villages were properly policed, no one would know the depth of relationship between peasants and enemy who still controlled large areas of South Vietnam. So long as guerrilla units continued to strike virtually at will without peasants warning government authorities, government did not either command peasant support or control peasants. And what of White House silence following Sir Robert Thompson's *second* visit to Vietnam in the autumn? What of *New York Times* reports " . . . asserting that Sir Robert had reported on the continuing failure of the South Vietnamese to uproot the Viet Cong's underground political structure?"[29]

The Administration's definition of combat forces was also suspect. American aircraft were interdicting Communist supply lines in Cambodia and were also furnishing close air support to Cambodian forces. Although South Vietnam was building an air force, it had a long way to go. As of November, its helicopter fleet counted two hundred and fifty machines compared to some four thousand American machines in the area, and Secretary of the Air Force Robert Seamans admitted that U. S. Air Force units would have to remain in Indochina for years.[30] Plans to remove *all* combat forces also changed. Two combat divisions, the 101st Airborne and the 1st Cavalry (Airmobile), would remain to provide security for bases such as Da Nang and Cam Ranh Bay.

Nor did the Administration confine MACV entirely to a defensive posture. American deaths may have been reduced but they did not cease—forty deaths a week is over two thousand a year. Installations suffered guerrilla attacks and patrols suffered casualties. The enemy shot down an American reconnaissance plane in North Vietnam and in late November the President authorized bombing strikes—"protective reaction"—to resume south of the 19th parallel. MACV at the same time launched a helicopter raid on an alleged prisoner-of-war camp near Hanoi. Ostensibly designed to free American prisoners, it also demonstrated American ability to penetrate North Vietnamese defenses. It failed on the first count and in so doing symbolized the over-all intelligence failure of American arms: no prisoners were in the camp. As for psychological effect, Hanoi already knew that American arms were capable of invading the North, just as its leaders knew that American atomic bombs could eliminate Hanoi. That wasn't the crux of the matter. Hanoi also knew that what happened subsequently might well end civilization.

The threat of renewed bombing of the North, obviously an attempt to influence intractable North Vietnamese negotiators in Paris, brought general outcry from around the world. In defending it, indeed in threatening to resume it in earnest, Defense Secretary Laird cited what he insisted was an "understanding" with the North when President Johnson stopped the bombing in late 1968. Hanoi predictably denied that any "understanding" existed. Laird should have read Kissinger's analysis of these negotiations in his celebrated *Foreign Affairs* article and respected the devastating effect of morbid linguistic behavior induced by the two countries' inability to identify with each other.

A more valid reason for threatening to resume bombing was embarrassing. American intelligence was reporting indications of a build-up from the North that scarcely jibed either with Hanoi's alleged state of exhaustion or Administration claims of "victory" in Cambodia. An Institute for Strategic Studies analysis of the Cambodian incursion concluded:

> ... The immediate effect was to reduce pressure on American forces in Vietnam and thus to ease the course of American withdrawal and "Vietnamization." But the North Vietnamese had not been crippled. Other supply routes, based not only on expanding the "Ho Chi-minh trail" but also on the Mekong and Sekong rivers, were developed with some speed to replace that through [the port of] Kompong Som [Sihanoukville]. At the same time, military efforts in both southern Laos and eastern Cambodia were stepped up.

The same analysis pointed out that in South Vietnam

> ... the leadership in Hanoi had openly reverted to a policy of "protracted struggle" by guerrilla forces and organized activity by major Viet Cong and North Vietnamese units was increasingly restricted to the sparsely populated fringes of the country.[31]

In mid-December, a Brazilian journalist reported from Hanoi that the North Vietnamese were preparing " ... a new and perhaps decisive round of fighting on the ground." He continued:

> ... There is every evidence to the visitor here that, for all the reports out of Washington and Saigon and even Moscow that the Viet Cong are exhausted and the North Vietnamese over-extended, preparations are under way for another push.[32]

As the year drew to a close, the enemy was fighting hard in Laos and Cambodia and remained uncomfortably evident in South Vietnam, as witness the shelling of Saigon. His negotiators in Paris showed little inclination to negotiate. In mid-December, Hanoi radio predicted "more complex" and "more violent" fighting throughout Indochina in 1971.

CHAPTER SEVENTY-SEVEN

1. Shawcross, 173.
2. Louis Heren, *The Times* (London), Washington, D.C., June 4, 1970.
3. *Newsweek*, July 5, 1971.
4. Frances Fitzgerald, 418.
5. Hackworth, 732–3.
6. Shawcross, 151.
7. Hackworth, 732–4.
8. Nixon, *Memoirs*, 467–8.
9. Shawcross, 214.
10. Louis Heren, *The Times* (London), Washington, D.C., June 29, 1970.
11. Ibid.
12. Blaufarb, 266–7.
13. Richard Hughes, *The Sunday Times* (London), Hong Kong, July 5, 1970.
14. Louis Heren, *The Times* (London), Washington, D.C., June 2, 1970. Vann would be killed in a helicopter crash in the central highlands in June 1972.
15. *The Times* (London), AP and Reuters, Saigon, July 23, 1970.
16. *The Times* (London), and AP, August 17, 1970.
17. Shawcross, 179.
18. Ibid., 194.
19. Ibid., 182.
20. Ibid., 183.
21. Ibid. 220.
22. Ibid., 221, 313 ff.
23. *The Times* (London), Bangkok, July 23, 1970.
24. Ian McDonald, *The Times* (London), Washington, D.C., July 14, 1970.
25. Karnow, 25–6.
26. James Reston, *The Times* (London), October 15, 1970.
27. Neil Sheehan, *The Times* (London), October 19, 1972.
28. Michael Hornsby, *The Times* (London), Saigon, October 26, 1970.
29. Fred Emery, *The Times* (London), Washington, D.C., January 17, 1971.
30. *The Times* (London) and AP, Saigon, November 5, 1970.
31. International Institute for Strategic Studies, *Strategic Survey 1970,* "Eastern Asia."
32. Henry Brandon, *The Sunday Times* (London), Washington, D.C., December 13, 1970.

CHAPTER 78

The Nixon administration's new strategy • Hanoi's position • The war in Cambodia • Opposition at home • ARVN invades Laos: "the golden opportunity" • Battlefield alchemy: disaster • Reasons why • Picking up the pieces • Flies in the Nixon ointment • The Calley case • Captain Daniels writes the President

IN EARLY 1971, two voices sounded words as prophetic as those uttered by Shakespeare's witches dancing around another devil's brew. One belonged to Secretary of Defense Melvin Laird, who announced that the U.S. combat role in South Vietnam would end within twelve months. More time would be needed, however, for the South Vietnamese " . . . to replace American air support, logistics and administration." By May, American strength in Vietnam would be reduced to 285,000 men.[1] Laird's brave words complemented Nixon's effort to close a political coffin before it claimed what rapidly was becoming an executive corpse. Militarily his statement was as flaccid as the rest of the Nixon Doctrine. Primarily a political ploy designed to ease anti-Administration pressures within the United States, it also was intended to allow the Administration certain strategic and tactical flexibility within South Vietnam and Cambodia. By tying American troop withdrawals to the progress of Vietnamization, it enabled the Administration to plead that overt military action against the enemy within South Vietnam, Cambodia, Laos, and North Vietnam was necessary to save American lives. It also established the notion of a large and expensive residual force remaining in South Vietnam (for the next hundred years). Politically it was cheap, militarily it was unsatisfactory, diplomatically it was meaningless.

The other voice emanating from the devil's brew belonged to Prime Minister Pham Van Dong, who announced from Hanoi that " . . . the Vietnamese people would insist on unconditional withdrawal by the Americans and that this point was not negotiable."[2] The prime minister's intransigence was reflected in Paris, from where Ambassador David Bruce continued to report no progress in peace talks, and also in Laos, Cambodia, and South Vietnam, where guerrillas and PAVN units continued to fight brisk if isolated actions. Le Duan, first secretary of Hanoi's Communist Party, emphasized this stand by announcing that the North's " . . . strategic guideline is to fight a protracted war, gaining strength as one fights." " . . . To engage in military struggle under unfavorable circumstances," he said, echoing Sun Tzu, "is a serious mistake."

Le Duan's words seemed to some Western observers to be an admission of defeat and in a sense they were. But they scarcely were tantamount to capitulation. They instead marked a shift in strategy, one predicated primarily on the realization that American public opinion was forcing American disengagement from the war. Where two years earlier Hanoi was ignoring internal damage in favor of prosecuting the war in the South, it now turned to repairing this damage as part of growing strong internally in order to carry on protracted warfare. A visiting Canadian journalist, Michael Maclear, found that the government had pulled all stops in the North. Not only were conscription-age men and women assigned to labor brigades, but the government was even offering such incentives as cash bonuses and home-building loans to further its program of repairing war damage and rebuilding the economy.[3] This shift in strategy represented a victory of sorts for the moderate factions in the Politburo—as we shall see, it was all too transitory.[4]

Internal stress did not mean an end to combat operations in the South. Despite U.S.-ARVN attacks of the previous spring, the Communist position in Cambodia remained strong, in part owing to increased aid from China. Sihanouk later wrote that by March 1971 seventy of the country's one hundred administrative districts had been "liberated" by the guerrillas and that 751 of 1,129 villages were in guerrilla hands. By September, guerrillas would claim control of four fifths of the country, which held five million of Cambodia's seven million population.[5] Supplies continued to flow south via the Ho Chi Minh trail in defiance of American air interdiction (at this point American planes had dropped more bombs on Indochina than it had on both the European and Pacific theaters during World War II).[6] In November, Communist units had occupied a strategic pass in Cambodia to cut Highway 4, the single road connection between the capital of Phnom Penh and Kompong Som (Sihanoukville), Cambodia's single deepwater port (see map on page 998). The capital soon suffered a fuel shortage. Convoys carrying fuel from South Vietnam on the Mekong River fell victim to guerrilla ambushes. In early January, a combined Cambodian-ARVN task force heavily supported by American planes moved to reopen the highway. When ground

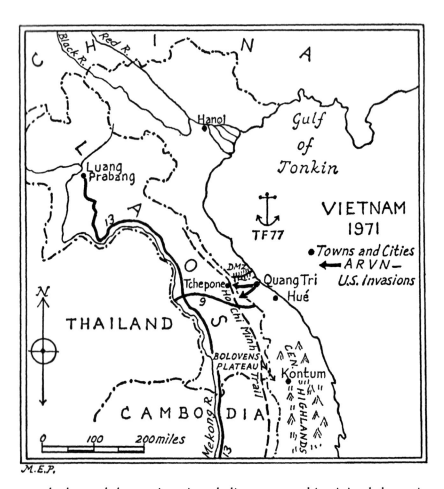

M.E.P.

attacks bogged down, American helicopter gunships joined the action. Although Cambodian troops captured the target pass, Viet Cong suicide squads a few days later struck Phnom Penh's airport, virtually eliminating the fledgling Cambodian air force, and shelled the capital to send morale plunging. MACV responded with massive airlifts of barbed wire, sandbags, and more arms and ammunition to Phnom Penh. Simultaneously in Laos, PAVN units knocked out a series of Meo guerrilla outposts in the important Bolovens Plateau area—outposts secretly organized and supported by the CIA.

The new action caused a furor in Congress. Opposition members including Republicans interpreted it as a violation of the Cooper-Church amendment, which prohibited the Administration from using funds for U.S. operations in Cambodia. The Administration justified the action as necessary to protect American troops as well as, in Melvin Laird's words, " . . . to supplement the efforts and the armed forces of our friends and allies who are determined to resist aggression."[7] Secretary of State Rogers repeated this theme to an angry Senate Foreign

Relations Committee and to a bewildered but restive American public. The Administration, he said, was prepared to use air power in Indochina " . . . to the fullest possible extent necessary."[8]

The powerful fumes of Congressional and public dissent had not yet dissipated when reports of another Nixon surprise began to reach American newsrooms. Despite a blackout imposed by MACV and the White House, the American public learned that some twenty thousand South Vietnamese soldiers, the elite of ARVN, were moving toward southern Laos. This task force, backed by an impressive armored task force of some ten thousand American troops, was said to be occupying once-familiar terrain in northwestern reaches of South Vietnam. A second ARVN task force was reportedly moving into eastern Cambodia. In early February, an uneasy world learned that South Vietnam had invaded the panhandle of southern Laos. American planes and artillery had prepared the way; American helicopters supported the action; American armor backed the effort but remained in South Vietnam.

ARVN Operation Lam Son 719 and U.S. Operation Dewey Canyon II were designed to sever the Ho Chi Minh trail leading to Cambodia—a "golden opportunity," according to advocates including Abrams and the JCS, to eliminate enemy supply lines and thereby shorten the war.[9] Vice-President Nguyen Cao Ky told correspondents in Saigon that ARVN forces would probably remain in Laos until the end of the dry season in May and would probably repeat the operation the next year. It might be necessary, he said, to bomb North Vietnam in the process. Nixon blithely announced in Washington that the operation was "consistent with international law." It was as well that attorney Nixon did not have to debate the legal issue. Congressional opponents such as Senator Mike Mansfield deplored the action as a "deepening of the tragedy." The Royal Laotian Government condemned it, as did UN Secretary-General U Thant "in strong terms."[10]

As in the case of the invasion of Cambodia the previous spring, front-line communiqués (issued from back-line headquarters) told of slight resistance with impressive captures of food and ammunition. According to General Hoang Xuan Lam, ARVN commander of the invasion, whose headquarters at Quang Tri, despite incredibly inefficient communications, were unbelievably located fifty miles from the Tchepone target area, " . . . the southward flow of North Vietnamese men and supplies down the Ho Chi Minh trail . . . has been completely halted." The general claimed that his forces were deployed along Highway 9 fifteen to twenty miles inside Laos and that 750 North Vietnamese had been killed at a cost of forty to fifty ARVN troops.[11] Abrams informed Washington that " . . . I am confident that the task that was initially laid out will be done."[12]

Ugly rumors were already creeping into newsrooms, however. *Time* magazine noted that in the first five days of combat, twenty-nine thousand troops supported by " . . . 493 gunship attacks, 216 air cavalry missions, and 4,025 separate lifts of troops and supplies . . . destroyed two trucks, exploded one ammunition storage area and found one 57-mm. recoilless rifle, the mount for a mortar and a few dozen 105-mm. artillery shells."[13] Although MACV announced the loss of twelve helicopters, journalist Michael Hornsby suggested that as many as fifty had been damaged or destroyed. If this was true, it followed that enemy resistance must be more than sporadic. Sure enough two days later President Nixon repeated a report from General Abrams that although ARVN was fighting in "a superior way," it had "run into heavy resistance."

Abrams' words precluded battlefield alchemy. In the harsh crucible of tactical reality, the "golden opportunity" was turning into base disaster: Operation Lam Son 719 was coming apart at the seams. Communist forces had fallen back only to snake around clanking ARVN armor columns to strike vulnerable lines of communication—a tactic as old as war. Once ARVN units occupied various positions, usually in battalion strength, VC and PAVN units joined to launch "suicide" attacks, exactly as they had done at Dien Bien Phu, Ia Drang, and elsewhere. As at Dien Bien Phu, they now sprang a tactical surprise in the form of tanks, old Russian PT-76s whose presence had gone undetected by American fliers (but was undoubtedly known to local peasants).

Washington attempted to break the truth as painlessly as possible. On February 22, the South Vietnamese Government, which earlier had spoken of minimum enemy forces in the area, changed its tune. President Thieu said the invasion was to prevent a North Vietnamese invasion of South Vietnam's five northern provinces. While Secretary of Defense Laird insisted that ARVN units were " . . . achieving their objective of major disruption of enemy supply routes," the enemy not only had shifted to western arteries beyond ARVN's reach but was overrunning ARVN positions in the vicinity of Highway 9. By February 25, the battle so wished for by MACV and ARVN was on. For ten days, ARVN seemed to be holding its own and then some. On March 7, Saigon proudly announced the capture of Tchepone, a major Communist staging and supply area. Vice-President Ky, never at a loss for the dramatic, told correspondents that his government was looking for a "Dien Bien Phu in reverse." General Lam claimed that his forces had cut "the main portion" of the Ho Chi Minh trail: the enemy was taking casualties twenty times heavier than his own and had lost about six thousand killed and hundreds more wounded by air strikes as well as 112,000 tons of ammunition, 245 vehicles including seventy-four tanks, and thirteen hundred tons of food.[14] In a dramatic Pentagon press conference,

Laird and Lieutenant General John Vogt, Jr., proudly displayed a piece of enemy pipeline used to bring gasoline from the North—but failed to mention that it had been captured weeks earlier by a commando raid.

ARVN losses were also heavy. In the week ending March 4, they reportedly amounted to 898 killed and over two thousand wounded. American deaths numbered sixty-nine. *Time* magazine stated that "... in three weeks, no less than five ARVN battalions had, for all practical purposes, been knocked out of action."[15] Journalist Derek Wilson reported fourteen helicopters shot down in one day; an American pilot had told him that "... we're being knocked off like flies."[16]

ARVN still seemed to claim the upper hand as further units slogged into battered Tchepone, twenty-five miles inside Laos. President Nixon continued to insist that the operation was a success. The fighting proved, according to General Abrams, that ARVN could "hack it" against top PAVN units.

Abrams apparently did not know that President Thieu had placed a casualty cap of three thousand on the operation.[17] Suddenly on March 11, General Lam began pulling units out of Tchepone only days after they had occupied it. And now ARVN units began yielding artillery fire bases one after the other, often destroying guns and vehicles to prevent capture by the enemy, before being evacuated by helicopters—or killed. American efforts to save ARVN units reached frantic proportions. One day's operations cost thirty-seven out of forty helicopters engaged.[18] By March 21, only four thousand ARVN soldiers remained in Laos. The day after television viewers around the world had watched desperate South Vietnamese soldiers clinging to helicopter skids in order to save themselves, Secretary of Defense Laird admitted that "withdrawal" was under way but that it was according to plan.[19] Three days later, ARVN had left Laos. A week later, enemy trucks were driving down the Ho Chi Minh trail.

Administration spokesmen now began singing new tunes. Lam Son 719 had not been designed only to cut enemy supply lines. Lam Son 719 had been designed to mass enemy troops and make them vulnerable to American air power. The world learned that over eleven thousand enemy soldiers had died and ten PAVN battalions had been annihilated by an operation that also relieved enemy pressure on Cambodia. The new paint was peeling before it dried. The cost of Lam Son 719 was tremendous. The Saigon government admitted to five thousand ARVN casualties (some observers thought ten thousand more likely) plus seventy American lives, thousands of ARVN deserters, morale shattered, perhaps 140 helicopters, thirty tanks, and scores of armored personnel carriers and artillery pieces lost.

What happened? Overconfidence played a major part. The earlier invasion of Cambodia, which had not provided an accurate test of ARVN's tactical effectiveness, had misled military commanders and experts whose optimism too often stemmed from second-hand observation and biased, often dishonest readiness reports. Sir Robert Thompson, Nixon's counterinsurgency guru, had given ARVN high marks and had agreed with Abrams that 70 percent of South Vietnam's army " . . . is on a fighting par with U.S. troops." Shortly after the debacle, Thompson in a report to Kissinger " . . . praised its military success and stated that the major factor in the war was now the question of South Vietnamese psychology and confidence."[20] Abrams, Thompson, and a good many others were continuing to confuse quality with quantity and were again ignoring General Gwynn's teaching that a lull in guerrilla warfare did not necessarily mean enemy impotence. ARVN found a flexibly organized and determined enemy willing to yield a branch or two of the Ho Chi Minh trail until the tactical position became clear. They found an enemy which had secretly brought down tanks and SAM missiles; an enemy that reinforced itself during battle with units from the DMZ; an enemy that skillfully employed guerrilla tactics to bewilder, slow, and isolate ARVN columns and outposts until they were ready for assault.

Divided command also came into play. ARVN and MACV together seem to have underestimated enemy strength—scarcely a new failing. Kissinger later wrote that on February 23, Westmoreland " . . . did not think that the forces assigned to the Laos operation were adequate; he himself [at an earlier point] had considered that four American divisions would be needed to seize and hold Tchepone; the South Vietnamese had allotted less than two to the operation."[21] But as army chief of staff, Westmoreland sat on the JCS and, according to Kissinger, had endorsed the plan " . . . together with the other Joint Chiefs of Staff."[22] Abrams allegedly urged Thieu to send in more forces than proposed, but Thieu refused. Thanks largely to U. S. Army indoctrination, ARVN commanders held almost mystical belief in the efficacy of air and artillery power, and this undoubtedly influenced Thieu's decision. Yet many Vietnamese air controllers could not speak English[23]—this after more than a decade and billions of dollars spent in trying to make ARVN a viable force. Once opposition developed, Abrams is said to have again urged Thieu to commit more troops but probably for domestic political reasons he refused and instead terminated the action.

Although Nixon and his aides attempted to present a satisfactory picture—Nixon later blamed MACV for providing inadequate air cover but insisted that the operation was a "success" with " . . . most of the military purposes achieved"[24]—the invasion itself let alone its obvious failure brought heavy criticism from within the United States.

Concurrent with its confused and contradictory course came a variety of other ills resulting from the American presence in Indochina. Despite reduction of American forces in the area and a claim that direct military expenditures in Indochina had decreased to $16 billion for the current fiscal year, over-all defense spending was to rise to $76 billion for fiscal year 1971–72. Even before the operation began, the American army reaped widespread opprobrium by dropping charges against Major General Samuel Koster for attempting to cover up the My Lai massacre. Koster was reduced in rank, given a letter of censure, and allowed to retire, the first of a series of mild punishments awarded for major dereliction of duty.[25] The operation was only just under way when a heart attack felled the Cambodian Prime Minister, Lon Nol, to confuse further that already confused situation. Then the story of bribery and corruption in American military clubs and post exchanges in South Vietnam (and elsewhere) broke; it would involve a brigadier general and the Sergeant Major of the Army, the most prestigious enlisted rank in the army.[26] ARVN's most able general, Do Cao Tri, was killed in a helicopter crash. On February 22, Lieutenant William Calley began a recital to a military court of his shocking actions at My Lai. A few days later, the army decided to court-martial his brigade commander, Colonel Oran K. Henderson. While fighting in Laos increased, four VC guerrillas blew up 75 per cent of Cambodia's oil refinery system. The American people next learned that so zealous was its army as to keep card files on 25 million American citizens. Sounding more like a police-state official than an American public servant, Assistant Secretary of Defense Robert Froehlke stated that

> . . . surveillance designed to cope with civil violence that might eventually require the use of army troops would continue. To protect people and property in an area of civil disturbance with the greatest effectiveness, he said, "military commanders must know all that can be learnt about that area and its inhabitants."[27]

Army agents might better have been employed studying their own establishment. While PX scandals mounted, the General Accounting Office accused American defense contractors of making wildly excessive profits. The public was also forcefully reminded that some soldiers in Vietnam, in addition to insubordination including refusal, on occasion, to fight and to drug addiction, had picked up the quaint habit of "fragging": eliminating overzealous officers with a hand grenade, in a word, murder. Writing of an army he had once considered " . . . the best Army the United States ever put into the field," Colonel Robert Heinl, a retired marine turned journalist, concluded in May 1971 that the "... United States armed forces, wrenched by seemingly insurmountable problems within and without, appear to have reached their lowest point in this century in morals, discipline and battleworthiness." After citing numerous incidents within and without Vietnam, Heinl quoted General Matthew Ridgway, former chief of staff of the army: "... Not before in my lifetime ... has the Army's public image fallen to such low esteem."[28] While army undercover agents continued to cover public gatherings in the United States and record covertly the words of American citizens, a military court at the end of March found William Calley guilty of callously murdering South Vietnamese civilians and sentenced him to life imprisonment.

The verdict set off still another internal domestic row. People had heard Calley describe the massacre at My Lai, yet some held that the young lieutenant was no more guilty than others. Bowing to pressures, President Nixon called the court to task and mitigated Calley's sentence to twenty years, later using the occasion to castigate further Congressional, media, and anti-war opponents.[29] Captain Aubrey Daniels, the twenty-nine-year-old army officer who had prosecuted, now wrote an open letter to his commander in chief. After expressing shock and dismay at the reaction of many people to the sentence, Daniels suggested that "... the war in Vietnam has brutalized us more than I care to believe" and that it must therefore cease. He continued:

> ... But how much more appalling it is to see so many of the political leaders of the nation who have failed to see the moral issue or, having seen it, to compromise it for political motive in the face of apparent public displeasure with the verdict.

Mouse Daniels then took lion Nixon to task:

> ... In view of your previous statements concerning this matter, I have been particularly shocked and dismayed at your decision to intervene in these proceedings in the midst of the public clamor. Your decision can only have been prompted by the response of a vocal segment of our population, who while no doubt acting in good faith, cannot be aware of the evidence which resulted in Lieutenant Calley's conviction.

Not only had the President "... damaged the military judicial system ... [and] subjected a judicial system of this country to the criticism that it is subject to political influence," but

...the image of Lieutenant Calley, a man convicted of the pre-meditated murder of at least 21 unarmed and unresisting people, as a national hero, has been enhanced.

He concluded:

...I would expect the President of the United States, a man whom I believed should and would provide the moral leadership for this nation, would stand fully behind the law of this land on a moral issue which is so clear and about which there can be no compromise.

For this nation to condone the acts of Lieutenant Calley is to make us no better than our enemies.

CHAPTER SEVENTY-EIGHT

1. Patrick Brogan, *The Times* (London), Paris, January 6, 1971.
2. Ibid.
3. Michael Maclear, *The Times* (London), January 19, 1971. See also, Shaplen, "We Have Always Survived," for developments in Hanoi after Ho's death.
4. Snepp, 21
5. Sihanouk, 180.
6. Frances Fitzgerald, 417.
7. *Time,* February 8, 1971.
8. *The Times* (London), Washington, D.C., January 29, 1971.
9. The operation was named after a Vietnamese victory over China in the seventeenth century, a belated attempt to profit psychologically as the North had been doing all along. Dewey Canyon was a misspelled code name.
10. *The Times* (London), New York, February 8, 1971.
11. Michael Hornsby, *The Times* (London), Quang Tri, February 15, 1971. See also, Davidson, 644–59, for an excellent analytical account of the battle.
12. Kissinger, *The White House Years,* 1004.
13. *Time,* February 15, 1971.
14. Derek Wilson, *The Times* (London), Khe Sanh, March 8, 1971.
15. *Time,* March 8, 1971.
16. *The Times* (London), Khe Sanh, March 8, 1971.
17. Kissinger, *The White House Years,* 1004. See also, ibid., 1008: " . . . As early as March 8 Abrams informed me that South Vietnamese commanders, having occupied the Tchepone area, considered their mission accomplished and were eager to retreat."
18. *Time,* March 15, 1971.
19. *The Times* (London), Washington, D.C., March 22, 1971. See also, Hackworth, 768.
20. Nixon, *Memoirs,* 499.
21. Kissinger, *The White House Years,* 1005.
22. Ibid.
23. Ibid., 1003.
24. Nixon, *Memoirs,* 428.
25. Hersh, "Coverup."
26. *The Times* (London), Washington, D.C., March 3, 1971. See also, Mollenhoff, 39–44; Shaplen, "We Have Always Survived":

... a conservative estimate is that fifteen thousand Americans, in uniform or out, have been involved in this process of corruption. These Americans have encouraged the black-marketing of all sorts of goods, have encouraged pilferage for payoffs, have raked huge profits from the smuggling of drugs and other goods, from the illicit trade in dollars, from the operation of night clubs, from the importation of American call girls and so on. . . .

27. Ian McDonald, *The Times* (London), Washington, D.C., March 2, 1971.
28. Heinl, "The Armed Forces: "Are they 'near collapse'?"
29. Nixon, *Memoirs*, 499–500.

CHAPTER 79

Medals on the White House lawn • Trouble in Saigon • The Pentagon Papers • Colonel Hackworth speaks out • The tottering U.S. economy • Kissinger goes to China • South Vietnam elections: Thieu plus Thieu equals Thieu • Fighting in Laos and Cambodia • New moves in Vietnam • Congress versus the Administration • Kissinger and the JCS • Yeoman Radford's busy camera • Operation Rolling Thunder resumes • Giap's spring offensive • ARVN's reverses • The war escalates • Nixon's new peace plan • ARVN's problems • Saigon's losses • Henry Steele Commager's salvo

To TRY TO bolster waning popularity, President Nixon in early April 1971 announced another large troop withdrawal and began to hint at a new diplomatic offensive which by restoring "the common purpose" would create "a new national unity." The words sounded somewhat forlorn in view of massive anti-war demonstrations including those by Vietnam veterans, some in wheelchairs, who flung their medals onto the White House lawn, and in less than a month their sentiments would be mocked by police batons cracking American citizens' skulls during a "May Day" demonstration in Washington. Nor was the President's posture strengthened by events in Saigon, where Vice-President Ky, openly breaking with President Thieu, not only called for a political solution based on coexistence with North Vietnam but also questioned Thieu's integrity and compared the country to a "sinking ship." In the polemics that followed, he stated what all critics had been saying for years: " . . . There is no social justice [in South Vietnam] right now."[1]

Military news was no better. A benumbed American public learned that large numbers of American troops in South Vietnam were using hard drugs in addition to widespread use of marijuana.[2] In mid-June, the nation began reading extracts from theretofore top-secret documents delivered to public media by a former analyst and RAND employee, Daniel Ellsberg. The first depressing revelations of extreme official dissembling published in what soon became famous as *The Pentagon Papers* were still rebounding when the General Accounting Office suggested that nearly two billion dollars budgeted for South Vietnam pacification programs from 1968 to 1970 could not be accounted for and listed ominously, among the problems, "misappropriation of funds."[3]

Worse was to come. Fury at the inane conduct of the war by supposedly professional generals had slowly been building in such able and immensely brave and qualified subordinates as Colonel David Hackworth. Hackworth had been trying for years to educate his seniors in order to save men's lives, generally without success. His own major tactical achievements, his increasingly critical articles in professional military journals, his not-so-subtle scorn for the rear-area commandos—all had combined to annoy army brass and deprive him of a well-earned brigade command. The illegal invasion of Cambodia had infuriated him; President Nixon's intervention in the Calley case sickened him. In an interview with ABC television in late June 1971, this battle-scarred combat leader, hero to many senior and junior officers, hard-bitten NCOs, and young soldiers in the field, was broadcast nationwide in America. A few of his answers told the American people the story of the incredibly inept military and civil performance in Vietnam.

On training:

" . . . in the main the training for Vietnam from the standpoint of the individual soldier, the young officer, and even the battalion, brigade, and division staff officers and senior commanders has been totally inadequate. . . . " As one result of poor training, Hackworth believed " . . . that our casualties were at least thirty percent higher . . . or even higher than that"; further, according to an official Pentagon classified study, 15 to 20 per cent of the casualties were the result of friendly fire—"one man shooting another man; friendly artillery firing on a friendly element; friendly helicopters firing on a friendly unit; tac[tical] air striking a friendly unit. . . ."

On American generals:

" . . . the average general that came to Vietnam did not have a good concept, good appreciation of the nature of guerrilla warfare. In most cases because of their lack of reading in depth about guerrilla warfare, they were not prepared for the war and they had to fall back on Korea and World War II." Without question this brought more casualties: " . . . one of the most classic examples is

Hamburger Hill. Here was a hill that had to be taken. Hundreds and hundreds of casualties occurred taking this hill. . . . [The Americans] had the hill for a few days and pulled off. So what was the reason for taking the hill? Why not stand back if the enemy is on it and bomb, but why use infantry to take the hill?"

Did senior commanders learn from mistakes and make appropriate changes?

" . . . I don't think so. I don't think that the top level ever developed a realistic strategic plan nor did they ever have tactics to support that strategic plan." Take, for example, the invasion of Laos: " . . . Conventional thinking put us in that operation rather than training a light, mobile guerrilla force . . . [to operate] in there like guerrillas." Echoing Roger Hilsman nearly ten years earlier, Hackworth wanted to fight guerrillas with guerrillas—small numbers " . . . well trained, highly motivated."

Asked if the silence of those officers who disagreed with MACV strategy and tactics was not in part responsible, Colonel Hackworth replied, " . . . That is right, and that is why perhaps we who have not been vocal should be charged for just criminal neglect."[4]

Not surprisingly, the President's popularity continued to decline and he was in serious political trouble. His Administration had recorded a fiscal-year deficit of over $23 billion, the second largest since World War II and one estimated to increase in the current fiscal year. The balance of trade also measured an unhealthy deficit, which meant, among other things, that the dollar's value stood in jeopardy. No less an authority than former chief presidential economic adviser Gardner Ackley warned

. . . that failure to act to stem inflation and unemployment "can threaten the stability of the social and political order." He said that inflation and unemployment were exaggerating the poverty problem to the point where current policies could provoke outright revolution.[5]

Although the Administration gained some hope from Henry Kissinger's secret mission to Peking (Beijing) followed by Nixon's state visit in February 1972, little encouraging news arrived from Indochina. As American, Thai, and Australian troop units continued to depart, President Thieu left no doubt that he headed a military dictatorship, a fact shortly emphasized when he alone ran for election. This was primarily the work of CIA, which spent "millions of dollars" in cowing and neutralizing Thieu's opposition in pursuing its policy of strengthening his government "at all costs." A senior CIA official in Saigon later wrote, ". . . By October 1972 . . . we had bought, bribed and sold so many South Vietnamese military and political figures that our spies and collaborators inside the government were mere extensions of ourselves."[6] Prime Minister Lon Nol in neighboring Cambodia added to the authoritarian air in mid-October by declaring a state of emergency and appointing ". . . a new government to rule by 'ordinance' rather than by constitutional law. He said that he no longer would 'play the game of democracy and freedom' since it stood in the way of victory."[7] Less than a month later, Field Marshal Thanom Kittikachorn overthrew Thailand's parliamentary government in favor of rule by revolutionary council.

Political issues seemed more clearly if unhappily settled than military issues. In Paris, the enemy had proposed in July a new seven-point peace plan unacceptable to either Washington or Saigon. As fighting receded inside South Vietnam, it continued to mount in Laos where the American government was spending hundreds of millions of dollars in fighting a clandestine war. In Cambodia, about thirty thousand PAVN troops supplemented by perhaps fifteen to twenty thousand Cambodian Communists, the Khmer Rouge, claimed control of about half the country. Morale in the Cambodian army continued to sink owing to confused communications (Lon Nol, as had Ngo Dinh Diem, insisted on commanding the army from Phnom Penh), corrupt and poorly trained officers (David Hackworth later wrote of the futility of trying to train "the playboy lackadaisical Cambodian officer" who had no intention of going to battle),[8] and political differences so pronounced between senior commanders that some who secretly sided with Sihanouk constantly sold arms and ammunition to the Khmer Rouge and PAVN units.[9] In October, an army task force relieved a besieged town north of Phnom Penh only to be cut to ribbons, two battalions decimated "by casualties and wholesale desertions," with huge losses of tanks, armored vehicles, artillery, machine guns, and rifles (all recently supplied by the American army).[10] As 1971 drew to a close, guerrillas were bombarding the capital, Phnom Penh, a threat that caused Saigon to send some twenty-four thousand troops across the border to bolster ARVN units already in Cambodia.

The situation in South Vietnam remained in flux. In September, a combined ARVN-U.S. task force hastily moved north against enemy activity in the demilitarized zone. Some two hundred American helicopters lifted thousands of ARVN troops to Quang Tri province where three brigades backed by about two thousand American troops began a giant "sweep" of the area. Enemy forces inside Cambodia continued to contest the border area. In the Mekong Delta, about forty thousand VC continued active. In mid-October, VC guerrillas slipped into an

American base eight miles from Saigon to blow up two helicopter gun-ships and damage three others.[11] Frank Snepp, the senior CIA analyst in Saigon, later wrote:

> ... The tone and content of the reporting [from Saigon] was be-coming increasingly ominous, and several colleagues and I con-cluded that a major North Vietnamese offensive was in the offing. Our over-cautious superiors at the CIA [in America], however, were not so sure and decided to check our conclusions with Kis-singer ... [who, preoccupied with negotiations] could not imagine the North Vietnamese might be preparing to revert to their old bad habits. ... Our superiors therefore dutifully blocked, qualified or modified any analyses that tended to suggest they were.[12]

In early 1972, " ... President Thieu and his staff drew up an assessment predicting a massive North Vietnamese drive across the demilitarized zone into the northernmost provinces of the country."[13]

The turbulent situation again brought dangerous Congressional an-tagonism. In late October, the Senate Foreign Relations Committee ap-proved an amendment that limited " ... all spending in Indochina to the single goal of withdrawing American troops."[14] The Administration loftily replied that it would continue operations necessary to protect American forces. A few days later, waves of B-52 bombers supple-mented by naval gunfire worked over enemy positions in the demilita-rized zone. About the same time, Secretary of Defense Laird announced that American troops might still be fighting long after the bulk of Amer-ican forces had been withdrawn. He told reporters in Saigon that he found the progress of Vietnamization " ... most encouraging ... that Saigon's position was militarily strong and the main problem facing South Vietnam was economic. It was one of strengthening and stabiliz-ing the economy so that the country could support its armed forces."[15] A few days later, President Nixon announced that another forty-five thousand troops would be withdrawn " ... and proclaimed the end of the U.S. offensive role in the war." Further withdrawals " ... would be determined by the level of enemy infiltration and combat activity, the success of Vietnamization, progress in securing release of American pris-oners in North Vietnam and obtaining an Indochina cease-fire." If no progress resulted from the Paris talks, " ... it will be necessary to main-tain a residual force" of American troops in the country, he said.[16] Ten days later he told newsmen, " ... Air power, of course, will continue to be used. We will continue to use it in support of the South Vietnam-ese until there is a negotiated settlement or, looking further down the road, until the South Vietnamese have developed the capability to han-dle the situation themselves." If the enemy increased infiltration,

". . . we will have to not only continue our air strikes, we will have to step them up."[17] No progress had resulted from the Paris talks, one reason probably being that General John Lavelle, commanding the U. S. Air Force in Vietnam, had taken it upon himself to open a secret air offensive against the North—in defiance of orders.[18]

Kissinger meanwhile had virtually eliminated Rogers and Laird from the policy-making process, and it is a matter of wonder why these two most important Cabinet members could be so dangerously spineless in publicly supporting the Administration when so many of their roles and responsibilities had been usurped by Kissinger's National Security Council. The villain in Laird's case was the JCS-NSC liaison office, an office that Laird had wanted eliminated since 1969, and with good reason:

> . . . According to J. Fred Buzhardt, the Pentagon's General Counsel . . . the Chairman [of the JCS] would actually send Kissinger the drafts of memoranda he was writing to Laird so that Kissinger could revise them, if he wished, to his own advantage.[19]

The love-match between Kissinger and the JCS received a major setback when Kissinger disagreed on such important topics as the strategic arms limitation negotiations. The JCS now installed a navy yeoman clerk in the liaison office to spy on Kissinger and " . . . to try to obtain any NSC documents that might interest the Chiefs and that Kissinger's staff might not provide." This was Yeoman Radford, who later testified to the Senate Armed Services Committee " . . . that he was ordered to obtain anything of interest to the Chiefs [JCS]—talk of troop cuts, agreements between the White House and Thieu, meetings with Swank [U.S. ambassador in Phnom Penh], assurances to Lon Nol . . . " Radford accompanied Kissinger's principal assistant, Colonel Alexander Haig, on several trips to Saigon and Phnom Penh, merrily photographing any documents of interest including those in Haig's briefcase. His greatest coup, however, came when he accompanied Kissinger to Pakistan, from where the latter departed for China and secret talks with Chou En-lai:

> . . . Radford rummaged through the burn bags in the plane and through Kissinger's briefcase. He read as much as he could of the transcript of Kissinger's meeting with Chou En-lai . . . [and] he obtained about 150 documents on the trip.[20]

The saga was exposed in December 1971 when columnist Jack Anderson " . . . published an account of an NSC meeting on the Indo-Pakistan war in which Kissinger had stressed that United States policy was to pretend neutralism but actually to 'tilt' towards Pakistan." The ensuing explosion in the White House caused one of Nixon's principal keepers, John Ehrlichman, to order a covert and highly illegal bunch of hood-lums—the so-called "plumbers"—to find the leak. Admiral Robert We-lander, who headed the liaison office, now informed Haig what Radford had been doing. To Kissinger's fury, Radford and Welander were trans-ferred "in silence."[21]

Beset by internal and external disorder in the extreme, the President could only play for time in the hope that overtures to Peking (Beijing) and Moscow would come to fruition. With the approach of an election year, he could not renege on repeated promises to withdraw the bulk of American troops from South Vietnam. Neither could he risk collapse of Thieu's government. He instead chose a middle course, that of using the American presence, particularly American air and naval power, to buttress ARVN until Vietnamization reached the point where Hanoi would see the light and come to the peace table willing to work a deal. To help Hanoi make up its mind, American planes made over a thou-sand raids on North Vietnam during December 26–30, 1971. No matter that neither Russia nor China contested the raids, no matter severe air interdiction in all areas, the enemy continued operations in Laos and Cambodia while MACV reported intense preparations for what ap-peared to be another Tet offensive.

Nixon put a brave face on failure to bring the enemy around. His insistence on the favorable progress of Vietnamization brought dissem-bling echoes from Administration officials, for example Melvin Laird testifying before the House Appropriations Committee in late February 1972 that

> ... the other side had been forced to switch from main-force to low-level guerrilla activity because of the "buildup of the South Vietnamese forces" and could not "conduct a large-scale military operation for a substantial period of time" because "they do not have the logistic support" or the "personnel."[22]

Five weeks later, Giap opened the spring offensive earlier predicted by CIA analysts in Saigon and ignored by Kissinger. Giap's effort involved elements of ten enemy divisions, some 150,000 troops whose armament, mainly from Soviet Russia's arsenals, included tanks, anti-aircraft and anti-tank heat-seeking missiles, MIG-21 aircraft and radar-guided an-tiaircraft guns.[23] In the North, two divisions spilled through the DMZ to fragment a newly formed ARVN division and chase it from Quang Tri, a task aided by poor weather which largely prevented interference from American aircraft. Units of two more divisions pushed in eastward from the Ho Chi Minh trail toward Hué while a fifth division remained north of the DMZ in close reserve. In the central highlands, elements of three PAVN divisions, already in control of the northern portion of II Corps area, began to push on Kontum. Another three divisions moved into III Corps area from Cambodia, besieging An Loc and controlling large areas north and west of Saigon.

The most serious threat existed in the northern part of the country. To defend Hué, President Thieu moved in his best units while Washington rushed naval and air support to the area. Abrams, who up to now had been boasting about ARVN's capabilities, cabled that " . . . it is quite possible that the South Vietnamese have lost their will to fight, or hang together, and that the whole thing may be lost." Nixon was appalled. "How can this have happened?" he asked Kissinger. "The South Vietnamese seem to go in cycles," Kissinger suggested. "They're very good for about a month, and now they're caving in on schedule."[24] Adding to Nixon's confusion was army chief of staff General Westmoreland's belief that the [enemy] drive would fade " . . . 'in a matter of days because the staying power of the enemy is not great.' " (The battle lasted well into June.)[25]

Whatever the prognosis, Nixon was determined that the new offensive would not succeed. If only sixty-nine thousand American ground troops remained in South Vietnam when Giap's drive started, he still held peripheral strengths. Within five weeks of the beginning of the offensive the U. S. Seventh Fleet was maintaining a task force in the Gulf of Tonkin that included six carriers, five cruisers, and forty destroyers, in all manned by forty-one thousand men. While air armadas including B-52 bombers struck enemy units throughout South Vietnam, MACV hastened to repair Thieu's material losses and to assure him and the world of continuing American support. Nixon's response at first seemed to produce a conciliatory diplomatic result but when this came to nothing, Nixon decided on the risky but dramatic move of mining North Vietnam's ports and increasing air strikes on North Vietnamese targets in accordance with Kissinger's suggested "November Option" of 1969, the "brutal blow" not then implemented because of political reasons.[26] This was now necessary, Nixon told the American people, to protect remaining American troops in Vietnam. As for total withdrawal of those troops, that would be to admit "an American defeat," which would " . . . encourage aggression all over the world." Sounding not unlike Lyndon Johnson at Baltimore seven years earlier, the President pointed to Hanoi's intransigence, which could only be surmounted by " . . . decisive military action to end the war." At the same time, he offered a new peace plan: total withdrawal of U.S. forces within four months in return for an internationally supervised cease-fire, return of American prisoners of war, and a political settlement negotiated by the Vietnamese themselves.

This was the sort of dramatic move favored by the Nixon-Kissinger psyche. As with past military escalations, notably the Cambodian and Laotian excursions, it brought national and international opprobrium marked by massive demonstrations and a host of new militant protesters inspired in part by publication of Frances Fitzgerald's Pulitzer prize-winning best-seller, *Fire in the Lake: The Vietnamese and the Americans in Vietnam*. The old curmudgeon I. F. Stone suitably epitaphed the new bombing in the North: " . . . air power had not given us victory" but "only prolonged the agony before defeat."[27] Neither did the effort produce a real political effect. Hanoi already had girded itself for resumption of bombing. Its Paris delegation claimed decided military advantages and spurned the President's latest proposals.

About all the escalation accomplished was to cheer a morose Saigon government. Gone was the earlier bravado. As reported by *Time* magazine:

> . . . Saigon's 492,000-man regular army is suffering from more than battered morale. There are fewer than 150,000 Communist soldiers committed to the invasion; nonetheless they have not only tied up all of ARVN's reserve strength but have also knocked out an ever-growing list of South Vietnamese units—one full infantry division, a third of another division, five infantry regiments, six armored regiments, three artillery battalions, nine ranger battalions, two airborne brigades and three battalions of marines, Saigon's best troops. The South Vietnamese have admitted to heavy casualties: 4,610 dead and 14,093 wounded. U.S. military men hope that, with unstinting American air support and Nixon's morale-boosting moves, ARVN can hold up at least through May, when monsoon rains are expected to dampen the action in the southern two-thirds of the country.[28]

To many observers it was a repeat of Chiang Kai-shek and China. Like General Lon Nol in Cambodia and Field Marshal Thanom Kittikachorn in Thailand, General Thieu now threw off the light cloak of Western-inspired democracy to declare martial law and ask the national assembly for emergency powers. Simultaneously, his new commander in the field, Lieutenant General Ngo Quang Truong, started probing attacks toward Quang Tri.

Having focused allied eyes on Quang Tri and Hué, Giap in late May opened a new offensive against An Loc, a furious action that again isolated the town's six thousand defenders. When a relief force stalled some miles south of the town on Highway 13, a helicopter lift brought in two regiments to reinforce the battered garrison. As battle slowed and partial lull claimed various areas, the American bombing effort intensified with thousands of tons of television- and laser-guided "smart" bombs dropping on North Vietnam, complemented by thousands of sorties that hammered enemy forces around Hué, Kontum, and An Loc.

Although ranking American officers claimed enormous damage to the enemy, it remained painfully clear that if ARVN was holding, it was only because of American air and naval power (over two hundred B-52 bombers were engaged by end of May). Giap's offensives had caused the Saigon command to strip the vital Mekong Delta of troops. The pacification effort there virtually ceased. VC cadres appeared as the government yielded control throughout the vast area. By end of June, the offensives had generated over one and a half million refugees and had cost ARVN over seventy thousand casualties. Thieu's secret police had arrested thousands of "suspected Viet Cong sympathizers" and would continue to arrest some fourteen thousand a month. Thieu continued to invoke emergency measures and in September, like Diem before him, abolished hamlet elections to return South Vietnamese government to the feudal days.

Still, his government had held together and in September an ARVN task force finally reoccupied Quang Tri, a city of rubble evacuated by the enemy, who continued to hover nearby. Similarly, key cities and towns in center and south felt the hot breath of enemy troops which controlled perhaps 50 per cent of South Vietnam and operated almost without opposition in Laos and Cambodia. Giap had taken heavy casualties but had achieved his primary goal of disrupting the highly vaunted Vietnamization and pacification of the South.

He had achieved a great deal more by causing a new surge in America's antiwar movement. In October, no less a person than the world-famous historian, Henry Steele Commager, fired a major salvo with his essay in *The New York Review of Books,* "The Defeat of America":

> ... Using the documents then available, a close examination of the long and gradual escalation of the war demonstrated the tremendous difficulty in finding any coherent logic or rational objective behind our involvement in Vietnam, beyond some vague "honor" that in any case we have forfeited. For Commager there was a "demented" quality to the American military effort in Vietnam; by 1972 with Nixon's trip to China and the thaw between Washington and Beijing, the original goal, if goal it was, of containing China had obviously been abandoned.
>
> Commager reviewed evidence and arguments from eight years of governmental deception ... [to show that] we Americans had blithely come to accept a double standard: German reprisals in World War II were seen as war crimes punishable by death, "but when we wipe out defenseless villages with 'incontinent ordinance', or engage in massacres as brutal as that at Lidice, these are mistakes or aberrations that do not mar our record of benevolence."

President Nixon, like his predecessor, was determined not to go down in history as presiding over the first American defeat, but Commager believed it was too late. America had unalterably been defeated, "not, to be sure, on the field of battle, but in the eyes of history." We have the power to destroy Vietnam and call it victory, but such insensate destruction would be madness, not victory. This is a war we cannot win and "a war we must lose if we are to survive morally." Commager contended that true patriots throughout this awful episode in American history had been the war resisters.[29]

CHAPTER SEVENTY-NINE

1. Derek Wilson, *The Times* (London), Saigon, May 2, 16, 1971.
2. Frances Fitzgerald, 423: "... In the spring of 1971 the U.S. command [in Vietnam] itself estimated that 10 percent of the troops in Vietnam were taking heroin, and that 5 percent were addicts."
3. *The Times* (London), Washington, D.C., July 11, 1971.
4. Hackworth, 776–7.
5. Harlow Unger, *The Sunday Times* (London), August 1, 1971.
6. Snepp, 14–15, 19 ff.: Most of the millions of dollars was "... pocketed by members of the Thieu regime."
7. *Time*, October 21, 1972. See also, Shawcross, 229.
8. Hackworth, 747.
9. Shawcross, 202.
10. Ibid., 203.
11. *The Times* (London), Saigon, October 13, 1971.
12. Snepp, 21.
13. Ibid., 22.
14. *The Times* (London), Washington, D.C., October 20, 1971.
15. Derek Wilson, *The Times* (London), Saigon, November 7, 1971.
16. Ian McDonald, *The Times* (London), Washington, D.C., November 12, 1971.
17. *Time*, November 22, 1971.
18. Ibid., June 26, 1972. Lavelle's action by disrupting peace talks may well have prolonged the war; at the very least it lent credence to enemy charges of American dissembling. Lavelle's punishment was retirement as a three-star general with a pension of $2,250 a month.
19. Shawcross, 205.
20. Ibid., 205–6.
21. Ibid., 206–7.
22. Stone, "Why Nixon Won His Moscow Gamble." See also, Kissinger, *The White House Years*, 1099–1100. Abrams had been warning of an "imminent enemy offensive" since early January 1972.
23. Shaplen, "Letter from Vietnam." As usual, Mr. Shaplen offers an excellent and detailed account of this action.
24. Nixon, *Memoirs*, 598.
25. Karnow, 642.
26. Woodward and Bernstein, 189. See also, Morris, 163–4.
27. Schalk, 154.
28. *Time*, May 22, 1972.
29. Schalk, 157.

CHAPTER 80

HANOI'S POLITICAL and military position was not as favorable in autumn of 1972 as it would have the world believe. Giap's offensives, which had begun to stall in July, had cost him dearly in men and matériel. The blockade of northern ports together with massive aerial interdiction of road and railroad transport and bombing of troop units had slowed supply to bring serious ammunition and other shortages. Hanoi had been especially alarmed by Nixon's summit meeting with Soviet Premier Leonid Brezhnev in Moscow in late May and by Russia's cooling attitude and Nixon's incipient rapproachement with China. Poll ratings in the United States clearly favored Nixon's re-election, which would mean continuing military and economic support to Saigon. The anti-war movement in America, comforting as it was to Hanoi, had noticeably weakened—the student protest sharply diminished when Nixon announced that no more draftees would go to Vietnam unless they volunteered. Hanoi could no longer win a military victory—but a political victory was still possible.

After a summer of intense diplomatic activity in which Kissinger persuaded the enemy to accept a cease-fire without prior approval of President Nguyen Van Thieu, Le Duc Tho met secretly with Kissinger in Paris in late September to present a new ten-point peace plan. When this was rejected, he followed with still another plan in October which, according to Nixon, " . . . met almost all our major requirements." That those "requirements" had been watered down so as to mean virtually nothing did not upset Nixon, who later claimed that the new plan " . . . amounted to a complete capitulation by the enemy. They were accepting a settlement on our terms"[1] (along with a promise of hefty economic aid to the North).[2]

Nixon responded to the new offer by reducing the bombing of the North while authorizing " . . . a massive airlift of military equipment and supplies" to Saigon, which would not be possible once the agreement was signed. Negotiations with the North continued throughout October, the chief stumbling block being the Thieu government in Saigon, which understandably would not accept the provision that North Vietnamese troops would remain in South Vietnam—nor was Thieu swayed by Kissinger's absurd argument " . . . that the Communist forces, already weakened by battle and deprived of reinforcements, would eventually wither away."[3] More to the point, Nixon informed Thieu that " . . . you have my complete assurance that if Hanoi fails to abide by the terms of this agreement it is my intention to take swift and retaliatory action."[4] Having good reason to believe that Nixon could not live up to a commitment that would keep American forces in Vietnam, Thieu did not buy this either, remaining so truculent as to be threatened with a cutoff of U.S. aid and a separate agreement between Washington and Hanoi with the South left out in the cold.[5]

Continued stalemate was driving Nixon frantic. His temper worsened considerably in October when the Nobel committee in Stockholm, instead of awarding him its peace prize, shared the prize with Kissinger and Le Duc Tho—which elicited Oriana Fallaci's succinct comment,

". . . Poor Nobel. Poor peace."[6] Kissinger's concept of "honor" allowed him to accept.[7] Le Duc Tho declined, notifying the committee that ". . . peace has not yet been established in Vietnam. In these circumstances it is impossible for me to accept."[8]

As Nixon had blamed Congress, the press, television, the American people, and even Kissinger's diplomacy for his failure to end the war, so now he struck out at the JCS, which was ordered in December to launch another massive B-52 bombing of the Hanoi area and to reseed the mines in Haiphong harbor, what James Reston called "war by tantrum," and what Senator Mike Mansfield termed a "stone-age tactic." Hanoi's signal for renewed negotiations was scarcely a capitulation brought on by the sacrosanct B-52 bombing, as Nixon later claimed. ". . . Its terms differed only very slightly from those that Hanoi had offered three months before," noted one observer,[9] and its attitude had probably been altered by a promise of over $4 billion in U.S. reconstruction aid.[10]

Negotiations resulted in an "Agreement on Ending the War and Restoring the Peace in Vietnam," signed by the principals in late January 1973. President Thieu, who had been shut out of the talks, was only slightly mollified by a second promise from Nixon: " . . . You have my assurance that we will respond with full force should the settlement be violated by North Vietnam."[11]

The cease-fire promised by the "Agreement on Ending the War . . . " was never to materialize. Nixon and Kissinger's "peace with honor" was as thin a piece of paper as ever was signed. Nowhere did the Paris agreement treat the basic problem of " . . . who would rule postwar South Vietnam."[12] Once the shooting stopped, Thieu's government was supposed to work with the Communist PRG to establish a Council of National Reconciliation and Concord that, by *unanimous* consent, would decide on the shape of the future South Vietnamese Government and arrange the requisite elections for it.[13]

This body was never formed because the shooting never stopped. The highly touted cease-fire was a sham. In theory, it was to be carried out with the help of two teams, one composed of members from the opposing sides, one of Hungarians, Poles, Indonesians, and Canadians. Since team decisions had to be unanimous, they were rarely made or, if made, were ineffective. Prior to the agreement being signed, both sides rushed to build up their forces and armament, which in the case of South Vietnam was accomplished by an enormous airlift of U.S. weapons and ammunition.

" . . . According to field statistics, more than 6,600 South Vietnamese soldiers were killed in the first three months of the truce"[14]—and that was only the beginning. To help cover Thieu's military vulnerability, Nixon ordered U.S. planes to open a prolonged B-52 and tactical aircraft bombing and strafing campaign that would probably still be going on had an enraged Congress not killed it a few months later. Owing to the agreement's muddled language, heavy fighting would continue in South Vietnam; owing to a vital omission of language, the agreement did not state a specific deadline for the withdrawal of foreign troops from either Cambodia or Laos. The senior CIA analyst in Saigon at the time summed it up well:

> . . . In sum, then, the peace of Paris was no peace at all. It imposed no limitation, or obligation on either side that could not be nullified through the unanimity principle, and apart from withdrawal of U.S. forces, all major provisions were subject to reinterpretation and further debate.[15]

In short, even the most dim-witted observer had to recognize that the Paris agreement would not end the war in Indochina.

The cease-fire in theory left President Thieu in control of " . . . roughly 75 percent of South Vietnam's territory and about 85 percent of its population."[16] Thanks to an overflowing cornucopia of American aid, his army numbered over a million men equipped with a variety of modern weapons, including 175-mm. guns and M-60 tanks, supported by the fourth largest air force in the world, which included modern fighters, gunships, and helicopters, and even by a small navy.[17]

Its endemic weaknesses were several, however. Thieu's national government along with numerous local governments were penetrated by Communist agents who reported virtually all secret plans and developments to Hanoi. Thanks to the professional ministrations of MACV over the years, the armed forces had never learned how to fight either an insurgency or a conventional war on their own. They had become almost totally dependent on American advisers, American artillery, and American air support. Despite years of expensive, even lavish, training, the officer corps lacked talent and motivation, largely the result of promotion by favoritism and purchase. The army, like the government, was corrupt from the highest-ranking general to the lowest-ranking private; payrolls were padded, rations diverted, arms and ammunition sold to the enemy—precisely as had been the case with Chiang Kai-shek's Nationalist army some years earlier.[18] That aside, in the early months of 1973, it was making substantial territorial gains (so much for the cease-fire) against a partially fragmented enemy, which in part explains why its fragile condition was not yet apparent to the outside world. But in large part continued deception was the work of the new American ambassador, a Thieu-fanatic named Graham Martin, and the Defense Attaché's Office (formerly MACV) whose $30-million-a-year budget maintained " . . . 400 civilian employees, 50 American military officers, and 2,500 American civilian contract workers," a combination that by means of biased reports often succeeded in preventing the ugly truth from reaching concerned policy makers in Washington.[19]

More apparent was Thieu's continued authoritarian rule. Instead of trying to develop a broader political base in order to support future travails, his government continued to jail thousands of dissidents of a dozen varieties. Opposition, however, continued to mount. Millions of refugees had no jobs, inflation soared, army desertions increased owing in part to pay problems brought on by a treasury drained by vast military expenditures and all-pervasive corruption.

The enemy also had problems. The 1972 offensive, although resulting in psychological and territorial gains, had been expensive. The economic condition in the North was " . . . in dreadful shape—poorer than any country in Asia," with future prospects bleak owing to greatly reduced support from Russia and China.[20] Serious disagreements existed in the top-level leadership, PAVN and the VC suffered from high desertion rates, there was a serious manpower shortage, relations with the Khmer Rouge insurgents were worsening—" . . . the Cambodians are even denying food to their Vietnamese allies and could not be trusted with any important combat assignment in our offensive."[21] In 1811, the French Marshal Bessières, who had just taken over an army command in Spain, ended his appreciation with these words:

> . . . Everyone allows that we are too widely scattered. We occupy too much territory, we used up our resources without profit and without necessity: we are clinging on to dreams.

In early 1973, a prominent North Vietnamese general described PAVN's condition:

> . . . We had not been able to make up our losses. We were short of manpower as well as food and ammunition, and coping with the enemy was very difficult.[22]

Party leaders eventually decided on a compromise policy of "no war, no peace,"

> . . . a careful balancing act that would enable them to husband resources at home while slowly building toward military parity in the south, behind the "shield" of the Paris agreement.[23]

Hanoi still owned precious assets (not least of which was strategic and tactical flexibility). The cease-fire confirmed Communist holdings in the South, both along the western border mountain country and some isolated areas in the Mekong Delta. Thirty thousand PAVN troops remained in Cambodia where, according to Prince Sihanouk, Khmer Rouge guerrilla units were commanded by PAVN officers. " . . . In Laos, PAVN field units, numbering perhaps 50,000, were stationed along the Ho Chi Minh trail, besides garrisoning the central Plain of Jars and several frontier districts." Combat troops in South Vietnam were beefed up after the cease-fire from an estimated forty thousand to 170,000 supported by some six hundred medium and light tanks and heavy artillery, not to mention the People's Liberation Armed Forces (PLAF) sixty thousand strong. While ARVN forces were wearing themselves out with search-and-destroy operations in the Mekong Delta and along the Cambodian border, the Communists were building twelve airfields, " . . . ten of them defended by surface-to-air missiles (SAM), and several all-weather roads were under construction in northern South Vietnam and along the Lao-Vietnam border."[24] While lying low tactically—commanders were instructed to " . . . attack only when they were clearly superior to Thieu's troops"[25]—the army simultaneously embarked " . . . on a huge logistical program designed to create a springboard for an eventual offensive of vast proportions." This included building an all-weather highway from Quang Tri province down to the Mekong Delta, a three-thousand-mile oil pipeline from Quang Tri to their headquarters seventy-five miles northwest of Saigon, which in time housed " . . . a modern radio grid . . . that enabled them to communicate directly with Hanoi and with their field units." As Stanley Karnow presciently concluded:

> . . . That the Communists could undertake such a stupendous enterprise testified to the failure of American bombings to destroy the equipment and fuel that they had amassed in North Vietnam over the preceding years.[26]

The amazing resilience of the guerrilla enemy showed itself in spring of 1973 when VC units began hitting isolated ARVN outposts and supply dumps. Taken with intelligence reports of Communist construction projects in the South, renewed VC activity brought a veiled threat from the White House of renewed American intervention in South Vietnam, a quaint notion that died in mid-August with the termination of the B-52 bombing campaign in Cambodia. Sir Robert Thompson allegedly had advised Thieu that Nixon would find a way around the Congressional bombing ban.[27] Hoping to impress the American people with his determination and capabilities, Thieu resumed offensive operations and did make some impressive gains. But any hope of renewed B-52 bombings were dashed by Nixon's increasing involvement in the filth and cover-up of the Watergate scandal.[28]

ARVN's stepped-up operations caused General Giap to demand increased PAVN attacks. Owing to North Vietnam's lack of allies, faltering economy and disagreement among senior Communist leaders (some of whom wanted priority given to rebuilding the North's economy), these were restricted to raids against isolated ARVN outposts and fuel and supply dumps, but escalation became so serious that in late October the American president, despite his increasingly perilous political position, warned North Vietnam " . . . against the resumption of major war and reminded it of past 'miscalculations' about American responses."[29] Those words died with the passage in early November of the War Powers Act (over Nixon's veto), which further restricted the executive's war-making powers.

By year's end, it was apparent that North Vietnam, although unable to mount a "general offensive," had radically improved its position in the South. It was just as apparent that Thieu's position had weakened owing to skyrocketing inflation, decreasing American interest in the country and thus a falling off of economic and military aid, increasingly corrupt civil and military officials, and greatly lowered army morale.

For the first time in many years, relative quiet reigned in Laos, the people and soil of which had been the recipients of over two million tons of bombs—" . . . two-thirds of a ton of bombs for every single man, woman, and child in Laos"—dropped by U.S. aircraft, "three-quarters of that after Nixon's inauguration."[30] A cease-fire had gone into effect in late February under the terms of a peace agreement that provided for " . . . the withdrawal of all foreign troops within ninety days, and the formation of a coalition government within thirty days. The Communist Pathet Lao controlled about 75 percent of the country but most of the people lived in the government-held portion."[31] Although a coalition government had not been achieved by year's end, the Communists were in the stronger position in that they completely controlled the border areas where the Ho Chi Minh trail had been converted into practically a superhighway " . . . dotted with truck rest and service areas, oil tanks, machine shops . . . all protected by hilltop antiaircraft emplacements."[32]

Matters were not so quiescent in Cambodia, which was rapidly being torn to pieces. Already in 1972, the Communist Khmer Rouge was moving toward what it termed the "Democratic Revolution." In some areas, peasants " . . . were henceforth forbidden to wear the traditional multicolored sarong; all were now required to wear the plain black shirt and trousers normally worn by peasants at work, which later became the uniform of Democratic Kampuchea."[33] Early in 1973, the Khmer Rouge " . . . began an intensified campaign to drive the Vietnamese from the country, in combination with a new purge of Sihanoukists and other dissident 'Third Force' cadres."[34] In February, the Khmer Rouge opened a new military offensive at once answered by an American B-52 bombing campaign, the planes flying over sixty missions a day,[35] from bases in Thailand and secretly orchestrated in part from the American embassy in Phnom Penh—an effort that would cost $7 billion before Cambodia's fall.[36] Owing in part to a lack of up-to-date large-scale maps, bombing inaccuracies caused thousands of civilian casualties even though killing sixteen thousand Khmer Rouge guerrillas (according to Seventh Air Force).[37] In destroying some Khmer Rouge units, it also brought a flow of recruits to the Communists and caused a good many moderate party members to move to the hard-line right and away from any co-operation with the North Vietnamese: " . . . The 'Democratic Revolution' was both a product of, and a capitalization upon, the U.S. aerial war . . . the bombing sowed a whirlwind which the CPK [Communist Party Kampuchea] Centre was ready to reap."[38] William Shawcross concluded that the campaign would " . . . destroy the old Cambodia forever."[39] Bombing or no, by April some fifteen thousand Khmer Rouge guerrillas had almost surrounded Phnom Penh, which probably would have fallen but for the B-52 strikes; Khmer Rouge command problems that prevented co-ordinated attacks; supply problems, in particular a shortage of ammunition occasioned by increasingly difficult relations with PAVN and VC troops; and the onset of the rainy season.

There seemed but one possibility of saving Cambodia and this was by a plan of the French ambassador in Peking (Beijing) for China to arrange a cease-fire and return Prince Norodom Sihanouk as ruler, a plan endorsed by American ambassadors in Saigon and Phnom Penh. Unfortunately, Henry Kissinger, who had refused to see Sihanouk on several occasions, felt that withdrawal of U.S. backing for the Lon Nol regime would be seen in Peking and other foreign capitals

> . . . as a sign of American weakness. . . . "I don't want to hear about Laos-type compromise," he told John Dean, the U.S. ambassador in Phnom Penh . . . "Your job is to strengthen the military position so we can negotiate from strength."[40]

As one result of this myopic policy, American military advisers had assumed virtually full control of American policy, to the fury of most embassy civilian officials. Incredibly, this policy included the import of enough weapons and supply to equip four conventional Cambodian divisions. Through summer and autumn of 1973, ships and planes brought in thousands of tons of arms: " . . . 105- and 155-mm. artillery; over a hundred armored personnel carriers; more heavy river craft; 81-mm. mortars; grenade launchers; recoilless rifles; 45,000 more M-16 rifles . . . equipment for the headquarters and the combat support elements of four divisions"[41]—most of which existed only on paper.

Contrarily, the Khmer Rouge numbered about sixty thousand well-disciplined and motivated men who again sprang into action when the rainy season ended in November. At year's end, Phnom Penh was holding out—the Communists controlled an estimated " . . . 70 percent of the country and 50 percent of the population."[42]

The situation did not essentially alter until late in 1974. Laos was the first to go under. The Communist hand was greatly strengthened by the emergence of a coalition government. That was soon destroyed by the Pathet Lao, which in early December abolished the monarchy in favor of the People's Democratic Republic. Prince Souvanna Phouma's illness was used as a pretext to replace him with his half brother, Prince Souvanouvong, veteran leader of the Pathet Lao guerrillas. Souvanouvong became president of the new government and immediately established diplomatic relations with Hanoi.

Cambodia held out a trifle longer. In November, Kissinger, having realized that he had made a major diplomatic blunder, appeared in Peking to ask for Chinese mediation, a fruitless attempt since he refused to abandon the Lon Nol regime and work for Sihanouk's restoration.[43] In late December 1974, Khmer Rouge guerrillas, aided by Chinese-supplied water mines and heavy artillery, launched a new offensive that soon cut Phnom Penh from its Mekong River supply line. The situation was similar to that in China in its last months of agony. Government forces held the capital and important cities and towns; Communist forces controlled the countryside and the major roads and waterways. Despite heavy fighting and horrendous casualties, isolated government garrisons fell one after the other while Khmer Rouge forces closed in on the capital. The end came in mid-April with the fall of Phnom Penh. The Khmer Rouge insurgents moved in quickly, executed all government officials it could find, and forcibly evacuated all residents to the countryside—the opening moves in what would become one of the ugliest bloodbaths in history.

South Vietnam came last. There the Communists continued their ambitious road and base program while keeping ARVN off balance by guerrilla hit-and-run raids. ARVN counterattacks slowed, the inevitable result of tying up too many troops in defense of fixed positions—the same error earlier made by American troops—and of the cutback in artillery and air firepower. That cutback was necessitated in part by the reduction of American military aid, in part by ARVN quartermasters knowing neither what type and quantities of ammunition they possessed nor where the stuff was located. Maintenance problems also increased with reduced American support, but there was still no sign of the major Communist offensive so feared by Thieu. Although PAVN troops scored significant gains in the central highlands, the Iron Triangle north of Saigon, and in the Mekong Delta, Thieu derived some comfort from President Gerald Ford, who succeeded the disgraced Nixon in August and who shortly after assured Thieu of "continued support."[44] Bolstered by military and economic grants of millions of dollars from Washington to answer the inflated needs supplied by the American embassy in Saigon, Thieu's government, though increasingly shaky, seemed as if it might survive. But Communist gains had whetted Communist appetites for more territory. In December, Communist forces from Cambodia struck in the Mekong Delta to disrupt the all-important rice harvest. Simultaneously, PAVN and VC units moved into Phuoc Long province, which bordered Cambodia only seventy-five miles north of Saigon. In early January 1975, the provincial capital of Phuoc Binh fell to the enemy, a severe blow to South Vietnamese military and civil morale and a portent of things to come.

Such was the continued Communist pressure that, once an entire ARVN division had disintegrated in the central highlands, Thieu in mid-March ordered the evacuation of the central and northern provinces, which he called the " . . . unproductive areas of the country."[45] By month's end, the enemy claimed thirteen of South Vietnam's forty-four provinces. Four of ARVN's thirteen divisions no longer existed and millions of dollars' worth of arms, aircraft, munitions, and equipment were in enemy hands. ARVN's strategy was Chiang Kai-shek's strategy: defend cities and towns. Giap's strategy was Mao Tse-tung's strategy: cut communications with cities and towns to force retreat or annihilation (and sometimes both).

The Ford administration was beside itself. The army's chief of staff, General Frederick Weyand, was sent to Saigon from where he reported that the capital could be held with more American military aid. Ford asked Congress for one billion dollars and Congress said no. With the capital almost surrounded and with his own divisions dispersed, Thieu resigned and the Americans and some South Vietnamese—some sixty thousand in all—were evacuated by helicopter to waiting U.S. ships. It was left to General Duong Van Minh to negotiate a settlement with the Viet Cong, whose leaders refused to negotiate. On the last day of April 1975, Van Minh unconditionally surrendered to end the war in Vietnam.

* * *

The division of Vietnam formally ended in July 1976 with the emergence of the Socialist Republic of Vietnam governed by Premier Pham Van Dong. Although armed resistance to the government was minimal, the administrative task of converting the South to the mysterious ways of Communist government was immense and was far from accomplished by year's end. Laos also faced severe difficulties owing in part to an exodus of government officials and businessmen necessary to revive a shattered economy, in part to continued resistance by royalist troops in the South. Cambodia, now renamed Kampuchea and governed by Khmer Rouge leader Pol Pot, was in the throes of a massive bloodbath brought on by the Khmer Rouge's genocidal campaign to eliminate the urban intelligentsia and re-educate the masses while turning the country back to the stone age, an incredible travesty of civilization graphically told by William Shawcross, among others.[46]

Although the emergent countries formed a new power structure in the region, it was anything but the monolithic empire that a host of U.S. conservatives feared would sweep through Thailand and down the Malaysian Peninsula to turn all of Southeast Asia into a Communist camp. Instead, centuries-old fears and hatreds began to assert themselves almost immediately. If the Khmer Rouge government was giving top priority to conducting massive genocide, its army still found time to clash with Thailand's security forces in trying to halt the flow of Kampuchean refugees from leaving the country, and with Vietnamese troops which continued to occupy areas along the eastern border. Continuing clashes reportedly escalated in 1977 " . . . into heavy fighting involving between 10,000 and 20,000 men . . . using heavy artillery and tanks."[47] On the last day of the year the Phnom Penh government charged Vietnam with "large-scale unwarranted aggression," broke off diplomatic relations, and refused to enter into negotiations to settle the border problem even though its one ally, China, along with other neighboring countries had urged it to do so.[48] Heavy fighting continued in January. Apparently believing that it had taught its bumptious neighbor a salutary lesson, Hanoi pulled out its troops and in early February proposed to settle matters by creating a three-mile-deep internationally policed cordon sanitaire on either side of the line. Rejecting this sensible proposal, Pol Pot continued to fight.

The lines were now clearly drawn: Kampuchea, client state of a China intent on preserving its influence in the area and only too happy to supply Kampuchea with arms and equipment, including tanks and artillery; Vietnam, client state of a Soviet Union intent on further expanding its influence in Southeast Asia and only too happy to supply massive military and economic aid to Vietnam; Laos, perhaps unwilling host to fifty thousand Vietnamese troops, but clearly in the Soviet-

Vietnam sphere of influence; the ASEAN nations (Indonesia, Malaysia, Philippines, Singapore, and Brunei) terrified of Chinese, Soviet Union, and Vietnamese aspirations, wringing their hands and wailing like banshees; the United States, finally appalled at having opened this Pandora's box of evil winds, a disconsolate spectator seemingly content to mutter platitudes about those evil Khmer Rouge savages.

The situation could only escalate. Vietnam signed a treaty of friendship with the Soviet Union and sent more forces south. China increased its troop strength along the China-Vietnam border, and began edging diplomatically toward its American enemy. In late December 1978, a Vietnam army about 120,000 strong stormed into Kampuchea. After a few disastrous stands against the intruders, Khmer Rouge forces wisely retreated into the interior in order to fight a guerrilla war. In less than two weeks, the Vietnamese owned Phnom Penh, and Kampuchea had a new government, the People's Republic of Kampuchea headed by a Pol Pot defector, Heng Samrin, who presided over a People's Revolutionary Council. By early summer, the invaders, now about two hundred thousand strong, controlled most of the country, having pushed an estimated thirty thousand surviving Khmer Rouge guerrillas into the northwest corner where they were given limited sanctuary in Thailand and supplied with weapons and equipment from China.[49]

The fallout from the Vietnamese blitzkrieg was intense. China could not accept the Vietnamese presence in Kampuchea, which by extension threatened to replace Peking's (Beijing's) traditional influence by that of the Soviet Union. In early 1979, in order to "punish" Vietnam, a Chinese army perhaps one hundred thousand strong crossed the border, pushed back local troops, seized a provincial capital, and in less than a month returned to Chinese soil, a seemingly pointless operation that cost the army an estimated twenty thousand casualties while failing to discourage Vietnamese operations in Kampuchea.[50] Hanoi, however, having captured a blood-soaked wasteland, was already discovering that it needed increased economic aid from the Soviet Union. Moscow gladly accommodated but in return claimed increased naval facilities at Cam Ranh Bay and Da Nang. In November 1979, the United Nations General Assembly passed a resolution " . . . calling for the immediate and total withdrawal of Vietnamese forces from Kampuchea,"[51] but this produced no more efficacious results than various regional attempts to contain the spreading fire.

Hanoi meanwhile was consolidating its position in Kampuchea, a task that in spring of 1980 caused its forces to make brief incursions into Thailand both to force refugee camps to be moved inland from the border areas and to discourage Thailand from giving further aid to the Khmer Rouge. The Vietnamese action caused an instant international outcry and brought large shipments of weapons, including tanks, anti-tank missile systems, aircraft, and helicopters from the United States to the Thai army.[52]

The diplomatic and military stalemate carried over into 1981. In an effort to improve its international reputation, Khmer Rouge leaders had replaced Pol Pot with Khieu Samphan, at least titularly. Khmer Rouge forces, thanks to China's largesse, had by now regrouped and numbered an estimated thirty to thirty-five thousand. In addition, the Khmer People's National Liberation Front (KPNLF), headed by Son Sann, a former prime minister in the old Sihanouk government, fielded perhaps five thousand guerrillas; Prince Norodom Sihanouk, the former quixotic ruler of Cambodia who in 1975 had enthusiastically endorsed the Khmer Rouge cause, was putting together what would become the non-communist Sihanouk National Army (ANS) with the aid of Chinese arms and equipment.[53] Grave differences abounded in the insurgent camps, however. Son Sann refused to work with the despised Khmer Rouge, nor would he serve under Sihanouk. The Khmer Rouge had dedicated itself to drive the Vietnamese and the puppet PRK government out of the country, a stance endorsed by its patron, China. Contrarily, Son Sann and Sihanouk favored a negotiated settlement that would keep the Khmer Rouge from returning to power. Despite these and other differences, the three groups in 1982 formed the Coalition Government of Democratic Kampuchea (CGDK) with Sihanouk as president, Khieu Samphan as vice-president and Son Sann as prime minister.

The war meanwhile had settled into a give-and-take affair with one side then the other gaining the upper hand. Vietnamese and PRK forces generally took the offensive during the dry season (November to May) but were unable to claim any outstanding victories. The rebel forces continued to grow. In 1984, the Khmer Rouge army counted an estimated forty thousand troops maintained by frequent large shipments of arms and equipment that arrived in Thailand by boat from China. Sihanouk's ANS numbered about ten thousand and Son Sann's force had also increased. Co-ordinated operations might have brought better results, but these were not to be. Each group occupied its separate enclaves and fought its own war, the Khmer Rouge being by far the most active.

The military stalemate radically altered in early 1985 when a series of large-scale attacks by twenty to twenty-five thousand Vietnamese and PRK troops, supported by heavy artillery, tanks and aircraft, methodically eliminated the guerrilla camps inside the Kampuchean border, forcing the insurgents to disperse and retreat into Thailand. Although they eventually regrouped, they were unable to resume normal operations for a considerable period.

The guerrillas nevertheless slowly recovered and, despite large numbers of enemy troops deployed along the border, resumed often effective hit-and-run raids that underlined the indisputable fact that an expensive stalemate existed. The Vietnamese Government in particular had made a serious error in embarking on a course of imperialistic expansion before putting its economic house in order. Unable to manage its own economy, it had been suddenly faced with having to manage Kampuchea's affairs, in essence of having to oversee and fund a rebuilding of the country. Russia at first was willing to make the heavy financial investment which seemed to be justified by the potential strategic return. Already in 1982, Vietnam was receiving from the Soviet Union about $3 million a day—$1.1 billion a year—and Kampuchea additional enormous sums, expenditures that continued for the next several years. In 1986, however, Mikhail Gorbachev made the Kremlin take a hard look at the Southeast Asia investment. The look hardened in 1987 when it was evident that the Soviet Union was on the verge of a financial crisis and, as one result, was almost desperately seeking rapprochement with Washington and Peking (Beijing). Since a major obstacle to this tack was the war in Kampuchea, the Kremlin now began to pressure Hanoi to withdraw its forces from Kampuchea as a first step in ending what had become an unwanted war.

Hanoi did not fail to grasp the significance of this development. For some time it had realized the cost of rampant imperialism. An empty treasury taken with a moribund economy had made survival almost totally dependent on the Soviet Union. If the Soviet goose dried up, Hanoi would find it difficult to keep alive, let alone sustain the Kampuchean venture. In 1987, the government announced that it was withdrawing twenty thousand troops from Kampuchea, a propitiatory move directed toward the U.S. and China in the hope of eventually attracting sufficient investment to compensate for waning Soviet patronage. In 1988, Hanoi removed another fifty thousand troops along with the Vietnamese senior command headquarters.[54] The economic situation was now so serious that in November, Hanoi decided to give priority to reshaping the economy, which could be done only by a 50 per cent cut in military spending in 1990.[55] In September 1989, the last forces were withdrawn (although some units may have returned in response to increased Khmer Rouge operations).

The message had become clear to the PRK government in Phnom Penh with the first departure of Vietnamese troops: the weight of the war would soon fall on its militarily weak shoulders. The same faults that had bedeviled Lon Nol's army—corrupt and unqualified commanders; inept tactics; communication and supply failures; low morale—made it doubtful if the government could survive a sustained Khmer Rouge offensive, a fear shared by a good many other governments. As one result, Hun Sen, who had replaced Heng Samrin, changed political direction by tilting toward a capitalist economy while murmuring soft words to the United States and China, indeed to the world, in the hope of gaining the political and financial support necessary if it came to peace negotiations with his opponents.[56]

Thailand too was tiring of the border war. Chatichai Chunhavan, who became prime minister in August 1988, wanted Indochina to change "from a battlefield to a marketplace," a goal he emphasized by a new political flexibility that included the unprecedented act of inviting Hun Sen to Bangkok, to the consternation of Thailand's ASEAN partners.[57] This promising initiative was abruptly canceled in early 1991 by a military coup and Chunhavan's fall from power, but at least it emphasized the need for direct talks with the principal parties.

Exploratory talks already had occurred in late 1987 and these led to a generally fruitless series of conferences and formal meetings. Hopes were high for a breakthrough at the Paris conference in July and August 1989, but once again stalemate resulted.

So it was that the hurdles leading to a negotiated peace were high, the runners slow and awkward. As one expert put it, " . . . Clearly, the best outcome for Cambodia would be a comprehensive political settlement that demilitarized the internal struggle, neutralized Cambodia as an arena for superpower and regional rivalry, and gave the Khmer people an opportunity for free and fair elections."[58] If few could fault this, the few included the three groups of the CGDK and the incumbent PRK. As president of the CGDK, Prince Sihanouk proposed a quadripartite formula that basically called for dissolving the CGDK and PRK in favor of sharing power on a four-party basis under United Nations supervision until elections could be arranged.[59] Prime Minister Hun Sen of the PRK, on the other hand, wanted a " . . . ceasefire in place and a continuation of the political status quo—the PRK regime—until general elections" that would be organized by a "steering committee" and held under United Nations supervision.[60] Neither proposal was accepted but each was getting warm.

The impasse was broken by two unlikely sources, a United States congressman from New York, Stephen J. Solarz, whose basic plan formed the foundation for a subsequent diplomatic initiative by Australia's foreign minister. As worked out, the plan essentially turned the problem over to the United Nations, which would arrange and police a cease-fire, install an interim government, demobilize and disarm the opposing forces, repatriate nearly four hundred thousand refugees, and, finally, organize and monitor a general election to take place in spring of 1993. Although this plan circumvented a number of earlier objections, it was faulted because of the very high cost (an estimated $2 billion) of UN participation and because there was no surety that the

UN was capable of running the government in the interim phase. It would probably not have been accepted by Prime Minister Hun Sen had Hanoi not put on the pressure and kept it on—in return for limited rapprochement with and a promise of economic aid from the United States if all went well.

All of course did not go well. The peace accords were signed in October 1991 after months of furious squabbling between the four factions and various concerned governments. The first troops—a contingent of about two hundred men—of the UN peacekeeping force arrived in early November, but owing to budgetary and other problems the build-up to ten thousand peacekeepers vital to the peace process was delayed until December. In mid-November, Prince Norodom Sihanouk returned to a warm welcome in the capital and took charge of a "national reconciliation council" (Supreme National Council) that would run the coalition government until elections were held in 1993.

It was scarcely a pacific atmosphere. Shortly after Sihanouk's return, the Khmer Rouge accused him of collusion with Hun Sen in an attempt to limit Khieu Samphan's influence in the new government. Khieu Samphan's arrival in Phnom Penh created new problems in that he was attacked, beaten, and nearly lynched by a furious mob which prompted him to flee only eight hours after he arrived.[61] Only upon Khieu Samphan's return did the Supreme National Council hold its first inaugural meeting, which seems to have been an exercise in futility. By February, Khmer Rouge agents were busily destabilizing Hun Sen's already wobbly government while its guerrillas were grabbing as much government land as possible in the central and northwestern provinces. In February, fighting broke out between government forces and the Khmer Rouge,[62] and had increased in intensity by late March.[63]

Although the arrival of the main body of the UN peacekeepers bolstered general morale, it did not rub off on the Khmer Rouge, which predictably displayed an openly obstructive policy, refusing to allow UN monitors into their areas and rejecting the second phase of the plan, which called for each group to demobilize 70 per cent of its strength.[64]

Khmer Rouge destructive tactics carried into autumn as UN strength rose above twenty thousand. A three-month boycott of the Council was broken only by a threat of UN sanctions, but few believed that renewed talks would lead to partial demobilization as called for by the Accords. By end of October, the Khmer Rouge was again boycotting Council meetings. In the following months, Pol Pot and Khieu Samphan did everything possible to sabotage the peace plan. Roads were mined, trains and bridges blown up, "traitors" shot, UN voter-registration teams fired on, UN personnel seized and held prisoners, UN teams kept from operating in Khmer Rouge–controlled areas. Also contributing to the mayhem were President Hun Sen's security forces doing all they could to intimidate supporters of Prince Norodom Ranariddh's royalist party, Funcinpec, several members of which were assassinated during the pre-election campaign.

All to no avail. Thanks to the determination and courage of the 22,000-man UN command, UNTAC, headed by veteran Japanese diplomat Yasushi Akashi, with its military arm commanded by the no-nonsense Australian Lieutenant General John Sanderson, and thanks to the overwhelming desire of the Cambodian people for peace, an amazing 4.6 million or 90 percent of eligible voters went to the polls in spring of 1993.[65]

Despite militant Khmer Rouge threats that continued to the last minute, the polls opened on schedule on May 23 and closed five days later, a "free and fair" election, according to UN observers (and a surprisingly peaceful one after all the Khmer Rouge bluster). The winner was Prince Norodom Ranariddh, the forty-nine-year-old son of Prince Norodom Sihanouk, the seventy-year-old former king, who returned to Cambodia from exile in China. Ranariddh's royalist party, Funcinpec, won a surprising 46 percent of the vote and fifty-eight seats in the new constituent assembly; Hun Sen's ruling CPP won 38 percent of the vote and fifty-one seats. Although the royalist party lacked the necessary majority to form a new government, Ranariddh managed to convene the constituent assembly, whose 120 members set about writing the new constitution that was called for in the 1991 peace accords.

When it had become apparent that Funcipec was winning the election, furious CPP leaders cried foul and demanded a new election in several provinces. Despite or perhaps because of the old Prince Norodom Sihanouk's somewhat convoluted ministrations as head of state, a new civil war loomed for several tense weeks as Hun Sen, refusing to accept election results, refused to leave office. If Sihanouk contributed to the confusion, he also in part resolved it by arbitrarily dissolving the government and proclaiming himself " . . . chief of state, prime minister and supreme commander of the Cambodian armed forces, reserves and police."[66] Although this declaration precipitated another series of crises, a kind of peace was reached by Sihanouk who appointed his son and Hun Sen "co-prime ministers," a power-sharing arrangement that disallowed the Khmer Rouge (which had boycotted the elections) any say in government.

Khmer Rouge guerrillas now began attacking army outposts. Simultaneously, however, Khieu Samphan (with Pol Pot looking over his shoulder) offered to merge his ten thousand guerrillas with the new national army and to yield control of his domains (about 20 percent of Cambodia) in return for a place in that government. This deal might have gone through in one form or another but for the adamant refusal of Western nations, in particular the United States, which threatened to cancel an $880 million aid program if the government accepted Samphan's proposal. Since the government was broke (civil and military wages being months in arrears), it had little choice but to back down. Intensified Khmer Rouge attacks followed, but in August the new army responded in strength to force the guerrillas from recently seized army outposts.

The next surprise came in September when Norodom Sihanouk and his son arbitrarily decreed that Cambodia was a constitutional monarchy with Sihanouk as king. Sihanouk at once appointed his son first prime minister and Hun Sen second prime minister, a coalition government approved in October by the new parliament, along with a new constitution. By this time, however, Sihanouk was in Beijing undergoing treatment for cancer and not expected to return to Cambodia until spring of 1994.

Although departure of most of the UN command during November passed without undue incident (excepting the theft of millions of dollars worth of its vehicles and other equipment),[67] the government must surmount a great many hurdles if it is to survive. Prince Ranariddh has continued trying to persuade Khmer Rouge leaders to break up their private army and yield control of their operational areas to the government. Sihanouk recently changed his tune, which is not unusual, and announced that selected Khmer Rouge officials would be given governmental posts if the Khmer Rouge surrendered,[68] an offer soon retracted owing to the objection of Prince Ranariddh.[69]

Despite its still significant strength, the Khmer Rouge should not be able to topple the government, providing that the latter's present strength (December 1993) is maintained, and it is possible that in time Khieu Samphan (but not Pol Pot) will be allowed a place in government. Considering the government's disparate elements, however, not to mention the widespread corruption that infests its ranks, the road ahead will be rocky, particularly if King Sihanouk should die. Sihanouk and his son nonetheless seem to be generally optimistic as regards the future. For the sake of the long-suffering Cambodian people, we must hope that this guarded optimism is not misplaced.

CHAPTER EIGHTY

1. Nixon, *Memoirs*, 691–2.
2. Shawcross, 261.
3. Nixon, *Memoirs*, 699. See also, Snepp, 78.
4. Nixon, *Memoirs*, 718. See also, Snepp, 88: " . . . It [the President's statement to Thieu] was the opening flourish in Washington's postwar commitment to South Vietnam, one on which the U.S. Congress would never be consulted."
5. Snepp, 29.
6. Fallaci, 30. See also, Haldeman, 84.
7. Kissinger, *Years of Upheaval*, 369.

8. Isaacs, 142.
9. Ibid., 61.
10. Snepp, 51.
11. Karnow, 658. See also, Shawcross, 260.
12. Snepp, 48.
13. Ibid., 48–9. My italics.
14. Isaacs, 84.
15. Snepp, 50.
16. Karnow, 657.
17. Isaacs, 49. The Vietnamese had more planes than pilots; according to a later U.S. Air Force study, the force of over 3,000 combat aircraft was " . . . completely beyond their ability to maintain."
18. Snepp, 103, who quotes from an official GAO report for the two years following the so-called cease-fire:

> . . . over $200 million of matériel had been lost or squandered by the South Vietnamese during the same period. . . . Large amounts of equipment, it said, had been stolen or sold illegally to the Communists. Among the items listed as "missing" or "unaccounted for": 143 small warships valued at $37 million; $2 million worth of ammunition, declared unusable because of poor storage; and $10 million in small arms which had simply disappeared from supply depots. . . . The Pentagon and the Defense Attaché's Office [in Saigon], in an effort to reconcile the separate balance sheets, simply wrote off $44 million in military aid. . . . The American taxpayer, in short, was asked to subsidize Saigon's corruption, and the Vietnamese foot soldier was obliged to die for it.

19. Ibid., 78, 99–101.
20. International Institute for Strategic Studies, *Strategic Survey 1973*, 73.
21. Ibid.
22. Karnow, 659.
23. Snepp, 55.
24. International Institute for Strategic Studies, *Strategic Survey 1973*, 70. See also, Snepp, 55–6.
25. Karnow, 659.
26. Ibid., 659–60.
27. Snepp, 91.
28. Woodward and Bernstein, 54 ff.
29. International Institute for Strategic Studies, *Strategic Survey 1973*, 73.
30. Isaacs, 161. " . . . This was approximately the tonnage dropped by U.S. air forces in all of World War II in both the European and Pacific Theaters of war."
31. International Institute for Strategic Studies, *Strategic Survey 1973*, 74. See also, Isaacs, 175–89.
32. Karnow, 663.
33. Kiernan, 338.
34. Ibid., 357.
35. Snepp, 51.
36. Shawcross, 350.
37. Kiernan, 390.
38. Ibid., 391.
39. Shawcross, 264, 271–2, 275–6.
40. Snepp, 97.
41. Shawcross, 313.
42. International Institute for Strategic Studies, *Strategic Survey 1973*, 74.
43. Snepp, 123.
44. Ibid., 113–14.

45. Ibid., 185.
46. Shawcross, 389.
47. The International Institute for Strategic Studies, *Strategic Survey 1977*, 84.
48. Ibid., 84–5. See also, Shawcross, 385 ff.
49. International Institute for Strategic Studies, *Strategic Survey 1979*, 57.
50. Ibid., 58.
51. Ibid. *1980–81*, 100.
52. Ibid., 99.
53. Shawcross, 378–80.
54. International Institute for Strategic Studies, *Strategic Survey 1988–89*, 114.
55. Ibid., 116.
56. Richburg, 118.
57. Ibid., 119.
58. Solarz, 99.
59. Ibid., 104.
60. Ibid.
61. *International Herald Tribune*, November 28, 1991.
62. *Newsweek*, February 10, 1992.
63. *International Herald Tribune*, March 27, 1992. See also, *The Independent* (U.K.), March 31, 1992.
64. *International Herald Tribune*, June 13–14, 1992. See also, *Newsweek*, June 29, 1992.
65. *International Herald Tribune*, April 17–18, November 15, 1993.
66. Ibid., June 9, 1993.
67. Ibid., September 3, 1993.
68. Ibid., November 23, 1993.
69. Ibid., December 2, 1993.

PART FOUR

THEN UNTIL NOW:
A SURVEY

Anyone is a criminal who promotes an avoid-
able war; and so is he who does not promote
an inevitable civil war.

JOSÉ MARTÍ—HERO OF THE 1895 CUBAN REVOLUTION

CHAPTER 81

The Latin American problem: poverty, guerrillas, and drug barons •
Venezuela's short insurgency • *The Guatemala experience* • *Raúl
Sendic's Tupamoros of Uruguay*

> It is the time of the furnaces, and it is only nec-
> essary to see the glow.[1]
>
> JOSÉ MARTI

ALTHOUGH THE twenty countries of Central and South America differ greatly in size, population and natural resources,
their peoples share a great many things in common, not least of which
is a growing desire to participate in the community of democratic
nations. They also share a tragic history of foreign rule that decimated
their peoples and reduced their resources. That was followed by economic exploitation by foreign interests whose governments did not hesitate to intervene militarily when necessary to preserve the political,
economic, and social status quo of a small, wealthy elite controlling a
repressive police and army. This explains in part many decades of authoritarian government, mostly by the military, with concomitant political assassinations, civil rights abuses, and some of the most
inefficient, corrupt, and ruthless dictators in the history of the world,
an unpleasant state of affairs difficult to contravene owing both to the
highly passionate Latin American temperament which frequently mili-
tates against political stability, and in most of the countries to the slow
growth of a stabilizing middle class with members intent on pursuing
a career of public service. As a young Argentinian diplomat recently
explained to me, suitably qualified persons such as university graduates
regard politics more "as an opportunity to improve one's financial and
social standing . . . rather than a chance to serve one's people."

This general middle class non-involvement in, indeed scorn of politics helps to explain the slow progress of today's reformist governments

in reversing a disastrous legacy: a tradition of corruption at all levels of government (including police and military); antiquated and wasteful farming production and distribution; massive child labor—at least " . . . 30 million children aged ten to fourteen" at work today, of whom perhaps fifteen million are working and often living in the streets;[2] rabbit-warren slums with no running water, no electricity, no toilets— " . . . an estimated 100 million people without adequate drinking water";[3] vast numbers of unemployed in the cities and countryside; landowning elites sufficiently rich and powerful to torpedo land distribution and other vital programs; an appalling shortage of elementary schools and qualified teachers, thus high rates of illiteracy; poor and in some cases no medical and social services (with noteworthy exceptions such as Uruguay), thus the inevitable rampant endemic diseases (including the present cholera epidemic, the first in a century); finally, the result in large part of Roman Catholic teachings to illiterate peasants, ever-mounting birthrates in countries where over half the population is living below the poverty line and which have a high percentage of the population under fifteen years of age—despite the death of nearly one million children " . . . under five years of age every year."[4] Should the reader think this is alarmist writing, I refer him or her to country-by-country statistics presented in the elegant 1991 edition of the *Encyclopaedia Britannica*, which, together with the indispensable *Annual Register and Record of World Events, Keesing's Contemporary Archives, Keesing's Record of World Events, Facts on File*, and the impressive publications of the prestigious International Institute for Strategic Studies, I have relied on heavily for this survey.

Adding to the burden of contemporary reformist governments is an understandable tradition of insurrections attempted and sometimes carried out by guerrilla warfare. Initially sporadic, these efforts were greatly encouraged by the successful Russian Revolution—during the last seven decades, scores of guerrilla bands and organizations have sprung into existence. Nurtured by Marxian seeds planted in the fertile ground of human hopelessness, watered by repression instead of weakened by reform, cultivated by Russian gold and Western greed, fertilized by Fidel Castro's seizure of Cuba in 1959, these rural guerrilla and urban guerrilla terrorist movements, by challenging established governments, have brought nightmares of violence to countries around the world.

It did not take long for the shock waves of the Cuban revolution to roll over Latin America. The fallout was intense. All the ingredients necessary for revolution were abundantly on hand in Latin America when Fidel Castro became Cuba's ruler and chief guru of guerrilla wars of liberation designed to turn Latin America into one gigantic Communist camp.

Most of the insurgencies that followed were not co-ordinated. They occurred at different times and places under different conditions and in a number of forms. At first, the emphasis was on Maoist-Castro rural strategy: " . . . In the underdeveloped Americas," Che Guevara wrote, "the countryside must be the basic formula for the armed struggle."[5] Guevara's failure in fomenting a rural guerrilla war in Bolivia (see Chapter 57) and the failure of other rural uprisings in Guatemala, Colombia, Peru, Venezuela, and Chile brought an insurgency turnaway from Mao Tse-tung back to basic Marxist-Leninist urban guerrilla warfare. " . . . Today the epicenter of the war must be in the great urban zones," the Spanish anarchist Abraham Guillén insisted.[6] "The urban guerrilla's reasons for existence," wrote Carlos Marighela, "the basic condition in which he acts and survives, is to shoot."[7]

A wave of urban insurgencies fueled by the New Left revolutionary thinking propounded by Herbert Marcuse, Guillén, Marighela, Régis Debray, and other radical commentators now swept over the hemisphere and indeed the world, its hallmark violence: robbery, extortion, kidnaping, assassination, airplane hijackings, mass murder by indiscriminate bombing. Techniques and goals varied. Headlines beginning in the late 1960s were claimed for a decade by groups consisting of social dropouts who practiced random terrorist acts with only nebulous goals such as a demand for world revolution: the Black Panthers, the Weathermen, and the Symbionese Liberation Army in the United States, the Japanese Red Army, the Red Army Faction (Baader-Meinhof) in West Germany, the Angry Brigade in Great Britain, the Red Brigades in Italy, Middle Eastern groups that splintered from the Palestine Liberation Organization such as the Popular Front for the Liberation of Palestine-General Command and Abu Nidal's terrorists based in and supported by Libya—to name only a few. Leroy Eldridge Cleaver, Angela Davis, Patty Hearst, Ulrike Meinhof, Andreas Baader, Daniel Cohn-Bendit, and others became the darlings of the militant radicals, but not for long. Society in general soon came to regard them as very dangerous criminals to be dealt with by law enforcement agencies, as indeed they were. After flourishing in the late 1960s and early 1970s, their activities slowed and frequently stopped as many of their leaders were imprisoned or killed, some by members of the same organization. A few remain active today, seemingly more interested in practicing terror for terror's sake than in bringing about world revolution.

This was only one category of urban guerrilla terrorist groups. The other category consisted of groups with specific goals, particularly those operating in conjunction with rural guerrilla movements, which lasted somewhat longer. Failure to build a secure political base—the *bête noir* of urban guerrilla groups—eventually caught up with the majority of them. If they made life hell for many citizens, if they toppled some governments, if they drastically damaged economies, they nevertheless often forced political, social, and economic reforms necessary if their countries were to enter the democratic mainstream to provide some hope for the millions of their peoples.

Generally they did not in the end prosper. Generally they either dried up or converted to legitimate political parties or remained a small, often fragmented force in being responsible for an occasional bank robbery or kidnaping or assassination—a challenge to security forces but not a major threat to government. There are exceptions: today they remain a serious threat to the governments of Colombia and Peru.

Now comes the irony. When most Latin American governments were gaining on the guerrillas, when some reforms were starting to take hold, when some guerrilla supporters and sympathizers were tiring of seemingly endless internecine warfare with its daily ration of bombs and corpses, a new element emerged to enlarge political, economic, social, and security problems a thousandfold. That element was drugs, at first to feed the huge North American market, where the same factors that fueled guerrilla movements in Latin America—unemployment, poverty, illiteracy, and disease—combined to provide one of the most lucrative markets for any product in world history.

Rather than recognize the problem at home and treat it as the crisis it is, rather than take emergency action (and damn the cost) to begin eliminating the desire and need for drugs, the American government in large part shifted the blame to the drug-producing and drug-trafficking countries, mainly to Peru, Colombia, Bolivia, and Panama, with tentacles all over the place. The school solution to the problem as seen in the Reagan and Bush administrations was to eliminate drug production. The U. S. Drug Enforcement Administration (DEA), which had nearly secreted itself out of existence, suddenly became a household word. Millions of dollars were given over to suppression programs. Teams of experts were sent to target countries; ships patrolled the seas, airplanes combed the skies—and they are doing so today.

The rise of the drug barons was a boon to Latin American guerrillas, who had been finding it not so easy to carry on, what with funds from extortion, robberies, and kidnapings shrinking, what with Castro's quasi-defection from their cause in 1983, what with increasingly effective government countermeasures and reduced popular support, what with Mikhail Gorbachev's turnaway from exported revolution followed by a bankrupt and crumbling Soviet Union. But by 1989, some guerrilla leaders had long since found a two-way bonanza, first in selling Mafia-style "protection" to peasant coca growers, second in selling services to drug barons, anything from murdering political opponents to protecting roads and hidden airstrips and processing and refining areas from government forces in return for heaps of hard cash, their perverted rationale presumably being that they were serving the revolutionary cause by contributing significantly to the decline of capitalist and Western society (and so they were—and are).

So it was that at an already difficult time a new and disturbing factor entered into the age-old challenge of fighting insurgency warfare. It will probably not be the last, and in time it will probably be countered if concerned governments and guerrilla movements will come to their senses, and if Western societies will open crash programs to get their children off the streets and back into schools and jobs. As will be seen in the following survey, in several Latin American countries guerrilla warfare is still alive and well or at least nascent; in other countries where it has been suppressed often at a great cost to political, economic, and social structures, the threat of renewed guerrilla outbreaks re-mains—this in proportion to the strength and achievements of reformist governments.

One of the early and certainly one of the most curious insurgencies inspired by Fidel Castro's seizure of Cuba in 1959 sprang up in Vene-zuela. In spring of 1960, a group of young militants in Caracas formed the Movement of the Revolutionary Left (MIR) under Cuban auspices. In addition to money received from extortion, the group embarked on a profitable series of robberies, kidnapings, and hijackings of ships and planes. Cuba supplied most of its arms, trained recruits in Cuban camps, and supplied veteran guerrilla "advisers" who fought in MIR ranks. In its formative years, the MIR insurgency was largely confined to terrorist acts in the cities but in 1962, the insurgency was joined by members of the Venezuelan Communist Party (PCV), which founded another guerrilla group, the Armed Forces of National Liberation (FALN), also Cuban-inspired since at this time Castro was intent on exporting revolution to Latin America and had hit upon Venezuela as a pilot model.

Castro's model did not turn out too well. Although MIR grew steadily in the 1960s, in particular attracting students to its banner, internal dissension was already weakening its effort. The villain was MIR excesses, which upset life in the cities to lose the movement much of its popular support. With public blessing, President Romulo Betan-court authorized a counterinsurgency campaign that severely blunted MIR operations. First to desert the movement was its founder. He was followed in the mid-1960s by a large number of rank-and file who believed that it was futile to continue armed violence. By 1970, the movement was moribund although a few splinter groups carried on guerrilla operations in one form or another. The MIR itself recovered politically and in the mid-1970s won representation in the national assembly. It remained radically left but did not return to guerrilla operations. The defection of Cuba from the goal of a Communist Latin America, the demise of Communist Russia, and the end of insurgencies in Nicargua and El Salvador damaged its political importance, but it remains a potential force in the turbulence of Venezuelan politics.

The FALN did not fare so well. A number of its members soon began to resent Communist Party emphasis on urban instead of guerrilla war. The break came in 1966 when its leader, Douglas Bravo, a former Politburo member, acted without PCV authority and was expelled from the party, taking most of the FALN guerrillas with him. Bravo's two major lieutenants did not share his faith in a rural strategy and a major rift soon developed. As with the MIR, other members grew disillusioned with the armed struggle and left the group. Once Castro's darling, Bravo grew increasingly distant from the Cuban leader, and by the end of the decade embraced a Maoist strategy while openly criticizing Castro in his widely disseminated writings. Around 1970, the FALN dissolved into a number of splinter groups which in one form or another carried on the struggle until the late 1970s, when it vanished from the scene.[8]

A third group appeared in 1969 with the fall of the MIR. That was the Red Flag Party (PBR) led by Gabriel Puerta Aponte and consisting of about a hundred guerrillas from the MIR. Never large, the PBR funded itself by bank robberies and ransoms derived from kidnaping wealthy Venezuelan ranchers; it was also supported by Cuba and by sympathetic South American revolutionary movements. It suffered a severe setback with Puerta's arrest in 1981 followed by a successful police operation two years later that netted thirteen of its "international terrorists." Factionalism also damaged its operations and public appeal. It is still alive, a member of Venezuela's leftist political group, and is believed to be working with the Colombian ELN in protecting the drug routes from Colombia into Venezuela, from where the cocaine is shipped to foreign markets.[9]

Drug trafficking in Venezuela has grown to the extent that in 1992 President Andrés Pérez ordered "all-out war" on the traffickers, a particularly courageous move considering his own precarious position as survivor of two recent military coup attempts. Unfortunately, his "war" dissolved into political scandal in spring of 1993 when he was forced from office to stand trial, along with several political associates, on charges of massive corruption. After months of political turbulence, including several bombings, December elections installed seventy-seven-year-old Rafael Caldera Rodríguez as the new conservative president. Considering the close election results, the meager election turnout (reportedly less than 10 percent of the eligible voters), and the weak state of the economy, the chances are that the PBR not only will survive but, in view of the power of the international drug barons, may even prosper.

Guatemala's insurrectionary problems go back nearly fifty years. Continued governmental failure to give the people a fair shake spurred the growth of liberal and Marxist movements until in 1944 a general strike toppled a weak interim government to place organized labor in a dominant political position. This social revolution, inherited by Guatemala's first popularly elected president, philosophy professor Juan José Arévalo Bermejo, brought a new labor code and some land reforms, but it was hindered by internecine quarrels and coup attempts, during which Guatemalan Communists captured the labor movement and helped to elect the leftist politician Jacobo Arbenz Guzmán to the presidency in 1951.

A need for land reform had long been obvious. The major villain was the United Fruit Company, a United States company which had kept numerous Guatemalan dictators in its pocket. In 1953, United Fruit owned 42 percent of Guatemala's land yet was growing bananas on only 139,000 of its three million acres.[10] This lopsided situation was threatened by an agrarian reform law that authorized the Arbenz government to expropriate 225,000 acres of uncultivated land for distribution to landless peasants.

The United Fruit Company is a very powerful organization with a lot of important friends. In 1953, these included John Foster Dulles, Eisenhower's Secretary of State; Allen Dulles, chief of CIA; retired army General Walter Bedell Smith, Under Secretary of State; Henry Cabot Lodge, U.S. ambassador to the United Nations; and John Moors Cabot, Assistant Secretary of State for Inter-American Affairs. In 1953, United Fruit spent a great deal of money in hiring public relations firms to circulate a total message to the effect that " . . . Guatemala was ruled by Communists bent on conquering Central America and seizing the Panama Canal."[11] The company's influential friends and a fair portion of an uninformed electorate readily accepted this warning. According to Eisenhower, John Moors Cabot convinced him that Guatemala was " . . . openly playing the Communist game,"[12] an assertion substantially reinforced by the new ambassador to Guatemala, John Peurifoy.[13]

Arbenz in reality was playing the reform game. Edward Rice, a retired senior American diplomat has recently pointed out that no Communists held cabinet-level or army command posts, and of fifty-one deputies in Arbenz's ruling coalition four were Communists. That there was a Communist influence at working levels and in labor unions was true enough. That was perfectly legitimate (and certainly understandable), and it was also true that Guatemala had consistently supported the United States on major cold war issues in the United Nations.[14]

This was the situation when Eisenhower authorized the CIA to open a covert campaign designed to overthrow Arbenz. It began with a misinformation campaign that put the Guatemalan government " . . . in a false light abroad and [created] fear and uncertainty within."[15] After bribing a suitable numer of Guatemalan army officers, the CIA sent in a force of Guatemalan dissident exiles and mercenaries commanded by dissident Carlos Castillo Armas with a small air cover provided by CIA. Castillo's "Liberation Army" invaded in June 1954 and probably would have failed in its mission had President Eisenhower not authorized additional air power.[16] Although there was no popular rising against the Arbenz government and no army mutiny, neither was there army support for Arbenz, who resigned and took refuge in Mexico. He was eventually replaced by Castillo. Backed by the Eisenhower administration, this "farseeing and able statesman" (in Eisenhower's words)[17] canceled all reform programs (and returned the expropriated land to the United Fruit Company). He was assassinated three years later. His replacement, General Miguel Ydígoras Fuentes, provided the CIA with secret training areas for the Cuban invasion, an unpopular move that precipitated an uprising of army officers in 1960, put down with CIA help. Some surviving officers fled to the hills, where they organized diverse guerrilla bands and called for a national revolution. The Guatemalan army put a stop to this—the bands were soon decimated, most of their leaders killed.

Guatemala was ruled by military government for the next nearly twenty-five disastrous years. All attempts at reform either failed or were so watered down as to be meaningless. Shrinking world markets and rampant inflation fueled in large part by inept administration and massive corruption increased general dissatisfaction until at times virtual civil war existed. Guerrilla terrorist murders of two U.S. military advisers and the U.S. ambassador in 1968 and of the German ambassador in 1970 were answered in kind by security forces. Violence escalated. Suspected dissidents, those who had earlier supported liberal presidents—students, trade unionists, doctors, lawyers, teachers—were hunted down by death squads composed of urban guerrilla terrorists of the right condoned and often encouraged by the security forces. Simultaneously, massive counterinsurgency campaigns cleansed the countryside to the extent that one official study put the number of children who had lost one or both parents at 110,000.[18] Such was the carnage that in 1977, President Carter cut off military aid to the government.[19]

That solved nothing. General Romeo Lucas García, who became president in 1978, at once turned loose paramilitary bands to wipe out " . . . the social democratic parties and the left-leaning labor and peasant organizations that had been allowed to emerge in the mid-1970s."[20]

It was not a good time for freedom. " . . . Literally hundreds of non-violent opposition leaders were murdered and many more were sent into exile."[21] By 1982, the killings totaled perhaps thirteen thousand.[22] That scarcely squelched the guerrilla opposition, " . . . which for the first time in history succeeded in mobilizing important sectors of the Indian community, which comprises over half of the total population. . . . As repression grew in the countryside, so did guerrilla strength and renewed activity."[23]

Fraudulent elections held in 1982 in an attempt to persuade Washington to renew military aid led to another coup that installed a born-again Christian, General Efraín Rios Montt, in the presidency. Montt managed to restrain the more violent activities of the death squads while launching a counterinsurgency offensive designed to bring the country-side under government control. In six months, this effort resulted in an estimated five thousand Indian deaths, some 250,000 Indians displaced from their villages, thirty thousand refugees who fled into Mexico, and fifty thousand villagers press-ganged into civil patrols whose mission was to kill any surviving dissidents.[24] Despite this abominable record, Rios persuaded President Ronald Reagan to lift the arms embargo and resume selling arms to the Guatemalan Government, albeit in limited quantities. As Christopher Dickey has pointed out, there seems little doubt that Rios' strong-arm methods coerced a great many villagers, at least temporarily, into passive acceptance of the regime.[25]

Leaving aside his failure to repair an ailing economy, Rios got into political trouble by yielding to the dictates of his California Protestant evangelists over those of his predominantly Catholic generals.[26] Ousted by a military coup in late 1983, he was replaced by his defense minister, who soon turned the government to shambles. In 1985, when thousands of peasants were dying from malnutrition and when Guatemala City was rocked by massive riots, the militarists finally bowed to regional and international protests and allowed an election.

The election was won by a political moderate member of the Christian Democratic Party, Marco Vinicio Cerezo, who had escaped three assassination attempts by death squads. Vinicio's efforts to demilitarize "a thoroughly militarized country" and to consolidate " . . . a democratic process in a country with almost no real civilian institutions"[27] were from the beginning hamstrung by military overseers working hand in hand with the country's economic elite.[28] The new president, who inherited the worst depression in half a century, instituted an austerity program that met with only partial success. Though officially proscribed, death squads continued their violence in the cities, where their activities were increasingly challenged by urban guerrilla terrorists until killings and counterkillings became the order of the day. Renewal of military aid by the Reagan administration, inspired in part by the growing insurgency in El Salvador and the CIA effort to topple the Sandinista government in Nicaragua, enabled the thirty-thousand man army to expand counterguerrilla operations. Various guerrilla bands responded by forming the Guatemalan National Revolution Unity (URNG) of perhaps a total of two thousand hard-core guerrillas. Some hope for an eventual compromise peace appeared in August 1987 when Guatemala joined with other Central American countries in signing the regional Arias peace plan that called for Central America to solve its own problems without the help of external powers.

This could not take place overnight. Vinicio's increasingly inept and corrupt government survived but could not tame military extremists, who continued political assassinations, kidnapings, and torture while remaining immune from prosecution.[29] In December 1989, a general officer told a graduating class of the army's elite counterinsurgency corps to " . . . forget all humanitarian principles and become war machines . . . because from now on, they will be called Masters of War and Messengers of Death."[30] Anyone suspected of being a leftist rebel was fair game for arrest and often execution; peasant villages suspected of aiding leftist rebels were wiped out.[31]

Vinicio's humiliating defeat in the November 1990 elections brought some important and hopeful changes to this ugly state of affairs. The new president, Jorge Serrano Elias, a right-wing Protestant evangelist, promised to end the thirty-year-old civil war that had cost an estimated 120,000 deaths and resulted in what he called "a culture of death." After surviving an assassination attempt shortly after taking office, Serrano started well by having government officials and military officers meet with guerrilla heads of the URNG (which unfortunately came to nothing). He also gained kudos by replacing the military head of the national police force with a civilian who fired three thousand policemen within ten months. Members of the armed forces "for the first time" were " . . . charged with violations of human rights."[32]

Unfortunately these reforms were more cosmetic than real. Serrano's reign ended in spring of 1993 when, beset by critics for failing to end the thirty-two-year-old insurgency, by a deteriorating economy, and by one of the worst human rights records in the world, he summarily dissolved congress and the supreme court—an *autogolpe,* or one-man coup, that at once caused the U.S. government to suspend a $30 million aid program. This action, taken with massive civil protests, caused military chiefs to back away from the self-proclaimed dictator, whose regime lasted only a week before a bloodless military counter-coup forced him into hurried exile. Within days, the Guatemalan congress elected a new president, a human rights activist, Ramon León Carpio.

Although Guatemala's fragile democracy had seemingly survived, Leon's new government has had its hands full in trying to right the country's many wrongs. Several thousand kids still roaming the streets are systematically beaten, tortured, and murdered by the police despite widespread international protests that culminated in sharp reductions of aid from several countries.[33]

Nor is the guerrilla situation comfortable. According to Michael Radu and Vladimir Tismaneanu, at least three major groups continue to operate. The Rebel Armed Forces (FAR), born circa 1960, almost eliminated in 1968 but responsible for the ambassadorial killings of that year and 1970, revived in 1978 and are today operationally active though with perhaps only two hundred hard-core members; the Guerrilla Army of the Poor (EGP), born circa 1972, was about two thousand strong a decade later but subsequently declined sharply; the Revolutionary Organization of the People in Arms (ORPA), born circa 1982, is estimated at about a thousand strong today and is operationally very active—" . . . in many ways its approach to revolutionary violence is similar to the Peruvian Sendero Luminoso."[34]

The comparatively small numbers of guerrillas should not be misinterpreted, because these groups are supported by thousands of sympathizers. But neither should the trappings of unity claimed by the UNRG be taken too seriously. Their essential weakness remains their failure to unite in one revolutionary ideology, be it Marxist-Leninist, Maoist, or a combination of the two with a touch of Castroism to lend it a social democratic flavor. Their individual and combined threat to the government is nevertheless very real and has recently increased owing to heavy drug trafficking across the northern part of the country. Since 1990, U. S. DEA agents allegedly have been working closely with the Guatemalan military to interdict this trade and its guerrilla support. The Catch-22 here is that this means U.S. financial support of the Guatemalan military, which is still violating human rights on a large scale while preventing necessary political and economic reforms from being carried out.[35]

One thing is certain: The guerrillas are not going to be either pacified or eliminated until proper reforms are instituted and respected, that is until the Guatemalan people are given decent housing, decent food, decent land plots, decent jobs, and decent health services. Although Guatemala is potentially the richest country in Central America, it also has " . . . the most extreme disparities between wealth and poverty . . . [with] religious and racial tensions . . . acute and growing."[36] The task of turning this around remains. Over a decade ago, a very astute journalist, Alan Riding, concluded, "No matter what fantasies are projected by idealism or ambition, in the end it is sheer underdevelopment—political, religious and cultural, as well as economic—that determines the limits of hope."[37]

Some three years after Castro's takeover of Cuba, a nationalist revolutionary organization called the National Liberation Movement (MLN) appeared in the sprawling capital of Montevideo, home to perhaps 50 per cent of tiny Uruguay's three million people. This group was known as the Tupamoros—the name deriving from an Inca prince who led a revolt against Spanish rule in the late eighteenth century—was led by Raúl Sendic, a young union organizer of sugarcane field workers, who had recently been released from prison.[38] Sendic and his fellows wished to set up a socialist state devoid of foreign economic and political entanglements, which they blamed for Uruguay's severe economic problems.

The insurgents faced a peculiar problem in that the sparsely populated countryside bereft of mountain or jungle sanctuaries did not offer a suitable *loco* for rural guerrilla warfare.[39] They perforce turned to the teeming capital and to urban guerrilla warfare with stress on terrorism as spelled out in the writings of Régis Debray, Abraham Guillén, and Brazilian Communist Carlos Marighella (whose rather pedestrian work, *The Minimanual of Urban Guerrilla Warfare,* was soon to become the bible of guerrilla terrorists everywhere).

Sendic's Tupamoros did not rush into action. Perhaps twenty in number, they recruited selectively from the professions, schools, universities, women's rights organizations, trade unions, the local Communist Party, the Roman Catholic clergy, and even from the military. By 1965, " . . . there were five hundred fully committed guerrillas, with more than five thousand people sympathetic to the movements."[40]

The movement came out of the closet in 1968 by publicly announcing its aim of bringing down the government. One of its first acts was to steal a loan company's books which revealed illegal currency speculations by several government officials.[41] The movement also gained favorable publicity and more adherents by stealing milk and food trucks and distributing the contents to the pitiful children of Montevideo's squalid barrios.

As its cellular organization in large part protected its activists and as intelligence, finance, and numbers improved, tactics expanded to robbing stores and warehouses for supplies (including chemicals with which to make bombs). Banks and post offices were robbed for money; intimidation of important persons and business executives extorted more money. Prominent citizens, foreign executives, and diplomats were kidnaped, often brutally (the British ambassador Geoffrey Jackson was held for eight months), both for political blackmail (release of guerrilla prisoners, improved factory conditions, publicity for the cause), and for ransom ($250,000 was paid for the Brazilian consul's release).[42] Foreign firms were sabotaged in the hope of making them leave the country and thus further damaging the economy; raids on police stations and army posts yielded weapons, ammunition—and publicity. Murder was a final tactic, the victims being policemen, government officials, politicians, and anyone else who opposed the insurgency (including a U.S. CIA police adviser who was kidnaped and killed in 1970, an act which did considerable harm to the guerrilla cause).[43]

There were setbacks. Equipped increasingly with modern technology and instructed by U.S. advisers, the police were gradually getting their act together and the military, theretofore quiescent, was also coming to life. In 1970, Raúl Sendic and eight hard-line Tupamoros were arrested and imprisoned.[44] Fueled in part by general dissatisfaction with the shrinking economy, the government's harsh austerity program and runaway inflation, the movement nonetheless continued to grow, perhaps to as many as 1,500 to three thousand members in 1971 when Tupamoros gangs carried off daring jailbreaks to free about one hundred fifty of their fellows (including Sendic). They seemed also to have won substantial sympathy if not support. A poll in 1971 showed that " . . . 59 percent of the Uruguayan public thought of them as an organization motivated by social justice and human motives."[45] That was perhaps true but at the time the average citizen did not know very much about the Tupamoros (one result of excessive secrecy and effective cellular security measures), much less about what the movement hoped to achieve. Toppling the government was one thing, building a new government was another. What did the Tupamoros intend? No one seemed to know. Robberies and kidnapings and killings went on. Those tactics had brought a rightist backlash and with it increasing activity of rightist death squads that included the police and military and which were turning Montevideo into a nightmare of counterkidnapings, torture, and murder.

Arrogance now caught up with the Tupamoros. In 1971, an attempt to spread the revolution to the countryside failed. A sharp decline in public sympathy already had occurred, owing in part to the kidnaping of the British ambassador, a Catholic, and his prolonged imprisonment, during which he displayed tremendous fortitude when exposed to journalists, and to the murder of the U.S. police adviser, Don Mitrione, a Catholic with nine children. This reversal showed in the national elections in which the left-wing coalition suffered defeat. In 1972, the Tupamoros made a major mistake by killing an army officer, which brought down the wrath of the traditionally non-political military.[46] A military coup the following year was followed by an army crackdown in which some three hundred Tupamoros were killed and three to five thousand jailed.

During the subsequent ten years of military dictatorship, thousands of political "suspects" were arrested and often tortured before being imprisoned or killed. The bloodbath, which had drawn the ire of the civilized world, fortunately was interrupted in 1985 by the election of a civilian government headed by the Colorado Party's candidate. President Júlio María Sanguinetti reinstituted democratic rule, amnestied all police and military personnel guilty of human rights violations from 1973 to 1985, pardoned Raúl Sendic (who died four years later from " . . . the effects of his torture while a prisoner,"[47] released many political prisoners (despite severe opposition), and allowed the Tupamoros to re-emerge as a legitimate political party. In 1989, the Colorado Party lost to the Blanco Party candidate, Luis Alberto Lacalle Herrera, an opponent of the blanket amnesty law, who subsequently has tried to revitalize the economy by privatization and other measures while respecting the legacy of democratic rule. Although the left-wing Broad Front coalition party came third in the presidential elections, it did carry Montevideo and thus remains a force to be reckoned with.

Just how long the new democracy will survive is a moot question, although to date, December 1993, President Luis Alberto Lacalle seems to have kept the army and most former guerrilla groups under control. If the latter, as members of the leftist *Frente Amplio* (FA) or Broad Front political party, have so far behaved, not all of them have rejected armed revolution as a means to secure still overdue reforms. For the moment, however, FA leadership seems to be upholding the democratic principle while frantically preparing for the scheduled November 1994 elections, which they hope will remove the traditional Blanco and Colorado ruling parties from power.

CHAPTER EIGHTY-ONE

1. Lavan, 44.
2. *Newsweek*, October 19, 1992.
3. Ibid.
4. Ibid.
5. Halperin, 8.
6. Ibid., 10.
7. Ibid.
8. Radu and Tismaneanu, 361–3. In preparing this survey, I have frequently relied on this scholarly and detailed compilation of guerrilla movements and their operations in Latin America.
9. Ibid., 365–8.
10. Rice, 39.
11. Ibid., 41.
12. Eisenhower, *Mandate for Change*, 422.
13. Ibid. Peurifoy informed Eisenhower and Dulles, " . . . It seemed to me that the man [Arbenz] thought like a Communist and talked like a Communist, and if not actually one, would do until one came along." See also, ibid., 423: In October 1954, Peurifoy testified before a U.S. Congressional committee

that "... the Arbenz government beyond any question was controlled and dominated by Communists. These Communists were directed from Moscow."

14. Rice, 42.
15. Ibid., 43.
16. Eisenhower, *Mandate for Change*, 426.
17. Ibid.
18. Rice, 49.
19. International Institute for Strategic Studies, *Strategic Survey 1982–83*, 126.
20. Riding, 653. See also, The International Institute for Strategic Studies, *Strategic Survey 1980–81*, 24.
21. Riding, 653.
22. International Institute for Strategic Studies, *Strategic Survey 1982–83*, 126.
23. Riding, 653.
24. Ibid. See also, International Institute for Strategic Studies, *Strategic Survey 1982–83*, 126–7; *Newsweek*, August 31, 1992.
25. Dickey, 685.
26. Ibid., 686.
27. International Institute for Strategic Studies, *Strategic Survey 1985–86*, 197.
28. Best, 99–117.
29. International Institute for Strategic Studies, *Strategic Survey 1989–90*, 185. See also, ibid., *1990–91*, 121–2.
30. Moss, 431.
31. Ibid. See also, *Newsweek*, August 31, 1992, "Subtle Clues in Shallow Graves."
32. *The Annual Register of World Events 1991*, 77.
33. *The Independent* (U.K.), March 31, 1992.
34. Radu and Tismaneanu, 235–68.
35. Moss, 453.
36. International Institute for Strategic Studies, *Strategic Survey 1990–91*, 122.
37. Riding, 643.
38. Goode, 72–3. See also, Radu and Tismaneanu, 348.
39. Rice, 58.
40. Goode, 76.
41. Ibid., 77.
42. Clutterbuck, *Living With Terrorism*, 36–7. See also, Jackson.
43. Halperin, 143.
44. *The Annual Register of World Events, 1971*.
45. Goode, 79.
46. International Institute for Strategic Studies, *Strategic Survey 1972*, 65.
47. *The Annual Register of World Events 1989*, 74.

CHAPTER 82

The Somoza dictatorship • Birth of the Sandinista Liberation Front Nicaragua (FSLN) • FSLN revolutionary aims • Stringent government suppression of civil liberties • FSLN guerrillas open fire • Government excesses • Somoza's fall • The FSLN Communist regime • The CIA and the Contras • Daniel Ortega's Sandinistas • CIA excesses • Contra reverses • Irangate • The stalemate war • 1990 elections won by Violeta Barrios de Chamorro • The reconstruction task • Revolt of the recontras *and* revueltos *• The hostage crisis • The secret arms cache • Continuing rebel threat*

THE MURDER of Nicaragua's famed guerrilla leader Augusto César Sandino in 1934 (see Chapter 23) was the work of Anastasio Somoza García, chief of the Nicaraguan National Guard and a favorite of U. S. Secretary of State Henry Stimson. In 1936, Somoza overthrew the civilian president to become president in an unopposed election, the beginning of a dictatorship that lasted until his assassination in 1956. The dictatorship was continued by his elder son, who died in 1963, and, after a brief interim government, by his brother, Anastasio Somoza Debayle, a 1946 West Point graduate who ruled until 1979. The Somoza dictatorship, supported by a series of American administrations on behalf of private commercial interests, formed one of the most corrupt and cruel regimes in the world. Somoza's personal fortune was estimated at $500 million;[1] he owned " . . . one fourth of Nicaragua's cultivatable land, 130 businesses and industries, vast quantities of rental property and, with officers of the 7,000 strong National Guard, monopolized gambling and prostitution."[2] Thanks to the elder Somoza much of Nicaragua's land was converted to such export crops as cotton and coffee, thus reducing growing areas for traditional staple crops essential to feed a rapidly growing population. The inevitable result was widespread hunger and malnourishment that brought a shockingly high infant mortality rate. The sudden demise of the Somoza regime surprised a great many Americans—the only surprise to observers of the area was why it had not come earlier.

In 1961, a small group of radical students founded an insurgent political party called the National Liberation Front (FLN), which under the aegis of three Marxist Nicaraguans soon was renamed the Sandinista Liberation Front (FSLN) in honor of non-Marxist César Sandino. The aim of the FSLN was to topple the Somoza government by an armed guerrilla group, the Sandinistas.[3] It was not a coherent movement, it lacked funds and direction, and its operations were repeatedly broken by the National Guard, whose officers had been trained in counterinsurgency warfare by the U. S. Army—by 1967 twenty-five American military advisers were stationed in Nicaragua teaching the Guard how to use the flow of weapons and equipment provided by Washington.[4] A distinguished diplomat named Edward Rice tells us that after ten difficult years the FSLN " . . . had no more than a score of men in the mountains undergoing military training and a handful of members in the cities."[5] Michael Radu and Vladimir Tismaneanu recently concluded that " . . . by 1970 the FSLN practically ceased to exist."[6] The movement probably would have collapsed but for continued governmental excesses.

The watershed occurred when a major earthquake in 1972 left some six thousand dead and over three hundred thousand without shelter. Instead of doing their job, National Guard soldiers often deserted their posts to join in widespread looting. American soldiers were flown in to restore order but could not prevent National Guard officers and civilian politicians from stealing quantities of medicines and relief supplies— " . . . about half of the $32 million supplied by the United States for reconstruction was never accounted for."[7] This rapacious behavior resulted not only in numerous peasant recruits for the Sandinista guerrillas but also considerable sympathy from other political parties including the important middle class liberal party, the Democratic Union of Liberation (UDEL) founded by Pedro Joaquín Chamorro, scion of an old liberal family and publisher of Managua's leading newspaper *La Prensa* (The Press).

Dissidence grew in 1974 when Somoza pushed through a new constitution, declared opposition parties illegal, abolished freedom of the press, threw the protesting Chamorro in jail, and was elected president. Shortly after he was sworn in, a small group of Sandinista guerrilla terrorists burst into the mansion of a wealthy businessman to seize and hold hostage a number of prominent dinner guests. They were released unharmed when Somoza paid a large ransom, freed fourteen political prisoners, published a Sandinista proclamation, and flew the rebels out of the country (cheered by crowds on their way to the airport).[8]

Somoza responded to this guerrilla derring-do by a ruthless counterinsurgency campaign in the countryside that would last for over three years. Among the victims was Carlos Fonseca Amador, one of the three founders of the FSLN (and a national hero today), whose death strengthened the hand of the single surviving founder, Tomás Borge, an adherent of the Cuban style of Marxism. The FSLN at this time was split into three factions: one small faction which proposed a dogmatic, class-centered approach . . . limited to isolated urban terrorist activities;[9] the Maoists, who wanted to wage guerrilla warfare designed " . . . to drain Somoza's resources in a long term but elusive military campaign," but " . . . never really established a popular line of support among the peasants";[10] and finally Borge's Terceristas, the largest faction, which held for immediate action, be it terrorism in the cities or guerrilla warfare in the countryside or both.[11] The Terceristas " . . . played a major role" in bringing the FSLN to power while openly advocating socialism and popular democracy and establishing " . . . extensive alliances and coalitions with groups on all sides of the political spectrum," a lesson learned from Castro's revolution.[12] The Terceristas gained an important ally, Costa Rica, whose government " . . . permitted the formation, arming and training on its soil of a Sandinista invasion force."[13] Other Sandinista recruits received military training in Cuba, which also supplied some arms.[14] In autumn of 1977, FSLN guerrillas attacked National Guard garrisons in five cities. Although the attacks were repulsed, they brought a show of support from prominent religious and professional leaders who demanded Somoza's removal.[15]

Somoza erred fatally in early 1978 by having the newspaper publisher Pedro Chamorro murdered. Chamorro's funeral drew thousands of mourners and was followed by widespread riots, a three-week general strike and the conversion of more prominent Nicaraguans to the revolutionary movement. The government suffered another serious setback in the autumn when a group of Terceristas led by Éden Pastora and wearing National Guard uniforms stormed the National Palace to seize fifteen hundred hostages including the country's legislators. Somoza was forced to pay another hefty ransom, release sixty prisoners (including Borge), publish FSLN decrees, and fly the escapees to Cuba. Fresh guerrilla attacks sparked off major insurrections in several cities and brought on a new round of bloodletting by National Guard forces—with an estimated three thousand rebels and sympathizers killed.[16] In spring of 1979, Pastora, now famous as Commander Zero, struck again, this time leading one thousand five hundred guerrillas from his Costa Rica base into Nicaragua, a final offensive that attracted thousands of local sympathizers to his banner. This time the National Guard lost. A panic-stricken Somoza fled the country in July (and was assassinated in Paraguay in 1980).

The Pyrrhic victory cost perhaps fifty thousand dead. An interim government headed by the FSLN looked on a ruined economy and about half a million homeless people. This tragic situation was soon worsened when it became increasingly obvious that the FSLN was not only infested with corruption but was determined to turn Nicaragua into a Communist state along Cuban lines complete with secret police, neighborhood surveillance, press censorship, and suppression of opposition political parties, anti-Sandinista religious groups, labor unions, and private business groups.[17] What had approached a heterogeneous insurgency now fragmented as UDEL and other political groups began turning their backs on the new government.[18]

Washington had watched these developments with a wary eye. Although President Carter had stopped military aid to Somoza after Chamorro's murder, he also treated the dictator with considerable moderation, a feckless stance that tended to bring Nicaraguan moderates into the radical camp. Where Carter liberals had been inclined to play both sides while hoping for a new and better day for Nicaragua, Reagan conservatives proclaimed the FSLN a major threat to democracy (as if the Somoza government had been a bastion thereof) and invoked the old shibboleth of falling dominoes which would result in a communist Central and South America, a charge which gained certain currency in the United States in view of the FSLN's support of an insurgency in neighboring El Salvador, as well as state visits to Managua by PLO leader Yasser Arafat and Fidel Castro, and by " . . . a trade and aid agreement with Soviet Russia."[19]

Fired by such hawks as Secretary of State Alexander Haig and his subordinate Thomas Enders and using Nicaraguan aid to the Salvadoran insurgents as justification, President Reagan in 1981 suspended all aid to the Nicaraguan Government, the first step in an attempt to topple the Sandinista regime. U.S. fleet units were to prepare to position off Central American coasts; the ubiquitous CIA was to begin destabilizing an already floundering economy and was to organize, train, and support a guerrilla force of counterrevolutionaries that would eventually fight under the flag of the Nicaraguan Democratic Force (FDN).

The Contras, as they were soon termed, were a rather unattractive, in some ways forlorn mixture of disaffected liberals, National Guard fugitives, polyglot mercenaries, and peasant *campesinos*—in all an estimated five thousand men being trained in camps spotted along Honduras border areas, an effort for which another $19 million was allocated to the CIA in 1982.

In Costa Rica, the disaffected hero of the revolution, Éden Pastora, headed the exiled Revolutionary Democratic Alliance (ARDE), which included other prominent Sandinista dropouts and which, once its demands for political reforms were spurned by the Sandinistas, would field its own guerrilla force. But Pastora would have nothing to do with FDN resistance training in Honduras because its military high command " . . . was mainly composed of former officers of Somoza's National Guard."[20]

For this and other reasons, Contra operations were initially disappointing although they did draw the support of some disaffected Miskito Indians who had been forcibly evicted from their homelands by the Sandinistas.[21] Early spring offensives met determined resistance from government forces. Inside Nicaragua, there was little evidence of popular support for the Contras and all attempts to seize a town and make it the capital of a liberated area (in the Mao-Guevara-Castro tradition) were bloodily repulsed.

Rumors of repeated Contra atrocities during raids inside Nicaragua were circulating in Washington, and these were suddenly polarized by *Newsweek* magazine's explosive revelation of America's newest "secret war." Suddenly, the American public became aware that U.S. aid to Honduras had tripled to $33 million in 1982 with another $13 million spent on building three air strips capable of handling large U.S. troop carriers; that U.S. military advisers were working with the Honduran army, which in July had participated in joint maneuvers with U.S. forces.[22] Was Reagan intent on merely interdicting Nicaraguan arms supply to El Salvador guerrillas—or was Reagan intent on building an army with which to invade Nicaragua? Suspicious U.S. lawmakers in December 1982 publicly approved the Boland Amendment (secretly passed four months earlier), which barred " . . . the Reagan administration from supporting military operations aimed at overthrowing the Sandinista government."[23] In an attempt to sway a hostile Congress, President Reagan in July 1983 announced with considerable fanfare that a bipartisan commission headed by Henry Kissinger would review U.S. strategy and policies in Central America, a brave effort since in a good many minds there did not seem to be a strategy that, as one expert put it, " . . . links a clear statement of national interests with a sober sense of national capabilities."[24] Also in July, two U.S. Navy carrier battle groups positioned off the Central American coast as prelude to combined ground maneuvers with the Honduran army—by year's end more than four thousand U.S. troops were still in Honduras where they would continue to participate in exercises with the Honduran military.[25] In late 1983, the on-again-off-again U. S. Congress yielded to presidential plea and authorized the CIA to spend another $24 million in military and non-military aid to the Contras, who now claimed perhaps ten thousand fighters,[26] but whose fresh offensives in the northern Nicaragua border area in 1983 had met with no more success than earlier efforts.

The Kissinger report released in January 1984 was a non-event recommending as it did supplementary aid to the tune of $400 million for fiscal year 1984–85 and a whopping $8 billion in aid for the next five years. Such a proposal had to be stillborn not alone because of the grotesque sums involved and because a large portion of those sums would merely enrich corrupt politicians and generals without bringing a change for the better, but also because, as a consultant to the Kissinger Commission later wrote, " . . . even this recommended level of assistance would hardly secure the Commission's goal of 'strong and free economies' in Central America."[27]

By early 1984, Contra funds were running out and the Reagan administration again turned to Congress. But now the story broke of the CIA's participation in mining Nicaraguan ports, a blatant act of war, followed by the Administration's refusal to accept jurisdiction of the International Court of Justice in a suit brought by Nicaragua.[28] This unacceptable act provoked a Congressional blanket shut-off of any "covert" aid to the Contras, a decision that hardened when the American public learned of other CIA excesses such as instructing Contra teams in how to assassinate Nicaraguan leaders.

Although the U. S. government prevented the Sandinista regime from securing large loans from such as the World Bank and the International Monetary Fund, it was subsidized by Russia (which by 1989 would have furnished some $3 billion in aid) and by Cuba (whose aid was sharply curtailed after the U.S. invasion of Grenada in October 1983), both countries sending weapons and large numbers of military advisers, and also by Communist-bloc countries in Eastern Europe and by Iran, France, and Libya. A general election in late 1984 although boycotted by some liberal parties was won by Daniel Ortega Saavedra with over 60 per cent of the vote. International observers judged the election to be fair but the Reagan administration called it a sham and greeted Ortega's inauguration by imposing a trade embargo to stifle further the Nicaraguan economy.

Contra reverses combined with a slowdown of military aid meanwhile had brought a return to small-unit guerrilla warfare, mostly in the northern and eastern regions where the Contras won some support from the Miskito Indians. Renewal of $27 million worth of "nonmilitary" aid to the Contras in August 1985[29] greatly improved their transport and communication capabilities, but that did not change the slow pace of and only minor gains from operations inside Nicaragua.[30]

But more help was on its way. In 1985, the Reagan administration was tacitly supporting Iraq in its prolonged war against Iran. Reagan now authorized his national security adviser, Robert McFarlane, to arrange for the secret sale of arms to Iran in an attempt to persuade the Iranian government to use its assumed influence on Shiite Hezbollah terrorists who were holding American hostages in Lebanon. This altogether fanciful scheme soon grew like the national debt—it was the perfect way to end-run Congress in order to get funds to the Contras. The scheme was for international weapon traffickers—those persons who rate just below drug traffickers on the sleaze scale—to secretly supply Israel with arms purchased from U.S. arsenals. Israel would then sell them to Iran through middlemen at vast profit. Not only would Iran gratefully arrange for the release of the hostages, so the argument went, *but* a share of the profits apparently to be determined by the weapon traffickers would be transferred to secret offshore Contra bank accounts for additional arms purchases by the traffickers using shell corporations in Switzerland, Portugal, Panama, and other countries. This Machiavellian operation—CIA director William Casey allegedly called it "the ultimate covert operation"[31]—was in the hands of McFarlane and his successor Vice-Admiral John Poindexter, who turned it over to one of his staffers, the young and zealous Lieutenant Colonel Oliver North, an Annapolis graduate and Marine Corps officer who undoubtedly saw silver leaves turning to silver stars. A further secret initiative, apparently the result of North's fecund if somewhat twisted mind, involved obtaining voluntary donations for the Contras from private supporters in the United States and abroad, the latter donors including the king of Saudi Arabia, the sultan of Brunei and the Taiwanese government, a matter of many millions of dollars deposited in secret bank accounts controlled by the arms traffickers.

Several things were wrong with this mickeymouse operation. Supplying the Contras with money to buy arms placed the national security adviser and certain co-operating officials in covert sections of CIA and the Departments of State and Defense in direct contravention of the Boland Amendment despite the Administration's later invocation of "executive privilege" (which constitutionally does not exist); a joint Congressional investigating committee concluded that " . . . the common ingredients of the Iran and Contra policies were secrecy, deception and disdain for law."[32] It violated the U. S. government's own embargo on arms sales to Iran. It made a mockery of the U. S. government's formal pledge to other Western nations that ransom would not be paid to guerrilla terrorist kidnapers. In the case of Saudi Arabia, Brunei, and Taiwan, it committed the Reagan administration to quid pro quo future favors; more directly, it lent itself to blackmail—according to Oliver North, one of the middlemen had to be paid $4.5 million to shut him up once he was cut out of the operation.[33] It contradicted U. S. Department of State and Department of Defense policies not to mention common sense: there was no assurance that the Iranian government controlled the Hezbollah guerrilla terrorists, which indeed it did not— during negotiations two *more* hostages were seized. Adding insult to injury, the bulk of the large profits accruing from supplying arms to a potentially dangerous enemy went to a group of amoral arms-trafficking mercenaries whose secret contracts called for open-end profits with no questions asked.[34] Of the estimated $12 million of illicit profits made from the arms sales, one authority believes that only $4 million reached the Contras, the rest going to various middlemen and their cohorts; the same authority believes that the Contras received some $30 million from Saudi Arabia and less than $4 million from private U.S. sources.[35] Finally, what could not possibly have been kept secret was not kept secret. In October 1986, Sandinista forces shot down a CIA aircraft that was flying a resupply mission to Contra forces in Nicaragua. Revelation of the arms sales followed. The subsequent Irangate (aka Iran-amok, Iranagua) scandal summarily ended Poindexter and North's cowboy nonsense but it also severely damaged the Administration's international prestige and ripped further the already tattered fabric of the American people's belief in their government.[36] Subsequent investigations, arrests, trials, sentences, and retrials that finally freed the miscreants cost millions of dollars in addition to raising serious questions in many citizens' minds as to the impartiality of American justice and the seemingly unlimited power of the executive branch of government to make a mockery of the law. The fiasco widened in December 1993 when President George Bush saw fit to pardon two former senior CIA officials, former Secretary of Defense Caspar Weinberger and former Attorney General Edwin Meese. Fortunately for the record Special Prosecutor Lawrence Walsh persevered with his extensive Contra-Iran investigations, a detailed report of which was published in early 1994 to leave little doubt as to presidential culpability in this scandalous deceit. Still unsettled is the question of George Bush's denial of the operation while serving as Vice-President, which could lead to serious charges.

Although the Contras received $100 million in U.S. aid in 1986 and were said to number fifteen thousand, they remained a " . . . largely cross border raiding party,"[38] and nowhere succeeded in holding a town or even a village. By year's end, they numbered only about a thousand active combatants. Operations nonetheless continued and even expanded. One observer claimed that by spring of 1987, there had been 372 rebel attacks in more than two thirds of the country and that the guerrillas were increasing attacks on electric power grids, bridges, communications facilities, fuel depots, and roads.[39]

This was no mean achievement since Ortega's army numbered over sixty thousand with another fifty thousand in the reserves and local militias. Units were increasingly well equipped with Soviet-supplied weapons including assault helicopters and gunships, tanks, armored vehicles, and heavy artillery, not to mention an estimated thirty-five hundred Cuban advisers, many of them veterans of guerrilla warfare in Angola and elsewhere. Ortega's problem was the Vietnam syndrome; in short, the Sandinistas were trying to fight a counterinsurgency with quantitative rather than qualitative tactics, for example, by relocating 160,000 villagers in 1987 without providing adequate facilities or compensation. Both sides practiced atrocities, but in so doing a large army makes more enemies than a small guerrilla force. Terrain more often than not favored the guerrilla, particularly in areas where César Sandino's guerrillas had led U. S. Marines a merry chase over half a century earlier.

Here was a war that no one was winning, a war that was impoverishing hundreds of thousands of Nicaraguans while driving the Ortega government into bankruptcy. The war had also caused a political crisis in the United States, where the Reagan administration was determined to topple the Sandinistas by military force and where Administration opponents believed negotiations to be the answer, a stance shared by many other governments, which further believed that the solution lay in purely regional negotiations by the Contadora Group (Mexico, Colombia, Panama, and Venezuela) backed by the Contadora Support Group (Peru, Argentina, Brazil, and Uruguay) and by more active support of the Organization of American States (OAS) and the United Nations—even though this combined effort had not made much visible progress in the past.[40]

Ortega's Marxist government responded to internal and external pressures in 1987 by coming up with a new constitution generally " . . . acknowledged to contain most of the principles of representative democracy" and by promising national elections in 1990.[41] This was followed by a renewed Central American peace initiative that in August led to the signing of Esquipulas II (the revised Arias Plan first presented the previous February by Costa Rica's President Oscar Arias) by Costa Rica, El Salvador, Guatemala, Honduras, and Nicaragua. This was a bold and imaginative initiative that " . . . attempted to bring peace and stability to the region by taking the initiative away from all of the external actors—the U.S., the USSR, Cuba and the Contadora Group and Contadora Support Group countries."[42] A provision of this agreement called for a ninety-day cease-fire to commence in April 1988.

Although a hoped-for extension of the cease-fire did not materialize—the fault largely of the Contras—the spark had gone out of the war. As peace appeared to be possible, the already divisive command of the Contras split, with authority seemingly left to the hard-liners. But Contra fortunes further deteriorated when the U. S. Congress again shut off military aid. On the Sandinista side, the economy continued to plunge until inflation was totally out of control (33,000 per cent).[43] Ortega's austerity programs, never popular, were leading to increasing unrest and stringent demands by four opposition parties, which recently had formed the National Opposition Union (UNO). Such were the pressures exacerbated by a serious earthquake, by Soviet aid drying up, by the U.S. blockade, and by the eclipse of Cuban influence that in 1990 Ortega honored a constitutional commitment to hold internationally supervised elections, which nearly all observers expected the FSLN to win. Instead, Violeta Barrios de Chamorro (widow of the murdered publisher), the UNO coalition party's candidate openly backed and financed by Washington, emerged as the victor. A 90 per cent voter turnout gave UNO 55 per cent of the vote against 41 per cent for the Sandinistas.[44] To almost everyone's surprise, the Sandinistas turned over the government to the new administration (with the dangerous proviso that the Sandinistas retained control of army and police) and swore allegiance to Chamorro and to the constitution.

As in 1979, victory was somewhat Pyrrhic. The economy was in shambles. A good many Contras did not take kindly to the cease-fire and subsequent turning in of their weapons by an estimated twenty thousand members; nor were they pleased when Chamorro kept certain Sandinista leaders in office. Vital economic reforms were also contested both by right-wing parties and by FSLN-dominated labor unions, which led a series of major strikes and a threatened insurgency in summer of 1990, an ugly situation resolved only by army and police. Despite considerable financial aid from the United States and other international sources—over $500 million in 1991—the economy continued to decline, largely the result of a weak and corrupt reformist government unable to overcome obstructionist tactics from left and right extremist parties.

As of this writing, December 1993, the poverty level is estimated to stand at 70 percent, illiteracy at 50 percent.[45] Unemployment is an estimated 60 percent;[46] social, medical, and educational services remain meager: Nicaragua is now judged to be the second poorest country in the hemisphere (after Haiti).[47]

Promises of land grants and financial assistance to Contra and Sandinista veterans who turned in their arms have not been kept. In 1991 bands of armed Contras known as *recontros* appeared in northwestern Nicaragua to demand both what had been promised them as well as the dismissal of Sandinista senior army and police officials who, they believed, were responsible for their plight.[48] Government failure to act on their behalf was followed by the outbreak of sporadic guerrilla warfare in the countryside by some three thousand Contra and Sandinista veterans—the *revueltos*. According to one source, in the first half of 1993 there were over eighty-five skirmishes with more than one hundred dead.[49] In July a rebel force of about 150 former Sandinista soldiers invaded a town in the north to rob banks and raid police stations before being rounded up by a sizable army force. The following month a group of disgruntled Contras seized thirty-seven government officials as hostages to their demands for land; pro-Sandinistas in Managua responded by seizing some fifty members of the rightist National Opposition Union, including the country's vice-president, a crisis thankfully resolved without bloodshed.[50]

An even more disturbing event embarrassed Chamorro's beleaguered government prior to the hostage crisis. In late May an explosion in a Managua automotive repair shop revealed an enormous secret cache not only of guerrilla arms, including surface-to-air missiles, but a horde of documents that connected the arms to the supposedly disarmed FMLN guerrilla organization in El Salvador, besides suggesting that the holding could be traced to a group of international guerrilla terrorists that included the Spanish Basque ETA. Over three hundred passports, many of them blank, from twenty-one countries, were seized along with the names of company executives and 150 prominent Latin American families who were to be kidnaped for ransom.[51] Although Chamorro's defense minister, General Humberto Ortega, disclaimed any knowledge of the exposed arsenal, skeptics found this difficult to believe, particularly when FMLN informants in El Salvador pinpointed several more secret caches in Managua. Particularly skeptical was the U.S. Senate which cut off $90 million in aid pending further investigation of an alleged Sandinista connection with international guerrilla terrorists.[52]

In partial palliation Violeta Chamorro announced in October that army commander Ortega would be replaced in 1994. Such is her loose control of government that this does not mean he will go—nor would his departure necessarily mean the end of what appears to be a seriously burgeoning rebel guerrilla movement.

CHAPTER EIGHTY-TWO

1. International Institute for Strategic Studies, *Strategic Survey 1979*, 80.
2. Rice, 31. See also, International Institute for Strategic Studies, *Strategic Survey 1979*, 108–9.
3. Radu and Tismaneanu, 292–3.
4. Rice, 32.
5. Ibid., 34.
6. Radu and Tismaneanu, 299.
7. Rice, 34. See also, International Institute for Strategic Studies, *Strategic Survey 1979*, 109.
8. Rice, 35.
9. Radu and Tismaneanu, 299.
10. Ibid.
11. International Institute for Strategic Studies, *Strategic Survey 1979*, 109. See also, Rice, 35.
12. Radu and Tismaneanu, 299–300.
13. Rice, 35.

14. International Institute for Strategic Studies, *Strategic Survey 1979*, 112.
15. Ibid., 109.
16. Ibid., 110.
17. Dickey, 671.
18. Riding, 650–2.
19. International Institute for Strategic Studies, *Strategic Survey 1980–81*, 24.
20. International Institute for Strategic Studies, *Strategic Survey 1983–84*, 116–17. See also, Riding, 649–50; Dickey, 672.
21. Dickey, 668 ff.
22. Riding, 673.
23. Ibid., 649.
24. Treverton, 128–38.
25. International Institute for Strategic Studies, *Strategic Survey 1983–84*, 116–17.
26. Purcell, 119. See also, North, 234.
27. Treverton, 135.
28. International Institute for Strategic Studies, *Strategic Survey 1984–85*, 32.
29. Purcell, 119.
30. International Institute for Strategic Studies, *Strategic Survey 1985–86*, 202–3.
31. North, 13.
32. International Institute for Strategic Studies, *Strategic Survey 1987–88*, 74.
33. North, 281.
34. Ibid., 21.
35. Purcell, 119. See also, North, 265: Owing to an administrative error, North tells us, the sultan of Brunei's hefty donation was placed in the wrong secret Swiss bank account and was apparently not used; International Institute for Strategic Studies, *Strategic Survey 1986–87*, 76–9.
36. International Institute for Strategic Studies, *Strategic Survey 1986–87*, 76–9.
37. *Newsweek,* November 2, 1992.
38. Shultz, 363.
39. Purcell, 122.
40. Treverton, 128–38. See also, Purcell, 110–11, for the alleged defects of the proposed Contadora treaty.
41. Best, 101.
42. Moss, 421. See also, ibid., 427–8, for details of the plan; Purcell, 111–13.
43. International Institute for Strategic Studies, *Strategic Survey 1989–90*, 186.
44. Ibid., 1990–91, 123.
45. *International Herald Tribune,* June 2, 1993.
46. *Newsweek,* August 2, 1993.
47. *International Herald Tribune,* June 2, 1993.
48. Ibid., August 3–4, 1991.
49. *Newsweek,* August 2, 1993.
50. *The Independent* (U.K.), August 22, 24, 26, 1993.
51. *International Herald Tribune,* July 15, 1993.
52. Ibid. August 20, 1993.

CHAPTER 83

Birth of the Brazilian insurgency • Early terrorist guerrilla successes •
Carlos Marighela's death • Guerrilla reverses and final failure of the
insurgency • Birth of the Argentinian insurgency • Montoneros
terrorist guerrilla aims • Early guerrilla successes • "The dirty war"
• Final guerrilla defeat • The Chilean scene: Allende and Pinochet •
Soviet Russia and Cuba end aid to the insurgents • Pinochet's electoral
defeat

BRAZILIAN INSURGENTS ALSO chose urban guerrilla warfare
in attempting to overthrow a military dictatorship and establish a Marxist-Leninist form of government similar to that in Fidel Castro's Cuba. The nucleus of three guerrilla groups that emerged in the
late 1960s came from a split in the Brazilian Communist Party (PCB)
which, guided by Moscow, was pursuing a reformist as opposed to a
militant policy.

First to rebel was a long-time member of the PCB Politburo and a
veteran revolutionary, Carlos Marighela, who together with a few other
dissidents broke away in 1967 to establish the National Liberation Action (ALN) in São Paulo. About the same time, another group of dissidents in the state of Rio Grande do Sul left the PCB to form the
October 8 Revolutionary Movement (MR-8)—named for the date that
Che Guevara was captured in Bolivia. Still other disillusioned members
of the PCB broke away to form the Revolutionary Brazilian Communist
Party (PCBR). Finally, a group of retired left-wing army officers
emerged in the Revolutionary People's Vanguard (VPR) whose leader
was Carlos Lamarca.[1]

The common denominator of these groups was revolutionary violence as propounded by Carlos Marighela in *The Minimanual of Urban
Guerrilla Warfare*. In 1968, the ALN opened a guerrilla terrorist campaign of robberies, kidnapings, and assassinations which the MR-8 and
PCBR groups quickly emulated. After such successes as the 1969 kid-

naping of a U.S. ambassador (released in exchange for fifteen political prisoners and publication of a guerrilla manifesto), it ran into serious trouble despite an impressive growth in members. A police ambush in 1969 eliminated its most aggressive leader, Carlos Marighela, as his group was carrying out a bank robbery. In 1970, the group kidnaped the German and Swiss ambassadors (released in exchange for forty and seventy prisoners respectively),[2] but Marighela's successor and several other leaders were killed. By 1972, the ALN was no longer a cohesive force although about fifty guerrilla terrorists remained active.[3]

MR-8 was considerably smaller than the ALN—perhaps less than a hundred members and about the same number of sympathizers—and it too soon came on hard times. Like the ALN, it confined itself to urban guerrilla terrorism and at times successfully worked with ALN guerrillas in robbing banks and in kidnapings. It suffered from slack security, however, and in 1969 was all but knocked out by the arrests of a large number of its members. It revived in the early 1980s as an adjunct to the PCB but its operations allegedly were hamstrung by PCB orthodoxy.[4]

The PCBR was the best survivor. Backed by Cuba, it enjoyed significant growth, but like the other groups it never did establish a solid base of operations (a major difficulty faced by most urban guerrilla terrorist organizations). After dimming out in the late 1970s, it revived in the 1980s and continues active today.[5]

The VPR suffered the ALN's fate when its leader Carlos Lamarca was killed in a shootout in 1971 from which the organization never recovered.[6]

The reason for the over-all failure of the Brazilian insurgent movement is twofold. First was the error in striking out against the establishment without being able to win the average citizen's support—the same error made by the Tupamoros in Uruguay. Government excesses, particularly the highly publicized accusations of torture, won the guerrillas some sympathy, but such were guerrilla excesses that in the end the average citizen was not sorry to see them go. Second was their failure to take the revolution to the countryside, to establish what Régis Debray called a *foco*—a secure base from which to expand revolution by converting Marshal Lyautey's *tache d'huile* concept to revolutionary goals. Marighela recognized this failure. As Michael Radu wrote:

> ... Early in 1969 ... he tried to work out a coherent interpretation of the relation between the urban and rural guerrilla, considering that the success of each type of strategy depended on the effectiveness of the other ... [but] "The whole urban struggle, whether on the guerrilla or mass-movement front, must always be seen as tactical struggle ... the decisive struggle will be in the rural area."[7]

It followed that guerrilla terrorism was an integral part of guerrilla warfare, "an arm the revolutionary can never relinquish."[8]

So the urbanists came and went, leaving the usual carnage of corpses and unrequited hopes for a more just social order behind them. Dreary military government followed dreary military government with corruption endemic at all levels. But then in 1990 along came a charismatic provincial governor named Fernando Collor de Mello, who in the first direct elections in twenty-nine years was overwhelmingly elected president on a reform ticket with a promise to end corruption and reduce a whopping inflation.

He started well enough by introducing an ambitious program designed to bring inflation under control, reduce public spending, and spur economic growth. Alas, the program was stillborn. He did not revitalize the economy nor did he do much about inflation, nor did he satisfactorily tackle such glaring social evils exemplified in a federal police report in Brasília which stated that

> . . . a total 4,611 children and adolescents had, it was estimated, been killed over the last three years and thousands more raped, abused, and sold into prostitution. Military personnel were reliably reported to have been implicated in the killings.[9]

What Collor did do was to turn his back on his promises and open his pocket to a massive corruption scheme amounting to an alleged $300 million, of which he is believed to have received a very satisfactory chunk. And for which, after months of roiling Brazilian politics, he was impeached, removed from office, and subsequently indicted on several charges before finally resigning in disgrace.

To everyone's relief, the army showed no inclination to take over government. In winning the day at least temporarily, Brazilian democracy can be congratulated—but only if it begins to eliminate the massive social inequities that inspired Marighella and his guerrillas to stop talking and start shooting.

Unusual violence erupted in Argentina with the assassination in 1970 of a former president of the country. This was the work of the Montoneros Perónista Movement (MPM), an urban guerrilla terrorist group whose leader was a professional terrorist, twenty-two-year-old Mario Firmenich. The following year, the Montoneros and another guerrilla group, the People's Revolutionary Army (ERP), threw down the urban guerrilla gauntlet by a series of robberies and kidnapings that soon turned to indiscriminate murders answered in kind by security forces and private murder squads to begin a terrifying decade still referred to in Buenos Aires as "the dirty war."[10]

The Montoneros, so named in an attempt " . . . to identify with the Andean pastoral hill-rebels in the nineteenth century,"[11] derived from the left-wing faction of the earlier Perónist regime. Their aim was to achieve revolution by violence, not alone in Argentina but throughout Latin America. Kidnapings in 1971 soon became big business conducted under the guise of humanitarian good works such as feeding and clothing the poor. Enormous ransoms were paid by international companies for the return of their executives; other companies paid huge ransoms for "protection" Mafia-style.[12] Guerrilla activities were temporarily dampened in 1973 with the return to power of the former exiled president, Juan Domingo Perón, who soon outlawed the ERP. Perón's death a year later brought his widow, Isabel Perón, to power. Although the Montoneros, who claimed a large union membership, helped her to be elected, she soon turned on them, a mistake in that her weak and vacillating government could not cope with this now-powerful movement:[13] some five thousand hard-core guerrillas; fifteen thousand active sympathizers;[14] several million dollars in funds; and close connections with Cuba and with several Latin American revolutionary movements and, eventually, with the PLO, the Spanish Socialist Party (PSOE), the Spanish Communist Party (PCE), Sweden's Social Democrats, and with several African revolutionary movements.[15]

The ERP evolved from Trotskyite extreme left-wingers of the Perónist regime. The movement was led initially by Mario Roberto Santucho, who in 1972 was forced into exile.[16] Led by Enrique Haroldo Gorriarán Marle, the ERP accumulated a war chest estimated at $30 million by spring of 1974, mostly from ransoms of kidnaped victims, a figure that may have tripled in 1975 when an Argentinian company allegedly paid $60 million for the release of three executives.[17] Despite the ban imposed by Perón, the ERP grew to perhaps three thousand active members and several thousand supporters. In 1975, it attempted to open a rural insurgency in Tucumán province, a two-year effort finally suppressed by security forces. Meanwhile, the ERP had attracted guerrilla refugees from failed insurgencies in Uruguay, Bolivia, and Chile. It now put up $5 million to form remnant rebel movements in those countries into an international revolutionary junta which would spread war to the countryside,[18] and in addition would send hit teams to assassinate Latin American diplomats in European embassies.[19]

In the next two years, urban guerrilla warfare turned many parts of the beautiful city of Buenos Aires into a murderous hell of terrorists waging all-out war with rightist death squads, police, and army. " . . . Right there," an Argentinian friend told me some years later, "right there I watched my best friend jumped by three men and thrown into a car—we never saw him again."

Failure of security forces to best ERP terrorists brought a military coup in 1976 and a repression that claimed an estimated ten thousand lives of guerrillas and "suspects"—or too often innocent civilians who failed to get out of the way of war. Brutal as it was, the counterinsurgency campaign spelled an end to organized guerrilla insurgency—at least to the present day.

Since its foundation in 1922, the Communist Party of Chile (PCCh) played an integral role in the political turbulence that long has characterized this elongated coastal nation of over twelve million people. After a good many ups and downs, the leftist heyday arrived in 1970 when the Popular Unity coalition candidate Salvador Allende Gossens was elected president in what most observers deemed to be a fair election. Trouble was: Allende was a dedicated Marxist Socialist (a founding member of the Chilean Socialist Party) burdened with an opposition-controlled congress. Although he nationalized a large number of companies and reduced unemployment, he failed to control inflation nor did he implement other promised reforms. His problems ended in 1973, courtesy of a military coup strongly supported if not planned by the CIA, during which he was killed. General Augusto Pinochet Ugarte was installed as dictator, a position he retained until 1989.

The Pinochet dictatorship proscribed the Communist and Socialist parties. Luis Corvalán, secretary-general of the PCCh, was jailed along with thousands of his fellows and eventually exiled. Largely owing to his efforts, the PCCh revived and in 1980 officially adopted a policy of violence to carry out its revolutionary strategy.

This decision was warmly greeted by members of the Movement of the Revolutionary Left (MIR), which had come to life in 1965 under the leadership of Dr. Miguel Enríquez, " . . . a fervent admirer of Fidel Castro and a supporter of the Cuban strategy of subversion in Latin America."[20] Violence was a basic tenet of this large revolutionary group, " . . . one of the main instigators of the unrest and antidemocratic actions that led to the military counter-reaction in 1973."[21] Enríquez was killed by a police raid in 1974. His replacement, Arturo Villavella, a Marxist fanatic, was captured in the same year, exiled after three years in jail, returned to Chile, and was killed in 1983. He was replaced by a left-wing extremist, the nephew of Salvador Allende, Andrés Pascal Allende, whose continuing commitment to terrorism alienated most of the more moderate political parties. The MIR never fully recovered from Pinochet's crackdown and has been limited to isolated guerrilla terrorist actions in the major cities, sometimes in conjunction with the FPMR.

Both the PCCh (FPMR) and MIR were generously supported by voluntary (and involuntary) contributions and by foreign sympathizers, notably Soviet Russia and Cuba. In 1986, Chilean security forces stumbled on an incredible find, a PCCh guerrilla camp disguised as a coastal fishing village and featuring a small airstrip, advanced communications, underground classrooms and an armory of over three thousand rifles, Soviet-made rocket launchers, American-made anti-tank weapons, two tons of TNT, and quantities of plastic explosives.[22]

MIR probably would have continued to re-establish itself but for improved counterinsurgency operations, along with Pinochet's defeat in the 1989 elections and, most important, the demise of the Soviet Union, the near bankruptcy of Cuba, and the end of insurgencies in Nicaragua and El Salvador.

CHAPTER EIGHTY-THREE

1. Radu and Tismaneanu, 115–27.
2. Halperin, 14.
3. Radu and Tismaneanu, 118. See also, Halperin, 8–9.
4. Radu and Tismaneanu, 123.
5. Ibid., 124.
6. Ibid., 127.
7. Ibid., 117.
8. Ibid.
9. *Annual Register of World Events 1991*, 70.
10. Clutterbuck, *Living with Terrorism*, 44–50, for details of the kidnapings.
11. Radu and Tismaneanu, 95.
12. Clutterbuck, *Living with Terrorism*, 45.
13. Pimlott, 125–7.
14. Radu and Tismaneanu, 94. See also, Halperin, 9.
15. Radu and Tismaneanu, 99.
16. Ibid., 102.
17. Halperin, 17.
18. Clutterbuck, *Living with Terrorism*, 45.
19. Laqueur, *Terrorism*, 187.
20. Radu and Tismaneanu, 140.
21. Ibid.
22. Ibid., 136.

CHAPTER 84

The background of revolution in El Salvador • The National Coalition Party (PCN) in power • José Napoleón Duarte's opposition party, the Democratic Nationalist Organization (ORDEN) • War with Honduras • Rise of the Communist guerrilla movement, the Farabundo Martí Popular Forces of Liberation (FPL) • The shooting starts • Guerrilla techniques and tactics • Formation of the Farabundo Martí National Liberation Front (FMLN) • Guerrilla setbacks and disunity • Duarte's new government • Rise of Roberto d'Aubuisson Arrieta's ultra-right party, the National Republican Alliance (ARENA) • ORDEN's right-wing death squads • U.S. military and economic aid to Duarte's junta • Soviet, Cuban and other external aid to the insurgents • Military stalemate • Insurgents lose external aid • The Arias peace plan • The United Nations peace offensive • The war ends • The United Nations peacekeeping force • The cost • Continuing government repression • The UN Truth Commission • President Cristiani objects • The secret FMLN arms cache in Nicaragua • The death squads strike again • Incriminating U.S. intelligence files • The last chapter is not yet written

... El Salvador is at war because it is one of the sickest societies in Latin America. Its archaic social structure remains basically colonial. Despite some efforts at change, a tiny urban elite and dominating cast of army officers essentially rule, but do not effectively govern, an illiterate, disease-ridden and frustrated majority of peasants and urban slum-dwellers. Order is often imposed by violence; there is not now, nor has there ever been, a just legal system. The rebels, in short, have had ample cause to lead a revolution.

JAMES LEMOYNE, 1989[1]

As with other Latin American countries, tiny El Salvador's five million people look back on a long history of rebellion, first from Spanish rule, then from the rule of poverty and hopelessness imposed by a small elite which owned 60 percent of the arable land and which controlled what was virtually a private army. Protest movements occasionally sprung up during the nineteenth and early twentieth centuries only to be suppressed by a harsh succession of authoritarian, usually military, governments, but not until 1932 did extreme violence begin to become a way of life.

In 1932, the secretary-general of the small Communist Party (PCES), Augustín Farabundo Martí, led a peasant insurrection put down by the summary execution of ten thousand people—the *matanza* (slaughter) never to be forgotten by the little people. More military governments followed, the dust settling in 1961 when a coup put Lieutenant Colonel Adalberto Rivera of the National Conciliation Party (PCN) in power. Rivera's six-year rule was repressive enough but he did improve the country's economy and increase its export trade. Rivera's administration saw the rise of the opposing Christian Democratic Party (PDC) whose candidate, José Napoleón Duarte, was elected mayor of the capital, San Salvador. Rivera attempted to counter the PDC and a growing Communist opposition by forming the Democratic Nationalist Organization (ORDEN)—" . . . a large, secretive paramilitary organization"[2] whose death squads ruthlessly attempted to eliminate *any* opposition.

Rivera's successor, Colonel Fidel Sánchez Hernández, ran into economic difficulties brought on by the fall of cotton and coffee prices and by the outbreak of a brief war with Honduras in mid-1969, a senseless dispute provoked by Salvador accusing Honduras of a genocidal policy toward some three hundred thousand mostly illegal immigrant Salvadoran workers in Honduras.[3] After several thousand lives were lost and a great deal of money spent, the shooting ended in a precarious truce.

At this time, the secretary-general of El Salvador's Communist Party, Salvador Cayetano Carpio, tried to persuade the party to open a Maoist-style protracted revolution, an effort that caused his expulsion from the party. Undeterred, Cayetano Carpio and a small band of guerrillas, after training in Cuba, Vietnam, and elsewhere, returned to El Salvador to establish the country's first guerrilla organization, the Farabundo Martí Popular Forces of Liberation (FPL), which commenced a series of guerrilla terrorist actions in San Salvador and soon grew in numbers and operation to form a formidable threat to the government.

In 1972, a patently fraudulent election, in which the coalition party's candidate, José Napoleón Duarte, made an unsuccessful challenge, placed Colonel Arturo Molino of the PCN in office. A postelection coup attempt by Duarte having failed, he was arrested and exiled to Venezuela.

Molina's regime was a disaster as was that of his PCN successor, General Carlos Humberto Romero, president from 1977 to 1979. Instead of trying to come to terms with rising opposition, the ruling junta was determined to eliminate it. Growing excesses committed by police, soldiers, and death squads of off-duty right-wing policemen and soldiers—in 1975, a dozen protesting students were shot to death—caused even Roman Catholic priests to defy superiors and become political activists, in some instances joining Cayetano Carpio's and other burgeoning guerrilla movements whose members, actively operating in cities and the countryside, were frequently at odds with each other as had happened in Nicaragua.[4]

The PCES, pressed by the Soviet Union, meanwhile had reversed course and in 1979 accepted armed struggle as the only means to achieve its revolutionary ends—as Carpio had insisted all along. At Fidel Castro's urging, its secretary-general, Schafik Jorge Handal, now turned to the task of uniting all revolutionary groups into one central organization.

At this time, five major guerrilla groups were operating in El Salvador: the PCES with some two thousand members, some of them guerrilla fighters soon to be formed into the Armed Forces of Liberation (FAL); Cayetano Carpio's FPL, which was allied with the Popular Revolutionary Block (BPR), a mass organization with perhaps fifty to eighty thousand members; Joaquín Villalobos' People's Revolutionary Army (ERP), a splinter group from the PCES which had grown to some two thousand guerrilla fighters; Fernan Cienfuegos' Armed Forces of National Resistance (FARN), a splinter group from the ERP which claimed one hundred thousand supporters; and Robert Roca's (probably an alias) Revolutionary Party of Central American Workers (PRTC) with only a few hundred activist, mostly urban, guerrilla terrorists.[5]

Disparate as were these groups, they shared a great many things in common. Semantics aside, their basic goal was to impose a Communist government on El Salvador along the lines of Castro's Cuba, although at least one leader, ERP's Villalobos, saw victory in El Salvador as a springboard to a Communist Central America.[6] All agreed that the only way to make the revolution succeed was by violence, be it in the cities or in the countryside.

To finance their operations, the groups depended initially on the traditional means of bank robberies and kidnapings for ransom, but such are the expenses of revolution that all groups were soon beholden to foreign countries which either donated or sold them arms and equipment: the Soviet bloc, Libya, the PLO, the Basque ETA, Cuba, Angola, Ethiopia, various Latin American revolutionary movements, and radical movements including those within the United States.

Marked similarities also showed in propaganda techniques, recruitment (middle-class intellectuals, students, workers, peasants), indoctrination (tough and merciless), organization, intelligence collection, use of front groups, security, training at home and abroad, the intransigent doctrinaire stance of leaders and lieutenants, and the preference of group leaders to conduct operations from Managua, capital of Nicaragua.

But grave differences existed in other spheres owing to capricious leaders, conflicting ideologies, incompatible strategy and tactics, cohesiveness, varying degrees of morale, discipline, security, and, most of all, operational effectiveness. Although a single revolutionary party, the Farabundo Martí National Liberation Front (FMLN) appeared in 1980, its guerrilla components were not going to change their ways even though urged to do so by moderates of the political front, the Democratic Revolutionary Front (FDR). Had they done so, there might well have been a coalition or even a Communist government in El Salvador today.

When Romero's government fell to a military coup by a short-lived junta of younger reformist officers, José Napoleón Duarte returned from exile to merge his Christian Democrats (PDC) with a new ruling junta dominated by senior generals, the majority of whom held no interest in promulgating what the PDC ostensibly championed—social and economic reforms, elimination of human rights abuses, negotiations with rebel leaders. The day after Duarte joined the PDC to the junta, seven PDC leaders left the party, declaring that a " . . . program of reform with repression runs contrary to the fundamentals of the Christian Democrats."[7] Although Duarte pushed through a land reform bill that initially " . . . redistributed about 20 percent of El Salvador's arable land," owing to right-wing obstructionism " . . . it had little of the sweeping social and political effect for which it was designed."[8] That did not deter the Carter administration, upset by the Sandinista victory in Nicaragua, from sending a team of U.S. military advisers to El Salvador and from preparing to resume "nonlethal" military aid which it had suspended in 1977.[9]

Violence occasioned by military, police, ORDEN, and guerrilla excesses was now routine. In early 1980, a right-wing death squad murdered powerful critic Archbishop Oscar Arnulfo Romero while he was saying mass. In June, soldiers stormed the National University, a left-wing stronghold, killed at least fifty students, and permanently closed the institution. Later in the year, six opposition party leaders were kidnaped and murdered and four Roman Catholic nuns, U.S. citizens, were murdered by right-wing goons (which caused a brief suspension of U.S. aid). Leftist terrorists countered with kidnapings and civil demonstrations, which led to more killings. By year's end, the fighting in cities and countryside would claim nine thousand lives in what was becoming all-out civil war,[10] recognized as such by the Carter administration which in October sent more U.S. military advisers.

Recruits meanwhile flocked to guerrilla banners, but the new umbrella revolutionary party, the FMLN, could not hold off the erosion of separatism. There was no central guerrilla command. The major guerrilla forces continued to run their own wars, some striking in the cities, some in rural areas, some in both, and they were also divided on the subject of protracted war versus negotiated peace.[11] Throughout 1980, these groups variously ambushed rural army units, raided garrisons to steal weapons and ammunition, and blew up roads and bridges both to disrupt army communications and to prevent export crops from getting to market. During this period, Nicaragua's Sandinistas were believed to be smuggling Russian- and Cuban-supplied arms to Salvadoran rebels via Honduras, though not in the quantities claimed by either San Salvador or Washington.

Early in 1981, the guerrillas opened a "final offensive" in the north and called for a general strike to bring down the government, a move correctly condemned by Cayetano Carpio as premature. This Salvadoran version of the Vietnam Tet offensive failed. The army sent guerrilla forces reeling, no major strike developed, and the insurgents, at that time particularly powerful in the cities, lost many of their urban bases and were forced to retreat to mountainous areas for temporary sanctuary. It is interesting to note that " . . . the United States sent no arms to El Salvador between 1977 and 1981; the San Salvador military thus defeated the guerrilla offensive of January 1981 *without* significant US assistance."[12]

The growing guerrilla threat taken with Romero and the PDC's fall from power had brought a hardening of the right that swung landowners and business executives to the support of Major Roberto d'Aubuisson Arrieta's ultra-right party, the National Republican Alliance

(ARENA). In early 1981, the lame-duck Carter administration authorized $5 million worth of military equipment to the junta.[13] The new Reagan administration, apparently having learned nothing from Vietnam and convinced that it could eliminate what it called the Cuban-Russian-inspired insurgency within a few months, chose to attempt to settle a social revolution by military power as opposed to seeking a political solution through regional diplomacy. Duarte's junta was given a total fifty-four U.S. military advisers who were to reorganize, train, and equip the Salvadoran military forces: $25 million worth of military aid was granted to supply modern weapons including a squadron of A-37 fighter planes; simultaneously, fifteen hundred officers and men were being trained at United States camps, a figure that would rise to nine thousand by 1983 and would result in doubling the size of an already inflated officer corps and more atrocities such as the massacre by the new Atlactl Battalion of a reported eight hundred people including forty-two children in a remote village.[14]

The refurbished Salvadoran army, largely trained in conventional warfare by U.S. advisers, more and more resembled the laggard South Vietnam ARVN of the sixties and seventies, including impossibly corrupt commanders, low morale, a rising desertion rate, and severe repressive measures against anyone suspected of aiding the insurgents. So blatant were human rights abuses that the U. S. Congress passed a law under which President Reagan had to certify that the Salvadoran government was making satisfactory progress in eliminating human rights abuses before military aid was provided. Reagan's grudging compliance was academic, his favorable pronouncements virtually meaningless; in late 1983, he ended certification by vetoing a bill that called for its continuation.

In 1982, the ultra-rightist Roberto d'Aubuisson was elected president of a constituent assembly whose members belonged predominantly to the right wing. At Washington's insistence, a conservative lawyer, Alvaro Magaña, was appointed interim president of the country while the assembly prepared a new constitution. During this period, Washington's hopes for a quick military victory were dashed by the continuing poor performance of the Salvadoran army. The guerrillas, on the other hand, had recovered in large part from the humiliating defeat of their 1981 "final offensive." In early 1982, a successful raid by an eight-man ERP guerrilla team trained in Cuba knocked out most of the fledgling air force (including several U.S.-supplied helicopters) at Ilopango Air Base. Attacks on isolated army garrisons increased to the extent that in 1983 " . . . the guerrillas could make credible claims that most of their weapons, including even mortars and artillery pieces, came from the United States by way of captured government troops."[15] Once emerged from mountain sanctuaries, the insurgents had begun carrying the revolutionary message to rural peasant areas, which increasingly fell under their control as they continued to ambush and attack government troops and to sabotage the infrastructure by blowing up roads, bridges and power lines, and burning cotton, coffee and sugar crops and factories. Simultaneously, the FMLN infiltrated San Salvador and other cities, where urban guerrilla terrorists functioned as the guerrilla equivalent of ORDEN's feared death squads. Yet such was the lack of the Communist political appeal that in many areas the guerrillas were suffered rather than enjoyed. In 1983, it was evident that a military stalemate existed, with some observers giving the edge to the insurgents.[16]

Insurgent morale suffered a major setback when Fidel Castro, as one result of the successful U.S. invasion of Grenada in October 1983, prudently announced that his client countries could not count on military assistance from Cuba in case they were attacked by the United States. Equally upsetting were the 1984 spring elections which brought a moderate Christian Democrat government led by José Napoleón Duarte to power and with that another hefty increase in U.S. military aid. A major split also occurred in guerrilla ranks. Salvador Cayetano Carpio, leader of the large FPL guerrilla force, had always insisted on a policy of "protracted war." When his second-in-command and former mistress, Mélida Anaya (Commandante Ana María), followed Cuban and Nicaraguan wishes in opting for a more conciliatory negotiating policy, Cayetano Carpio had her murdered and soon after committed suicide. The cause was further damaged when one of Cayetano Carpio's urban groups killed a U.S. naval officer, as well as by the highly publicized murder of thirty captured soldiers by his guerrillas.[17]

These and other guerrilla aberrations hindered but did not halt operations. One experienced observer noted that at year's end, " . . . the Salvadoran army allowed the most modern U.S. designed garrison in the nation to be overrun by a guerrilla force that it had not even known was in the area. Two days later, in the first hours of 1984, the rebels blew up the largest, and supposedly the most heavily guarded bridge in the country."[18]

More mobile tactics introduced by an army now numbering forty-two thousand equipped with helicopters and gunships seemed to favor government chances, but it soon became apparent that the army could not divorce itself from U.S.-imposed conventional strategy and tactics.[19] Although the guerrillas suffered heavy casualties, including those from aerial bombing attacks which also produced counterproductive civilian casualties, these were replaced and guerrilla strength remained at an estimated nine to eleven thousand.[20] Search-and-destroy missions inside guerrilla country in the northern and eastern areas accomplished little more than to cause the enemy to regroup in small units, which carried the war to the central and western areas and to the cities in the form of guerrilla terrorist attacks. To the government's consternation, the guerrillas retained sufficient mobility to mass their forces for large-scale attacks on military garrisons and other key targets. Since government forces failed to hold guerrilla areas, the guerrillas continued to be supported by large numbers of peasants who, often under duress, furnished money, food, and information.

Rebel tactics changed considerably in 1985. ERP leader Joaquín Villalobos despite opposition from subordinates ordered his guerrillas to plant large numbers of antipersonnel mines within rebel-controlled areas, a promiscuous tactic believed to have accounted for 70 per cent of army casualties (807 dead and 1,885 wounded from July 1984 to June 1985) and also civilian casualties, which of course cost the guerrillas some support.[21] Although the guerrillas continued on occasion to attack in strength, they relied increasingly on urban terrorism: an attack in June killed four U. S. Marines and some civilians; local mayors were kidnaped and some were killed; President Duarte's daughter was kidnaped and released in return for freeing a number of important prisoners. Government forces and secret death squads answered this offensive with the usual repressive measures—and the war went on.

Duarte was in trouble. His attempts at reform had been stymied in almost every direction by rightist opposition. Meetings with guerrilla leaders led to nothing. Inflation and unemployment stood at over 50 per cent; labor unrest continued to grow. This unsatisfactory situation continued into 1986 and 1987 with only slight changes, although a further increase in the size of the military forces and an additional $111.5 million in U.S. military aid allowed some pressure to be put on the insurgents. Hope for peace briefly revived in 1987 with the announcement of a regional peace plan worked out by Costa Rica's President Arias, but its eminently sensible provisions brought an immediate backlash from the right that was marked by significant gains of d'Aubuisson's ARENA party in the legislative and municipal elections in early 1988, as well as by a sharp increase in violence caused by renewed death squad murders and guerrilla car-bombings in the cities and greatly increased insurgent activity in the countryside.

The rebels also were in trouble. Soviet Premier Mikhail Gorbachev's diplomatic initiative designed to win great-power backing for a new Russia boded ill for further Soviet-Cuban support, already reduced to a trickle; nor did the Sandinistas seem any longer overly enthusiastic in fomenting Central American rebellions. Neither was their position inside El Salvador all that favorable. The top command remained split as to whether to continue protracted war or to join peace negotiations; almost no rational leader believed that a general uprising was possible or even that the insurgents could win a general election. This left a negotiated peace that was anathema to hard-liners convinced that such would sound the death knell for the revolution. There remained but one course. Documents captured by the army in 1988 revealed " . . . the most rigid, arid Marxist analysis imaginable and outline[d] a strategy of revolutionary war based on sabotage, terrorism, military attack and negotiation [as a tactic to win power]."[22] That was precisely the form of warfare that the Salvadoran army was least able to fight. As a later report " . . . by four senior U.S. Army officers notes: 'despite ESAF's [Salvadoran armed forces] improved battlefield skills, failure to develop a proper framework for counterinsurgency operations led to a deadlock. . . . As of April 1988, a tough, resourceful opponent remains in the field . . . showing no inclination to give up.' "[23]

This strategy was confirmed during the two months prior to the 1989 elections. With the victory of Alfredo Cristiani, a businessman and the ARENA candidate, the government swung further to the right although Cristiani himself headed a group of "moderates" within this ultra-right party. Cristiani's early measures, which included steep price increases in public transport and electricity, the return of banks to private ownership, unpopular modifications in the land reform program, and increased arrest of left-wing political activists, were guaranteed to insure continued violence. But Cristiani also named " . . . a national commission for contacts with the FMLN" that he hoped would lead to peace talks.[24]

After a summer of murder, preliminary talks between government and FMLN representatives in Mexico and Costa Rica produced little more than an airing of previous intransigent stands before being broken off during another violent orgy of fighting that led to intensive bombing of the poorer portions of San Salvador occupied by FMLN units, declaration of a state of siege, new anti-terror laws, mass arrests, and more death squad murders including the shocking killing of six Jesuit priests. By year's end, the fighting had claimed 401 guerrilla, 476 military, and over two thousand civilian lives and of course thousands more wounded and homeless.[25]

The standoff continued into 1990 but, as had happened earlier in Nicaragua, internal and external pressures weighed heavily on both sides. President Cristiani was in a very uncomfortable position. It was all too clear that his armed forces had acted impetuously and stupidly in the recent fighting, to the extent that some heretofore sympathetic members of the U. S. Congress now considered motions to curtail or even withdraw military aid. This antagonism softened somewhat when a colonel and eight soldiers were charged with murder for killing the Jesuit priests and when Cristiani fired his chief of the air force. At the end of January, he was received in the White House where President Bush reiterated his complete support although stressing the necessity of military and other reforms vital to any renewal of negotiations and indeed to continuing U.S. aid. All this, however, did not lessen the fact of a seemingly determined enemy bent on destroying a wavering state.

But this enemy was in an even more precarious position than Cristiani's government. Guerrilla units had suffered heavy casualties in the recent fighting, losses no longer easily replaced. The Soviet Union's disintegration taken with the newly elected Chamorro government in Nicaragua spelled a virtual end to external arms support (which the government would continue to receive). Recent security force round-ups had severely damaged urban guerrilla terrorist movements and had sent sympathetic left-wingers scurrying for cover and even escape from the country. Even the most intransigent FMLN leaders could not deny the movement's increasing isolation with concomitant loss of resources and morale.

These various factors combined to open the door to a new United Nations peace initiative in 1990. The UN had long been concerned with the war and with the various regional and U.S. initiatives that one after another had come to nothing. Backed now by Russia and the U.S., in April it brought Salvadoran Government and FMLN representatives to Geneva where each side agreed to accept further negotiations under UN auspices. The UN's goal was a cease-fire in September but that was not achieved owing to the old conundrum—which came first, the chicken-and-egg: the refusal of the military to accept reforms including a major reduction in size and the refusal of the FMLN to accept a cease-fire and give up its arms before those reforms were accomplished. The U. S. Congress showed its displeasure with the military's intransigence by voting to halve the current $85 million in military aid,[26] but the FMLN also earned displeasure by conducting a series of co-ordinated attacks against military targets (for the first time using surface-to-air missiles supplied by Nicaragua). Undeterred and strongly backed by other isthmus countries as well as by the U.S., Mexico, Venezuela, Colombia and Spain, the UN continued its paternal efforts. Legislative elections in March 1991 cost the ARENA party its majority and were taken as an encouraging sign of political moderation necessary if peace was ever to be achieved. Negotiations continued during summer of 1991 with each side moderating its demands and agreement reached on a number of sweeping constitutional and institutional (particularly military and police) reforms that had been major stumbling blocks in past talks. As had been the case in Vietnam, a great deal of fighting accompanied the negotiations, inspired in large part by the FMLN wanting to control more territory as chances for a cease-fire improved.

Nonetheless, negotiations proceeded with one issue settled here, another there. Although the year ended with no agreement, only two weeks later the last hurdles were overcome and a peace settlement signed. Under its terms the Cristiani government agreed to a series of human rights reforms including a purge of those members of the army and police forces who had involved themselves with the infamous death squads. The FMLN guerrillas, on their part, agreed to turn in all their arms and to form a legitimate political party. The agreement also included a very welcome cease-fire on the first day of February 1993 that was followed by the arrival of a United Nations peace-keeping force (ONUSAL) and pledges by Western nations to help rebuild the country.

Thus the end of a twelve-year guerrilla war that cost at least seventy-five thousand killed, perhaps a million refugees, billions of dollars in property damage and a shattered economy.

Well, not quite.

In September 1992 ONUSAL officials and those of the human rights group Americas Watch said that ". . . the end of the war has reduced human rights violations but that summary executions, arbitrary arrests and cruel treatment of police suspects continue."[27] As increasing evidence pointed to continuing army and police complicity in human rights violations, suspicious UN officials sponsored a three-member Truth Commission, which ". . . found the state and military responsible for most of the atrocities of El Salvador's civil war," and which recommended, among other things, "the dismissal of the nation's supreme court and the immediate dismissal of forty officers accused of human rights abuses."[28]

President Alfredo Cristiani, who had singularly failed to carry out the purge of the military and police agreed to in the peace terms, was still not to be moved. The report, in his words, did not fulfill "the desires of the majority of Salvadorans." Sounding like the leading members of the U.S. Republican Party after the fall of Vietnam, he went on: "That desire is to forgive and forget the painful past that has caused us so much suffering."[29]

The UN effort received another major setback in May, this time from the Farabundo Martí Liberation Front (FMLN). Only days after FMLN leaders told UN Secretary General Butros Butros-Ghali that all guerrilla arms had been destroyed or turned in, an accidental explosion in the Nicaraguan capital of Managua revealed an enormous arsenal of diverse FMLN weapons, probably hidden with the connivance of Nicaraguan Sandinista leaders. Butros' protests to the FMLN caused voluntary informants to pinpoint fifteen more arsenals in Managua, after which embarrassed FMLN leader Schafik Jorge Handal insisted that *now* all arms had been destroyed.[30]

Cristiani's subsequent attempts to dampen criticism by announcing the relief of his defense minister General René Emilio Ponce—the person said to have ordered the murder in 1989 of six Jesuit priests—failed to satisfy disgruntled liberal critics while infuriating extreme rightists. In November rightist death squads assassinated two prominent FMLN party leaders, killings at once denounced by Cristiani, who promised "serious investigations."[31]

The Cristiani government, facing elections in March 1994, suffered another blow in November when the U.S. government released twelve thousand heretofore secret documents that both confirmed and enlarged the unpalatable facts of Salvadoran death squad activities from the early 1980s onward, activities known to but overlooked by both the Reagan and Bush administrations. They also confirmed the participation of some of Cristiani's current political colleagues, including officeholders, in these activities.[32]

As of this writing, December 1993, the U.S. Congress is pressing the Clinton administration to force the release of still more pertinent documents that undoubtedly will greatly embarrass the Cristiani government (not to mention Messrs. Reagan and Bush), but just may cause it to get serious about implementing promised reforms before the March elections. Sadly enough, a great deal more violence will undoubtedly occur. As Jorge Castañeda has pointed out in his informative book *Utopia Unarmed*, El Salvador is one of the Latin American countries where a last chapter is yet to be written.[33]

CHAPTER EIGHTY-FOUR

1. LeMoyne, 106–7.
2. *Encyclopaedia Britannica,* 1991, Vol. 15, 694.
3. International Institute for Strategic Studies, *Strategic Survey 1968,* 55 ff.
4. Rice, 106. See also, Thomas Anderson; LeMoyne.
5. Radu and Tismaneanu, 187–8, 189, 194, 205, 220–1, 228–9.
6. Ibid., 219.
7. Bonner, xvi.
8. Dickey, 680.
9. Bonner, xv.
10. International Institute for Strategic Studies, *Strategic Survey 1980–81,* 22–7.
11. Riding, 645–6.
12. Treverton, 137.
13. International Institute for Strategic Studies, *Strategic Survey 1980–81,* 24.
14. *Newsweek,* November 2, 1992.
15. Dickey, 677.
16. Gleijeses, 1060–61.
17. Dickey, 681–2.
18. Ibid., 683.
19. Shultz, 362.
20. International Institute for Strategic Studies, *Strategic Survey 1984–85,* 198.
21. Ibid, *Strategic Survey 1985–86,* 198. See also, Radu and Tismaneanu, 214.
22. LeMoyne, 116.
23. Shultz, 362.
24. International Institute for Strategic Studies, *Strategic Survey 1989–90,* 190.
25. Ibid., 191.
26. *International Herald Tribune,* June 26, 1991.
27. *The Independent* (U.K.), September 3, 1992.
28. *International Herald Tribune,* March 20, 1993.

29. Ibid., March 20, 1993.
30. *Newsweek*, July 26, 1993. See also, *International Herald Tribune*, November 9, 1993.
31. *International Herald Tribune*, November 9, 1993.
32. Ibid., November 10, 1993.
33. Castañeda.

CHAPTER 85

Spread of Communist insurgency in Colombia • Divergent terrorist guerrilla groups • Varying guerrilla fortunes • The drug equation • Government counterinsurgency measures • The guerrillas strike back • The government declares war on the drug-guerrilla alliance • Cartel king Pablo Escobar Gaviría's imprisonment and escape • Escobar's death • Continuing guerrilla activity • Security forces and human rights abuses • Turbulent Peruvian politics • Emergence of terrorist guerrilla groups in the 1960s • Governmental disasters • Rise of Abimael Guzmán Reynoso's terrorist guerrilla party, Sendero Luminoso (SL), or Shining Path • The guerrilla alliance with the cocaine cartels • Guzmán's gains • Peru's economic decline • The refugee problem • Enter President Alberto Fujimori • Fujimori cleans the government's house • Guzmán goes to jail • Guzmán's about-face • The SL's decline • Remaining guerrilla strength • The task ahead

SPURRED BY economic dissatisfaction and the stunning success of Fidel Castro's revolution, a flurry of guerrilla groups emerged in Colombia in the 1960s. The first group, the National Liberation Army (ELN), was formed by dissident young members of the Colombian Communist Party (PCC) in 1964. Operating primarily in rural northeastern Colombia and financed by robberies, kidnapings, voluntary contributions, extortions and " . . . continual and substantial report from Cuba,"[1] it grew to a few hundred active guerrillas by the late 1960s.

A second group, the Revolutionary Armed Forces of Colombia (FARC), appeared in 1966 as the militant branch of the PCC. Initially it was a rural movement of a few hundred peasants led by a thirty-six-year-old peasant activist Pedro Antonio María (aka Manuel Marulanda Vélez). Based mainly in the south and funded similarly as the ELN, it continued to grow during the 1960s though failing to establish Régis Debray's concept of a revolutionary *foco,* that is a liberated area secure from the intrusion of security forces. A third guerrilla group, the People's Liberation Army (EPL), was formed in 1967 as the militant arm of a splinter Communist Party, the Communist Party of Colombia-Marxist-Leninist (PCC-ML), which pledged fealty to Chinese communism and was supported in part by China. It remained small, perhaps 250 guerrillas, and enjoyed only limited success in its Maoist-inspired insurgency in the provinces north-northwest of Medellín. A fourth group, the 19 of April Movement (M-19) appeared in southern Colombia only in 1974.[2] Aided by the now-standard means of financing— robberies, kidnapings, voluntary contributions, extortion, aid from Cuba, and, increasingly, payments from drug traffickers—M-19 grew rapidly to number perhaps five thousand members within a few years.

These divergent groups might have operated for years without gaining undue prominence and strength had it not been for the multibillion-dollar traffic in a drug called cocaine. Cocaine has been around for a long time—in the 1890s it was openly sold by Parke Davis in the United States and it has always been a suspected ingredient of Coca-Cola[3]— but it only started to become big business when markets expanded in Western nations beginning in the late 1960s and 1970s (a residue of the Vietnam War in the case of the United States). Cocaine comes from the humble coca leaf, of which tons are grown and processed into coca paste in remote areas of Peru, Bolivia, and Colombia for refining into cocaine and marketing by two Colombian cartels, the Cali cartel some 150 miles southwest of Bogotá and the Medellín cartel about the same distance to the northwest. As demand in the United States increased, so did cultivation. In 1981, Colombian peasants produced twenty-five hundred tons; in 1985 about eighteen thousand tons. In 1985, " . . . the street value of cocaine exported from Colombia to the U.S.A. was estimated to be $80 billion a year."[4]

This pernicious industry affected Colombian guerrilla groups in several ways. During the 1970s, guerrilla leaders homed in on peasant coca growers and in Mafia style demanded 10 per cent of crop sales " . . . in exchange for 'protection' from the police and military."[5] For the FARC, this eventually brought in about $40 million a year. Another vast sum came from the cartels, which hired guerrillas to protect refinery operations from army and police raids. It was primarily drug money that enabled M-19 to grow so rapidly and expand northward, setting up guerrilla terrorist groups in the principal cities. These groups soon sold their services to the drug barons in the form of hit operations against dangerous opponents in government, the judiciary, police, and army.

It was not all easy going for the guerrillas. The Colombian police and army contained a great many well-trained men loyal to the government. As these organizations received advisers and improved equipment such as helicopters, mainly from the United States, their operations improved. By 1979, ten of the ELN's top leaders had been killed. If in the same year M-19 guerrillas made headlines by tunneling into a Bogotá armory to seize nearly six thousand weapons,[6] an ensuing army operation captured an estimated hundred of its members. In 1984, a raid on a cocaine-refining complex netted the government nearly fourteen tons of cocaine (street value $1.2 billion).[7] Another challenge came from disgruntled policemen and soldiers who formed death squads which mercilessly eliminated anyone even suspected of left-wing affiliations (a campaign all too familiar to other Latin American governments which reaped international opprobrium and in some cases either a decrease or a cutoff in aid as a result). The groups also suffered from internal dissension and from failure to establish secure liberated areas essential for a successful rural insurgency.

In spring of 1984, these and other factors resulted in President Belisario Betancur Cuartas' government bringing about a truce with M-19, EPL, and FARC (the diehard ELN refused to deal). It soon broke down and violence increased. In 1985, cartel leaders had the minister of justice murdered. Betancur declared a state of siege—detention of terrorists without bail, trial by military courts, even possible extradition to the United States for trial.[8] A few months later, M-19 terrorists stormed the Palace of Justice in Bogotá, undoubtedly upon order of the cartels. The ensuing shoot-out cost about a hundred lives including those of the president of the Supreme Court, several of his justices, and all of the terrorists, among whom were a number of important leaders.

This was the mess inherited by the new president, Virgilio Barco Vargas, in 1986. At first the guerrillas, urban and rural, had things their own way, as did the drug barons. The ELN had been hurt but it was still strong and rich enough to carry out several urban and rural operations culminating in 1986 when it opened a campaign to drive foreign oil companies out of northeastern Colombia, mainly by sabotage and raids on installations. In time this would total $50 million in damages and seriously threaten oil production in Colombia and Venezuela.[9] M-19 was also hurt but still managed to establish and maintain contacts with revolutionary groups in Peru, Ecuador, Venezuela, El Salvador, Guatemala, Nicaragua, and Panama.

The guerrilla operations that were designed to turn Latin America into a socialist paradise were increasingly taking a backseat to the drug war. In early 1987, a massive police operation pulled in over seventy important drug cartel members, their arrogance frighteningly demonstrated by one who declared that " . . . his supporters would kill a judge a week in Colombia or the USA until he was released."[10] In late 1988, Alan Riding reported from Bogotá:

> ... So far this year, 3,000 people have died in the political violence in this country of 31 million, including almost 800 soldiers and policemen and 700 guerrillas. More than 300 have been kidnapped by leftists or criminals, while one of the country's six loosely allied rebel groups has bombed a pipeline carrying the country's oil exports on at least sixty occasions this year.

But Riding also wrote that:

> ... with the country exhausted by violence, the front line of the war has become the battle for peace, with the main leftist guerrilla groups and the government blaming each other for continuation of the conflict.[11]

Only in 1989 did the government agree to open talks with M-19 and other guerrilla groups. Although these led to the temporary breakup of M-19, they scarcely stemmed the omnipresent killings (for some years one murder every three hours in Medellín) that led up to the 1990 presidential elections.

By now the guerrillas were no longer the major security threat to the country. The drug traffickers were. Aided by massive assistance from the United States, President Barco opened war. The cartels responded predictably. Another wave of terrible violence covered the stricken country. Cartel thugs, many of them guerrillas, killed judges and local officials, journalists were taken hostage, newspaper offices burned, a commercial aircraft blown up with 107 killed. Three anti-cartel presidential candidates were murdered. Nevertheless, the anti-cartel candidate of the Liberal Party, César Gaviría Trujillo, was elected president, a clear mandate to continue the war.

At first it seemed as if the government was gaining the upper hand. In early 1991, the joint leader of the Medellín cartel, Jorge Luis Ochoa, surrendered. Two months later, the Maoist guerrilla group (EPL) converted into a legal political party. But in February, a blast in the center of Medellín City killed twenty-two and injured 135 persons, apparently in retaliation for Jorge Luis Ochoa's surrender. In the same month, as protest to the opening of the new Constituent Assembly, FARC and ELN guerrillas struck a variety of targets to produce a new round of heavy fighting. But a congressional decision in May to repeal the law that permitted extradition of drug traffickers (primarily to the United States) brought the unexpected surrender of the Medellín cartel leader,

Pablo Escobar Gaviría. A terrorist amnesty law in the summer was said to prove effective and new anti-terrorist laws passed that autumn seemed to presage at least a partial solution of the cartel problem.

This hope died shortly after birth. Escobar's imprisonment only enhanced the Cali cartel's operations, which, despite new laws and millions of dollars of aid from the United States, not only continued to flourish but to expand to new large markets in Europe.

This was bad enough, but then came the horrible truth that Escobar had jobbed his own arrest. Escobar's "prison" (which he helped to design) included a luxury complex, " . . . the work of a professional interior designer for a rich bachelor."[12] According to British journalist Tim Ross, Escobar's new home included a richly furnished salon with bar, TV, Jacuzzi, waterbed (soon familiar to imported whores), and an office full of the latest communications technology (supplemented by fifty carrier pigeons) necessary to run his international drug empire as if he were sitting in Medellín. When life palled, he could retreat to a nest of luxury cabins secluded in the woods.[13] Guards were a joke. He was surrounded by his own security force (Ross who supplemented his article by detailed photographs speculated that fears of assassination may have prompted Escobar's surrender). This was the secure prison cosmeticized by barbed-wire fences, searchlights, and even a minefield to reassure the public that Enemy Number One was safely out of harm's way.

The blowup came when the government, stung by publicized allegations of Escobar's luxurious life- and business-style while a guest of the nation, announced that he would be transferred to another prison. In July 1992, the prisoner, who may have undergone plastic surgery to disguise himself, escaped along with seven "guards" after a shoot-out with the army. Although his escape made little difference to the drug traffic, which the Cali cartel had largely taken over, his capture at once became a point of honor with the greatly embarrassed Gaviría government. After months of concentrated police work by a special unit, aided by a CIA intelligence team, the quarry was run to ground in early December—not surprising in view of a $5 million price on his head—and was killed in a police shootout.[14]

This was something of a Pyrrhic victory. Despite President César Gaviría's assurances in July 1993 that the Cali cartel would soon be broken up, and despite a warrant that has been issued for the arrest of the Cali boss, Miguel Rodríguez Orejuela, the Cali organization continues to prosper.[15] As of this writing, December 1993, there are disturbing rumors of a possible deal being made between the government and the cartel whereby the latter would be dissolved in return for its bosses retaining their billions of dollars and being accepted as legitimate businessmen.

Nor do the two major guerrilla organizations, ELN and FARC,

seem to be on the point of surrender, as Gavíria also suggested was the case.[16] In 1992 oil lines were blown up over sixty times, which cost the state oil company millions of dollars; twenty more such attacks had occurred by mid-1993.[17] As of December 1993 guerrillas still control large areas in the countryside and are active in the cities. In going after them, Colombia's security forces, along with the infamous death squads, have reaped considerable, apparently justified opprobrium from diverse human rights groups, which claim that far more opponents of the Gavíria regime have been eliminated than either guerrillas or members of the drug cartels.[18] Should Gavíria ever succeed in eliminating major drug trafficking—no easy task—his next job will be to return his country to the democratic processes that he claims to embrace.

The Republic of Peru is the third largest and one of the most backward countries in South America and, from the standpoint of guerrilla warfare, by far the most perverse. It also has one of the most turbulent political records in Latin America, which helps to explain the problems of its twelve-year-old attempt to fashion a democratic government.

A major insurgency against a military dictatorship occurred in 1961 with the emergence of the Revolutionary Front of the Left (FIR). This Trotskyite group after mobilizing an estimated three hundred thousand peasants in the Cuzco area nearly four hundred miles southeast of Lima began seizing the enormous haciendas and distributing their hundreds of thousands of acres of land to the Indian peasants. The movement was broken by the army in 1962 and its leader, Hugo Blanco, was imprisoned. But now a splinter group from the Peruvian Communist Party (PCP) organized the more militant National Liberation Army (ELN), while still another splinter group of young rebels created the Movement of the Revolutionary Left (MIR), both movements being Castro-inspired and -funded, and both eliminated in 1965 as serious threats with the arrest of one leader and the death of the other.

In 1963, another military dictatorship gave way to the election of Fernando Belaúnde Terry as president. During the next five years, Belaúnde pushed through important reforms that included expropriation and distribution to landless Indians of half a million acres of farmland, a major factor in ELN and MIR's failure to bring off a successful rural insurgency.

Belaúnde was forced from office in 1968 by a leftist military junta led by Juan Velasco Alvarado, a self-styled "revolutionary nationalist."[19] For seven years, the Velasco government pushed Peru back to an economic stone age by expropriating foreign (mainly U.S.) companies, breaking up vast haciendas, and, inevitably, forcing large sums of gold and foreign capital from the country. Heavy military expenditures did improve the combat potential of the army but only to fight conventional, *not* counterinsurgency warfare.

In 1975, still another coup, led by General Francisco Morales Bermúdez, resulted in a new constitution and, in 1980, the return of Belaúnde to the presidency. Belaúnde inherited an economic disaster, the dimensions of which can be judged from inflation rising to 3,240 per cent in five years. As if that weren't sufficient, he also inherited a new insurgency.

The threat was twofold. It came first from a Maoist group that had splintered from the PCP in 1964 and after many twists and turns finally consolidated itself as the Sendero Luminoso, or Shining Path (SL). Based primarily at the University of San Cristóbal in Ayacucho about two hundred miles southeast of Lima, the movement's leader was Abimael Guzmán Reynoso (aka Chairman Gonzalo), a messianic professor of philosophy who had built a disciplined cult of young disciples into a militant guerrilla movement. Guzmán's revolutionary goal was to replace capitalist rule by the ancient agricultural system of the Incas, a "pure" socialism that had appealed to Mao and Castro and would in time be emulated by Pol Pot in Cambodia (Kampuchea).[20]

The second threat came from a small Socialist splinter group of mostly university radicals and surviving members of the MIR. The Túpac Amaru Revolutionary Movement (MRTA) emerged as an urban guerrilla terrorist group in 1982 when it commenced a prolonged bombing campaign against international companies and foreign banks, probably in collusion with if not control of the SL, the idea being to drive pernicious foreign influence and capital out of the country.[21]

SL members amounted to perhaps two to three thousand in 1983, of which about half were Indians speaking only the Quechura language. Training was rudimentary. The guerrillas lacked weapons, depending for the most part on those bought or stolen from the army or taken from wounded or dead policemen and soldiers, and on dynamite stolen from the numerous mines in the area. Guzmán's attempt to establish liberated areas proved to be an expensive failure—in 1983 security forces claimed three thousand guerrilla casualties including a thousand dead.[22] Although this hurt the SL, it in no way terminated their operations, which soon expanded into the cities. Kidnapings and assassinations brought reprisals both by security forces and allied death squads. Human rights abuses rose as did Guzmán's own allies, inflation, and unemployment.[23]

And always those damn guerrillas. And coca.

The situation was this: Peru grows over 60 per cent of the world's supply of coca leaf, which is processed into coca paste and smuggled to drug cartels in Colombia and Mexico where it is refined to the white cocaine vicariously sold on North American (and increasingly European) streets. Long a staple commodity, coca's legal production is fixed at an annual eighteen million kilograms but " . . . illegal production is estimated to be in excess of fifty million kilograms."[24] According to one authority, James Anderson, " . . . the arable land devoted to growing coca" in the Tingo María area " . . . increased from 4,800 acres in 1970 to over 40,000 by the mid-1980s, the legal [cultivated] limit for the entire country."[25] By 1987, sixty-two thousand acres were reportedly under cultivation in the Upper Huállaga Valley alone.[26] When the government, pushed by the United States, attempted to wean peasants from coca cultivation in favor of other crops, it was met by blanket hostility, understandable in that *each* local resident in the producing areas was paid around $400 a month, virtually a fortune.[27] Nor was the government entirely enthusiastic about the program. Anderson estimates that in 1986 illegal exportation of cocaine amounted to $4 billion, of which " . . . some $1 billion found its way into the Peruvian economy."[28] Even worse, drug barons had bought a good many public servants including judges, administrators, mayors, police, and army personnel at all levels—in 1985, security forces smashed a huge drug smuggling operation run by personnel in the Peruvian Ministry of the Interior,[29] and this was probably just the tip of the iceberg. Either corrupt or intimidated judges have released an estimated 85 percent of guerrillas or guerrilla suspects seized by the military.

Add to this the guerrilla factor. Guzmán, a fanatic revolutionary who believes in the violent destruction of representative government in order to bring about world revolution, was welcomed by both coca-growing peasants and coca-paste-exporting drug barons. Despite the Belaúnde government's claim of guerrilla suppression, by 1984 the SL had expanded into the Tingo María area some 220 miles northeast of Lima on the "cocaine highway" to Colombia. Its presence there was no accident. In 1984, the coca trade was threatened by the U.S.-sponsored " . . . largest crop substitution program in South America."[30] SL guerrillas attacked the main camp near Tingo María, killed the local employees, and with them the program. On the one hand, SL guerrillas "protected" peasant growers and processors from thieves, for which they received a satisfactory "contribution"; on the other hand, they "protected" the processors and shippers from police and army intrusions in return for an alleged $500 million a year. This enabled Guzmán to fund his ever-expanding organization that cost a great deal of money to run and also to equip his guerrillas with more-modern weapons. The more cocaine paste exported the better in Guzmán's mind—for nothing could have been of greater assistance in toppling what he considered to be the already decadent Western society than hard drugs.

Belaúnde was replaced in the 1985 elections by the populist party APRA's candidate, Alan García Pérez, whose radical economic and financial policies eventually cost Peru international funding without drastically improving the over-all situation. As with Belaúnde so with García—Peru isolated from the international finance community, a stagnant economy, an 8,000 per cent inflation, massive unemployment, murders around the clock, corrupt and intimidated judges, a feckless and corrupt military, general strikes, more than two hundred thousand peasant refugees living in shantytown squalor, elected officials resigning for fear of the guerrillas, and all the while the SL growing stronger and expanding operations. Although security forces claimed some six thousand guerrilla causalties in 1987, the movement was still estimated to number ten thousand,[31] and had established liberated areas in the Andes Valley northwest of Ayacucho, key provinces that the SL would control in 1989 when, according to one report, half of the nation was " . . . living in emergency zones in which the army is given wide powers to combat the guerrillas."[32]

This was the scenario inherited by Alberto Fujimori, the son of immigrant Japanese parents who unexpectedly won the 1990 presidential election on a reformist ticket. Backed by a comfortable majority, Fujimori turned to the Peruvian equivalent of cleansing the Augean stables. Amazingly, he made considerable progress. He reduced human rights violations by the police, military, and death squads, he engineered an austerity budget that brought inflation under control, he resumed payments to the World Bank and thus regained eligibility for further loans, he stirred a reluctant army into organizing armed peasant patrols to defend villages against the SL guerrillas, and he supported a radical "new town" project. By means of government assistance, displaced migrants to the cities were given 90 square meter plots in theretofore "waste" areas on which to build their own brick houses and develop and run their own communities—the *pueblos jóvenes,* settlements of about five thousand people.[33]

He did none of this gracefully. Not being a politician, Fujimori did not hide his contempt for opposition congressmen; nor for corrupt judges, whom he called "jackals"; nor for a supine Roman Catholic Church hierarchy, which he called "medieval and recalcitrant"; nor for President Bush's anti-drug campaign, which he correctly criticized for being aimed more at the growers than at the users in the United States.[34] In running what was basically a one-man show, he continued to have both popular and military backing. But there was a price tag. To maintain popular backing, he had to secure a better way of life for his people. To retain military backing, he had to coddle the armed forces not only by overlooking a good many abuses but by allowing the military to rule its own house in the hope of persuading far too many reluctant officers to move determinedly against Abimael Guzmán's ever-expanding and richer SL.

Guzmán's SL gained far more than it lost in the first two years of Fujimori's presidency. It had forged more links in the "iron belt" around Lima. Recruiting was brisk in refugee-crammed shantytowns; assassinations and killings rose as more officials were intimidated or bought off. Operations in coca-growing areas were more profitable than ever, too often unimpeded by army units most of whose officers were either in Guzmán or the traffickers' pay or both. By now, Guzmán had expanded his propaganda effort to the major cities of the Western world, where agents, operating under a "Sun-Peru" logo, sold " . . . books, leaflets and posters" depicting the SL as saviors of Peru who would ultimately achieve world revolution—an invidious campaign which Fujimori was unable to stop despite urgent appeals to foreign government heads.[35]

But already a tiny cloud had appeared on Guzmán's horizon. Early in Fujimori's presidency, he had concentrated his meager anti-terrorist resources on the single task of capturing Guzmán. A newly formed special unit almost succeeded in doing that in spring of 1990 and in January 1991, the quarry escaping only by minutes.[36]

Fujimori meanwhile was chafing under congressional restraints while SL guerrillas were closing in on Lima. Feeling himself hamstrung by an opposition Congress and by a corrupt judiciary, he startled the world in April 1992 by carrying off an *autogolpe*—a one-man coup (backed by police and military). Congress was dissolved overnight, political opponents arrested, civil liberties suspended, journalists detained, and heavy censorship imposed on the capital.[37] Reaction from abroad was instant and harsh. President Bush suspended aid; Spain and Japan made threatening noises to do so; the OAS spoke of imposing sanctions. Within Peru, 71 per cent of the people approved his dissolving Congress and 89 per cent approved his plan to reorganize the judiciary.[38]

Guzmán's SL reacted by opening a guerrilla terrorist campaign against the middle class. In late July, SL terrorists exploded a car bomb—six hundred kilograms of dynamite—in a prosperous Lima suburb killing over twenty people and wounding some 150. A series of indiscriminate car bombings and assassinations followed as some experts believed the SL was moving in for the kill.

And indeed it was. In mid-September, the president's counterterrorist task force raided a house in a quiet Lima suburb. Within minutes, the work of years paid off. Arrested were Guzmán and three key subordinates who were completing plans for an enormous October offensive. Other documents soon led to the arrest of two hundred more members of the movement.[39]

Guzmán's arrest brought a new wave of optimism to the jaded Peruvian people, most of whom blamed him personally for an estimated twenty-three thousand deaths and $20 billion of property destruction in the last twelve years. Without question, the SL movement experienced violent shock waves at the loss of its leader. More shock waves followed in October 1993 when in a televised broadcast from jail Chairman Gonzalo stated his desire for a peace settlement and " . . . praised the political and economic policies of Fujimori." This startling about-face was apparently engineered by Fujimori's behind-the-scenes intelligence guru, Valdimiro Montesinos, who was said to have "broken" Guzmán to the extent that he followed his broadcast by issuing brief communiqués in praise of the government (in return for additional prison comforts).[40]

Qualified observers point to a loss of three thousand SL militants and cadres since Guzmán's arrest; to a leadership crisis brought on by 80 percent of the 1992 Central Committee being in jail or dead;[41] to a considerable increase in SL desertions; and to the cautious return of natives to abandoned villages around Ayacucho, once Guzmán's private fiefdom, and of farmers and ranchers to estates north of Lima, an area no longer considered a "red zone." Peruvian experts claimed in late 1993 that the SL has lost " . . . about fifty percent of its firepower, of its capacity to carry out major operations."[42]

Perhaps so, but this does not necessarily prove that Guzmán's defection is decisive. SL leaders insist that he has been tortured and drugged—indeed, he was reportedly cut from nearly all human contact, placed under a restricted food diet and deprived of books, magazines, television, or radio—all to make him amenable to the alleged psychological ministrations of Montesinos.[43] There are probably still between fifteen and twenty thousand guerrillas operating from a number of military "regions," each with its own command and staff organization to control a "principal force" along with militia forces maintained in zones and villages. These organizations are backed by a cleverly constructed series of "support bases" and are funded from an estimated $20 to $100 million annual income derived from the drug cartels but also from extortion, bank robberies, and "revolutionary taxes" collected from the people.[44]

SL guerrilla terrorists remained uncomfortably active in 1993, as witnessed by urban and countryside offensives in May, August, September, and October that killed over one hundred civilians and wounded several hundred more.[45] Only half as many people died from political violence in the year following Guzmán's arrest as in the previous year, but the figure still reached over sixteen hundred. Taken with guerrilla losses, the tally for the thirteen-year-old war is now twenty-seven thousand dead and $23 billion of property destruction.

Although Fujimori has improved police and army morale and, with that, counterinsurgency effectiveness, the army's senior commanders remain divided as to the best counterinsurgency strategy. The "French school" insists on a strictly military-dominated administration in contested areas, the method employed by the French army in Algeria, a war the French ultimately lost (see Chapters 54, 55). The "British school" holds for a counterinsurgency campaign conducted by military-police-civil committees which first must ensure that villages are protected in order to obtain intelligence necessary to identify and eliminate the SL support organiztion,[46] the successful strategy employed in Malaya (see Chapter 46). Although Fujimori is said to prefer the latter strategy—he reportedly plans to appoint civil governors in the contested areas—he is not going to reform the army overnight, particularly when its senior commanders remain prone to corruption by the drug cartels. I am informed that he is currently under pressure by some senior generals to choose the French school's approach, and it would appear from the series of attacks on remote villages in 1993 that these villages are not being adequately protected. One must hope that, being an intelligent man, Fujimori sees the inherent fallacy in this approach and is strong enough to insist on that of the proven British school.

Even if the movement should be neutralized eventually, there remains the immense problem of eliminating the coca growers, processors, and traffickers. Then there is the even more immense task of bringing about a more equitable society by at least narrowing the gulf between the haves and have-nots (the basic reason for all guerrilla wars)—and when all that is accomplished, there is the vital matter of resuming democratic government.

CHAPTER EIGHTY-FIVE

1. Radu and Tismaneanu, 160.
2. Ibid., 156, 149, 162, 168.
3. *Newsweek,* November 16, 1992.
4. Clutterbuck, *Terrorism and Guerrilla Warfare,* 90–2.
5. Ibid., 92.
6. Radu and Tismaneanu, 171.
7. Clutterbuck, *Terrorism and Guerrilla Warfare,* 93.
8. Ibid., 94.
9. Ibid., 121.
10. Ibid., 95.
11. Alan Riding, *International Herald Tribune,* December 17–18, 1988.
12. Tim Ross, *The Sunday Times* (London), August 9, 1992.
13. Ibid.
14. *Newsweek,* December 13, 1993.
15. *The Independent* (U.K.), July 28, 1993.
16. Ibid.
17. Ibid.
18. See, for example, *The Independent* (U.K.), July 26, 1993.
19. International Institute for Strategic Studies, *Strategic Survey 1970,* 62.
20. Clutterbuck, *Terrorism and Guerrilla Warfare,* 115–20, for a more detailed exposition.
21. Radu and Tismaneanu, 339–43.

22. Ibid., 325.
23. Ibid.
24. James Anderson, 46.
25. Ibid.
26. *International Herald Tribune,* December 19, 1991.
27. James Anderson, 46.
28. Ibid.
29. Ibid.
30. Ibid., 47.
31. Radu and Tismaneanu, 325.
32. *International Herald Tribune,* June 13, 1989.
33. *Newsweek,* April 20, 1992. See also, Clutterbuck, "Peru: How to Defeat SL?"
34. Ibid.
35. *International Herald Tribune,* December 19, 1991.
36. *Newsweek,* September 28, 1992.
37. *The Independent* (U.K.), April 8, 1992.
38. *Newsweek,* April 20, 1992.
39. Ibid., September 28, 1992.
40. *International Herald Tribune,* October 23–24, November 30, 1993.
41. Ibid., November 30, 1993.
42. Ibid.
43. Ibid.
44. Clutterbuck, "Peru: How to Defeat SL?"
45. *International Herald Tribune,* May 18, October 23–24, 1933. See also, *The Independent* (U.K.), August 21, 1993.
46. Clutterbuck, "Peru: How to Defeat SL?"

CHAPTER 86

Ireland divided by treaty • Rise and fall of the Irish Republican Army (IRA) • The "Protestant Ascendancy" in Ulster • IRA survival • Failure of political, social, and economic reforms in Ulster • The 1969 riots: Catholics versus Protestants • The British army takes over • The IRA splinters: Officials versus Provincials • Internment of IRA members and "suspected" members • Violence escalates • Bloody Friday • Loyalist Protestant death squads • British army operations • IRA setbacks • Failure of political solutions to the conflict • IRA and Loyalist Protestant excesses • 1993: Violence continues • Tentative peace discussions • The Hume-Adams talks • Britain's secret talks with the IRA • The Major-Reynolds peace plan • The situation in December 1933

> ... out of this national liberation struggle a new Ireland will emerge, upright and free ... this then is our aim, an independent, united democratic Irish Republic. For this we shall fight until the [British] invader is driven from our soil and victory is ours.
>
> IRISH REPUBLICAN ARMY (IRA) PROCLAMATION,
> DECEMBER 11, 1956[1]

OUR CHAPTER 17 left an Ireland ravaged by war, first against the British, which resulted in the partition treaty of 1921; then between rebel guerrillas of the Irish Republican Army (IRA), who wanted to abrogate it, and the legitimate government of the Irish Free State, which was equally determined to uphold it. The treaty was scarcely ideal in that it created a sore spot by forming six of the north-

1121

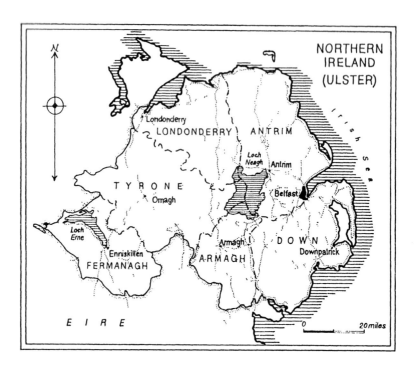

ern counties into the Protestant-dominated separate government of Northern Ireland (Ulster), which had its own parliament but remained part of the United Kingdom.

The IRA at this time numbered about a hundred thousand members but was scarcely a cohesive organization, being split into pro- and anti-treaty factions, the latter wanting to resume war against England. In 1922, dissident IRA guerrillas kidnaped a member of the Dail (Senate), which brought down governmental wrath—in two months, twelve thousand IRA militants were in jail and seventy-seven were executed by firing squad.[2] By spring of 1923, the IRA irregulars were defeated "politically and militarily," but a few extremists kept the movement alive. Patrick Bishop and Eammon Mallie in their excellent book *The Provisional IRA* wrote that by end of the 1920s the organization " . . . had been reduced to a dedicated rump of conspirators, bound together by a sense of betrayal, in the service of an invisible republic"[3]—and by a belief that extreme violence was the sole method to drive the British out of Northern Ireland.

Thanks to strong government measures, the IRA decline continued, nor did its fortunes improve when the Free State evolved into the independent Republic of Ireland in 1937. During World War II, Eamon de Valera's government locked up four hundred of its members. In 1947, its strength was estimated at two hundred active members. The following year it concluded an alliance with the Sinn Fein (Republican)

Party before deciding " . . . to launch a guerrilla war against the British troops occupying Northern Ireland."[4]

The next four years were devoted to obtaining weapons, mostly from raids on police stations and military camps, but also from sympathizers in the Irish Republic, including some civil officials and military personnel. By late 1965, units were being recruited and trained in the North, an effort complemented by armed teams crossing the border to carry out sabotage missions mainly in the South Armagh border area. It soon became clear that the projected operations were overly ambitious. The Protestant-dominated North—the six counties which contain one third of Ireland's population and in which the Catholics are in a minority one third—was controlled by a Unionist parliament at Stormont Castle outside Belfast. Over the years, the Royal Ulster Constabulary (RUC) had become an efficient police force backed by a twenty-five-thousand-man anti-Republican auxiliary called the Ulster Special Constabulary—the "B" Specials, which later would be replaced by the Ulster Defense Regiment (UDR).[5] After IRA teams began blowing up bridges, railroads, power stations and other facilities in the border areas, Stormont passed an internment law which enabled the RUC to sweep up hundreds of Ulster Republicans. Even without the support of Catholics North and South, the campaign lasted into 1962, when a discouraged IRA headquarters in Dublin publicly terminated it.

IRA failure brought a change in strategy engineered by a new Marxist chief of staff, Cathal Goulding. Influenced by the Campaign for Nuclear Disarmament in Britain and the civil rights movement in America, Goulding hoped to bring Catholics and Protestants in Ulster together in a civil rights campaign, the first step in melding the workers in North and South into a revolutionary force that would bring about a united Communist Ireland.[6]

Considering IRA factionalism and general inactivity outside Dublin, this grand design would probably not have got off the ground but for two factors. One was the patently unfair treatment of Catholics by the "Protestant Ascendancy" government of Northern Ireland. Stormont was controlled by Protestant Unionists including such extremists as the Reverend Ian Paisley and William Craig, who had no intention of allowing Catholics to have a place in the sun. Little or no attempt had been made to bring them into a predominantly Protestant society. Catholic children attended Catholic schools, Protestant children Protestant schools. Far too many Catholics lived in segregated, generally poor areas of cities and towns; they got the crumbs from the civil jobs table, their education was often sparse with limited access to university places; they were discriminated against in housing, unemployment ran high, resentment deep. Admittedly their status was slowly improving by the 1960s, and probably a large majority and certainly most of the growing middle class were opposed to violence. In 1965, large numbers of Catholics and Protestants had welcomed the Ulster prime minister's efforts to eliminate discrimination, efforts ruthlessly blocked by Ian Paisley and his fellow extremists.[7]

The other factor stemmed from the blocking of Prime Minister Terence O'Neill's attempted reforms. This was a Catholic non-violent civil rights campaign for reform, which in 1967 emerged as the Northern Ireland Civil Rights Association (NICRA).[8] Violence had entered the previous year when a march by Catholic protesters was physically disrupted by the Ulster Volunteer Force (UVF), an illegal right-wing Protestant paramilitary group in Belfast. Infiltration of the civil rights movement by left-wing trade unionists and Communists soon exacerbated matters as did the formation of the republican Catholic Nationalist Party and an insurgent People's Democracy, a group of far left student militants whose member Bernadette Devlin won passing headline fame.[9] In 1968, civil rights marchers were being routinely harassed by Protestant mobs, which on occasion also attacked Catholic shops and homes. It was a pivotal year, for had the RUC not made " . . . the fatal error of failing to protect the right to demonstrate," as counterinsurgency expert Richard Clutterbuck pointed out, the IRA would have had no grounds to assert its traditional role in protecting the trod-upon Catholics.[10] That the campaign largely succeeded showed in November when the Stormont government belatedly announced a program that met most of the demands of the movement and in 1969 even transcended them by passing housing and electoral reforms and by establishing a Ministry of Community Relations " . . . responsible for ensuring equality of opportunity in all fields,"[11] reforms fought tooth and nail by right-wing Unionists, who were further infuriated by the Westminster-inspired decision to disarm the RUC in an attempt to convert it from a paramilitary to a regular police force, thus in theory making it less resented by the Catholic population, but in fact turning the subsequent response role to IRA attacks over to the army in direct contradiction to valid counterinsurgency strategy.

In this period of increasing violence, the IRA played a minimal role. The movement was already split, Dublin headquarters still nonsectarian, still demanding caution, Ulster members definitely sectarian and increasingly militant but not yet in a position to open effective fire. In 1969, active members in Belfast counted less than sixty; inactive members probably numbered about forty with about three hundred to five hundred mostly middle-aged sympathizers. In Londonderry, probably no more than ten persons " . . . regarded themselves as members."[12] Nevertheless, some of them already had infiltrated the NICRA leadership and inevitably grew more involved as violence increased.

The British army also had played a minimal role. But now Protestant sabotage of key installations had caused Westminster to order garrison soldiers to protect electric power plants and water reservoirs. Their pacific role ended in July. Unemployed youths in Bogside, Londonderry's Catholic area, reacted to a commemorative march of ultra-Unionists celebrating the unsuccessful siege of Londonderry by the Catholic Stuart, James II, in 1689 by hurling bricks and petrol bombs, then burning cars and looting shops, a riot broken up by RUC police using water cannon and tear gas. A subsequent three-day riot resulted in heavy fighting between the rioters, the RUC, Paisleyite mobs, and eventually the "B" Specials, a donnybrook brought under control only by the arrival of a British army battalion, but with a large number of wounded and several million pounds' worth of property damage.[13] A simultaneous five-day riot in West Belfast was finally suppressed by British troops, the toll being seven killed, 750 wounded, and fifteen hundred Catholic and three hundred Protestant families forced to abandon their homes.[14]

A major result of these riots was to splinter the IRA, its militant members forming the Provisional IRA (named in commemoration of the Provisional Government proclaimed in Dublin in 1916). The new organization at once gained money, arms, and training facilities through the connivance of certain Irish Republic politicians, including two government ministers, civil officials, and army and customs officers, who apparently feared the Communist objectives of the Official IRA while sympathizing, at least in part, with the insurgent aims of the Provisional IRA, chiefly that of eliminating the British presence in Northern Ireland.[15] The Provisionals' Army Council in Dublin was headed by Chief of Staff Sean MacStiofain with Rory O'Brady's non-Marxist Provisional Sinn Fein Party (opposed to the Marxist Sinn Fein) as its political front. Traditional IRA aims, " . . . to beat the Protestants to their knees, drive out the British and reunify Ireland," were to be carried out by a three-phase program of violence, first in defending Catholic areas against Protestant, RUC, and British army incursions; second in eye-for-an-eye retaliation if an IRA member was killed; finally in an all-out offensive against the British "occupation" of Ulster.[16]

At this point, the British army was not the villain of the scene in most Catholic eyes; indeed the soldiers had been welcomed in Londonderry and Belfast as protectors against the RUC and Protestant extremist groups during the 1969 riots. This attitude began to change in 1970 when increasingly severe IRA-instigated riots brought on army house-to-house searches by often overzealous troops along with overly harsh military strictures such as "anyone seen with a petrol bomb was liable to be shot dead."[17] Riot control is never an easy task, even with trained troops. With untrained troops, excesses are almost impossible to avoid, particularly when a tired, uncertain, and often frightened young soldier is unduly provoked by having to dodge a petrol bomb or a brick or by being cursed, spat upon, or shot at. The rule of self-preservation can often surmount the wording of a regulation. But provocation works both ways. Stormont's announcement that any rioter arrested would be given a six-month mandatory jail sentence brought swift reaction as did overenthusiastic employment by security forces of nausea-producing CS gas followed by swinging nightsticks. Both IRA factions, the Officials and the Provisionals, were swamped with recruits, mostly young Catholic males looking for a supposedly adventurous escape from all-too-familiar poverty and unemployment. As early as 1970, the theretofore small Belfast Provisional IRA, now called the Belfast Brigade, had built fourteen operational units and divided the city into three combat "battalion" areas from which they carried out 153 bombings of shops and factories by year's end.[18] Weapons were still in short supply, as was money, but dynamite and gelignite were easily stolen from quarries and turned into bombs, and empty milk bottles filled with petrol and fitted with a jury-rigged fuse produced formidable results. The explosions frightened and intimidated people, cost jobs when stores and factories were blown up, and, perhaps most important, brought an increased army presence in the form of patrols, vigorous house searches, and time-consuming vehicle checkpoints to upset the daily life of the average citizen—and of course headlines to keep the movement in the public eye. Army house-to-house searches discovered pistols, rifles, automatic weapons, shotguns, home-made bombs, and explosives. Driblets of arms were arriving from sympathetic Irish Americans and would soon increase as the result of an IRA propaganda campaign carried out by American sympathizers who formed the Northern Aid Committee (NAC). This was fertile ground. There are about twenty-two million Irish Americans, the result of the embittered emigrations of the last century. NAC soon boasted a hundred chapters across the U.S., which raised about $600,000 a year for the cause.[19] In Belfast, IRA guerrillas robbed banks and post offices for money to buy more arms, and as the movement grew in strength, it resorted to extortion Mafia-style and even opened legitimate businesses.

Insurgency breeds its own escalatory dynamics. The flow of recruits to the IRA was matched by the flow of recruits to right-wing paramilitary groups. Excesses on one side produced excesses on the other side. The situation could only deteriorate further unless someone changed the rules. Brigadier Frank Kitson, an innovative veteran of several counterinsurgencies (see Chapter 52), arrived in Belfast in September 1970 as commanding officer of a British brigade. It was at once evident to him that the rules had to be changed, his plan being to defuse the situation by persuading moderate Catholic and Protestant elements to support the government. Once isolated and properly combated, Kitson argued, the extremists would slowly run out of steam and eventually the authorities would restore peace and order while the Stormont government came to its senses and legislated further necessary reforms.[20]

This very sensible plan of "deescalation and attrition," in effect the *raison d'être* for the army's presence, fell victim to overwhelming circumstances. British army tactics, higher command intransigence, RUC and "B" Special operations, and right-wing guerrilla terrorist acts already had turned a majority of Catholics against the government and its security forces to make them either sympathizers with, supporters of, or participants in IRA operations.

As matters stood, violence could only escalate. In early 1971, the Official IRA in Belfast had grown to perhaps twelve companies and in January defied Dublin policy by opening its own armed offensive marked by selective as opposed to indiscriminate assassinations, an effective tactic that intimidated some judges, most jury members, and not a few potential defectors from the cause. Simultaneously, the Provisionals, who were receiving more and more arms from the United States, turned to attacks on army posts and RUC stations, killing where possible, and to indiscriminate bombing of pubs, a nasty business answered by the government bringing in more troops and by increasingly severe army countermeasures. In December 1970, there were six thousand British troops in Ulster; a year later, over fourteen thousand.[21] By mid-July 1971, ten British soldiers had been killed. The Provisional IRA in Londonderry meanwhile had remained relatively quiescent until two Catholic youths were shot and killed by soldiers in July to bring a fresh flow of volunteers to take up arms.

To try to dampen the violence, Prime Minister Brian Faulkner's government introduced Eamon de Valera's old weapon of internment—detention without trial of anyone suspected of IRA activities. In Belfast darkness, army and police teams swept into Catholic ghetto areas, an ill-planned operation that snatched up about fifty low-level IRA members; a similar raid in Londonderry fared better by picking up most of the active Provisionals.[22] The haul was meager compared to the public relations disaster.[23] Within thirty-six hours of the raids, seventeen people had been killed, hundreds of houses set on fire, extended attacks opened on soldiers and police, and an all-out bombing campaign ordered by Dublin headquarters.[24] Official and Provisional IRA units were again inundated with young volunteers all too eager to start shooting; most of the remaining Catholic moderates swung to support of the IRA; the Roman Catholic Church publicly condemned the new law; the Catholic Social Democratic and Labor Party (SDLP) opened a major campaign of civil disobedience—by year's end, twenty-two thousand Catholic households were refusing to pay municipal rent, which in some cases brought on a collapse of local government.[25]

This dismal picture darkened in 1972 with a steady increase in bombings and killings. In late January, a march in Londonderry turned into a riot quelled in part by British paratroopers at a cost of thirteen Catholic lives. What at once was termed Bloody Sunday added to the "climate of sympathy" created by internment and sustained by punitive counterinsurgency tactics, chiefly overaggressive street patrols, hot pursuit into Catholic areas, and often overzealous, and generally ineffectual house-to-house searches by British soldiers, as many as twenty-five hundred in one month.[26] Although patrols and house searches from time to time uncovered small caches of arms, they rarely caught important IRA members. Children were posted to report on intruders and housewives warned of intrusive patrols by banging garbage lids together thus giving IRA guerrillas time to evade patrols or, in some instances, to set up ambushes.

Stormont's failure to get its act together and implement additional reforms brought about Brian Faulkner's resignation. In March, Prime Minister Edward Heath's Conservative government prorogued the Stormont parliament, its responsibilities taken over by a Secretary of State for Northern Ireland, William Whitelaw. This in effect made the British army responsible for law and order, a questionable but perhaps unavoidable move that relegated the RUC to the sidelines in a situation where police should always play the predominant role, *supported* by the army when necessary. On the other hand, the abrupt end of fifty years of Stormont rule exercised a propitiatory effect on Catholic public opinion, which saw in it the seeds of constitutional reform, and it marked the beginning of IRA decline that increased as Whitelaw worked to bring all political parties together in order to fashion a politically viable Northern Ireland.

IRA operations were already slowing. A major change in British army policy was lowering military visibility, thus reducing friction with the civil population. British army intelligence was improving, mainly the work of Brigadier Frank Kitson who, as in Kenya and Cyprus, insisted on the value of low-level intelligence and covertly inserted his soldier agents into Catholic areas to obtain information that, once properly evaluated, collated and distributed, led to the arrest and imprisonment of often important IRA members by the RUC Special Branch. A series of senseless IRA bombings had caused a good many Catholics to question their support of the organization. Incipient challenge of IRA rule began growing in Catholic areas only to be countered by the invidious practice of "kneecapping": the victim was shot through the back of the knee, often to be crippled for life. Young ladies who fraternized with British soldiers were routinely tarred and feathered; people who were not easily intimidated were shot dead. Reappearance of Protestant death squads formed by members of the Ulster Defense Association

(UDA) was met by IRA indiscriminate killings of Protestants, which solved nothing but added to an increasing war-weariness. By spring of 1972, Catholic housewives were circulating petitions that called for peace. In May, the Official IRA, reverting to its original doctrine, called a cease-fire against the security forces and condemned the brutal violence of the Provisionals, terming them " . . . little more than racketeers."[27] Stung by this criticism, the Provisionals declared a cease-fire in June and attended an official conference in London, which came to nothing owing to impossible IRA demands, an egregious error that suggests the Provisionals were now fighting for fighting's sake rather than for achievement of political aims.

Then came Bloody Friday in late July, an insensate one-day IRA car-bombing campaign in Belfast which killed nine and wounded 130 citizens, mostly women and children. In response to public protest, the army was reinforced to a total twenty-one thousand troops and with the RUC, its members once again carrying arms, stormed theretofore no-go Catholic enclaves in Belfast and Londonderry. This coup markedly reduced IRA intimidation in these areas, which in time resulted in an increased flow of intelligence. Intimidation of juries was also checked when Westminster suspended trial by jury of arrested guerrilla terrorists and suspects in favor of one-judge verdicts—the highly controversial but very effective Diplock courts. By October and November, "leading members of the IRA were being arrested at the rate of one a day,"[28] and contributions from the United States had sharply lowered.[29] IRA excesses also brought a change of heart in Dublin, whose government declared the IRA to be illegal and jailed a large number of its members including Chief of Staff Sean MacStiofain. Minister Whitelaw meanwhile had been courting both the strongly Catholic SDLF and Brian Faulkner's Unionist Party in trying to win support for a concessionary compromise that among other things would guarantee Catholic politicians a place in government.

Though somewhat improved, the situation was still dicey from the security forces' standpoint. As if police and army did not have enough on their hands, a new element of sectarian killings emerged in 1972, the result not so much of conflicting religious and political ideologies as of gang warfare. In financing operations, both the IRA and Protestant guerrilla and paramilitary groups had built up lucrative incomes derived from robbery and extortion, in the case of the IRA an estimated £1 million in 1972.

The IRA had now to recognize that Britain had no intention of relinquishing its governmental responsibilities. Any doubts of IRA leaders on this score were soon banished by the arrival in Belfast in early 1973 of a hard-charging commander in chief of British forces, Lieutenant General Frank King. Following Kitson's line, King concentrated more on low-level intelligence collection by covert surveillance on which to base overt action by small, mobile units that replaced large foot patrols. Improved intelligence brought a significant increase in the identity, arrest, and conviction of guerrilla terrorists. Sixteen Provisionals were picked up in June in Belfast, among them the Belfast Brigade's commanding officer, young Gerry Adams. One report stated that "in Belfast a Provisional unit was forced to suspend operations due to lack of arms"; in Londonderry the Provisionals were reduced from three "brigades" to about fifty gunmen, "most of whom operated as nomadic terrorist groups with a loose military structure." The Provisional IRA now had to depend on Active Service Units (ASUs) consisting in theory of five to eight men "but often nothing more than a single gunman."[30] King also emphasized individual training and community relation activities, which considerably alleviated the sting of the unpopular house-to-house searches.

The results were dramatic. In 1972, 467 people were killed in Northern Ireland: 103 British soldiers, 17 police, 26 UDR soldiers, and 321 civilians. In 1973, 250 people were killed: 58 British soldiers, 13 police, 8 UDR soldiers, and 121 civilians. The situation further improved in 1974 (a total 215 dead) when a policy change placed emphasis on "police primacy" in all operations. Although the numbers killed in 1975 and 1976 increased to 247 and 297 respectively, the bulk of these were civilian deaths attributed in large part to IRA operations being challenged by various Protestant paramilitary groups.[31] Guerrilla terrorist tactics practiced by the Ulster Defense Association (UDA), the UVF and a new group called the Ulster Freedom Fighters (UFF) for some time had been as much of a challenge to security forces as to the IRA. It was now apparent that the UVF and UFF operated more for bloodthirsty revenge and monetary gain than for political reasons—indeed the RUC estimated that over 75 per cent of their members were criminals.[32] From 1977 to late 1992, death totals ranged from a low of 54 to a high of 113, the majority resulting from sectarian shootings. (Deaths from automobile accidents during this same period ranged from a low of 173 to a high of 355.)

The IRA was to be further hurt. In March, the Irish Republic navy intercepted a cargo ship carrying five tons of arms intended for the IRA, the first shipment of a total $5 million worth of arms supplied by Libya's Muammar al-Qaddafi. Minister Whitelaw's political maneuverings had in large part weaned SDLP support from the IRA and with that Irish-American contributions dropped from $600,000 to an estimated $160,000 a year.[33] Provisional IRA operations in the border area of South Armagh caused the Dublin government to increase the number of Irish Republic soldiers assigned to border duties. Increased cooperation with the RUC and British forces followed, though scarcely to the desired degree, as did the arrest in Dublin of the IRA Chief of Staff Seamus Twomey.

This combined initiative brought some unfortunate spinoffs. One was increased IRA recruitment of ten- to sixteen-year-olds, who found violence more fun than school and soon became able enough assassins, bombers, and arsonists.[34] Another was the shift of the major guerrilla effort to the South Armagh countryside, which, in view of a three-hundred-mile-long border and limited number of army and police brought an awkward challenge; despite the most strenuous efforts, the security forces never entirely blocked the supply of smuggled arms from Eire to the North. Still another was an extension of operations to England proper where the first car bombs were detonated in March to cause one dead and 180 wounded.[35] Older readers will remember the savage Birmingham pub bombings and the activities of the notorious Balcombe Street gang, which planted bombs in some private clubs and one exclusive school to kill six people and earn each perpetrator over thirty years in jail. Then came the Guildford pub bombings that killed five and wounded 54 civilians. Those efforts were complemented by similar bombings in Ulster. In addition to bombs detonated in parked cars, the "proxy bomb attack" appeared: a private car was stopped, loaded with a bomb and the driver " . . . forced to drive to a specific target" for detonation.[36] Fire bombings also increased with the development of an incendiary device the size of a cigarette package.

Headlines generated by these acts could not disguise IRA setbacks. Owing to the British Government's initiative, a proposal for power sharing by Ulster Protestants, Ulster Catholics, and the British Government had emerged along with various proposals for constitutional and electoral reforms necessary for such a system to work. After several months of severe political turbulence, an agreement of sorts resulted in the election of a new Ulster parliament and a cabinet consisting of six Protestant and five Catholic members serving under Prime Minister Brian Faulkner, thus in theory bringing together for the first time " . . . Catholic and Protestant leaders in an effort at conciliation and reconstruction."[37] This optimistic development was followed by a British incentive to establish a Council of Ireland designed to improve relations between Eire and Ulster. This plan backfired because a large Protestant majority regarded it as " . . . the prelude to a sell-out to Southern papists," a massive indignation shown at the polls in early 1974 when eleven of the twelve members elected to represent Northern Ireland at Westminster actively opposed the agreement.[38] Owing to this backlash, incited principally by Ian Paisley and other extremists and exemplified by a ten-day strike that brought virtual paralysis to Ulster, and by massive car bombings in Dublin and Monaghan that in one evening killed thirty-six and wounded over two hundred persons, the attempt to produce "conciliation and reconstruction" had failed by spring of 1974. Brian Faulkner resigned and the Ulster parliament and cabinet collapsed to leave government again in the hands of Westminster.[39]

Despite these setbacks, Wilson's new minister for Ulster, Merlyn Rees, pressed on with power sharing in local government (by 1977, Catholics would sit on all but three of twenty-six local councils), and he also persuaded the army to lessen the number of the despised house searches. In addition, he offered to phase out internment and gradually release detainees provided the IRA co-operated by ending violence.* This policy coerced the IRA to co-operate and in December 1974 its leaders agreed to a brief cease-fire that in 1975 was expanded in return for the release of all the remaining IRA detainees, though not to the particular pleasure of the security forces.[40]

If not yet moribund, the entire IRA apparatus was in trouble. The Official IRA suffered a major blow in late 1974 when a Trotskyite splinter group formed the Irish Republican Socialist Party (IRSP), which in time fielded the guerrilla Irish National Liberation Army (INLA). This led to war among the Official IRA, the IRSP, and the Provisional IRA, which, when they weren't killing each other, were killing and being killed by Protestant members of the UVF and UDA.[41] In 1974, 215 people were killed in Northern Ireland. In 1975, the year of the cease-fire, 247 persons were killed and over a thousand were charged with shootings, bombings, robberies, and other terrorist-related crimes.[42] Catholic sympathy with the IRA was at an all-time low, not only in Northern Ireland but in Eire and the U.S. Ordinary citizens seemed equally disgusted with the atrocities perpetrated by Protestant groups: 60 per cent of those arrested were thugs, many with criminal records.[43] Continued violence in 1976 brought the emergence of the Women's Peace Movement with huge marches that included Protestant women in Belfast and Dublin (a noteworthy effort that unfortunately had faded from the scene by 1980).

By the end of the cease-fire, the British army had fine-tuned its technical skills, particularly in the collection of intelligence, although a great deal remained to be done in improving RUC collation and analysis techniques and in strengthening the all-important RUC Special Branch, whose members were operating without vital technology such as computers. The RUC gained much sharper teeth in 1976, however, with the passage of the Emergency Powers Act. IRA suspects could now be held for seven days before being charged. Harsh, often brutal, interrogations

---

* This was not altogether altruistic. Public opinion had forced the government to categorize interned IRA members as "political prisoners" with concomitant privileges. Once released, they could be rearrested if they returned to their old ways—this time as common criminals with few if any perquisites.

so increased the flow of intelligence that " . . . between 1976 and 1979 about three thousand people were charged with terrorist offenses, most of them on the basis of confessions obtained under interrogation."[44] But relations between the RUC and the army remained strained, with each wanting operational control over the other, a conflict that greatly hampered the intelligence process described by one commentator as being in 1979 " . . . still an uncoordinated mess."[45] What was needed was a completely co-ordinated security effort commanded by one person as had been the case with previous successful British counterinsurgencies. A succession of army commanders had asked for the right of direct communication with the Irish Republic army as well as the right of "hot pursuit" of terrorists using Eire as a sanctuary, requests predictably denied on constitutional grounds.

The Provisional IRA was also changing. Its leaders were now younger members who were putting greater emphasis on training and on co-ordinated operations. There was also increased emphasis on gaining political control " . . . with an Armalite [rifle] in one hand and a ballot box in the other."[46] Provisional IRA leaders were in contact with West German, Libyan, Iranian, and Spanish Basque guerrilla terrorists, the latter advising them to stop killing low-level soldiers and concentrate on " . . . judges, generals and top ministers." Although these organizations supplied some arms, the bulk still came from the U.S., as did perhaps $150,000 a year in cash, but the IRA's main income derived from armed robbery, extortion, and racketeering, which continued to bring in $1 million or $2 million a year or more.[47]

It soon appeared that the new leaders had profited but little from past errors in trying to build a popular power base without offering the Catholic public a coherent political philosophy which included a statement of realistic aims. Not only were the Provisionals fighting the Official IRA, the INLA, the RUC, Protestant paramilitary groups, and the British army, but increasingly they had been forced to use intimidation to retain support inside the Catholic areas. It seemed almost as if they went out of their way to increase their isolation by courting general condemnation. In 1976, an IRA hit team murdered the British ambassador to Eire.[48] In 1977, IRA guerrilla terrorists carried out a firebombing campaign against tourist hotels in twenty Northern Ireland towns, of course putting a lot of their own people out of work. In early 1977, an ASU team murdered the British ambassador to The Hague. A month later, the Conservative Party spokesman for Northern Ireland, Airey Neave, was blown up in London in his booby-trapped car. Later in the year, a commando team murdered Lord Louis Mountbatten of World War II fame to reap further opprobrium (another team killed a British officer and seventeen soldiers the same day). Two years later, a team detonated a bomb in a pub frequented by soldiers and their Irish girlfriends—sixteen killed, sixty-six wounded. In 1982, bombs were exploded in London parks—eight killed, fifty-three wounded. In 1983, car bombs were exploded behind Harrods department store in London—eight killed. In the same year, thirty-eight hard-core terrorists escaped from a maximum security prison (five years later, ten escapees were still at large).[49]

Criticism of these tactics was somewhat muted in Ireland when IRA prisoners went on a hunger strike that in one form or another lasted from 1981 to 1983. The death of ten IRA prisoners from starvation brought a tremendous outpouring of sympathy from the Catholic populations of both Eire and Ulster. As one result, the Sinn Fein Party grew considerably in membership. Gerry Adams, now out of prison and head of the Provisional IRA's Army Council, for some time had been steering the movement in a political direction by again fronting it with Sinn Fein. In 1982, Sinn Fein won five of seventy-eight seats in the short-lived Ulster National Assembly. In the 1983 general elections, it won 13.4 per cent of the vote and Adams was elected a member of parliament for West Belfast.[50]

This did not spell real prosperity for the cause. By 1984, IRA guerrilla activists were reduced to an estimated 250 diehards, but this was an experienced, highly disciplined, and ideologically devout group supported by a large number of sympathizers. Nor did the figure presumably include "sleeper" agents who had infiltrated Irish communities in England to lie dormant until called upon to launch new terrorist campaigns such as those of 1991–92. On the other hand, intelligence collection was momentarily improved by the recruitment of highly placed IRA and republican officials—supergrasses—who informed on their fellows in return for a new life abroad, a project only partially successful since appeals courts began overturning convictions based on testimony of the supergrass informers, most of whom were dangerous criminals with but slight credentials of probity. Not only were a large number of prisoners convicted on supergrass testimony released by appeals courts, but some of the supergrasses in turn were tried for and convicted of murder.[51] Continued IRA guerrilla terrorist operations eventually told on Sinn Fein, which lost considerable ground in the 1986 elections, a development that only brought more violent attacks by the Provisionals.

Meanwhile, the political situation had radically changed. In late 1981, the Westminster and Dublin governments had established the Anglo-Irish Inter-Governmental Council (AIIC), designed to improve relations between the two countries and to find a political solution to the Northern Ireland problem. Progress was slow but in November 1985, Prime Ministers Margaret Thatcher and Garret FitzGerald signed an Anglo-Irish agreement which " . . . affirmed that any change in the status of Northern Ireland would only come about with the consent of the majority of the people of Northern Ireland" (that is, the Protestants). The agreement promised regularly scheduled conferences between Dublin and Stormont to deal with " . . . political matters, with security and related matters, with legal matters (including the administration of justice), and with the promotion of cross-border cooperation."[52] The first conference was followed by another in early 1986 and included discussion on improved cross-border co-operation. Meanwhile, the Republic of Ireland signed the European Convention on the Suppression of Terrorism and the U. S. Government approved an assistance package of $250 million in support of the Anglo-Irish agreement.[53]

The agreement was immediately attacked by both Catholics and Protestants in Northern Ireland, the former infuriated by Dublin's seeming recognition of England's continued presence in Ulster, the Protestants by the introduction of the Irish Republic in the affairs of Ulster. Massive demonstrations of both sects, boycotting of the National Assembly, civil disobedience campaigns—all combined to topple the fragile Northern Ireland Assembly, which was dissolved in spring of 1986. Once again direct rule was invoked and anarchy threatened. New Protestant guerrilla terrorist groups appeared. Armed robberies rose to 724 for the year with sixty-one recorded deaths and 1,450 wounded.[54]

It was all-out war once more. In spring of 1987, a major IRA attack on a police station in County Armagh was frustrated with eight IRA members shot, " . . . the worst loss suffered by the IRA since the 1920s," Gerry Adams reportedly complained.[55] In reprisal, the IRA planned a large bombing, which in the event misfired to kill eleven and wound sixty-one innocent civilians in Enniskillen.[56] Anglo-Irish conferences seemed to produce more words than action. Arms continued to reach the IRA, including a new plastic explosive, Semtex, reportedly " . . . almost invisible to security scanners."[57] Security forces in Armagh routinely stumbled on arms and explosive dumps. The French navy intercepted a ship carrying 150 tons of arms including Soviet-built SAM-7 missiles and rocket launchers intended for the IRA. The RUC gained another five hundred men to put it above thirteen thousand and units of Britain's crack counterterrorist organization, the Special Air Service Regiment (SAS), were reportedly deployed to the provinces.

In early 1988, a SAS team shot three IRA terrorists to death in Gibraltar. The IRA retaliated with a series of attacks on security forces in Ulster and British garrisons in Germany, a campaign continued into 1989 and 1990. In 1991, the IRA opened another offensive in England with a mortar attack on Number 10 Downing Street, which caused some property damage but no fatalities and was followed by a bomb exploded in Victoria Station—one killed, forty wounded.[58]

The almost hopeless scenario was challenged by a new Secretary of

State for Northern Ireland, Peter Brooke, who for over a year had been leading a political offensive involving all major political parties in Ulster. All-party talks in the spring were quickly sabotaged by right-wing Unionist leaders Paisley and Molyneaux and were soon terminated. Following Prime Minister John Major's intervention, the talks resumed in March only to be suspended until after the British general election. The Provisional IRA celebrated Major's re-election by exploding a large bomb in London's financial district—three killed, over ninety wounded, £1.5 billion worth of structural damage to buildings.[59] All-party talks resumed in May, but were stymied by Unionist refusal to allow the Dublin government to participate. In an effort to curb sectarian violence, Westminster declared the Ulster Defense Association (UDA) to be illegal. Members of the largest Protestant paramilitary group in Ulster can now be summarily imprisoned for up to ten years.[60] In August, an Ulsterman won the sad distinction of becoming the three thousandth fatality of the insurgency.[61] In September, all-party talks resumed only to be boycotted by Ian Paisley's party. Also in September, the Provisionals exploded an enormous bomb, which destroyed the forensic science laboratory outside of Belfast; miraculously, no one was killed but property damage was estimated at £20 million and essential police work seriously delayed. Guerrilla terrorists closed out the year with a series of bombings in Manchester and London.

This violent scenario but slightly changed in 1993. Commencing in April, Britain's Prime Minister John Major and Northern Ireland Secretary of State Sir Patrick Mayhew tried unsuccessfully to revive the suspended peace talks. The political spectrum broadened in July when the Irish Republic's Prime Minister Albert Reynolds talked about asking President Bill Clinton to intervene if the talks were not resumed.[62] At work here was the intransigent stance of Protestant Ulster diehards who refused to negotiate unless the Irish Republic canceled its constitutional claim to the sovereignty of Ulster, a demand that as of December 1993 has prevented the talks from resuming.

Although British officials claimed that the Provisional IRA guerrilla terrorists were hurting, the latter continued to carry out terrorist operations in the cities and countryside, and in waging virutally open warfare with Loyalist paramilitary groups (now considered by many army and police officials to be a more serious threat than the IRA). In truth, the violence potential of both sides is enormous, as witness the recent security-force seizure of a three-thousand-pound IRA bomb; or the finding of an immense IRA bomb under Bournemouth pier in England that would have taken hundreds of holiday-makers' lives; or the IRA September bombing of a Belfast supermarket to cause £1 million damage; or the intercepted shipment from Poland of two hundred assault rifles, two tons of explosives, and thousands of rounds of ammunition intended for Protestant guerrilla terrorists in Northern Ireland; or the random Protestant killings of five Catholics in eight days in September; or the Halloween massacre by a UFF Protestant terrorist of seven people in a bar in November.

Is there an end in sight for what some regard as a twenty-three year-old, others as a three-hundred-year-old, insurgency? Last year the answer would have been no, and there are still a great many people on both sides who foresee an endless war. In 1993, however, there have been some positive signs that the concerned governments are facing up to an increasing groundswell of public demand for an end to the senseless killing.

The IRA can claim credit for part of the initiative by having secretly approached the British government in February 1993 with a peace feeler. Subsequent talks apparently hinged on the IRA's willingness to abandon violence, but the content of the talks is murky owing to conflicting statements by Sinn Fein chief Gerry Adams and British government spokesmen, the latter greatly embarrassed when the world learned in the following November of the secret meetings. The substance is probably similar to that of more open talks begun by John Hume, leader of the SDLP's 650,000 Catholics, and Gerry Adams last spring, the idea apparently being to persuade IRA militants to lay down their arms in return for an official position at the negotiating table. Hume subsequently briefed Prime Minister Major and Prime Minister Reynolds on these discussions, the latter greeting the peace effort as a first step toward a "just and lasting solution" to the war. Major was sufficiently impressed to appeal to Adams to renounce terror " . . . and join the dialogue on the way ahead,"[63] and to want to keep the talks going.[64] Both Dublin and London governments seemed to be showing new flexibility, Major stating that "some cherished positions will have to be modified" in the "quest for peace,"[65] and Reynolds allegedly suggesting that the Irish Republic would consider altering its constitutional claims to sovereignty of Northern Ireland.[66] According to one report, in early December IRA spokesmen said " . . . they were, and remain, interested in a cease-fire leading to substantive talks."[67]

Despite the recent conciliatory words flowing from Dublin, a meeting between the prime ministers in early December merely emphasized the dichotomy in official thinking.[68] But then came the bombshell, when at a subsequent meeting Major and Reynolds put on the table a specific peace plan that, inter alia, offered self-determination to Northern Ireland and a position at the peace table for the IRA after it had carried out a no-nonsense cease-fire for three months.

All well and good, but the momentum will not be easy to maintain. Reverend Ian Paisley predictably greeted the Major-Reynolds plan with accusations that the British were betraying Ulster Protestants. Protestant moderates of the Ulster Unionists party, which is larger than Paisley's, are however showing an interest in these events, motivated in part by an increasing war weariness displayed by both Catholic and Protestant civic groups. But the Paisleyites and other extremist groups are well organized, financially strong, totally obdurate, and utterly ruthless. The same may be said of the militant IRA guerrilla terrorists, and there is certainly no guarantee that Gerry Adams, even if so inclined, could bring them to heel.

The rising Ulster middle class, though tired of the brutal and senseless killings and costly, disruptive bombings, is still neither sufficiently aroused nor organized to assert the political clout necessary to change things. Unlike many other insurgencies, this one is relatively easy to accept—anything from 54 to 113 deaths a year are not very many in a shooting war (in 1992 there were 800 gang-related homicides in Los Angeles). The U.K. and Irish Republic governments have not overly exerted themselves in pursuit of peace in the past, but again, an increasing war weariness in both countries, as well as an annual cost of $3 to $5 billion to Britain, appears to have shaken off their lethargy.

As 1993 closes, then, the hope for an eventual peace is brighter than it has been for a quarter of a century. Virtually everything hinges on the IRA's acceptance or rejection of the Anglo-Irish proposal. The debate in IRA circles will be acrimonious, but there must be many militants who realize that the odds in the long run are against them, particularly as police intelligence techniques improve and as security forces increasingly win the cooperation of a general public sickened by the shameful and revolting violence of what more often than not is gang warfare with religious overtones.

CHAPTER EIGHTY-SIX

1. Bishop and Mallie, 26.
2. Ibid., 21.
3. Ibid., 22.
4. Ibid., 23.
5. Bruce, 2–7.
6. Bishop and Mallie, 33–5. See also, Clutterbuck, *Guerrillas and Terrorists*, 64–5; International Institute for Strategic Studies, *Strategic Survey 1988–89*, 100.
7. Clutterbuck, *Guerrillas and Terrorists*, 65.
8. Goode, 129–30.
9. Institute for the Study of Conflict, *Conflict Studies Number 36*, June 1973, 2.
10. Clutterbuck, *Guerrillas and Terrorists*, 66.
11. Institute for the Study of Conflict, *Conflict Studies Number 36*, June 2, 1973 See also, ibid., *Conflict Studies Number 50*, October 1974, 27.
12. Bishop and Mallie, 73, 108.
13. Ibid., 68. See also, Bell, 364.
14. Bishop and Mallie, 83, 88.
15. Joe Jackson.

16. Bishop and Mallie, 106–7. See also, Clutterbuck, *Guerrillas and Terrorists,* 67.
17. Bishop and Mallie, 116.
18. Ibid., 109–10, 120–7.
19. Ibid., 235. See also, Institute for the Study of Conflict, *Conflict Studies Number 36,* June 1973, 18, which estimates that the NAC raised £1 million between 1969 and 1973.
20. Hamill, 41–2.
21. International Institute for Strategic Studies, *Strategic Survey 1971,* 68.
22. Bishop and Mallie, 144–5.
23. Clutterbuck, *Guerrillas and Terrorists,* 69. See also, International Institute for Strategic Studies, *Strategic Survey 1971,* 69–70.
24. Bishop and Mallie, 145: There had been 157 IRA bombings in 1970, a figure that rose to over a thousand by end of 1971.
25. International Institute for Strategic Studies, *Strategic Survey 1971,* 69.
26. Bishop and Mallie, 159.
27. Institute for the Study of Conflict, *Conflict Studies Number 50,* October 1974, 10.
28. Ibid., *Conflict Studies Number 36,* June 1973, 7. See also, Goode, 133–4.
29. Clutterbuck, *Guerrillas and Terrorists,* 70.
30. Institute for the Study of Conflict, *Conflict Studies Number 50,* October 1974, 7.
31. Clutterbuck, Private letter to the author. See also, Hamill, 143.
32. Institute for the Study of Conflict, *Conflict Studies Number 50,* October 1974, 11. See also, *Conflict Studies Number 36,* June 1973, 8.
33. Bishop and Mallie, 241.
34. Goode, 135.
35. Bishop and Mallie, 198–9.
36. Institute for the Study of Conflict, *Conflict Studies Number 50,* October 1974, 9.
37. Ibid., 2.
38. Ibid., *Conflict Studies Number 108,* June 1979, 4.
39. *Irish Times,* May 12, 1974, and May 17, 1990. See also, *NOW in Ireland,* May 1990; Raymond Murray, 108–21.
40. Clutterbuck, *Guerrillas and Terrorists,* 72.
41. Bishop and Mallie, 221.
42. Ibid., 255.
43. Clutterbuck, *Guerrillas and Terrorists,* 74. See also, Institute for the Study of Conflict, *Conflict Studies Number 108,* June 1979, 19.
44. Bishop and Mallie, 255.
45. Hamill, 242.
46. Ibid., 228.
47. Ibid., 235, 239. See also, Clutterbuck, *Terrorism and Guerrilla Warfare,* 160.
48. Goode, 137.
49. *Keesing's Record of World Events,* Vol. 34, 1988. December 1988, 36,238.
50. Bishop and Mallie, 305–7.
51. *Keesing's Record of World Events,* Vol. 31, 1985. October 1985, 33,939.
52. Ibid., Vol. 36, 1990. December 1990, 34,070.
53. Ibid., Vol. 37, 1991. April 1991, 34, 315–18.
54. Ibid., May 1991, 35,156.
55. Ibid., Vol. 34, 1988, October 1988, 36,327.
56. Ibid.
57. Ibid., 36,238.
58. *The Independent* (U.K.), April 11, 1992.
59. *Keesing's Record of World Events,* Vol. 38, 1992. April 1992, 38,869.
60. *The Independent* (U.K.), August 11, 1992.
61. Ibid., August 28, 1992.

62. *The Independent* (U.K.), July 4, 1993.
63. *New York Times,* November 23, 1993.
64. *International Herald Tribune,* December 1, 1993.
65. *New York Times,* November 23, 1993.
66. *International Herald Tribune,* December 2, 1993.
67. Ibid., December 2, 1993.
68. Ibid., December 4–5, 1993.

CHAPTER 87

The Basque legacy • Rise of the ETA • The "armed struggle" • Government countermeasures • The ETA splits: ETA-PM versus ETA-M • Franco's death • ETA refusal of government's amnesty and limited autonomy offer • Increased violence • The French connection • ETA setbacks • The drug factor • Continuing ETA guerrilla attacks • The situation in late 1993

TUCKED AWAY in the coastal mountain country of northwest Spain are four provinces which, taken with three French provinces on the other side of the Pyrenees, comprise an ancient ethnic community whose language bears no relation to other European tongues. This is Basque country, home of some of the finest cooking in Europe and home also of a long-standing insurgency carried out by the ETA and other guerrilla terrorist groups dedicated to winning total independence for the province from Spain. Although that goal is not shared by a large proportion of the region's 2.3 million inhabitants, of whom 65 per cent are native Basques,[1] there seems little doubt that the majority do want greater autonomy than the Madrid government to date has granted. There also seems little doubt that the majority do not accept ETA's doctrine of guerrilla terrorist violence to accomplish the stated goal although some are certainly in sympathy with the goal and apparently are willing to overlook ETA excesses in trying to accomplish it.

The Basques stem from the seventh century if not earlier. They have always occupied a unique position on the Iberian Peninsula, their semi-autonomous position guarded by mountains and sea and by a series of provincial *fueros*, or special local statutes such as that authorizing them to maintain their own customs posts. This began to change in the nineteenth century, owing to the encroachment of political centralization and the industrial age, during which most of the *fueros* were abolished. Adept as always, the coastal Basques soon established important in-

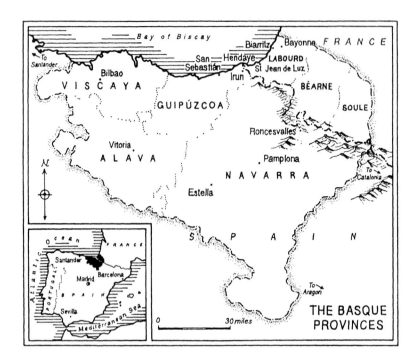

THE BASQUE PROVINCES

dustrial centers, but by attracting foreign capital and workers from the poorer Spanish provinces, these began to dilute the homogeneous quality of Basque life. These changes led to a rise of nationalism and in 1895 to the founding of the Basque Nationalist Party (PNV) by Sabino de Arana, who, as Edward Moxon-Browne tells us,

> ... gave shape to the course of Basque nationalism by baptizing the new state Euzkadi, designing its flag, and working to encourage the dissemination of the Basque language. Arana laid the foundation of the Basque nationalist ideology which, among other things, comprised a dedication to the Catholic religion, the espousal of non-violent methods to achieve political goals, the belief that all Basques should be united across the Pyrenees, and the assertion that language should be the defining characteristic of the Basque race. With a few modifications, and with a flexible view on the appropriate political structures to underpin these goals, those principles have remained the core of PNV orthodoxy up to the present time.[2]

Matters might have remained thus had it not been for the Spanish civil war (1936–39) and the dictatorship of Generalissimo Francisco Franco (1939–75). Franco loathed the coastal Basques, who fought as Republicans in the civil war. He not only banned the language, he banned its teaching and he ordered the burning of Basque books. Repression is not easily accepted by an intelligent people. In the early

1950s, a group of young nationalists splintered from the PNV to form the Euzkadi ta Azkatasuna (ETA—Basque Nation and Liberty), " . . . a simple nationalist movement with Basque independence as its sole objective."[3] The ETA did not advocate armed struggle but nevertheless it was treated as a subversive movement, and in the early 1960s its leaders went underground, moving to France, Belgium, Algeria, Ireland, and Venezuela.[4] Continued police repression brought a militant *cambio de sentido*, a change of mind, in 1966, at least to thirteen of the forty-five members who attended the movement's Fifth Assembly and who opted for violence—the "armed struggle"—to achieve their aim of turning the provinces into a Communist country. A series of bank robberies, attacks on military and police posts, and the murder of a provincial Basque police chief in 1968 were met with emergency decrees that enabled Franco's police to disarm the armed struggle by locking up hundreds of Basque dissidents (including several Roman Catholic priests), many of them receiving long prison sentences handed down by *military* courts in the best fascist tradition, a highly controversial affair that culminated in the 1970 Burgos trials in which six militants were sentenced to death for the murder of the Basque police chief.*[5] These hotly criticized trials, which attracted world attention, probably more than any single factor insured the growth of the movement—hundreds of young Basques flocked to revolutionary banners to continue a campaign of robberies, bombings, kidnapings (both for ransom and an improvement of working conditions), and killings. The government, encouraged by pro-Franco demonstrations such as a turnout of five hundred thousand in Madrid, evoked further emergency decrees including the right of the police " . . . to detain arrested persons for up to six months without trial."[6] In 1972, four ETA guerrilla terrorists struck on the unlikely but imaginative plan of kidnaping Franco, who would be exchanged for 150 ETA prisoners.[7] Once this proved infeasible, they killed Franco's new prime minister and presumed successor, Admiral Carrera Blanco, in late 1973 by tunneling under a street, packing the tunnel with high explosive and blowing admiral, bodyguard, chauffeur, and car over a five-story building, an incredibly bizarre operation well told by Peter Janke.[8] A few months later, the ETA's Sixth Assembly, attended by only thirty-six members, split into two factions, the ETA-PM (political-military), which stuck to the original goal of achieving Basque autonomy by building a powerful political base but also by using violence when necessary, and the ETA-M (military) whose proclaimed objective " . . . was the establishment of a Basque socialist state by armed action."[9]

---

* Such was the domestic and foreign outcry that Franco commuted the sentences to thirty years.

Unlike many guerrilla terrorist organizations, ETA-M believed in selective killing, " . . . symbolic attacks cumulatively expressing a coherent message to the public and the government," as Moxon-Browne elegantly put it.[10] Of an estimated 240 victims of ETA-M between 1968 and 1980, two thirds were soldiers or police, the Guardia Civil " . . . accounting for one third of all fatalities and a quarter of all those wounded. National and local policemen accounted for 23 percent of the fatalities. . . . "[11] Other victims included the governors of Madrid and of the Basque province of Guipuzcoa, leading opposition figures, mayors of several Basque towns, and, inevitably, a considerable number of luckless bystanders. The ETA was not fighting alone. In 1975, five terrorists belonging to ETA-M and to the Revolutionary Anti-Fascist and Patriotic Front (FRAP) were found guilty of murdering police officers and were executed by firing squad, an event that caused widespread international protest.[12]

Two major events now affected the ETA's campaign of violence. One was Franco's death in 1975, the other the establishment of a parliamentary democracy under the popular King Juan Carlos and the election by the people of a *Cortes,* or parliament. These major changes greatly improved PNV chances for gaining increased autonomy and undoubtedly would have resulted in further gains but for ETA intransigence. The *Etarras,* as ETA members were called, would have nothing to do with the new government, in their eyes a "pseudo democracy" that did not alter the status of the "real powers . . . the military, the financial oligarchy, the Church."[13] That the ETA did not stand alone was made clear in 1978 by the hostile reception in Basque country of the new constitution. Although this document, endorsed by a majority of Spaniards, effectively ended Franco-style fascism in favor of democratic government, 63 per cent of Basque voters rejected it on grounds that it failed to restore traditional Basque rights and did not grant sufficient autonomy to the provinces. Two more militant parties, the Euzkadika Eskcrra (EE) and the Herri Batasuna (HB), the latter the political front for ETA-M, surfaced to advocate " . . . the compulsory teaching of Basque in schools, the withdrawal of Spanish troops from Basque soil and various measures against 'capitalism.' "[14] As a sign of the times, each party won significant representation in Basque parliamentary elections held in 1980 at the height of ETA-inspired violence.

So violence it was, and violence it would remain. The targets were selective but diffuse, members of the Guardia Civil and the National Police being favorites. Token bombings were carried out at resort towns along the Mediterranean coast in unsuccessful efforts to disrupt the financially all-important tourist trade. Prominent persons were kidnaped and held for ransom. Army officers and soldiers stationed in Basque country were killed and also became targets in other places such as Madrid, where in 1986 an ETA-M "Spanish Commando" began to operate. A provincial military governor was killed as were a few business executives.

The government had tried to ward this off. As opposed to Franco's rigid policy of centralized government, the new government in principle had agreed on limited autonomy not only for the Basque provinces but also for Catalonia, Galicia, and Andalucia. Under the provisions of the 1978 constitution, the Basques and Catalans were to obtain full autonomy in 1980, including, in the case of the Basques and only after acrimonious argument, a favorable tax situation and an all-Basque police force as guaranteed in the 1979 Statute of Guernica.[15] The government, however, refused to withdraw the generally detested Guardia Civil.

When the ETA refused to accept this conciliatory policy, the government replied in kind. The year 1980 brought new anti-terrorist laws. Suspected terrorists could be jailed for ten days; security forces had the right to search houses without a warrant, intercept mail, and tap telephones. Tougher laws followed in 1981 and still tougher laws two years later when specially trained Guardia Civil police were assigned to the Basque provinces and given what amounted to combat pay.[16] With the advent of Felipe Gonzalez's socialist (PSOE) government in 1984, ETA sanctuary in France also was further compromised.

France was in a difficult position vis-à-vis Spain. Neither the French Government nor large numbers of the French people had been sympathetic to the Franco regime; nor was the "new democracy" at once accepted as genuine. The three French Basque provinces contained a large number of sympathizers with the ETA and its demand for an all-Basque independent state. The French Government prided itself on upholding the nation's traditional acceptance of political refugees.[17] Although ETA excesses had caused the French to ban the ETA organization in 1972, these factors not only resulted in an open tolerance of ETA activities on French soil but also in a refusal to extradite Spanish Basque ETA-suspects, who were termed "political refugees," to Spanish custody. According to one report, in 1980 two hundred Spanish guerrilla terrorists were based in the French border provinces. Covert efforts by Spanish intelligence to penetrate the Basque network were resented by France while French intransigence angered Madrid. A further complication arose when some Basque industrialists, tired of paying extortion to ETA militants, began to support a rightist paramilitary organization, the Anti-Terrorist Liberation Group (GAL), which concentrated on murdering suspected ETA members operating in France.

The new socialist government in Spain began to change the French attitude. Although François Mitterrand's socialist government still refused to extradite ETA suspects to Spain, it did begin to get them out of harm's way by deporting them to such countries as Uruguay and

Venezuela. Madrid in time also offered new terms to ETA-M members, including a policy of "social reintegration" by which terrorists in Spain and abroad could gain amnesty in return for " . . . renouncing all future acts of violence."[18] The offer was followed by a brief slowdown in ETA operations while Spanish government officials secretly met with a leader of the "nationalist ETA" (as opposed to the Marxist ETA in France) in Algeria, talks broken off when this man was killed in February. ETA kidnapings, bombings, and killings began again in March.

The ETA-M suffered a major setback some months later when a French court ruled in favor of sending four Spanish ETA members suspected of "criminal" as opposed to political activities back to Spain, an act that brought an immediate ETA offensive against the French presence in Spain. ETA-M tactics also sharply altered with the introduction of the car bomb (as had been the case with the IRA in Northern Ireland) and the advent of regional commando groups such as the Barcelona Commando, the Madrid Commando, the Itinerant Commando, which often acted, sometimes unwisely, on their own initiatives. Even loyal ETA sympathizers found it difficult to accept a car bomb explosion in Madrid " . . . in which five civil guards were killed and a further eight people injured."[19]

Despite persistent ETA operations, it was increasingly clear in 1986 that the security forces were slowly winning the battle. In April, ETA-M's military chief was arrested in France and deported to Gabon. Other ETA-M guerrilla terrorists received heavy sentences in French courts: some were deported to far away lands, others handed over to Spanish authorities without formal extradition proceedings. One French raid in Hendaye swept up six ETA activists, an arsenal of weapons, about a million French francs, and " . . . plans for attacks in Madrid and Barcelona."[20] Security forces continued to score in 1987, breaking up several ETA-M commando groups in Basque country and badly hurting the Spanish Commando by the arrest of its members and seizure of arms, explosives, and papers.

These setbacks understandably brought dissension in ETA ranks, the Marxist element in France holding out for prolonged war, the nationalist element in Algeria favoring negotiations with Madrid. In July 1987, government officials again met secretly with ETA-M leaders in Algeria, talks designed according to government sources only " . . . to bring an end to violence and not negotiation on the Basque region's political future."[21] French co-operation was also increasing as a result of guerrilla activities of a French Basque organization called Imparretarrak (Those of the North). In pursuing members of this organization, French police uncovered a Spanish ETA-M supply dump and arrested a man " . . . believed to have been ETA's supreme commander for the past two years, directing the activities of its commandos."[22] A Franco-

Spanish operation in October resulted in the arrest of over a hundred ETA suspects. In November, Spanish police claimed to have " . . . dismantled almost the entire infrastructure in Guipuzcoa [province]" and in December French police picked up another senior leader.

The ETA-M fought back hard, if not wisely. In June, the Barcelona Commando exploded a car bomb underneath a supermarket, killing twenty-one citizens, wounding thirty, and bringing out five hundred thousand Catalans of all political persuasions in a protest march. Continued killings of Guardia Civil and other policemen culminated in December when an ETA-M commando exploded a car bomb outside a police barracks, killing four Guardia Civil plus two women and five children to bring public indignation to a boil in Basque country as well as in the rest of Spain.[23]

This sordid pattern continued throughout 1988, which brought two new complications. One was French anger at the criminal activities of the Spanish rightist group, GAL, a quarrel duly settled with the socialist Mitterand government. The other was the wholesale importation of cocaine, one ton of which was seized by police in the Basque border town of Irun, the beginning of a massive problem that eventually would move the ETA to second place on the villain list. While violence dominated the mainland, talks continued with ETA-M in Algeria. Hopes for a settlement rose in early 1989 when ETA-M announced a cease-fire, but these were soon dashed by the extravagance of ETA-M demands and fighting began again in March.

So it was one step forward, two steps backward. Violent excesses continued to capture headlines. A Madrid court sentenced *each* of four ETA members to 2,232 years of imprisonment for having blown up a police bus three years earlier.[24] An ETA commando kidnapped a Pamplona industrialist, held him for eighty-four days, and released him for a ransom believed to have been close to $3 million.[25] Early in 1990, the Basque parliament passed a resolution " . . . proclaiming the right of the Basque people to self-determination and to decide fully and democratically on its political, economic, social and cultural status." Self-determination, however, " . . . could only come about gradually and democratically and with due regard to 'historical context.' "[26] The ETA responded by mailing five parcel bombs. Security forces arrested the leader of ETA-M's Itinerant Commando, who rather unwisely was carrying over six hundred pounds of explosive in his car, which was intended to blow up the colorful Sevilla *feria*—one of the most revered fairs in Spain. That arrest led to seventeen more in France—and the *feria* was saved. ETA-M next declared war on the World's Fair and Olympics scheduled for 1992 in Spain, a declaration emphasized by exploding a car bomb near Barcelona, killing six policemen and wounding eight.[27]

1991 brought more of the same: a car bomb exploded outside a Guardia Civil barracks, leaving nine dead including four children. ETA teams bombed Spanish diplomatic and commercial buildings in Rome, Milan, Bologna, Munich, Düsseldorf; in August, for the third year running, bomb threats against the Spanish rail system disrupted travel plans of over two hundred thousand people.[28]

These were desperate acts of desperate men. Arrests throughout the year continued to fragment the ETA organization. But the hard-core movement was not ready to die, nor was it entirely isolated. ETA deaths in prison or from shootouts invariably brought protests in the form of demonstrations or even strikes in the Basque country. To those within the movement who believed that " . . . the armed struggle was lost, was senseless and was damaging the Basque Nationalist left, and that ETA must face up to defeat," the hard-core leadership replied that " . . . the armed struggle remained the decisive factor in the process of attrition against the 'political enemy,' " a proclamation followed by the arrest of thirty ETA suspects, which in turn was followed by a bomb exploding under an army bus in Madrid to kill four soldiers and a bystander and wound seven passers-by.[29] More arrests of senior leaders occurred in spring and summer.[30]

Expo-92 in Sevilla and the World Olympics at Barcelona opened and closed without visible interference—a psychological disaster for what was left of ETA.

The organization was undoubtedly hurting, but was scarcely moribund. In June 1993 ETA guerrilla terrorists exploded two car bombs in Madrid that killed six senior military officers and wounded twenty-five civilians,[31] an action that caused a shocked minister of the interior to realize that the ETA could still murder "when and where they want."[32] In July guerrillas kidnaped a Basque industrialist (eventually released for a reported ransom payment of $4 million). In August four bombs were exploded in Barcelona, wounding five innocents; the following month ETA gunmen killed a Spanish army general.

These and other acts have turned public opinion in the Basque country sharply against the ETA. Elections in June 1993 returned only two members of the ETA political front, the Herri Batasuna, to the national parliament. In September thousands of demonstrating *vascos* identified themselves as ETA opponents by wearing blue lapel ribbons.

This is not to suggest that ETA will die overnight. There is still a stong nationalist movement in the Basque provinces, and the ETA militants, although sharply reduced in number, still have numerous sympathizers and a good deal of money. Presumably they will require both if they are to survive as an organized threat to the state.

CHAPTER EIGHTY-SEVEN

1. Moxon-Browne, 1.
2. Ibid., 2.
3. Ibid.
4. Janke, 7.
5. *Keesing's Contemporary Archives*, Vol. 18, 1971. January 1971, 24,405–8, for an interesting digest of these events including the Burgos trials.
6. Ibid., 24,406.
7. Janke, 2.
8. Ibid., 2–3.
9. Ibid., 6.
10. Moxon-Browne, 6.
11. Ibid., 7.
12. *Keesing's Contemporary Archives*, Vol. 21, 1975. November 1975, 27,463. See also, *The Times* (London), September 5, 1975; International Institute for Strategic Studies, *Strategic Survey Autumn 1975*, 72–4.
13. Moxon-Browne, 5.
14. Ibid., 4.
15. *Keesing's Contemporary Archives*, Vol. 26, 1980, April 1980, 30,181.
16. Ibid., Vol. 30, 1984. August 1984, 32,802.
17. Ibid., Vol. 19, 1983. May 1973, 25,907.
18. *Keesing's Record of World Events*, Vol. 32, 1986. February 1986, 34,182.
19. Ibid., December 1986, 34,825.
20. Ibid.
21. Ibid., Vol. 34, 1988. April 1988, 35,851.
22. Ibid.
23. Ibid., 35,852.
24. Ibid., Vol. 35, 1989. November 1989, 37,050.
25. Ibid., Volume 36, 1990. February 1990, 37,263.
26. Ibid.
27. Ibid., April 1990, 37,330, 37,387.
28. Ibid., Vol. 37, 1991. August 1991, 38,300, 38,356, 38,402. See also, *International Herald Tribune*, August 10–11, 1991.
29. *Keesing's Record of World Events*, Vol. 38, 1992. February 1992, 38,783.
30. *The Independent* (U.K.), March 30, 1992.
31. *International Herald Tribune*, June 26, 1993.
32. *Daily Telegraph* (U.K.), June 22, 1993.

CHAPTER 88

The 1947 partition of Palestine • The birth of Israel in 1948 • Arab League armies invade Israel and are defeated • The refugee problem • A shaky peace • Increasing guerrilla warfare • The Suez Canal fiasco and Israeli gains • Rise of the Palestine Liberation Organization (PLO) • Guerrilla warfare intensifies • PLO's guerrilla terrorist elements • Israeli countermeasures • The 1967 six-day war • United Nations Resolution 242 • The occupied territories • 1973 invasion of Israel • The Camp David Accords • The Lebanon war and Israeli occupation • Yasser Arafat's defeat • Decline of the PLO • Israeli departure from Lebanon • Outbreak of the intifada *• Yasser Arafat's renascence • Israeli conflict with the U.S. Government • Israel expels Islamic Hamas guerrillas • Peace talks resume • Israel's secret talks with the PLO • The new Israeli-PLO peace plan • The problems ahead*

> . . . life for life, eye for eye, tooth for tooth, hand for hand, foot for foot, burning for burning.
>
> EXODUS 21:23–5

WE LEFT PALESTINE ON the verge of being partitioned between Jews and Arabs (see Chapter 45), the details to be worked out by a special United Nations committee. The committee's solution was reluctantly adopted by the Jewish Agency (the executive body of the international Zionist organization) once the British Government made it clear that it intended to yield the mandate and withdraw its troops in the near future. The resolution was passed by UN General Assembly vote, by no means unanimous, in late 1947. The Arab League responded by ordering attacks against Jewish settlements not only in Palestine but throughout the Middle East.

The partition was immensely complicated and rather unrealistic, thus a fitting supplement to the Balfour Declaration of 1922, which set the scene for the interminable guerrilla wars prior to World War II. As Sydney Bayley wrote of the 1947 partition in his excellent book, *Four Arab Israel Wars and the Peace Process:*

> ...the Jewish state was to comprise 56 percent of the area of Palestine and would have a Jewish population of 449,000 and an Arab population (including Bedouin) of 510,000. The Arab state would comprise 43 percent of the area, with an Arab population (including Bedouin) of 747,000 and about 10,000 Jews. The international enclave [the city of Jerusalem together with Bethlehem] would total about 68 square miles and have about 100,000 Jews and 100,000 Arabs. A Palestine Commission of five members [from Bolivia, Czechoslovakia, Denmark, and the Philippines] was given responsibility for implementing the partition plan, under the guidance of the Security Council.[1]

It is doubtful that a more powerful time-bomb has ever been constructed. Not unnaturally the Palestinian Arabs and other Arab states—Egypt, Iraq, Lebanon, Saudi Arabia, Syria, Transjordan, and Yemen—regarded the plan as an attempt to settle a Western-created problem at their expense, and they rejected it as "illegal and unjust."[2] While the Arab League recruited and trained an Arab Liberation Army, Palestinian and Egyptian guerrillas began attacking Jewish motor convoys and isolated Jewish settlements busy turning desert sands into profitable farming communities. Jewish Haganah (Defense Organization) counterattacks of Arab villages followed. In this opening exchange, the Jews had the upper hand. Neither the Arab Liberation Army nor local Arab militias in Palestine were well-trained or well-organized forces. The Haganah and its Palmach assault units, on the other hand, had been fighting Arabs and the British for nearly three decades. World War II saw the birth of two guerrilla terrorist groups, the Irgun Tsvai Leumi (Etzel)—the National Military Organization—and the Lokhammei Kherut Israel (Lehi)—Fighters for the Freedom of Israel—better known as the old Stern Gang (see Chapter 45), which now conducted independent operations against the Arabs. Isolated Jewish settlements had long since been providing their own protection in much the same way pioneers in nineteenth-century America had protected their settlements against Indians. When a kibbutz was violated, retaliation by Haganah and guerrilla units was swift and harsh. Perhaps inevitably, this led to pre-emptive strikes against Arab targets, the ar-

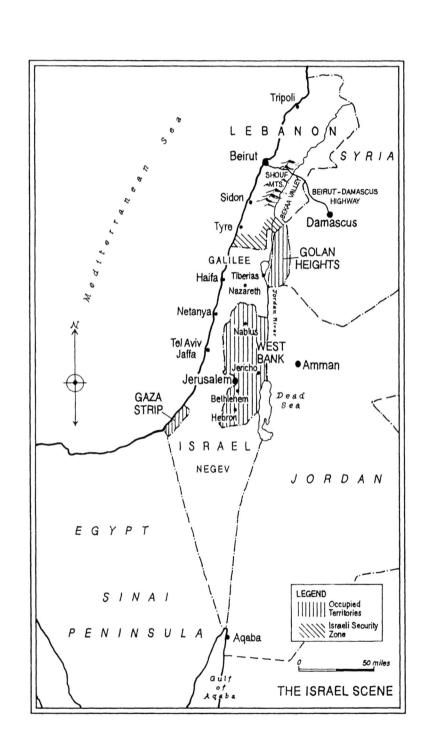

THE ISRAEL SCENE

gument being that these were "defensive"[3]—a semantic perversion historically known as "preventive war" and practiced by, among other aggressors, Frederick the Great and Eric Ludendorff. Some of the strikes were unnecessarily harsh, for example that by Israeli guerrillas who in 1948 put one village to the torch after killing 250 Arabs, half of them women and children.[4] Arab guerrillas at once retaliated by ambushing a convoy and killing seventy-seven Jews, but it was the village massacre that captured headlines and led not only to international opprobrium but also to the Arabs leaving their villages in increasing numbers, the beginning of what grew to be an unmanageable and enormously tragic refugee problem.[5]

Unable to stem escalating violence the UN Palestine Commission, supported by the Jewish Agency, asked for an international military force to intervene, but nothing came of this largely because of U.S. resistance,[6] nor was the dispirited British army scheduled for departure about to help. The British mandate ended in May 1948, whereupon David Ben-Gurion declared that the Provisional Government of Israel had come into being. It was a stormy birth at once contested by Arab League armies invading from Egypt, Lebanon, Syria, and Jordan. UN special envoy Count Folke Bernadotte of Sweden somehow managed to arrange a cease-fire policed by a force of UN observers, but guerrilla forces refused to accept it and when fighting resumed in July, the Israeli army soon gained the upper hand. Bernadotte's repeated efforts to achieve a compromise settlement by granting Israel western Galilee and the Arabs the Negev led to his assassination by Israeli guerrilla terrorists in September 1948. Despite the pleas of UN envoy Ralph Bunche, who had replaced Bernadotte, Israeli forces continued to push into Galilee and the Negev, routing the Arab Liberation Army and even briefly pushing into Egypt before year's end.

Bowing to U.S. demands, Israel pulled back from Egypt early in 1949 and accepted a cease-fire that left it with more land than it had been granted by the partition. It had been quite a year: over half a million Arabs had fled their Palestinian villages; an estimated one hundred thousand Jewish immigrants had arrived in Palestine and many more were to come.[7] The Arab League was in disarray. In January, what was now the Government of Israel signed an armistice with Egypt; similar agreements followed with Lebanon and Syria, and in spring of 1949 Israel was admitted to the United Nations. Under UN auspices, Armistice Demarcation Lines supervised by UN personnel were established. In July 1949, Ralph Bunche informed the Security Council that fighting had ended in Palestine.[8]

This happy event was not long lasting. As Israel consolidated its territorial gains, as Israeli citizens "made the desert bloom," as the young nation grew in confidence and manpower—over half a million immigrants, many of them from Arab countries, received with open arms between 1949 and 1956—the Arab states festered in disunity, refusing to recognize Israel's place in the sun yet unable to challenge it by other than pinprick raids by guerrillas, the *fedayeen,* answered rapidly and roughly by an increasingly mobile Israeli army equipped with modern U.S. weapons to defend its vulnerable borders with Egypt, Jordan, Syria, and Lebanon. The refugee problem, roughly one million Arabs jammed into camps in Jordan, Lebanon, Syria, and the Gaza Strip, went unheeded. Israel did not want them back, indeed David Ben-Gurion washed his hands of any responsibility for their plight; the Arab states did not want them, and those who managed to escape the camps and settle in those states were shabbily treated.[9] Each side was too busy feeding hatred to allow humanitarianism to interfere. For Arabs, it was a matter of revenge; for Israelis, preservation. Border raids increased; Egyptian suicide teams were sanctioned by Egypt's Gamal Abdul-Nasser; Israeli retaliation followed; armistice agreements bent and broke; Jordan grew antagonistic and seized the West Bank;* superpowers entered the fray; Russia replaced U.S. influence in Egypt; the U.S. continued to support Israel; wanting to isolate Israel economically, Gamal Abdul-Nasser closed the Suez Canal to Israeli use and blockaded the Gulf of Aqaba; Nasser nationalized the Canal; to retrieve it, Britain and France supported by Israel launched a surprise attack during which Israeli troops seized the Sinai Peninsula and passed into Egypt—an ill-planned, ill-executed, and very costly fiasco that terminated in November 1956, the UN sending in a six-thousand-man force to police up the mess while the principals withdrew their troops. Though pressed by the U.S., Israel refused to yield either the Gaza Strip or the western coast of the Gulf of Aqaba. In 1958, Egypt and Syria formed the United Arab Republic; Moslems in Christian-dominated Lebanon started a civil war; Iraq and Jordan formed a union that lasted for six months, ending with King Faisal's murder . . . and so it went. As Julian Becker put it: " . . . Manifestly the desire for Arab unity was the chief cause of Arab disunity."[10]

Nearly a decade passed before the next decisive development in the Arab-Israeli conflict, not that there was a lack of regional crises during this period. Although Egypt stopped sending guerrilla teams into Israel, partly owing to UN observation posts along the border, such attacks continued from Jordan, Syria, and Lebanon. Some of these were made by Syrian guerrillas recruited from Palestinian refugee camps in Leba-

---

* The West Bank of the Jordan River is inaptly named. The area containing the biblical lands of Judaea and Samaria and such cities as Jerusalem, Nablus, Jericho, and Bethlehem measures nearly eighty miles north to south and thirty miles east to west, thus amounting to a considerable portion of Palestine. Its western border is only about nine miles from the sea at its nearest point.

non, some by factions of Ahmed Shuqairi's Palestine Liberation Organization (PLO), a new movement formed by six Palestinian groups at Egyptian President Nasser's instigation, its goal the "liberation" of Palestine.[11] The principal group, the Movement for the Liberation of Palestine, or al-Fatah, was organized in 1957 by, among others, twenty-six-year-old Yasser Arafat, a Palestinian refugee and an officer in the 1956 war. Al-Fatah guerrillas first went into action in 1964, small raids that publicized the group and won financial support from the Arab world.

As Israel again moved toward war with its neighbors—this time the *casus belli* was a dispute over Israeli use of water from the Jordan river—the PLO became increasingly active but was temporarily eclipsed by Israel's overwhelming military victory in June 1967—the famous six-day war which left Israel in possession of the Sinai Peninsula, Gaza, the West Bank of the Jordan, and the Golan Heights, a land area three times the size of Israel.[12]

But victory is an illusory word. The new lands included "a million hostile Arabs," in the words of one realistic Israeli politician.[13] Israel's victory and subsequent harsh military occupation of the West Bank and Gaza guaranteed implacable hatred that could not but result in another war.[14] In an attempt to forestall this, the UN in November 1967 passed Resolution 242, which called for " . . . Withdrawal of Israeli armed forces from 'territories occupied in the recent conflict . . . [and] a just settlement of the refugee problem,' " the latter exacerbated by the addition of another three hundred thousand refugees to a total 1.5 million.[15]

As superpower positions polarized, the U.S. supporting Israel, the Soviet Union supporting Egypt and Syria, it was apparent to the Palestinians that an impasse had developed. In their minds, their only recourse was guerrilla warfare, and it was not long before PLO guerrillas of the Palestine Liberation Army (PLA) were striking Israeli positions from Jordan and Lebanon with Israeli forces retaliating in kind.

The PLO was gaining in strength, drawing on the immense pool of young refugees and a horde of youthful volunteers from Arab countries for its guerrilla recruits and on rich Arab states such as Saudi Arabia, Libya, and Kuwait for money to buy arms. Shuqairi's death late in 1967 was followed by the young Yasser Arafat's ascendancy.[16] In early 1969, Arafat was elected chairman of the PLO's executive committee. Of the organization's several guerrilla groups, Arafat's al-Fatah with about seven to nine thousand guerrillas was the most important and also the least militant. More recently formed groups included Dr. George Habash's Popular Front for the Liberation of Palestine (PFLP), a Marxist guerrilla terrorist group of about five hundred members formed in 1968; and two splinter groups from the PFLP, Ahmed Jibril's Popular Front for the Liberation of Palestine—General Command (PFLP-GC), and Naif Hawatmeh's Popular Democratic Front for the Liberation of Palestine (PDFLP).[17] In addition to these groups was a large Syrian Ba'ath guerrilla organization founded in 1968 and called Vanguards of the Popular Liberation War, its military arm being al-Saiqa (Thunderbolt), led by Zuhayr Muhsin.[18] Of these organizations, Arafat's Fatah, Hawatmeh's PDFLP, and Muhsin's Saiqa " . . . wanted political negotiation and territory for Palestinian self-determination wherever it could be won."[19] The remaining groups, refusing these notions in favor of an all-out "armed struggle" to annihilate Israel, formed the Rejection Front, itself of fragile lasting power.[20] Indeed, had it not been for the intense factionalism that led to countless quarrels between the Arab guerrilla groups, it is doubtful that Israel could have survived.

By 1969, several thousand Saiqa and PLO guerrillas were based in southern Lebanon where they infiltrated refugee camps that held some one hundred thousand Palestinians and " . . . were turning the camps into centers for guerrilla training and indoctrination."[21] Arafat's major guerrilla force in Jordan had expanded sufficiently to control large areas of the kingdom and there was talk that he was planning a coup against King Hussein.

In 1969, guerrillas based in Lebanon and Jordan carried out an estimated thirty-nine hundred guerrilla actions against Israel and in 1970 were averaging about five hundred a month including raids from Lebanon as far into Israel as Haifa.[22] Israel did not take this lying down, and most observers give the army high marks for its counterguerrilla tactics. When an El Al plane was hijacked, Israel responded by an airborne commando raid on the Beirut airport that destroyed thirteen planes belonging to Arab countries. Ground forces were authorized to make "hot pursuits" into Lebanon and Jordan and also to make preemptive strikes against suspected guerrilla concentrations.

George Habash's PFLP terrorists made world headlines in May 1970 by blowing up the pipeline that carried Saudi Arabian oil to Mediterranean ports.[23] Later in the year, PFLP terrorists hijacked four Western commercial aircraft and held passengers and crew hostage until the release of some imprisoned guerrillas. After releasing the hostages, they blew up the planes. That action, coupled with increasing encroachments by the PLO in Jordan and two attempts by PFLP terrorists to assassinate Hussein, led to what the PLO would remember as Black September: its forceful eviction by the Jordanian army after heavy fighting which cost the guerrillas perhaps three thousand dead before the groups retreated dispiritedly into Syria and southern Lebanon.[24] Guerrilla terrorists of the PFLP and of a new group, the Black September Organization operating out of Syria, now began claiming headlines by such operations as the murder of nine Israeli athletes at the Olympic Games in Munich in September 1972 (after previously carrying out a series of assassinations in Europe).

What few people seemed to realize was that the PLO could not exist without Palestinian refugees.[25] It was all very well to have forced those people from their lands, but surely it was incumbent on the responsible parties—Britain, the U.S., Israel, Egypt—to find them a new homeland and in conjunction with their oil-rich fellow Arabs—Saudi Arabia, Libya, Iraq, Kuwait, Yemen—to give them the money necessary to build new livelihoods. It was not as if the Israelis had been given or had taken the world—" . . . in 1984," wrote one commentator, "the size of the Jewish State is less than a quarter of 1 percent of Arab territory, and the Arabs have some two dozen states."[26] There is almost no mention of this collective responsibility. In 1972, King Hussein did come up with a plan to build a federated United Arab Kingdom with Jordan, a plan immediately denounced by Israel, Egypt, and Syria,[27] and soon forgotten. Yet almost everyone in a responsible position stressed again and again that there could never be a suitable peace between Israel and the Arab world until the "Palestinian question" was satisfactorily resolved.

Various attempts to bring about Israeli evacuation of the vast Sinai Peninsula having failed, in 1973 Egyptian and Syrian armies opened a surprise invasion of Israel which caught its army off guard. Although the October war ended favorably for Israel, it also deepened Arab hostility and for the first time opened Arab eyes to the value of oil as a weapon against the West. We should take note that the war could not have been fought without massive U.S.-Soviet military aid to the belligerents; indeed it very nearly provoked a clash between the two superpowers.

The war left the Palestinian refugee problem unsolved. It was, however, becoming better recognized thanks in part to headlines engendered by PLO terrorist attacks abroad. In 1974, the UN General Assembly, ignoring Israel and U.S. protests, listened to Yasser Arafat talk about Middle East problems, an impressive performance that helped win the PLO an observer's role in the United Nations, full membership in the Arab League, and general recognition that the Palestinian refugees must be provided with a homeland.

In mid-1977, Prime Minister Menachem Begin (whose Irgun guerrilla terrorists had helped to force Britain from Palestine) visited America's new President, Jimmy Carter, who

> . . . made it clear that there was no hope for a settlement in the Middle East without a homeland for the Palestinians. . . . Carter stressed that the establishment of Jewish settlements in the occu-

pied territories was a serious obstacle to peace, but Begin insisted that there was no way of stopping Jews from settling in biblical Israel. . . . Begin ruled out any contact with the PLO and said that Israel would never agree to a Palestinian homeland or entity."[28]

Carter's determined attempts to break the deadlock, notably by sending veteran negotiator and now Secretary of State Cyrus Vance to the troubled area, finally brought an unprecedented meeting between President Sadat of Egypt and Prime Minister Begin under the auspices of President Carter. This resulted in Israel and Egypt signing the Camp David accords and subsequently a formal peace treaty in 1977. Under its terms, Israel agreed to a phased withdrawal from the entire Sinai Peninsula. The treaty also affirmed " . . . the legitimate rights of the Palestinian people and their just requirements." Although the Israel Knesset, or parliament, approved the accords, Israeli right-wingers vigorously opposed them. President Sadat for his part won only open censure from the Arab world and Egypt was expelled from the Arab League. As for "the legitimate rights of the Palestinian people," no action was taken and little more was heard for the next few years.

An important casualty of the Middle East deadlock was Lebanon, whose once-prosperous facade had been shattered by continual political turbulence compounded by the presence of Zuhai Mohsen's Syrian-backed Saiqa guerrillas and the influx of PLO guerrillas evicted from Jordan. Early in 1975, a new civil war broke out between Christians and Moslems, the left-wing Druze groups of the latter being supported by Palestinian guerrillas. By early 1976, the almost defunct Lebanese army and the Maronite Christians, whose main military strength rested in Pierre Gemayel's Phalange militia, were on the verge of defeat by Arafat's PLO guerrillas and socialist Kamal Jumblatt's Druze militia (themselves in conflict with the Rejection Front of splinter guerrilla groups). Not wanting this to happen, Syria's Hafez Assad sent in an armor division to support the Maronites and Israel began supplying them with weapons. Owing largely to the leadership of Gemayel's son Bashir, the war ended in October in the Maronites' favor, a hollow victory in view of the casualties—at least forty thousand killed, one hundred thousand wounded and half a million people displaced from their homes.[29] Syrian armies remained in northern Lebanon and in the Bekáa Valley "as a peacekeeping force" and most of the PLO bases in Beirut and in northern and southern Lebanon remained intact, their presence formally accepted by the Lebanese Government.[30]

This was anathema to Bashir Gemayel, who, supported by the slippery Phalange patriarch Camille Chamoun, eventually persuaded Israel to guarantee " . . . the safety of the Lebanese Christian community."[31] Begin did not encourage Gemayel's bellicose intentions of ejecting the Syrians from Lebanon. Gemayel's desire for a confrontation with Syrian troops in the Bekáa Valley probably would have been frustrated by Begin's government had it not been for the PLO presence in southern Lebanon, the supportive presence of Secretary of State Alexander Haig in Washington, and the hawkish presence of Ariel Sharon, the Minister of Defense in Begin's cabinet.

Ironically, Yasser Arafat's presence in southern Lebanon resulted from the mass of refugees caused by Israel's victories over the Arab states. Arafat's guerrillas had easily infiltrated the refugee camps eventually to build "a state-within-a-state," gathering the support of Shiite Moslems in the countryside and Sunni Moslems in the cities: " . . . the PLO had become by 1976 the sole instrument of rule in the western sector of Lebanon stretching from Beirut to the Israeli border,"[32] from where PLO guerrillas stole into Galilee and elsewhere. Israeli troops retaliated by striking PLO camps in Lebanon—in early 1978, twenty-five thousand Israeli troops pushed across the border and, aided by Major Sa'ad Haddad's expanding Christian militia, burned dozens of Palestinian villages and left some seven hundred dead before withdrawing.[33]

In 1981, Menachem Begin was taking an even stronger line against the PLO enemy. With the exception of a surprise air raid that knocked out Saddam Hussein's nuclear reactor plant in Iraq and the abrupt annexation of the Golan Heights later that year (actions that infuriated his U.S. ally), Begin's main thrust was against the PLO. A host of raids by land and sea accompanied by heavy aerial bombing raids of PLO camps in Beirut and southern Lebanon brought prolonged PLO artillery shelling of the Galilee settlements, a duel interrupted by a cease-fire in July. But Begin and his closest advisers had decided that the PLO had to leave southern Lebanon if Israel's northern flank was ever to be secure, the plan being to clear the area of enemy and establish a twenty-five-mile-deep security zone north of the border. But now a secret plan was hatched by central players Ariel Sharon, Foreign Minister Yitzhak Shamir, and a few military hawks, who intended not only to drive Arafat's PLO and Assad's Syrians out of Lebanon but to install Bashir Gemayel as president. This fitted in nicely with Alexander Haig's current vendetta against Syria although the extent of his encouragement to Sharon (against Reagan's wishes) has not yet been fully revealed; that it was considerable is suggested by his quarrel with Reagan and subsequent removal from office.

The Machiavellian details of Sharon's double-dealing and the subsequent mainly conventional and very cruel war that began on June 6, 1982, by Israeli forces pushing into Lebanon are not pertinent to this survey. It is enough to say that Israeli soldiers and fliers won an overwhelming victory against both Syrian and PLO armies.[34] Arafat was forced into asylum in Tripoli and an estimated eight thousand of his followers were dispersed in various Arab states.[35] This was a solid enough gain for Israel but it was tempered by the majority of three hundred thousand Palestinian refugees, including several thousand guerrillas, remaining in their squalid Lebanon camps; by a large Syrian army based in the Bekáa Valley, from where it controlled over half the country; by a strong Druze militia holed up in the Shouf Mountains, where Bashir Gemayel's Phalange militia suffered a serious defeat in attempting to evict them; by the precarious position of Bashir Gemayel's new government; by his assassination in September; and by the opprobrium heaped on Israel from Cairo, Washington, and other capitals for invading Lebanon and then carrying out a prolonged and bloody occupation.

Suddenly aware that Sharon's war had placed him in a vulnerable position, Menachem Begin decided that both Israeli and Syrian troops must vacate the country, leaving the Lebanese responsible for policing the border security zone. Here Israel-manned surveillance posts would be supported by Major Sa'ad Haddad's Christian militia of fifteen hundred to two thousand troops. Washington agreed with the plan, a "simple and logical" solution in Secretary of State George Shultz's words, but one that depended on Christian Maronite control of the country.

Amin Gemayel, who had replaced his brother as president, did not control the country. The steps taken by the Reagan administration to gain him control did not sufficiently respect either the intense religious and political factionalism in Lebanon or the political acumen of Syria's Hafez Assad generously supported by an extremely anti-Israel Soviet Union.

The basis of the plan was a multinational armed force to keep the peace while Gemayel relied on U.S. economic and military aid to build a strong army. Meanwhile, Arafat's remaining forces in Lebanon would be given sanctuary in Iraq and Jordan. A Lebanese-Israeli-PLO treaty would further isolate Syria. The Reagan administration had made the supreme error of underestimating Assad. Increasing aid to the Moslem Druze militia, he reinforced his army in Lebanon to a total twelve hundred tanks, increased his Soviet military advisers to five thousand, and surrounded Damascus with batteries of SAM-5 ground-to-air missiles.[36]

What of the PLO? There was no doubting that it had suffered " . . . the worst blow in its eighteen-year existence."[37] It had lost heavily in numbers—estimates vary from one to five thousand—and it also had lost its corporate "homeland." Its various groups were widely dispersed. Arafat and about a thousand guerrillas finally ended up in Tunisia. Leaders of small terrorist groups found refuge in Damascus but their fighters had to go as far as South Yemen and Algeria. An estimated two thousand guerrillas remained secretly in Beirut while others joined the three to four thousand guerrillas still in the Bekáa Valley and in north Lebanon.

Yasser Arafat remained chairman of the PLO and, after beating off a rebellion in his own Fatah Party, was soon touring the Arab states, pulling the strands together.[38] If the PLO had been weakened, it certainly was not moribund, and such countries as Saudi Arabia and Libya continued to contribute generous amounts of money. Arafat's task was daunting, not only organizationally and logistically but politically. The big question was, what next? Some within the organization wanted to intensify " . . . the armed struggle for the total liberation of Palestine." Others realized that Israel was there to stay and believed that the solution lay in an independent state comprising the West Bank and Gaza.[39] Some Arab countries agreed with this, others did not. In September 1982, President Reagan, borrowing from King Hussein's 1972 proposal, called for an end of Israeli settlements in the occupied territories, refused the notion of converting these lands into an independent Palestinian state, and concluded: " . . . it is the firm view of the United States that self-government by the Palestinians of the West Bank and Gaza in association with Jordan offers the best chance for a durable, just and lasting peace." Considering that the PLO still refused to recognize Israel's existence, that Israel refused to negotiate with the PLO, that Jordan did not recognize Israel, that any thought of Jordan mixing into PLO affairs was anathema to Syria and the PLO splinter groups in Damascus, neither Reagan's nor any other plan was to be even debated, much less accepted. Israel rejected the plan outright. Although Arafat did not directly reject it, he effectively neutered it by insisting on " . . . the national rights of the Palestinian people 'under the leadership of the PLO, its sole legitimate representative' and demanded the setting up of 'an independent Palestinian state with Jerusalem as its capital.' "[40]

In mid-September, Israeli troops in the shattered city of Beirut joined with Amin Gemayel's Phalangist militia in storming PLO refugee camps in West Beirut which were believed to be harboring militant guerrillas, a two-day operation that turned into a sickening slaughter of an estimated three thousand Palestinians.[41] World-wide condemnation of the action was shared within Israel by protest marches of up to four hundred thousand people and by the emergence of a Peace Now movement. It also brought harsh words from President Reagan and it cost Israel a great many former friends including some important Jewish figures.[42]

The unhappy occupation continued throughout 1983. In September, Prime Minister Begin resigned, reportedly distraught by the occupying army's high casualty rate, but such was the power of the military that occupation continued into 1984. In April, the government announced that its forces would stay in Lebanon until the South Lebanese Army

(SLA)—formerly the Christian militia commanded by Major Sa'ad Haddad (and after his assassination by Antonio Lahad)—was ready to replace them.[43] This decision was tempered later in the year when a Jordan-PLO initiative based on UN Resolution 242 called for Israel to respect " . . . the principle of territory in exchange for peace" and withdraw from the West Bank and Gaza.[44] Wiser heads now recognized that the political priority had to shift southward (where it had always been despite Sharon's costly frolic into Beirut) and a three-stage withdrawal from Lebanon commenced in early 1985. Owing to guerrilla interdiction, this was a slow and painful operation completed only in June.

Such was the perpetual turmoil in the Middle East that one crisis was scarcely over before another began. While members of the major factions continued to kill each other in Lebanon and while the Jordan-PLO initiative was making tentative approaches to Israel's new "national unity" Labor government headed by Shimon Peres, the world's attention shifted to the Iran-Iraq war which ended only in 1987. By then, Hussein and Arafat's attempt to bring Israel into peace negotiations had come to naught. Also by then, the long-suffering Palestinian refugees living under Israeli rule in the occupied territories had had enough.

In 1987, rumbles of civil revolt heard for years turned to thunder. When an Israel taxi driven by a Jew crashed into and killed four Palestinian laborers, the storm boke. The ensuing Arab uprising, or *intifada,* in the West Bank, Gaza, and the Golan Heights was carried out on the one hand by youths hurling stones and petrol bombs, on the other by passive resistance in the form of general strikes, resignations of Arab officials and policemen, refusal of Arabs to pay taxes and boycott of Israeli-owned shops and Israeli-made goods.

The Israeli government moved fast and hard to quell the uprising. Prime Minister Yitzhak Shamir's "iron fist policy" was spelled out by Minister of Defense Yitzhak Rabin as giving priority to "might, power and beatings."[45] This resulted in several hundred Palestinian deaths, seven to eight thousand wounded and twenty-two thousand imprisoned in 1988.[46] It also resulted in massive official protests by the U. S. and U. K. governments, the European parliament, the UN Security Council, and not least by the general Israeli public. As the rebellion spread in 1989, Israeli security forces began firing plastic bullets in carrying out an official policy of "shoot-to-wound,"[47] to achieve Rabin's announced goal of "hurting them . . . leaving scars."[48] By year's end, the number of Arab deaths from military action had risen to six hundred plus 150 caused by Arab vigilantes killing suspected Arab collaborators. Jewish deaths numbered forty. Although some schools reopened in the West Bank, the intifada was becoming a way of life: " . . . The government, army and the public had settled into an attitude of acceptance of the level of violence and a pattern of attrition was established."[49]

The intifada apparently caught the PLO by surprise, although Arafat hastened to support it politically and financially. Arafat's authority, however, was seriously challenged by Palestinian members of Hamas, a growing militant Islamic resistance movement which advocated " . . . an Islamic state in all of Palestine (including Israel) and rejected the PLO's giving growing reliance on political struggle and a compromise solution."[50] The gulf between Arafat's PLO and other guerrilla terrorist groups widened visibly in late 1988 when, in presenting a peace plan to the UN, he " . . . condemned terrorism in all its forms," later telling journalists, " . . . I repeat for the record that we totally and absolutely renounce all forms of terrorism."[51] Secretary of State Shultz took the next important step in agreeing to open talks with the PLO, though without recognizing it as a Palestinian state. Shultz's successor, James Baker, openly criticized the Israeli Government for continuing its policy of armed struggle. Shamir shrugged off his words, the PLO committed itself to more not less violence, the Islamic Hamas gained in strength and influence, and the intifada intensified.

Once again, the "Palestinian problem" was shunted aside by war, this time brought on by Saddam Hussein's invasion of Kuwait in August 1990 and the ensuing Gulf War. That crisis resolved (at least in part), the intifada regained center stage as the Israeli government expanded its settlement program, which, according to an official U.S. report, had established " . . . over 200,000 Israeli settlers . . . in some 200 settlements in the occupied territories" and was growing as much as 10 per cent annually.[52] Hoping to halt the program, the Bush administration delayed approval of $10 billion in promised loan guarantees to Israel, but at the same time pushed ahead on bringing Israelis and Palestinians to the negotiating table, no mean feat that was accomplished in Madrid in late 1991. More talks ensued, intransigence prevailed, intifada violence reached a new high as Israel's relations with Washington reached a new low, the Bush administration holding firm in refusing to release the loan guarantees until the settlement program was halted.

In February 1992, Prime Minister Shamir publicly reneged on Israel's commitment to the Camp David Accords.[53] Seemingly nothing could alter conservative Likud intransigence, that is until mid-1992 when, *mirabile dictu,* the conservative government gave way to Yitzhak Rabin's center-left coalition. The new government held out the olive branch to Washington by canceling future settlement building. In mid-August, Rabin opened peace negotiations with Syria, going so far as to offer Hafez Assad a portion of the Golan Heights in return for a peace treaty between the two governments—tacit acceptance of the "land for peace" formula originally set forth in UN Resolution 242.[54] At peace talks in Washington in late August, Israeli Foreign Minister Shimon Peres did not offer much more than some form of Arab autonomy in the occupied territories, but he subsequently stated that he wanted a political settlement, a goal that he realized could be achieved only by pursuing the "land for peace" formula.

Negotiations came to an abrupt halt in December 1992 when the Israeli government summarily expelled 415 Palestinian Islamic fundamentalists—suspected Hamas guerrilla terrorists—from the West Bank. Because no other country offered sanctuary, the unfortunates, some of whom were *not* guerrilla terrorists, were consigned to a bleak hillside in Israeli-occupied Lebanon, there to spend a cold winter in tents with neither adequate food nor medical care—a TV spectacular that, although blackening the Israeli image, failed to change the government's stance until spring of 1993. Indeed, the government in March again moved firmly when, in an attempt to end Palestinian guerrilla attacks inside Israel, it closed the borders of the West Bank and the Gaza Strip, thus preventing over 100,000 Arabs of the 1.8 million in these territories, from keeping their jobs in Israel.[55]

These events, taken with frequent riots and killings in the occupied territories, did not encourage a resumption of peace talks, and it was only by a superhuman diplomatic effort that Secretary of State Warren Christopher brought delegations from the concerned parties—Israel, Syria, Jordan, Lebanon, and the Palestinians—together in Washington for the ninth round of talks. This time a new and important face appeared at the table, that of Faisal Husseini, the leader of the Palestinian team, who heretofore at Israeli insistence had not been permitted to attend the talks. For this slight plus, however, there was a very large minus, and that was the absence of the well-known scruffy face of the all-time guerrilla survivor, Yasser Arafat, a political pariah in the eyes of Washington and Israel. The ninth round of what Clyde Haberman aptly termed "the stutter-start negotiations" ended three weeks later with the usual whimper, the all-important question of Palestinian self-rule in the occupied territories no closer to a solution than ever.[56]

The tenth round of talks that resumed in mid-June, again without the presence of Yasser Arafat, ended "with such gloom there was not even talk of a date to talk again."[57]

Matters might well have remained in limbo had it not been for fourteen rounds of secret talks in an isolated Norwegian farmhouse that had begun in May. A month earlier the doughty political columnist Flora Lewis had called attention to Yasser Arafat's appeal to end the violence and hold elections in the occupied territories. More important, he "accepted that the first stage of negotiations be linked to 'self-government,' without reference to the later goal of statehood."[58] This became the basis for the ultra-secret talks between Yasser Arafat and

Israeli Foreign Minister Shimon Peres under the aegis of the Norwegian government.

Without revealing the existence of the talks, Peres in late June ". . . joined the growing number of Israeli politicians . . . urging that the Israeli-occupied Gaza Strip be turned over to Palestinians 'as soon as possible' and that the Israeli army retreat from most of the area."[59] Concurrent with this development, certain Israeli cabinet ministers realized that the bête-noire of the Washington negotiations was the absence of Yasser Arafat and, contrary to Washington's policy, that the time had come for direct talks with the PLO—a feeling that gained weight during a summer of heavy fighting and the increasing threat from Islamic guerrilla terrorists in the West Bank and Gaza, not to mention a dangerous stalemate with Syria over the Golan Heights and Syrian support of guerrilla terrorists in Lebanon.

Although Prime Minister Yitzhak Rabin still refused to recognize either Yasser Arafat or the PLO, that decision was forced on him in late August when the story broke of Shimon Peres' secret negotiations having produced ". . . a radical new peace formula under which Palestinians hope independence would be tested first in the Gaza Strip and in the West Bank town of Jericho."[60]

This was the concept, an *Arab* concept, that won almost instant approval by the members of the eleventh round of peace talks then taking place in Washington. Within a week the logjam of years had been broken: Israel and the PLO formally recognized each other; the U.S. recognized the PLO; Yatzik Rabin and Yasser Arafat not only signed the agreement at a special White House ceremony but *publicly shook hands*.

The ratified agreement called for a withdrawal of Israel troops by December 13, 1993, from the Gaza Strip and the town of Jericho, security to be taken over by Palestinian police. An interim Palestinian government is to be replaced by election of a Palestine Council in spring of 1994. It was anticipated that the agreement would pave the way for separate agreements between Israel and Jordan (accomplished), and between Israel and Syria-Lebanon (not accomplished), and would lead eventually to Israel's turning over all of the West Bank to Palestinian rule.

The agreement was at once denounced by powerful factions both in Israel and the PLO. The Israeli right-wing Likud Party pronounced it a betrayal of Israel's interests as did the 100,000 or so Jewish settlers in Gaza and the West Bank. The Israeli army grumpily announced that it had not been consulted and pointed to security dangers that would accrue from an Israeli troop-police evacuation. Yasser Arafat faced an incipient rebellion in the PLO, whose governing council nevertheless approved the agreement.

Scarcely a day has passed since ratification without a crisis developing in the occupied territories, all to the delight of the gloom-and-doom factions on each side. As fighting intensified between Jewish settlers and Palestinian Arabs in late November and early December, Prime Minister Rabin warned of a possible delay in troop evacuation, much against the wishes of Yasser Arafat. Sure enough, the day arrived—and the troops remained. The world must hope that this is only a temporary setback now that the way has at last been opened for peace.

CHAPTER EIGHTY-EIGHT

1. Bayley, 1.
2. Ibid., 4.
3. Ibid., 3.
4. Goode, 90–1.
5. Bayley, 12–13.
6. Ibid., 8.
7. Ibid., 44.
8. Ibid., 66–70.
9. Becker, 2.
10. Ibid., 37.
11. Bayley, 187.
12. Ibid., 240.
13. Ibid.
14. Cobban, 36–9.
15. Bayley, 270–1, 243. See also, Clutterbuck, *Guerrillas and Terrorists*, 79.
16. Cobban, 21–35, is excellent on the origin and growth of Arafat's al-Fatah and the PLO.
17. Becker, 73, for biographical details of the various leaders.
18. Ibid., 72–3.
19. Ibid., 82.
20. Cobban, 15.
21. Goode, 102.
22. Ibid., 101.
23. International Institute for Strategic Studies, *Strategic Survey 1970*, 45.
24. Cobban, 49–52. See also, Becker, 75–6.
25. Cobban, 7–8, 38–42.
26. Becker, 30.
27. Bayley, 293.
28. Ibid., 351.
29. Becker, 136.
30. Cobban, 81.
31. Schiff and Ya'ari, 29.
32. Ibid., 79.
33. Cobban, 94–5.
34. Becker, 205–7.
35. Cobban, 3.
36. Schiff and Ya'ari, 295.
37. International Institute for Strategic Studies, *Strategic Survey 1982–83*, 75.
38. Cobban, 4–5.
39. International Institute for Strategic Studies, *Strategic Survey 1982–83*, 77.
40. Ibid., 78.
41. Cobban, 129–30.

42. International Institute for Strategic Studies, *Strategic Survey 1982–83*, 71–2, 75–7.
43. *Keesing's Record of World Events* Vol. 31, 1985. February 1985, 33,438.
44. Ibid., March 1985, 33,494.
45. Ibid., Vol. 34, 1988. April 1988, 35,859.
46. International Institute for Strategic Studies, *Strategic Survey 1988–89*, 157–8.
47. *Keesing's Record of World Events* Vol. 35, 1989. December 1987–December 1988, 36,436.
48. International Institute for Strategic Studies, *Strategic Survey 1988–89*, 159.
49. *The Annual Register and Record of World Events 1989*, 197–8.
50. International Institute for Strategic Studies, *Strategic Survey 1988–89*, 159.
51. *Keesing's Record of World Events*, Vol. 35, 1989. December 1987–December 1988, 36,438.
52. Ibid., Vol. 37, 1991. April 1991, 38,168.
53. *International Herald Tribune*, February 8–9, 1992.
54. *Newsweek*, March 2, 1992.
55. *International Herald Tribune*, April 12, 1993.
56. Ibid., June 8, 1993.
57. *The Independent* (U.K.), July 6, 1993.
58. *International Herald Tribune*, April 16, 1993.
59. Ibid., June 29, 1993.
60. *The Independent* (U.K.), August 29, 30, 31, 1993.

CHAPTER 89

Emperor Haile Selassie of Ethiopia toppled • The Dergue's Marxist-oriented urban and rural guerrilla opposition • The Eritrean challenge • War in Ogaden province • Soviet and Cuban military presence • Guerrilla reverses • The massive refugee problem • Lieutenant Colonel Mengistu Haile Mariam's regime • Widespread famine • Guerrilla gains • Mengistu's fall • 1993: Independent Eritrea • The divided Sudan: Moslem versus Christian • Guerrilla warfare in Equatoria • The 1972 Addis Ababa accord • Colonel Mohammed al-Numiery's rule • John Garang's guerrilla army • 1990 Sudan: "a human rights disaster" • Lieutenant General Hassan al-Bashir's Islamic government • Pope John Paul II protests • Starvation • Bashir's Islamic fundamentalist state • Anarchy in the South

IN 1941, ETHIOPIAN GUERRILLAS supported by British troops delivered the first defeat to the Axis powers in World War II by forcing the Italian invaders to retreat from their country. Emperor Haile Selassie thereupon returned from exile to resume rule of this vast land (some 472,000 square miles) that held forty-six million people of diverse ethnic, tribal, and religious beliefs. Although preaching a policy of modernization, the emperor failed to introduce vital political and economic reforms; nor did his autocratic command of the army insure undivided loyalty. In 1974, he was deposed by a military coup after forty-four years of rule. He was replaced by a military dictatorship carried out by the Provisional Military Administrative Council, or Dergue, one of whose leaders was a Marxist lieutenant colonel, Mengistu Haile Mariam.

The new government, like that of Mohammed Daud in Afghanistan, lorded over what essentially was an impoverished agrarian society, a

tribal nation, one of the poorest in the world, life expectancy forty years, high illiteracy, a host of killing endemic diseases, few schools, hospitals, or clinics. To put this right, the Dergue socialist government nationalized industries and banks, implemented a radical land reform program—and jailed or executed any members of the former regime who stood in its way.

The new government faced several threats to its existence. One came from urban middle-class members of the largest ethnic group, the Amharas, who formed the Ethiopian People's Revolutionary Party (EPRP), a Marxist group whose guerrilla terrorists began eliminating important government and trade union officials, army officers, and police to bring on the harshest possible countermeasures in the form of thousands of arrests and large-scale executions to the extent that the movement was largely neutralized by 1978.[1]

Another threat came from the enormous semidesert province of Ogaden, home to some two million Somali-speaking traditionally unruly nomads, in the form of a large guerrilla group called the Western Somali Liberation Front (WSLF) supported by Somalia. In 1977, the WSLF went to war against the government, the vanguard of an invasion by the Soviet-trained Somali army. The invaders made good progress initially but then bogged down and in 1978 were forced from the country by Ethiopian troops supported by a large Cuban contingent. This was only a victory of sorts in that it left a simmering insurgency that would challenge Ethiopian-Cuban forces for many years.

Other threats were not so easily neutralized coming as they did from a number of insurgent guerrilla groups: the Eritreans and Tigreans in the north, the Afars in the east, the Harrars in the southeast, and the Oromos (Gallas) in the south, all wanting independence for their provinces.

The coastal province of Eritrea with its six-hundred-mile coastline on the Red Sea had been a problem since 1952. A former Italian colony, it was forced into federation with Ethiopia by the United Nations in order to provide Ethiopia with access to the sea. Subsequently a trouble spot, Haile Selassie sought to solve the problem by abrogating the treaty and making Eritrea an Ethiopian province,[2] an act that brought on a full-scale guerrilla insurgency. The major guerrilla group was Ahmed Mohammed Nasser's Eritrean Liberation Front (ELF), which was supported financially by Somalia, Libya, Iraq, and South Yemen.[3] The ELF fought government forces from 1960 on, eventually becoming a " . . . well-armed, well-trained, well-disciplined and highly motivated" force some twenty-two thousand strong.[4] Two other guerrilla groups emerged in time: Ramadan Mohammed Nour's Marxist Eritrean People's Liberation Front (EPLF), which split from the ELF in 1971 and numbered about twelve thousand; and Oosman Saleh Sabbe's ELF-Popular Liberation Forces (ELF-PLF), about two thousand strong. In 1977, these forces controlled most of the province, and had it not been for intense internecine squabbling, they might well have claimed the entire province. Once the Somalis were expelled from Ogaden province, however, army reinforcements arrived in the north and the guerrilla offensive was temporarily checked. Another insurgency sprang up in the neighboring province of Tigre, where guerrillas of the People's Liberation Front (PLF) were in control of most of the province. A third challenge came from the Oromo Liberation Front (OLF), which was also fighting for independence. More fighting took place in the northwest province of Begemder, where Ethiopian refugees in the Sudan formed a guerrilla group that enjoyed only limited success. But in the east, Afar guerrillas systematically cut road and rail lines connecting Addis Ababa with the Djibouti outlet to the sea.

To counter these insurgencies and fight the war in Ogaden, the Dergue maintained an army of about three hundred thousand (including militias). This force had received $400 million worth of U.S. military aid since 1953 and was being trained by a three-hundred-man U.S. military advisory group. Washington continued to support the government for the first two and a half years of Dergue rule, a nebulous relationship that noticeably cooled as Mengistu clawed his way up the leadership rostrum, his way cleared by his executing scores of former comrades and others accused of "counterrevolutionary crimes." Mengistu became chairman of the Dergue in 1977 and announced that henceforth only socialist countries would supply weapons to Ethiopia. The U.S. canceled its aid program and soon withdrew its advisers. Soviet arms and Cuban soldiers were now arriving in quantity. By early 1978, an estimated one thousand Soviet and two thousand Cuban military advisers were working with the greatly expanded Ethiopian army.[5] During 1978, the army received " . . . some 600 tanks and over 90 combat aircraft, including twenty of the sophisticated MiG-23s."[6] There were now an estimated fifteen thousand Cuban troops in the country. In late 1978, Mengistu was received in the Kremlin, where he signed a twenty-year treaty of friendship. At year's end, Ethiopian and Cuban forces were more than holding their own in the continuing guerrilla war in Ogaden. Eritrean guerrillas had been forced to disperse to bases in Sudan; the ELF had been particularly hard hit, leaving the EPLF " . . . as the main force for Eritrean independence."[7] In the east, both the Tigrean and Afar guerrilla groups were badly damaged and in the west the guerrillas were almost out of business.[8] A "red terror" campaign against the urban EPRP killed an estimated twenty-five hundred insurgents with tens of thousands arrested and sentenced to "political reeducation"[9] to virtually end the movement.

The new government nonetheless continued to face massive problems as famine swept the land and as revitalized guerrilla groups in Eritrea and Tigre continued to fight. By 1984, more than six million people were believed to be starving and at least half a million close to death.[10] A massive program that resettled six hundred thousand northerners to the south had to be halted because of widespread protests that sent thousands more refugees into Somalia and Sudan. Once the rains came and harvests improved, Mengistu renewed the program. He also introduced a new constitution, which was accepted by 81 per cent of the vote. Under its terms, Ethiopia became the Popular Democratic Republic theoretically run by an 835-member parliament, the Shengo. The republic came into being in late 1987 with Mengistu as president assisted by a cabinet of twenty members, seventeen of whom came from the old Dergue.[11]

The new government had no sooner taken office than another famine struck that would affect up to five million people. Both the army and guerrilla groups would as in the past obstruct relief efforts by holding up food convoys when it suited their political purposes. By February 1989, the TPLF occupied all of Tigre province and the EPLF held all of western Eritrea. Together with the perilous state of the economy and the famine crisis, these gains brought on an unsuccessful coup attempt by fourteen senior military officers including five major generals.[12] The Shengo now voted unanimously to start peace talks with the EPLF in London and the TPLF in Rome, something the somewhat apprehensive

Soviet Union had been pressing Mengistu to do for some time.

Heavy fighting meanwhile continued in both provinces. In early 1990, EPLF forces seized the vital port of Massawa and had encircled the Second Army of about one hundred thousand men holding the Eritrean capital Asmara.[13] Mengistu earlier had been forced to pull his best units out of Eritrea to counter the TPLF's advance on Addis Ababa, a combined effort with several smaller guerrilla groups fighting under an umbrella organization, the Eritrean People's Democratic Revolutionary Front (EPDRF). In a radio broadcast in March, Mengistu admitted the failure of his socialist regime and announced a number of liberal reforms of more capitalist than socialist thrust. His old socialist party was now renamed the Ethiopian Democratic Unity Party (led by Secretary-General Mengistu and an eleven-man Politburo), in which opposition groups were welcome to participate.[14] The guerrilla groups scorned his proposals, rightly identifying them as a play for time. Nor did Mengistu's chief patron, the Soviet Union, seem impressed, suggesting coldly that he lay " . . . particular emphasis on promoting talks on peace and national reconciliation."[15] Apparently unimpressed with this paternal advice, Mengistu in June refused a cease-fire offer by the EPDRF in return for the establishment of a broad-based transitional government. He next called for general mobilization in order to win the war.[16]

Peace talks between the government and EPLF in Washington in early 1991 brought a renewed offer of autonomy for Eritrea similar to the one sabotaged by Haile Selassie in 1960—an offer countered by the EPLF with a demand for a referendum on Eritrean independence.[17] While EPLF guerrillas continued to fight in the northwest, OLF units were fighting west of Addis Ababa and EPDRF forces, moving in from the northwest, were only thirty miles from the capital in late March.[18]

The end was drawing near. On April 19, in a three-hour broadcast Mengistu offered to resign " . . . if that will preserve the unity of the country," but in the same speech he attacked " . . . tribal secessionists . . . mercenaries and traitors."[19] Two days later, he presented the Shengo with a resolution to set up a " . . . peace forum with all opposition parties and unity forces" in order to form a transitional government.[20] In early May, he was making frantic peace moves, which went generally unheeded. Then on May 21, he suddenly disappeared (reportedly to be given asylum in Zimbabwe).

A week later, EPDRF guerrillas moved into Addis Ababa against almost no opposition, its leader Meles Zenawi announcing " . . . that a transitional government would be formed in consultation with other groups, pending elections"; EPLF leaders who set up a provisional government in Eritrea promised to co-operate with the EPDRF administration in Addis Ababa.[21]

In July, acting head of state Meles Zenawi called a conference of hundreds of delegates from twenty-five political parties, to whom he presented a transitional charter of government that was to remain in force until a future general election. The provisional government of Eritrea announced that a referendum on independence would be held in 1993.

In April 1993 over 99 percent of the Eritrean electorate voted for separation from Ethiopia in a UN-declared "free and fair" election, the first step toward a promised democracy for the new state.

> The [Sudanese] rebels will be crushed by the end of the year.
>
> PREMIER MOHAMMED AHMED MAHGOUB,
>
> NOVEMBER 1965[23]

The Republic of the Sudan was born in 1956. A former British possession, Sudan is the largest country in Africa, nearly a million square miles complete with mountain ranges, timbered hills, grassy plains, swamps, rain forests, and deserts. Home of the Mahdi, of Omb-durman and General Gordon's ill-fated stand at Khartoum, home also to the famous White Nile and Blue Nile, whose histories are so wonderfully told by Alan Moorehead, home also to 572 tribes speaking 114 languages, all of which spell intense poverty, ignorance, and misery.[24]

Under British control, the country for all practical purposes was divided into the larger Arab Moslem North of about 7.5 million people and the Negro Christian-Animist South of 2.75 million, of whom 250,000 were Christian converts. The North continued to grow, the South to lie dormant. Arabic became the official language, which closed most civil servant jobs to blacks—the Southerners were given exactly six of eight hundred positions made vacant by the British exodus in 1954.[25] Political differences abounded in the new government. One important northern party wanted an independent unified Sudan, another an alliance if not union with Egypt. The southern party wanted autonomy for the South in a federated union. Militarily, the North also dominated the South. The Sudan Defense Force was officered by northerners. The older Equatoria, or Southern Corps, was staffed by twenty-four northern officers with only nine junior southern officers, and a similar imbalance existed in the police and civil administration.[26]

The trouble started in August 1955, when a southern infantry company ordered to the North mutinied. More mutinies followed, all put down in a few weeks with some of the leaders executed and the Southern Corps disbanded, many of its soldiers slipping off into the bush with their weapons. The uneasy relationship continued after independence, southern resentment growing as northern politicians and army officers moved swiftly to autocratic rule. Such were the constant crackdowns on southern political aspirations that in 1966 their political leaders fled to Uganda, Kenya, and Ethiopia, where they established the Sudan African National Union (SANU).

Up to this point, the fugitive members of the disbanded Southern Corps had been relatively quiescent, stealing food from luckless natives while evading government forces, supplementing their meager number of rifles with " . . . bows and arrows, spears and machetes."[27] In 1968, however, these disparate groups merged into the Land Freedom Army (LFA), which soon was renamed Anya-Nya (Snake Poison).[28] Working from base camps in frontier areas, the guerrillas attacked police and army posts, gradually growing in strength as northern repression caused southern dissidents to join their ranks. By 1965, they would number perhaps five thousand but would still lack weapons.

The North meanwhile had plunged into a sort of controlled anarchy, with premiers resigning, coalition governments coming and going, riots, strikes, corruption, inflation—the usual fate of any country governed by the few for the profit of the few. In the South, SANU, never united, splintered into various groups. The gulf between North and South remained as wide as ever, the southerners demanding self-government, the northerners refusing to consider more than regional reforms. In remote southern areas, the guerrillas struck where possible, then retreated into jungle or mountain camps to leave frustrated soldiers burning villages and killing indiscriminately as famine and disease covered the land. In other areas, guerrillas controlled the countryside, imposing taxes, even setting up their own administrations. But there was neither military nor political unity. Guerrilla leaders ruled their fiefs and political leaders squabbled as parties formed and dissolved. In 1969, there were three governments in the South with one in exile. The guerrilla movement lacked any co-ordination and often deteriorated into savage tribal wars.

The semianarchic picture North and South changed in 1969 when thirty-eight-year-old Colonel Mohammed al-Numiery led a successful coup against the Khartoum government, set up a revolutionary council to govern the new Democratic Republic of Sudan, and dissolved all political parties to rule as military dictator of a socialist government suppressing all "liberation movements," including Yasser Arafat's Palestine Liberation Organization.[29]

Shortly after Numiery had taken over the government, the guerrilla movement began to achieve cohesion. That was the work of Joseph Lagu, an army lieutenant who defected to the Anya-Nya and eventually commanded the Eastern Equatoria region. In August 1971, Lagu formed the Southern Sudan Liberation Movement (SSLM), but in December a government drive by some fourteen thousand troops and six thousand police chased the guerrillas into Uganda. In March 1972, both sides agreed to a cease-fire and subsequently signed a treaty, the Addis Ababa accord, that in theory guaranteed the South's autonomy and offered generous concessions to the guerrilla insurgents, many of whom were absorbed into the regular forces.

After several years of relative quiet on the shooting front, increased friction between Moslem settlers and indigenous southerners caused Numiery (recently elected to a third six-year term by a 99.6 per cent vote)[30] to renege on the Addis Ababa agreement by dividing the South into its former three separate regions, which the Southerners interpreted as an abrogation of autonomy. Tempers were already short owing to the government's international exploitation of southern oil fields that resulted in the presence of numerous foreigners intruding into what the Southerners regarded as their own land. Khartoum's recent failure to ameliorate serious food shortages—by 1983 the Numiery government was awash in a sea of domestic and foreign relations crises—was also a bone of contention as was Numiery's mutual defense agreement with Egypt, regarded by many as prelude to political-military integration with Cairo and thus a further strengthening of Moslem power. Hostility increased in October 1983 when Numiery announced that " . . . the penal code had been revised in order to link it 'organically and spiritually' with Islamic law (sharia)."[31]

A revitalized guerrilla movement now emerged to fight what was regarded as injustices, the Sudanese People's Liberation Front (SPLF) and its militant guerrilla wing, the Sudanese People's Liberation Army (SPLA), led by John Garang. The guerrilla aim was to overthrow Numiery's government and install a "people's democratic government."[32] In early 1983, veterans of the old Anya-Nya group re-formed into Anya-Nya II (allegedly controlled by the SPLF) and began attacking police and army posts, operations subsequently expanded to sabotage of railroads and bridges and kidnapings of foreign oil company employees.[33] In December, the army reported that in breaking a guerrilla siege of a town it had killed 480 guerrillas.

Real trouble had begun in February 1983, as it had in 1955, with a mutiny by a southern army unit which refused to be transferred to the North. Fighting soon flared between southern and northern army units. In May, a southern battalion mutinied and in the ensuing battle seventy-eight soldiers were reportedly killed.[34] Sporadic fighting continued as guerrilla strength grew. In spring of 1984, Numiery declared a state of emergency and moved additional troops to the South to fight a new civil war.

It was more a tragic war than an interesting one, at least from the guerrilla standpoint. It was expensive, costing an estimated $1 million a day (30 per cent of the budget) when the country faced a $12 billion external debt.[35] It was a war interrupted by turbulent political change and meaningless cease-fires. In 1985, a military coup deposed Numiery to put government in the hands of a Transitional Military Council. Colonel John Garang's SPLA declared a brief cease-fire, which led to nothing. Elections in 1986 resulted in a coalition government headed by Prime Minister Sadeq el-Mahdi, but peace talks with Garang soon broke down and the war continued, a war of protest but also a war of bloodthirsty tribal feuds fought against a background of almost unimaginable human suffering occasioned by widespread famine and the subhuman behavior of both guerrilla and government forces. As in Ethiopia, both sides used food as a weapon, often holding up and even seizing urgently needed food supplies in order to score politically with one or another tribe.

Garang's SPLA, armed now with surface-to-air missiles, scored a series of notable victories in 1987 to leave government forces in shaky control of southern provincial capitals and little else. Further government reverses in 1988 produced a crisis in Khartoum, political intervention by the United States, and a demand from Sudanese army leaders that the government make peace.[36] As sieges and countersieges of towns and cities continued and as rapacious soldiers and guerrillas ravaged the countryside, the flow of refugees, many of whom were near starvation, jammed camps within and without the country. Conditions in North and South worsened; repression increased. By 1990, according to Africa Watch, Sudan was "a human rights disaster"—civil war and famine had taken more than five hundred thousand lives " . . . while thousands of women and children in the south had been sold into slavery."[37]

There seemed to be no end to this Dantesque nightmare. In June 1989, the government was deposed by a coup and replaced by Lieutenant General Hassan al-Bashir's fundamentalist Islamic military dictatorship. Not surprisingly, peace talks between government and southern leaders broke down at year's end—as the specter of another far more violent famine hovered over the land.

Disaster struck in early 1990 when an estimated eight million Sudanese (roughly one third of the population) were facing starvation. Far from co-operating with relief efforts, the Bashir government downplayed the severity of the famine while continuing to consolidate its power by torturing and executing hundreds and probably thousands of political, military, and religious opponents, real or imagined. In the midst of this chaos, Bashir definitively tipped his political hand by supporting Iraq in the Gulf War and by establishing a National Islamic Front that called for a *jihad* or holy war against the West.

Trouble meanwhile had broken out in John Garang's guerrilla army, whose leaders had split over whether the revolutionary goal was that of "a united, secular Sudan" (Garang's belief) or that of "an independent black state" (the dissident Nasir group's belief).[38] The schism and subsequent severe fighting between the two factions caused postponement of further peace talks. It also allowed government forces to open a large offensive in February 1992 that succeeded in overrunning a number of towns formerly held by the SPLA.

Peace talks that finally began in late May did not halt the fighting. By October, government forces had regained control of a dozen towns, while Garang's increasingly hard-pressed guerrillas were tied up in besieging the provincial capital of Juba.[39] Elsewhere in the South, Bashir's troops were continuing a campaign of civil murders that some observers compared with the Serbian "ethnic cleansing" of Bosnia-Herzegovina. The pogrom worsened during the winter to the extent that Pope John Paul II publicly scolded the Sudanese leader, Lieutenant General Omar Hassan al-Bashir, " . . . who called allegations of human-rights abuses 'grotesque fabrication,' " this at a time when according to a United Nations' estimate, " . . . 800,000 Sudanese faced imminent starvation,"[40] in part owing to brutal factional fighting in the South.

This unhappy situation continued into spring of 1993, the fate of Sudan's nearly eight million non-Moslem peoples growing more hopeless as Bashir and the Islamic National Front continued to try to convert the country to a strict fundamentalist Moslem state. This activity was supported by Iran, which has helped Bashir turn his country into the world's major terrorist-training center as well as into an international pariah. Bashir's government is not only at odds with its neighbors, dangerously so in the case of Egypt, but also with the U.S. government, which in August 1993 placed Sudan on its list of terrorist nations (Iran, Iraq, Syria, Libya, Cuba, and North Korea), for both supporting and at times harboring Abu Nidal's guerrilla terrorist organization, the Lebanese Hezbollah, and the Palestinian Islamic Hamas group.[41]

Fighting in the South meanwhile intensified to the extent that the United Nations has had increasingly to suspend its relief operations.[42] There is no sign of a letup in this guerrilla war. In June peace talks between Garang's SPLA and the government came to nothing. With the advent of the dry season in September, government forces opened a new offensive against SPLA guerrilla units. That, taken with increasing food shortages, can mean only more massive starvation in the months ahead.

CHAPTER EIGHTY-NINE

1. International Institute for Strategic Studies, *Strategic Survey 1977*, 24.
2. Makinda, 13.
3. International Institute for Strategic Studies, *Strategic Survey 1974*, 87.
4. Ibid. *1977*, 22.
5. Ibid., 20.
6. Ibid., *1978*, 94.
7. Ibid., 97.
8. Ibid., *1979*, 97.
9. Ibid.
10. Ibid., *1984–85*, 100.
11. Ibid., *1987–88*, 188.
12. *Keesing's Record of World Events*, Vol. 36, 1990. January 1990, 37,173.
13. Ibid., February 1990, 37,239. See also, International Institute for Strategic Studies, *Strategic Survey 1990–91*, 230.
14. *Keesing's Record of World Events*, Vol. 36, 1990. March 1990, 37,310.
15. Ibid., April 1990, 37,368.
16. Ibid., Vol. 37, Supplement February 1991, 38,053.
17. Ibid., 37,996.
18. Ibid., March 1991, 38,089.
19. Ibid., 38,137.
20. Ibid.
21. Ibid., News Digest for May 1991, 38,174.
22. Ibid., July 1991, 38,322.
23. O'Ballance, *The Soviet War in the Sudan: 1955–1972*, 79.
24. Ibid., 18.
25. Ibid., 37.
26. Ibid., 40.
27. Ibid., 57–8.
28. Ibid., 59.
29. Ibid., 105.
30. *Keesing's Contemporary Archives*, Vol. 39, 1983. July 1983, 32,292.
31. Ibid., Vol. 30, 1984. July 1984, 33,009. See also, International Institute for Strategic Studies, *Strategic Survey 1985–86*, 182–3.
32. *Keesing's Contemporary Archives*, Vol. 30, 1984. July 1984, 33,010.
33. Ibid.
34. Ibid., Vol. 29, 1983. July 1983, 32,293.
35. International Institute for Strategic Studies, *Strategic Survey 1986–87*, 183–4.
36. Ibid., *1988–89*, 184–5.
37. *Keesing's Record of World Events*, Vol. 36, 1990. April 1990, 37,367.
38. Ibid., Vol. 37, 1991. September 1991, 38,426.
39. *Newsweek*, October 5, 1992.
40. *Newsweek*, February 22, 1993.
41. *International Herald Tribune*, August 20, 1993. See also, *The Independent* (U.K.), August 19, 1993.
42. *Newsweek*, July 19, 1993.

CHAPTER 90

The Western (Spanish) Sahara partitioned between Mauritania and Morocco • Decision contested by the Popular Front for the Liberation of the Sequiet el-Hamra and Rio de Oro (Polisario) guerrillas • Algerian-Libyan backed Polisarios force Mauritania from the war • Polisario's continued successes • Reagan government backs Morocco • The "Hassan Wall" • Polisario's setbacks • The United Nations proposed referendum • Morocco agrees but refuses scheduled elections • The Western Sahara in limbo

AT FIRST GLANCE, the future of the Spanish Sahara, subsequently known as the Western Sahara, did not seem of much importance—something over 102,000 square miles of desert detritus providing a forlorn existence for some sixty thousand Saharan Arabs, a few thousand foreign settlers, and as many Spanish legionnaires. Bowing to a United Nations resolution passed in 1973, Spain agreed to yield its control until a future plebiscite decided whether the area should become independent or be ruled by Spain or Morocco. Not trusting a vote, King Hassan II of Morocco pre-empted matters by sending 350,000 of his people into the area in 1975—the famous "Green March" that briefly claimed world headlines. This dramatic gesture was intended to bolster the king's popularity at home, insure the security of his southern flank, and, not least, give him possession of the rich Bu Craa phosphate mines, which, taken with his own extensive phosphate holdings, would give him a near world monopoly.[1]

Spanish forces peremptorily stopped the Moroccan march a few miles inside the country, but a subsequent private agreement with Spain gave Morocco control of the larger northern sector that included Bu Craa, and Mauritania control of the southern portion. This agreement pleased neither the local Saharans nor Morocco's immediate neighbor, Algeria, which wanted an independent Western Sahara that eventually

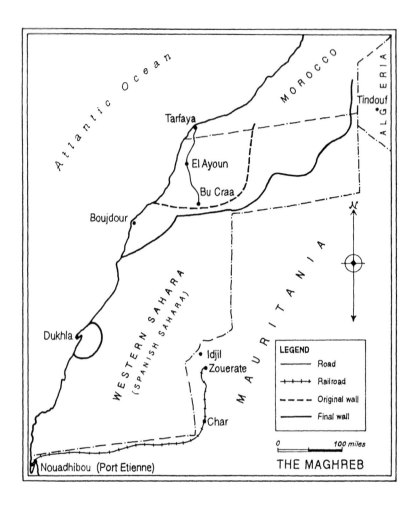

THE MAGHREB

would fall into Algeria's sphere of influence. Toward this end, the Algerian government had backed a guerrilla movement, the Popular Front for the Liberation of the Sequiet el-Hamra and Rio de Oro (Polisario), which in 1973 began attacking Spanish desert garrisons. In 1976, an emboldened Polisario headquarters in Algeria claimed the Western Sahara as the Sahara Arab Democratic Republic (SADR).

This was no ragtag guerrilla army. One authority wrote that it consisted " . . . of about 10,000 guerrillas armed with recoilless rifles, Soviet-made heavy mortars, and SAM-7 missiles mounted on Land Rovers . . . highly mobile, well organized and well trained troops with a close knowledge of the terrain."[2]

The ensuing war was a disaster for Mauritania. Polisario guerrillas almost at once struck its long and vulnerable railroad that carried vital iron ore exports to the sea. In a futile effort to protect the line, the small Mauritanian army expanded tenfold and was soon devouring 65 per cent of the national budget.[3] A beaten and financially stricken Mauritania left the war in 1979—and left the Western Sahara to Morocco.

Owing to Libyan Colonel Qaddafi's largesse buttressed by Syria and Iraq, Polisario guerrillas received so many arms and so much equipment, including armored vehicles and even tanks, that they began tilting toward conventional tactics. In 1979, Polisario smelled victory. Thirty-five states, mostly African, had recognized the SADR, the Office of African Unity in Addis Ababa supported it, and the United Nations General Assembly passed a resolution in its favor. By 1981, Moroccan forces were increasingly on the defensive, but in that year the new Reagan administration in the United States provided the first shipments to King Hassan of $400 million worth of arms including combat aircraft and helicopters. In 1982, a military stalemate had developed, a typical insurgency situation with regular forces holding about 10 per cent of the territory including cities and towns, the insurgent forces the rest. But also in 1982, the Moroccan army had stumbled on what proved to be the winning formula.

Earlier in this book, we commented on the general uselessness of walled barriers as a valid counterinsurgency weapon, for example the Morice Line used by the French in Algeria (see Chapter 55) or the multimillion-dollar fiasco built by the Americans in Vietnam (see Chapter 66). Conditions were uniquely different in the Western Sahara, however. Here there were fixed flanks, one being the Moroccan border guarded by static defenses, the other the sea. In 1982, with ample sand, rocks, and labor on hand, Moroccan army engineers built a four-hundred-mile-long wall to protect the northwestern part of the area that included the Bu Craa phosphate mines. The ten- to twelve-foot-high wall, holding sensors and radars that detected enemy presence several miles away, was defended by units from the eighty-thousand-man Moroccan army now based in Western Sahara.

The results were dramatic in the best tradition of Marshal Lyautey's *tache d'huile* concept (see Chapter 13). Not only did the Polisario fail to breach the line but the land behind the line became alive. The Bu Craa mine reopened, investment poured in, general prosperity followed.[4] Following *tache d'huile* tactics, a second line followed in late 1983 to enlarge the protected area. Moroccan fortunes rose even further in 1983 when King Hassan startled the diplomatic world by opening a dialogue with Colonel Qaddafi. A resultant agreement called for Qaddafi to halt arms shipments to the Polisarios if Hassan gave him a free hand for his foray into Chad in support of Goukouni Queddeï's Forces Armées Populaires, which was again challenging Hessène Habré's shaky regime.

Diplomacy was all very well but the secret of Hassan's success was the expanding fortified lines—a third one in spring of 1984, a fourth in October, a fifth in 1985. The net external result of what became known as the "Hassan Wall" was to slowly push the guerrillas back into Algeria despite their frantic attempts to blast through using mortars, rockets, and even tanks. The net internal result was $2 billion worth of foreign investments in the protected area.[5]

Hassan's position had improved so much in 1986 that he abrogated the treaty with Qaddafi (who that spring had been temporarily *hors de combat* as a result of a major U.S. air strike) and " . . . stated his willingness to abide by a unilateral ceasefire and accept a UN-sponsored plebiscite."[6] Despite repeated Polisario attacks, Moroccan army control of Western Sahara continued to expand. In 1988, Hassan restored diplomatic relations with Algeria, itself in a state of severe economic decline, and in June joined the four other Maghreb leaders in their first meeting for a quarter of a century (the prelude to the founding of the Arab Maghreb Union in 1989). Along with SADR leaders, he also agreed to a United Nations plan which called for " . . . a vote by residents of the former Spanish colony either to set up an independent state or to become part of Morocco."[7] In early 1989, King Hassan received Polisario leaders for "discussions" of the peace plan.

Following a year of on-again-off-again fighting, Polisario offered a unilateral cease-fire provided that Morocco agreed to an early referendum. That did not begin to materialize until spring of 1991, when United Nations officials came up with a plan: once a large number of Western Sahara refugees had been repatriated (estimated cost $34 million), Morocco would withdraw two thirds of its armed forces; a carefully supervised registration of voters, based on a 1974 Spanish census, would follow and voting would take place in January 1992.[8]

What happened next to this $200 million project?

A great deal. The 1974 Spanish census listed seventy-four thousand eligible Saharans but the Polisario claimed that the figure had risen to two hundred thousand. Hassan for his part sent in tens of thousands of troops and settlers who he claimed were eligible voters.[9] Despite the confusion, UN officials were about to get preparations under way in early August 1991 when Moroccan forces broke a relatively peaceful two-year lull by aerial bombing and strafing of a Polisario base.[10] Hassan defended the action on grounds that Polisario guerrillas were infiltrating Western Sahara in order to sabotage the elections. Moroccan soldiers simultaneously began "cleaning-up operations" in the area between the protective wall and the border. Then, in late August, King Hassan, having apparently concluded that Morocco would not win the plebiscite, disputed the UN's approved list of seventy-four thousand "eligible" voters while rejecting 120,000 names deemed eligible by Morocco.[11]

Further clashes aside, a formal UN cease-fire came into effect in September as UN preparations for the election continued. More trouble followed, including a threat by Moroccan forces to fire on UN monitors. January 1992 came and went as Hassan pulled one delaying tactic after another.

Direct talks between Morocco and the Polisario guerrillas in July 1993 proved humiliating to the latter when Moroccan delegates refused even to discuss the referendum.[12]

As of this writing, December 1993, and after the expenditure of millions of dollars, the UN-engineered referendum has still not taken place—the fault in large part of Morocco's obdurate King Hassan, in part of members of the UN Security Council for letting him get away with it.

CHAPTER NINETY

1. International Institute for Strategic Studies, *Strategic Survey 1975*, 45–6.
2. Ibid., *1979*, 95.
3. Ibid., 93.
4. Ibid., *1983–84*, 108.
5. Ibid., *1988–89*, 193.
6. Ibid., *1986–87*, 184.
7. *New York Times*, December 28, 1988.
8. *Keesing's Record of World Events*, Vol. 37, 1991. April 1991, 38,169.
9. *New York Times*, December 28, 1988.
10. *Daily Telegraph* (U.K.), August 8, 1991.
11. *Keesing's Record of World Events*, Vol. 37, 1991. August 1991, 38,410.
12. *The Independent* (U.K.), July 23, 1993.

CHAPTER 91

Portuguese colonial rule in Africa • Origin of the African National Council • Colonial rule challenged in the 1950s • The Angolan black uprising • Guerrilla shortcomings • Rise of Jonas Savimbi's National Union for Complete Independence of Angola (UNITA) • The Liberation Front of Mozambique (FRELIMO) • Hard-pressed Portugal grants independence to its colonies • War between Agostinho Neto's Popular Movement for the Liberation of Angola (MPLA), Helden Roberto's Popular Union of Angola (UPA—later FNLA), and Savimbi's UNITA • The Soviet-Cuban presence in Angola • Rise of black nationalism in South West Africa (renamed Namibia in 1968) • Sam Nujoma's South West African People's Organization (SWAPO) opens guerrilla campaign • Civil war in Angola • Pretoria and Washington's military and financial aid to UNITA • Namibia wins independence • Angolan peace agreement signed in 1991 • Savimbi loses 1992 elections and renews the war • Mozambique's war against Rhodesia and the Republic of South Africa • Rhodesia becomes Marxist Zimbabwe • Mozambique's political changes • Effects of widespread famine

OF A GREAT many execrable colonial governments, those of the Portuguese in Africa must stand near the top of the list. Beginning in 1505, the Portuguese presence was purely exploitive in the worst sense. Two and a half centuries of social crimes were compounded in the 1950s by a claim that Angola and Mozambique were " . . . overseas provinces . . . an integral part of the Portuguese state."[1]

These provinces-to-be were peopled largely by African natives, the *indigenes,* ruled by the *non-indigenes,* a polyglot mixture of *mestizos* or half-castes, *assimilados* or "civilized" Africans, and preponderantly by Portuguese nationals. The widely separated colonies had one thing in

THE PORTUGUESE LEGACY

common: the miserable state of their African native populations owing to penurious white governments unwilling to support even basic social services. Such was the lack of schools, for example, that by 1961 barely 1 per cent of the natives had reached "civilized"-African status.[2]

Colonal rule in Africa had for long been challenged by spasmodic, usually disorganized, black uprisings put down sooner or later by government forces, often with immense losses of native lives. The first major political challenge to white rule came in 1912 with the emergence of the African National Congress (ANC) " . . . aimed at eliminating all color bars and obtaining black representation in [the South African] parliament."[3] Spreading the political gospel by protest marches and strikes, the party managed to survive and indeed to spawn other opposition groups before World War II. Its flowering came after the war when South Africa's dominant National Party pledged itself to apartheid and white supremacy. In 1952, ANC membership counted one hundred thousand and was rapidly growing. Simultaneously, colonial rule elsewhere was challenged by the emergence of nationalist, usually tribal-based leftist parties, in the case of Angola and Mozambique Eduardo Mondlane's Liberation Front of Mozambique (FRELIMO), Helden Roberto's Popular Union of Angola (UPA) and Agostinho Neto's Popular Movement for the Liberation of Angola (MPLA).

Real trouble started in Angola in 1961 when an estimated six thousand UPA guerrillas from northeastern Angola massacred several hundred whites and several thousand *mestizos* and *assimilados,* a revolt supported by the Soviet Union and carried into the next year (when the UPA became the Liberation Front of Angola or FNLA). In 1963, the FNLA's rival, the MPLA, joined the action.

The rebels had several advantages. They were recognized politically by the Organization of African Unity and a number of members of the United Nations General Assembly were sympathetic to their cause. Neighboring countries, themselves in throes of self-determination, provided convenient sanctuary for the FRELIMO and the MPLA in Zambia and Tazmania, the FNLA in Zaire. The Soviet Union, China, Cuba, North Korea, and eventually the United States offered economic and military support, a decidedly mixed blessing that began the insidious process of removing revolt from a local and regional to a superpower plane with concomitant damage to social infrastructures—we are still paying the price today.

The rebels also suffered disadvantages. As with guerrilla groups in Ethiopia, Sudan, and some Latin American states, the African guerrillas lacked a valid aim other than to throw out the foreigners and gain a self-ruled independence with which they were in no way prepared to cope. They also lacked weapons—in the early stages, there were more machetes and spears than rifles—and they faced a determined foe: a few thousand Portuguese troops in 1961 grew to 130,000 (including blacks) in 1964 armed with modern weapons and supported by tanks, artillery, aircraft, and helicopters. Nor did the guerrilla groups claim undivided tribal loyalties. Recruitment of blacks into the army rose significantly with the abolition of the hated indigenes–non-indigines classification system.[4]

In relatively short order, counterinsurgency programs were resettling tribes in protected villages and providing long-overdue social services. Security forces in Angola had regained control of most of the northeast by late 1961, the guerrillas having suffered heavy casualties while being pressed back into Zaire. Neither did MPLA operations particularly prosper, its estimated five to seven thousand guerrillas being forced to utilize Zambian bases with operations confined largely to eastern border districts. The guerrillas nonetheless survived and in 1966 were joined by Jonas Savimbi's recently founded National Union for Complete Independence of Angola (UNITA), a splinter group from the FNLA of which Savimbi had been secretary-general. UNITA's few hundred guerrillas operated in central and eastern Angola where in time they would establish a viable political base among the large Ovimbunda tribes which accounted for 40 per cent of the total population.[5]

FRELIMO guerrillas in Mozambique, who had opened fire in 1964, also experienced mixed fortunes owing to the immensity of the country (some 308,000 square miles, home to nineteen major tribes, hundreds of subtribes, and seventeen languages plus dialects) and to several pro-Portuguese tribes including the Macuas, which made up about 40 per cent of the population. The guerrillas operated mainly in the north, usually conducting hit-and-run raids against military and police posts while trying to win over the diverse tribes. In 1969, FRELIMO leader Eduardo Mondlane was assassinated and was replaced by a diehard Marxist, Samora Machel. Aided by arms from Russia and China, Machel branched out and by late 1973 was fighting in the south and east.[6]

His was an uphill battle. The Portuguese command had removed the most exposed tribes into defended villages and in 1972 opened a massive civil program that included construction of schools, medical clinics, roads, and railroads. Captured guerrillas were given the choice of joining the government's forces or returning to their guerrilla unit, and a reported 90 per cent chose government. But it was all too little and too late. The war had become almost prohibitively expensive to Portugal. By 1974, the military forces had suffered an estimated eleven thousand dead and thirty thousand wounded.[7] More and more veterans lacking arms, legs, eyes, and minds filled Portugal's streets. The country's defense budget had risen as its international standing dropped. In 1974, a coup by disaffected left-wing army officers ousted the government and attempted to find a political solution to the insurgencies. Following six months of political turmoil, a replacement government finally decided to leave the war. Mozambique was given its independence under FRELIMO rule in 1975. Angola gained independence in late 1975 but only after a vicious civil war fought more on conventional than guerrilla lines, on the one side Agostinho Neto's MPLA, backed by Soviet Russia and supported by three thousand recently arrived Cuban ground troops and probably by guerrillas from the Southwest People's Organization (SWAPO) of Namibia; on the other side Helden Roberto's FMLA and Jonas Savimbi's UNITA, supported by South African ground troops. The war ended (briefly) with Neto's victory in 1976. Under communist MPLA rule the country became the People's Republic of Angola.

Aided by fifteen thousand Cuban troops and large shipments of arms from the Soviet Union, the indirect result of South African troops intervening in Angola in October 1975, Agostinho Neto moved rapidly to consolidate his victory. Large-scale military operations in 1976 forced FNLA and UNITA guerrillas to leave their strongholds and take to the bush to fight guerrilla warfare. South African troops, which had moved into Angola initially to protect a large hydroelectric project earlier undertaken with Portugal, and which in subsequent fighting had penetrated up to two hundred miles inside Angola, were withdrawn to South Africa's neighboring colony of South West Africa (Namibia) early in 1976. In February, the Organization of African Unity recognized Neto's government and general international recognition followed.

Neto's problems were scarcely over. Jonas Savimbi, the forty-one-year-old leader of UNITA, now claimed to command anywhere from two to ten thousand guerrillas who were fighting in central and south eastern Angola. Among other accomplishments, this effort prevented the government from opening the all-important Benguela railroad that runs over twelve hundred miles from the port of Lobito to Zambia and Zaire. In late 1976, Savimbi claimed to control four provinces and to have killed fifteen hundred Cubans and more than two thousand MPLA troops.[8] A new guerrilla group based in Zaire, the Front for the Liberation of the Enclave of Cabinda (FLEC), announced that it had killed three hundred Cuban soldiers who were protecting the oil fields (from which Angola derived 90 per cent of its income).[9] So effective was this guerrilla resistance that Fidel Castro, instead of beginning to withdraw his soldiers as he had stated, committed more troops—by summer twenty thousand Cuban troops were in the country.[10]

The situation could only escalate. From Neto's standpoint, the key factor was the strong military support from Russia and the presence of Cuban troops. The key factor from the opposition's standpoint was South Africa's determination to topple the communist MPLA regime in Luanda in order to prevent the Soviet-Cuban virus from spilling over the twelve-hundred-mile-long border into Namibia, and by projection into South Africa itself. Missing from the equation was U.S. support for the insurgents. After a brief period of U.S. aid and despite fervent pleas by President Ford and Secretary of State Kissinger, the latter wanting to send U.S. troops to Angola, Congress voted overwhelmingly in 1976 " . . . to refuse funds for arms in support of the 'pro-Western' liberation movements in Angola."[11]

South West Africa (renamed Namibia in 1968) had been a problem area for some time. Two thirds the size of the Republic of South Africa, its 318,000 square miles held an estimated 1.3 million people, mostly unenfranchised tribal blacks.[12] It had fallen under Germany's control in 1884, an unhappy experience demonstrated by a major native rebellion which, lasting into 1908, was broken by the army at an estimated cost of fifty-four thousand native lives. Thenceforth the country was administered in typical colonial fashion, its peoples exploited to Pretoria's profit while remaining impoverished and uneducated. In 1920, the League of Nations mandated the area to South Africa but in 1946 the

United Nations rejected Pretoria's claim to incorporate it into the Union of South Africa. The spreading wave of nationalism soon engulfed the unenfranchised blacks. Thanks largely to the African National Congress, the first black resistance organization in South West Africa was formed in 1958 and in 1960 became the South West African People's Organization (SWAPO), aimed at achieving independence from South Africa. Led by Sam Nujoma, this was a rural group of several hundred guerrillas, some of whom had been trained in Eastern-bloc countries.[13] In 1964, the UN ended South Africa's mandate. Two years later, the Pretoria government refused an order from the UN to withdraw from the country. Meanwhile, SWAPO guerrillas, having achieved little by relatively peaceful means, converted to the Marxist armed struggle. A guerrilla insurgency rapidly developed. In its formative stages, SWAPO's military wing, the People's Liberation Army of Namibia (PLAN), established bases in Zambia and Angola from where they infiltrated into Namibia to attack outposts of the South African Defense Force (SADF) along with police stations, from which they derived arms and ammunition.

When civil war broke out in Angola in 1975, South Africa allied itself with Jonas Savimbi's UNITA guerrilla group, which at that time was receiving U.S. military aid. SADF units from Namibia and from a large garrison that was guarding a hydroelectric project about twenty miles north of the border now began raids, some in conjunction with UNITA guerrillas, that penetrated as far as two hundred miles inside Angola, the pretext being "hot pursuit" of SWAPO guerrillas, whose forays into Namibia had become frequent and increasingly difficult to counter.

The civil war in Angola soon reached stalemate: the FNLA in general control of the north, the MPLA in control of the north-central, and UNITA generally dominant in the central-southeast. Buttressed by Cuban troops, MPLA forces contested FNLA and UNITA by frequent search-and-destroy missions that led to heavy but scarcely decisive fighting during 1976–83. By 1981, a reported ninety-five thousand South African troops (including Namibian levies) were in Namibia, units were frequently fighting in Angola, and South African planes were actively supporting Savimbi's guerrillas and bombing suspected SWAPO camps.

South African control of Namibia, however, was being increasingly challenged by African and Western nations, to the extent that in 1978 the UN General Assembly passed Resolution 435, which called for an independent Namibia, something Pretoria refused to consider so long as Cuban troops remained in Angola.

Up to 1982, peace talks had come to nothing. But with Angolan government forces generally on the defensive, the economy shattered, and with South Africa's heavy expenditure of men and money and increasing political isolation, both sides had good reason to reach a peaceful settlement. Hopes for this rose in 1984 when U.S. mediators persuaded the two governments to agree to a cease-fire to be followed by South Africa withdrawing its troops. Initial enthusiasm soon waned as accusations of cheating thundered back and forth. Nor did the cease-fire cover UNITA, whose guerrillas continued to harass MPLA troops while SWAPO guerrillas continued to fight their war against South Africa. In protest Pretoria slowed, then stopped the withdrawal of its troops, which were still twenty-five miles inside Angola in early 1985 and did not finally leave the country until April. Subsequent government offensives against Savimbi's stronghold in southeastern Angola brought renewed support from the SADF, which also continued "hot pursuit" of SWAPO guerrillas inside Angola.[14]

The war escalated in 1986 in part owing to the U. S. Congress lifting the ban on supplying arms to one side or the other in southern Africa's numerous conflicts. The Reagan administration had long wanted to topple the Luanda government, which after Agostinho Neto's death was headed by José Eduardo dos Santos, and now began reinforcing Savimbi's UNITA with $30 million worth of ground-to-air and anti-tank weapons, thus allying itself with South Africa to the discomfiture of many Congressional and other liberals. As the U. S. State Department had warned Reagan, this returned the war to superpower level. Soviet Russia responded by sending more fighter-bomber planes, tanks, armored personnel carriers, helicopters, advanced radar equipment, ground-to-air missile batteries and additional Cuban troops—a total fifty thousand in 1988. Despite this largesse, government offensives met no better success than formerly thanks in part to continuing U.S. military aid to UNITA of about $15 million a year and to SADF operations including air strikes and heavy artillery support of UNITA guerrillas.[15]

The costly stalemate might have continued but for the rise of Mikhail Gorbachev. Not only was the war in Angola costing the Soviet Union over $1 billion a year, it was seriously impeding his diplomatic initiatives in the West. As in 1985, both Luanda and Pretoria also had good reason to end the war. It had shattered Angola's economy and had made the government's survival almost totally dependent on the Soviet Union and the presence of Cuban troops. It was costing Pretoria millions a year in direct expenses, $80 million a year in subsidies to UNITA, millions more in grants to Namibia and, perhaps worse, was instrumental in keeping South Africa an international pariah.

In our day, and perhaps earlier, it almost seems that political settlement of an insurgency depends on mutual exhaustion of opposing sides. After months of U.S.-sponsored negotiations, Angola, Cuba, and South Africa agreed on a cease-fire in August 1988. Later in the year, the three countries called for Cuban troops to leave Angola and for South African troops to withdraw from Angola and Namibia; a cease-fire between the SADF and SWAPO was to begin in spring of 1989 to be followed by elections for a constituent assembly, the first step toward promised independence, in November. Meanwhile SADF forces would be restricted to barracks and SWAPO forces to their Angolan camps, this arrangement to be enforced by a UN contingent of seventy-five hundred troops.[16]

Owing to UN delay in deploying its peacekeeping force (reduced to forty-five hundred to save money),[17] the agreement came into force two months late and then only after considerable bloodshed.[18] After further serious clashes cooled by UN mediation, SWAPO leader Sam Nujoma returned to his homeland amidst much fanfare in September. In November, 670,000 Namibians—90 per cent of those eligible to vote[19]— elected a constituent assembly, 41 of its 72 seats going to SWAPO. Since SWAPO needed a two-thirds majority to implement its own constitution, Nujoma had to write one acceptable to all parties. That was done and in March 1990, Nujoma was sworn in as independent Namibia's first president.

Matters did not similarly prosper in Angola, in part because of the Bush administration's decision to continue supplying Jonas Savimbi's UNITA with arms while refusing to recognize José Eduardo dos Santos' MPLA until Dos Santos agreed to enter into direct talks with Savimbi. Supported by Washington, Savimbi in early 1989 refused Dos Santos' offer of a general amnesty. In June, both sides finally agreed to a cease-fire but fighting soon broke out, and in September Savimbi backed off from signing the agreement. Owing in part to further supplies of arms by the Soviets to MPLA and by the U.S. to UNITA, the fight-talk-fight syndrome ran its costly course during 1990 and into spring of 1991 when both sides signed a peace agreement brokered by the U.S., Portugal, and Russia. The accord called for MPLA and UNITA forces to meld into a single national army while the parties prepared for UN-monitored multiparty general elections.

The national army was never formed. Elections were held in September 1992 following more than two years of frantic political maneuvering during which UNITA forces, an estimated thirty-five thousand regular and auxiliary guerrilla fighters, remained intact in southeastern Angola. Although Jonas Savimbi seemed confident of victory, he suffered from a poor press that resulted from his own autocratic manner, and from well-founded charges that he had murdered opponents within the UNITA leadership and had condoned if not encouraged barbaric UNITA excesses that accounted for thousands of civilian deaths. Perhaps his greatest weakness was his failure to organize a strong political base. José Eduardo dos Santos by contrast enjoyed good press relations despite the known corruption of his government. Aware of Russia's decline and his own precarious economy, he adroitly abandoned his Communist stance and began moving toward the capitalist West, even changing the country's name to the comfortable-sounding Republic of Angola. An election in which 90 per cent of nearly five million voters participated and which was deemed fair by some eight hundred UN observers gave Dos Santos 49.6 per cent of the vote to about 40 per cent for Savimbi. Because Dos Santos did not receive over 50 per cent of the vote, a runoff was necessary. Savimbi, however, shouted fraud and reopened the shooting war only a few weeks after the election. Although both sides agreed to new talks, this came to nothing and the violent civil war continued into 1993 with Savimbi and the UNITA guerrillas getting the worst of it, although finally recapturing their traditional stronghold of Huambo in the central highlands (after two months of fighting that cost an estimated ten thousand dead).[20]

A new round of UN-sponsored talks between the MPLA and UNITA in April failed when the Dos Santos government accepted and Savimbi refused to accept a UN-brokered peace plan. Savimbi faced further isolation when President Clinton reversed traditional U.S. policy by recognizing the Dos Santos government in Luanda.

Fighting once again escalated. In July the United Nations reported that "more than one thousand people are dying every day from war and its consequent starvation";[21] "that 100,000 people have been killed in fighting since October [1992 when Savimbi refused to accept election results] and two million more are in danger of starvation."[22] A cease-fire offer from Savimbi in August went largely unheeded, not surprisingly, since his troops had hurled some three thousand shells into the besieged city of Kinto in the two previous days.[23] That the almost constant fighting was telling on UNITA forces was suggested by a still stronger offer from Savimbi in September, prompted, according to observers, by a desire to prevent a UN-embargo on supplies, especially oil, to the rebel organization.

It is possible that Savimbi will be forced back to the negotiating table. The Luanda government has gained some important allies. U.S. spy satellites are feeding intelligence to the MPLA army;[24] Britain has lifted its arms embargo on Luanda;[25] South Africa is reportedly permitting a private force of five hundred veteran guerrilla fighters to bolster MPLA forces.[26]

In November the Angolan government stated that two thousand people a day were being killed in what nearly all experts consider to be a stalemate war.[27] As of this writing, December 1993, the war continues—to the cost of millions of long-suffering blacks who must deserve something better.

As Portugal's hasty withdrawal from Angola plunged southwest Africa into prolonged war, its departure from Mozambique brought profound conflicts with the Republic of South Africa and Rhodesia, not unnaturally since President Samora Machel declared Mozambique to be a Leninist-Marxist state dedicated to improving the livelihood of the masses. Machel certainly had his hands full. Almost the size of Namibia, this oddly elongated, potentially rich country supported about 13.5 million people, mostly Bantu-speaking blacks practicing Islamic, Christian, and animist religions. Portuguese colonists had not been kind to the country. Few schools or hospitals existed; illiteracy and illness were widespread; life expectancy was forty-five years. The country was virtually bankrupt, food was short in many towns, and famine was looming in the central and northern regions. The guerrilla war had damaged an already inadequate infrastructure. Roads and railroads needed extensive repairs, port facilities at the capital Lourenço Marques (soon to become Maputo) and Beira needed overhaul and expansion, the economy was at a standstill—and the people necessary to start the country running again for the most part had fled. Although China delivered some military aid, it soon pulled out of the area, leaving it to Russia, which supplied mostly small arms, and to Cuba which furnished numerous military instructors.

To worsen matters, Machel had a very determined enemy on the other side of his eight-hundred-mile-long western border. That was Rhodesia, whose white government headed by Ian Smith was being threatened by a black nationalist insurgency. The trouble had started when Rhodesia was still a British colony. In 1957, the black nationalist Joshua Nkomo had founded the Rhodesian African National Congress. Three years later, he joined with four other nationalists—the Reverend Malabaningi Sithole, Robert Mugabe, and Herbert Chitipo—in forming the National Democratic Party, a militant group that wanted an independent Rhodesia with one-man, one-vote government.[28] In 1961, Great Britain implemented a new constitution for the colony that suggested the possibility of future majority rule, albeit very gradually. That was not to the liking of the ruling white minority—220,000 out of well over four million. Angry (and frightened) whites now formed the conservative Rhodesian Front Party, which, determined to remain in power, cracked down hard on the black nationalist movement.

Had the black National Democratic Party remained intact, it possibly could have brought about desired reforms—liberal world opinion was certainly on its side. Instead, it split into two parties, Joshua Nkomo's Zimbabwe African People's Union (ZAPU) and Malabaningi Sithole's Zimbabwe African National Union (ZANU). In 1964, Great Britain granted independence to Northern Rhodesia, which became Zambia, and to Nyasaland, which became Malawi. Also in 1964, Ian Smith's government in Southern Rhodesia outlawed both the ZANU and the ZAPU, whose members fled to Zambia. To Smith's demand for independence, the British government replied that the whites would have to bring blacks into the governing process. In 1965, a furious Smith backed by a majority of whites declared a unilateral independence. That made Rhodesia a political pariah second only to the Republic of South Africa and brought it heavy political and economic sanctions levied by Britain and later the United Nations to increase further its isolation.

ZANU recruits meanwhile were being trained and armed by Russian and Cuban instructors in Zambia and Eastern-bloc countries. Small guerrilla groups now began to infiltrate into Rhodesia, where for the next four years they were effectively neutralized by a small but efficient army buttressed by Rhodesian police and some two thousand paramilitary South African police. Tactical failure only increased the friction between ZANU and ZAPU leaders. In 1969, Sithole and his lieutenants, deciding to wage a rural war in the Maoist style, formed the Zimbabwe African National Liberation Army (ZANLA), whose recruits were trained by Chinese instructors in Tanzanian camps. Posted to camps in northern Mozambique (with FRELIMO blessing), they began infiltrating into northeastern Rhodesia. Rhodesian security forces responded with large-scale raids into Mozambique, a campaign so successful that according to one authority there were only a hundred ZANLA guerrillas still fighting in 1974.[29] The war slowed the following year when the South African Government attempted to negotiate a peace—without success. When fighting resumed in 1976, the Rhodesian Government faced two guerrilla threats, one from ZANU, led now by Robert Mugabe, in the east, the other from Joshua Nkomo's ZAPU based in Zambia. The two organizations meanwhile had formed a Patriotic Front—more a truce than a party—to fight a guerrilla war with forces greatly strengthened by thousands of recruits trained in Tanzania, Zambia, and Angola and armed with modern Russian and Chinese weapons. ZANLA guerrillas continued to be based in northern Mozambique, from where they were to open a "front" along the eight-hundred-mile border. ZAPU's military arm, ZIPRA, which counted eight to ten thousand guerrillas, was based in Zambia, from where it would open "fronts" in both east and west.

This then was the situation in spring of 1976 when Samora Machel, using Rhodesian army raids into Mozambique as pretext, closed the border to Rhodesia, a desperate act since it was possible that it would cause Rhodesia to invade Mozambique and since it deprived financially strapped Mozambique of millions of dollars a year in customs, port dues, and railway charges formerly incurred by landlocked Rhodesia. In partial palliation, Machel signed a twenty-year Treaty of Friendship with the Soviet Union and with the help of Russian, Cuban, and North Korean military advisers began converting his FRELIMO force into a conventionally organized army. He also sent FRELIMO guerrilla units to work with Rhodesian guerrillas based in Mozambique.

The ensuing war was hideous in the extreme. As ZANLA and ZIPRA guerrillas attempted to block Rhodesian communications by cutting road and rail networks, a process accompanied by kidnaping or killing any whites or blacks who refused to support them, Rhodesian security forces replied in kind by making large-scale attacks against camps in Zambia and Mozambique, claiming (probably accurately) to have killed hundreds of guerrillas. As part of this counterinsurgency effort, the Rhodesian army in 1977 sponsored the Mozambican National Resistance, or RENAMO, group led by Afonso Dblakama. This polyglot guerrilla force was composed of former white settlers, Portuguese soldiers, army deserters, juvenile delinquents, renegades from FRELIMO, and other dissentient blacks, just the sort of mixture that spells unbridled brutality—which henceforth was the case. By 1978, Rhodesian security forces numbered some 115,000 including eight thousand regular and thirty-five thousand reserve policemen.[30] Despite an all-out counterinsurgency campaign, the guerrillas appeared to be on top and they probably would have toppled the government had there been a unified insurgent political and military command. There was nothing remotely resembling this. As it was, a transitional government, which the Smith regime had had to accept in early 1978, a prelude to majority rule, was not accepted by Mugabe and Nkomo's Patriotic Front whose own internal rivalries led to serious armed clashes between ZANLA and ZIPRA guerrillas in 1979. By then, however, a new constitution had been approved and the first one-man, one-vote elections held for a multiparty house of assembly. The elections, in which 63 per cent of an estimated two million electorate had voted, were won by the Rhodesian African National Congress, whose internal branch was led by Bishop Abel Muzorewa who was now prime minister of what had become Zimbabwe/Rhodesia.[31] In 1980, a second election was won by the Patriotic Front and the former colony became the nation of Zimbabwe with Robert Mugabe, a dedicated Marxist, its first president.

Although the insurgent victory in Rhodesia eased Samora Machel's military position, it did not alter his deteriorating economic situation. The war had cost Mozambique dearly. Incessant raids had not only taken thousands of civilian lives, they had created hundreds of thousands of civilian refugees. Thousands of farms had been abandoned and many of those that survived had fallen victim to inept management of Russian and Cuban "experts" who had also run the meager industrial plant into the ground. The Soviet Union had not proved to be the hoped-for generous patron; indeed Machel's fervent Marxist rhetoric had noticeably softened as he started edging toward the West. The conversion was encouraged by drought and famine that from 1982 to 1984 displaced and killed hundreds of thousands, a period in which the Soviet Union's limited aid contrasted sharply with generous Western and United Nations relief efforts. But now Machel faced another problem in the form of a guerrilla campaign designed to end his regime.

This was the work of the RENAMO group operating from bases in South Africa's Transvaal. With the fall of the Smith regime in Rhodesia, RENAMO had been adopted by the South African Government and army; other important donors were former Portuguese colonial landowners, Oman, Brazil, Saudi Arabia, and right-wing organizations in Germany and the United States (reportedly the American Heritage Foundation in Washington, where RENAMO was said also to maintain a lobbying organization).[32]

After infiltrating Mozambique, RENAMO guerrillas, operating in units of up to a hundred men, employed tactics similar to those used by Salvadoran guerrillas, that is striking communication lines, blowing up bridges, burning farms, slaughtering livestock, blocking wells, demolishing schools and health clinics, all to force the people to leave the land to seek refuge in overburdened camps,[33] tactics that in time would drive five million subsistence farmers from the land. Despite the best efforts of the army, theoretically inspired by Machel's strident call for a revival of "people's war,"[34] the guerrillas prospered, partly because of the immensity of the land and mounting RENAMO strength, estimated at eight to ten thousand by late 1983 when its guerrillas " . . . had succeeded in removing large areas of Mozambique . . . from any vestige of government control."[35] So overstrained were Mozambique's inadequate defenses that in this same period South African commandos successfully carried out air and ground strikes against suspected African National Congress offices in the capital, Maputo.[36]

Faced with this new threat and trying to cope with a widespread famine, looking at a moribund economic and agrarian future, increasingly removed from Russian aid, Machel now approached his South African enemy. Pretoria was also having difficulties as a result of the worst drought in memory, the heavy costs of the war in Angola, and the widespread sabotage of vital installations by ANC and FRELIMO guerrillas. The result was the Nkomadi Accord of 1984, a non-aggression pact hammered out with the help of U.S. mediators. In brief, Pretoria would cease support of RENAMO in return for Mozambique closing down African National Congress offices in Maputo. The accord also called for committees to be set up to provide various joint economic development ventures in Mozambique. Hailed by President P. W. Botha as having " . . . set a new course in the history of South Africa,"[37] the accord was more a victory for Pretoria than for Mozambique. Theretofore none of the Front Line States (Angola, Botswana, Mozambique, Tanzania, Zambia, Zimbabwe) had recognized apartheid government by opening diplomatic relations with Pretoria. Machel's decision to do so was resented not alone by these governments but also by powerful factions in the FRELIMO party. Even worse, although he dutifully set about expelling ANC officials and guerrillas, he could not expel all of them. Pretoria on the other hand made a big show of cutting its links with RENAMO, but not until a large supply drop had been made to its units inside Mozambique and not before another fifteen hundred to two thousand trained and equipped guerrillas had slipped into Mozambique.[38] It then transpired that elements in South Africa's army refused to accept the agreement and continued to supply RENAMO forces. The result was an *increase* in RENAMO operations during the rest of 1984—and a rapid deterioration in Mozambique-South African relations. These worsened as RENAMO attacks increased in 1985 and as ANC sabotage revived in South Africa. Such was the growing threat from RENAMO that Mozambican and Zimbabwean paratroops attacked what was believed to be its headquarters in the western mountains. Here sufficient evidence of South Africa's continued support of the insurgents was found to elicit an admission of guilt from Pretoria. In palliation, South Africa's public loans to and private investment in Mozambique increased in 1985. Machel's temper was further softened by $2 million worth of military equipment from Pretoria, a million dollars of U.S. aid,[39] by the U.S. and eleven other countries imposing economic sanctions on South Africa,[40] and by his being cordially received at the White House by President Reagan.

The war continued into 1986 as the government tried to counter RENAMO's increasing gains. In part it was a case of poacher turned gamekeeper. RENAMO guerrillas were officially called "armed bandits" and all stops were pulled to eradicate them. As the FRELIMO had taught the Portuguese army, this was difficult if not impossible. An amnesty offer brought no dramatic result. Machel might well have gone under but for reinforcement by the vanguard of twelve thousand soldiers from Zimbabwe and three thousand from Tanzania deployed to assist Mozambican forces in guarding the vital 180-mile road, railroad, and pipeline corridor that stretched from the Rhodesian border to the Mozambique port of Beira. In September, Machel, supported by Zimbabwe and Tanzania, forced Malawi to expel all RENAMO forces with the result that ten thousand enemy guerrillas debouched into the northern province of Zambezia, " . . . capturing, and for the first time holding, major bridges and several towns."[41] At this crucial point, Machel was killed in an air crash believed by some observers to have been arranged by pro-RENAMO elements in the South African army.[42] Machel was replaced by Joaquim Chissano, who, supported financially by Western nations and the Front Line States, pledged himself to pursue victory over RENAMO while continuing to build a socialist state, a task aided by additional troops from Zimbabwe who helped to clear the Zambezia valley of RENAMO guerrillas. As is so often the case in counterinsurgency warfare, this resembled putting a finger on a drop of mercury—in short order, fugitive guerrilla units reassembled in central Mozambique where, presumably supplied from South Africa, they continued offensive operations, in July killing over four hundred civilians including women and children in one attack, and in October hitting a truck convoy to kill over three hundred people and wound hundreds more,[43] all in the most bestial way such as reportedly boiling children in front of their parents—the ghastly story is told in William Finnegan's *A Complicated War*. RENAMO also declared war on Zimbabwe and began "hot pursuits" across the border, actions that drove thousands more civilians into perilously overcrowded refugee camps.[44]

The hideous situation gradually altered in 1988 owing in part to the world-shaking change in Soviet policies evoked by Mikhail Gorbachev, but also in part to President Joaquim Chissano's realization that government forces could not defeat the guerrillas, that his country was rapidly approaching bankruptcy, and that all indications pointed to the prospect of an appalling famine. Using the occasion of a FRELIMO congress in July, Chissano presented a twelve-point peace plan and announced that the government would enter into "indirect" negotiations with RENAMO providing that the group would "renounce violence and agree to abide by the Constitution."[45] Congressional delegates next learned, undoubtedly to their astonishment, that the base of the FRELIMO party was to be expanded, thenceforth to include " . . . private property owners and members of the business community" as well as members of all religious faiths.[46] In fact, Chissano, like Mikhail Gorbachev, was admitting socialist defeat as shown by a new constitution " . . . which provided for a multiparty system, direct elections and a free-market economy."[47]

Predictions of a horrible famine proved all too accurate. In 1990, nearly two million Mozambicans were approaching starvation, and severe fighting had forced another quarter million to leave their lands.[48] Nevertheless, direct talks were held in Rome in July, August, and September. Owing to RENAMO delaying tactics—it needed time to form a political party—progress was slow, but in November when the new constitution was introduced the government recognized RENAMO's status as a political party. In March 1992, at the ninth round of peace talks, an electoral system was agreed on. The two sides edged closer to agreement during the eleventh round of peace talks in July, during which progress was made concerning the composition of a future army.[49]

CHAPTER NINETY-ONE

1. Pimlott, 80.
2. Ibid.
3. *Encyclopaedia Britannica*, 1986, Vol. 1, 135.
4. Pimlott, 83.
5. International Institute for Strategic Studies, *Strategic Survey 1975*, 9.
6. Pimlott, 85.
7. Ibid.
8. *Newsweek*, November 1, 1976.
9. International Institute for Strategic Studies, *Strategic Survey 1976*, 45. See also, ibid., *1988–89*, 147.
10. *Keesing's Contemporary Archives*, Vol. 22, 1976. May, 1976, 78,072.
11. International Institute for Strategic Studies, *Strategic Survey 1975*, 2.
12. *Encyclopaedia Britannica 1991*, Vol. 8, 494.
13. Pimlott, 13.
14. International Institute for Strategic Studies, *Strategic Survey 1985–86*, 186–9.
15. Ibid., *1987–88*, 194. See also, ibid., *1988–89*, 197; *International Herald Tribune*, June 27, 1989.
16. International Institute for Strategic Studies, *Strategic Survey 1989–90*, 75. See also, *New York Times*, December 22, 1988; *International Herald Tribune*, June 7, 1989.
17. *International Herald Tribune*, December 22, 1988.
18. *USA Today*, International Edition, April 5, 1989.
19. *Encyclopaedia Britannica 1991*, Vol. 11, 46.
20. *New York Times*, March 7, 1993.
21. *The Independent* (U.K.), July 9, 1993.
22. Ibid., July 23, 1993.
23. Ibid., August 13, 1993.
24. Ibid., August 30, 1993.
25. Ibid., August 10, 1993.
26. *Newsweek*, October 25, 1993.
27. *International Herald Tribune*, November 10, 1993.
28. Pimlott, 88.
29. Ibid., 92.
30. *Keesing's Contemporary Archives*, Vol. 24, 1978. April 28, 1978, 28,948.
31. Ibid., Vol. 25, 1979. August 10, 1979, 29,757, 29,759.
32. *Keesing's Record of World Events*, Vol. 34, 1988. February 1988, 35,686.
33. Ibid., 35,685.
34. International Institute for Strategic Studies, *Strategic Survey 1982–83*, 108.
35. Jaster, 258. See also, International Institute for Strategic Studies, *Strategic Survey 1984–85*, 107.
36. Jaster, 259.
37. International Institute for Strategic Studies, *Strategic Survey 1984–85*, 107.
38. Jaster, 260.
39. Ibid., 262.
40. International Institute for Strategic Studies, *Strategic Survey 1985–86*, 185.
41. Ibid., *1986–87*, 190.

42. Ibid., *Adelphi Papers Number 227, 1987–88,* 18: *Pravda* openly charged South Africa with the crime.
43. Ibid., *Strategic Survey 1987–88,* 197. See also, Finnegan.
44. *Keesing's Record of World Events,* Vol. 34, 1988. January 1988, 35,628: One camp administrator reported that by the end of October, there were over 22,000 refugees in a camp built for 10,000 and that 1,000 were arriving every month. See also, ibid., August 1988, 36,084: The United Nations reported in July that there were already 570,000 Mozambican refugees in Malawi with 20,000–40,000 arriving every month.
45. Ibid., Vol. 35, 1989. July 1989, 36,804. See also, *International Herald Tribune,* October 10, 1989.
46. Ibid.
47. *Keesing's Record of World Events,* Vol. 37, 1991. February 1991 Supplement, 38,044.
48. Ibid., January 1991, 37,945–6.
49. *Newsweek,* July 27, 1992.

CHAPTER 92

Afghanistan old and new • Political disunity • Prime Minister Mohammed Daud's rise and fall • The Soviets install Nur Mohammed Taraki's Marxist government • The jihad (holy war) declared by mujaheddin guerrillas • Collapse of the Afghan army • The Soviet army versus the guerrillas • Soviet military deficiencies • Mujaheddin disunity • Pakistan's role • U.S. military aid to the mujaheddin • Military stalemate • The Mohammed Najibullah regime • Mikhail Gorbachev pulls out • The war continues: Gulbuddin Hakmatyar versus Ahmed Shah Massoud • The drug factor • United Nations attempts to end the fighting fail • The war continues

Oh Gods! From the venom of the Cobra, the teeth of the Tiger, and the vengeance of the Afghan—deliver us.

OLD HINDU SAYING[1]

AFGHANISTAN'S PRESENT TROUBLES began in 1839 when Great Britain, intent on preventing Russian expansion southwards, invaded the land, the first of three wars that did much to increase a traditional xenophobia in what became known as "the hermit's kingdom,"[2] an undisciplined group of tribal fiefdoms squeezed between British India and czarist Russia.

The country remained under British hegemony until 1919, when it won full independence, to be governed in theory by young King Mohammed Zahir but in fact by the king's ultraconservative Pashtun uncles. It did not begin to come of age until a non-violent political revolution ushered in Mohammed Daud as Prime Minister Lieutenant General Daud Khan, who intended to rule *sans* the royal uncles. A cousin of the king, Daud was a latter-day Kemal Ataturk determined to lead his country into the modern world by an extensive program of economic development—an extremely ambitious if highly laudable goal.

His task was complicated not only by a politically fragmented nation, but also by quarrelsome, aggressive neighbors: in the north a seven-hundred-mile border with the former Soviet Central Asian republics marked for hundreds of miles by the Amu Darya River (the Oxus River of antiquity crossed and recrossed by Alexander the Great in his pursuit of Bactrian guerrillas—(see Chapter 1); in the west and southwest, Islamic Iran; in the east, Pakistan; and in the south, Pakistan's desert pendant Baluchistan. Afghanistan's backbone, the formidable Hindu Kush mountain range, stretches 450 miles from southwest to northeast, the stern parent of wildly undisciplined fertile valleys sloping to river-cut plains and deserts that are home to nearly 90 per cent of an estimated fifteen million people who are as diverse as their landscape. Of the several ethnic and religious groups, the Pashtuns, the traditional rulers, are the largest with about seven million spread into fiercely independent tribes and clans " . . . varying in size from a thousand to a million."[3] Pashtun cohesion is further obstructed by Afghanistan's arbitrarily drawn border with Pakistan, the Durand Line imposed by Britain that cut a number of Pashtun tribes in half, part of them living in Afghanistan, part in the Northwest Frontier province of Pakistan. Farsi and Turkic are the two principal languages but numerous other tongues vie with each other and with a feast of dialects often foreign to a neighboring tribe. The country people are poor but proud. Illiteracy is high, serious illnesses and epidemics abound, only 20 per cent of the drinking water is safe, life expectancy is low.

So it was that Mohammed Daud set himself a Herculean task. Ironically, his rise to power occurred in 1953 at the height of the cold war between Soviet Russia and the West. Fearful of Soviet expansion southward as imperial Britain had been before him, U. S. Secretary of State John Foster Dulles knocked together a "northern tier" defensive coalition, the Central Treaty Organization (CENTO) of Pakistan, Iran, Turkey, and Iraq, an unlikely alliance of capricious rulers if ever there was one. The alliance did not include Afghanistan and Daud's request for arms was turned down: Washington was afraid that Afghanistan wanted to invade pet-of-the-moment Pakistan or at least prevent Pakistan from merging the Northwest Frontier province, home to a large number of Pashtuns, with the rest of the country.[4] Daud in reality wanted an efficient army in order to control his country's diverse tribes. Washington's limited amount of economic aid only partially ameliorated the resentment felt in Kabul.

While U.S. diplomacy vis-à-vis Afghanistan stumbled, Soviet diplomacy soared. Where the U.S. spent a few million dollars on educational

AFGHANISTAN

and engineering projects, the Soviet Union spent over $200 million to modernize the army and build new roads.

Daud's ambitious reforms continued as he attempted to follow a foreign policy of non-alignment even though tilting toward Moscow. By 1959, he had largely eliminated the traditional veil and the *purdah*, or seclusion of upper-class women from public view.[5] But in relying on the new and young educated elite to carry out his reforms, he over-looked the importance of the diverse ethnic and tribal elements that formed the real if splintered power of the land. As progress faltered and criticism increased, his regime grew more oppressive. Instead of respecting traditional rule by joining it to government rule he ignored it and since traditional rule governed about 90 per cent of the land, that meant that he was making the cardinal error of failing to establish a political base necessary to support his reformist program.[6] Here was the basic reason for his ultimate failure, indeed for the fragmented non-government of today's Afghanistan.

As if there weren't sufficient problems at home, Daud challenged Pakistan over the Northwest Frontier province. Continued friction there led to Iraq's summary closing of the border, which shut off Afghanistan's trade routes to the east, ended his policy of non-alignment, cut off most U.S. aid, and committed him to the Soviet sphere of influence. In 1963, controlled anarchy became uncontrollable and Daud resigned. Government returned to King Mohammed Zahir. A new constitution did little to quiet political turbulence that brought five prime ministers between 1965 and 1972 and also brought into existence in 1965 the People's Democratic Party of Afghanistan (PDPA) with its two opposing factions, the very radical Khalq (Peoples) Party and the more moderate pro-Moscow Parcham (Banner) Party, the latter supporting Daud. In 1973, Daud regained power in a bloodless coup, abolished the monarchy, wrote a new constitution, and made tentative peace with Pakistan. Again he failed to establish a strong political base, relying instead on opportunistic sycophants to run an ineffectual but repressive government. In 1978, following a violent period of assassinations, antigovernment demonstrations and wholesale arrests, pro-Soviet extremists within the two factions of the PDPA brought off another coup that cost Daud his life and established the pro-Soviet Democratic Republic of Afghanistan.

The central government of Afghanistan was now in the hands of a revolutionary council formed by members of the Marxist-Leninist PDPA headed by Nur Mohammed Taraki, a power group so extreme that even the Kremlin advised modification of its policies.[7] The PDPA soon split as Taraki, a member of the Khalq faction, consolidated his position by dismissing such opposition leaders of the Parcham faction as Deputy Prime Minister Babrak Karmal (sent to Prague as ambassador). Taraki's intensified reform program, which included a highly controversial land distribution scheme, alienated more tribal leaders and mullahs (Islamic priests) as it filtered down to the countryside; a major literacy campaign that included teaching women how to read and write drew instant condemnation from conservative males.[8]

The first armed revolt by guerrilla *mujaheddin* (holy warriors) occurred in the central provinces in late summer of 1978 and soon spread to other parts of the country, the start of a declared *jihad,* or holy war. Guerrilla terrorists were soon exploding bombs in the cities and in early 1979 they murdered the U.S. ambassador in Kabul. In March, guerrilla riots in Herat were suppressed by troops but only after the deaths of perhaps five thousand people. The split in the PDPA widened. Deputy Prime Minister Hafizullah Amin, who replaced Taraki as prime minister, ordered a bloodbath in which thousands of political opponents were jailed or executed. Meanwhile, the Afghan army was folding under guerrilla onslaught. In September, Taraki, supported by the Soviet Union, tried to oust Amin and was murdered.

Russia's stake in Afghanistan had grown considerably and for good reason. Soviet hegemony would mean exclusive access to the rich un-derdeveloped northern gas fields and in time to undeveloped copper, chrome, iron, and bauxite deposits. It would also move Russia five hun-dred miles toward the warm waters of the Arabian Sea and its pros-perous parent, the Indian Ocean, whose waters lapped the major oil-producing nations of the world. Beyond Afghanistan lay Pakistan's desert province, Baluchistan, with its two-hundred-mile coastline and three ports and with many of its sixty tribes not overly fond of Pakistan rule.[9] By late 1978, thousands of young officers had been trained in the Soviet Union and the Kremlin had supplied an estimated $3.5 billion in economic and military aid, the latter including tanks, jet fighters, and helicopter gunships:[10] additional military aid was promised under the terms of a twenty-year Treaty of Friendship signed that year.

Now, in 1979, as four to five thousand Soviet military advisers were in Afghanistan, as the Afghan army continued to disintegrate, and as Amin continued his repressive police actions (more than a thousand mullahs had been killed during his regime),[11] the Kremlin was faced with an either/or situation: either to continue supporting a client state with the hope of eventually profiting from its investment or to abandon it and thereby lose face at a crucial time in the cold war.

Probably without realizing the innate if unco-ordinated strength of the mujaheddin jihad, the Kremlin chose not so much to support the client state as to rule it. Amin was no longer acceptable. His radical reforms and vicious purges had alienated far too many important Af-ghans and were held to be partly responsible for what appeared to be a losing counterinsurgency campaign. A coup arranged by Moscow brought Amin's murder and replacement in late 1979 by Babrak Kar-mal. Using the patently flimsy pretext that Karmal had invoked the Treaty of Friendship to call for help, the Kremlin sent in an expedition-ary force and the war was on.

By the time the dust cleared, several thousand Soviet military advisers in Kabul had been joined by five thousand airborne troops complete with armored vehicles, tanks, and artillery. Simultaneously, the van-guard of a fifty-thousand-man army moved in from the north. Once Karmal's government was secure, Soviet forces occupied the major cit-ies, towns, and airfields in order to offer the Afghan army safe garrisons from which to fight the mujaheddin.[12] Karmal meanwhile attempted to gain popular support by releasing thousands of prisoners and promising extensive reforms—words ignored by thousands of key officials who either fled the country or joined the mujaheddin.

We should keep in mind that the Soviet high command was about as familiar with the realities of counterinsurgency warfare as the U.S. command had been in Vietnam. Among its many mistakes was that of underestimating the fighting capabilities of what it derisively termed "counterrevolutionary bandits." Few preparations had been made, linguistically or otherwise, to use the indigenous population as a source of intelligence. That probably explains why troops from the Central Asian republics were used to occupy the northeastern provinces and were then hastily replaced when they struck up too strong a kinship with the locals. Still another error was to suppose that the Afghan army, already reduced from ninety thousand to about thirty thousand by casualties and sickness but mainly by desertion (in some cases of entire brigades), could wage a successful counterinsurgency. Its increasingly dismal performance perforce turned the Soviets themselves to the task, where they at once erred by deploying large airborne and armor formations in mountain country with troops neither tactically nor technically trained for that type of warfare.[13] Repeated failures eventually brought tactical modifications and a change " . . . to combined operations involving motorized infantry, tanks and helicopter gunships."[14]

Who were the enemy?

The mujaheddin comprised several hundred groups of variously armed guerrilla fighters generally isolated from each other not only by rugged terrain but by important tribal differences—one thinks in passing of T. E. Lawrence and the Arab tribes (see Chapter 16). What happened in one province or even part of a province did not often affect events elsewhere. This isolation taken with generally inadequate arms in the opening phase of the insurgency should have made those groups easy game for the hunters, but such was not the case.

The guerrilla groups came in different sizes and colors. Seven of the main organizations were headquartered in Peshawar, a town about forty miles inside Pakistan that marks the western end of the Khyber Pass. Dominant among these was the Hezb-i Islami, an Islamic fundamentalist group headed by a Pashtun, Gulbuddin Hakmatyar, an Islamic extremist who repeatedly clashed with leaders of more moderate fundamentalist beliefs such as the Hanafi sect of Sunni Islam, but who managed to garner an estimated 70 per cent of the arms and money received from foreign sources.[15] Other major groups based inside Afghanistan fought independently of the Pakistan-based groups. Some were large such as Ahmed Shah Massoud's rival coalition, the Islamic Jihad Council, which controlled the Panjshir Valley area; some were small such as the Hazaryat guerrillas in central Afghanistan. Together the mujaheddin numbered about ninety thousand. Had one leader harnessed this vast potential, the security forces would have been overwhelmed. As it was, the Soviets were able to fight a tough protracted war with a relatively small number of men.

What were the mujaheddin fighting for? Principally to remove the PDPA communist regime and with it the Soviet army before returning to their own way of life. What was to replace the regime? Most of the mujaheddin did not know or care. Certain of their leaders did care but only in a power-grabbing sense as opposed to establishing a legitimate civil government capable of homogenizing a dispersed, illiterate, and fiercely independent population. This was the essential weakness of the insurgents. No one had anything positive to offer politically.

Despite disunity and lack of arms, the guerrillas more than held their own in 1980, even challenging government control of such important cities as Kandahar and Herat. Additional weapons were acquired from dead and wounded soldiers, from deserters and in time from China and Egypt (using U.S. and Saudi Arabian money to buy them). Millions of dollars also came from extensive cultivation of the opium poppy, which was refined into heroin for sale in the U.S. and Europe.[16]

In early 1981, the Kabul government insisted " . . . 'the main band of rebels' had been destroyed, and that it only remained to mop up the small groups which had survived,"[17] a matter of six months—this at a time when the Afghan army had been reduced to thirty thousand men and Russian construction teams were working overtime to build a road and rail bridge across the Amu Darya River in the hope of clearing seriously clogged supply lines. Although counterinsurgency tactics had improved by decentralization of command authority—the motorized rifle battalion was now the basic maneuver unit—and by increased use of helicopter gunships, Soviet military analysts had begun complaining about the efficacy of guerrilla sniper fire, frequent ambushes of convoys, guerrilla-made forest fires and avalanches, the blowing up of bridges and mining of roads, and infiltration from Pakistan where " . . . a solid barrier has been set up against the bandits, but [insurgents] keep coming through."[18] Co-ordinated ground-helicopter assaults such as those in the Panjshir Valley north of Kabul often yielded short-term gains, but these were costly: Russian casualties rose from an estimated fifteen to seventeen hundred in 1979 to a total five thousand by end of 1981.[19] They were also expensive in money and they solved very little, since there were not sufficient troops to hold the seized areas, but by destroying everything in sight they did force many locals to join refugee camps in the cities and thus increase already serious food and power shortages. To compensate for tactical failures, Soviet commanders introduced a scorched-earth policy carried out both by ground troops burning villages and crops and slaughtering livestock, and by indiscriminate bombing of cities, towns, and villages in order to create more refugees and to deprive guerrillas of food and information—a deliberate attempt to make "terror reign."[20]

The picture did not radically change in 1983, although Soviet casualties rose to about ten thousand with large numbers down from typhoid fever, dysentery, and pneumonia.[21] Soviet troop strength rose to an estimated 105,000 and the Afghan army to perhaps thirty-five thousand but the government was no closer to victory. The stalemate continued throughout 1984, the sixth year of the increasingly expensive Soviet occupation, with all sides hardening their positions. Since 1982, the United Nations envoy Diego Cordovez had been trying to start talks between the Kabul government and Pakistan and Iran but with no success, nor would Kabul negotiate directly with the mujaheddin. Guerrilla bombings and assassinations continued in the cities, particularly in Kabul, and some mujaheddin groups received ground-to-air missiles, ground-to-ground rockets, anti-tank weapons and radio equipment. Mujaheddin leaders continued to squabble in Peshawar, but some commanders inside Afghanistan began to co-ordinate local military actions, with considerably improved results. Continued guerrilla offensives caused the Kremlin to up the manpower ante to 115,000. Although Soviet forces received improved equipment, sick-lists remained long and individual morale lower, with the troops frequently using drugs. Casualties also rose. Total Soviet losses from 1979 were " . . . estimated at 20–25,000 (roughly one-third of them killed)"; total financial cost to the Kremlin was reportedly $12 billion.[22] Food and fuel shortages increased in cities and towns and so did serious epidemics, with little or no medicines for the ill. Afghan army morale was low; the conscription age was now sixteen. Karmal had won some favor by adopting a pro-Islamic stance, by softening and even discarding some of the more stringent Amin reforms, by releasing some political prisoners, and by extending the franchise, but his increasingly fragmented regime was believed to control just over 20 per cent of the population.[23]

In 1985, the first year in which Western journalists were legally allowed to enter Afghanistan, the war seemed to tilt in the government's favor as security forces gained control of most cities and towns and began pushing guerrillas back to the mountains. Karmal established a Ministry of Islamic Affairs, announced elections for local assemblies, and convened large meetings of tribal, religious, and political elders as well as of frontier tribesmen, in an effort to win their support in the crucial Pakistan border areas. In addition to adding non-party persons both to the Council of Ministers and the Revolutionary Council, he made other conciliatory moves designed to win over businessmen, mullahs, and intelligentsia. Behind this facade of Islamic democracy, Sovietization proceeded apace. The teaching of the Russian language was now compulsory from an early age and thousands of youngsters were sent to Central Asian provinces for ten years of schooling.[24] On the military side, the policy of terror against villages suspected of guerrilla sympathies was changed to a policy of coercion, which in many areas resulted in the formation of local militias that guarded villages and gave information on guerrilla movements and location to the Khad, the Afghanistan secret police. An amnesty program brought in a large number of defectors, including one group of a thousand guerrillas which was organized into a local defense militia.[25]

Despite some of the biggest Soviet/Afghanistan drives of the war, the killing of large numbers of mujaheddin, and the capture of guerrilla arms dumps, the fighting was scarcely decisive. More weapons were flowing into mujaheddin camps—the U.S. reportedly supplied $250 million worth in 1985—and nowhere did the resistance seem broken. In truth, both sides were tiring of the war but now the mujaheddin gained a new and totally expected ally in the form of Russia's Mikhail Gorbachev. To the outspoken Gorbachev, who was staring encroaching national bankruptcy in the face, the Afghan insurgency was a "bleeding wound." It had cost thirty-five thousand Soviet casualties (including fifteen thousand dead) to date; it was costing $15 million a day; it was standing in the way of detente with the West, China, and the Arab states; and it was bringing increasing domestic dissatisfaction in Russia.[26]

As a first step in extricating Russia from the war, Gorbachev selected Dr. Mohammed Najibullah, chief of the secret police, to head a program of "national reconciliation." That was a somewhat odd choice in that, as head of Khad, Najibullah personally had been responsible for many thousands of deaths from torture of political prisoners. Nevertheless, he replaced Karmal as head of the PDPA and ruler of the country and offered a six-month cease-fire during which the government would organize a "coalition of national unity," write a new constitution, and oversee the election of a national assembly. Gorbachev himself promised the phased withdrawal of six Soviet regiments to begin in 1987 and to continue providing the mujaheddin joined the cease-fire and co-operated with the policy of national reconciliation.[27]

The mujaheddin were not interested. They had largely recovered from tactical setbacks in 1985 and were again in front militarily, having received some $500 million worth of arms in 1986, about half of which were furnished by the U.S., including ground-to-air Stinger missiles.[28] Nor were they interested in "national reconciliation" or even in a new constitution which made Islam the official religion. Despite the political window-dressing, it was all too obvious that Najibullah was running a Soviet-dominated dictatorship. When the Soviet regiments, some seven thousand troops, began to depart in 1987, it was also obvious that Russia was tiring of the war. Mujaheddin military successes continued to mount as the flow of foreign arms increased—over $600 million worth from the U.S. and many more millions from China and Saudi

Arabia in 1987. Increasingly, the Soviet forces and what remained of the Afghan army were on the defensive in the cities and countryside, to the extent that in early 1988 Gorbachev no longer tied Soviet troop withdrawal to perpetuation of the PDPA regime in Kabul, stating that " . . . Soviet troops would leave the country in less than ten months, beginning on 15 May provided that there was no interference from Pakistan and the U.S."[29] Confirmed by the UN-sponsored Geneva Accords, which Gorbachev signed in April, the withdrawal began on schedule and was completed in mid-February.[30]

Most Western experts predicted that the Najibullah regime would fall and be replaced by a mujaheddin government.[31] Nothing of the sort happened. The Kremlin continued to supply Najibullah with arms (including long-range Scud missiles), food, and fuel brought in by air— " . . . nearly $2 billion in military equipment by mid-October."[32] To general surprise, the hard core of the Afghan army, perhaps ten thousand veterans, more than held its own in the battle for the cities. Conversely, the increasingly fragmented mujaheddin fought either spasmodically or not at all. This was owing first to the nature of the beast, second to a massive failure brought on by U.S./Pakistan interference. In late 1988, the U.S. and Pakistan decided to form an Afghan Interim Government (AIG), which would replace the Kabul regime. To hasten this event, an offensive commanded by Pakistan's Inter-Service Intelligence organization was opened against government garrisons at Jallalabad and Khost, battles fought much more along conventional than guerrilla lines and as a result ending in stalemate with a large loss of guerrilla lives.[33] Meanwhile, members of the AIG were elected but these came from the Sunni Party alliance in Peshawar and excluded field commanders, the eight Shiite guerrilla groups based in Iran and most moderates, thereby insuring continued diversity and strife. This spilled over to other governments, with Iran and the Soviet Union holding for a coalition government in Kabul, Pakistan and Saudi Arabia pushing for an extreme fundamentalist government controlled by Hekmatyar's Hezb-i Islami.

The political and military impasse continued into 1989, but each side was hurting. In February, Najibullah declared a state of emergency and in May offered the Pakistan-based mujaheddin, addressed now as "brothers" not "bandits," a series of important concessions including an invitation to join the government in return for a cease-fire. The coalition was in greater disarray than ever. A ten-week siege of Islamabad had been defeated, the guerrillas again suffering heavy casualties.[34] In July, a faction of Hekmatyar's Hezb-i Islami ambushed and killed thirty mujaheddin including several of Ahmed Shah Massoud's commanders, an act that caused AIG President Mojadiddi to call Hekmatyar a "criminal" and a "terrorist,"[35] and cost the Hezb-i Islami, already suspected of selling Stinger missiles to Iran, U.S. support. Hekmatyar in turn accused Massoud of the crime and broke with the AIG. Massoud responded by attacking Hekmatyar's strongholds in Afghanistan. A second siege of Islamabad in November also failed, again with heavy casualties.

Najibullah had scant cause to rejoice. The PDPA was as divided as the mujaheddin. In March 1990, dissident army and air force officers led an unsuccessful attack on the presidential palace.[36] Najibullah not only survived but such was the tepid performance of the enemy that in spring of 1990 he called an end to the emergency and presented still another peace plan at once rejected by the mujaheddin.[37]

Subsequent events bear a curious resemblance to those that finally brought an end to the stubborn civil war in El Salvador. The United Nations had been trying to bring about a peace since 1982 with little progress until the signing of the Geneva Accords in 1988. In late 1989, a small UN force was created " . . . to monitor the withdrawal of foreign troops from Afghanistan as well as other aspects of the Geneva Accords of 1988."[38] In 1991, after a major mujaheddin offensive had captured the garrison city of Khost, UN Secretary-General Perez de Cuellar announced a peace plan based in part on proposals by the exiled Afghanistan King Zahir Shah. Its basic points were a cease-fire, an end to external influence, including the supply of arms to either side, and a UN-supervised election. Although Najibullah, who had lost considerable Soviet support after the fall of Gorbachev, accepted the plan, the hard-core mujaheddin—Hekmatyar's Hezb-i Islami and the AIG—refused to consider it: " . . . if Najibullah is there, there can be no cease-fire."[39] Hekmatyar's stance sparked off another round of internecine war, but the moderate groups representing an estimated 90 per cent of all mujaheddin agreed to consider the plan. Subsequent talks between the Iran-based groups, four of the seven AIG Pakistan groups and Pakistan and Iran representatives came to nothing. The picture changed radically in September with a U.S.-Soviet decision to end all weapon deliveries to the opposing sides. After more fighting and more talking, the mujaheddin majority met with Soviet Union officials in November. The battered Soviets, their own empire crumbling around them, agreed to end support for the Najibullah regime, which would be replaced by an interim government until elections could be held. That demarche was followed by further UN action which resulted in Najibullah's resignation and the establishment of an interim government in Kabul despite hard-core fundamentalist rejection of the resolution.[40] In theory the fifteen-year-old war, which had taken an estimated 1.5 million lives and had torn over five million Afghans from their homes, was over.

Well—not quite. The interim council, composed of representatives from the ten major guerrilla groups and headed by President Burhanuddin Rabbini, the non-Pashtun leader of the Jamait-i Islami group of fighters, was not universally applauded. While it was being organized, Hekmatyar's Pashtun guerrillas and Massoud's non-Pashtun guerrillas were securing control of their respective areas. Najibullah's fall from power in mid-April sent these groups racing to Kabul, Hekmatyar's troops moving in from south and east, Massoud's men from the north, a victory march on Massoud's part joined by scores of local government militia forces before he reached Kabul.[41] Prior to their arrival, Najibullah had attempted to escape the country but was intercepted by Major General Abdul Rashid Dostam, the non-Pashtun Uzbek leader of a strong government militia that had defected to the new government. When Hekmatyar and Massoud's forces reached Kabul in late April, a series of bloody battles followed. Massoud supported by Dostam forced the Hezb-i Islami fighters from the city to the southern hills. Reinforced by tanks and artillery brought up from his rear area base, Hekmatyar opened an artillery attack on the capital, killing seventy-three people and wounding nearly four hundred.[42] In late May, the two leaders signed a peace agreement but it was soon vitiated when the government not only refused to disband Dostam's force but incorporated it into the army.

The sides were now drawn for what has become a second civil war, this time Moslem Afghans fighting Moslem Afghans. The key players are Hekmatyar, supported by some powerful Pashtun leaders and reportedly by some Pakistani and Saudi Arabian officials; and Massoud, supported by most Shiite and other non-Pashtun leaders. Each side has ample stocks of weapons and ammunition, courtesy of Russia, the U.S., China, and Saudi Arabia. The result is stalemate, neither force being able to militarily defeat the other. The war has turned Kabul into virtually a ghost town, with no hospitals, no medicines, no electricity, no telephones, intermittent water supply, severe food shortages, embassies deserted, thousands of houses and shops buried in rubble. Various guerrilla factions are constantly at each other's throats, stealing and murdering. Hekmatyar's artillery shells and rockets fall on the city with maddening frequency. By late August, over two thousand people had been killed: " . . . more citizens of Kabul have died since the mujaheddin took power than during fourteen years of civil war."[43]

As a final crime, heroin production and distribution in the eastern border areas has grown so that it is now " . . . beyond the control of all the regionally interested governments, not only of Kabul and Islamabad, but also of Teheran and Moscow."[44]

Unfortunately, the anarchic situation continued in the following months as regional guerrilla leaders lorded it over independent fiefdoms such as the enclaves belonging to Sayer Jaffer Naderi and Rashid Dostum in the north. Despite almost constant fighting in and around Kabul, all attempts to bring about meaningful peace negotiations have failed.

As of this writing, December 1993, the war goes on—and with it the probable dissolution of Afghanistan as we have known it.

CHAPTER NINETY-TWO

1. Fletcher, 7.
2. Ibid., 1.
3. Ibid., 2, 5, 289 ff.
4. Ibid., 266–8.
5. Ibid., 272–3.
6. Rubin, 153 ff.
7. Ibid., 152.
8. Urban, 28.
9. Riencourt, 423–4.
10. International Institute for Strategic Studies, *Strategic Survey 1979*, 53.
11. Ibid, *1985–86*, 131.
12. Ibid., *1980–81*, 64. See also, Urban, 51–3.
13. Hart, 61.
14. International Institute for Strategic Studies, *Strategic Survey*, 64. See also, Urban, 66–8.
15. Schultheis.
16. Urban, 56–8, 77–8.
17. International Institute for Strategic Studies, *Strategic Survey 1981–82*, 93.
18. Hart, 63. See also, International Institute for Strategic Studies, *Adelphi Papers Number 259*, Summer 1991, 46–7; Urban, 98–9.
19. Ibid., *Strategic Survey 1981–82*, 94.
20. Malhuret, 428.
21. International Institute for Strategic Studies, *Strategic Survey 1982–83*, 87. See also, Urban, 128.
22. Ibid., *1984–85*, 73.
23. Ibid.
24. Ibid., *1985–86*, 131–3.
25. Ibid., 137.
26. Ibid., *Adelphi Papers Number 259*, 47.
27. Ibid., *Strategic Survey 1986–87*, 135.
28. Ibid, 138.
29. Ibid., *1987–88*, 137.
30. *USA Today*, International Edition, February 1, 16, 1989.
31. Ibid., February 15, 16, 1989.
32. Rubin, 162.
33. See, for example, *International Herald Tribune*, May 6–7, 1989.
34. Rubin, 156–9, for what went wrong.
35. Ibid., 159–60.
36. *Keesing's Record of World Events*, Vol. 36, 1990. March 1990, 37,314–5.
37. Ibid., May 1990, 37,453.
38. Ibid., March 1990, 37,355.
39. Ibid., Vol. 37, May 1991, 38,194.
40. *International Herald Tribune*, March 20, April 11–12, 1992.
41. *The Independent* (U.K.), April 15, 1992. See also, *International Herald Tribune*, April 24, 1992.
42. *Newsweek*, May 18, 1992.
43. *The Independent* (U.K.), August 28, 1992.
44. International Institute for Strategic Studies, *Strategic Survey 1989–90*, 163–4.

SELECTED BIBLIOGRAPHY

Abel, E. See Kalb, M.L.

Abernathy, M. Glenn, Dilys Hill, and Phil Williams, eds. *The Carter Years: The President and Policy Making.* London: Francis Pinter, 1984.

Acheson, Dean. *Present at the Creation: My Years in The State Department.* New York: W.W. Norton, 1969.

Adcock, F.E. *The Roman Art of War Under the Republic.* Cambridge, Mass.: Harvard University Press, 1940.

Alastos, Doros. *Cyprus Guerrilla: Grivas, Makarios and the British.* London: William Heinemann, 1960.

Alba, Victor. *The Mexicans: The Making of a Nation.* New York: Frederick A. Praeger, 1967.

Alden, J.R. *The American Revolution, 1775–1783.* New York: Harper and Brothers, 1954.

———. *A History of the American Revolution: Britain and the Loss of the Thirteen Colonies.* London: MacDonald, 1969.

———. *The South in the Revolution, 1763–1789.* Baton Rouge, La.: State University Press, 1957.

Aldington, R. *Lawrence of Arabia: A Biographical Enquiry.* London: Collins, 1955.

Alleg, Henri. *The Question.* London: John Calder, 1958.

Alsop, S., and T. Braden. *Sub Rosa: The OSS and American Espionage.* New York: Reynal and Hitchcock, 1946.

Altamira, Rafael. *A History of Spain.* New York: D. Van Nostrand, 1949.

Amery, Julian. *Sons of the Eagle: A Study in Guerrilla Warfare.* London: Macmillan, 1948.

Anders, W. *An Army in Exile.* London: Macmillan, 1949.

Anderson, James. *Sendero Luminoso: A New Revolutionary Model?* London: Institute for the Study of Terrorism, 1987.

Anderson, Thomas P. *Politics in Central America: Guatemala, El Salvador, Honduras, and Nicaragua.* New York: Frederick A. Praeger, 1982.

The Annual Register of World Events. London: Longman, 1975–91.

Anon. *An Historical Account of the Expedition Against the Ohio Indians in the Year MDCCLXIV Under the Command of Henry Bouquet, Esq.* London: n.p., 1766.

Appian, *Appian's Roman History,* Vol. 1 of 4 vols., tr. Horace White. London: William Heinemann, 1964.

Armbrister, Trevor. *A Matter of Accountability: The True Story of the Pueblo Affair.* London: Barrie and Jenkins, 1970.

Armstrong, J.A., ed. *Soviet Partisans in World War II.* Madison, Wis.: University of Wisconsin Press, 1964.

Armstrong, J.A., and K. DeWitt. "Organization and Control of the [Soviet] Partisan Movement." In Armstrong, op. cit.

Aron, Robert. *De Gaulle Before Paris: The Liberation of France June–August 1944*, tr. H. Hare. London: Putnam, 1962.

Arrian, *Anabasis Alexandri*, Vol. 1 of 2 vols., tr. P.A. Brunt. London: William Heinemann, 1929.

Arthur, George. *Life of Lord Kitchener*, Vol. 1 of 2 vols. London: Macmillan, 1920.

Asprey, Robert B. "The Peninsular War" and "Wellington at Waterloo," *Army Quarterly*, Vols. 77–78, April and July, 1959.

———. "Waller of Samar," *Marine Corps Gazette*, May and June, 1961.

———. "Special Forces: Europe," *Army*, January, 1962.

———. "Small Wars—1925–1962," *Leatherneck*, 1962.

———. "Guerrilla Warfare," *Encyclopaedia Britannica*, 1969.

———. "Jungle Warfare," *Encyclopaedia Britannica*, 1969.

———. "Tactics," *Encyclopaedia Britannica*, 1971.

———. *War in the Shadows: The Guerrilla in History*, 2 vols. Garden City, N.Y.: Doubleday, 1975.

———. *Frederick the Great: The Magnificent Enigma*. New York: Ticknor and Fields, 1986.

———. "Guerrilla Warfare," *Encyclopaedia Britannica*, 1991.

Atkin, Ronald. *Revolution: Mexico 1910–1920*. New York: John Day, 1969.

Atkinson, Rick. *The Long Gray Line*. London: Collins, 1990.

Azan, Paul, ed. *Par l'Epée et par la Charrue: Écrits et Discours de Bugeaud*. Paris: Presses Universitaires de France, 1948.

Badian, E. "Alexander the Great and the Unity of Mankind." *Historia*, Vol. 7, pp. 425–44. Wiesbaden: Franz Steiner Verlag, 1952.

Baker, Carlos. *Hemingway: The Writer as Artist*. Princeton, N.J.: Princeton University Press, 1967.

Baldwin, Hanson. "The Case for Escalation," *New York Times Magazine*, February 27, 1966.

———. "The Foe is Hurting." *Reader's Digest*, March 1968.

———. "To End the War in Vietnam, Mobilize!" *Reader's Digest*, October 1966.

Ball, George W. *The Past Has Another Problem: Memoirs*. New York: W.W. Norton, 1982.

Barclay, C.N. "The Western Soldier Versus the Communist Insurgent," *Military Review*, February 1969.

Barea, A. *The Track*, tr. Ilsa Barea. London: Faber and Faber, 1943.

Barker, Dudley. *Grivas: Portrait of a Terrorist*. London: Cresset Press, 1959.

Barnett, Donald L., and Katari Njama. *Mau Mau from Within: Autobiography and Analysis of Kenya's Peasant Revolt*. New York: Monthly Review Press, 1966.

Barrett, David D. *Dixie Mission: The United States Army Observer Group in Yenan, 1944*. Berkeley, Calif.: University of California Press, 1970.

Bass, Robert D. *Swamp Fox: The Life and Campaigns of General Francis Marion*. London: Alvin Redman, 1959.

Batista, Fulgencio. *Cuba Betrayed*. New York: Vantage Press, 1962.

Bayley, Sydney D. *Four Arab-Israeli Wars and the Peace Process*. London: The Macmillan Press, 1990.

Beaufre, André. "Prospects for the New General," *The Sunday Times* (London), March 24, 1968.

Becker, Julian. *The PLO: The Rise and Fall of the Palestine Liberation Organization*. London: Weidenfeld and Nicolson, 1984.

Beckett, J.C. *The Making of Modern Ireland 1603–1923*. London: Faber and Faber, 1966.

Beeler, John. *Warfare in England, 1066–1189*. Ithaca, N.Y.: Cornell University Press, 1966.

———. *Warfare in Feudal Europe, 730–1200*. Ithaca, N.Y.: Cornell University Press, 1971.

Behr, Edward. *The Algerian Problem*. London: Hodder and Stoughton, 1961.

Bell, J. Bowyer. *The Secret Army: The IRA 1916–1979.* Dublin: The Academy Press, 1979.

Bennett, Richard. *The Black and Tans.* London: Hulton, 1959.

Bennoune, Mahfoud. *The Making of Contemporary Algeria 1830–1987.* New York: Cambridge University Press, 1988.

Berman, Larry. *Lyndon Johnson's War: The Road to Stalemate in Vietnam.* New York: W.W. Norton, 1989.

———. *Planning a Tragedy. The Americanization of the War in Vietnam.* New York: W.W. Norton, 1983.

Bernard, Stéphane. *The Franco-Moroccan Conflict, 1943–1956.* New Haven, Conn.: Yale University Press, 1968.

Bernstein, Carl. See Woodward, Bob.

Bertrand, L., and C. Petrie. *The History of Spain.* London: Eyre and Spottiswoode, 1934.

Best, Edward. "An Alternative American Policy for Nicaragua." *Survival* March/April 1987. International Institute for Strategic Studies.

Besterman, Theodore. *Voltaire.* London: Longmans, Green, 1969.

Béthouart, Hilaire. "Combat Helicopters in Algeria." In Greene, T.N., ed., op. cit.

Bianchi, A. See Seers, D.

Bigelow, John. *Principles of Strategy.* Philadelphia: J.B. Lippincott, 1894.

Billias, George A., ed. *George Washington's Opponents.* New York: William Morrow, 1969.

Bird, M.J. *The Secret Battalion.* London: Muller, 1965.

Bishop, Patrick, and Eamonn Mallie, *The Provisional IRA.* London: William Heinemann, 1987.

Black, Eugene R. *Alternative in Southeast Asia.* London: Pall Mall Press, 1969.

Blair, C.N.M. *Guerrilla Warfare.* London: Public Records Office WO 231/80.

Blanch, Leslie. *The Sabres of Paradise.* London: John Murray, 1960.

Blaufarb, Douglas E. *Counterinsurgency Era: U.S. Doctrine and Performance. 1950 to the Present.* New York: The Free Press, 1977.

Bleicher, Hugo. *Colonel Henri's Story,* ed. Ian Colvin. London: William Kimber, 1954.

Blow, Rex. "With the Filipino Guerrillas." *Australian Army Journal,* 1966.

Bohannan, C.T.R. See Valeriano, N.D.

Bohlen, C.E. *The Transformation of American Foreign Policy.* New York: W.W. Norton, 1969.

Bonner, Raymond. *Weakness and Deceit: U.S. Policy and El Salvador.* New York: Times Books, 1984.

Boswell, James. *The Journal of a Tour to Corsica; and Memoirs of Pascal Paoli,* with an Introduction by Morchard Bishop. ed. London: Williams and Norgate, 1951.

Bouchier, E.S. *Spain Under the Roman Empire.* Oxford: Blackwell, 1914.

Boyle, Andrew. *Trenchard.* London: Collins, 1962.

Brandon, Henry. *Anatomy of Error: The Secret History of the Vietnam War.* London: André Deutsch, 1970.

Brett-James, Antony. *Wellington at War 1794–1815.* London: Macmillan, 1961.

Bridgland, Fred. *Jonas Savimbi: A Key to Africa.* Edinburgh: Mainstream Publishing, 1986.

Brown, Malcolm, and Julie Cave. *A Touch of Genius.* London: J.M. Dent, 1988.

Browne, Malcolm. "Why South Viet Nam's Army Won't Fight." *True* magazine, October 1967.

Bruce, Steve, "Northern Ireland: Reappraising Loyalist Values." *Conflict Studies Number 249,* March 1992. Institute for the Study of Conflict.

Brzezinski, Zbigniew. *Power and Principle: Memoirs of the National Security Adviser (1977–1981).* New York: Farrar, Straus and Giroux, 1983.

Bucher, Lloyd M. *Bucher: My Story.* Garden City, N.Y.: Doubleday, 1970.

Bullitt, W.C. "A Report to the American People on China." *Life,* October 13, 1947.

Bundy, McGeorge. "The End of Either/Or." *Foreign Affairs*, June 1967.

Bundy, William P., "The Path to Vietnam." *Survival*, October 1967. International Institute of Strategic Studies.

Burchett, W.G. *Vietnam: Inside Story of the Guerrilla War*. New York: International Publishers, 1965.

Burn, A.R. *Alexander the Great*. New York: Macmillan, 1947.

———. *Persia and the Greeks*. London: Edward Arnold, 1962.

Burne, A.H. *The Agincourt War*. London: Eyre and Spottiswoode, 1956.

———. *The Crecy War*. London: Eyre and Spottiswoode, 1955.

Burton, Sandra. "Aquino's Philippines: The Center Holds." *Foreign Affairs, America and the World*, 1986.

Bury, J.B. *A History of the Eastern Roman Empire*. London: Macmillan, 1912.

———. *A History of Greece: To the Death of Alexander the Great*. London: Macmillan, 1959.

———. *History of the Later Roman Empire*, 2 vols. London: Macmillan, 1923.

Bushell, A.H. "Insurgency and the Numbers Game," *Army Quarterly*, April 1967.

Butler, J.R.M. *History of the Second World War, Grand Strategy*, Vol. 2. London: Her Majesty's Stationery Office, 1957.

Butterfield, Fox. See Sheehan, Neil.

Buttinger, Joseph. *Vietnam: A Dragon Embattled*, Vol. 1 of 2 vols. New York: Frederick A. Praeger, 1967.

Byford-Jones, W. *Grivas and the Story of EOKA*. London: Robert Hale, 1959.

Cabezas, Omar. *Fire from the Mountain: The Making of a Sandinista*. New York: Crown, 1985.

Caesar, Julius. *Commentaries on the Gallic War*. 2 vols, tr. T. Rice Holmes. London: Macmillan, 1908.

Caird, L.H. *The History of Corsica*. London: Unwin, 1899.

Callinan, Bernard. *Independent Company*. London: William Heinemann, 1953.

Callwell, C.E. *Small Wars: Their Principles and Practice*. London: Her Majesty's Stationery Office, 1899.

———. *The Armed Strength of Roumania*. London: Her Majesty's Stationery Office, 1888.

———. *Hints on Reconnaissances in Little Known Countries*. London: Her Majesty's Stationery Office, 1890.

———. *Handbook of the Armies of the Minor Balkan States*. London: Her Majesty's Stationery Office, 1891.

———. *Handbook of the Turkish Army*. London: Her Majesty's Stationery Office, 1892.

Calvert, Michael. *Prisoners of Hope*. London: Jonathan Cape, 1952.

Calvert, Peter. *The Mexican Revolution, 1910–1914: The Diplomacy of Anglo-American Conflict*. London: Cambridge University Press, 1968.

Cameron, James. *The African Revolution*. New York: Random House, 1961.

Campbell, Arthur. *Jungle Green*. London: Allen and Unwin, 1953.

Campbell, John Franklin. " 'What Is to Be Done?' Gigantism in Washington." *Foreign Affairs*, October 1970.

Cannon, Lou. *President Reagan: The Role of a Lifetime*. New York: Simon and Schuster, 1991.

Cannon, M.H. *The War in the Pacific—Leyte: Return to the Philippines*. Washington, D.C.: U.S. Government Printing Office, 1954.

Capps, Walter. *The Vietnam Reader*. New York: Routledge, 1991.

Caputo, Philip. *A Rumor of War*. New York: Holt, Rinehart and Winston, 1977.

Carr, E.H. *Karl Marx: A Study in Fanaticism*. London: J.M. Dent and Sons, 1934.

———. *Studies in Revolution*. London: Macmillan, 1950.

Carr, Raymond. "Spain and Portugal—1793 to c. 1840." *The New Cambridge Modern History*, Vol. 9 of 12 vols. London: Cambridge University Press, 1965.

Carter, James. *Keeping Faith: Memoirs of a President*. New York: Bantam Books, 1982.

Carver, George A., Jr. "The Real Revolution in South Viet Nam." *Foreign Affairs,* April 1965.

Casella, Alessandro. "The Militant Mood." *Far Eastern Review,* May 16, 1968.

Castanáneda, Jorge 6. *Utopia Unarmed: The Latin America Left After the Cold War.* New York: Alfred A. Knopf, 1993.

Caulaincourt, Duke of Vicenza. *Memoirs,* 3 vols., ed. Jean Hanoteau, tr. Hamish Miles. London: Cassell, 1950.

Cave, Julie. See Brown, Malcolm.

Chanda, Navan. *Brother Enemy: The War After the War.* New York: Collier Books, 1986.

Chapelle, Dickey. "How Castro Won." In Greene, T.N., ed., op. cit.

Chapman, Leonard. "Remarks." U.S. Marine Corps release, n.d.

Charters, David A. *The British Army and Jewish Insurgency in Palestine 1945– 1947.* London: Macmillan, 1989.

Charles, First Marquis Cornwallis. *Correspondence,* Vol. 1 of 3 vols., ed. Charles Ross. London: John Murray, 1859.

Chauvet, P. See Deschamps, H.

Cheetham, Sir Nicolas. *A History of Mexico.* London: Rupert Hart-Davis, 1970.

Cheshire, H.T. "The Great Tartar Invasion of Europe." *The Slavonic Review,* Vol. 5. London, 1926.

Chester, Edmund A. *A Sergeant Named Batista.* New York: Henry Holt, 1954.

Chorley, K.C. *Armies and the Art of Revolution.* London: Faber and Faber, 1943.

Christiansen, Eric. *The Origins of Military Power in Spain—1800–1854.* London: Oxford University Press, 1967.

Churchill, Peter. *Of Their Own Choice.* London: Hodder and Stoughton, 1952.

Churchill, Randolph S. *Winston S. Churchill,* Vol. 1 of 2 vols. London: William Heinemann, 1966.

Churchill, Winston S. *Marlborough:—His Life and Times,* Vol. 1 of 2 vols. London: G.C. Harrap, 1933.

———. *The World Crisis,* Vol. 5. London: Thornton Butterworth, 1929.

Clark, Mark W. *From the Danube to the Yalu.* New York: Harper and Brothers, 1954.

Clark, Ramsey. "On Violence, Peace and the Rule of Law." *Foreign Affairs,* October 1970.

Clark, R.W. *The Birth of a Bomb.* London: Phoenix House, 1961.

Clarke, H.B. *Modern Spain 1815–1898.* London: Cambridge University Press, 1906.

Clausewitz, Carl von. *The Campaign of 1812 in Russia.* London: John Murray, 1843.

———. *On War,* Vol. 2 of 3 vols., tr. J.J. Graham. London: Routledge and Kegan Paul, 1968.

Clement, David A. "Le May: Study in Counter-Insurgency." *Marine Corps Gazette,* July 1967.

Clery, C.F. *Minor Tactics.* London: Kegan Paul, Trench, 1887.

Clifford, Clark M. "A Viet Nam Reappraisal: The Personal History of One Man's View and How It Evolved," *Foreign Affairs,* July 1969.

———. *Counselor to the President: A Memoir.* New York: Random House, 1991.

Clinton, Sir Henry. See Willcox, William B.

Clutterbuck, Richard L. *The Long Long War—Counter-Insurgency in Malaya and Vietnam.* New York: Frederick A. Praeger, 1966.

———. "Peru: How to Defeat SL?" *Army Quarterly and Defense Journal,* October 1992.

———. *International Crisis and Conflict.* London: Macmillan, 1993.

———. *Guerrillas and Terrorists.* Athens, Ohio: Ohio University Press, 1980.

———. *Living With Terrorism.* New Rochelle, N.Y.: Arlington House, 1975.

———. *Conflict and Violence in Singapore and Malaysia 1945–1983.* Singapore: Graham Brash (PTE), 1984.

————. *Protest and the Urban Guerrilla.* New York: Abelard-Schuman, 1974.

————. *Kidnap, Hijack and Extortion.* London: Macmillan, 1987.

————. *Terrorism and Guerrilla Warfare.* London and New York: Routledge, 1990.

————. *International Crisis and Conflict.* London: Macmillan, 1993.

Cobban, Helena. *The Palestinian Liberation Organisation: People, Power and Politics.* Cambridge, U.K.: Cambridge University Press, 1989.

Cohan, Leon. "Intelligence and Viet-Nam." *Marine Corps Gazette,* February 1966.

Cole, D.H., and E.C. Priestley. *An Outline of British Military History, 1660–1936.* London: Sifton Praed, 1936.

Collier, Ellen C. See Library of Congress.

Colonial Office (Corfield, F.D.). *Historical Survey of the Origin and Growth of Mau Mau.* London: Her Majesty's Stationery Office, 1960. (Command Paper 1030.)

Commager, Henry Steele. "A Limit to Presidential Power?" *The New Republic.* Quoted in International Institute for Strategic Studies, *Survival,* July 1968.

————. See Morison, S.E.

Coogan, Tim P. *Michael Collins.* London: Hutchinson, 1990.

Cookridge, E.H. *Inside SOE: The Story of Special Operations in Western Europe 1940–45.* London: Arthur Barker, 1966.

Cooper, Chester L. *The Lost Crusade: The Full Story of U.S. Involvement in Vietnam from Roosevelt to Nixon.* London: MacGibbon and Kee, 1970.

Corfield, F.D. See Colonial Office.

Cornwallis, First Marquis. See Charles.

Corson, William R. *The Betrayal.* New York: W.W. Norton, 1968.

Costigan, G. "The Anglo-Irish Conflict, 1919–1922." *University Review,* Dublin, Spring 1968.

Cowell, Alan. *Wars of Power and Freedom from Zaire to South Africa.* New York: Simon and Schuster, 1992.

Crosthwaite, Charles. *The Pacification of Burma.* London: Edward Arnold, 1912.

Cumberland, Charles C. *Mexico: The Struggle for Modernity.* New York: Oxford University Press, 1968.

Dallin, Alexander. *German Rule in Russia, 1941–1945.* London: Macmillan and Co., 1957.

————, R. Mavrogordato, and W. Moll. "Partisan Psychological Warfare and Popular Attitudes." In Armstrong, op. cit.

Dalton, H. *The Fateful Years.* London: Muller, 1957.

Davidson, Basil. *Partisan Picture.* London: Bedford Books, 1946.

————. *Africa in Modern History. The Search for a New Society.* London: Allen Lane, 1978.

————, Lionel Cliffe, and B. H. Selassie, eds. *Behind the War in Eritrea.* London: Spokesman, 1980.

Davidson, Phillip B. *Vietnam at War: The History: 1946–1975.* London: Sidgwick and Jackson, 1988.

Davies, Edmund F. *Illyrian Venture: The Story of the British Military Mission to Enemy-Occupied Albania 1943–1944.* London: Bodley Head, 1952.

Davis, Leonard. *Revolutionary Struggle in the Philippines.* London: Macmillan Press, 1989.

Deakin, F.W.D. *The Embattled Mountain.* London: Oxford University Press, 1971.

Deakin, James. "Big Brass Lambs." *Esquire,* December 1967.

Dean, John W. III. *Blind Ambition: The White House Years.* New York: Simon and Schuster, 1975.

De Beer, Gavin. *Alps and Elephants: Hannibal's March.* London: Geoffrey Bles, 1955.

————. *The Struggle for Power in the Mediterranean.* London: Thames and Hudson, 1969.

Debray, Régis. *Revolution in the Revolution?—Armed Struggle and Political Strug-*

gle in Latin America. New York: Monthly Review Press, 1967.

de Gaulle, Charles. *Memoirs of Hope,* Volume 1 of 2 vols., tr. Terence Kilmartin. London: Weidenfeld and Nicolson, 1970.

———. *The War Memoirs of Charles de Gaulle,* Vol. 3, *Salvation 1944–1946,* tr. R. Howar. New York: Simon and Schuster, 1960.

Deschamps, H., and P. Chauvet. *Gallieni Pacificateur.* Paris: Presses Universitaires de France, 1949.

Devillers, Philippe, and Jean Lacouture. *End of a War: Indochina, 1954.* New York: Frederick A. Praeger, 1969.

Devine, Alex. *Montenegro in History, Politics and War.* London: T. Fisher Unwin, 1918.

DeWitt, K. See Armstrong, J.A.

DeWitt, K., and W. Moll. "The Bryansk Area." In Armstrong, op. cit.

Dickey, Christopher. "Central America: From Quagmire to Cauldron?" *Foreign Affairs, America and the World, 1983.*

Dictionary of National Biography 1922–30. London: Oxford University Press, 1937.

Dodge, T.A. *Hannibal,* vol. 1 of 2 vols. Boston: Houghton Mifflin, 1891.

Donovan, James A. *Militarism, U.S.A.* New York: Charles Scribner's Sons, 1970.

Donovan, James A. See Shoup, David M.

Douhet, Giulio. *The Command of the Air,* tr. D. Ferrari. London: Faber and Faber, 1943.

Dowas, Frederick. *The Killing Zone: My Life in the Vietnam War.* New York: W.W. Norton, 1978.

Draper, Theodore. *Castroism: Theory and Practice.* London: Pall Mall Press, 1965.

———. *Castro's Revolution: Myths and Realities.* London: Thames and Hudson, 1962.

Duncan, Donald. *The New Legions.* New York: Random House, 1967.

Duncan, H.L. "Does China Want War?" *Army Quarterly,* July 1967.

Duncanson, Dennis J. *Government and Revolution in Vietnam.* London: Oxford University Press, 1968.

———. "The Vitality of the Viet Cong." *Encounter,* December 1966.

———. See Tanham, George K.

Durrell, Lawrence. *Bitter Lemons.* London: Faber and Faber, 1959.

Earle, E.E., ed. *Makers of Modern Strategy.* Princeton, N.J.: Princeton University Press, 1941.

Eden, Anthony. *The Memoirs of Anthony Eden: Full Circle.* Boston: Houghton Mifflin, 1960.

———. *Towards Peace in Indo-China.* London: Oxford University Press, 1966.

Éditions G.P. *La Merveilleuse Histoire de l'Armée Française.* Paris, 1947.

Edmonds, James E. "Jomini and Clausewitz." *Army Quarterly,* April 1951.

Ehrlich, Blake. *The French Resistance.* London: Chapman and Hall, 1966.

Eisenhower, Dwight D. *Mandate for Change 1953–1956.* London: William Heinemann, 1963.

———. *Waging Peace 1956–1961.* London: William Heinemann, 1966.

Eldridge, F. *Wrath in Burma.* New York: Doubleday, 1946.

Ellsberg, Daniel. *Escalating in a Quagmire.* Boston: Center for International Studies, MIT, 1970.

Encyclopaedia Britannica, 33 vols. Chicago: Encyclopaedia Britannica, 1991.

Enthoven, Alain C., and K. Wayne Smith. *How Much Is Enough?* New York: Harper and Row, 1971.

Evans, D.L. "Civil Affairs in Vietnam," *Marine Corps Gazette,* March 1968.

Fagg, J.E. *Latin America: A General History.* London: Macmillan, 1969.

Falk, Pamela S. "Cuba in Africa." *Foreign Affairs,* Summer 1987.

Fall, Bernard. *Hell in a Very Small Place: The Siege of Dien Bien Phu.* London: Pall Mall Press, 1967.

————. *Street Without Joy*. London: Pall Mall Press, 1963.

————. *The Two Viet-Nams: A Political and Military Analysis*. London: Pall Mall Press, 1963.

————. "Viet Nam in the Balance." *Foreign Affairs*, October 1966.

Fallaci, Oriana. *Interview with History*, tr. John Shepley. New York: Liveright, 1976.

Falls, Cyril. *A Hundred Years of War*. London: Gerald Duckworth, 1953.

————. See MacMunn, G.

Fellowes-Gordon, Ian. *Amiable Assassins: The Story of the Kachin Guerrillas of North Burma*. London: Robert Hale, 1957.

Fergusson, Bernard. *Beyond the Chindwin*. London: Collins, 1962.

————. *Trumpet in the Hall*. London: Collins, 1970.

————. *The Wild Green Earth*. London: Collins, 1946.

Finnegan, William. *A Complicated War. The Harrowing of Mozambique*. Berkeley, Calif.: University of California Press, 1993.

Fischer, Louis. *The Story of Indonesia*. New York: Harper and Row, 1959.

Fisher, H.A.L. *Europe: Ancient and Medieval*. London: Eyre and Spottiswoode, 1938.

Fitzgerald, Frances. *Fire in the Lake*. London: Macmillan, 1972.

Fitzgibbon, Constantine. *Out of the Lion's Paw*. London: MacDonald, 1970.

Fletcher, Arnold. *Afghanistan Highway of Conquest*. Ithaca, N.Y.: Cornell University Press, 1965.

Foley, Charles. *Island in Revolt*. London: Longmans, Green, 1962.

————, and W.I. Scobie. *The Struggle for Cyprus*. Stanford, Calif.: Hoover Institution Press, 1975.

Foot, M.R.D. *SOE in France*. London: Her Majesty's Stationery Office, 1966.

————. *Resistance: An Analysis of European Resistance to Nazism 1940–1945*. London: Eyre Methuen, 1976.

Ford, Gerald R. *A Time to Heal: The Autobiography of Gerald R. Ford*. London: W.H. Allen, 1979.

Fortescue, John. *Wellington*. London: Ernest Benn, 1925.

Fox, Guy. See Scigliano, Robert.

Fox, Robin Lane. *Alexander the Great*. London: Allen Lane, 1973.

Franke, Wolfgang. "The Taiping Rebellion." In Franz Schurmann, op. cit.

Frédéric II, *Oeuvres (Histoire de Mon Temps)*, Vol. 2 of 30 vols., ed. J.D.E. Preuss. Berlin: Decker, 1846.

————. *Oeuvres (Militaires)*, Vols. 28 and 30 of 30 vols., ed. J.D.E Preuss. Berlin: Decker, 1856.

Frizzell, Donaldson D. See Thompson, W. Scott.

Fulbright, J. William. "In Thrall to Fear." *The New Yorker*, January 8, 1972.

————, ed. *The Vietnam Hearings*. New York: Vintage Books, 1966.

Fuller, J.F.C. *British Light Infantry in the Eighteenth Century*. London: Hutchinson, 1925.

————. *The Conduct of War, 1789–1961*. New Brunswick, N.J.: Rutgers University Press, 1961.

————. *The Decisive Battles of the Western World*, Vols. 1 and 2 of 3 vols. London: Eyre and Spottiswoode, 1956.

————. *The Generalship of Alexander the Great*. London: Eyre and Spottiswoode, 1958.

Furneaux, Rupert. *Abdel Krim: Emir of the Rif*. London: Secker and Warburg, 1967.

Galay, N. "The Partisan Forces." In Liddell Hart, B., ed., *The Soviet Army*, op. cit.

Galbraith, John K. *How to Get Out of Vietnam*. New York: Signet, 1967.

Gallery, Daniel V. *The Pueblo Incident*. Garden City, N.Y.: Doubleday, 1970.

Gallieni, General. *La Pacification de Madagascar (Opérations d'Octobre 1896 à Mars 1899)*. Paris: Librairie Militaire R. Chapelot, 1900.

García, Mauro. *Documents on the Japanese Occupation of the Philippines*. Manila: Philippines Historical Association, 1965.

Gardner, Brian. *German East*. London: Cassell, 1963.

Garnett, David, ed. *The Letters of T.E. Lawrence*, London: Jonathan Cape, 1927.

Garthoff, R.L. *Soviet Military Doctrine*. Glencoe, Ill.: The Free Press, 1953.

Gavin, James. *Crisis Now*. New York: Random House, 1968.

———. "A Soldier's Doubts." *Harper's Magazine*, February 1966.

Gaxotte, Pierre. *Frederick the Great*. London: G. Bell and Sons, 1941.

Gettleman, Marvin E., ed. *Viet-Nam: History, Documents, and Opinions on a Major World Crisis*. New York: Fawcett, 1965.

Gheusi, P.B. *Gallieni et Madagascar*. Paris: Éditions du Petit Parisien, n.d.

Giap, Vo Nguyen. *Big Victory, Great Task*. New York: Frederick A. Praeger, 1968.

———. *People's War, People's Army*. New York: Frederick A. Praeger, 1967.

———. "The Strategic Role of the Self-Defense Militia Force in the Great Anti-U.S. National Salvation Struggle of our People." Foreign Broadcast Information Service, April 1967.

Gilbert, Felix. "Machiavelli: The Renaissance of the Art of War." In Earle, op. cit.

Gillespie, Joan. *Algeria: Rebellion and Revolution*. London: Ernest Benn, 1960.

Gilpatric, Roswell W. "Vietnam and World War III." *New York Times*, May 30, 1965.

Giraldus Cambrensis. *The Autobiography of Giraldus Cambrensis*, ed. and tr. H.E. Butler. London: Jonathan Cape, 1937.

Giskes, H.L. *London Calling North Pole*. London: Arthur Barker, 1966.

Gleijeses, Piero. "The Case for Power Sharing in El Salvador." *Foreign Affairs*, Summer, 1983.

Goldenberg, Boris. *The Cuban Revolution and Latin America*. London: Allen and Unwin, 1965.

Goode, Stephen. *Guerrilla Warfare and Terrorism*. New York: F. Watts, 1977.

Goodhart, Philip. See Henderson, Ian.

Goodrich, L.C. *A Short History of the Chinese People*. London: Allen and Unwin, 1969.

Gordon, C.D. *The Age of Attila*. Ann Arbor, Mich.: University of Michigan Press, 1960.

Gowers, Andrew, and Tony Walker. *Behind the Myth: Yasser Arafat and the Palestinian Revolution*. London: W.H. Allen, 1990.

Grant, Zalin. "What Are We Doing in Thailand?" *The New Republic*, May 24, 1969.

———. *Facing the Phoenix: The CIA and the Political Defeat of the United States in Vietnam*. New York: W.W. Norton, 1991.

Graves, Robert. *Lawrence and the Arabs*. London: Jonathan Cape, 1927.

Greene, Graham. *The Quiet American*. London: William Heinemann, 1955.

Greene, T.N., ed. *The Guerrilla and How to Fight Him*. New York: Frederick A. Praeger, 1962.

Grier, S.L. "Black Pajama Intelligence." *Marine Corps Gazette*, April 1967.

Griffith, Samuel B. *The Battle for Guadalcanal*. Philadelphia: J.B. Lippincott, 1963.

———. *The Chinese People's Liberation Army*. New York: McGraw-Hill, 1967.

———. "Guerrilla." *Marine Corps Gazette*, August 1950.

———. *Sun Tzu: The Art of War*. London: Oxford University Press, 1963.

———. *In Defense of the Publick Liberty*. London: Jonathan Cape, 1977.

Grivas, George. *General Grivas on Guerrilla Warfare*, tr. A.S. Pallis. New York: Frederick A. Praeger, 1965.

———. *The Memoirs of General Grivas*, ed. Charles Foley. New York: Frederick A. Praeger, 1964.

Grossman, David, "Guests Can Be Shown the Door." *New York Times Magazine*, December 13, 1992.

———. *Sleeping on a Wire: Conversations with Palestinians in April*, tr. Haim Watzman. New York: Farrar, Straus and Giroux, 1992.

Groves, Leslie. *Now It Can Be Told.* London: André Deutsch, 1963.

Guedalla, Philip. *Wellington.* New York: Harper and Brothers, 1931.

Guevara, Ernesto Che. *Bolivian Diary,* tr. Carlos Hansen and Andrew Sinclair. London: Jonathan Cape, 1968.

———. *Che Guevara on Guerrilla Warfare,* ed. Harries-Clichy Peterson. New York: Frederick A. Praeger, 1961.

———. *Che Guevara Speaks: Selected Speeches and Writings,* ed. George Lavan. New York: Grove Press, 1967.

———. *Reminiscences of the Cuban Revolutionary War,* tr. V. Ortiz. New York: Grove Press, 1963.

Gurtov, Melvin. *The First Vietnam Crisis: Chinese Communist Strategy and United States Involvement 1953–1954.* New York: Columbia University Press, 1967.

Hackworth, David. *About Face.* New York: Simon and Schuster, 1989.

Haig, Alexander. *Caveat.* New York: Macmillan, 1983.

Halberstam, David. *The Making of a Quagmire.* New York: Random House, 1965.

———. *The Best and the Brightest.* New York: Random House, 1972.

Haldeman, H.R., with Joseph DiMona. *The Ends of Power.* New York: Times Books, 1978.

Hall, D.G.E. "Thailand (History)." *Encyclopaedia Britannica,* Vol. 21. 1968.

Halperin, Ernst. *Terrorism in Latin America.* Beverly Hills, Calif.: Sage Publications, 1976.

Hamill, Desmond. *Pig in the Middle: The Army in Northern Ireland 1969–1984.* London: Methuen, 1985.

Hammer, Ellen J. "Genesis of the First Indochina War: 1946–1950." In Gettleman, op. cit.

———. *The Struggle for Indochina 1940–1955.* Stanford, Calif.: Stanford University Press, 1966.

Hammond, J.W. "Combat Journal." *Marine Corps Gazette,* July and August 1968.

Hargreaves, Reginald. *Beyond the Rubicon.* New York: New American Library, 1966.

Harries, Owen. "Should the U.S. Withdraw from Asia?" *Foreign Affairs,* October 1968.

Harrison, H.D. *The Soul of Yugoslavia.* London: Hodder and Stoughton, 1941.

Harrison, John A. *China Since 1800.* New York: Harcourt, Brace and World, 1967.

Harrison, J.P. *The Endless War: Fifty Years of Struggle in Vietnam.* New York: The Free Press, 1982.

Hart, Douglas M., "Low Intensity Conflict in Afghanistan: The Soviet View." *Survival,* March/April 1982. International Institute for Strategic Studies.

Hart, Robert. *These from the Land of Sinim: Essays on the Chinese Question.* London: Chapman and Hall, 1903.

Harvey, Frank. *Air War: Vietnam.* New York: Bantam Books, 1967.

Haukelid, Knut. *Skis Against the Atom.* London: William Kimber, 1954.

Hayes-McCoy, G.A. *Irish Battles.* London: Longmans, Green, 1969.

Heelis, J.E. "Triumph in Malaysia." *Marine Corps Gazette,* January 1967.

Heilbrunn, Otto. "Counter-Insurgency Intelligence." *Marine Corps Gazette,* September 1966.

———. "Counter-Insurgency Tactics: A Question of Priorities." *Army Quarterly,* January 1967.

———. *Warfare in the Enemy's Rear.* New York: Frederick A. Praeger, 1963.

Heinl, Robert D. *Soldiers of the Sea.* Annapolis, Md.: U.S. Naval Institute, 1962.

———. "The Armed Forces: Are They 'Near Collapse'?" Detroit *Sunday News,* May 23, 1971.

Hemingway, Ernest. *For Whom the Bell Tolls.* London: Penguin Books, 1955.

Hemphill, Marie de Kiewiet. "The British Sphere 1884–94." In Oliver and Mathew, eds., op cit.

Henderson, G.F.R. *Stonewall Jackson and the American Civil War.* London: Longmans, Green, 1961.

Henderson, Ian, with Philip Goodhart. *The Hunt for Kimathi*. London: Hamish Hamilton, 1958.

Henderson, William. "South Vietnam Finds Itself." *Foreign Affairs,* January 1957.

Henisart, Paul. *Wolves in the City. The Death of French Algeria.* London: Rupert Hart-Davis, 1970.

Heren, Louis. *No Hail, No Farewell.* London: Weidenfeld and Nicolson, 1971.

Herodotus. *The History of Herodotus,* Vol. 1 of 2 vols., ed. A.J. Grant, tr. George Rawlinson. London: John Murray, 1897.

Herr, Michael. *Dispatches.* New York: Alfred A. Knopf, 1978.

Herring, George C. *America's Longest War: The United States and Vietnam, 1950–1975.* New York: John Wiley and Sons, 1979.

———. "America and Vietnam: The Unending War." *Foreign Affairs,* Winter 1991/92.

Herring, H.A. *A History of Latin America.* London: Jonathan Cape, 1955.

Hersh, Seymour M. "Coverup." *The New Yorker,* January 22 and January 29, 1972.

———. "My Lai 4." *Harper's Magazine,* May 1970.

———. *The Price of Power: Kissinger in the Nixon White House.* New York: Summit Books, 1983.

Heymann, Frederick G. *John Ziska and the Hussite Revolution.* Princeton, N.J.: Princeton University Press, 1955.

Hiebert, Murray. "Pessimism for Peace." *Far Eastern Economic Review,* May 30, 1991.

Higgins, Marguerite. *Our Vietnam Nightmare.* New York: Harper and Row, 1965.

Hilsman, Roger. *To Move a Nation: The Politics of Foreign Policy in the Administration of John F. Kennedy.* Garden City, N.Y.: Doubleday, 1967.

Ho Chi Minh. *Prison Diary,* tr. Aileen Palmer. Hanoi: Foreign Languages Publishing House, 1962.

———. *Ho Chi Minh on Revolution. Selected Writings 1920–1966,* tr. Bernard Fall. New York: Frederick A. Praeger, 1967.

———. *Ho Chi Minh: Selected Articles and Speeches, 1920–1967,* ed. Jack Woddis. London: Lawrence and Wishart, 1969.

Ho Kan-chih. "Rise of the Working Class Movement." In Schurmann, op. cit.

Hodges, D.C., ed. *Philosophy of the Urban Guerrilla: The Revolutionary Writings of Abraham Guillén.* New York: William Morrow, 1973.

Hodgkin, Thomas. *Vietnam: The Revolutionary Path.* London: Macmillan, 1981.

Holt, Edgar. *Protest in Arms: The Irish Troubles 1916–1923.* London: Putnam, 1960.

Hoopes, Townsend. *The Limits of Intervention.* New York: McKay, 1969.

Hoover Institution on War, Revolution, and Peace. *France During the German Occupation, 1940–1944,* 3 vols., tr. P.W. Whitcomb, Stanford, Calif.: Stanford University Press, 1957.

Hordern, Charles. *Military Operations East Africa 1914–1916,* Vol. 1. London: Her Majesty's Stationery Office, 1941.

Horne, Alistair. *A Savage War of Peace: Algeria 1954–1962.* London: Macmillan, 1977.

Horowitz, David. *Containment and Revolution.* Boston: Beacon Press, 1967.

Hosmer, S.T. (Chairman). *Counterinsurgency: A Symposium—April 16–20, 1962.* Santa Monica, Calif.: RAND Corporation, 1963.

Howard, Michael. "Jomini and the Classical Tradition in Military Thought." *Studies in War and Peace.* London: Maurice Temple Smith, 1970.

Howard-Johnston, James. "Studies in the Organization of the Byzantine Army in the Tenth and Eleventh Centuries," Ph.D. thesis. Oxford: 1971.

Howe, Sonia E. *Lyautey of Morocco.* London: Hodder and Stoughton, 1931.

Hoyt, Robert S. *Europe in the Middle Ages.* New York: Harcourt, Brace and Company, 1957.

———. *Life and Thought in the Early Middle Ages.* Minneapolis: University of Minnesota Press, 1967.

Htin Aung, Maung. *A History of Burma.* New York: Columbia University Press, 1967.

———. *The Stricken Peacock: Anglo-Burmese Relations 1752–1948.* The Hague: Martinus Nijhoff, 1965.

Huberman, Leo, and Paul Sweezy. *Cuba: Anatomy of a Revolution.* London: Routledge and Kegan Paul, 1960.

Hughes, Richard. "After Ho, Watch for Giap and a Tougher Line in Hanoi." *The Sunday Times* (London), September 7, 1969.

Hull, Cordell. *Memoirs.* New York: Macmillan, 1948.

Ibarruri, Dolores. *They Shall Not Pass.* London: Lawrence and Wishart, 1966.

Insor, D. Thailand. *A Political, Social and Economic Analysis.* London: Allen and Unwin, 1963.

Institute for the Study of Conflict. "Ulster: Politics and Terrorism." *Conflict Studies No. 36.* London: June 1973.

———. Janke, Peter. "Ulster: Consensus and Coercion." *Conflict Studies No. 50.* London: October 1974.

———. "Ulster: A Decade of Violence." *Conflict Studies No. 108.* London: June, 1979.

———. "Spanish Separatism: ETA's Threat to Basque Democracy." *Conflict Studies No. 123:* London: October 1980.

International Institute for Strategic Studies. *Strategic Survey, 1968–92.*

———. *Survival, 1975–92.*

———. "The Lessons of the Soviet/Afghan War." Adelphi Paper 259, Summer 1991.

Isaacs, Arnold R. *Without Honor. Defeat in Vietnam and Cambodia.* Baltimore: Johns Hopkins University Press, 1983.

Isaacs, Harold. *The Tragedy of the Chinese Revolution.* Stanford, Calif.: Stanford University Press, 1962.

Isaacson, Walter. *Kissinger: A Biography.* New York: Simon and Schuster, 1992.

Ivanov, Miroslav. *The Assassination of Heydrich,* tr. Patrick O'Brian. London: Hart-Davis, MacGibbon, 1974.

Izady, Mehrdad R. *The Kurds: A Concise Handbook.* London: Crane Russak, 1992.

Jackson, Geoffrey. *People's Prison.* London: Faber and Faber, 1973.

Jackson, Joe, "Lawyers, Guns and Money," *Magill Monthly Magazine* (Eire), May 1980.

Jacoby, A. See White, T.H.

James, Daniel. *Che Guevara: A Biography.* London: Allen and Unwin, 1970.

———, ed. *The Complete Bolivian Diaries of Ché Guevara: And Other Captured Documents.* London: Allen and Unwin, 1968.

Janke, Peter. See Institute for the Study of Conflict.

Jaster, Robert S. "The Security Outlook in Mozambique." *Survival,* November/December 1985. International Institute for Strategic Studies.

Jenkins, Brian. "The Unchangeable War," RAND Corporation, n.d.

Johnson, Lyndon B. *Public Papers of the President,* 10 vols. Washington, D.C.: U.S. Government Printing Office, 1965–70.

———. *The Vantage Point: Perspectives of the Presidency.* New York: Holt, Rinehart and Winston, 1971.

Jolly, R. See Seers, D.

Jomini, Baron de. *The Art of War.* Philadelphia: J.B. Lippincott, 1862.

Jules, Roy. *The Battle of Dienbienphu,* tr. Robert Baldich. London: Faber and Faber, 1965.

Jumper, Roy, and M.W. Normand. "Vietnam: The Historical Background." In Gettleman, op. cit.

Just, Ward. *To What End. Report from Vietnam.* Boston: Houghton Mifflin, 1968.

————. *Military Men.* New York: Alfred A. Knopf, 1971.

Kahin, George M. *Nationalism and Revolution in Indonesia.* Ithaca, N.Y.: Cornell University Press, 1952.

————, and John W. Lewis. *The United States in Vietnam: An Analysis in Depth of America's Involvement in Vietnam.* New York: The Dial Press, 1967.

Kahn, Herman. "If Negotiations Fail." *Foreign Affairs,* July 1968.

Kalb, M.L., and E. Abel. *Roots of Involvement: The U.S. in Asia 1784–1971.* New York: W.W. Norton, 1971.

Karnow, Stanley. *Vietnam: A History.* London: Century Publishing, 1983.

————. *In Our Image.* New York: Random House, 1989.

Keesing's Contemporary Archives, 1970–1987.

Keesing's Record of World Events, 1988–present.

Kellen, Konrad. "Fourth Round or Peace in Vietnam?" RAND Corporation, 1968.

Kendall, P. *The Story of Land Warfare.* London: Hamish Hamilton, 1957.

Kennan, George F. *American Diplomacy, 1900–1950.* London: Secker and Warburg, 1952.

————. *The Decision to Intervene.* London: Faber and Faber, 1958.

————. *Memoirs.* London: Hutchinson, 1968.

————. *Russia Leaves the War.* London: Faber and Faber, 1956.

See also x.

Kennedy, John F. *The Strategy of Peace.* New York: Harper and Brothers, 1960.

————. *Public Papers of John F. Kennedy,* Vol. 1 of 2 vols. Washington, D.C.: U.S. Government Printing Office, 1962.

Kenworthy, E. W. See Sheehan, Neil.

Kenyatta, Jomo. *Facing Mount Kenya: The Tribal Life of the Gikuyu.* London: Secker and Warburg, 1938.

Kiernan, Ben. *How Pol Pot Came to Power: A History of Communism in Kampuchea, 1930–1975.* London: Verso, 1985.

Kirby, S.W. *The War Against Japan: The Loss of Singapore.* London: HMSO, 1957.

Kirkpatrick, F.A. *The Spanish Conquistadores.* London: Adam and Charles Black, 1934.

Kissinger, Henry. *Nuclear Weapons and Foreign Policy.* London: Oxford University Press, 1957.

————. *The White House Years.* London: Weidenfeld and Nicolson and Michael Joseph, 1979.

————. *Years of Upheaval.* London: Weidenfeld and Nicolson, 1982.

Kitson, Frank. *Gangs and Counter-Gangs.* London: Barrie and Rockliff, 1960.

————. *Low-Intensity Operations.* London: Faber and Faber, 1971.

————. *Bunch of Five.* London: Faber and Faber, 1977.

Knightly, P., and C. Simpson. *The Secret Lives of Lawrence of Arabia.* London: Nelson, 1969.

Kochan, Lionel. *Russia in Revolution 1890–1918.* London: Weidenfeld and Nicolson, 1966.

Koestler, Arthur. *Promise and Fulfilment: Palestine, 1917–1949.* London: Macmillan, 1949.

Kohl, J., and J. Lift. *Urban Guerrilla Warfare in Latin America.* Cambridge, Mass.: MIT. Press, 1974.

Kovic, Ron. *Born on the Fourth of July.* New York: McGraw-Hill, 1976.

Krausnick, H. *Anatomy of the SS State.* London: Collins, 1968.

Krepinevich, Andrew F., Jr. *The Army and Vietnam.* Baltimore, Md.: Johns Hopkins University Press, 1986.

Kriegel, Richard. "Revolutionary Development." *Marine Corps Gazette,* March 1967.

Krulak, V.H. "Address to Western Newspaper Industrial Relations Bureau . . . ," U.S. Marine Corps release, n.d.

Kun, Ernst, and Joseph Kun. "North Vietnam's Doctrine." *Survival*, February 1965. International Institute for Strategic Studies.

Laber, Jeri, and Barnett Rubin. *A Nation is Dying: Afghanistan Under the Soviets.* Chicago: Northwestern University Press, 1988.

Lacouture, Jean. *Vietnam: Between Two Truces*, tr. K. Kellen and J. Carmichael. London: Secker and Warburg, 1966.

———. *Ho Chi Minh*, tr. Peter Wiles. London: Allen Lane/The Penguin Press, 1968.

Lacroix, Paul. *Military and Religious Life in the Middle Ages and the Renaissance.* London: Bickers and Son, c. 1874.

Lafeber, Walter. *Inevitable Revolution: The United States in Central America.* New York: W.W. Norton, 1983.

Laffan, R.G.D. *Select Documents of European History*, Vol. 1 of 2 vols. London: Methuen, 1930.

Lancaster, Donald. *The Emancipation of French Indochina.* London: Oxford University Press, 1961.

Lansdale, Edward G. "Viet Nam: Do We Understand Revolution?" *Foreign Affairs*, October 1964.

———. "Viet Nam: Still the Search for Goals." *Foreign Affairs*, October 1968.

Lapp, Ralph E. *Arms Beyond Doubt: The Tyranny of Weapons Technology.* Chicago: Cowles Book Company, 1970.

Laqueur, Walter. *The Guerrilla Reader: A Historical Anthology.* New York: The New American Library, 1977.

———. *Terrorism.* Boston: Little, Brown, 1977.

Lartéguy, Jean. *The Centurions*, tr. Xan Fielding. London: Hutchinson, 1961.

Lavan, George. See Guevara, Ernesto Che.

Lawrence, T.E. "Guerrilla Warfare." *Encyclopaedia Britannica*, Vol. 10. 1957.

———. *Revolt in the Desert.* London: Jonathan Cape, 1927.

———. *Seven Pillars of Wisdom.* London: Jonathan Cape, 1973.

Leakey, L.S.B. "Colonial Administration from the Native Point of View." *Comparative Methods of Colonial Administration.* London: Chatham House, 1930.

———. *Defeating Mau Mau.* London: Methuen, 1954.

———. *Kenya: Contrasts and Problems.* London: Methuen, 1936.

———. *Mau Mau and the Kikuyu.* London: Methuen, 1952.

———. *White Africa.* London: Hodder and Stoughton, 1937.

Lederer, William. *Our Own Worst Enemy.* New York: W.W. Norton, 1968.

———. *The Ugly American.* New York: W.W. Norton, 1958.

Lees, Michael. *The Rape of Serbia: The British Role in Tito's Grab for Power 1943-1944.* New York: Harcourt Brace Jovanovich, 1991.

Leftwich, William G. "Decision at Duc Co." *Marine Corps Gazette*, February 1967.

Le Moyne, James. "El Salvador's Forgotten War." *Foreign Affairs*, Summer 1989.

Lenin, V.I. *Selected Works*, Vol. 3 of 3 vols. Moscow: Foreign Languages Publishing House, c. 1961.

Leonard, R.A. *A Short Guide to Clausewitz on War.* London: Weidenfeld and Nicolson, 1967.

Leopold, Richard. *The Growth of American Foreign Policy.* New York: Alfred A. Knopf, 1965.

Lettow-Vorbeck, General von. *My Reminiscences of East Africa.* London: Hurst and Blackett, 1920.

Lewis, John W. See Kahin, George M.

Lewy, Guenter. *America in Vietnam.* New York: Oxford University Press, 1978.

Li, D.J. *The Ageless Chinese.* New York: Charles Scribner's Sons, 1965.

Library of Congress, Congressional Research Service. "Instances of Use of United States Armed Forces Abroad, 1798-1989," ed. Ellen C. Collier. Washington, D.C.: Congressional Research Service, 1989.

———. *U.S. Low-Intensity Conflicts 1899-1990.* Washington D.C.: U.S. Government Printing Office, 1990.

Liddell Hart, B.H. *The Decisive Wars of History: A Study in Strategy.* London: G. Bell and Sons, 1929.

———. *T.E. Lawrence.* London: Jonathan Cape, 1934.

———, ed. *The Soviet Army.* London: Weidenfeld and Nicolson, 1956.

Lift, J. See Kohl, J.

Lilienthal, David E. "Postwar Development in Viet Nam." *Foreign Affairs,* January 1969.

Lippmann, Walter. *The Cold War: A Study in U.S. Foreign Policy, 1947.* New York: Harper and Brothers, 1947.

Lloyd, E.M. *A Review of the History of Infantry.* London: Longmans, Green, 1908.

———. "The Third Coalition." *The Cambridge Modern History,* Vol. 9 of 13 vols. London: Cambridge University Press, 1904.

Lohbeck, Don. *Patrick J. Hurley.* Chicago: Henry Regnery, 1956.

Longford, Elizabeth. *Wellington: The Years of the Sword.* London: Weidenfeld and Nicolson, 1969.

Lorch, Netanel. *The Edge of the Sword: Israel's War of Independence, 1947–1949.* New York: G.P. Putnam's Sons, 1961.

Lowenthal, Richard. "Russia and China: Controlled Conflict." *Foreign Affairs,* April 1971.

Luce, Siméon. *Histoire de Bertrand du Guesclin et de Son Époque.* Paris: Librairie Hachette, 1867.

Lyautey, H. "Du Rôle Social de l'Officier" and "Du Rôle Colonial de l'Armée." *Revue des Deux Mondes* (1891 and 1900).

———. *Lettres du Sud de Madagascar (1900–1902).* Paris: Librairie Armand Colin, 1935.

———. *Lettres du Tonkin,* 2 vols. Paris: Éditions Nationales, 1928.

———. *Lettres du Tonkin et de Madagascar (1894–1899).* Paris: Librairie Armand Colin, 1933.

Lyautey, Pierre. *Lyautey L'Africain: Textes et Lettres du Maréchal Lyautey Présentés par Pierre Lyautey,* 4 vols. Paris: Librairie Plon, 1953.

MacDonald, J.R.M. "The Terror." *The Cambridge Modern History,* Vol. 8 of 13 vols. London: Cambridge University Press, 1904.

Mack, R.E. "Ambuscade." *Marine Corps Gazette,* April 1967.

———. "Minbotrap." *Marine Corps Gazette,* July 1967.

Mackenzie, A.M. *Robert Bruce King of Scots.* London: Oliver and Boyd, 1934.

Mackesy, Piers. *The War for America 1775–1783.* London: Longmans, Green, 1964.

Maclean, Fitzroy. *Disputed Barricade.* London: Jonathan Cape, 1957.

———. *Eastern Approaches.* London: Jonathan Cape, 1949.

Maclear, Michael. *The Ten Thousand Day War. Vietnam: 1945–1975.* New York: St. Martin's Press, 1981.

MacMunn, G., and C. Falls. *Military Operations: Egypt and Palestine,* Vols. 1 and 2. London: Her Majesty's Stationery Office, 1928, 1930.

Madariaga, Salvador de. *The Fall of the Spanish American Empire.* London: Hollis and Carter, 1947.

Mahan, A.T. *The Influence of Sea Power upon the French Revolution and Empire 1783–1812,* 2 vols. London: Sampson, Low, Marston, 1892.

———. *The Influence of Sea Power upon History 1660–1783.* London: Sampson, Low, Marston, 1900.

———. *Sea Power in Its Relations to the War of 1812.*

Mahon, Lord. *The Life of Belisarius.* London: John Murray, 1829.

Mailer, Norman. *Armies of the Night: History as a Novel. The Novel as History.* New York: New American Library, 1968.

Makinda, Samuel, "Shifting Alliances in the Horn of Africa." *Survival,* January/February 1985. International Institute for Strategic Studies.

Malaya, Department of Information. *Communist Banditry in Malaya.* Kuala Lumpur: Department of Information, n.d.

Malhuret, Claude. "Report from Afghanistan." *Foreign Affairs*, Winter 1983–1984.

Mallie, Eamonn. See Bishop, Patrick.

Mao Tse-tung. *On Guerrilla Warfare*, tr. and with an Introduction by Samuel B. Griffith. New York: Frederick A. Praeger, 1962.

———. *Selected Works*, Vol. 1. Peking: Foreign Languages Press, 1964.

———. *Basic Tactics*, tr. and with an Introduction by Stuart R. Schram. New York: Frederick A. Praeger, 1966.

Marcum, John A. "Angola." *Survival*, January/February 1988. International Institute for Strategic Studies.

Marighela, Carlos. *For the Liberation of Brazil*. London: Penguin, 1971.

———. *The Minimanual of Urban Guerrilla Warfare*. San Francisco: People's Press, 1970.

Markham, Felix. *Napoleon*. London: Weidenfeld and Nicolson, 1963.

Marlowe, John. *The Seat of Pilate: An Account of the Palestine Mandate*. London: Cresset Press, 1959.

Marshal, Bruce. *The White Rabbit*. London: Evans Brothers, 1964.

Marshal, S.L.A. *Battles in the Monsoon*. New York: William Morrow, 1967.

Martin, David. *The Web of Disinformation: Churchill's Yugoslav Blunder*. New York: Harcourt Brace, 1990.

Masaryk, G.T. *The Spirit of Russia*, Vol. 1 of 2 vols. London: Allen and Unwin, 1919.

Mathew, Gervase. See Oliver, Roland.

Matthews, Herbert L. *Castro: A Political Biography*. New York: Simon and Schuster, 1969.

———. *Revolution in Cuba*. New York: Charles Scribner's Sons, 1975.

———. *The Cuban Story*. New York: George Braziller, 1961.

Matthews, Tanya. *Algerian ABC*. London: Geoffrey Chapman, 1961.

Mavrogordato, R., and E. Ziemke. "The Polotsk Lowland." In Armstrong, op. cit.

May, E.S. *A Retrospect on the South African War*. London: Sampson, Low, Marston, 1901.

Mazour, A.G. *Russia: Tsarist and Communist*. New York: D. Van Nostrand, 1962.

McBeth, John. "Electronic Warfare." *Far Eastern Economic Review*, May 23, 1991.

McCarthy, Eugene. *The Limits of Power*. New York: Dell, 1967.

McCuen, John J. *The Art of Counter-Revolutionary War*. London: Faber and Faber, 1966.

McLaren, Moray. *Corsica Boswell*. London: Secker and Warburg, 1966.

McCutcheon, Keith B. "Air Support for III MAF." *Marine Corps Gazette*, August 1967.

McGaffin, William, and Erwin Knoll. *Scandal in the Pentagon: A Challenge to Democracy*. Greenwich, Conn.: Fawcett, 1969.

Mecklin, John. *Mission in Torment*. Garden City, N.Y.: Doubleday, 1965.

Meinertzhagen, R. *Kenya During 1902–1906*. London: Oliver and Boyd, 1957.

Menenger, Charles. *Northern Ireland: The Troubles*. London: Hamlyn, 1985.

Mijatovich, Chedo. *Servia of the Servians*. London: Putnam and Sons, 1911.

Miksche, F.O. *Secret Forces: The Technique of Underground Movements*. London: Faber and Faber, 1950.

Millar, George. *Horned Pigeon*. London: William Heinemann, 1946.

———. *Maquis*. London: William Heinemann, 1945.

Miller, John G. "From a Company Commander's Notebook." *Marine Corps Gazette*, August 1966.

Miller, Judith. "Terrorism around the Mediterranean." *Adelphi Paper No. 230*, Spring 1988. International Institute for Strategic Studies.

Mills, C. Wright. *Castro's Cuba*. London: Secker and Warburg, 1960.

Mitchell, Philip. *African Afterthoughts*. London: Hutchinson, 1954.

Moll, W. See DeWitt, K.

Mollenhoff, Clark R. *The Man Who Pardoned Nixon.* London: St. James Press, 1976.

———. *Game Plan for Disaster: An Ombudsman's Report on the Nixon Years.* New York: W.W. Norton, 1976.

Mommsen, Theodor. *The History of Rome,* Vols. 2 and 3, tr. W.P. Dickson. London: Macmillan and Co., 1906.

Montross, Lynn. *U.S. Marine Operations in Korea 1950–53,* Vol. 3 of 3 vols. Washington, D.C.: U.S. Government Printing Office, 1957.

Moorehead, Alan. *The Russian Revolution.* New York: Harper and Brothers, 1958.

Morison, S.E. *Leyte: June 1944–January 1945,* Vol. 12 of 15 vols. London: Oxford University Press, 1958.

———. *The Oxford History of the United States 1783–1917.*

———, and H.S. Commager. *The Growth of the American Republic,* Vol. 2 of 2 vols. New York: Oxford University Press, 1962.

———, and M. Obregón. *The Caribbean as Columbus Saw It.* Boston: Little, Brown, 1964.

Morris, J.E. *The Welsh Wars of Edward I.* London: Oxford University Press, 1901.

Morris, Roger. *Uncertain Greatness. Henry Kissinger and American Foreign Policy.* New York: Harper and Row, 1977.

Morrock, Richard, "Revolution and Intervention in Vietnam." In Horowitz, op. cit.

Mosley, Leonard. *Duel for Kilimanjaro.* London: Weidenfeld and Nicolson, 1963.

Moss, Ambler H., Jr. "Peace in Central America." *Survival,* September/October, 1990. International Institute for Strategic Studies.

Mountbatten, Vice-Admiral the Earl. *Report to the Combined Chiefs of Staff by the Supreme Allied Commander South-East Asia, 1943–1945.* London: Her Majesty's Stationery Office, 1951.

Moxon-Browne, Edward. "Spain and the ETA. The Bid for Basque Autonomy." *Conflict Studies No. 201,* 1987. Institute for the Study of Conflict.

Moyers, Bill D. "One Thing We Learned." *Foreign Affairs,* July 1968.

Mulligan, Hugh A. *No Place to Die.* New York: William Morrow, 1967.

Munro, D.C. See Strayer, J.R.

Munslow, B. *Mozambique: The Revolution and Its Origins.* London and New York: Longmans, 1983.

Murphy, John F. *State Support of International Terrorism.* London: Mansell, 1989.

Murray, M. *Hunted: A Coastwatcher's Story.* London: Angus and Robertson, 1967.

Murray, Raymond. *Special Air Service in Ireland, 1969–89.* London: Mercier Press, 1990.

Murtha, John P. "Combat Intelligence in Vietnam." *Marine Corps Gazette,* January 1968.

Myers, E.C.W. *Greek Entanglement.* London: Rupert Hart-Davis, 1955.

Myrdal, Gunnar. *Asian Drama: An Inquiry into the Poverty of Nations,* 3 vols. London: Allen Lane/The Penguin Press, 1968.

Nasution, Abdul Haris. *Fundamentals of Guerrilla Warfare.* New York: Frederick A. Praeger, 1965.

Navarre, Henri. *Agonie de l'Indochine.* Paris: Librairie Plon, 1956.

Neave, Airey. *Saturday at MI-9.* London: Hodder and Stoughton, 1969.

Neustadt, Richard E., and Ernest R. May. *Thinking in Time: The Uses of History for Decision-Makers.* New York: The Free Press, 1986.

Newman, Robert P. *Owen Lattimore and the "Loss" of China.* Berkeley, Calif.: University of California Press, 1992.

Nixon, Richard M. "Asia After Viet Nam," *Foreign Affairs,* October 1967.

———. *Public Papers of the President.* Washington, D.C.: U.S. Government Printing Office, 6 vols., 1971–75.

———. *The Memoirs of Richard Nixon.* London: Sidgwick and Jackson, 1978.

Njama, K. See Barnett, Donald L.

1230

Nolff, M. See Seers, D.

Norman, M.W. See Jumper, Roy.

Nuechterlein, Donald E. *Thailand and the Struggle for Southeast Asia.* Ithaca, N.Y.: Cornell University Press, 1965.

Nutting, Anthony. *Lawrence of Arabia.* London: Hollis and Carter, 1961.

O'Ballance, Edgar. *The Soviet War in the Sudan: 1955–1972.* London: Faber and Faber, 1977.

———. *The Kurdish Revolt 1961–1970.* London: Faber and Faber, 1973.

———. *The Algerian Insurrection 1954–1962.* London: Faber and Faber, 1967.

———. *The Greek Civil War, 1944–1949.* London: Faber and Faber, 1966.

———. *The Red Army.* London: Faber and Faber, 1964.

Oberdorfer, Don. *Tet!* New York: Doubleday, 1971.

Obregón, M. See Morison, S.E.

O'Donnell, Kenneth. "LBJ and the Kennedys." *Life,* August 7, 1970.

Ogburn, Charlton. *The Marauders.* New York: Harper and Brothers, 1959.

O'Hea, Patrick. *Reminiscences of the Mexican Revolution.* Mexico City: Editorial Fournier, 1966.

Olcott, C.S. *William McKinley,* Vol. 2 of 2 vols. New York: Houghton Mifflin, 1916.

Oldenbourg, Zoé. *Catherine the Great.* London: William Heinemann, 1965.

Oliver, Roland, and Gervase Mathew, eds. *History of East Africa,* Vol. 1 of 3 vols. London: Oxford University Press, 1963.

Oman, C.W.C. *A History of the Art of War in the Middle Ages,* Vol. 1 of 2 vols. London: Methuen, 1924.

———. *A History of the Peninsular War,* 7 vols. London: Oxford University Press, 1902.

O'Neill, Robert J. *Vietnam Task.* Melbourne: Cassell Australia, 1968.

Otway-Ruthven, A.J. *A History of Medieval Ireland.* London: Ernest Benn, 1968.

Paget, Julian. *Counter-Insurgency Campaigning.* London: Faber and Faber, 1967.

Palmer, Dave R. *Summons of the Trumpet: A History of the Vietnam War from a Military Man's Standpoint.* New York: Ballantine Books, 1978.

Palmer, Dave Scott, ed. *Shining Path of Peace.* London: Hurst and Co., 1992.

Palmier, Leslie. *Indonesia and the Dutch.* London: Oxford University Press, 1962.

Pares, Bernard. *A History of Russia.* New York: Alfred A. Knopf, 1933.

Paret, Peter. *Yorck and the Era of Prussian Reform.* Princeton, N.J.: Princeton University Press, 1966.

———. *French Revolutionary Warfare from Indochina to Algeria: The Analysis of a Political and Military Doctrine.* London: Pall Mall Press, 1964.

———, and John Shy. *Guerrillas in the 1960s.* London: Pall Mall Press, 1962.

Parker, H.M.D. *The Roman Legions.* Cambridge, U.K.: W. Heffer and Sons, 1958.

Parry, Albert. "Soviet Aid to Vietnam." *The Reporter,* January 12, 1967.

Paul, Elliott. *Life and Death of a Spanish Town.* London: Peter Davies, 1939.

Paul, Roland A. "Laos: Anatomy of an American Involvement." *Foreign Affairs,* April 1971.

Payne, Robert. *The Civil War in Spain.* London: Secker and Warburg, 1962.

———. *Lawrence of Arabia: A Triumph.* New York: Pyramid Books, 1963.

———. *Mao Tse-tung.* London: Abelard-Shuman, 1967.

Pearson, C.H. *History of England During the Early and Middle Ages.* London: Bell and Daldy, 1867.

Perlez, Jane. "A New Chance for a Fractured Land." *New York Times Magazine,* September 22, 1991.

Perroy, E. *The Hundred Years War,* tr. W.B. Wells. London: Eyre and Spottiswoode, 1951.

Petrie, C. See Bertrand, L.

Pflaum, Irving. *Tragic Island: How Communism Came to Cuba.* Englewood Cliffs, N.J.: Prentice-Hall, 1961.

Phillips, Ruby Hart. *Cuba: Island of Paradise*. New York: McDowell, Obolensky, 1959.

Pike, Douglas. *Viet Cong: The Organization and Techniques of the National Liberation Front of South Vietnam*. Cambridge, Mass.: MIT Press, 1967.

Pimlot, John, ed. *Guerrilla Warfare*. New York. The Military Press, 1985.

Piquet-Wicks, Eric. *Four in the Shadows*. London: Jarrolds, 1957.

Pisor, Robert. *The End of the Line: The Siege of Khe Sanh*. New York: W.W. Norton, 1982.

Platonov, S.F. *History of Russia*, tr. E. Aronsberg. London: Macmillan, 1925.

Plutarch. *Lives*, Vol. 3 of 5 vols., tr. A.H. Clough. London: Macmillan, 1902.

Pokrovsky, M.N. *Brief History of Russia*, 2 vols., tr. D.S. Mirsky. London: Martin Lawrence, 1933.

Polo, Marco. *The Travels of Marco Polo*, tr. Ronald Latham. Harmondsworth, Middlesex, U.K.: Penguin Books, 1958.

Polybius. *The Histories*, Vol. 2 of 6 vols., tr. W.R. Paton. London: William Heinemann, 1922.

Ponteil, Félix. *L'Eveil des Nationalités et le Mouvement Libéral*. Paris: Presses Universitaires de France, 1968.

Poole, A.L., ed. *Medieval England*, Vol. 1 of 2 vols. London: Oxford University Press, 1958.

Pratt, Fletcher. *Ordeal by Fire*. London: Bodley Head, 1950.

Prescott, William H. *The History of the Conquest of Mexico*. Chicago: University of Chicago Press, 1966.

Preston, R.A. *Men in Arms*. London: Thames and Hudson, 1962.

Priestley, E.C. See Cole, D.H.

Proxmire, William. *Report from the Wasteland: America's Military-Industrial Complex*. New York: Frederick A. Praeger, 1970.

Purcell, Susan K. "The Choice in Central America." *Foreign Affairs*, Fall 1987.

Pushkin, A.S. *The Captain's Daughter*. Moscow: Progress Publishers, 1954.

Pye, Lucien W. *Guerrilla Communism and Malaya: Its Social and Political Meaning*. Princeton, N.J.: Princeton University Press, 1956.

Radu, Michael, and Vladimir Tismaneanu. *Latin American Revolutionaries*. London: Pergamon-Brassey's, 1990.

Rankin, Hugh F. "Charles Lord Cornwallis: Study in Frustration." In Billias, op. cit.

Rapoport, Anatol, ed. *Clausewitz on War*. London: Penguin Books, 1968.

Raskin, Marcus G., and Bernard B. Fall. *The Viet-Nam Reader: Articles and Documents on American Foreign Policy and the Viet-Nam Crisis*. New York: Random House, 1967.

Ray, J.K. *Transfer of Power in Indonesia 1942–1949*. Bombay: P.C. Manaktala and Sons, 1967.

Reagan, Ronald. *An American Life*. New York: Simon and Schuster, 1990.

Reeves, Richard. *A Ford, Not a Lincoln: The Decline of American Political Leadership*. London: Hutchinson, 1976.

Reichley, James A. *Conversations in an Age of Change*. Washington, D.C.: The Brookings Institution, 1981.

Reischauer, Edwin O. *Beyond Vietnam*. New York: Alfred A. Knopf, 1967.

Rice, Edward E. *Wars of the Third Kind: Conflict in Undeveloped Countries*. Berkeley, Calif.: University of California Press, 1988.

Richburg, Keith. "Back to Vietnam." *Foreign Affairs*, Fall 1991.

Ridgway, Matthew B. "Indochina: Disengaging." *Foreign Affairs*, July 1971.

———. *Soldier: The Memoirs of Matthew B. Ridgway*. New York: Harper and Brothers, 1956.

———. *The Korean War*. Garden City, N.Y.: Doubleday, 1967.

Riding, Alan. "The Central American Quagmire." *Foreign Affairs, America and the World*, 1982.

Riencourt, Amaury de. "India and Pakistan in the Shadow of Afghanistan." *Foreign Affairs*, Winter 1982–1983.

Rings, Werner. *Life with the Enemy: Collaboration and Resistance in Hitler's Europe 1939–1945*, tr. J. Maxwell Brownjohn. London: Weidenfeld and Nicolson, 1979.

Roberts, Adam, ed. *The Strategy of Civilian Defense*. London: Faber and Faber, 1967.

———. "Lessons of Geneva 1954." *The Times* (London), April 23, 1968.

Roberts, Chalmers M. "The Day We Didn't Go to War." *The Reporter*, September 14, 1954.

Robinson, Linda. "The End of El Salvador's War." *Survival*, September/October 1991. International Institute for Strategic Studies.

Robinson, R.E.R. "Reflections of a Company Commander in Malaya." *Army Quarterly*, October 1950.

Roeder, Franz. *The Ordeal of Captain Roeder*, tr. and ed. Helen Roeder. London: Methuen, 1960.

Rolo, Charles J. *Wingate's Raiders*. London: G.C. Harrap, 1944.

Romanus, C.F., and R. Sunderland. *The China-Burma-India Theater: Stilwell's Problems*. Washington, D.C.: U.S. Government Printing Office, 1956.

Rose, J.H. "The Second Coalition." *The Cambridge Modern History*, Vol. 8 of 13 vols. London: Cambridge University Press, 1904.

Ross, Stanley K. *Francisco I. Madero: Apostle of Mexican Democracy*. New York: Columbia University Press, 1955.

Rostow, W.W. *The United States in the World Arena*. New York: Harper and Brothers, 1960.

Rovere, Richard H. *The Eisenhower Years*. New York: Farrar, Straus and Cudahy, 1956.

Roy, Jules. *The Battle of Dien Bien Phu*. New York: Carrol and Graf, 1984.

Royal United Services Institution Seminar. *Lessons from the Vietnam War*. London: RUSI, 1969.

Ruark, Robert. *Something of Value*. London: Hamish Hamilton, 1955.

Rubin, Barnett R. "The Fragmentation of Afghanistan." *Foreign Affairs*, Winter, 1989–1990.

——— see Laber, Jeri.

Salinger, Pierre. *With Kennedy*. Garden City, N.Y.: Doubleday, 1966.

Salisbury, Harrison E. *Behind the Lines: Hanoi*. New York: Harper and Row, 1967.

Sansom, Robert L. *The Economics of Insurgency in the Mekong Delta of Vietnam*. Cambridge, Mass.: MIT Press, 1970.

Schalk, David. *War and the Ivory Tower*. New York: Oxford University Press, 1991.

Schandler, Herbert Y. *The Unmaking of a President: Lyndon Johnson and Vietnam*. Princeton, N.J.: Princeton University Press, 1977.

Schell, Jonathan. *The Military Half*. New York: Alfred A. Knopf, 1968.

———. *The Time of Illusion*. New York: Alfred A. Knopf, 1975.

Schell, Orville. See Schurmann, Franz.

Schevill, F. *History of the Balkan Peninsula*. New York: Harcourt Brace, 1922.

Schiff, Ze'ev, and E. Ya'ari. *Israel's Lebanon War*, ed. and tr. Ina Friedman. London: George Allen and Unwin, 1985.

Schlesinger, A.M. *Political and Social History of the United States*. New York: Macmillan, 1926.

Schlesinger, Arthur M., Jr. *The Bitter Heritage: Vietnam and American Democracy 1941–1966*. Boston: Houghton Mifflin, 1967.

———. *A Thousand Days*. Boston: Houghton Mifflin, 1965.

Schoenbrun, David. "Journey to North Vietnam." *The Saturday Evening Post*, March 1968.

Schram, Stuart R. *Mao Tse-tung.* New York: Simon and Schuster, 1967.

Schulten, A. "The Romans in Spain." *The Cambridge Ancient History,* Chapter 10 of Vol. 8. London and Cambridge, U.K.: The University Press, 1930.

Schultheis, Rob. "In Afghanistan, Peace Must Wait." *New York Times Magazine,* December 29, 1991.

Schurmann, F.L. *Russia Since 1917.* New York: Alfred A. Knopf, 1957.

Schurmann, Franz, and Orville Schell, eds. *China Readings 1 (Imperial China: The Eighteenth and Nineteenth Centuries).* New York: Penguin Books, 1967.

———. *China Readings 2 (Republican China: Nationalism, War, and the Rise of Communism, 1911–49).* New York: Penguin Books, 1968.

Scigliano, Robert. *South Vietnam: Nation Under Stress.* Boston: Houghton Mifflin, 1964.

———, and Guy Fox. *Technical Assistance in Vietnam: The Michigan State University Experience.* New York: Frederick A. Praeger, 1965.

Scobie, W.I. See Foley, Charles.

Scullard, H.H. *Scipio Africanus, Soldier and Politician.* London: Thames and Hudson, 1970.

Seers, D. et al. *Cuba: The Economic and Social Revolution.* Chapel Hill, N.C.: University of North Carolina Press, 1964.

Ségur, Philippe-Paul de. *Napoleon's Russian Campaign,* tr. J.D. Townsend. London: Michael Joseph, 1958.

Servan-Schreiber, Jean-Jacques. *Lieutenant in Algeria,* tr. Ronald Matthews. London: Hutchinson, 1958.

Seton-Watson, Hugh. *The Decline of Imperial Russia, 1815–1914.* London: Methuen, 1952.

———. *The East European Revolution.* London: Methuen, 1956.

Shaplen, Robert M. "Letter from Vietnam." *The New Yorker,* May 13, 1972.

———. *The Lost Revolution.* New York: Harper and Row, 1966.

———. *The Road from War.* New York: Harper and Row, 1970.

———. "Viet-Nam: Crisis of Indecision." *Foreign Affairs,* October 1967.

———. "We Have Always Survived." *The New Yorker,* April 15, 1972.

Sharp, U.S. Grant. "We Could Have Won in Vietnam Long Ago." *Reader's Digest,* May 1969.

Shawcross, William. *Sideshow: Kissinger, Nixon and the Destruction of Cambodia.* London: Andre Deutsch, 1979.

Sheean, Vincent. *Personal History.* New York: Doubleday, Doran, 1936.

Sheehan, Neil. *A Bright Shining Lie: John Paul Vann and America in Vietnam.* New York: Random House, 1988.

———. "Annals of War, An American Soldier in Vietnam." *The New Yorker,* June 27, 1988.

——— et al. *The Pentagon Papers.* New York: Bantam Books, 1971.

Sherwood, Robert E. *Roosevelt and Hopkins.* New York: Harper and Brothers, 1948.

Shoup, David M., and James A. Donovan. "The New American Militarism." *The Atlantic,* April 1969.

Shoup, Lawrence H. *The Carter Presidency and Beyond: Power and Politics in the 1980s.* Palo Alto, Calif.: Ramparts Press, 1977.

Shultz, Richard H., Jr. "Low Intensity Conflict: Future Challenges and Lessons from the Reagan Years." *Survival,* July/August 1989. International Institute for Strategic Studies.

Sidey, Hugh. *John F. Kennedy, President.* New York: Atheneum, 1963.

Sihanouk, Norodom, as related to Wilfred Burchett. *My War with the CIA: Cambodia's Fight for Survival.* London: Penguin Books, 1973.

Skeen, Sir Andrew. *Passing It On: Short Talks on Tribal Fighting on the North-West Frontier of India.* London: Gale and Polden, 1932.

Skidmore, Thomas E., and Peter H. Smith. *Modern Latin America.* New York: Oxford University Press, 1984.

Skobeleff, General. *Siege and Assault of Denghil-Tépé*, tr. J.J. Leverson. London: Her Majesty's Stationery Office, 1881.

Skodvin, Magne. "Norwegian Non-Violent Resistance During the German Occupation." In Adam Roberts, op. cit.

Slane, P.M. "Tactical Problems in Kenya." *Army Quarterly*, 1954.

Slessor, Sir John. *The Central Blue*. London: Cassell, 1956.

Slim, William R. *Defeat into Victory*. London: Cassell, 1956.

Slimming, John. *Malaysia: Death of a Democracy*. London: John Murray, 1969.

Smith, Earl E.T. *The Fourth Floor: An Account of the Castro Communist Revolution*. New York: Random House, 1962.

Smith, Hedrick. See Sheehan, Neil.

Smith, R.B. *An International History of the Vietnam War*, 2 vols. London: Macmillan, 1987.

Smith, R. Harris. *OSS: The Secret History of America's First Central Intelligence Agency*. London: University of California Press, 1972.

Smyth, John. *Percival and the Tragedy of Singapore*. London: MacDonald, 1971.

Snepp, Frank. *Decent Interval: An Insider's Account of Saigon's Indecent End Told by the CIA's Chief Strategy Analyst in Vietnam*. New York: Random House, 1977.

Snow, Edgar. *The Other Side of the River: Red China Today*. New York: Random House, 1961.

———. *Random Notes on China 1936–1945*. Cambridge, Mass.: Harvard University Press, 1957.

———. *Red Star over China*. New York: Random House, 1938.

Soedjatmoko. "South-East Asia and Security." *Survival*, October 1969. International Institute for Strategic Studies.

Solarz, Stephen J. "Cambodia and the International Community." *Foreign Affairs*, Spring 1990.

Sorensen, Theodore C. *Kennedy*. New York: Harper and Row, 1965.

Special Operations Research Office (American University). *Casebook on Insurgency and Revolutionary Warfare*. Washington, D.C.: American University, 1962.

Spencer-Chapman, F. *The Jungle Is Neutral*. London: Chatto and Windus, 1949.

Standing, Percy Cross. *Guerrilla Leaders of the World: From Charette to Delvet*. London: Stanley Paul, 1912.

Stanford, R.K. "Bamboo Brigades." *Marine Corps Gazette*, March 1966.

Stenton, F.M. *Anglo-Saxon England*. London: Oxford University Press, 1943.

Stephens, Robert. *Cyprus: A Place of Arms*. London: Pall Mall Press, 1966.

Stilwell, Joseph W. *The Stilwell Papers*, ed. T.H. White. New York: William Sloane, 1948.

Stolfi, Russel H. *U.S. Marine Corps Civic Action Efforts in Vietnam—March 1965–March 1966*. Washington, D.C.: U.S. Marine Corps, 1968.

Stone, I.F. "Why Nixon Won His Moscow Gamble." *The New York Review of Books*, June 15, 1972.

Strauss, Lewis. *Men and Decisions*. New York: Doubleday, 1962.

Strayer, J.R., and D.C. Munro. *Middle Ages, 395–1500*. New York: Appleton-Century, 1942.

Strong, Simon. *Shining Path: The World's Most Deadly Revolutionary Force*. London: HarperCollins, 1992.

Stschepkin, E. "Russia Under Alexander I, and the Invasion of 1812." In *The Cambridge Modern History*, Vol. 9 of 13 vols. London: Cambridge University Press, 1904.

Sukhanov, N.N. *The Russian Revolution, 1917*, ed. and trans. Joel Carmichael. London: Oxford University Press, 1955.

Sulzberger, C.L. *The Test: De Gaulle and Algeria*. London: Rupert Hart-Davis, 1962.

Summers, Harry G., Jr. *On Strategy: A Critical Analysis of the Vietnam War*. Novato, Calif.: Presidio Press, 1982.

Sunderland, R. See Romanus, C.F.

Sutherland, C.H.V. *The Romans in Spain*. London: Methuen, 1939.

Sweet-Escott, Bickham. *Baker Street Irregular*. London: Methuen, 1965.

Sykes, Christopher. *Orde Wingate*. London: Collins, 1959.

———. *Cross Roads to Israel*. Bloomington, Ind.: Indiana University Press, 1975.

Szulc, Tad. *The Illusion of Peace: Foreign Policy in the Nixon Years*. New York: Viking Press, 1978.

Taber, Robert. *M-26: Biography of a Revolution*. New York: Lyle Stuart, 1961.

———. *The War of the Flea*. London: Paladin, 1970.

Talbott, John. *The War Without a Name. France in Algeria, 1954–1962*. London: Faber and Faber, 1981.

Tanham, George K. *Communist Revolutionary Warfare: From the Vietminh to the Viet Cong*, rev. ed. New York: Frederick A. Praeger, 1967.

———. *Trial in Thailand*. New York: Crane, Russak, 1974.

———. *War Without Guns*. New York: Frederick A. Praeger, 1966.

———, and Dennis J. Duncanson. "Some Dilemmas of Counterinsurgency." *Foreign Affairs*, October 1969.

Tannenbaum, Frank. "The United States and Latin America," *Political Science Quarterly*, June 1961.

Tarlé, Eugène. *Napoleon's Invasion of Russia, 1812*, tr. G.M. London: Allen and Unwin, 1942.

Tarleton, Banastre. *A History of the Campaigns of 1780 and 1781, in the Southern Provinces of North America*. London: T. Cadell, 1787.

Tarn, W.W. *Alexander the Great and the Unity of Mankind*, Vol. 1 of 2 vols. London: Oxford University Press, 1933.

Taruc, Luis. *He Who Rides the Tiger*. New York: Frederick A. Praeger, 1967.

Taylor, Alistair M. *Indonesian Independence and the United Nations*. London: Stevens and Sons, 1960.

Taylor, L.A. *The Tragedy of an Army: La Vendée in 1793*. London: Hutchinson, 1913.

Taylor, Maxwell. *Responsibility and Response*. New York: Harper and Row, 1967.

———. *The Uncertain Trumpet*. New York: Harper and Brothers, 1960.

Taylor, Telford. *Nuremberg and Vietnam: An American Tragedy*. New York: Quadrangle Books, 1970.

Tee, W.S. "Solutions in Counter-Insurgency Operations." *Army Quarterly*, October 1967.

Temperley, H.W.V. *History of Servia*. London: G. Bell and Sons, 1917.

Thayer, Charles W. *Guerrilla*. New York: Harper and Row, 1965.

Thayer, George. *The War Business*. London: Weidenfeld and Nicolson, 1969.

Thomas, Hugh. *Cuba or The Pursuit of Freedom*. New York: Harper and Row, 1971.

———. *The Spanish Civil War*. New York: Harper and Brothers, 1961.

Thompson, Robert. *Defeating Communist Insurgency: The Lessons of Malaya and Vietnam*. New York: Frederick A. Praeger, 1966.

———. "Feet on the Ground." *Statist*, February 4, 1966.

———. "My Plan for Peace in Vietnam." *Reader's Digest*, March 1970.

———. *No Exit from Vietnam*. London: Chatto and Windus, 1969.

———. "On the Way to Victory." *The Sunday Times* (London), December 21, 1969.

———. *Revolutionary War in World Strategy 1945–1969*. London: Secker and Warburg, 1970.

Thompson, Virginia. *French Indo-China*. London: Allen and Unwin, 1937.

Thompson, W. Scott, and Donaldson D. Frizzell, eds. *The Lessons of Vietnam*. London: Macdonald and Jane's, 1977.

Thucydides. *History of the Peloponnesian War*, Vol. 2 of 4 vols., tr. Charles F. Smith. Cambridge, Mass.: Harvard University Press, 1953.

Tillion, Germaine. *Algeria: The Realities*. London: Eyre and Spottiswoode, 1958.

Tinker, Hugh. *South Asia: A Short History*. London: Macmillan, 1989.

Tismaneanu, Vladimir. See Radu, Michael.

Tolstoy, Leo. *War and Peace*, tr. Constance Garrett. London: William Heinemann, 1971.

Toy, Sidney. *A History of Fortifications*. London: William Heinemann, 1955.

Trager, Frank. *Why Viet Nam?* New York: Frederick A. Praeger, 1966.

Tran Van Dinh. "Elections in Vietnam." *The New Republic*, July 2, 1966.

Trevelyan, George. *George the Third and Charles Fox*, 2 vols. London: Longmans, Green, 1914.

Treverton, Gregory F. "U.S. strategy in Central America." *Survival*, March/April 1986. International Institute for Strategic Studies.

Trinquier, Roger. *Modern Warfare: A French View of Counter-Insurgency*. New York: Frederick A. Praeger, 1964.

Truman, Harry S. *Year of Decision 1945*. London: Hodder and Stoughton, 1955.

———. *Years of Trial and Hope*. Garden City, N.Y.: Doubleday, 1956.

Tse-tung. See Mao Tse-tung.

Tsiang Ting-fu. "The English and the Opium Trade." In Schurmann, op. cit.

Tuchman, Barbara W. *Stilwell and the American Experience in China—1913-45*. New York: Macmillan, 1971

U.S. Air Force. "The U.S. Air Force in Southeast Asia." Washington, D.C.: Headquarters, U.S. Air Force, 1967.

U.S. Congress. "The Candidates' Views." *Congressional Quarterly*, May 3, 1968.

U.S. Department of the Army. *German Antiguerrilla Operations in the Balkans (1941-1944)*. Washington, D.C.: U.S. Government Printing Office, 1954.

U.S. Department of Defense. "Working Paper on the North Vietnamese Role in the War in South Vietnam." Washington, D.C.: 1968.

U.S. Department of the Navy. "Riverine Warfare." Washington, D.C.: U.S. Government Printing Office, 1967.

———. "Chinfonote 5721." Washington, D.C.: U.S. Navy, March 28, 1968.

U.S. Department of State. *Viet Nam: The Struggle for Freedom*. Publication 7724 (Department of Defense, Gen.-8). Washington, D.C. U.S. Government Printing Office, 1964.

———. *United States Relations with China—With Special Reference to the Period 1944-1949*. Washington, D.C.: U.S. Government Printing Office, 1949. Subsequently published as *The China White Paper—August 1949*, Stanford, Calif.: 2 vols. Stanford University Press, 1967.

U.S. Government. *The United States Strategic Bombing Survey—Over-all Report*. Washington, D.C.: U.S. Government Printing Office, 1945.

U.S. Marine Corps. "III Marine Amphibious Force—The Mission—And How It Is Fulfilled." Washington, D.C.: Headquarters, U.S. Marine Corps, October 1967.

———. "The Battle for Hills 861 and 881." N.p., n.d.

———. "Khe Sanh Wrap-Up." N.p., n.d.

U.S. Senate. *Refugee Problems in South Vietnam*. Washington, D.C.: U.S. Government Printing Office, 1966.

———. *Role of Dr. Henry A. Kissinger in the Wiretapping of Certain Government Officials and Newsmen*. Washington, D.C.: U.S. Government Printing Office, 1974.

———. *Hearings Before the Committee on the Philippines of the United States Senate in Relation to the Philippine Islands*, 2 vols. Washington, D.C.: U.S. Government Printing Office, 1902.

U.S. Senate Committee on Foreign Relations. *Background Information Relating to Southeast Asia and Vietnam*. Washington, D.C.: U.S. Government Printing Office, 1967.

———. *United States-Vietnam Relations 1945-1967*, 12 vols. Washington, D.C.: U.S. Government Printing Office, 1971.

U.S. Senate Republican Policy Committee. *The War in Vietnam.* Washington, D.C.: Public Affairs Press, 1967.

U.S. Seventh Fleet. "Cruisers and Destroyers in Vietnam." N.p., n.d.

———. "Task Force 77." N.p., n.d.

Urban, Mark. *War in Afghanistan.* London: The Macmillan Press, 1988.

Uris, Leon. *Exodus.* London: Allen Wingate, 1959.

Urrutia Lleó, Manuel. *Fidel Castro and Company, Inc.: Communist Tyranny in Cuba.* New York: Frederick A. Praeger, 1964.

Usborne, C.V. *The Conquest of Morocco.* London: Stanley Paul, 1936.

Utley, Freda. *Last Chance in China.* Indianapolis: Bobbs-Merrill, 1947.

Vagts, Alfred. *Defense and Diplomacy: The Soldier and the Conduct of Foreign Relations.* New York: Kings Crown Press, 1956.

Valeriano, N.D. and C.T.R. Bohannan. *Counter-Guerrilla Operations: The Philippine Experience.* New York: Frederick A. Praeger, 1962.

Vance, Cyrus. *Hard Choices: Critical Year in American Foreign Policy.* New York: Simon and Schuster, 1983.

Vandegrift, A.A., and R.B. Asprey. *Once a Marine.* New York: W.W. Norton, 1964.

Vandenbosch, A., and M.B. Vandenbosch. *Australia Faces Southeast Asia: The Emergence of a Foreign Policy.* Lexington, Ky.: University of Kentucky Press, 1967.

Vandenbosch, M.B. See Vandenbosch, A.

Vernadsky, George. *A History of Russia.* New Haven, Conn.: Yale University Press, 1945.

Vidal-Naquet, Pierre. *Torture: Cancer of Democracy.* Harmondsworth, Middlesex, U.K.: Penguin Books, 1963.

Vlekke, B.H.M. *Nusantara: A History of Indonesia.* The Hague: W. van Hoeve, 1959.

Volckmann, R.W. *We Remained.* New York: W.W. Norton, 1954.

Wagner, David H. "A Handful of Marines." *Marine Corps Gazette,* March 1968.

Waley, Arthur. *The Book of Songs.* London: Allen and Unwin, 1937.

Walker, Lannon. "Our Foreign Affairs Machinery: Time for an Overhaul." *Foreign Affairs,* January 1969.

Walker, Walter. "How Borneo Was Won." *The Round Table,* January 1969.

Wallace-Hadrill, J.M. *The Barbarian West, 400–1000.* London: Hutchinson, 1952.

Walsh, W.B. *Russia and the Soviet Union.* Ann Arbor, Mich.: University of Michigan Press, 1958.

Walt, L.W. "Are We Winning the War in Vietnam?" Washington, D.C.: Headquarters, U.S. Marine Corps, n.d.

———. "Khe Sanh: The Battle That Had to Be Won." *Reader's Digest,* August 1970.

———. "The Nature of the War in Vietnam." Washington, D.C.: Headquarters, U.S. Marine Corps, n.d.

———. *Strange War, Strange Strategy.* New York: Funk and Wagnalls, 1970.

Ward, Christopher. *The War of the Revolution,* Vol. 2 of 2 vols., ed. J.R. Alden. New York: Macmillan, 1952.

Warnke, Paul, and Leslie Gelb. "Security or Confrontation." *Foreign Policy,* Winter 1970–71.

Watteville, H. de. *Lord Kitchener.* London: Blackie and Son, 1939.

Webb, James. *Fields of Fire.* Englewood Cliffs, N.J.: Prentice-Hall, 1978.

Webster, Graham. *The Roman Imperial Army of the First and Second Centuries A.D.* London: Adam and Charles Black, 1969.

Wedemeyer, A.C. *Wedemeyer Reports.* New York: Henry Holt, 1958.

Wehl, David. *The Birth of Indonesia.* London: Allen and Unwin, 1948.

Weigley, R.F. *History of the United States Army.* New York: Macmillan, 1967.

———. *The American Way of War: A History of United States Military Strategy and Policy.* New York: Macmillan, 1973.

Weinberg, G.L. "The Yelna-Dorogobuzh Area of Smolensk Oblast." In Armstrong, op. cit.

Weinberger, Caspar. *Fighting for Peace.* New York: Warner Books, 1991.

Weller, Jac. "The U.S. Army in Vietnam: A Survey of Aims, Operations, and Weapons, Particularly of Small Infantry Units." *Army Quarterly,* October 1967.

Welles, Sumner. *The Time for Decision.* New York: Harper and Brothers, 1944.

West, Francis J. "Small Unit Action in Vietnam." Washington, D.C.: Headquarters, U.S. Marine Corps, 1967.

West, Rebecca. *Black Lamb and Grey Falcon,* Vol. 1 of 2 vols. London: Macmillan, 1942.

Westmoreland, W.C. *A Soldier Reports.* New York: Da Capo Press, 1989.

White, Lynn, Jr. *Medieval Technology and Social Change.* London: Oxford University Press, 1962.

White, T.H. *The Making of the President 1960.* New York: Atheneum, 1961.

———. *The Making of the President 1968.* New York: Atheneum, 1969.

———, and A. Jacoby. *Thunder Out of China.* New York: William Sloane, 1946.

———. See Stilwell, Joseph W.

Wickwire, Franklin, and Mary Wickwire. *Cornwallis: The American Adventure.* Boston: Houghton Mifflin, 1969.

Wickwire, Mary. See Wickwire, Franklin.

Wighton, Charles. *Heydrich: Hitler's Most Evil Henchman.* London: Odhams Press, 1962.

Wilcken, U. *Alexander the Great,* tr. G.C. Richards. London: Chatto and Windus, 1932.

Willcox, William B., ed. *The American Rebellion: Sir Henry Clinton's Narrative of His Campaigns, 1775–1782, with an Appendix of Original Documents.* New Haven, Conn.: Yale University Press, 1954.

———. *Portrait of a General: Sir Henry Clinton in the War of Independence.* New York: Alfred A. Knopf, 1962.

———. "Sir Henry Clinton: Paralysis of Command." In Billias, op. cit.

Williams, Phil. See Abernathy, W. Glenn.

Williamson, R.E. "A Briefing for Combined Action." *Marine Corps Gazette,* March 1968.

Wilson, Harold. "The Night LBJ Wrecked Our Secret Manoeuvres for Peace." *The Sunday Times* (London), May 16, 1971.

Wingate, Ronald. *Wingate of the Sudan.* London: John Murray, 1935.

Winstedt, R.O. "Malaysia (History)." *Encyclopaedia Britannica,* Vol. 14. 1968.

Wolfert, Ira. *American Guerrilla in the Philippines.* New York: Avon Books, 1945.

Wolff, Leon. *Little Brown Brother.* Garden City, N.Y.: Doubleday, 1961.

Womack, John. *Zapata and the Mexican Revolution.* London: Thames and Hudson, 1968.

Wood, Bryce. *The Making of the Good Neighbor Policy.* New York: Columbia University Press, 1961.

Woodhouse, C.M. *Apple of Discord.* London: Hutchinson, 1948.

———. *The Story of Modern Greece.* London: Faber and Faber, 1968.

Woodhouse, J.M. "Some Personal Observations on the Employment of Special Forces in Malaya." *Army Quarterly,* April 1955.

———. *The Struggle for Greece 1941–1949.* London: Hart-Davis, MacGibbon, 1979.

Woodruff, Philip. *The Men Who Ruled India: The Guardians,* Vol. 2 of 2 vols. London: Jonathan Cape, 1954.

Woodward, Bob, and Carl Bernstein. *The Final Days.* New York: Simon and Schuster, 1976.

Woolman, David. *Rebels in the Rif.* Stanford, Calif.: Stanford University Press, 1969.

Wooten, James T. "How a Supersoldier Was Fired from His Command." *New York Times Magazine,* September 5, 1971.

Anti-Imperialist League (U.S.), 126–7
Anual, 268–9
Ap Bac, battle of, 738, 758
Ap Bia, battle of, see Hamburger Hill
Appian, 15
Aqaba, Gulf of, 1154
Aquino, Benigno, Jr., 538
Aquino, Corazon, 538–40
Arab-Berber tribes, 96, 657
Arab Bureau, Algeria, 658
Arab-Israeli peace talks, 1164–6
Arab rebellion against Turkish rule,
    179–91; see also Lawrence, Col.
    T.E.
Arafat, Yasser, 1080, 1155, 1157,
    1159, 1161, 1163–6, 1174
Aragon, 82
Arakan offensives, 421, 432, 434
Arana, Sabino de, 1142
Arango, Dorotheo, 163
Aranjuez, 77
Arbenz Guzmán, Jacobo, 1068
Archangel, 215
Archbishop of Canterbury, 196
ARDE, Nicaragua, 1080
Ardennes, 296
Arévalo Bermejo, Juan José, 1068
Argentina, 1085; insurgency, 1091–3
Argoud, Col. Antoine, 672
Arias, Pres. Oscar, 1085, 1102
Arias Peace Plan, 1071, 1085
Armstrong, Brig., 345
Armstrong, Prof. John A., 329–30
Arnett, Peter, 898
Arnulfo Romero, Archbishop Oscar,
    1099
Aron, Robert, 319
Arp Arslan, 34
Arrian, 4
ASEAN, 1049
Asia Youth Conference (1948), 564
Asquith, Pr. Min. Herbert H., 193
Assad, Hafez, 1158, 1160, 1163
Associated Press (AP), 831
Association of Ulemas, Algeria, 659
Atkin, Ronald, 167
Atlantic Charter, 563
Atlantic magazine, 972
Atomic bomb, 301–3, 353, 449, 470,
    589, 611, 724, 749, 772, 906, 931,
    935–6, 945, 958, 986, 989, 993–4
Aung Htin, Prof. Maung, 142–3, 416,
    435–7
Aung San, Maung, 416, 435–7

Auriol, Pres. Vincent, 425–6
Australia: coastwatchers, 371;
    independent companies, 373; Timor
    guerrilla force, 373–4; training of
    British Commandos, 373; forces in
    Vietnam, 823–4, 864, 953
Auténtico party, Cuba, 691–2
Autumn Uprising of 1927 (China), 293
Avars, 30, 32
Ayala, Plan of, 165
Aziz, Mazri el-, 180, 182
Azrak, 186

Baader, Andreas, 1064
Baader-Meinhof guerrilla terrorists,
    1064
Bactria, 4, 6–7
Bagandae, 21
Bailey, Col., 344
Baker, James, 1163
Bakunin, Mikhail, 203
Baldwin, Hanson, 858–9, 901
Balfour Declaration, 551, 1151
Balkans, 9, 319 ff.
Ball, George, 721, 786, 806–8, 858,
    908, 932
Balliol, John, 43
Balsha, George, 339
Balsome Street gang, IRA guerrilla
    terrorists, 1131
Ba Maw, Dr., 435–6
Bangkok, 390
Bannockburn, battle of, 46
Bao Dai, Emp., 392, 400, 402–3, 482,
    486, 503; fall of, 403, 512, 595,
    599–601, 607; restoration of, 482
Barbarians, 22–34, 58
Barco Vargas, Virgilio, 1110–1
Baring, Sir Evelyn, 634, 636
Barker, Gen., 557
Barnes, Maj. Gen. John, 970
Barnes, Lt., 118–9
Barnett, Dr. Donald L., 632
Barr, Maj. Gen. David, 463–4
Barrett, Col. David D., 444, 463
Barri, Gerald de, see Giraldus
    Cambrensis
Barrientos government, 712, 714
Bases Aéro-Terrestres, 512
Bashir, Gen. Hassan al-, 1176–7
Basque insurgency, see Spain
Bass, Mr., 128
Bataan, 378, 384

Bragg, Gen. Braxton, 105–6
Brandon, Henry, 907
Bravo, Douglas, 1067
Brazil, 1085; insurgency, 1089–90
Breasted, Prof., 4
Brest-Litovsk, treaty of, 219
Bretons, 46–7
Brezhnev, Prem. Leonid, 1039
Briand, Aristide, 273
Briggs, Gen. Sir Henry, 568–9; Briggs
   Plan, Malaya, 568
British Commandos, 313
British East Africa, see Kenya
British East India Company, 232
Brittany, 46–7, 74–6
Brooke, Gen. Sir Alan, 425, 427
Brossolette, Pierre, 316
Browne, Malcolm, 760
Browne, Lt. Col. Thomas, 69
Brozovich, Josip, see Tito, Marshal
   Josip (Broz)
Bruce, David, 1007, 1010, 1027
Bruce, Robert, 44–6
Brunei, sultan of, 1083
Brussels Conference (1874), 110
Buchan, Alistair, 890
Bucher, Capt. Lloyd, 896
Buck, Pearl, 230
Bu Craa mines, Western Sahara, 1179,
   1181
BUDC, Philippines, 529
Buell, Gen. Don C., 105
Buford, Col., 64
Bugeaud, Gen., 97–100, 111, 658
Bulgaria, 27, 30, 32; World War II,
   338, invaded by Germany, 297
Buller, Gen. Sir Redvers, 143–4
Bunche, Ralph, 1153
Bundoola, 102
Bundy, McGeorge, 74, 787, 793–4,
   852, 857–8, 888, 908, 919, 921,
   960
Bundy, William, 771–2, 778, 783,
   788, 793–5, 801, 876, 920;
   preparation of Congressional
   resolution, Tonkin Gulf, 771;
   escalation "scenario," 771
Bunker, Amb. Ellsworth, 870–2, 892,
   908, 966, 995
Burchett, Wilfred, 737
Burgoyne, Gen. John, 60–1
Burguete, Gen. Ricardo, 269–70
Burma, 102–3; map, 420; British
   conquest (1820–1825), 102, 140,

second war (1852), 140, pacification
   of Upper Burma (1885–1890), 140–3;
   British administration (1890–1941),
   415–6; World War II: British retreat,
   414–5, Burma rifle regiments, 419,
   anti-British attitude, 415, Allied
   ground operations, 421, 433–4,
   Allied/Burmese guerrilla operations,
   417–8, 425–7, 431–5; see also Slim,
   Gen. Sir William; Stilwell, Gen.
   Joseph; Wingate, Maj. Gen. Orde
Burma Road, 396, 415–6
Burmese National Army, 435–6
Burn, Prof. A.R., 4
Bury, Prof. J.B., 4
Bush, Pres. George, 1065, 1084, 1103,
   1106, 1116–7, 1163
Bussaco, battle of, 80
Butros-Ghali, Butros, 1105
Buttinger, Joseph, 151–2, 595, 615,
   759
Buzhardt, J. Fred, 1032
Byrnes, James, 483
Byzantine Empire, 29–34; map, 31

Cabot, John Moors, 1068
Caesar, Julius, 9–11, 20, 58
Cairo Conference, 431
Cajeme, 163
Caldera Rodríguez, Pres. Rafael, 1067
Calenzana, battle of, 53
Cali drug cartel, Colombia, 1109,
   1112
Calleo, David, 981
Calley, Lt. William, 1023–5
Callinan, Maj. Bernard, 373
Callwell, Gen. Charles E., 76, 137–40,
   150, 282, 751, 846, 986
Calvert, Michael, 425–7
Cambodia (Kampuchea), ix, 395, 397,
   582, 596, 816, 865, 911, 1114;
   map, 478; fall of Sihanouk, 994–5;
   U.S. bombing of, 876, 962–7, 974,
   992, 1018; Geneva Agreements, 963;
   Viet Minh guerrilla attacks, 582;
   Lon Nol government: 994–5, 1030;
   peasant repression, 995; army, 1030;
   U.S. support, 995–6, 1045–6; Lon
   Nol's fall, 1046; PAVN/VC
   sanctuary, 902–4, 962–4, 993–4,
   1030; U.S./South Vietnam invasion
   of, 996–1003, 1019; guerrilla war,
   1017–8, 1049–55: Khmer Rouge,
   963, 1043–6; Khmer Serai, 963,

Cambodia (*continued*)
996; air war, 1017–8, 1045; ground war, 1017–8; Pol Pot government, 1048: genocidal campaign, 1046–8, "Democratic Revolution," 1044–5, fall of, 1046; CIA operations, 963, 966, 994–5, 1000; Vietnam invasion, 1048–51; Heng Samrin government, 1049–52; Hun Sen government, 1052–5; refugees, 1048; resistance groups: ANS (Sihanouk), 1050, NLF (Son Sann), 1050; Khmer Rouge (Khieu Samphen),1050–5; Vietnam withdrawal, 1051; UN intervention, 1052–5; Sihanouk's return, 1053, becomes king, 1055; elections, 1054; Prince Ranariddh's coalition government, 1054–5

Camden, battle of, 67–8
Campbell, Gen. Sir Archibald, 102
Campbell, Arthur, 572
Camp David Accords, 1158, 1163
Can, Ngo Dinh, 605
Cannae, battle of, 27, 29
Cantabria, 17, 21
Cao Dai, 395, 472, 600–1, 619, 849
Caputo, Philip, xi, xiii, 834, 836–7, 844, 951
Caravelle Manifesto, 619–20
Carlson, Col. Evans, 372
Carnot (decree), 74
Carpentier, Gen., 498, 500, 503
Carr, E.H., 202
Carranza, Venustiano, 166–70
Carrera, Adm. Blanco, 1143
Carter, Pres. Jimmy, 1069, 1080, 1098–9, 1157–8
Carthaginians, 9, 13–5, 29
Carver, George, 908
Casey, William, 1083
Cassivellaunus, 10–1
Castañeda, Jorge, 1106
Castillo Armas, Carlos, 1069
Castriotes, George "Scanderbeg," 339
Castro, Raúl, 695, 700, 702, 706, 708–9
Castro Ruz, Fidel, xi, 715, 1063, 1066, 1080, 1093, 1097, 1101, 1108, 1113–4, 1188; background, 694–5; early revolutionary activities, 685, 695; imprisonment, 695–6; preparation for insurgency, 698, Mexico, 698–9; Cuba landing, 700; Sierra Maestra base, 700–4; Matthews interview, 701–3;

strength, 686, 699–700; guerrilla operations, 705–6, 708–9; victory, 710; revolutionary theory, 711–12; *see also* Batista, Fulgencio; Cuba; Guevara Lynch, Ernesto (Che)
Cat Bi, 479, 588
Cathelineau, Jacques, 74
Catholic National Party, Ulster, 1124
Cato, M. Porcius, 15
Catroux, Gen. Georges, 663
Caulaincourt, Amb. Count Armand de, 85–7, 89
Cayetano Carpio, Salvador, 1096–7, 1099, 1101
Cédile, Col. Jean, 472
Celts, 9, 13
Central Intelligence Agency, *see* United States: Central Intelligence Agency
Central Treaty Organization (CENTO), 1202
Cerides, Pres. Glafcos, 655
Céspedes, Pres. Carlos de, 115, 690–1
Chaffee, Gen. Adna, 131–2
Challe, Gen. Maurice, 675–8; Challe Plan, 676–7
Chalons-sur-Marne, battle of, 29
Chamberlain White Paper, 552–4
Chambrun, Gen., 273–4
Chamorro, Pedro, Joaquín, 1078–9
Chamorro, Violeta Barrios de, 1086–7
Chamoun, Camille, 1158
Champa kingdom, 38
Chang Chihtung, 237
Chang Hsueh-liang, Marshal, 252
Chaouen, 265
Chapelle, Dickey, 706
Charlemagne, 27
Charles, *see* Cornwallis, Lord Charles
Charles IV, king of Spain, 76–7
Charles V, king of France, 46–7
Charles VI, 50
Charles X, king of France, 96
Charles XII, king of Sweden, 50
Charleston, S.C., 64, 66, 68–70
Chasseurs d'Afrique, 157
Chataigneau, Gov.-Gen., 659
Chattanooga, Tenn., 105–6
Chávez, Julio, 162
Chechens, 100
Cheka, 212–3, 215
Chekiang province, 241, 260
Chennault, Gen. Claire, 440, 442, 444, 447
Ch'en Yi, Gen., 463–4

Ebro River, 14, 77
Eden, Anthony, 313, 399, 516, 590, 648, 652
EDL, Colombia, 809–11
Edmonds, Sir James E., 93–4
Edson, Col. (Red Mike), 288
Edward I, king of England, 39–44
EE, Spain, 1144
Ehrlichman, John, 1033
Einsatzgruppen, 324, 326
"Einstein letter," 301
Eisenhower, Pres. Dwight D., 577, 582–3, 587, 589–92, 701, 704, 709–10, 719, 748, 919, 922, 1068–9; Geneva Conference, 594–6; Cuba, 692; South Vietnam, 599, 601–2; Diem, 599, 601–2, "row-of-dominoes," 590; French Indochina, 577, intervention in Vietnam, 589–92, 726, Ridgeway report, 592
Elgin, Lord, 236
Eliot, Sir Charles, 628–9
Elizabeth I, queen of England, 51
Ellsberg, Daniel, 1028
ELF, Eritrea, 1170–1
ELN, Colombia, 1102, 1110–2
ELN, Peru, 1113
El Salvador, 1096–1106; map, 1062; repressive governments, 1096 ff.; growth of guerrilla movements, 1096–8; guerrilla insurgency, 1097 ff.; guerrilla tactics, 1100–2; counterinsurgency tactics, 1100–1; atrocities, 1099, 1101–3; cease-fire and peace, 1104–6
El Sordo, 292
Ély, Paul, 587, 589, 592
Élysée Agreements, 486
Emergency Regulations Act, 565
Emerson, Lt. Col. Henry, 843–4, 882
Emery, Fred, 985, 987
Emporiae (Ampurias), 13
ENA, Algeria, 659
enclave theory, 853–4
Encounter magazine, 890
Encyclopaedia Britannica, 1063
Enders, Thomas, 1080
Engels, Friedrich, 467
England: maps, 39, 57, 65, 73, 146, 177, 187, 401, 406, 420, 626, 655, 1122; Afghan War (1837–1842), 137; American Revolution, 63–70; Egypt, 180; Arab revolt, World War I, 179–91; Africa: First Boer War

(1881), 137; Second Boer War (1899–1902), 140, 143–8; Burma: conquest of (1820–1825), 102, 140, second war (1852), 140, pacification of Upper Burma (1885–1890), 140–3, 236; World War II, *see* England: World War II; Wales, pacification of, 39–43; Scotland, pacification of, 43–6; Corsica, 54; China, 232–3, 236–7; Vietnam, 403, 803, postwar occupation, 471–2; RAF, 473; refuses Allied intervention, Dien Bien Phu, 590; Afghanistan, 1201–2; Greece, 515–8, 520; Indonesia, 543–6; Malaya: prewar, 408–9; World War II, *see* Malaya; postwar, 563–74; Mexico, 161, 166–7; Kenya, 624–42; India: 72–4, 280, 284–5; Indian Mutiny (1857), 137; German East Africa, 172–4, 176–8; Palestine, *see* Lawrence, Col. T.E.; Ireland, 92–101, 1121–4; Ulster, 1121–38; Mesopotamia, 277–80; Cyprus, 643–55; Portugal, 76–83; Spain, 76–83; Russia, 209–10, 215–6, 219–22; World War II: SOE operations, 299, 300, 305, 307–8; 310–4, 316–9, 342–8, 352–3, 359–63, 390–1, 750; Malaya: 407–12; defense of, 405–7; Spencer-Chapman, 408–13; France, 310–9; Yugoslavia, 342–7, 351–4; Norway, 299, 308; Greece: defense of, 357; guerrilla resistance, 359–63; Albania, 365–6; Burma: retreat from, 414–5; Allied ground operations, 421, 433–4; long-range penetration, 425–7, 436–8; SOE operations, 300, 415, 417, 435; Allied/Burmese guerrilla operations, 417–8, 433–6; Slim's achievements, 418–21, 430–1, 435–6; Wingate's folly, 423–7, 431–2; Ethiopia, 423–4
English, Brig. Gen. Lowell, 822
English East India Company, 408
Enosis, Cyprus, 643–5, 652, 654
Enríquez, Dr. Miguel, 1093
Enthoven, Dr. Alain, 877, 903
EOKA, Cypriot guerrillas, 646–53
EPLF, Ethiopia, 1170–2
EPRF, Eritrea, 1172
EPRP, Ethiopia, 1169
Eremenko, Stepan, 88
Eritrea, 1170–2

Eroglu, Pr. Min. Dervis, 655
ERP, Argentina, 1091–3
ERP, El Salvador, 1097, 1100, 1102
Erskine, Gen. Sir George, 637–8
Escobar Gaviría, Pablo, 1112
Esquipulas II, treaty of, 1085
Estrada Palma, Tomás, 116, 688–9
ETA, Basque guerrilla terrorists, 1141, 1143–7
ETA-M, 1143–7
ETA-PM, 1143
Ethiopia, 1168–73; map, 1169; Haile Selassie deposed, 1168; Mengistu's Dergue dictatorship, 1168–72; U.S. aid, 1170–1; Soviet Union/Cuban aid, 1171; opposition, 1169–70; Eritrea, 1170, 1172; Ogaden, 1169–70; Tigre, 1171–2; Mengistu deposed, 1172; Eritrea wins independence, 1173
Etzel, Jewish guerrillas, 554
Ewell, Lt. Gen. Julian, 880, 985, 987–8
Exodus 1947, 559

Fabian tactics, 22, 47
Fabius Maximus, Quintus, 22, 69
Facts on File, 1063
Faisal, King, 1154
Falkenhausen, Gen. von, 250
Falkirk, battle of, 45
Fall, Bernard, 397, 587, 615, 619, 755, 834–5, 841
FARC, Colombia, 1108–12
Far Eastern Agreement, 449–50
Faulkner, Brian, 1127–9, 1131–2
FDN, Nicaragua, 1080
Feisal, king of Mesopotamia, 279
Feisal, Prince, 180–3
Feland, Brig. Gen. Logan, 287
Feldt, Comdr. Eric, 371
Fellowes-Gordon, Ian, 426
Felt, Adm. Harry, 771–2, 774
Fêng Yü-hsiang, Gen., 242–3
Ferdinand, Prince, 77
Ferdinand I, Emp., 50
Ferguson, Maj. Patrick, 68–9
Fergusson, Bernard, 425–7, 432
Fertig, Col. Wendell, 381–3
FEU, Cuba, 689, 699
Fez, 223–4; treaty of, 155
FFI, France, 318
Fierro, Rudolfo, 167
Finnegan, William, 1198

FIR, Peru, 1113
Fishel, Wesley, 604–5, 622, 832
Fitzgerald, Prof. C.P., 920–1
Fitzgerald, Francis, xi, 1035
Fitzgerald, Garret, 1134
Flippen, William, 759
FLN, Algeria, 661, 663, 666, 668–9, 671–3, 675–9
Flores Magón brothers, 163
Flying Tigers, 440
FMLN, El Salvador, 1098–9, 1101, 1103–5
FNLA, Angola, 1186
Foch, Marshal Ferdinand, 222, 930
Foco insurreccional revolutionary concept, 711, 714
Foley, Charles, 648–9, 653
Fonseca Amador, Carlos, 1079
Foot, Sir Hugh, 652
Foot, Prof. M.R.D., 298, 310
Foreign Affairs magazine, 921, 925, 960–1
Forrest, Gen. Nathan Bedford, 105–8, 110
Forrestal, Michael, 721; Forrestal-Hilsman Report, 758
Fourier, Charles, 162
Fowler, Henry, 903
Fox, Charles James, 70
France, 43–7, 50, 72, 101, 1082; intervention in Rif rebellion, 272–5; pacification of Algeria: 96–100, 154–7, map, 98; China, 236–7; Corsica (1768–1769), 53–5; Spain and Portugal (1808–1812): 76, 83–102, map, 79; Vendée (1793): 74–6, map, 75; Tyrol (1809): 84–5, map, 85; Russia (1812): 85–91, map, 87; Algeria, *see* Algeria; Indochina: pacification of, 150–3; colonization of, 391–6; World War II, French surrender of, 397, Decoux's dictatorship, 397–8; rise of Communist nationalism, 393–6, 400, 402–3; postwar, *see* France: Vietnam; intervention in Russian Revolution (1917–1918), 209–10, 215–222; Spanish Civil War, 290; Vietnam: maps, 478, 491, 499, 576; postwar condition of, 473–4; French claims to, 472–3; occupation of, 472; DRV opposition, 473; outbreak of war, 477–9; (1946–1949): the military situation, 481–2, the

France (continued)
political situation, 482, 485–8;
(1950–1953): the military situation,
497, 502, 508–9, French defects,
497–8; the political situation, 499–
500, 503–6; strategic errors, 508–9,
512, 514; political failure, 509–10;
tactics, 473, 475, 477, 480–1, 508–
9, 512, 514; continuing political
failure, 575; (1953): the military
situation, 576; Navarre's mission,
575; strategy, 577; tactics, 577;
increased U.S. aid, 577–8, 582; the
"Navarre Plan," 582; fortified
airheads, 582; Dien Bien Phu, 582–
5, battle of, 587–9, casualties, 592;
Navarre on policy, 585; French
withdrawal, 585; World War II:
map, 311; German invasion and
occupation, 296; guerrilla resistance,
303, 305, 310–19, Communist
element, 314; postwar: 470–1;
Communist threat, 471
Francis, Ahmed, 663
Francis, Amb. David, 215
Franco-Bahamonde, Gen. Francisco,
265, 270–1, 289, 892, 1142–5
Frank, Gov. Gen. Hans, 306
Franke, Prof. Wolfgang, 233
Franklin, Lt. Col. J. Ross, 970
Franks, 27, 32–3, 36
Fredericksburg, battle of, 110
Frederick the Great, king of Prussia,
guerrilla opposition, 50, 56, 58, 854
Frederick William, elector of
Brandenburg, guerrilla opposition,
51–3; map, 52
Frederick William III, king of Prussia,
88
Freeman's Journal, 193
Freikorps, French and Prussian
irregulars, 53
FRELIMO, Mozambique, 1185–7,
1194–8
French, Gen. Sir John, 143, 145–6
French and Indian War, 56–64; map, 57
French maquis, 308, 315–9
French Revolution, 74
French Union, 486
Fridigern, 27–8
Friedman-Yellin, David, 555
Froehlke, Fred, 1023
Frunze, Gen. Mikhail V., 321
FSLN, Nicaragua, 1078–80, 1096

Fuchs, Klaus, 464
Fujimori, Pres. Alberto, 1116–9
Fukien province, 247, 250
Fulbright, Sen. William J., 804–5, 853,
890, 987, 991, 1000
Fuller, Maj. Gen. J.F.C., 4, 105
Funston, Gen. Frederick, 130–1, 535
Furneaux, Rupert, 269

Gage, Gen. Thomas, 59–60, 835
Gaillard government, 673–4
GAL, Basque insurgency, 1145, 1147
Galba, Servius, 18
Galbraith, John Kenneth, 889–90, 932
Galilee, 1153, 1159
Gallieni, Gen. Joseph, 136, 152–3,
156, 392, 752
Gambiez, Gen., 678
GAMO, 510
Gandhi, Mahatma, 284
Gapon, Georgi, 205–6
Garang, John, 1175–7
García, Calixto, 116
García Pérez, Alan, 1115–6
Gardner, Arthur, 692, 701, 704
Gatacre, Sir William, 143
Gates, Gen. Horatio, 66–8
Gaul, 7, 13, 58
Gauss, Clarence, 442
Gavin, Gen. James, on Dien Bien Phu,
720; Laos, 720; Vietnam, 853–4,
856, 882, 889, 904, 918, 953
Gaviría Trujillo, César, 1111–3
Gaza Strip, 1154–5, 1161–2, 1164–5
Gazelle Force, 418
GCMA, 502–3, 512, 583, 585
Gégêne torture, 670
Gemayel, Amin, 1160–1
Gemayel, Bashir, 1158–60
Gemayel, Pierre, 1158
Geneva Accords, Soviet Union/
Afghanistan, 1210–1
Geneva Conference, 584, 590, 594–6,
610
Genghis Khan, 36–7
Genocide: French in Algeria (1830–
1844), 99; Germans in Russia
(World War II), 324–6; Nazi
Germany, 326; Douhet's concept of
aerial warfare, 931
Gent, Sir Edward, 565
George III, king of Greece, 356
Georgia, 63–4, 108
Germain, Lord George, 64

Hunan province, 235, 245–7, 250
Hundred Years' War, 46
Hungarian irregulars, 51–2
Hungary, World War II, 338; invaded by Germany, 297
Hung Hsiu-ch'üan, 233–6
Hung Wu, Emp., 231
Huns, 24–5, 27, 29; map, 26
Hunt, Brig. Kenneth, 955
Huong, Tran Van, 789–90, 983
Hupeh province, 250
Hurley, Maj. Gen. Patrick: China mission, 445–8, 451, 454–6; resignation, 458–9
Husein, Prince (sherif of Mecca), 180
Hussein, king of Jordan, 1156–7, 1161–2
Hussein, Sadam, 1159, 1163
Husseini, Faisal, 1164

Ia Drang, battle of, 841
Ibarruri, Dolores (La Pasionaria), 289
I Ho Ch'üan societies, 237
Ilaga guerrilla terrorism, Philippines, 538
Imphal, 412
India, 37, 103, 113, 136, 281, 415–6, 421–22, 930; map, 73; World War II: Indian troops retreat from Burma, 414–5; in first Arakan offensive, 419–21; in brigade operations, 425–7, 432; in Fourteenth Army, 430–1; in second Arakan offensive, 432–3
Indian Empire, 141
Indians (North American), 56–64; Indian Wars, U.S.: map, 112; 102–3, 111–3
Indibilis, Spanish guerrilla leader, 14–5
Indochina: map, 401; French colonization of, 391–6; Vietnamese resistance to, 391–6; rise of Ho Chi Minh, 393–6; World War II: French surrender to Japan, 397; Decoux's dictatorship, 397; resistance movements, 398–400, 402–3; Japanese takeover, 399–400; Japan declares independent Vietnam, 400; U.S. involvement, 396, 398–9; Communist element, 400–3; Viet Minh guerrillas, 402; postwar: international importance of, 481–2; U.S. estimate of importance, 578; see also France: Indochina; France: Vietnam; United States: Vietnam

Indochinese Communist Party, 396, 402–3, 474–5
Indochinese Union, 391
Indonesia: map, 543; Japanese occupation, 388–90; Dutch overlords, 389; nationalist movements, 389; Japanese brutality, 389–90; proclamation of independence, 390; postwar: conditions, 470, 543; Allied return, 544–5; peace negotiations, 545–6; Dutch pacification campaign, 546–8; guerrilla warfare, 547–50; Indonesian victory, 550
Industrial Revolution, 92
International Institute for Strategic Studies, 898, 955, 1014, 1063
International Monetary Fund, 1082
Intifada, Arab uprising, 1162–3 ff.
Iran, 1082–3, 1208
Iraq, 270, 930, 1082
IRB, 192–3
Ireland, 41, 50, 1133; Revolution (1916–1921), 192–201; Dail, 194; Free State, 196; Republic, 1122; role in Ulster insurgency, 1121–38; see also Irish Republican Army; Ulster
Irish Free State, 1121–2
"Irish Question, the," 195
Irish Republican Army, 194–6, 1121–38; aim, 1121; formation of, 194; growth, 1122–5; Provisional IRA, 1125–6; opens Ulster insurgency, 1125; funding, 1126, 1130, 1133; guerrilla warfare, 1125 ff.; Protestant factor, 1123 ff.; British counterinsurgency campaign, 1127 ff.; peace negotiations, 1136–8
Irgun-Etzel, Palestine Jewish guerrillas, 554–9, 561
Iron Triangle, 865
Irrawaddy River valley, 102, 417
Isaacs, Prof. Harold, 240
Islamic fundamentalism, 680–2, 1164–5; 1176–7, 1206, 1208, 1210–2
Islamic Jihad Council, 1206
Isle of Pines, Cuba, 695–6
Isly, battle of, 99
Israel: map, 1152; postwar: guerrilla war against Arabs, 1151–5; declaration of statehood, 1153; Suez Canal war, 1154; the six-day war, 1155; territorial gains, 1155; refugee problem, 1154–5, 1157; UN

Little Missouri area, 111
Liu Po-ch'eng, Gen., 463–4
Livy, 15
Llewellyn ap Gruffydd (Prince of
Wales), 39–42
Lloyd George, Pr. Min. David, 193,
196, 551, 644
Loan, Gen. Nguyen Ngoc, 849, 898
Lockhart, Bruce, 313
Lockhart, Sir William, 136
Loc Ninh, battle of, 865
Lodge, Henry Cabot, 115
Lodge, Henry Cabot, Jr., 744, 759,
761, 767–8, 771, 826, 849, 857,
908, 1068; ambassador to South
Vietnam, 743, 774; Paris peace
talks, 959
Lombards, 32,
London, 42, 77–8
Long, Nguyen Van, 503
"Long-Hair Rebels," China, 234, 236–
7
Long March, 250–1
Long Range penetration operations,
425–7, 431
Long Wall, Constantinople, 30
Lon Nol, Premier, 994–7, 1001, 1009,
1023, 1030
Lords Marchers, 41
Loudoun, Lord, 59
Louis XIII, king of France, 50
Louis XIV, king of France, 49–50
Louis Philippe, king of France, 96, 99
Luang Prabang, 583
Lucas García, Gen. Romeo, 1069
Luce, Henry, 461
Lucullus, Lucius, 18
Luftwaffe, 297, 930
Luna, Gen., 123, 127
Lusitanians, 13, 18–19
Luyên, Ngo Dinh, 605
Luzon, Philippines, 123, 128–30, 378,
384–5
Lyautey, Marshal Hubert, 136, 150,
270–4, 392, 480–1, 752, 835, 884,
949, 954, 1090; Indochina, 150–3;
Madagascar, 153; Algeria/Morocco,
154–7

MAAG, U.S., 611–3, 622
Macado, Gerardo, 689–90
MacArthur, Gen. Douglas, 378, 380,
386, 457, 578, 591, 749, 949
McCain, Adm. John S., Jr., 995

McCarthy, Eugene, 890, 908, 923
McCarthy, Joseph, 465, 692
Macco, Antonio, 116
McCone, John, 767, 798, 920
McCuen, Col. John, 480, 509
McDonald, Ian, 1000
Macea, José, 116
Macedonia, 6–7, 27
McFarlane, Robert, 1082–3
McGovern, Sen. George, 992
Machado, Gerardo, 116
Machel, Samora, 1187, 1193–8
Machiavelli, Niccolò, x, 48–9
MacKenzie, A.M., 47n.
McKinley, Pres. William, 115, 119–20;
Cuba, 115, 119, 688–9; Philippines,
123, 125, 127, 130–1
Maclean, Bill, 364–6
Maclean, Brig. Sir Fitzroy, 345–7,
351–3
Maclear, Michael, 1017
Macmillan, Harold, 652
McNamara, Robert, 719, 721, 725,
736–7, 742, 748, 759, 761, 767–8,
770–2, 775, 784–5, 793, 801, 834,
842, 849, 857–61, 864, 875, 877–9,
891–2, 902, 931–2, 919, 935, 946;
pessimism, 767; recommendations,
767–8; reports, 761, 767–8; volte-
face, 761
McNaughton, John, 778, 780, 784,
793–4, 802, 876
Macready, Nevil, 195–7
MacStiofain, Sean, 1125, 1129
MACV, U.S., 736, 755
Madagascar, 102, 137, 153
Madani, Abessi, 681
Mad Mullah, 270
Madras, 284
Mafeking, South Africa, 143
Magana, Alvaro, 1100
Magoon, Charles, 689
Magsaysay, Ramon, 536–7, 541
Mahan, Capt. Alfred T., x, 114–5,
124, 472
Maharbal, Gen., 29
Mahgoub, Mohammed Ahmed, 1173
Mahi ed Dine, 96
Mailer, Norman, 907
Maillebois, Marquis de, 53
Maine, USS, 119
Major, Pr. Min. John, 1136–7
Makarios III, archbishop of Cyprus,
645–8, 651–4

1262

Mountbatten, Adm. Lord Louis, 430, 432, 435–6, 448, 543–4, 1133
Moxon-Browne, Edward, 1142, 1144
Moyers, Bill, 926–7
Mozambique, 1185–7, 1193–9; map, 1185; guerrilla warfare under Portuguese rule, 1185–7; Machel's government, 1193: guerrilla war with Rhodesia and South Africa, 1194–7; shifts allegiance to the West, 1198–9
MPL, Philippines, 530–1
MPLA, Angola, 1185–7, 1191–2
MPM, Argentina, 1091–2
MR-8, Brazil, 1089–90
MRLA, Malaya, 567, 569, 571
MRTA, Peru, 1114
MTLD, Algeria, 659–60, 662, 668
Mugabe, Robert, 1193–5
Muhsin, Zuhayr, 1156, 1158
Mujaheddin guerrillas, Afghanistan, 1204–11
Mukden, siege of, 463
Murat, Gen., 77
Muraviev, Col., 214
Mus, Paul, 399
Muskie, Sen. Edmund, 999
Mussolini, Benito, 293, 297
Muzorewa, Bishop Abel, 1195
Myers, Gen. Samuel, 622
Myitkyina, 446
My Lai massacre, see South Vietnam
Myrdal, Gunnar, 578–9

Naderi, Sayer Jaffer, 1212
Naegelen, Marcel Edmond, 660
Nagasaki, 931
Nairobi, 173
Najibullah, Dr. Mohammed, 1209–12
Nanking, 235–6, 238, 242, 253, 259
Nantes, 314; battle of, 74
Napier, "Fagin," 136
Napoleon, Emp. (Napoleon Bonaparte), 54, 76, 80–92, 339, 882
Napoleon III, Emp., 161–2
Napoleonic wars, 113
Naranjo, Jr., Francisco, 165
Narses, Gen., 29–30
Nasser, Ahmed Mohammed, 663, 1170
Nasser, Gamal Abdul-, 1154–5
Nasution, Gen. Abdul Haris, 549
National Broadcasting Company (NBC), 759

National Defense Council, Greece, 518, 521, 523
National Democratic Front, Philippines, 538–40
National Democratic Party, Rhodesia, 1193
National Front, Indonesia, 546
National Islamic Front, Sudan, 1177
National Liberation Committee of Vietnam, 403
National Security Council, U.S., see United States
Nation magazine, 920
NATO, 673, 678
Naulin, Gen., 274
Navarre, Gen. Henri-Eugène, 514, 575–7, 582–5, 587–8, 592; Navarre Plan, 582, 589
Neave, Airey, 313, 1133
Nedić, Gen., 338, 341, 343
Negev desert, 1153
Nelson, Donald, 445–6
Nenita operations, Philippines, 533
Neo-Destour Party, Tunisia, 658
Neri, 164
Nero, Claudius, 14
Neto, Agostinho, 1185, 1187–8, 1190
New Delhi, 429, 433
New Guinea, World War II, 371, 373, 389
New Republic magazine, 889
Newsweek magazine, 759, 865, 961–2, 988, 1081
New Yorker magazine, 821, 926
New York Review of Books, 853, 887, 889
New York Times, 701–3, 771, 831, 852–3, 938–9, 945–6, 966, 972, 983, 996, 1000, 1011, 1013
New York Times Magazine, 858
Nez Percé Indians, North America, 113
Nhu, Mme. (Tran Le Yuan), 605, 727, 743–4, 759, 791, 887
Nhu, Ngo Dinh, 605, 607, 727, 739, 741, 743–4, 750, 754, 923
Nicaragua, 1085–6, 1094, 1099, 1104; map, 1062; Somoza dictatorship, 1077–9, guerrilla opposition, 1077–9, Communist Sandinista Liberation Front (FSLN), 1078–80: successes, 1078–9, factions, 1079, overthrow of government, 1079; condition of country, 1080; Sandinista

Robinson, James, 759
Robles, Gen. Juvencio, 165
Rochejacquelein, Count Henri de la, 75–6
Rockefeller, Nelson, 960
Roeder, Capt. Franz, 87, 89, 882
Rogers, Robert, 59, 62n.
Rogers, William, 966, 975, 992–3, 997, 1032
Rolling Red Horde theory, 581
Roman Empire, 9–11, 24–34; maps, 10, 14, 26; invasion and occupation of Spain, 13–21; Britain, 9–11; Celtiberians, 78; Hannibal, 7–9
Romania, invaded by Germany in World War II, 297
Romans, 72, 78, 103
Romanus, 34
Rome, sack of, 28
Romero Humberto, Gen. Carlos, 1097
Rommel, Fld. Marshal Erwin, 297, 359
Ronda, 290
Roosevelt, Pres. Franklin D., 301–2, 312, 354, 398–9, 429, 438, 440, 445–6, 449–50, 453, 461–2, 469, 690
Roosevelt, Theodore, 115, 688–9
Root, Elihu, 210
Rorke's Drift, battle of, 137
Rose, Gen. Hugh, 136
Rosenberg, Alfred, 324
Rossignol, 74
Rostow, Walter, 719, 721–3, 725–6, 736, 748, 785, 788, 795, 803, 858, 876–7, 885, 888, 902–3; "aggression from the North" theme, 721, 768, 919, 935
Rousseau, Jean Jacques, 59
Routiers, Brittany, 46–7
Rovera, Dr., 79
Roxane, 7
Roxas, Pres., 530–1
Royal Air Force, 277–82, 473; Somaliland, 277; World War II, 296–7, 426, 930–1
Royal Irish Constabulary, 194; Auxiliary Division (Auxies), 195–6, 1123, 1125, 1127–30, 1132–3, 1135
Royal United Service Institution, 137
Ruark, Robert, 624
Runciman, S., 595
Rundstedt, Fld. Marshal Gerd von, 316–7

Rusk, Dean, 721, 726, 742, 748, 771, 785–7, 793, 800–1, 803, 852, 854; "aggression from the North" theme, 721, 854, 857, 872, 887, 903, 906–8, 919–20
Russell, Sen. Richard, 965
Russia, x, 37; maps, 37, 87, 101, 216; French invasion (1812), 85–91, map, 87; pacification of Daghestan, 100–1, map, 101; Manchuria, 236; Revolution: 202–24, Russian Duma, 207–9, Lvov-Kerensky provisional government, 209–12, Russian Soviet of Workers' and Soldiers' Deputies, 209–12, Bolshevik consolidation of victory, 213–4, Allied intervention, 215–7, map, 216

Saadi, Yassef, 670
SADA, 1180–2
Sadat, Muhammad Anwar el-, 1158
Safire, William, 996
Saguntum, 14
Saigon, 151, 473, 577
Saint-Arnaud, Gen., 99
Sainteny, Jean, 474–6
Saiqa, al-, Syrian guerrillas, 1156, 1158
Salan, Gen. Raoul, 509–13, 583, 675–6, 678
Salazar, 164
Salinger, Pierre, 925
Salisbury, Harrison, 831, 938–40
Salmond, Marshal of the RAF Geoffrey, 279
Salvia the Soothsayer, 9
Samar, Philippines, 131, 378
Samrin, Heng, 1049
Sánchez, Julián, 79
Sanderson, Lt. Gen. John, 1054
Sandinistas, Nicaragua, 1078–87
Sandino, Augusto César, 287–9, 1077–8, 1085
San Luis Potosí, Plan of, 163
Santa Anna dictatorship, 161
Santee River, 66, 68
Santo Domingo, 116; United States in, 285–6
Santucho, Mario Roberto, 1092
SANU, Sudan, 1154
Sapia, Friar, 79
Saracens, 32–3
Saraphis, Col., 357, 360–2, 516
Saratoga, N.Y., 61, 66

781, 800, 875, 962, new tactics, 787, high morale, 787, fresh offensives, 782–3, 792–3, 803–4, administration, 800, strength, 800, 834, 848, 901, 1006, infiltration of refugees, 803–4, logistics, 835, 875, 936, tactics, 845–6, continuing gains, 850, propaganda, 852, retreat, 865, capabilities, 944, peace talks, 975, alleged desertions, 984–5, Viet Minh cadres, 606, 612–3, 617–8, guerrilla terrorist tactics, 618–9, 755; Washington lobby, 623; strategic-hamlet program, 722, 736, 739–41, 758, 760, failure, 739–42, 756–7, abandoned, 769; Chieu Hoi (defector) program, 754; policy, 559–60, 610–3, 615–6; provisional government, 767, political disunity, 766–7; Khanh government (1964–February 1965): 767, 769–71, 774, 778–80, 789–90, Program of Action, 769, New Rural Life Hamlets, 769, Advanced People's Action Groups, 769, 827, deterioration of government and army, 777, anti-American display, 790, dictatorship, 789, fall of, 790; Thieu-Ky government (1965–1974): 803, 826–8, 840, pacification program, 826–8, elections, 827, 859, 871, Revolutionary Development Groups, 827, 871, failure of, 848–51, 858–60, corruption, 849–50, 886–7; repressive government, 849–50, 988–9, 993, 1010, Montagnard defection, 849, Guam Conference, 871, new constitution, 871, civilian casualties, 875, 897, 909, VC/PAVN Tet offensives, 897–900, 909, 948, psychological effect of, 906–7, Phoenix program, 910–1, Honolulu meeting, 913, quarrel with U.S., 913–4, overall casualties, 914, effect of U.S. bombings, 941–2, Midway Island conference, 976–7, disclosure of Communist espionage ring in government, 982, Communist infiltration of government, 1011–2, invasion of Cambodia, 996–1000, 1002, continued ARVN presence in Cambodia, 1007, invasion of Laos, 1019–22, failure of, 1020–2, casualties, 1021, Thieu/Ky quarrel,

1027, elections, 1029–30, Thieu declares martial law, 1035, cease-fire, 1040, PAVN/VC gains, 1042, unconditional surrender to North Vietnam, 1047

Southwest Africa (Namibia), 1188–91; background, 1188; insurgency, 1188–91; UN intervention; 1190–1, given independence, 1191

Souvanouvong, Prince, 1046

Soviet Union, 454, 919–20, 922, 924–5, 931, 1065, 1094, 1104; maps, 216, 333; following World War I: consolidation of the revolution, 213–24, Red Terror, 213–4, Allied intervention, 215–6, 218–22, Red Army, 217–8, 220, NEP, 223–4, Comintern, 223–4, in Chinese Revolution, 240–3, in Chinese civil war, 249–50, 252, aid to Spanish Nationalists, 291–4; World War II: 321–37, German invasion, 297, 321–2, German occupation policy, 324–6; guerrilla resistance, 303, 321–3, 325–7, 331–2, 334–6, German countertactics, 327–30; postwar: Poland, 306–7, Manchuria, 458, China, 458, 578, recognition of DRV, 486, aid to, 616, Geneva Conference, 594–6, aid to North Vietnam, 616, 834, 875, 936, 992, 1006, reduces aid, 1042, 1048–9, 1051; aid to: Nicaraguan insurgency, 1079, 1082, Chilean insurgency, 1094, El Salvador insurgency, 1097–8, Egypt and Arab countries, 1154, 1157, Ethiopia, 1171, Angola, 1186, 1190–1, Mozambique, 1193, 1195–6, Afghanistan government, 1202–3, 1205–10

Spaatz, Gen. Carl, 931

Spain, 72, 103; maps, 13, 79, 117, 268, 1142; Roman invasion and occupation, 13–21; Celtiberians, 13–4, 17–8, 78; French invasion and occupation, 76–83, "the Spanish Ulcer," 84–5; Spanish-American War, 111, 688; Cuban insurrection, 115, 116–20; the Tercios, 265, 269, 271, 289; Philippines, 123, 125–6; Morocco, see Rif rebellion; Civil War, 74, 289–94, 930, 1142, Communist element, 291 ff., guerrilla warfare, 291–4; Spanish

1271

Spain (*continued*)

Morocco, *see* Western Sahara; Basque insurgency, 1098, 1141–8, map, 1142, background, 1141–3, ETA terrorist group: emergence, 1143, aims, 1141, 1143, allied guerrilla terrorist groups, 1143–4, operations and tactics, 1143–8, counterinsurgency operations and tactics, 1145–8, public disapproval of, 1148

Spartacus, 9

Special Forces (Green Berets), U.S., *see* United States: Vietnam

Speckbacker, Joseph, 84

Speer, Albert, 302

Spencer-Chapman, 373, 408–13

Spinoza, Benedict de, 922

Spitamenes, Gen., 6–7

Spock, Dr. Benjamin, 889

Spotsylvania, battle of, 110

SSLM, Sudan, 1175

Staley, Prof. Eugene, 722, 739

Stalin, Joseph, 222, 243, 252–3, 293–4, 306–7, 322, 331, 353, 449–51, 454–5, 457, 462, 467, 469–70

Statute of Guernica, 1145

Stauffenberg, Claus von, 331

Steinwehr, Gen. von, 108

Stennis, Sen. John, 965, 997

Stern, Abraham, 554–5, 1151

Stern Gang, Jewish guerrillas, 554–9

Stettinius, Edward, 455

Steuben, Gen. von, 61

Stilwell, Gen. Joseph (Vinegar Joe), 414–5, 421–3, 433–4, 440–2, 451, 453; quarrel with Chennault, 442–3, 447; relations with Chiang Kai-shek, 441–3, 445–8, dismissal, 445, 448

Stimson, Henry L., 287, 1077

Stirling, battle of, 44

Stolypin, Premier, 208

Stone, I.F., xi, 1035

Stormont Castle, 1123–4, 1135

Storrs, Ronald, 180

Stoughton, Gen., 107

Strategic Bombing Survey, 932–3

Strategic-hamlet program, *see* South Vietnam

"strategic key" versus "strategic convenience," 579–81, 621, 652, 747, 773, 879

Strauss, Lewis, 301–3

Strecker, Maj., 89

"Stronghold" concept, 431–2, 512

Stuart, Gen. Jeb, 107

Stuart, Amb. J.L., 459–60

Stump, Adm. Felix, 622

Subutai, Gen., 37–8

Sudan, 1173–7; background, 1173; guerrilla wars, 1173–7; political parties; 1174–7, Numery dictatorship, 1174–7; Basher fundamentalist Islamic dictatorship, 1176–7

Suez Canal, invasion of, 1154

Sukarno, Achmed, 389–90, 543–6, 548–9

Sully, François, 759

Sulzberger, Arthur H., 760

Sulzberger, C.L., 664

Sumatra, 389, 544–7, 549

Summer Palace, 236

Summers, Col. Harry, xi

Sumter, Thomas, 66–7

Sunni Moslems, 1159

Sung dynasty, China, 38, 231

Sun Tzu, x, 32–3, 40, 49, 138, 257, 405, 754, 1017

Sun Yat-sen, 238–41, 259

SWAPO, Namibia, 1187, 1189–91

Swedish Social Democrats, 1092

Sweet-Escott, Bickham, 360

Switzerland, 1083

Sykes, Christopher, 423, 426, 429

Symbionese Liberation Army, 1064

Symington, Stuart, 983

Syria, 33, 183, 188, 1156

Szechwan province, 238, 250

Szilard, Leo, 301

Tache d'huile (oil spot) technique, 153, 155, 481, 672, 711; *see also* Lyautey, Marshal Hubert

Tafileh, 186

Tafilelt, 154

Taft, Pres. William Howard, 166, 528; Philippines, 131–3

Tai Li, Gen., 443–5

Taiping Rebellion, 233–6

Talavera, battle of, 80

Tam, Nguyen Van, 512–3

Tampico incident, 168

Tanga, German E. Africa, 172–3, 176

Tanganyika, 172

Tangier, 272; Treaty of, 100

Tanham, Dr. George K., 890

Tan Malaka, 545–6, 548

1272

1273

Trinquier, Maj. Roger, 502, 512, 585, 669–70
Trong, Huynh Van, 982
Trotsky, Leon, 207–8, 210–1, 214–5, 243
Truehart, William, 758
Truman, Pres. Harry S., 453, 461–2; postwar: 470, 483, 510, 517, 527, 557, China, 453, 455, 461–4, Truman Doctrine, 471, 517–20, Greece, 517–20
Trung, Tran Nam, 743
Truong, Lt. Gen. Ngo Quang, 1035
Truong Chinh, 395, 489
Tsalderis government, Greece, 518
Tsarskoe Selo, 209
Tseng Kuo-fan, Gen., 235–6
Tuchman, Barbara, 421
Tugela River, 143–4
T'ung Meng Hui, 238–9
Tunisia, 657–8, 663, 666, 668, 671–4, 676, 682, 1160
Tupamaros, 1072–4, 1090
Turenne, Gen., 49
Turgenev, Ivan, 203
Turkestan, 37
Turkey, 96, 652; World War I, 179–91
Turkish Cypriotes, 643–4, 651, 654–5
Turkomans, 137
Tu Ve, 480
Tuyen, Dr. Tran Kim, 613
Twain, Mark, 239
26th of July Movement, Cuba, 695, 705
Twomey, Seamus, 1131
"Tyranny of the Dead," 297
Tyrol: map, 85; French conquest of, 84–5; guerrilla defense, 84–5
Tyrone's rebellion, 50–1

Ucles, 79
UDA, Ulster, 1128–30, 1132, 1136
UDEL, Nicaragua, 1078, 1086
UDMA, Algeria, 639, 668
UDR, Ulster, 1123, 1130
UFF, Ulster, 1130, 1137
Ukraine, 213, 221, 321, 326
Union Pacific railroad, 111
UNO, Nicaragua, 1086
Ulster (Northern Ireland), 1121–38; map, 1122; background, 1121–4; early riots, 1125; IRA role, 1125–6; Provisional IRA insurgency, 1125 ff.;

British counterinsurgency tactics, 1125–8; Protestant guerrilla groups, 1129 ff.; casualties, 1130; IRA tactics, 1125–7, 1131, 1133–4; cease-fire, 1132; peace negotiations, 1134–8
Ulster Special Constabulary, 1123
UNITA, Angola, 1186–92
United Arab Kingdom, 1157
United Arab Republic, 1154
United Fruit Company, 288, 708, 968–9
United Nations, 450, 461, 469–70, 594, 712, 854, 1019, 1157; intervention in: Cyprus, 647, 652, 654–5; Greece, 515, 517–9; Indonesia, 547–9; Palestine, 559, 561, Palestine Commission, 1153; Vietnam, see South Vietnam; United States: Vietnam; Nicaragua, 1085; El Salvador, 1104–6; Israel, 1150, 1153–4, 1162, Resolution 242, 1155, 1162–3; Ethiopia, 1170; Angola, 1186, 1192; Namibia, Resolution 435, 1189, 1191; Afghanistan, 1208, 1210–1; Sudan, 1177; Western Sahara, 1179, 1181–3
United States: Afghanistan, 1202–3, 1204–12; air force, ix, 432, 750–1, see also United States: Vietnam; Angola, 1188–91; army: American Revolution, 63–70, Seminole Indian War, 102–3, Civil War, 104–8, 110, Cuba, 120, Philippines, 124–33, Mexico, 169–70, Russia, 215–6, World War II: Philippines, 378–87, China, 440–8, 455–6, postwar: Greece, 520–2, Philippines, 530–1, Indochina, see United States: Vietnam, Nicaragua, 1078, Honduras, 1081, El Salvador, 1100–1; Bolivia, 714; Burma, 414, 421–3, 433–4, guerrilla operations, 433–4; Cambodia, see United States: Vietnam; Central Intelligence Agency: Vietnam, see United States: Vietnam, Guatemala, 1069, Uruguay, 1074, Nicaragua, 1080–4, Chile, 1093, Colombia, 1122; China, 233, 236–7, 239, World War II: aid to, 440, Flying Tigers, 440, Nationalist China lobby in Congress, 442, 455, U.S. Naval Group, China,

442-5, OSS (Far East), 442-4; Sino-American Cooperative Association (SACO), 443-4, Dixie Mission: 444, report on Communist military capabilities, 447, Hurley Mission, 445-8, Stilwell repoort, 448, Stilwell recalled, 448, Wedemeyer mission, 448, 450, 453, 455, 458, 461, U.S. policy, 438, 440-2, 445-6, 448-50, 453-5, 457-60, 462, postwar, 457, Marshall mission, 459-60, Stuart report, 460; Colombia, 110, CIA, 112; Congress, 103, 120, 130, 462-3, 527, 577, 589-90, 688, 691, 706, 722, 747, 771-2, 775, 804, 841, 872, 895, 907, 909, 966, 984, 991-2, 996, 1000-1, 1007, 1010, 1018, 1047, 1081-3, 1085, 1100, 1103-4, 1188, 1190, Platt Amendment, 688, Teller Amendment, 688, Southeast Asia Resolution (Tonkin Gulf), 775, Cooper-Church Amendment, 1007, 1018, Boland Amendment, 1081, 1083; Cuba, 686, 688-92, 694-5, 701, 704-10; Cyprus, 645; Department of Defense, see United States: Vietnam; Department of State, 123-4, 448, 453, 455, 458-9, 464-5, White Paper on China, 464, Vietnam, see United States: Vietnam; Drug Enforcement Administration, 1065, 1072; El Salvador, 1098-1104; Ethiopia, 1170-1; Greece, 517, 519-22; Grenada, 1101; Guatemala, 1068-9, 1071-2, CIA, 1069; Indonesia, 545, 547-9; Israel, see Israel, Palestine; Joint Chiefs of Staff, ix, World War II, 429, 449-50, postwar, 457, 589, Vietnam, see United States: Vietnam; Laos, see United States: Vietnam; marines: Cuba, 629, Nicaragua, 287-9, 930, Santo Domingo, 285-6, World War II, 372, 957-8, Vietnam, see United States: Vietnam; massive retaliation policy, 585, 749; Mexican Revolution, 159, 161, 166-70; Military Advisory Council Vietnam (MACV), see United States: Vietnam; Mozambique, 1196; National Security Council, 589, 760, 786, 961-2, 986, 1032; navy, World War II, China, 443-5, postwar, Latin America, 1081; Nicaragua, 287-9,

930, 1080-4, CIA support of Contras, 1080-4, cost, 1081, 1084, illegal funding of, 1082-4, aid to Chamorro government, 1086; Office of Strategic Services (OSS), 299-300, 307-8, 317-9, 362, 390-1, 402-3, 474; Palestine, 1153, see also Israel, Palestine; Peru, 1117; Philippines, 127-33, 378-87, 525, 528, 530-1; Senate, 987, 992, 1087, Foreign Relations Committee, 834-5, 853-4, 907, 937, 991, 1018-9, Armed Services Committee, 965-6, 980; Uruguay, 1074; Vietnam: Truman Administration, 469, 507, postwar policy, 396, 398-9, 402-3, 471-2, 474, 482-8, 497-506, 510-1, 577, 584, 599-60, OSS, 474, military aid to French forces, 505, criticism of French policy, 512-3; Eisenhower Administration, 508-623, increased aid to French, 577-8, 582, military aid group arrives in Saigon, 577, military estimate, 578, debate on intervention, 589-92, Geneva Conference, 594-6; Kennedy Administration, 718-64; Johnson Administration, 765-956; Nixon Administration, 957-1057; army: morale, 1024, training, 1024, leadership, 1028, attrition strategy, 812, 834-5, 882, 903, 943; quantitative tactics, 812, 816-26: search-and-destroy, 816-8, economy of force, 882, clear-and-hold, 823, "spoiling," 822, 882, 909, critique of, 831-3, Operation Crazy Horse, 817-8, 842-3, 101st Airborne Division, 840, 970, 1013, Ap Bia (Hamburger Hill), 970-2, 977-8n., 1029, Delta Force, 844, 1st Cavalry (Airmobile) Division, 812, 816-8, 837, 880, 936, 946, 999, 1013, 1st Division, 865, 883, My Lai, 950-1, 987, 1010, 1023-5; Special Forces, 739, 756, 982, 1040-1; armed forces: commitment, 726, 736-7, 741, state of, 814-6, 944, training, 836, 944, doctrine, 719-20, 722-7, 736-7, 748-51, 753-5, 758, 944, rules of engagement, 813, 836, logistics requirement, 836-7, 880-1, ammunition expenditure, 836-7, 880-1, supply shortages, 836-7,

United States (*continued*)

844, rear area life-style, 837–9, 880, strategy, 812, 816–26, 863, 911, 943–4, 949 ff., tactics, 817–26, 865, tactical challenge, 840, 847–8, tactical failures, 841–3, 942–8, 951, tactical successes, 843–4, 864–5, 952–3, 912, troop build-up, 792–3, 795, 812, 857, 859–61, 863–6, 900–1, 909, tactical alteration, 962, interservice rivalry, 962, use of drugs, 1027, withdrawal of troops, 976, 983, 986, 993, 1016–7, 1031, 1033; Administration optimism, 736–7, 742, 759, 891–2; Administration dissent, 786–8, 806–8, 876–7, 889–91, 902–4, 908, 918–9, 961–2, 987; Civilian Irregular Defense Corps (CIDG), 816–7, 843; Demilitarized Zone (DMZ), 814, 821–3, 825, 832, 866–7, 883, 898, 940, 974, 980, 1033, electronic barrier, 859; helicopters, 736–7, 755–6, 815–8, 1023, medical evacuation, 816, 837, losses, 874, 880, 914, 946, 1020–1, logistic requirements, 946–7, shortcomings, 1019, 1021–2; hawks, 858–61; fictitious "victories," 840–3, 882, 970; critical voices, 758–9, 852–6, 857–8, 890–1; public opinion, 840, 887–9, 918, 925, 943, 972–3, 977, 981, 991, 993, 1028–9; casualties, 812, 823, 830, 836, 841, 866–7, 874, 897, 903, 909, 914, 971–2, 980, 984, 999, 1013; claimed enemy casualties, 818, 865–6, 882–3, 970–1, 986, 999; policy, 719–26, 736, 742–4, 769–75, 793–5, 801–2, National Security Action Memorandum, 917–8; aims, 783–4, 879, 917–9, 1045–6, 957–8, 976–7, 981, 1013, critique of, 917–28; strategy, 770–3, 958–9, 972, 976–7, 981, 984, 993, 1008; Vice-President Johnson's mission, 720–1; Staley mission, 722; Taylor-Rostow mission, 722–4; Hilsman-Forrestal mission, 757–8; Krulak-Mendenhall mission, 760; McNamara mission, 767, volte-face, 878–80, Pentagon report, 879; escalation, 726, 736–7, 741, 768–9, 777–8, 783, 793–5,

796–8, 802–3, 969, option to use nuclear weapons, 771, Operation Plan 34-A, 768–72, covert operations, 774–5, 778, 785–6, contingency offensive plans, 779–82, 787–8, Jorden mission, 771; cost, 736, 741, 770, 790, 804, 864, 874, 879, 881, 903, 914, 980–1, 983, 991, 1009, 1023–4, 1039, 1045; civil/military corruption, 1023–4, 1028; navy, 589, 768, 774–5, 793, 821, 824–6, 864, 870, 982, air operations, 771, 774, 777, 825–6, 865, 870, 1033–4, riverine warfare, 825, 865; air force, 771, 774, 794, 815–6, 824–6, 897, 965–7 1032–6, 1039–41, 1043–5; marines, 795, 798, 801, 803, 818–21, 970, mission, 818, pacification programs, 818–20, 847–8, 868–8, 883–4, 954–5, Combined Action Platoons (CAP), 820, 867, 954–5, tactics, 818, 844–5, 868–70, intelligence failure, 819, 846–7, rules of engagement, 819, 836, Khe Sanh, 866, 883, 896–9, 906, 909, 913, 948, 970, Buddhist riots, 821, Viet Cong, 867 ff., PAVN, 821, 866, casualties, 812, 823, 866–7, claimed enemy casualties, 812, 822–3, 866–7, 870, 875, 896–7, 899, 903, 907–9, 914, air operations, 818, 867, helicopters, 755–6, 818, 867, 946; anti-war movement, 852–6, 887–9, 898, 907, 925, 970, 972, 974, 980–1, 984, 1001–2, 1010, 1027, 1029, 1035–7, Kent State killings, 1001; refugees, 832–3, 883; "the other war," 826–8, 870–1, 883–6, 906–7, CORDS, 871, 885–7; Clifford Group, 902–6; the Wise Men, 908; proliferation of agencies, 758, 826, 852; Congressional hearing, 853–6, 991, Cooper-Church Amendment, 1007, 1018, Boland Amendment, 1081, 1083; World War I syndrome, 834, 857; Paris peace talks, 909, 959, 974–5, 1007, 1010–1, 1017, 1031–2, 1035, 1039, secret talks, 975, 981, 1010; Pentagon Papers, 783, 921, 1028 ff.; press/TV, 742, 757–60, 888–9, 912, 973, 980, 1000; Cooper mission, 783; McGeorge

Bundy mission, 793–4; enemy sanctuaries, 962–3, 987–8, 993, 1008–9, CIA-organized ground raids in, 966, 994–5, 1005, alleged PAVN/VC headquarters, 963–5; Vietnamization, 976–7, 981, 984, 993, 1006, 1011, 1016, 1031, pacification progress, 984, 993; Cambodia, alleged PAVN/VC headquarters, 963–5, Bowles mission, 964, secret bombing, 965, 969, 974, 992, results, 966–7, invasion of, 997–1000, 1005, results, 999–1000, military support of Lon Nol government, 995–6, 1045–6; Laos: CIA, 750, 992, secret bombing of, 992, 1044, ground forces in, 992, invasion of, 1019–22; Allied troops, 823–4, 864, 953; Central Intelligence Agency (CIA), 591, 599, 726–7, 736, 739, 743, 750, 756, 769, 773, 798, 802, 830, 876, 903, 906, 910, 920, 963, 966, 982, 992, Laos air strikes, 768, 992, 1044, refutation of domino theory, 773, Phoenix program, 982, 984; JCS, 762–9, 771–2, 775, 779, 783–5, 795, 798, 802–6, 828, 834, 850, 857, 859–61, 875–6, 879, 898, 900–1, 903, 919–20, 934–5, 943, 945, 949, 955, 1005, 1040; MACV, 736, 738, 755, 758, 760, 767, 811–2, 833–4, 840–1, 850, 871, 880, 909, 944–6, 954–5, 963, 965, 970–1, 982, 993, 995, 1000, 1005, secret air war, 961, 980, 1007; Department of State, 757, 964, 1005, White Paper: "Aggression from the North," 795; Department of Defense, 779, 783–4, 980, 993, 999, 1005, 1042; National Security Council, 786; air war, 771, 774, 777, 793–5, 796–8, 802–4, 812, 824–6, 830–1, 865, 870, 874–5, 900, 905–6, 909, 913–4, 969, 971, 974, 1009, 1013, 1017–8, 1031–6, 1039, 1041, 1045, Operation Rolling Thunder, 797, 803, 812, 824, 830–1, 858–60, losses, 860, 874, 914, 936–7, critique of, 929–42; ground war, 802–6, 811–2, 815–26, 831-4, 836–8, 840–8, 864–70, 891, 896–8, 912, 969–72, 974,

1009, 1013–4, 1017–8, 1030–6, 1041; naval war, 825, 865, 969, 1033–6, 1038–9, *see also* United States: air war; defoliation program, xi, 982–3

UNRRA, *see* United Nations
UPR, Brazil, 1089–90
Upton, Gen. Amery, 113–4, 120
Urbina, Tomás, 167, 169
Uris, Leon, 561
URNG, Guatemala, 1071–2
Uruguay, 1085, 1090; map, 1062; insurgency, 1073–4
Usborne, Adm. C.V., 96–8
USS *Maddox,* 774–5
USS *New Jersey,* 825, 982
USS *Pueblo,* 896, 981–2
USSR, *see* Soviet Union
Ustasi militia, 343
U Thant, 1019
Utrecht, Treaty of, 50
UVF, Ulster, 1124, 1130, 1132

Václav I, 38
Vadbolsky, 89
Valée, Gen., 97–8
Valens, Emp., 27
Valeriano, Col., 530, 535
Valley Forge, 61
Valluy, Étienne, 477, 480–1
Vance, Cyrus, 1158
Vandals, 29–30
Vandegrift, Gen. A.A., 371–2
Van Fleet, Gen., 521
Vann, Lt. Col. John, 758, 841, 886, 1008–9
Vaphiadis, Markos, 517–25
Vasilyev, Ermolai, 88
Vaslov, Gen., 330
Vauban, Marshal de, 49
Velasco Alvarado, Juan, 1113
Vélez, Pedro Antonio Mariá, 1108
Veliamonif, Gen., 100
Vendée rebellion, 74–6, map, 75; Hoche's counterinsurgency tactics, 75–6
Venezuela: insurgency, 1064, 1066–8, 1085; map, 1062
Vera Cruz, 161, 169
Vernadsky, Prof. George, 211
Vetilius, Gaius, 18
Vichy France, 310, 315, 396–8
Victor, Gen., 80

1277

Vidal-Naquet, Pierre, 671
Viet Cong, *see* South Vietnam; United States: Vietnam
Viet Minh, 402–3, 476, 664, 944; maps, 478, 491, 499, 576; World War II: foreign aid, 402, proclaim the new Democratic Republic of Vietnam (DRV), 403, British occupation, 403, return of French, 403; postwar: demand for independence, 473, position, 473–4, military-political organization, 490, tactics, 490–6, revolutionary teams, 491–6, offensives, 497–8, 500–1, casualties, 501, 512, infiltration tactics, 509–10, mobility, 509–10, Laos, 513–4, interdiction tactics, 577, Chinese aid, 577, military strength, 577, battle of Dien Bien Phu, 583–5, 588, 592, political settlement and French withdrawal, 592–3; *see also* Giap, Gen. Vo Nguyen
Vietnam, *see* North Vietnam; South Vietnam; United States: Vietnam; Viet Minh
Vietnam Communist Party, 620
Villa, Francisco (Pancho), 163–5, 167–70, 287
Villalobo, Joaquín, 1097
Villanueva, Lt., 382
Villavella, Arturo, 1093
Vilna, 86
Vimiero, battle of, 78
Vincent, John, 455
Vinh Yen, 500–1
Vinicio Cerizo, 1070–1
Virginia, 56, 108
Virginia Company (British), 55
Viriathus, 18–20
Visayan Islands, 378, 382
Visayan Republic, Philippines, 123–4
Visigoths, 29
Vitebsk, 86–7
Vladivostok, 215
Vogt, Lt. Gen. John, Jr., 1021
Voitinsky (Comintern agent), 240
Volckmann, Col., R.W., 384–7, on guerrilla warfare, 385–6
Vong, King Sisavang, 400
Voroshilov, Gen. Clement, 214, 331
Vouza, Sgt. Major, 371–2

Wales: map, 39, English pacification of, 39–43

Wallace, Vice-Pres. Henry, 445
Wallace, William, 44–5
Waller, Maj. Gen. L.W.T.W., 131–3
Walpole, Horace, 70
Walt, Lt. Gen. Lewis, 812–22, 848, 867, 871, 896, 913, 945–6, 948, 954, 973
Wapshare, Maj. Gen., 176
War of Succession, 50
Warrene, earl of, 43
Warring States (China), 23
Warsaw, battle of, 307
Waruhiu, Itote (Gen. China), Kenya, 638
Washifa, battle of, 113
Washington, Pres. George, 56, 60–1, 64, 66, 68
Washington Post, 124, 973
Washington Watch, 889
Watergate, 966
Wavell, Fld. Marshal A.P., 188, 414, 425
Weathermen, guerrilla terrorists, 1064
Weber, Max, 206
Wedemeyer, Lt. Gen. Albert, 445, 450, 453, 455, 458–9, 461–2; replaces Stilwell, 445; report on China, 455–6
Wehrmacht, 296, 324, 335
Weichs, Gen. von, 348
Weigley, Prof. Russel F., 56, 61
Weinberger, Caspar, 1084
Weizmann, Dr. Chaim, 553, 556
Wejh, 182–3, 186
Welander, R. Adm., 1033
Welles, Sumner, 690–1
Wellington, Duke of: India, 74; Napoleonic wars, 78–83; use of Portuguese and Spanish guerrillas, 78–83
Wemyss, Adm. Rosslyn, 182
Wergha Line, 273
Wergha River, 272
West, Capt. Francis J., 837, 845
West Bank, 1154–5, 1162, 1164–5
Westerling, Capt. "Turk," 547
Western Sahara: insurgency, 1179–83; map, 1180
Westmoreland, Gen. William, x xi, 792, 798, 801–2, 804–5, 812–3, 822–3, 828, 831, 835, 838–9, 840–2, 857, 859–61, 871–2, 874–6, 879–81, 883–4, 891–2, 895–903, 906, 908–9, 911–3, 919, 945–6,

948–50, 955, 993, 1022; background, 814; replaces Harkins, 774; attrition strategy, 812; 816–26, 863–4; failure of strategy and tactics, 832–4; critique of, 836–9, 840–8, 879–83, 943–56
Weyand, Lt. Gen. Frederick, 865, 896, 1047
Weyler, Gen., 116, 118–19
Wheeler, Gen. Earle G., 724, 787, 801, 805, 842, 876, 896, 900–1, 903, 920, 940, 980
White, Maj. Gen. George, 141–2
White, T.H., 421–2
Whitelaw, William, 1128–9
White Terror, China, 242–3, 248
White Terror, Russia, 208
Wickwire, Franklin and Mary, 71n.
Wildman, U.S. Consul, 123–4
Williams, Maj. Gen. Samuel, 611
Wilson, Pr. Min. Harold, 789, 803, 875, 888
Wilson, Amb. Henry Lane, 166–7
Wilson, Pres. Woodrow, 159, 166–9, 213, 239
Wingate, Maj. Gen. Orde, 423–7, 429–33, 512, 553, 583
Wingate, Sir Reginald, 182
Wise Men, 908
Wolfe, Gen. James, 89
Wolfert, Ira, 379
Women's Peace Movement, Ulster, 1132
Woodhouse, C.M., 358–9, 361–3
Woolman, David, 269, 271, 273
World Bank, 541, 1082

Yalta Conference, 449–51, 458, 461, 472
Yamashita, Gen., 386
Yangtze River, 235, 260, 447; Valley, 238, 242
Yaqui uprising, 162–3

Ydígoras Fuentes, Gen. Miguel, 1069
Yellow River, 251
Yelui Chutsai, 37
Yenan, 252, 445–6, 460
Yen Bai, 393, 512
Yenbo, 182–3, 186
Yeo-Thomas, Cmdr., 316
Yishuv, 552, 558
Yoke Force, 422, 434
Yorktown, battle of, 70
Yüan-chang, Chu, 231
Yüan Shih-k'ai, 238–9
Yucatán, 163
Yudenich, Gen., 221
Yugoslavia, x; map, 347; German invasion and occupation of, 338–9 ff.; guerrilla resistance, 338–54, Chetnik guerrillas, 341–5; Partisan guerrillas, 341–8; SOE mission to Tito's Partisans, 342–8; analysis of guerrilla effectiveness, 348–54; postwar: supports Greek Communist insurgents, 517, 519–20, breaks with Soviet Union, 578

Zabegern, 30
Zacharias, R. Adm. Ellis, 450
Zagoria, Prof. Donald S., 615, 732, 922, 941
Zahir, King Mohammed of Afghanistan, 1201, 1204, 1211
Zakhariadis, Nikos, 517, 522–3, 525
ZANU, Zimbabwe, 1193–4
Zariaspa, 6
Zayas, Pres. Alfredo, 689
Zeid, Prince, 180–2
Zeller, André, 678
Zervas, Col., 357, 360
Zoco el Telata, 266
Zog, king of Albania, 363
Zones excentriques, 582
Zouaves, 157
Zubatov, Col., 205
Zulu war, 137

0-595-22594-2

Printed in the United States
60173LVS00003B/6